The Bajío Revolution

The Bajío Revolution

Remaking Capitalism, Community,
and Patriarchy in Mexico,
North America, and the World

JOHN TUTINO

DUKE UNIVERSITY PRESS
Durham and London
2025

Library of Congress Cataloging-in-Publication Data
Names: Tutino, John, [date] author.
Title: The Bajío revolution : remaking capitalism, community, and patriarchy
in Mexico, North America, and the world / John Tutino.
Other titles: Remaking capitalism, community, and patriarchy in Mexico,
North America, and the world
Description: Durham : Duke University Press, 2025. | Includes bibliographical
references and index.
Identifiers: LCCN 2024050928 (print)
LCCN 2024050929 (ebook)
ISBN 9781478031932 (paperback)
ISBN 9781478028703 (hardcover)
ISBN 9781478061014 (ebook)
Subjects: LCSH: Capitalism—Mexico—Bajío Region—History. | Silver industry—
Mexico—Bajío Region—History. | Green Revolution—Mexico—Bajío Region—
History. | Capitalism—New Spain—History. | Silver industry—New Spain—History. |
Green Revolution—New Spain—History. | Bajío Region (Mexico)—Economic
conditions. | New Spain—Economic conditions.
Classification: LCC HC137.B38 t88 2025 (print) | LCC HC137.B38 (ebook)
DDC 330.972/402—dc23/eng/20250511
LC record available at https://lccn.loc.gov/2024050928
LC ebook record available at https://lccn.loc.gov/2024050929

Cover art: Manuel Serrano, *Vendedora de Buñuelos*. 19th century.
Oil on canvas, 49.5 × 57 cm (19.4 × 22.4 in.). Museo Nacional de
Historia, Instituto Nacional de Antropología e Historia (INAH),
Mexico City. Image: Wikimedia Commons.

For Mexicans everywhere
still working to make livable families and communities,
and for
Jane,
María, and Israel,
and
Gabriela,
my core family pursuing the same goals at home and beyond

CONTENTS

ILLUSTRATIONS

Maps

Figures

Between Silver and Maize

New Spain and Mexico in the World, 1550–1880

In 1802, "las muchachas"—the girls—occupied the home of manager don José Antonio Rico at Puerto de Nieto, a large landed estate set between the mining center of Guanajuato, then the world's top producer of silver, and Querétaro, the Americas' leading textile city, in the rich basin northwest of Mexico City known as the Bajío. The families of Puerto de Nieto lived by paid labor and tenant cropping, making maize and more to sustain cities, towns, and mines—and the global trade that Guanajuato's silver fueled. The Bajío was a primary engine of commercial capitalism, driving trades that linked China and India to Africa and the Euro-Atlantic World. Its social relations were precociously capitalist. Producers were drawn to work in mines, in textile workshops, and at landed estates by commercial relations of production. The families living and laboring at Puerto de Nieto negotiated patriarchal ways of work to sustain mines, textile towns, and global capitalism.

Don José Sánchez Espinosa, a priest, landed patriarch, and agrarian capitalist based in Mexico City, held estates from the outskirts of the capital, through the Bajío, north to San Luis Potosí. Since the early 1790s, in times of silver boom and imperial wars, he had instructed manager Rico to cut workers' salaries and maize rations at Puerto de Nieto—constraining lives to maximize profit. In 1802, Rico prepared a list of tenants, ready to demand higher rents and begin evictions. While men kept working and women struggled to sustain families, the girls saw futures at risk. Rico reported the invasion of his home and office and the muchachas' demand that evictions end. He said nothing about negotiating to end the occupation, a silence suggesting that concessions were made. Still, estate maize planting rose 20 percent that year, indicating that evictions happened.[1]

The people of Puerto de Nieto carried on as their lives deteriorated until September 1810. Then don Miguel Hidalgo y Costilla, pastor at Dolores just north, proclaimed his famous *grito* demanding rights to local rule as Napoleon occupied Spain, breaking Spain's empire at its center. Seeing power challenged, thousands of men struggling to sustain families on estate lands, including dozens of the muchachas' fathers, brothers, and neighbors at Puerto de Nieto, raised machetes to claim maize standing ripe in the fields. The rising came laden with contradictions: Hidalgo sought power in defense of property; the throngs around him fought for sustenance—and attacked property to gain it. Together they invaded the mining city of Guanajuato: Hidalgo claiming silver to fund his fight; popular rebels, rural and urban, taking maize to feed insurgents and families.

When Hidalgo faced political defeat early in 1811, rebels from Puerto de Nieto and estates all around Guanajuato returned home to press a decade of popular insurgency, taking estate lands to make maize to feed families and sustain guerrilla bands. While men fought, women (including muchachas who were now young adults) joined in cultivation to sustain families and communities in a decade of revolution that broke Guanajuato mining and the historic Asian trades it sustained.

Guerrillas fed by insurgent communities ruled the lands around the Guanajuato mines into 1820. Then, exhausted military powers set a pacification that recognized estate property—and family rights to cultivate estate lands. Rico returned from refuge in Querétaro to find commercial cropping gone. Families held strong at Puerto de Nieto, some living as prosperous rancheros, others making sustenance and a bit more. Women were more than 30 percent of leading rancheros, better rancheras, some surely former rebel muchachas. They unsettled patriarchy in a community that made maize to feed families first. With neighbors all around, they remade life in the Bajío.[2]

They also remade world trade. During the decade of revolution, rural insurgents repeatedly invaded Guanajuato. Joined by urban rioters, they sacked mines, shops, and the homes of the wealthy. Mining collapsed, cutting New Spain's silver flows in half by 1812—a devastating 30 percent fall of the global money supply. Historic trades in fine Indian cottons and Chinese silks broke, opening the world to industrial cloth made in English mills using cotton made by enslaved hands in the US South.

By 1820, anonymous insurgents had claimed new lives making maize to sustain families at Puerto de Nieto and across Guanajuato. In their fight, they took down silver production and cut key global trades. They undermined the Spanish regime restored after Napoleon's defeat in 1814, setting the stage for the difficult birth of Mexico as a nation in 1821. And

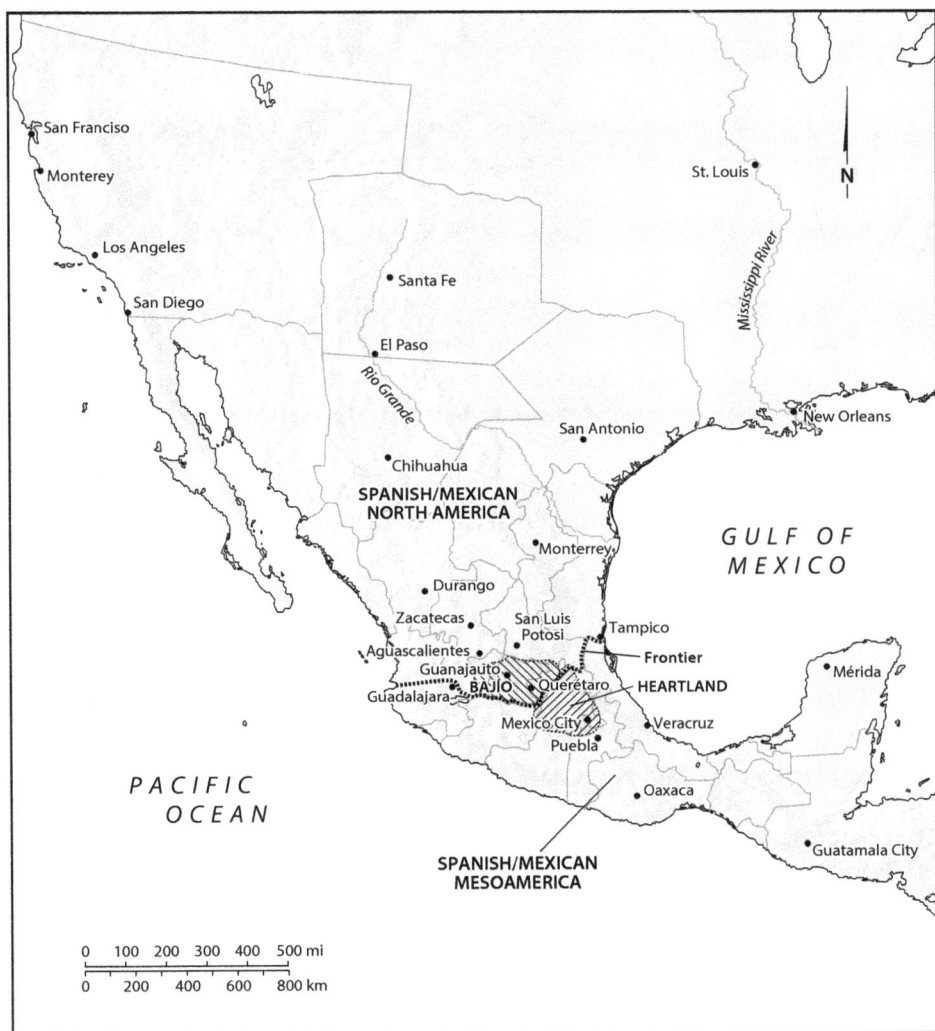

Map P.1 The Bajío and the Mesoamerican heartland, 1550–1880.

they opened the world to a new industrial capitalism drawing women and children to labor in English mills while forcing enslaved hands to plant cotton on US southern lands. Unknown people made a revolution in the Bajío and remade the world. Popular insurgents, men and the women who sustained them, drove a pivotal turning point in Mexican, North American, and world history.

History at the Intersection of
Capital and Sustenance

The Bajío was pivotal to the origins of global capitalism from the sixteenth century. A new world began in the 1550s when the emperor of Ming China declared silver the only money for trade and taxation in the world's largest and richest domain.[3] Half a world away in regions newly claimed by Spain, mines at Taxco and Pachuca near Mexico City, at Guanajuato and Zacatecas to the north (and at Potosí in the Andes), turned to make silver to meet rising Chinese demand. The opening to profit was unprecedented. The challenge was to find producing peoples. Europeans had arrived in the Americas carrying smallpox, plague, typhus, and other diseases unknown in the hemisphere, setting off a great dying among native people without immunities. In the Mesoamerican regions becoming New Spain, nearly 70 percent had died when the stimulus of silver came in the 1550s. The dying neared 90 percent as silver soared after 1600.[4]

Silver promised unimagined profit, while people who might work in mines and make maize for sustenance became scarce. That contradiction defined the origins of New Spain and shaped early capitalism. It reminds us that history is made at the intersections of pursuits of power and profit and necessities of work and sustenance, mediated by social relations of production. Drives to power and debated legitimations have long focused historical visions. Studies of social relations of production emphasize how producing peoples have been drawn to serve power. The ways of sustenance essential to power, production, and life rarely gain primary attention. Yet they are essential to capitalism and regime powers, communities and family life everywhere.[5]

From the 1550s to the 1870s, in New Spain and Mexico, silver drove pursuits of power and profit while maize sustained life. That long history frames the Bajío revolution—and demands a rethinking of the origins and transformations of global capitalism. While silver was pivotal to global capitalism from 1551 to 1873, maize had fed Mesoamerica and much of the Americas long before the rise of silver. It continues to feed Mexico and the world long after silver's demise—in radically changing ways.[6]

For millennia, Mesoamerican families made maize and more to sustain themselves and their communities, while regimes from early Olmecs, through imperial Teotihuacán, to the late-rising Mexica (Aztecs) forged military power backed by religious legitimations to extract the staple as tribute to maintain temple cities, armies, and trades.[7] When Iberians came to the Americas, Mesoamerican ways held through the first decades of Spanish attempts to rule New Spain. Facing depopulation and social dissolution, European power seekers allied with surviving native lords to claim maize and work as tributes from family growers while tributaries and tributes became ever scarcer. Native work gangs were sent to pan for gold—which quickly panned out. For decades after don Fernando Cortés' imagined conquest in 1521, people vanished, power waned, and land became vacant.[8]

The Chinese turn to silver in 1551 brought unprecedented chances to profit in a world opening to global trades. Natives knew silver deposits at Taxco south of Mexico City; they began mining in the 1530s, taking small gains in limited trades. With the Chinese turn, mining accelerated at Taxco and rose at Pachuca, northeast of the capital. But making silver on a global scale required tunneling, milling, and refining to profit. The *patio* process that used mercury to extract silver from midgrade ores was perfected at Pachuca in the 1550s—drawing mercury from mines at Almadén in Spain. Globally integrated extractive and industrial processes required capital, technology, and labor—which was often skilled and always faced risks, whether underground in mines prone to collapse and flooding, in mills that crushed ore and limbs, or in refineries working with poisonous mercury.

Still, in times of pandemic dying, indigenous and mixed men proved ready to take risks to gain unprecedented pay that often included ore shares. European and African newcomers joined native survivors in mining centers and in Mexico City, the capital of finance and trade, administration and justice, religion and education, crafts and more that tied New Spain to rising global trades. The challenge was sustenance. Maize had been made for millennia across Mesoamerica, feeding families, communities, and temple cities. Now, after waves of death, land was open, people were scarce, and survivors had little incentive to make maize to feed mining centers or the rising global city.

Profit seekers and regime builders had to adapt. In the Mesoamerican heartland surrounding Mexico City and the Taxco and Pachuca mines, Spanish officials and clergy worked with native lords to found self-governing indigenous republics granted lands more than sufficient to sustain themselves and make surpluses to feed the capital and the mines. Vacated lands were granted to Spaniards who built estates to raise wheat, sugar, and livestock—staples of European life. Most surviving native families remained in communities, making maize to feed themselves while sending men to labor seasonally at nearby estates, gaining cash making old-world crops in a new commercial economy. Working family land to make maize and estate lands to gain cash, men in reconsolidated Mesoamerican communities sustained surviving families—and a rising silver capitalism.[9]

Just north of the militarized states and maize-making communities of Mesoamerica, the Bajío had remained home to independent peoples who hunted, gathered, and made maize free of state powers before 1520. Then, from the 1550s, in the face of Chinese demand for silver, Spanish profit seekers came north aiming to exploit silver at Guanajuato and Zacatecas beyond, joined by Mesoamerican allies who maligned the region's independent peoples as Chichimecas, sons of dogs. True to their history, Chichimecas mounted decades of guerrilla resistance while diseases drove a dying that all but vacated the basin by the 1590s. As mining took off, Spaniards (and a few Otomí allies) claimed lands to build commercial estates, aiming to profit by feeding mining centers and new textile towns. Mesoamerican commoners came too, some to work in mines and workshops, most to try life on estate lands—where landlords paid ample salaries and guaranteed maize rations to men who labored to make maize and more for estate profit.[10]

Around 1600, New Spain solidified a dynamic silver economy set in two distinct regional ways of making maize. In the Mesoamerican heartland, native survivors kept land to make sustenance in self-governing republics, with men working seasonally for wages at nearby mines and estates. In the Bajío, Mesoamerican migrants became resident laborers on estate lands, gaining secure employment and sustenance to make maize and more in service of growers who profited by feeding mining centers, textile towns, and grazing estates in the basin and across the arid lands stretching north. Two ways of making maize sustained the silver capitalism that fueled global trades after 1600.

In both, hierarchies of patriarchy cemented social relations of production, tying working men to Spanish powers and silver capitalism. In heartland republics, native nobles, nearly always men, ruled local councils and raised maize to supply urban markets; commoners, mostly men, made maize on family plots to sustain household. In addition, local notables, always men, organized labor gangs enabling men and boys to gain wages in estate fields. In the Bajío, landlords, most men plus a few inheriting women, set only men to manage the men who labored as dependents on estate lands. Adult men gained salaries, maize rations, and chances to rent small plots to plant more. Sons gained wages as seasonal hands. Contrasting patriarchal structures locked in men's primacy making and/or gaining the necessities of life.

Still, women were essential producers everywhere: they made and raised children; they labored hours every day to grind maize and make the tortillas essential to meals; they kept gardens and small animals; they made cloth and clothing; they traded in local markets. Women worked endlessly, more than most men, to sustain families and communities—subsidizing estate profits and silver capitalism. Facing scarce producers, profit seekers enabled viable lives among working survivors in two variants, one in independent communities, the other on estate lands—both structured by patriarchy; both sustained by women's endless essential labors.[11]

In parallel yet distinct ways, men and women made maize and more to sustain the silver capitalism that fueled a rising world of commercial capitalism. About a third of Spanish American silver crossed the Pacific to Spanish Manila, where Chinese merchants gained pesos in exchange for fine silks and porcelains and Indian cottons. The rest crossed the Atlantic to Seville, dispersed across Europe and the Islamic world, with a major part flowing to India, where pesos bought the fine printed cotton cloth demanded by African princes and merchants as the price of humans bound into slavery. That silver capitalism sustained by maize boomed to 1640 and carried on in times of recession and still-sparse population to 1680. Then silver soared to new heights while population began to grow, generating rising profits and new pressures on producing families.

In the heartland after 1700, men in self-governing republics made maize to the extent they could while population growth left families with land ever less sufficient to sustenance. To compensate, men increased their seasonal labors at nearby estates that began planting maize to feed mining centers and Mexico City. The maize still made on family lands and the wages of seasonal labor combined to supply women with the essentials to make sustenance. Heartland families became less independent yet remained in landed republics, still negotiating patriarchy within families to keep sustainable lives through the eighteenth-century silver boom.[12] When heartland communities faced rising land and labor conflicts after 1750, they gained mediations in viceregal courts.[13] When Bajío insurgents challenged regime power and silver capitalism after 1810, the people in most heartland communities stayed at home and at work.

In the Bajío, the eighteenth century saw silver soar and population grow while families still lived as estate dependents and gained secure sustenance. Then, from the 1790s, amid imperial wars, landlords cut salaries and maize rations, raised rents, and pressed evictions on tenant families—knowing that new population pressures made them replaceable. Deepening social predations corroded men's access to the necessities of sustenance and threatened women's ability to maintain families across the basin that sustained the world's leading silver mines.[14] Without community rights, estate residents faced landlord power with little access to judicial mediation. The muchachas protested at Puerto de Nieto; others resisted as they could. Most struggled and adapted—frustrated and angry as once secure patriarchal ways of sustenance dissolved.

Then, in 1810, amid imperial wars, regime crisis, and drought-driven scarcities, Hidalgo's political revolt called men to arms to challenge Spanish imperial rule. Seeing power shaken and uncertain, thousands of men across rural Guanajuato took arms to claim maize—and in time, land to make it. In a decade of revolution, they gained estate land for family production while women took new roles making maize to feed families, communities, and guerrillas. Men fighting to restore patriarchy relied on women making maize—rattling patriarchy. With pacification in 1820, family growers, women prominent among them, ruled maize making on estate land. The insurgent men and sustaining women of Puerto de Nieto and estates all around the Guanajuato mines claimed new lives. Family autonomies making maize were the means, goal, and gain of the Bajío revolution.[15] Women's efforts in support of those goals challenged patriarchy. Families gained autonomy making maize while women claimed new participations in production and community life.

In their fight for family rights to make maize, Bajío revolutionaries broke mining at Guanajuato and rattled it across New Spain. China's exports collapsed; and the once dominant global empire became an importer of opium delivered from India by British merchants who drained China's historic stocks of silver. India's exports of fine cottons broke too, opening markets to industrial cloth made in English mills using cotton raised by enslaved hands in the US South.[16] Fighting to gain autonomous lives on the land, Bajío revolutionaries opened the world to an industrial capitalism grounded in slavery.[17]

In that world of change, in 1821 military men who had fought for a decade to contain the Bajío revolution proclaimed an independent Mexican empire.[18] Silver broken, trade fallen, state revenues scarce, and maize makers entrenched on the land, independence brought decades of conflictive politics to an imagined Mexican nation. Without silver, power seekers flailed; with maize, families held strong on the land.

Still, silver remained valuable in the world of early industrial capitalism. British capital came to Mexico in the 1820s, funding a regime without revenues and aiming to revive the mines. Regime debts soared, mines never profited, and British investors retreated. Then, in the 1830s, Bajío capitalists revived mining and built new industries, forging a new silver-industrial capitalism fed by family growers. New possibilities opened for Mexico and Mexicans: capitalists found profit while adapting to families strong on the land; women kept active roles in maize-making families as mining rose to historic heights at Guanajuato in the 1840s and 1850s—led by doña Francisca de Paula Pérez Gálvez.

The silver-industrial capitalism fed by family maize makers prospered in the Bajío through the war that took the lands from Texas to California into the United States in the 1840s. The new Bajío was rattled when battles provoked by the French invasion of the 1860s focused there. Still, the new silver-industrial capitalism grounded in family maize making only broke in 1873—when the United States joined England and Germany on a gold standard, ending silver's role generating capital made in Mexico.

The power of silver as capital in trade was set by imperial China in the 1550s. The United States joined its industrial-imperial allies to break silver's power in the 1870s. Maize makers across Mexico pressed on. Heartland communities faced corrosions of autonomies as populations grew while liberal powers privatized their lands. They joined Emiliano Zapata to drive a second revolution in 1910, gaining land to make maize to sustain families—and a new national industrial capitalism. Then, after 1950, medical capitalism delivered antibiotics that fueled unprecedented population explosions and urban growth, followed by a "green revolution" that made maize with machines and chemicals, driving families off the land. A century after the industrial powers broke the power of silver as capital, a new globalizing capitalism ended family maize making in Mexico and across the world.[19]

Maize, Mesoamerica's great contribution to human sustenance, remains essential—now made by capitalist growers in the United States who profit feeding a world of people crowded in burgeoning cities where they face lives of dependence laced with insecurities. In urbanizing globalizing times, patriarchy, too, has collapsed as a way to sustenance in Mexico and across the world. Yet too many men cling to once-entrenched, long-contested, and now impossible primacies, becoming violently assertive while women struggle to sustain families facing marginality and insecurity. Our world of globalization concentrates power while soaring numbers of women and men search for sustenance in times of social insecurity and proliferating violence.[20]

Bajío revolutionaries remade capitalism in New Spain as it became Mexico. They broke lives of dependence newly laced with insecurities and claimed ways and means for families to make maize to sustain themselves—rattling patriarchy in the effort. They opened the way to a new silver industrial capitalism that would flourish for decades—led by a power-ful woman. Simultaneously, the global reverberations of their revolution opened the world to a new Anglo-American industrial capitalism grounded in slavery that in time would lash back to block Mexico's historic capital independence set in silver—and later turn into a globalization that under-mined family maize making in Mexico and around the world. Knowing the Bajío revolution—locally and globally—is essential to understanding Mexico, the United States, and a world driven by concentrating capitalist powers and fed by capitalist maize.

The Revolution(s) That Remade Global Capitalism

The Bajío revolution remade New Spain as it became Mexico. It rerouted capitalism in North America and the world. Yet it remains unknown. It does not appear in histories of New Spain becoming Mexico, in studies of the Age of Revolution from 1770 to 1850, or in works exploring revolutionary conflicts in world history. Why? Historical studies have long focused on leaders and ideologies—and the popular risings that transformed the Bajío after 1810 produced no recognized or remembered leaders. No ideologues proclaimed grievances or visions for a better future. No leaders or factions emerged to claim roles in the struggles to make a Mexican state that began in 1821.

People in communities on estate lands, like the muchachas and their families at Puerto de Nieto, facing deepening predations in times of imperial war and regime breakdown, took arms in 1810 to press shared visions of justice without plotting or planning. They acted in families and communities, women meeting at home, in fields, and local markets; men entrenched in mountain bastions to ready attacks and avoid retaliation. They fought long and hard, men in guerrilla bands, women in sustaining communities to claim control of maize making to sustain families first—without leaders or manifestos and without a state defining their gains.[1] They did not seek political power or ideological fame while fighting to claim autonomous lives making maize on the land. They succeeded and forced local powers and global capitalists to adapt—to be condemned and then erased from history.

A Revolution Foretold, Documented, Despised, and Erased

There is ample record of their risings. Hidalgo's 1810 political revolt is celebrated by Mexicans as the start of their fight for national independence. His *grito* opened the way to mass rural risings. During four violent months, he dreamed of political rights while struggling to contain his followers' attacks on property. Power holders mobilized in defense of property, crushing the revolt early in 1811. An enduring focus on Hidalgo and his politics has deflected history from the popular risings he unleashed. A close reading of his brief revolt, however, documents the beginnings of a revolution he helped begin and could not contain.[2]

Unlike Hidalgo, Epigmenio González remains all but unknown.[3] A storekeeper with a shop on the plaza across from Querétaro's great Franciscan church, he joined debates in the summer of 1810 led by corregidor (magistrate) don Miguel Domíguez; councilman, merchant, and landlord don Pedro de Septién; and Hidalgo, too—provincial men seeking political rights in times of imperial crisis. While they talked, González wrote a plan to force estates to lease lands to family growers. He would preserve property while delivering production to families—precisely the outcome of revolution in 1820.

Domínguez, Septién, and Hidalgo all rejected González' plan. When viceregal forces broke their debates on September 15, the storekeeper was arrested, his papers confiscated, the plan hidden away through years of insurgency and long after. González had heard laments of evictions and knew the dreams of family planting shared by so many who came to his counter. Arrested before Hidalgo's rising began, González could not join or guide the revolution. He did foresee its goals and outcomes.

Don José Sánchez Espinosa knew everything González knew, and more. A priest and landed oligarch, he cut salaries and rations and pressed the evictions that raised the muchachas' ire at Puerto de Nieto in 1802. He learned from manager Rico's letters that local men took arms with Hidalgo in 1810, taking maize to feed families, and that in 1811 they rose again to forge guerrilla bands. In 1820, the priest-patriarch acquiesced in tenant family production as women kept leading roles in a much less patriarchal community—all documented in Rico's endless letters and detailed accounts.

Meanwhile, Sánchez Espinosa kept production and patriarchy alive at La Griega, east of Querétaro. Parallel letters and accounts detail how his managers first armed a small troop of Hispanic men, then delivered rising salaries, rations, and maize lands to an Otomí majority, keeping the peace, maintaining production, and holding patriarchy by undoing the impositions that provoked insurgency at Puerto de Nieto. After 1820, Sánchez Espinosa tried to revive commercial cropping at La Griega, but with mining collapsed and markets flooded with family maize, profit never returned.

Don José Sánchez Espinosa helped provoke the Bajío revolution, resisted it, and kept records detailing its origins and conflicts, limits and reverberations. His correspondence and accounts detail the rising's popular bases, women's new powers, and enduring social inversions at Puerto de Nieto. They also record the concessions that blocked insurgency at La Griega, and his inability to revive agrarian capitalism at estates famously profitable before 1810.[4] Arguably, the landed priest-patriarch knew the Bajío revolution better than anyone but its popular protagonists. In his efforts to thwart their fights and gains, he documented their struggles and transforming impacts.

Lucas Alamán despised the Bajío revolution. Born in 1792 to a Guanajuato mining family, he lived the fruits of silver capitalism. He avoided the violence of revolution by staying in Europe from 1810 to 1820. Returning to join the efforts to make a Mexican nation, he helped draw British capital to mining in the 1820s, then led Mexico's turn to industry in the 1830s. In the 1840s and 1850s, he saw silver revive at Guanajuato and industry rise at Querétaro while he struggled to forge a national regime set in New Spain's Catholic traditions.

Celebrated or reviled as the father of Mexican conservatism, in the early 1850s Alamán wrote a five-volume *Historia de Méjico*, detailing the conflicts of 1808 to 1824.[5] Honoring the silver riches and Catholic culture of New Spain, he narrated the long struggles that led to Mexican independence. He saw popular insurgents' violence as purely destructive, undermining silver and breaking the trades that made New Spain a kingdom of wealth and power. Taking land to make maize and feed families ate estate profits. Yet as Alamán wrote in the 1850s, Guanajuato silver reached historic heights while industry flourished at Querétaro. Why was he so angry? Surely because the revolutionary turn to family cropping broke the power of the landed oligarchs he admired, longed to join, and expected to back the regime of his dreams.

The Bajío revolution was foretold by González, opened by Hidalgo, recorded by Sánchez Espinosa, and despised by Alamán. In the 1820s, English emissary Henry Ward came to Mexico hoping to revive silver in service of British trade. He recognized the conflicts of 1810 to 1820 as a disruptive revolution and labeled them as such.[6] The social war that remade the Bajío and New Spain was seen as revolutionary in its time—lamented and rejected by the powerful.

Then liberals took control of Mexican politics and intellectual life from the 1850s. They saw no greatness and little good in the Spanish Catholic past honored by Alamán. They would not credit Bajío revolutionaries with breaking Mexico's landed oligarchs, even as their fall facilitated the liberals' rise to power. As free traders linked to British interests, they opposed Alamán's industrial project. The one vision liberals and Alamán shared was that families making maize on the land ate profit. Conservatives and liberals saw Epigmenio González' dream as a nightmare imposed by popular revolutionaries.

Refusing to see the dynamism of the silver economy honored by Alamán and Ward, Mexican liberals blamed an imagined Spanish imposition of a closed, anti-economic society for long difficulties of nation making.[7] Denying the reality of New Spain's dynamic silver capitalism, no revolution breaking its power and remaking the world was imaginable. Liberal myths erased the Bajío revolution.

Anglophone observers versed in black legends of Spanish cruelties easily adopted Mexican liberal visions. There was no need to explain Mexican independence: people powerful and poor fought to escape the horrors of Spanish rule. Then, left incapable by Hispanic Catholic legacies, they could neither rule nor prosper. Fixated on political conflicts, global liberals would not see the new silver-industrial capitalism set in family maize making—the legacy of the Bajío revolution. The revolution imagined by González, opened by Hidalgo, documented by Sánchez Espinosa, recognized by Ward, and despised by Alamán vanished. There was no need to explore how it opened the world to British industry and drove the expansion of slavery in the United States. There could be no call to explain how rising US power later blocked the promise of a Mexican capitalism fed by families making maize on the land.

Bajío insurgents made a revolution within Hispanic capitalism, keeping Catholic cultural ways in all their diversity. They forged new lives on the land, opened new roles for women, forced changes on powers above—and opened markets for capitalists beyond. Their revolution was not political or ideological, not state-made in a state-making world, not secular in a secularizing world. For pushing against that world, the Bajío revolution was fought, denigrated, and erased.

Revolution Silenced, Revolution Erased:
Haiti and the Bajío

The Bajío revolution was not the first rising of people facing deepening predations to break a new-world engine of early global capitalism, claim the land to make family sustenance, and turn the course of history. In 1790, French Saint-Domingue was the leading center of a plantation capitalism still rising across Atlantic America. It generated soaring profits from sugar made by enslaved hands, drawing unprecedented numbers of bound Africans, mostly men, but women too, to brutal labors in cane fields and refining mills. Social predations defined plantation slavery. They deepened as growing numbers of captives taken in African wars came bound to labor in Saint-Domingue.

A long history led to the Haitian Revolution. Europeans first made sugar with bound hands on the Mediterranean islands of Crete and Cyprus, aiming to sustain crusading invasions into lands holy to Muslims and Christians. Crusaders planted cane from East Africa and set Muslim captives taken in marches through the Balkans to labor in fields and mills. Sugar and slavery (the bound workers were Slavs) began to serve European power around 1000. After the Crusades, production spread west along Mediterranean shores where Africans taken in war and sent in caravans across the Sahara labored in bondage. When plantations came to Atlantic islands in the fifteenth century, sugar and slavery served Portuguese planters and Genoese financiers—with bound Africans the primary working hands.[8]

Sugar crossed the Atlantic early in the sixteenth century, planted in small scales on Caribbean islands and in New Spain. It flourished in northeastern Brazil after 1570, again led by Portuguese planters and Genoese financiers. Early on, enslaved Africans came in small numbers, bought for the knowledge of cane cultivation and sugar making gained in Atlantic islands. Native Tupí taken in armed raids were bound to serve as permanent workers. Others living in Jesuit missions fed themselves while laboring seasonally in cane fields. Sugar proved profitable while natives making cane fell to deadly old world diseases. Around 1600, with profits rising and natives dying, Genoese financiers and Portuguese planters turned to buying growing numbers of enslaved Africans to labor in Brazil as coerced sugar makers. The plantation complex reset in slavery proved enduringly profitable in Atlantic America.[9]

The silver capitalism that relied on indigenous producers in Spanish America and the plantation capitalism driving enslaved laborers in Portuguese Brazil rose together from 1580 to 1640 while Hapsburg kings set in Madrid led both Iberian empires. That integration mattered, as silver was essential to sugar and slavery. The African princes and merchants who took captives in war and sold them into slavery demanded South Asian cottons as primary payment, and Indian merchants demanded silver to sell cloth to Europeans. Spanish American silver fueled Portuguese trade during the decades of merged empires. Silver capitalism and plantation capitalism rose together, distinct yet inseparable.

In 1630, Dutch forces invaded northeastern Brazil, challenging Hapsburg power while looking to join sugar and slave trades. In response, Portugal broke with Madrid in 1640 and Brazilians reclaimed the northeast in the 1650s (as the first sugar boom waned). The Dutch then took the capital, machines, and enslaved hands key to sugar capitalism to the Caribbean, first to British Barbados, then to Jamaica.[10] Plantation ways spread northward, leaving rising empires fighting to gain access to the silver still monopolized by Spain and pivotal to the slave trade. The famous Atlantic triangular trades linking Europe, Africa, and the Caribbean were framed and sustained by larger global trades linking Spanish American silver, South Asian cottons, and African slave sellers. Plantation empires and slave traders seeking access to silver fueled wars that escalated after 1750.

After the Seven Years' War of 1757 to 1763 and through the war for US independence, sugar and slavery soared to new heights of profit and predation in British Jamaica and French Saint-Domingue. In both, the enslaved exceeded 90 percent of the population; in both, new racial restrictions limited the chances of free people of color. There were differences too: Jamaica remained focused on sugar while Saint-Domingue added coffee and cotton; in Jamaica, free men of African ancestry were blocked from roles as landed slaveholders, while in Saint-Domingue the *affranchi* might prosper, often making coffee on modest plantations.[11] Meanwhile, in times of war and peace, access to New Spain's silver remained essential to the rising slave trades that dragged growing numbers of captured African warriors to Caribbean plantations. Britain and France competed over access to silver and Indian cottons, ultimately increasing the debts that broke the French monarchy and opened the way to revolution in Paris and soon in Saint-Domingue.[12]

Dynamic growth drove predations that set deepening grievances upon the enslaved in both Jamaica and Saint-Domingue. Regime breakdown only came to Paris. And that breakdown opened the way to revolutionary risings in the French colony—with the *affranchi*, unique to Saint-Domingue, key actors demanding rights. In 1791, amid the early conflicts of the French Revolution, declarations of rights ricocheted across Saint-Domingue. On rich northern plains, groups of the enslaved took arms to fight for freedom. When Paris assemblies offered rights to French men in Saint-Domingue, French planters aimed to monopolize new participations. When *affranchi* planters claimed the same rights, they armed enslaved Africans, offering limited freedom to men who might serve their masters' power. As conflicts spread, growing numbers turned on masters to make fights over rights as Frenchmen a war for rights as men. Through years of conflict, the enslaved fought for freedom—and the right to make sustenance on the land: "Throughout the colony, a new kind of life was taking root, one based on independence and subsistence, one that for many ex-slaves embodied true freedom."[13] Production for family sustenance on the land became the means, goal, and gain of Haitian revolutionaries.

As Haiti became an independent Black nation in 1804, armed ex-slaves built lives of family sustenance on former plantation lands. Liberators who proclaimed freedom yet pressed freedmen to return to labor as sugar workers, from the agents of revolutionary France to the once-enslaved Toussaint L'Ouverture, could not sustain power. State builders saw exports as essential to state revenues; former enslaved people saw freedom as incomplete without lives making sustenance on the land. Armed ex-slaves had their way. They broke plantation production to set families on the land, joined by women who refused to return to cane fields and sugar mills.[14]

Saint-Domingue was the Americas' leading buyer of bound people and exporter of sugar, coffee, and cotton. In independent Haiti, families turned to making sustenance on the land, some raising coffee as a complement. Rejecting Haitians' self-liberation and destruction of plantations and trades, the Atlantic powers isolated the Black nation—while sugar and slavery boomed in Cuba, coffee and slavery remade Brazil, and cotton and slavery expanded to shape the United States.

The reverberations of Haiti's revolution came in a different way to New Spain. Saint-Domingue and its revenues lost, in May 1808 Napoleon invaded Spain, aiming to claim the silver flows still rising in New Spain. He captured Madrid and its Bourbon monarchs, breaking Spain's imperial regime.[15] He failed to gain New Spain's silver and faced guerrilla resistance in Spain that corroded his power in Europe.[16] Without a legitimate monarch in Madrid, political debates consumed Mexico City until a September military coup toppled the viceroy to ensure that silver kept flowing to fight Napoleon in Spain. Mining boomed for two more years while drought-driven profiteering in scarce maize deepened outage in families facing predations across New Spain.[17]

As in Saint-Domingue two decades earlier, imperial breakdown and social predations merged to provoke the revolution that exploded in 1810 in the Bajío. There, free, often ethnically mixed people made silver, cloth, and maize as dependent producers. Now, in times of surging silver, imperial war, and the Haitian Revolution, new predations assaulted patriarchal ways of sustenance, driving the 1810 insurgency that broke silver capitalism and claimed family production on estate lands by 1820.

The sequential revolutions that broke commercial cultivation and entrenched family production in Saint-Domingue and the Bajío from 1790 to 1820 illuminate pivotal processes and key tensions in the rise of global capitalism. Long ago, Fernand Braudel emphasized the dominant trajectory that shaped the long course of capitalism: profit-seeking powers concentrated capital and wealth by linking diverse producing and consuming peoples across an ever more integrated world of trade. Early on, dispersed centers of production and nodes of trade were sustained locally by families and communities on the land: rice growers in China and South Asia; maize makers across the mainland Americas; wheat and meat makers in Europe. In early commercial capitalism, a world of profit and trade was fed by family growers who produced for sustenance and took small gains from the commercializing world they fed.[18] Then, during centuries of change, capitalist powers drew growing numbers across the globe to lives of dependent production in service of profit and trade. Before 1800, such lives remained exceptional, even in Europe. They became more prevalent in the nineteenth-century industrial world—and the norm in our times of globalizing urbanization.

Plantation America and the Bajío developed as precocious historic exceptions—in radically different ways. Both profited by building lives of laboring dependence, the former mobilizing the coercions of slavery, the latter drawing producers to lives of commercial dependence. Then, when dependent people pivotal to capitalist power faced deepening predations after 1780, enslaved producers in Saint-Domingue and commercial dependents in the Bajío took arms to claim autonomies on the land. Their revolutions broke engines of early global capitalism and built communities making sustenance on the land. They turned the course of capitalism—without derailing its long-term rise.

The end of slavery and plantation production in Haiti opened the way for their expansions in Cuba, Brazil, and the southern United States—all supporting the rise of the industrial capitalism emerging in England and the northern United States. A decade later, the fall of silver in the Bajío opened global markets to Anglo-American industrial textiles. New Spain's silver gone, Chinese exports collapsed and the South Asian cottons historically bought with silver and sold in Africa to buy people enslaved to work on Atlantic plantations fell to British industrial cloth made of cotton raised by soaring numbers of enslaved hands in the US South.[19] The ultimate sign of Asia's fall: China's stores of silver were drained by British merchants who delivered opium from India to people facing imperial collapse.[20]

In unimagined and unintended ways, the revolutionaries who broke plantation capitalism in Haiti and silver capitalism in the Bajío opened the world to new industrial powers drawing women and children to mechanized mills—and enslaved men and women to labor across the Americas.[21]

One global trade held. Rattled by the scarcity of silver, the Atlantic slave trade fell 17 percent in the decade beginning in 1811, saving perhaps 140,000 Africans from bondage and transport to New World plantations—another gain delivered by Bajío revolutionaries. The international trade in bound humans rebounded in the 1820s, nearing the peaks set before the Haitian Revolution.[22] As machine-made cottons flowed to Africa to pay for enslaved people, trade in humans revived, despite British and US treaties calling for its demise. Rising numbers of Africans were dragged to Cuba and Brazil while a burgeoning internal trade sent hundreds of thousands from the Chesapeake to the cotton South. People sold in bondage neared a historic peak, an old predation sustaining a new industrial capitalism.

The Haitian Revolution was long known for its assault on slavery yet "silenced" in mainstream histories.[23] The Bajío revolution remains unknown, erased from history. There were complex reasons for the silencing and the erasure. But ultimately, historians and citizens have refused to see that popular revolutionaries fighting to end predatory dependencies and build lives of family autonomy on the land turned the course of history after 1790. Recent scholars have detailed the popular bases and radical outcomes of the Haitian Revolution at home and the spread of plantation slavery in its wake. It is time to recognize the anonymous people who made the Bajío revolution, claimed new lives on the land, broke silver-driven global trades, and opened the world to an industrial capitalism set in expansions of plantation slavery.

People Making Revolution—and Remaking Capitalism

Revolutionaries without leaders, without ideologies, and without aspirations to power are not easy objects of study. Transformations forced from below without formal plan or regime sanction often seem lost in chaos or a result of chaos. Yet recovering the lives and actions of anonymous revolutionaries and the changes they forced without a plan, yet with clear logic, brings new historical understanding. Pervasive presumptions of the dominance of power holders and power seekers become untenable as histories as contested and negotiated between powerful and producing peoples, men and women, come to the fore.[24]

The pursuit of such understanding requires a search for everyday people: the men and women who took the risks of fighting to gain and maintain sustainable lives—and their neighbors who stood aside to negotiate in less violent and risky ways. In the search, power holders imposing predations and struggling to keep land, profits, and eminence appear in new light. So do global actors turning Mexico's challenges to their own advantage. The Bajío revolution opens histories in which the people act and the powerful react. The sources that reveal the lives and goals of each group differ, yet they intersect to reveal contested power relations and complex histories often laden with contradictions.

The lives of producing people and insurgent communities often appear only in fragments—in land records and estate accounts, in managers' letters and reports of counterinsurgency commanders, in state builders' archives and census counts, in ideologues' visions and economic promoters' plans. More detailed if skeletal histories of laboring lives and maize-making families can be reconstructed from the accounts of work and rents kept at Sánchez Espinosa's Bajío estates. Notably, the sources that open glimpses of producing peoples' lives also reveal state makers' and profit seekers' struggles.

The fragmented sources that open the lives of the people who drove the Bajío revolution and shaped its outcomes are complemented by narratives written from perspectives of power. In the 1820s, US emissary Joel Robert Poinsett and British diplomat Henry Ward came to Mexico with outsiders' eyes—and hopes of turning Mexican challenges to US and British advantage.[25] They had much to learn and wrote detailed reports easily recognized as prejudiced. Yet read in the context of the conflicts between the people who made a revolution and power seekers struggling to contain its transformations, the outsiders illuminate key Mexican challenges.

In the late 1830s, Frances "Fanny" Calderón de la Barca, Scottish wife of Spain's first ambassador to Mexico, came to live among the women of Mexico City's struggling oligarchy. She recorded their attempts to keep eminence alive with eyes sympathetic to power, wary of the people, and open to women's assertions. She joined in private engagements and public encounters that reveal much about insecure socialites, assertive crowds, and women's will to endure.[26]

Then, in the 1850s, two Mexican political intellectuals, the liberal Guillermo Prieto and the cleric José Guadalupe Romero, detailed life in the Bajío as the new silver-industrial capitalism peaked and began to face challenges.[27] Lucas Alamán sent Prieto to exile in conservative Querétaro, where the liberal's opposition to industry and Catholicism made him almost as much an outsider as the Anglophone visitors of the 1820s. A cathedral canon, Romero detailed life in his home state of Guanajuato, where deeply religious peoples had made a revolution, built new lives on the land, and sustained a new capitalism driven by silver and generating new industries. He honored Catholic Guanajuato and resented liberal intrusions. Both showed their prejudices— yet read in the light of local power struggles, changing economic trajectories, and the lives of the people who sustained everything, they illuminate the Bajío remade in revolution.

The protagonists of the Bajío revolution long remained anonymous, seen only in fragmentary records of productive lives and rebellious acts, condemned by those they threatened, deposed, and forced to adapt. The analysis that follows relies on critical engagements with distinct and often contradictory sources to uncover the lives, reconstruct the struggles, and reveal the transformations driven by the unknown people who made the revolution that transformed New Spain as it became Mexico—and turned the course of global capitalism.

This history recognizes and insists that capitalism is as much about people as about ways and means of power. The chapters that follow focus on reconstructing peoples' lives. Too often, we only know the women and men who worked to sustain capitalism and then forced it to change in fragments. But by seeking out those fragments in diverse records—estate accounts and amnesty lists, property records, censuses, and more—we can reconstruct revealing patterns. People in-between—estate managers, counterinsurgent commanders, clergy, and more—set to serve the powerful, yet dealing daily with producing people, insurgents, and people making new lives generated letters and reports that revealed their own lives, the goals and actions of those they aimed to manage or control, and the long struggles and adaptations that led to revolutionary outcomes. Power holders—people seeking power, people clinging to power, and others living among them, men and women—generated private letters, detailed accounts, and published texts that reveal their goals, their adaptations to people pressing from below, and their struggles in times of regional conflicts, national challenges, and global reconstructions.

Over centuries, powerful people, producing people, and people in-between built a dynamic silver capitalism, locked together in productive inequality as profit seekers negotiated to deliver lives of patriarchal security to scarce producers on rich Bajío basin lands. When that scarcity waned after 1790 in times of imperial wars and silver boom, profit seekers pressed new predations that undermined producers' lives, setting off conflicts in 1810 as producing men and women mobilized to take control of production for family sustenance. They forced the powerful to adapt—and opened the world to a rising industrial capitalism grounded in enslaved labor. In the wake of the Bajío revolution, producers entrenched on the land forced Mexican nation builders to adapt. From the 1830s, they jostled to build a new silver-industrial capitalism sustained by family maize makers—until the imperial capitalism built on industry and slavery in the United States lashed back to block its way forward.

A People's History of the Bajío Revolution—and Global Capitalism: A Preview

Exploration of the Bajío revolution must begin with an understanding of the region's pivotal role in founding global commercial capitalism, the goal of part I. Chapter 1 introduces the ecology of the Bajío, it's Otomí-Spanish foundations before 1550, and the changes that began with China's turn to silver in the 1550s: Europeans opened mines at Guanajuato and built estates across the basin, dragging Africans to serve while Mesoamericans came to work the land.

Two Bajíos rose: greater Querétaro remained deeply Otomí as European merchants, estate builders, and manufacturers joined Otomí magistrates, landlords, and cultivators to forge a bicultural society that shaped the southeastern Bajío. Just west around Guanajuato, Spanish power ruled upland mines and estates built on basin lands. There, landlords set enslaved African minorities among Mesoamerican majorities, leading in time to free amalgamating communities. To 1760, silver promised profit while people held scarce, enabling the Querétaro Otomí and the amalgamating people around Guanajuato to gain solid earnings, maize rations, and access to land in patriarchal ways of commercial production while women worked to sustain families, communities—and the mines that fueled global trades.

Chapter 2 turns to the imperial challenges, silver dynamism, and population pressures that merged to generate the predations that would drive the risings of 1810. It examines the imperial impositions that led to local riots at Guanajuato in 1766 and 1767. It follows the revival of silver in the 1770s and the challenges of sustenance that came with the deadly drought and famine of 1785 and 1786. It focuses on the predations imposed on estate communities after 1790 as silver drove to new peaks in times of population growth, imperial war, and Haitian revolution. From 1800, revenue demands set new pressures on mine operators and estate owners. Then, in 1808, Napoleon broke the empire at its center, setting off political debates that rattled Mexico City while silver drove to peaks and drought, famine, and profiteering in maize fueled popular outrage, setting the stage for revolution.

Part II explores the decade of revolution. Chapter 3 details the origins, contradictions, and collapse of the Hidalgo revolt. It began in political debates at Querétaro in the summer of 1810. Talk of political rights rose as Epigmenio González dreamed of redistributions. Fears of popular risings stymied political action—until Hidalgo called his parishioners at Dolores took arms on September 16. He demanded political rights—to see thousands of men raise machetes to assault landed power. Hidalgo's revolt was marked by contradictions: leaders demanding political autonomy defended property while hungry and angry insurgents sacked estates, claimed food, and pressed for family autonomies.

Hidalgo's rebels sacked Guanajuato, taking silver and maize in the siege of the Alhóndiga. They marched to the edge of Mexico City—to face indifference among people in landed republics. Rebels retreated to sack Guanajuato again, then assembled west around Guadalajara. As Hidalgo defended property and refused popular demands for redistribution, the revolt broke at Puente de Calderón early in 1811. The rising he began shook viceregal power and silver capitalism—and fell to united defenders of power, property, and silver capitalism. Revolution had just begun.

Chapter 4 looks to the heart of the Bajío revolution. Many among Hidalgo's base, including men from Puerto de Nieto, returned home to take control of estate lands and join guerrilla bands while women sustained the fight by taking new roles in production and community life. Rebels again invaded Guanajuato, joining locals to sack mines and stores. As production fell and profit vanished, the mines turned to *buscones*, independent workers who sold ore to bidding refiners. Rural commanders reported endless chases, rarely able to contain guerrillas fed by rebel communities. Silver capitalism broke by 1812; agrarian capitalism dissolved as production to sustain families and insurgents ruled basin lands.

Insurgents carried on while the 1812 Cádiz constitution offered liberal political rights. They continued after Fernando VII reclaimed power in 1814 and blocked those rights. They fought through 1817, when Spanish liberal Francisco Javier Mina invaded with a gang of US freebooters declaring liberty, seeking silver, and disrupting insurgency and counterinsurgency. In 1818, regime forces saw the impossibility of victory and turned to pacifying amnesties that granted insurgents rights to cultivate estate lands as tenants—and keep arms to defend their gains. Amnesty lists detail settlements across Guanajuato; accounts from Puerto de Nieto in 1820 reveal gendered social outcomes. Commercial cropping gone, tenants paid rents to plant maize while women remained leading growers. Silver capitalism and agrarian capitalism collapsed—and patriarchy was shaken.

While insurgents remade Guanajuato, their neighbors around Querétaro stayed at home and at work. Chapter 5 explores how Spanish-Otomí divisions and material concessions inhibited revolt at La Griega. An estate troop kept local order while managers delivered rising incomes and maize rations and new access to land to keep men at work. Spanish and Otomí families first regained secure sustenance, then lands to plant in hierarchies of tenant production, gaining autonomies while restoring the patriarchal dependencies that kept women at sustaining labors. For a decade, a mix of estate cropping and family maize making funded counterinsurgency—at costs that blocked profit. Then, with pacification in 1820, the estate cut back on secure employment and tenant cropping while agrarian capitalism failed to revive.

Facing insurgents pressing existential threats to property and profit, Mexico City oligarchs mobilized. Chapter 6 details efforts that blocked political rebels, preserved property—yet could not save silver capitalism. Don José Sánchez Espinosa backed don Juan Nepomuceno Oviedo, manager of his grazing estates north of the Bajío, to fight Hidalgo and then chase José María Morelos—until Oviedo gave his life blocking the political rebel's route to the capital in 1812. The priest-patriarch then set his son, the Conde de Peñasco, to lead troops defending the regime, first near the capital, then north in San Luis Potosí. Father and son preserved property by fighting insurgents and conceding production to working families. Profit stayed scarce.

Other oligarchs led parallel efforts. Doña María Josefa de Velasco y Ovando set her manager at Tulancalco, between the capital and the Real del Monte mines, to resist insurgents. The Conde de la Cortina raised a troop at nearby Tlahuelilpan to chase insurgents into 1816. Property held while profit vanished. The widowed Condesa de Regla, with great mines at Real del Monte and vast estates stretching north from the capital, set men and resources to defend the regime and family properties through the decade of insurgency. She, too, kept property while profit dissolved and debts mounted.

Bajío revolutionaries cut New Spain's silver flows in half by 1812, breaking global trades while opening markets for industrial England, driving cotton and slavery across the US South. A new industrial capitalism began while the fall of silver and agrarian capitalism left the future of New Spain uncertain as families consolidated lives of autonomy making maize on the land—changes consolidated as pacification came to the Bajío in 1820.

Then, military commanders in Spain refused to sail to defend the empire in South America until Fernando VII restored the liberal Constitution of 1812.[28] Opposed to the restoration, royalist commander don Agustin de Iturbide, famous for defeating Morelos and brutalizing popular insurgents across the Bajío, called struggling elites to oppose the return to liberal rule. He allied with surviving political insurgent Vicente Guerrero in the Iguala rising that broke with Spain and proclaimed a Mexican empire in 1821. Military forces imposed an imagined new polity while silver and regime revenues were scarce—and families held strong on the land.

Part III turns to the challenges faced by people proclaimed Mexicans in the new world of Anglo-American industrial capitalism and Mexican nation making that came in the wake of the Bajío revolution. Chapter 7 explores the difficulties faced by the political few as they attempted to found a Mexican empire in 1821, then a Federal Republic in 1824. Silver and state revenues held low while military powers and costs stayed strong, foundational challenges reported by Poinsett. Nation builders invited British capital to fund the republic while profit seekers drew British partners aiming to revive mining at Guanajuato and beyond. The linked efforts failed, as Ward detailed. He learned to appreciate the dynamism of silver capitalism before 1810, saw the challenges left by the decade of revolution, and came to understand how British capital imposed costs and rigidities that blocked profit as mines struggled to revive. In the end, British loans created soaring debts that drained state revenues while mines slowly increased production—without yielding profit. Economic collapse fueled political instabilities. There would be no quick revival of silver capitalism.

Meanwhile, families entrenched on the land in the new State of Guanajuato carried on making maize, consolidating autonomies, and limiting patriarchy—the gains of insurgency. Chapter 8 returns to Puerto de Nieto in the 1820s as a growing tenant community mixed prosperous rancheros and families making solid sustenance, paying modest rents when they could, refusing when crops failed. Women remained leading tenants, often overshadowing male kin. The community made in insurgency held strong while church and state faced new challenges. Some clergy saw impudent worshippers; a "ranchero" priest adapted to local devotions to serve Puerto de Nieto and nearby communities. The first governor of Guanajuato, unable to revive mining or commercial planting, complained of ignorant and re-calcitrant people—and insubordinate women.

As silver held low, agrarian capitalism gave way to family production in widening regions of the new Mexican nation. Chapter 9 focuses on the emerging State of Querétaro, a commercial, textile, and agricultural region pivotal to silver capitalism before 1810, where insurgency was limited after 1810 and where the fall of silver led to a consolidation of family cultivation in the 1820s.

Landlord distress spread across Querétaro while Sánchez Espinosa and his managers tried and failed to revive agrarian capitalism at La Griega. Profit gone, debts rose as many leased out properties seeking income that rarely came. Lead leaseholders struggled too, while family growers, Hispanic and Otomí, made maize as tenants, sharecroppers, and squatters. Census reports from 1826 show family cropping spreading across Querétaro. After Sánchez Espinosa's death in 1827, La Griega, too, turned to tenant produc-tion, favoring Hispanics and displacing Otomí—many of whom found new lives at nearby estates welcoming family growers. The family maize making claimed by insurgents across Guanajuato before 1820 ruled rural Querétaro by 1830—where, without insurgency, patriarchy held stronger.

With family growers dominant in Guanajuato and taking root across Querétaro in the 1820s, people long dependent on estate power in regions north and south pressed for parallel gains. With silver slow to revive and families feeding themselves and selling surpluses at low prices, oligarchs tried to resist, repeatedly failed—often challenged within by insistent women, as chapter 10 details. After his father's death in 1827, the Conde de Peñasco was the leading landed proprietor in San Luis Potosí. He flailed as families took control of cultivation and grazing on his lands, leading his wife to insult his efforts and challenge his power. When later attempts to revive profits at pulque estates between the capital and the Real del Monte mines failed in the face of resistant communities, a second wife took con-trol, aiming to limit losses—with limited success. Frances Calderón de la Barca saw Peñasco's new bride as crass and scheming; she reported Cortina and Adalid women as nobly struggling; she honored Fagoaga women for keeping estates prosperous while doing charitable work among the urban poor—notable exceptions in times of oligarchic decline.

Into the 1830s, silver struggled while the family cultivation long en-trenched in the heartland took hold across the Bajío and regions north. Upon that base, Mexican capitalists revived silver and built new industries, forced to adapt to family growers—the enduring triumph of Bajío revolutionaries. The new postrevolutionary capitalism sustained by family maize makers focuses part IV.

Chapter 11 begins with the resurgence of mining at Guanajuato, led by don Juan de Dios Pérez Gálvez and his widowed sister doña Francisca de Paula, heirs to the once-rich Valenciana mines that had flooded as insurgency ended in 1820. In the 1830s, they raised capital locally to drain tunnels, gaining silver to fund a bonanza that came high above at La Luz in the early 1840s. New industries also began in the 1830s, promoted by Lucas Alamán and the Banco de Avío, the world's first development bank. Cayetano Rubio took capital from trade in silver to build Hércules at Querétaro, a great cotton mill drawing women to its machines. Meanwhile, ranchero and tenant growers fed families, mining centers, and industries while estates faced enduring debts, scarce profits, and fragmenting operations. Into the 1840s, mining revived and industry began, landlords struggled and families made maize on the land to sustain themselves and a new, more socially distributive capitalism.

The new Bajío flourished from 1845 to 1860, as chapter 12 details. Mining, industry, and family growers thrived during the war provoked by the United States in 1846. Invading armies never neared the basin as national authorities took refuge at Querétaro to gain revenues in Mexico's richest region. After the war, mining soared to new heights in the 1850s, led by doña Francisca de Paula Pérez Gálvez (her brother died in 1848). At her funeral in the 1860s, father Ignacio Montes de Oca, kin of the governor who condemned assertive women in the 1820s, credited her with reviving Guanajuato's mines—and Mexico's economy. Meanwhile, industry consolidated at Querétaro and spread across the Bajío while landed proprietors flailed—and family growers ruled on the land.

In 1853, Guillermo Prieto came to Querétaro, exiled by Antonio López de Santa Anna and Lucas Alamán. The liberal expected to see tradition set in exploitation. He met industrial dynamism, commercial lives, and Otomí family *huertas* (urban gardens). He praised rancheros—and saw their wives rule family finance. Awed by the plenty made and sold by family growers, Hispanic and indigenous, he lamented their diverse devotions. Then, in 1860, don José Guadalupe Romero surveyed life across Guanajuato. The cleric honored mining and lamented raucous lives at La Luz, then detailed production and worship across the basin. Families made maize everywhere; *huertas* blossomed where water permitted. Plenty reigned to sustain popular devotions often led by women. The liberal Prieto and the clerical Romero confirmed that the silver-industrial capitalism fed by family growers flourished through the 1850s.

It would not hold. The conclusion outlines how the global industrial capitalism enabled by Bajío revolutionaries struck back to break the new Mexico. While silver rose to new heights, industry spread, and family cropping held strong in the Bajío and beyond, the US invasion of 1846 took vast lands to forge an American West, blocking any resumption of the northward drive that marked silver capitalism before 1810. Taking Texas opened lands to the cotton and slavery that sustained British and US industries. Taking California gave the United States gold—capital to drive a capitalism less dependent on silver.

None of that inhibited the rise of the new Bajío before 1860. Still, conflicts fueled by the US incursion led to political wars that brought liberals to power in Mexico in 1860, while debates over the incorporation of once Mexican territories with or without slavery led the United States to Civil War in 1861. During that conflict, Mexican conservatives invited Napoleon III to mount the invasion that brought Maximilian of Hapsburg to an imagined Mexican Empire from 1864 to 1867. French forces and the emperor saw the silver-industrial wealth of the Bajío as essential to rule. They pressed battles to take Guanajuato during 1864 and 1865, breaking the dynamism of silver while troops took maize from family growers in years of drought, driving a crisis of sustenance. Then, in 1867, the fight to restore Mexican liberal rule brought a long siege to Querétaro, rattling industry, commerce, and life there.

Yet while the Bajío faced war, silver-industrial capitalism had spread across Mexico: silver peaked nationally while industry held across wide regions as liberals retook power in 1867. The Mexico forged by the Bajío revolution, shaken in its homeland, seemed poised to revive nationally. Then, in 1873, the United States—funded by gold mined in lands taken from Mexico—joined England and Germany on a gold standard. Radically devaluing silver, the leading industrial powers ended Mexico's capital independence. The capitalism financed by silver, energized by industry, and fed by family maize makers collapsed.

The epilogue outlines the challenges Mexicans faced after the fall of silver. With independent capital gone, family maize makers pressed to carry on in the face of new challenges. US capital and markets shaped Mexico's prospects, limiting industry and favoring exports. Liberal rulers pressed land privatizations as the population grew, corroding family cultivation. A second revolution began in 1910, leading to an experiment in national-industrial capitalism reset in patriarchal family maize making. It held strong amid depression in the 1930s—and supported the United States in World War II.

Then, in a postwar, Cold War world, US pharmaceutical capitalism delivered antibiotics that saved generations of Mexican children, unleashing a population explosion fed by "green revolution" maize made by machines and chemicals. Families pressed off the land faced urban lives marked by poverty and insecurity while migrants sought new lives *al norte* in lands once Mexican. Mexicans everywhere now live dependent on maize made by capital, machines, and chemicals in the United States.[29]

Our world has no memory of the laboring people who long sustained silver capitalism across the Bajío, faced assaultive predations from the 1790s, took arms to claim family sustenance in 1810—and made a revolution that turned the course of their own lives and global capitalism. Still, the dreams of family autonomy, challenges to patriarchy, and struggles to keep communities strong that drove the Bajío revolution shaped a new Mexican capitalism and set off global transformations.

We need histories that break the silencing, erasures, and deflecting concepts that mask and legitimate power. We need histories that link global capitalisms and changing regimes, their regional powers and local predations. We need histories that seek out the adaptations and negotiations, rebellions and revolutions that have made producing people, men and women, pivotal and at times powerful in struggles that have remade local lives, turned the powers that constrained them, and shaped the course of history. And we need to know the lives of autonomy that Bajío revolutionaries fought to claim, worked to sustain, and ultimately lost. Only then will we understand the world of dependencies that globalizing capitalism ultimately made.

PART I

Making Silver Capitalism,
1500–1810

1.

A New World in the Bajío

Silver, Capitalism, and Patriarchy,
1550–1760

A new world began in the Bajío in the 1550s. As disease devastated the Americas and China made silver the primary money in a rising world of trade, the fertile basin saw its original peoples erased by death and displacement as it became a place of capitalist promise marked by economic dynamism, cultural amalgamations, and patriarchal ways.[1] Capitalists took profit from mines, textile workshops, and commercial estates worked by diverse peoples drawn to the basin. Europeans pursued profit and power. Africans came bound to serve. And diverse Mesoamericans migrated north seeking new chances on the land—to find lives of secure patriarchal dependence.

Silver soared to 1640, stabilized to 1680, then rose again as the population began to grow. The Bajío economy of mining, textiles, and commercial cultivation held strong and productive stability marked everyday lives for two centuries. Then imperial demands brought conflicts that rattled the mining center of Guanajuato in the 1760s, followed by population pressures and social predations that assaulted patriarchal ways of work and sustenance on the land from the 1780s. An exploration of the founding centuries of silver dynamism and social stability in the Bajío is essential to understand the late eighteenth-century challenges that brought the region to revolution in 1810.

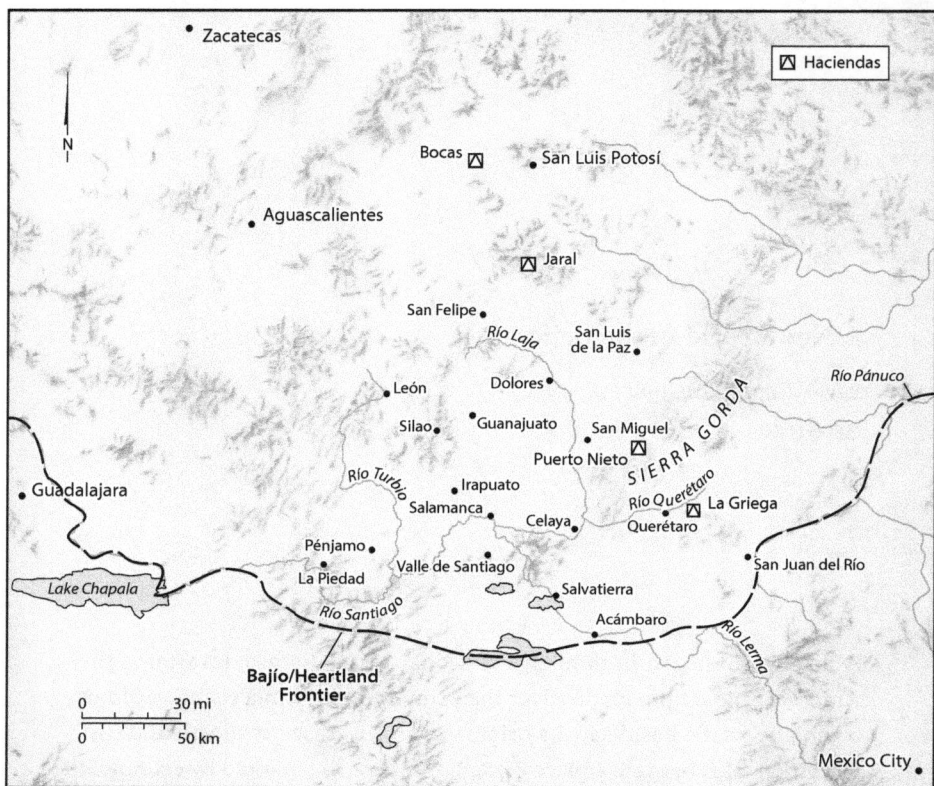

Map 1.1 The Bajío in New Spain.

Contested Foundations, 1520–1600

The Bajío begins around the city of Querétaro, 200 kilometers northwest of Mexico City, to extend a similar distance west across the modern state of Guanajuato. Set between sierras that rise on both coasts, its rich lands lie below 6,000 feet, watered by multiple rivers. The name Bajío, literally the depression, marks the contrast that struck travelers from the south as they descended into a lower, warmer, and wetter place. Around Mexico City the valleys are high, cool, and dry, ranging from 7,000 to 9,000 feet; north of the Bajío aridity rules as rains and rivers are scarce. The Bajío promised to sustain life.

Before Europeans came, the basin was home to sparse, state-free, and mobile peoples: Jonaces and Pames, Guamaraes and Guachichiles, lumped together and maligned by the Mexica (Aztecs) as Chichimecas—sons of dogs. They hunted deer and more, gathered fruits of the land, and cultivated maize, too, blocking the northward expansion of Mexica and Tarascan states, warring Mesoamerican regimes built on sedentary cultivating communities and dreaming of imperial hegemony—like the European societies of the time. In 1500, the Bajío was doubly distinct: a basin of rich agricultural potential, it was occupied by state-free, independent peoples.[2]

The new Bajío began soon after Iberians came to Mesoamerica. After smallpox struck the Mexica capital at Tenochtitlan in 1520, it fell to Cortés and his Tlaxcalan allies in 1521. In its first deadly wave, the disease devastated centers of power and production while spreading outward in community contacts, market visits, and long-distance trades. In the Mesoamerican core, about half of everyone was infected and two-thirds of the infected died: lords and commoners, commanders and warriors, priests and worshippers, men and women, adults and children. Equally devastating, smallpox assaulted prevailing truths. Established gods did not protect or cure. Survivors struggled to carry on, making maize while old truths crumbled and newcomers claimed power and promoted a new God.[3]

Amid the devastation, Otomí lords and cultivators living north of the Mexica capital looked to escape disease and powers in disarray. Connín, a noble merchant from Xilotepec who had traded in Chichimeca country, recruited settlers to trek north accompanied by a few Franciscans. No Spanish force was involved. The newcomers settled where the Amazcala River exited its canyon to water the expanding Bajío plain, founding Querétaro by the early 1530s.[4]

Connín ruled the rise of Querétaro as an Otomí-Christian community. He distributed land along the river to Otomí families who built irrigated urban *huertas*. They raised maize, frijol, chile, and other native staples, soon adding citrus and other old-world fruits and vegetables brought by Franciscans. Connín, soon baptized as don Fernando de Tapia, and other native lords claimed outlying lands to raise wheat and graze livestock, also old-world imports. They built a mill to grind wheat, adding bread to tortillas in local diets; they sent flour, hides, and wool south to Mexico City.

Querétaro thus began as an Otomí-Franciscan-Christian-cultivating-commercial community. It anchored the northern frontier of New Spain when, in 1546, native guides trekking with Spanish warrior-entrepreneurs across dry uplands north of the Bajío revealed silver deposits at Zacatecas. Parallel encounters led to silver in 1554 at Guanajuato, in mountains rising above the basin lands west of Querétaro. Between the "discoveries," in 1551 imperial China made silver the preeminent money in Asia-linked global trades.[5]

Mining took off first at Potosí, in Andean domains long under Inca rule, and at Taxco and Pachuca, in the Mesoamerican heartland around Mexico City. In both regions, silver production latched onto reconstituted indigenous communities to draw labor and sustenance—drafted by native lords in the Andes; negotiated by community leaders in New Spain.[6] In the 1570s, regular fleets began to deliver silver from Acapulco to Manila, traded to Chinese merchants for the silks and porcelains of China, spices from Southeast Asia, and South Asian cottons. Over time the Manila galleons sent about a third of Spanish America's silver directly to Asia. The rest went to Spain, where Genoese and other Italian merchants fed silver to markets across Europe, through the Middle East, and on to South Asia and China. Spanish American silver rose to drive global trades before 1600.[7]

Silver began slowly in the Bajío as independent Chichimecas fought to defend homelands from newcomers surging north. Europeans learned what Mesoamericans knew: Pames, Jonaces, Guamaraes, and Guachichiles would neither welcome nor serve outsiders; they fought in guerrilla bands to keep profit seekers and settlers off their lands. Into the 1590s, the Bajío lived times of war: Spaniards, Otomí led by Connín-Tapia, and diverse Mexica and Tarascan forces allied to fight Chichimecas. State-based people fought state-free peoples to claim lands rich in silver and maize-making potential.[8]

Chichimeca resistance slowed mining and settlement in the Bajío for four decades, until disease and war led some survivors to accept pacification, others to take refuge in mountain enclaves, still others to flee north beyond the commercial world driving into their homelands. All but vacated of original peoples, the Bajío would be built as a new society, stimulated by silver and global trade, settled by newcomers: a few Europeans, more enslaved Africans, a majority Mesoamericans.

From the Stimulus of Silver, Two Bajíos, 1590–1700

As war waned in the 1590s, mining accelerated at Zacatecas, Guanajuato, and San Luis Potosí, stimulating cultivation and cloth making across the Bajío. Settlement came in two variants: one built on Otomí foundations at Querétaro; the other led by Spaniards and worked by amalgamating African and Mesoamerican people around Guanajuato. Socially distinct, they were always linked: stimulated by silver, sustained by maize, focused on commercial ways, and structured by patriarchal hierarchies.

Querétaro became the commercial pivot of New Spain's new north. Connín-Tapia reinforced his power in campaigns against Chichimecas while Querétaro made maize and more to sustain the fight. On his death, his son don Diego de Tapia became Querétaro's leading lord and landlord. Other estate builders, Otomí and Spanish, joined him raising wheat and grazing livestock. European merchants, Spanish and Portuguese, many of them "new Christians" (recently Jewish, their presence facilitated by the union of Spanish and Portuguese crowns from 1580 to 1640), took profit linking mines, cultivators, and cloth makers to the Mexico City financiers who sent silver to the world.[9]

Otomí families remained entrenched on rich irrigated *huertas*. Governed by an Otomí council, they worshipped together in the San Sebastián parish. In the 1630s, they joined a local friar in devotion to El Cristo de la Huertecilla, Christ of the Little Huerta, who served the community as commercial powers rose all around. Thanks to their *huertas* and their Christ, the Querétaro Otomí held strong as a community making maize and more to eat and supply city markets.

In the city center, Hispanic entrepreneurs built *obrajes*, workshops employing dozens of workers to make cloth from local wool. They drew Mesoamerican migrants from the south to labor. Wage advances proved essential to gain workers; as the shops expanded into the seventeenth century, wages and advances rose. Workers came and went, rarely completing obligations contracted by advance payments. When courts tried to force compliance, they discounted debts—and still workers came and went. In times of disease and dying, with silver stimulating demand in a city of trade and textiles, and with most Otomí making maize and more on *huertas*, cloth makers had to adapt to scarce workers.[10]

Patriarchy ruled. Only six women appeared among more than four hundred men contracted to labor in the *obrajes*; thirteen more shared accounts with working husbands (likely spinning). A few guaranteed husbands' obligations, revealing women with shops and market stalls. Men labored while women traded. Nearly all were indigenous, local Otomí mixing with migrant Otomí, Mexica, and Tarascans. Around 1600, many spoke Spanish at work and in court, where neither employers nor judges could curtail their negotiations of work and life.

In time, frustrated *obraje* operators turned to buying enslaved Africans, easier to control in locked workshops. Bound Africans also worked in transport and tended livestock at outlying estates, where control proved more difficult. As a mostly male minority surrounded by an Otomí-Mesoamerican majority, enslaved Africans reproduced with native women, freeing their offspring (by Spanish law, children of indigenous mothers were free). In time, free mulatto men took the roles vacated by their bound fathers making cloth in *obrajes* and tending livestock at rural estates.

Querétaro pioneered a dual system of work that long shaped the Bajío. Mesoamerican migrants were drawn to service (labeled *sirvientes*) by advances against salaries. Many gained and kept earnings beyond their salaries; others departed, taking advances with them as they pursued new options. Secure employment enabled indigenous men to assert patriarchal rule over women and family households. Meanwhile, enslaved Africans were set to work in cloth making and other crafts, in transport and stock raising. They, too, knew their value in times of commercial expansion and scarce producers. Living among indigenous majorities and knowing that the offspring of native women were by law free, many coupled with native women to free their children. Some offspring identified as mulattoes, spoke Spanish, and labored in the commercial world. Others joined their mothers in the Otomí world on the *huertas*.

As Europeans took control of commerce, Otomí power endured at Querétaro. When don Diego de Tapia died without a male heir in the early 1600s, he left his rich estates to found the Convent of Santa Clara. His daughter doña Luisa ruled as abbess as the convent became the leading mortgage bank in the Bajío, funding purchases and improvements for an increasingly Hispanic landed elite. In another Otomí-Christian assertion, in the 1630s, a priest at nearby San Francisco Galileo, *el pueblito* (the little town), joined Otomí parishioners to found devotion to Our Lady of Pueblito. She focused Otomí life around Querétaro, parallel to Our Lady of Guadalupe then taking precedence around Mexico City.[11]

To 1665, the Otomí council remained the only government at Querétaro, leading an Otomí republic with dominion over *huertas* and jurisdiction over the Otomí majority. When the city's Spanish minority won a council that year, it gained jurisdiction only over the center and its Hispanic minority. Querétaro began as an Otomí society. Sustained by family *huertas* and Christian on its own terms, it was deeply commercial. Spanish power came slowly, bolstered by links to the world of capitalism. Enslaved Africans and their free mulatto children lived in-between, hispanized dependents serving Spanish enterprises. Querétaro began and endured as a bicultural society: Spanish and Otomí councils shared power; Spanish and Otomí leaders pursued profit; a Hispanic-mulatto minority labored in the city; the Otomí majority made maize and more on urban *huertas* and at outlying estates— all sustaining the silver capitalism rising west at Guanajuato.

Guanajuato began later: more Spanish in foundations; more amalgamating among its producing families; still structured by patriarchy. Settled minimally during decades of war, it developed rapidly from the 1590s.[12] Everything pivoted around the mines. Spanish prospectors led by native guides found veins of silver and gained rights to mine from a regime in search of revenues. The regime supplied the mercury essential to refine midgrade ores, taken from Almadén in mountains north of Seville—the monopoly a way to stimulate and account for production. Mexico City and Querétaro merchants financed mines; after minting and paying taxes of 12 to 15 percent, they gained pesos to trade across the globe. Financiers, merchants, and mine operators were always men.

Early on, the dangerous work of tunneling and refining with mercury fell to indigenous men who came north to claim wages four times higher than those available in any other work. Enslaved Africans, too valuable to risk in mines or with poisonous mercury in refineries, were set to labor in ironworks, transport, and other essential and often skilled work. Women came too—keeping taverns and inns, making and selling sustenance and drink. The mining town was a place of dangerous work, labor prosperity, and search for release. And there, too, enslaved African men had children with native women, producing generations of free mulattoes. In time, they became the primary labor force, risking limbs and lives in mines and refineries to gain high wages. Workers facing maiming disabilities made the silver that fueled global trades.

Patriarchal family formation proved challenging in the mineworking community. Men risking death took high wages and sought lives of comfort and release. Women sustained life and leisure, more often in informal marketing than household dependence. Lives of risk promised gain yet delivered insecurity and disabilities; men dreamed of primacy in the face of uncertainty; women made and sold sustenance in a place of fleeting opportunity and rampant insecurity. Men imagined patriarchy; women could not count on sustaining provision. Mining and its risks defined life in the upland canyon.

Meanwhile, Spanish landlords ruled the surrounding basin lands. They led Spanish councils, claimed lands along the rivers, built irrigation canals, and drew Mesoamerican migrants to settle. Estate builders aimed to profit by supplying the mines. With producers scarce, they offered lives of secure sustenance to dependent families. They drew indigenous men to work as *sirvientes* taking advances against salaries and gaining ample maize rations. Some rented plots to plant more maize. Boys worked seasonally for wages planting and harvesting estate crops. Estate operators enforced men's monopoly of employment as *sirvientes* with access to maize rations; only men and boys gained of wage work; nearly all tenants were men. They set men as patriarchal providers. Women produced and raised children, made cloth and clothing, and turned maize into tortillas for daily meals. Locked in gendered dependencies, they, too, labored to sustain households—and silver capitalism.

Enslaved Africans came to rural Guanajuato too, still a minority (about 20 percent of early arrivals). Again, they were set to guard livestock, work in transport, and learn diverse crafts. Again, they were mostly men set among an indigenous majority. Again, they mixed to generate free mulatto children. As Mexica, Otomí, and Tarascan migrants settled in towns and at estates, they, too, mixed; in the 1650s, native ethnic identities gave way to life as *indios*, a marker of inter-Mesoamerican *mestizaje*.[13] Guanajuato forged a world of amalgamations—risk laden and insecure in the mining city; dependent yet secure on estate lands.

The life of don Diego de la Cruz Saravia reveals much about the dynamic, amalgamating, patriarchal world that shaped the Guanajuato bottomlands. An estate builder around Valle de Santiago, he was all but certainly the son of the Diego de la Cruz who planted wheat outside town in the 1630s—and by his name and the absence of the *don* was surely of African ancestry. By the 1660s, don Diego had married doña Ynez María de Vergara y Moncayo and moved to an elegant home in Celaya with two children who eschewed their father's patronym—another sign of his African roots.[14]

Don Diego's 1669 will listed property worth nearly 60,000 pesos. The Celaya home was valued at 6,000 pesos; nearby lots and houses totaled 550 pesos. Ten slaves totaled 1,800 pesos, including the mulatta Ana, worth 350 pesos, and her three enslaved sons—Diego, eight, worth 200; twins Joseph and Francisco, two, valued at 100 each. The landed descendant of slaves kept slaves for household service. Don Diego's legacy also included 3,000 pesos in luxuries worn by doña Ynez: gold jewelry inlaid with emeralds; silk clothing embroidered with gold and silver; pearls, and more—much drawn from Asia to shine in the Bajío. A carriage worth 300 pesos carried the family in the streets of Celaya.

That eminence built on estate operations at Valle de Santiago, sixty kilometers west—far enough to separate don Diego and his children from his roots. He worked properties worth 40,000 pesos, raising wheat and maize on estate account, more maize on rented plots, while other tenants grazed livestock. He employed twenty-seven men as *sirvientes*. They gained monthly salaries set in pesos, part paid in cash, part delivered in cloth and goods, all backed by weekly rations that guaranteed sustenance. Men gained maize, cloth, and more to supply women who labored to make families, meals, clothing, and more. Ten *sirvientes* were mulatto; seventeen were *indios* of mixed Mesoamerican ancestries. The mulattoes earned a bit more, yet many were owed sums by the estate. *indios* formally earned less, yet most gained and never repaid advances well beyond salary levels.

Nearly fifty tenants paid rents. One commercial operator paid 250 pesos yearly: 100 in cash, 150 in improvements. Most owed 10 to 20 pesos, with many in arrears. Everything was negotiated. De la Cruz drew tenants to gain income and expand cultivation; he lowered rents for those clearing fields for new plantings. Everything was calculated in cash—except the rations that guaranteed sustenance. And everything was patriarchal: Don Diego only recruited men, Hispanic and indigenous, as workers and tenants. Only men gained access to the means of life—salaries, maize, and the means to produce them. The women who labored long and hard to turn staples into sustenance lived locked in dependence. Still, men, families, and a consolidating silver capitalism could not survive without women's constant labors. Unseen negotiations of patriarchal power and women's production lurked unrecorded.

By the middle of the seventeenth century, the Bajío had built a silver capitalism led by mining at Guanajuato, fueled by trade and manufacturing at Querétaro, sustained by commercial estates making maize and more, and by Otomí *huertas* at Querétaro. It was one regional economy: mines, textile workshops, and artisans sought profit. Otomí families with *huertas* fed themselves—and sold fruits and vegetables in city markets. Estates sought profit too, paying monthly salaries set in pesos backed by maize rations to permanent workers, collecting rents from tenants making maize, and paying wages to seasonal hands harvesting wheat and maize. Hispanic-Otomí divisions marked Querétaro; amalgamations shaped Guanajuato. Across a basin of scarce people, capitalist ways of making silver to profit in global trades built on patriarchal social relations guaranteeing secure sustenance set in maize.

The Bajío also drove New Spain's northward expansion. The mines just north at Zacatecas and San Luis Potosí were sustained by crops and cloth made in the Bajío. The search for silver and cultivable land reached the pueblos of the region named New Mexico before the sixteenth century ended. Traders there formed the northmost outpost of Spanish North America, engaging independent peoples far beyond in exchanges that brought sheep and woolen weaving to Navajos, horses, metal tools, and firearms to many others engaged in conflict and trade on a dynamic frontier.

Through the seventeenth century, warrior entrepreneurs and pacifying clergy drove north across the vast arid spaces between the Bajío and New Mexico, searching for silver, irrigable lands, and people to work. Finding mostly dry lands, they set off explosive expansions of herds of sheep, goats, and cattle. Where cultivation was enabled by streams, settlement reached Saltillo and Monterrey in the northeast, while missions drove north along the Pacific coast. When silver waned at Guanajuato and Zacatecas after 1640, mines at Parral on the road to New Mexico kept the northward drive of silver capitalism strong—still sustained by crops and cloth made in the Bajío.

The Bajío and Spanish North America emerged from interactions among entrepreneurs pursuing profit; migrants seeking chances in mines and on newly opened lands; and a regime that reacted to sanction regional powers, ways of production, and social relations negotiated to keep silver flowing, regime coffers full, and people at work—all sustained by maize. The regime did not design the Bajío nor the settlements driving north. It adapted to sanction and stabilize profit-seeking ways, drawing revenues from a rising silver capitalism pivotal to global trades and imperial aspirations.

In contrast with the Mesoamerican heartland regions just south, the Bajío had few indigenous republics outside of Querétaro with its *huertas*, and a few towns along the southern margins. Without community lands, rural majorities—Otomí around Querétaro, amalgamating across Guanajuato— lived as estate dependents. Still, as long as silver capitalism held and producers were scarce, hierarchies of patriarchal dependence guaranteed secure sustenance to stabilize lives across the Bajío's rich lands.[15]

Silver Surges; Stability Holds, 1690–1760

The eighteenth century brought rising silver production and renewed population growth to New Spain. Before 1760, the Bajío saw dynamic growth, enduring social stability, and new northward expansions as New Spain's silver flows rose from 4 million pesos yearly in the 1690s, to 8 million by the 1720s, reaching 12 million in the 1750s—growth sustained in great part by maize, cloth, and more made across the Bajío.

That growth began amid imperial uncertainty and years of war. The last Spanish Hapsburg, Carlos II, died in 1700 without an heir. He named as successor his nephew Felipe d'Anjou—a Bourbon backed by Louis XIV. Fearing a Franco-Spanish alliance, an Anglo-Dutch coalition backed an Austrian

Hapsburg claimant. From 1701, French and British coalitions fought on Iberian soil to set a preferred prince on the Spanish throne—with access to New Spain's silver the prize. The war broke in 1711 when the Hapsburg claimant died. Felipe V would be Spain's first Bourbon king. The 1713 Treaty of Ryswick aimed to balance the outcome by blocking any fusion of the French and Spanish regimes while granting England *asiento* rights to deliver enslaved Africans to Spanish America in exchange for silver. Still, viewed from Europe, the war forged a Bourbon alliance that threatened Dutch-British aspirations.[16]

The view from the Americas reveals more. During the war, production and demand for silver rose. The viceregal regime carried on in New Spain, solidifying the power of Mexico City merchants and financiers, Bajío mine operators, cloth makers, and landed capitalists.[17] Early in the war, the 1703 Methuen Treaty tied Portugal to the British war effort, giving England favored access to the gold flowing from the hills beyond Rio de Janeiro—panned by enslaved Africans.[18] France took control of western Santo Domingo, opening the way for Saint-Domingue to rise as a plantation colony competing with British Jamaica. Demand for enslaved Africans was set to soar—and the slave trade required silver, as did continuing Asian trades. France gained solid access to New Spain's pesos thanks to Bourbon trade links; Britain gained some selling enslaved people in Spanish America. New Spain flourished.[19]

From 1690 to 1750, its silver production tripled, a dynamism too often credited to "Bourbon reform." But the boom began before the war that brought Bourbons to power, and reforms rarely reached the Americas before 1740, and then proved more disruptive than stimulating. How, then, to explain the new dynamism of silver? The simultaneous booms of gold in Brazil and New Granada (now Colombia) and silver in New Spain from 1700 to 1750 are revealing. Historically, gold and silver, the world's leading money metals, alternated eras of rise and decline. Growing production of one led its value to fall relative to the other—in time leading to a reverse cycle. The eighteenth century proved a rare era when silver and gold rose together in the Americas. Chinese and South Asian demand for silver held strong, as did their global trades, while accelerating Atlantic trades in sugar, enslaved humans, and more added to rising demand for hard money—silver and gold.

That intersection came as global population growth shaped a world more commercially integrated than ever before. In Western Europe and across East and South Asia, seventeenth-century times of commercial stagnation and limited demographic growth gave way to sustained expansions around 1700. Simultaneously, the Americas depopulated by disease in the sixteenth century saw growth resume in the eighteenth. Global population entered a long era of sustained growth, raising the numbers of producers and consumers in a world of profit-seeking trades.

That world demanded specie. New flows of gold from Brazil favored England, while rising flows of silver from New Spain fueled resurgent trades with China and India and the slave trades that soared as Caribbean plantation economies claimed surging numbers of bound humans.[20] The African princes and merchants who sold captives to European slave traders still demanded fine cottons from India as primary payment. Europeans—Portuguese and Dutch, British and French—needed silver to purchase that cloth.[21] As the century began, fewer than 40,000 enslaved people were bound out of Africa yearly; by the 1740s, 60,000 exited annually, most sold to British and French plantations. Prices jumped from 5 to more than 10 pounds sterling per person after 1700, rose to nearly 20 pounds around 1740, then fell back to 15 pounds by 1750. The price of enslaved people tripled while numbers rose 50 percent.[22]

New Spain's silver output rose from 4 million to 12 million pesos yearly in the same decades, funding the rising trades in Indian cloth and African peoples that sent bound workers to Caribbean planters. As China trades also expanded, the stimulus of silver again energized the Bajío, while producing people remained scarce. Reports of silver output at Guanajuato begin in 1716, just after the war of succession ended. Mean production held under 1.2 million pesos yearly to 1720, then rose to more than 3.2 million pesos by 1746–50—tripling the economic stimulus of silver in the region.[23]

Populations grew across the Bajío. The mining city and its district held 43,000 people in 1743, 57,000 by 1755, always amalgamating.[24] The commercial, textile, and cultivating center of Querétaro approached 30,000 in 1743, still half Otomí.[25] San Miguel el Grande rose as a third urban pivot; the textile town saw its population approach 20,000 in 1743 and 25,000 by 1755. When no town in British America passed 15,000, three cities in the Bajío combined to exceed 100,000 in the 1750s, matching Mexico City, the capital of silver capitalism and largest city in the Americas.[26] Still, the Bajío remained mostly rural. The region grew from nearly 185,000 people in 1743 to more than 323,000 in 1755, led by a rise to 125,000 in the Celaya district set on the basin's richest irrigated bottomlands.[27]

Urban growth reflected expansions of mining, textile manufacturing, and the trades they stimulated. Rural populations rose to sustain the profit-seeking cultivation that fed people in the Bajío and across arid regions north (where mining boomed without parallel increases in cultivation). Rising global demand for silver stimulated mining, manufacturing, and a growing demand for maize and more. Populations also rose, as did local tensions, yet social stability held until the 1760s.

Urban Dynamism and Ferment

The three leading Bajío cities grew, boomed, and faced new social challenges, none disrupting local or regional dynamism. Querétaro remained a Spanish-Otomí city, with a council for each community. Immigrant Spaniards ruled commerce and textile production, the latter via large *obrajes* and putting-out to artisan households. American-born Spaniards operated most of the estates that expanded outside the city, still relying on the Santa Clara Convent, heir to Connín-Tapia wealth, for mortgage funding. Otomí family *huertas* still raised maize, fruits, and vegetables to feed themselves and supply local markets. The economy expanded, tensions rose—and the social order held.

From the early seventeenth century, Our Lady of Pueblito had focused Otomí devotions, offering assistance in everyday trials of cultivation, reproduction, and health—and compassion when assistance failed. Like Guadalupe around Mexico City, Our Lady of Pueblito aided and protected indigenous peoples. In the 1680s, don Juan Caballero y Ocío, a Jesuit-educated priest and rich Bajío landlord, built a shrine to Guadalupe in Querétaro. Few Otomí came. When he took the Christ of the Huerta precious to the urban Otomí to Guadalupe's church, they came to honor their patron, not the Virgin imported from the Mesoamerican heartland. When the sisters of Santa Clara drew Our Lady of Pueblito to their city chapel, seeking aid in times of drought or disease, they sanctioned her power. Sooner or later, she returned to the Otomí at Pueblito. Otomí cultural independence held strong.

From Querétaro's founding in the 1530s, the Otomí ruled the water that sustained city life. The river that fell out of the canyon to the west flowed north of the center, irrigating *huertas* before flowing east to Celaya and the bottomlands. As the Spanish center grew after 1700, its privileged residents feared water shortages. Don Antonio de Urrutía y Vergara, son of a Mexico City merchant and titled Marqués de la Villa de Villar del Águila, saw a solution. He campaigned in the 1720s to build a great aqueduct to draw water from the river high in the canyon and carry it across lowlands to the center, diverting it from Otomí *huertas* to supply Spanish mansions, convents, and *obrajes* (figure 1.1).

The Marqués claimed credit for the towering structure, though he provided only part of the funds. The work took from 1726 to 1738. When a parade inaugurated the aqueduct, the Otomí marched to proclaim that

Figure 1.1 Querétaro aqueduct.

"indios do prodigious things, . . . indios make everything." They reminded their Spanish neighbors that they had founded the city, fed it, and that their hands built the aqueduct that delivered water to the Spanish center. As it turned out, there was enough water for both Otomí and Spanish Queré-taro. The two communities jostled together in worship and work, rule and sustenance, carrying on as a dual society: separate and unequal, divided yet inseparable, and productively stable.[28]

San Miguel saw its own conflicts. Long a small market and craft town, it became a center of cloth making and landed wealth after 1700. Sons of Spanish immigrants who took profit in mining came to San Miguel in the 1720s and 1730s, opening *obrajes* to make cloth, building estates stretching north to graze sheep and supply wool. Led by don Manuel Tomás de la Canal, they forged integrated textile enterprises to profit from mining booms at Guanajuato, Zacatecas, and San Luis Potosí.

As they prospered, San Miguel oligarchs drove a religious revival to an-nounce their power. The city's small Otomí population and growing num-

Figure 1.2 Atotonilco sanctuary, San Miguel. Author photo.

bers of mulattoes kept local devotions to the Virgin and diverse saints who proffered protection and consolation to people struggling through daily life. No single devotion ruled. Rising oligarchs promoted a different Christianity focused on Christ, personal prayer, penance, and charity. It began with the Oratorio de San Felipe Neri, where a community of priests prayed, did penance, and led devotions in a chapel taken from a mulatto brotherhood. Don Luis Felipe Neri de Alfaro joined the Oratorio in 1730. Son of a Mexico City merchant, he came to San Miguel with capital—and a religious vision. He attached a chapel devoted to Nuestra Señora de Salud to the Oratorio. People seeking the Virgin in times of disease would come to her through the Oratorio devoted to penitential commitments.

Then, in the 1740s, Alfaro founded the sanctuary of Jesus of Nazareth at Atotonilco, north of town. He dammed a stream to irrigate lands for maize and more, then built a sanctuary-church focused on the passion and crucifixion of Christ (figure 1.2). Penitential retreats drew San Miguel oligarchs. Alfaro led passionate self-flagellations, while promoting acts of charity to assist the poor in times of dearth. Men profiting from estates and textile workshops focused on personal prayer and commitment to Christ. Their religious individualism offered a stark contrast to popular devotions seeking community integration, protection, and compassion. Yes, the oligarchs offered limited charity to sustain those who produced their wealth. Still, they forged a "Catholic ethic in the spirit of capitalism" that contrasted with community devotions to virgins and saints who delivered help and consolation.

Penitential fervor did not inhibit oligarchs' drive for profits. As silver production plateaued and cloth markets slowed in the 1750s, the Canal clan turned on don Baltasar de Sauto. Arriving in the 1720s, Sauto married into a merchant family and built an *obraje* and estate complex. By 1750, his *obraje* was the largest at San Miguel, challenging the combined enterprises of the Canal clan. When the economy slowed, they challenged Sauto, pressing investigations after a worker was murdered in his *obraje*. They aimed to break his role in the regional economy. A Querétaro judge ruled that the killing was personal—and that Sauto's labor relations were no different from his competitors. He survived, but when the economy revived, he was a secondary participant, leaving Canal family rule unchallenged.[29] Oligarchic power legitimated by penitential devotions held strong at San Miguel.

In the mining center of Guanajuato, riches and risk still shaped everything.[30] Production revived in the 1690s, before the war and Bourbon accession. It rose to 1750, when a limited downturn set in. During the boom, mine operators took credit from Mexico City financiers to expand operations, drawing workers to risky work cutting veins of ore ever deeper into torch-lit tunnels. Others carried heavy loads; still others waded through poisonous mercury to refine ores. The most consistent gains went to Mexico City financiers: the Fagoagas, Valdiviesos, and Sánchez de Tagles, who funded mines, delivered bullion to the mint, paid taxes to the crown, and sent pesos into global trade. Mine operators faced bankruptcy more often than bonanzas. Those who did find profit invested in estates, seeking steadier profit supplying the staples of life. A few struck riches to gain fame, titles, and great properties: Bustos as Marqueses de San Clemente; Sardanetas as Marqueses de San Juan de Rayas.

For the thousands of men and boys who dug, carried, and refined the ore to make the silver that drove global trades, the risks were physical, yet the rewards could be real. Men who wielded picks to follow veins of silver gained shares of ore in addition to wages still four times higher than any other work in New Spain. Those who hauled ore and labored in refineries earned less, yet more than any other laboring men. High pay rewarded work essential to

Figure 1.3 Rayas mine and Mellado chapel, Guanajuato. Author photo.

the world, done by men facing constant risks of collapse and flood, maiming and death—and the promise of mercury poisoning in the refineries.

Working lives fusing risk and prosperity fueled an economy of daily pleasure. Futures were uncertain at best; gains must be enjoyed today, for tomorrow was improbable. Women ran boarding houses and food stalls, taverns and gaming dens—and sites of sexual commerce. Silver drove lives premised on the probability that the mine or the body would fail sooner or later—often sooner. Live and spend today, for tomorrow promised more risk. Workers rarely lasted, yet others came to risk life and limbs for gains beyond other working men's chances.[31] By the 1750s, the people of Guanajuato were increasingly classed as mulatto. Of mixed Mesoamerican and African ancestry, most labored hard, spoke Spanish, and forged devotions while facing the risks of mining—men physically in mines and refineries, women socially in lives of commerce without security.

As mining soared, local powerholders worried about their inability to rule life in a raucous community essential to their prosperity—and the world economy. They sought a Jesuit solution. Doña Josefa Teresa de Busto y Moya, sister of the Marques de San Clemente, held shares in family mines and owned a refinery and rural estates left by her late husband. She pledged a fifth of her wealth, 60,000 pesos, to build a Jesuit college. Her titled brother added 10,000 pesos, as did a local refiner. Eighty thousand pesos was a large sum, but not enough. Don José de Sardaneta y Legaspi, councilman and operator of the Rayas mine, saw a solution. He gave nothing but called on mine operators to require workers to deliver part of their ore shares to fund the Jesuits. In the end, workers paid the most.

The goal was education for the prosperous, pacification for workers. Doña Josefa saw Jesuits bringing "spiritual sustenance." The local pastor saw "rude people" who were "poor mineworkers." Another priest declared that with Jesuit oversight "there would not be so many shiftless vagabonds, nor so many crimes and evils . . . committed repeatedly and atrociously by these ignorant people." The Marqués de San Clemente saw "base people" in need of instruction "to flee from vice." A treasury official insisted that only Jesuits could end mineworkers' "wanton lives of vice and lewdness." The powerful maligned the men who made the silver that drove global capitalism.

Before the college was finished, Jesuits came in 1760 to nurse the sick, offer sacraments, and bury the dead in a time of smallpox and floods. They returned in 1762 when typhus ravaged the city, leading parades drawing throngs to march with crowns of thorns, some bleeding from self-flagellation, all calling for penitence to cure the city's ills. Atotonilco came to Guanajuato. Would mine workers turn from lives of vice? In trying times, the Jesuits achieved a religious reckoning.[32]

In the long run, little changed. In 1764, a new parish priest called Guanajuato a "refuge of the poor drawn into entrails of silver, the den of vice-ridden men who by their numbers cause confusion and disorder; they recognize no law other than desire, fearlessness, and audacity; a tangle of men drawn together by infamy, they make a mountain town of brute customs." Workers faced constant risk, gained fleeting luxuries, and rarely solidified patriarchal family lives. Facing crisis, they tried penitential devotions; crisis past, they returned to lives of risk and revelry. The world depended on them. At the end of his damning portrayal, the pastor pivoted to promote Guanajuato as an "opulent vein of endless treasures, rich minerals deposited by God Omnipotent to enrich the public."[33]

Don Francisco de Ajofrín, a Capuchin friar, came a year later and witnessed that "workers gamble, spend, and lose all they have without end or limit; there is no pickman or blastman who is not prodigious, spending on luxuries, irrelevancies, and vices every treasure they take from the mines. It is laughable to see these smudged men, faces like devils, black apes ugly to the extreme, dressed in velvet trousers, a coat inlaid with silver and edged with gold over a ruffled Dutch shirt."

He told of a "debauched mulatto" who had taken 12,000 pesos from a small mine. He held a fiesta for "a rabble of wretched nobodies. . . . There were almost two thousand, yet no one lacked food or drink, thanks to the great liberality of the mulatto, whose name I don't recall. . . . There was such an abundance of bread, wine, pulque, meat, fruits, and maize tortillas, so much ten women got paid."[34] Was Ajofrín more upset that a mulatto gained wealth, that he shared it with his working colleagues, or that he paid women to deliver rich sustenance? Through jaundiced eyes, he saw community among Guanajuato mine workers. Gaining a small fortune, the "debauched mulatto" shared his bonanza with a community of fleeting wealth and endless risk. The people of Guanajuato made their own ways in times of insecurity, keeping silver capitalism strong in the face of endless inequities—until the regime turned to impose on their lives of labor, risk, and release in 1766 and 1767.

Agricultural Growth and Patriarchal Stability

While Bajío cities grew and faced tensions, commercial cultivation and patriarchal ways kept rural communities at work, sustaining silver capitalism as it soared to midcentury heights. Across Querétaro, Otomí families worked *huertas*, feeding themselves and a vibrant city. Nearby basins saw a few pueblos—San Francisco Galileo, el Pueblito, home of the Virgin; San Pedro de la Cañada, where the river passed through the canyon before reaching the city; Santa Rosa northwest on the road to San Miguel—surrounded by estates expanding irrigation and cultivation while worked by growing numbers of Otomí residents. Mulattoes still tended shrinking herds of livestock.[35]

Across the bottomlands around Celaya, Salamanca, Salvatierra, and Valle de Santiago, estates remained modest in area yet productive thanks to irrigation waters drawn from the confluence of rivers. Most operators lived in local towns. As mining boomed, men who profited still invested in bottomland estates, a secure way to escape the risks of mining—and to profit feeding the people living those risks. Most rural families, some classed as mulattoes, most as *indios*, all descended from amalgamating Mesoamerican and African ancestors, still lived as estate dependents. *Sirvientes* still gained monthly salaries plus rations, still took advances, still rented small plots—

still locked in patriarchal dependence keeping wives at work. As irrigation, cultivation, and population expanded across the bottomlands after 1700, making maize and more to sustain silver capitalism, stability held.

Across the basins framing Querétaro, San Miguel, and Guanajuato in a northern arc, large properties long devoted to grazing turned to cultivation as populations and markets grew. Estate records document changing lives and new stabilizations. Don Juan Caballero y Ocío, Guadalupe's sponsor in Querétaro, was the Bajío's leading estate entrepreneur around 1700. Heir to commercial wealth invested in land, he studied with Jesuits in Querétaro and Mexico City, took Holy Orders as a priest (not a Jesuit) in 1680, and settled in Querétaro to operate estates in the Bajío and regions north.[36]

He owned La Griega and Puerto de Nieto. A 1689 will and 1707 inventory detail economic operations and labor relations as the century began. La Griega lay in the Amascala basin, along the river before it fell through the canyon to water Querétaro. Lands once devoted to grazing now planted wheat and maize. A granary stored grain to sell when prices peaked; a chapel called residents to worship. Thirty Otomí men labored year-round for salaries set in cash and paid by distributions of cloth and other goods in advance—plus guaranteed maize rations. Other Otomí gained small plots of land in expectation they would take wages as seasonal hands in estate fields. The estate leased out Coyotillos for 100 pesos yearly, La Venta for 56. After 1700, La Griega operated much like don Diego de la Cruz' bottomlands properties in 1660—while keeping Querétaro's Spanish-Otomí divide.

Puerto de Nieto lay in the upland basin east of San Miguel. As the century began, it remained a center of livestock operations. "A great country house with great halls" (later occupied by muchachas) announced power; granaries held 2,000 fanegas of maize raised to sustain grazing properties north across San Luis Potosí. Otomí residents made maize; enslaved Africans herded livestock; "Domingo el mulatto" leased a rancho. And every year, herdsmen drove 20,000 sheep south from northern pastures for shearing at Puerto de Nieto, suppling wool to *obrajes* in San Miguel and Querétaro.

Men and boys proudly Otomí ruled cultivation set in patriarchal dependencies at La Griega; others of mixed ancestry lived parallel lives at Puerto de Nieto. At the latter, 140 enslaved men of African origins drove great flocks of sheep across open spaces stretching north. In open lands far from estate centers, how were they kept in bondage? Puerto de Nieto provided a home, sustenance, and shares of the herds' annual increase. Guaranteed sustenance, mobility, and chances to own livestock, bound men built families with free wives, liberating their children. Men enslaved and free, mixed and Otomí, negotiated power and patriarchy in productive Bajío communities as the eighteenth century began.

The records of Ciénega de Mata, a great property north of Guanajuato owned by the Rincón Gallardo family, detail evolving social relations of production after 1700.[37] Before the revival of silver, in the 1680s maize-making tenants ruled cultivation, feeding themselves and the estate community while 123 enslaved hands tended livestock. The estate sold sheep for mutton in Zacatecas, San Luis Potosí, across the Bajío, and in Mexico City; it supplied wool to *obrajes* in San Miguel and Querétaro. When surging silver stimulated regional markets after 1700, the enslaved at Ciénega de Mata fell below 30 in 1704, then rose to 50 in 1715—mostly male, mostly mulatto, still tending livestock. The number held to midcentury while estate dependence on their labor waned as many of the able fled.

Meanwhile, the estate took on rising numbers of *sirvientes*, paid monthly salaries to raise crops on estate accounts: 134 in 1720, 171 in 1727, 250 in 1734, nearly doubling in fifteen years of agricultural expansion. Most earned four pesos monthly, forty-eight pesos yearly—plus maize rations. Ciénega de Mata had a population of more than a thousand by the 1740s. Shared surnames indicate family ties; the repetition of de la Cruz and de los Reyes suggests that many *sirvientes* were mulattoes descended from former slaves.

Patriarchy held. Only two women appear in the lists of *sirvientes*, likely recent widows. Far from town markets, most recompense came in annual shipments of goods: cloth, shoes and hats, candles, metal wares, and tools, and a few small luxuries too—all accounted precisely in pesos. Men gained goods to supply wives who turned crops into meals, cloth into clothing, and much else to keep a family home. The system locked in patriarchal power: only men gained maize, cloth, and more, while women still worked long hours every day to sustain the families that sustained silver capitalism.

With the annual shipment, a man claimed most of the value of a year's labor—in advance. Obligated to work, often he did not. Annual accounts show that most *sirvientes* owed up to a half-year's earnings never repaid in labor. And every year, 20 percent of the *sirvientes* fled owing similar sums. Advance pay enabled *sirvientes* to sustain families and claims to patriarchy. There is no sign of attempts to reclaim advances, force returns, or enforce work. The system entrenched working men's patriarchy, enabling them to negotiate work and remuneration—as long as producers remained scarce.

The largest advances went to managers, supervisors, and craftsmen, who gained and failed to repay more than the average worker. In the language of capitalism, unpaid advances served as incentives and bonuses, ample to managers and the skilled, modest but real to everyday workers, unavailable to women. The enslaved gained no advances; they were paid in food rations, clothing allotments, and shares of their flocks' increase—none accounted against work. In 1734, another Domingo el mulatto, enslaved, oversaw the craftsmen and herdsmen who remained enslaved.

Why did so many free *sirvientes* "flee" and so many enslaved men remain at an isolated property where escape was easy? Among *sirvientes*, advances and rations drew many to the estate. They claimed earnings beyond salaries and work performed, keeping the excess as they formed families and kin-based communities. Men gained patriarchal power as providers; women worked long and hard to sustain families and communities. Many who left were young, still looking to form families; not finding a mate or a family to join, they took advances and moved on. Obligated labor solidified patriarchy and family sustenance without blocking men's mobility in times of agricultural expansion, community formation, and sparse population.

For enslaved men, estates offered secure sustenance tied to lives of everyday independence tending livestock far from estate centers. A few joined the ranks of managers or skilled craftsmen. Many gained property in livestock. Most stayed to marry free women, freeing children to form families in amalgamating communities. In the effort, enslaved men and free sons also claimed patriarchy.[38]

The first half of the eighteenth century saw silver production soar at Guanajuato, Zacatecas, and across regions north. Demand for sustenance rose apace. Successful merchant financiers and mine operators invested in Bajío estates, expanding irrigation and cultivation while driving livestock north to dry grazing lands. They planted wheat on irrigated fields and maize on rain-fed lands, employing growing numbers of *sirvientes* who gained maize rations; they let additional maize lands to tenants who with their sons worked as seasonal wage hands planting and harvesting estate crops. Populations and staples production grew together. Maize prices held steady and perhaps declined a bit; the periodic peaks of draught years held limited. *Sirvientes'* salaries and maize rations held steady, as advances often grew.

Productive stability endured. A powerful few took profit in mining, manufacturing, cultivation, and the trades that linked them. Dependent men negotiated patriarchal production and family relations at estates across the Bajío. Women remained essential to turning men's earnings into sustenance. Producers increased in numbers yet held scarce in the face of rising demand for staples. Men took gains in unpaid advances—or moved on. Women negotiated to ensure that men's earnings enabled them to do the work of sustaining families and communities. Patriarchal dependencies adapted to sustain silver capitalism deep into the eighteenth century—as its northward drive accelerated.

Driving North

After 1700, the Bajío's dynamic silver capitalism fueled new drives deep into North America. The first step was to stabilize the New Mexico frontier. The Pueblo revolt of 1680 had turned on Spanish officials, traders, and missionaries, killing some, expelling many, and ending Spanish rule. The rising came as mining fell at Parral, cutting trades that tied the Pueblos and northern independent peoples to Spanish silver. As the break persisted, some communities and outlying peoples felt the loss: at the edge of silver capitalism, they relied on Spanish traders to gain horses and other livestock, metal weapons and tools, and to sell hides, cloth, and more. Despite claims of reconquest, New Mexico rejoined Spanish North America by 1700 as silver revived and native peoples sought trade. Native alliances of resistance broke as frontier trades revitalized.[39]

The eighteenth-century revival was led by mines at Santa Eulalia, near the city of Chihuahua, far north of Parral.[40] With the boom at Santa Eulalia and the reincorporation of New Mexico, northward drives accelerated. Don Juan Caballero y Ocío founded missions in Baja California and donated estates to fund them. When traders from French Louisiana pressed into Texas, Querétaro capitalists funded settlements and missions around San Antonio. Jesuits set missions along the Pacific from Sinaloa to Sonora, engaging Yaqui people who trekked regularly to work in northern mines. And in the 1740s, don José Escandón led excursions based in Querétaro, first seeking to pacify independent people entrenched in the nearby Sierra Gorda, then driving north to build estates along the Gulf from the Pánuco River north to the Rio Grande.[41]

To 1760, silver capitalism boomed, driving global trades and northward expansion, sustained by maize and more made by dependent producers across the Bajío. Then when the 1760s brought global war and new imperial demands, they provoked riots that rattled life and mining at Guanajuato—where lives of risk kept patriarchy weak. Maize makers still secure in lives of patriarchal dependence carried on. Bajío silver capitalism was shaken in the 1760s, yet not broken until after 1810.

Shaking the New World

Global Wars, Capitalist Predations,
Imperial Crises, 1760–1810

New challenges came to the Bajío beginning in the 1760s. The Seven Years' War of 1757 to 1763 left postwar debts that led authorities in Madrid to impose taxes on Guanajuato mine workers, provoking riots in 1766 and 1767 that threatened silver production, Spain's empire, and global trade. After pacification, the regime negotiated with the men who made the pesos that filled its coffers. Streams of silver from Guanajuato and New Spain rose from the 1770s, enabling Spain to fund the US war for independence. Mining dipped in the face of drought in the 1780s, to revive in the 1790s as European empires and global trades entered more disruptive decades of war.

From 1770 to 1810, Spain, its imperial allies, and foes, too, gained funds. Wars and contested trades carried on while Bajío producers faced new pressures—first, the drought crisis of 1785–86; then the wartime disruptions that began in the 1790s; culminating when war, imperial crisis, and drought came together from 1808 to 1810. Aiming to profit in times of disruption and uncertainty, mine operators cut ore shares and wages. Estates cut salaries and rations, raised rents, and forced evictions—aided by new population pressures that made producers expendable and replaceable. After 1790, drives to profit became predatory, assaulting patriarchy and family sustenance.

Then, in 1808, Napoleon invaded Spain, took Madrid, and captured the reigning Bourbon monarchs. On learning the news, officials and oligarchs in Mexico City debated ways forward while people took to the streets pressing for new participations—until a September coup imposed military power, ended political debates, and blocked popular ferment, all to ensure that New Spain's silver flowed to the fight against Napoleon. For two years, silver production rose and landed capitalists profited while drought-driven hunger plagued people across the Bajío, the heartland, and beyond.

When news came in 1810 that the fight against Napoleon was lost, the authorities imposed by the 1808 coup lost legitimacy. In September 1810, two years after the coup, Hidalgo called a revolt at Dolores demanding political rights, opening the way for popular insurgents to assault power and property. Imperial war and social predations merged to set off risings that became a revolution. Silver capitalism and the trades it fueled broke after 1810. The Bajío and the world would never be the same.

War, Imperial Demands, and Mine Worker Riots in the 1760s

War and militarized trades marked global capitalism from its beginnings.[1] Into the eighteenth century, the Pacific trades that linked New Spain, China, and Asia held strong, while Atlantic trades in sugar and enslaved people soared as empires fought wars to gain access to the silver that funded everything. A key turn came in 1750 when the Treaty of Madrid ended the *asiento* that gave British merchants rights to deliver slaves to Spanish America in exchange for silver. Plantation production and the slave trades still rose while wars intensified. The Seven Years' War began in 1756 in conflicts between England and France in North America, to soon extend across Europe, the Americas, and South Asia. The status quo held in British Jamaica and French Saint-Domingue, the leading Atlantic plantation colonies, while Britain claimed new power in India. Toward the end, in 1762 and 1763, British forces took Havana and Manila, the key Atlantic and Pacific ports of transit for New Spain's silver. The goal: gain specie to fund trade in Indian cottons and enslaved Africans.

The gambit failed. Silver could wait or take new routes. The British exited Havana and Manila after a year. In the 1763 Treaty of Paris, Britain gained Canada; Britain and France kept key Caribbean plantation colonies; Britain gained new sway in the ports of India; and Spain gained New Orleans and the west bank of the Mississippi to Saint Louis. The settlement resolved everything—and nothing. New Spain remained the source of silver essential to global trades. Britain still competed with France to rule the trade in Indian cottons essential to trades in enslaved humans—with no sanctioned way to gain silver to pay. For decades after the war, New Spain's silver soared while Atlantic wars raged.

In the short term, all the belligerents faced burdensome debts. In 1765, England imposed new taxes and sent military powers to enforce them in North America, provoking resistance that became a war for independence led by merchants and landed elites, declared in 1776 and won in the 1783 Treaty of Paris that ended a second round of global wars.[2] Britain lost North American colonies that supported Caribbean plantations with flour, fish, and ships. It kept primacy in Indian ports—if it could gain silver to pay for the cottons made there. Support for the United States left France with rising debts while demand for enslaved Africans soared as Saint-Domingue became the leading Caribbean plantation colony. Those debts would lead to revolutions in France and Saint-Domingue.

Spain, too, faced postwar debts, fueling political conflicts in Madrid. Reformers saw a solution in new taxes on New Spain, the richest kingdom in the empire and supplier of silver to the world. Visitor General don José de Gálvez arrived in 1765, sent to enforce policies parallel to those driving resistance in British North America. Taxes would rise on maize and the pleasures of life (alcohol, tobacco, and playing cards). While rural people still made maize or gained rations for family consumption, escaping new taxes, urban consumers would pay. Notably, the mine workers who daily risked life to buy food, drank to dull the dangers of work, and gambled in dreams of gain beyond the pains of labor—the men who made silver—would pay. Reformers also ordered militia enrollments, long open to free mulattoes. Guanajuato mine workers might appreciate the option of joining militias when they chose; they resisted forced enrollments that would subject them to discipline and orders to control unruly crowds—meaning themselves. In the summer of 1766, they left the mines and took the streets; gaining concessions from local authorities they returned to work.

The summer of 1767 brought new orders to impose taxes and militia service, drawing workers to shut down Guanajuato's mines and take the city. Rioting spread to mines around San Luis Potosí, to upland San Luis de la Paz at the edge of the Sierra Gorda, and to Pátzcuaro—a center of Tarascan power south of the Bajío. The commercial-textile cities of Querétaro and San Miguel stayed at peace and at work. So did the residents of estate communities across the Bajío, where lives of patriarchal security kept families at work. Don Francisco de Mora, a miner, landlord, and militia commander at San Luis Potosí, restored order there. Then Gálvez came to announce repressions. The sequence repeated at Guanajuato: regional militias pacified the city, then Gálvez asserted power in public rituals. He executed nine rebel leaders, their heads displayed as gruesome warnings; another 170 rioters were sent to northern presidios or coastal ports. Peace returned to the city of silver.

Mine operators and city leaders knew that only ample salaries, ore shares, affordable sustenance, and chances at recreation and release would draw workers back to lives of risk in mines and refineries. They revoked the taxes that had provoked the risings and pressed the regime to reduce the cost of mercury—subsidizing the revival of mining. By 1770, silver surged again. Profit-seeking mine operators and rowdy workers reminded Gálvez of a truth he should have known: Guanajuato silver was essential to Spain's empire and global trade.[3]

Silver Capitalism in a World of War, 1770–1810

After conflicts quieted, mining and commercial life revived in the Bajío. Held below 3 million pesos yearly in the late 1760s, Guanajuato silver rose to near 5 million in the late 1770s. It fell to 4.5 million pesos in the 1780s, cut by famine crisis in 1785–86. Then, another crisis past, output rose to hold above 5 million pesos yearly through the 1790s as new wars set in. Guanajuato produced 25 percent of New Spain's silver; much of the rest came from regions north sustained by Bajío grains and textiles.[4]

Commercial life energized in step with mining. Across the Bajío, taxed commerce rose to 5 million pesos yearly in the early 1780s, fell below 4 million during and after the crisis of 1785–86, to approach 6 million pesos yearly from 1801 to 1805. A dip to 5.5 million from 1806 to 1809 reflected wartime drains on capital and social predations that constrained popular consumption. North of the Bajío, San Luis Potosí markets mirrored the Bajío, rising to 1805, receding to 1809; at Zacatecas, mining and trade rose to 1809. Trade was less dynamic around Durango and Chihuahua while it rose 10 percent in northwestern Sinaloa and Sonora, more than 25 percent in the northeast around Saltillo and Monterrey, and energized in Texas, New Mexico, and California, too.[5] Silver capitalism boomed from 1770 to 1810 while wars came, ended, and came again.

When the conflicts in British North America became a war for US independence in 1776, New Spain's silver flows approached 20 million pesos yearly. Mexico City merchants and oligarchs soon delivered 4.5 million pesos in donations and loans to support the fight to exit Britain's empire—beyond Spain's contributions from regular revenues. When the Andean risings linked to Túpac Amaru broke out in 1780, New Spain funded Pacific trades to hold Spain's power in South America. Silver capitalism funded the merchants and slave owners who took British North America out of empire while sustaining the fight that held Spanish rule in the Andes.[6]

Peace returned in the mid-1780s, just as drought and famine struck New Spain. Silver flows dipped, then recovered to rise above 23 million pesos as the 1790s began. China's trade held strong and silver remained pivotal to gaining Indian cottons to pay for enslaved Africans.[7] A stark contradiction marked the latter: from the 1780s, Britain held privileged access to Indian cotton goods while France gained silver via traders in Bourbon Cádiz. After the 1783 Treaty of Paris set US independence, Britain focused on ruling exports from India while merchants and officials in France founded a New East India Company, seeking access to the cottons essential to the slave trade to Saint-Domingue.[8] Should the new company contest British power in India or buy from British traders there? British and French regimes and East India companies jostled in years of conflict and collaboration. In the end, English primacy in India held, leaving French traders to face limited access to cottons, rising costs, and soaring debts. The financial crisis that provoked the French Revolution in 1789 began with debts built to back US independence, then peaked with the rising costs of gaining slaves for Saint-Domingue.[9]

Desperate for revenue, Louis XVI called an Assembly of Notables in 1787, then the Estates General in 1789. Their debates led to a revolution that broke the French monarchy, proclaimed national sovereignty, beheaded the king, and expropriated Church wealth—fueling political conflicts, popular risings, and global wars. Debts built defending slavery in British North America and funding the slave trade to Saint-Domingue brought revolution to Paris.

With news of conflicts and liberating promises arriving from Paris, in 1791 slaves began to rise in Saint-Domingue while slave owners, French and mixed, debated who among them earned rights to participate in French governance. Persistent conflicts led them to arm enslaved men—who quickly turned on their masters to pursue their own freedom and claim access to sustaining land. More than a decade of social war ended slavery, French rule, and plantation production. The French slave trade collapsed. British merchants might dominate—if they could gain Spanish American silver. As sugar and slavery rose in Cuba, British traders delivered bound Africans, gaining silver to buy the Indian cloth to pay for them. The global circuit of silver and slavery revived as British trades peaked after 1790.[10]

The French and Haitian Revolutions drove Atlantic wars with global consequences. Britain dreamed of gaining Saint-Domingue. The United States held neutral, seeking trade with France and Saint-Domingue as it became

Haiti—while dreaming of containing the example of enslaved people taking arms to gain freedom, land, and independence. Spain, too, was drawn into long wars, while New Spain's silver held over 23 million pesos yearly from the 1790s past 1800 as wartime demand overrode disruptions of trade.[11]

Spain faced rising debts while shifting alliances led to diversions of silver and revenues. From 1793, Spain joined Britain against revolutionary France—a reversal of long-standing ties caused by the Jacobin beheading of a Bourbon king. New Spain's silver then flowed toward England, funding war, slave trades, and more. After a brief peace, when war resumed in 1798 Spain returned to ally with France, to face British hegemony at sea. Complex deals involving British and US merchants became essential to ship silver to Europe—sharing New Spain's wealth. After 1800, Spain gained only 30 percent of New Spain's silver. Another 30 percent went to its ally France. Britain, their foe, gained 40 percent, again funding war and trade.[12] As New Spain's silver peaked, it flowed to all the contenders in Atlantic wars. Spain could not pay the rising costs of endless conflicts even as Mexico City financiers, merchants, and oligarchs raised donations and loans to bolster revenues flowing to the regime.

Desperate, the monarchy called in the wealth of Church institutions in Spain, to be compensated with bonds that promised to sustain Church activities—necessary given the people's deep Catholicism and the Crown's condemnation of revolutionary attacks on Church wealth in France.[13] Collections proved limited and debts mounted. In 1804, the Crown turned to take Church wealth across the Americas in a Consolidation of Royal Bonds—again promising to fund ecclesiastical operations.

In Spain, Church institutions relied on direct landholding; in New Spain, most lived on income from mortgages on rural estates and city real estate. The Consolidation called property owners, used to paying only annual interest of 5 percent, to redeem the full capital, paid directly to the Crown. Church lenders were promised future funding; estate operators were not. Many saw an assault on the economy that sustained New Spain and Spain's empire.

Don Miguel Domínguez, corregidor (royal magistrate) at Querétaro since 1801, protested in 1805. Claiming concern for the economy and the common good, he argued that convent banks such as Otomí-founded Santa Clara were pivotal to mining and cloth making, cultivation and trade. He emphasized that clerical mortgages were essential to estate operators in Querétaro and the Bajío, where provincials used loans to buy estates and expand irrigation, raising harvests to serve the common good in times of drought and scarcity. He did not note that recent expansions of irrigated cropping came tied to pay cuts and evictions that drove poverty and insecurity onto producing families. He promoted the welfare of the landed capitalists who sustained silver production, trade, and imperial revenues. The corregidor's common good required profitable planting on the land.[14]

Power and protests led to negotiated collections. Don José Sánchez Espinosa, heir to the rich Bajío estates assembled by don Juan Caballero y Ocío, paid nothing. Don Miguel Hidalgo, priest at Dolores, saw his small estate embargoed. Overall, great landlords paid little, thanks to limited mortgages and power to negotiate settlements; provincials paid more and saw more estates embargoed; clerical lenders lost most. Of 10.5 million pesos collected from 1805 to 1808, the Encarnación Convent in Mexico City paid 250,000 pesos; Santa Clara in Querétaro paid 200,000 pesos, the second-largest redemption in New Spain, fueling resentment among convent bankers and regional landlords.[15] Meanwhile, silver held near historic peaks and predations deepened on families across the Bajío.

Urban Challenges: Mine Workers, Tobacco Women, Cultural Contests, 1780–1810

In times of war, silver boom, and trade disruptions, new demands struck producing people across the Bajío. The canyon city of Guanajuato remained the motor driving silver capitalism. As demand rose, mine operators aimed to profit by cutting producer earnings. They tried to reduce or eliminate *partidos*, the ore shares that gave pick men incentive to risk all for their own and mine operators' gain. They cut the wages paid less skilled workers. They turned to boys paid little to do heavy hauling. And they drew hundreds of women to sort ores for refining, asserting women's greater dexterity yet paying them less. Still, everything was negotiated as silver soared.

The attempts to cut the gains of the men who did the most dangerous work underground failed. Skilled risk-takers knew their value—and could stay away, shift to another mine, or move to a new mining center. Hiring women cut costs and offered new chances at income. Overall, the men essential to cut ores deep underground held strong—still highly paid, still facing maiming risks, still unlikely to lead patriarchal households. Boys took on dangerous work for pittances, hoping for richer futures. Women found new access to paid labor, a way forward in a city with few patriarchal households; others still traded in sustenance, luxuries, and sex—surviving as best they could.

Guanajuato remained a place of rich and deadly insecurity; predations had long defined the work that drove silver capitalism and global trades.

Cycles of boom and bust continued in times of war: rich veins appeared, then vanished; promising mines might produce for years, then flood. The Sardaneta's San Juan de Rayas led Guanajuato through the 1770s; the Obregón's Valenciana boomed from 1780 to 1810. Both families gained titles, honored for driving silver capitalism forward through decades of demand, challenge, and predatory insecurity. Producing people carried on.[16]

The cloth making long centered at Querétaro and rising at San Miguel faced years of challenge, revival, and dislocation after 1770. The industry operated in two variants: *Obrajes*, large workshops concentrating dozens of male weavers and relying on women spinning at home, made woolens. Cotton production came in artisan households where men wove, wives and daughters spun, and sons helped as they could. Owner-operators ran *obrajes*; merchants ruled cottons by funding family producers and marketing their cloth.

Into the 1780s, wool prices rose as herds of sheep drove north; the drought of 1785–86 made it impossible for herds to travel at any price. Many *obrajes* closed; most cut production. Operators lost profit; workers lost secure employment. Cotton makers faced different challenges: Catalan regions in Spain began to industrialize, their exports favored by a regime aiming to draw silver home. In the Bajío, family workshops kept working while merchant financiers took more to deliver cotton from lowland growers and paid less for finished cloth, a predation that imposed poverty while preserving patriarchy.

Then, in 1793, the wars set off by the French and Haitian revolutions cut cloth imports to New Spain. *Obrajes* revived and family workshops found rising markets. Cycles of war, peace, and war again brought boom, constraint, and revival to Bajío cloth makers. The industry carried on in *obrajes* and family workshops, the former living cycles of expansion, layoffs, and rehiring that rattled patriarchy, the latter struggling with enduring poverty and endless insecurities that confirmed patriarchy while keeping provision uncertain.[17]

A new tobacco factory came to Querétaro in the 1780s, offering employment to thousands, in time mostly women. The Crown had claimed a monopoly in the 1760s, one of the revenue-seeking impositions that provoked rioting in Guanajuato. The regime built a large factory in Mexico City that in 1774 employed more than 5,000 men and 1,000 women, most paid piece rates that managers pressed down to cut costs. Worker resistance led to the creation of a mutual aid society, the Concordia, funded by worker contributions, allowing withdrawals to cover costs of marriage, illness, injury, or death.

Resistance also led the regime to disperse production to regional factories while turning to women workers. In the early 1790s, the Mexico City factory employed 7,000 workers, more than 3,000 women. Querétaro's factory employed 1,400 in 1794, then 3,700 by 1809, with 2,600 (70 percent) women. They, too, gained piece rates and mutual aid, plus day care for children. The turn to women's labor in the tobacco factories brought revenues to the regime—4 million pesos yearly after 1800, second only to silver.[18]

The turn to employment of thousands of women in silver refining in Guanajuato and tobacco manufacturing in Querétaro earns reflection. We do not know their ethnicities; surely many were mulatta in Guanajuato, Otomí in Querétaro. Managers saw women as less costly and more docile—though they required child care and other benefits to take on factory work. The larger question is what led women to lives of paid labor. In the world of risk and insecurity that defined life at Guanajuato, working men's lives were always insecure and often short; women rarely found security in patriarchal families. Refinery work added to the menu of ways to get by. At Querétaro, cycles of pressure and insecurity in the textile economy made patriarchal families ever less secure there too. The flow of women to paid labor in Guanajuato refineries and the Querétaro tobacco factory after 1790 rattled patriarchy while opening new avenues to sustenance for women. Stability held.

Cultural contests continued. During the first half of the eighteenth century, while popular devotions to serving and consoling virgins and saints held strong at Pueblito and beyond, sacramental worship became emphatically penitential at Atotonilco, where San Miguel oligarchs grappled with guilt as profit seekers in a world that honored justice and the common good. Then, after 1780, worship among the powerful at San Miguel turned "enlightened," asserting a "rational" Christianity of individual action and accountability while maligning popular devotions as "superstitions."[19]

A religious divide compounded deepening social polarities. The powerful had every reason to see themselves in control: they drove mines deep underground and took profit; they expanded irrigation to raise production and profits; inoculations began to protect a favored few from smallpox. For them, a religion of rational individualism legitimated lives of power and prosperity. The same profit seekers pressed predations spreading poverty and insecurity among growing majorities who saw devotion to powers promising aid and comfort ever more essential: Our Lady at Pueblito still ruled Otomí life around Querétaro; diverse virgins and saints focused popular devotion across Guanajuato.[20] The powerful found moral sanction in rational religion as they assaulted the common good; women and men struggling to survive found solace in powers offering aid and comfort.

Facing distress, the powerful might turn to popular devotions. The Conde de Colombini, don Francisco María de Colombini y Camayori, was an Italian nobleman educated in enlightenment and serving Spain in the Caribbean. In the 1790s, he faced a malady incurable until he landed in New Spain and met Our Lady of Pueblito. She saved him, and he penned a long ode to her powers and services, published in Mexico City in 1801.[21] Soon after, don José María Zeláa, a priest in Querétaro's congregation devoted to Guadalupe, wrote a reply. He noted Guadalupe's service in the face of disease and drought, exalting her promotion of charitable service funded by the powerful in hard times. He claimed Guadalupe for a religion of rational action and social legitimation.[22] The two texts surely set off debates among the powerful, prosperous, and literate few. Among the people, the many at Pueblito and the few at Guadalupe's Querétaro shrine told everything.

Struggles in the Countryside: A New Agrarian Ecology

Across the Bajío countryside, as silver soared to new heights, generating market demand and chances for profit, new population pressures enabled estate operators to press profit-seeking predations. Since the sixteenth century, sparse numbers had favored producing families and communities in negotiations that solidified secure patriarchal ways of provision on the land. Protections faded as population rose after 1770. A region with fewer than 325,000 people in 1755 rose to 430,000 by 1790, to approach 500,000 in 1810.[23] Estate operators saw populations grow beyond the needs of production, enabling them to cut pay and rations, raise rents, and evict those who could not pay.

Population growth generated a new ecology of production that prejudiced families on the land. Once devastating pandemics like smallpox became childhood maladies, leading to demographic expansions that began in the late seventeenth century and continued until typhus struck in the late 1730s. Growth resumed from the 1740s into the 1790s.[24] Infant death, faced inequitably, still limited numbers. In Querétaro's central parish, from 1789 to 1795, 20 percent of infants recorded as Spaniards died in their first year, while 30 percent died among mestizos and mulattoes and nearly 40 percent among Otomí. Among the Otomí on the *huertas* at San Sebastián, infant death approached 50 percent.[25] Painful and inequitable, infant mortality limited but did not block population growth.

In 1797, smallpox returned, leading Guanajuato intendant don José Riaño to bring inoculations to the city that drove silver capitalism. More than 11,000 were inoculated in the center where the powerful and the prosperous lived but only 4,800 in outlying mining camps. One percent of the inoculated died; 20 percent died among those denied. Few outside the mining center gained inoculation. Towns close to Guanajuato saw 1,500 to 2,000 inoculations each, with few in rural zones. The poorest regions of the intendancy around San Miguel, Dolores, San Felipe, and San Luis de la Paz were excluded. Outside the mining center, more than 92,000 cases of smallpox left a 20 percent death rate—striking mostly the young in estate-dependent rural communities.[26] Still, the population grew. And inoculations reinforced beliefs in enlightened rationality among the favored few—while those watching children die across the countryside knew to seek the aid and comfort of consoling virgins or saints.

Given that history, solid sustenance accounts for the Bajío's steady, if periodically interrupted, population growth. Into the 1780s, men gained secure salaries of 4 pesos monthly plus maize rations of 10 fanegas yearly, enough to ensure family sustenance, backed by their sons' seasonal wage work and often supplemented by rental access to small maize and garden plots. Such lives sustained nutrition—at the cost of women's endless labors. Through decanal cycles of plenty and dearth, maize harvests rose and fell. Estates harvested plenty in years of ample rains, delivering rations to the men that made the maize, storing surpluses awaiting times of drought and rising prices. For decades, the system fed families on the land and town consumers, too, sustaining population growth and silver capitalism.

During the same decades, irrigation had expanded on rich bottom-lands and across the upland basins around Querétaro, San Miguel, and León. Livestock left the region for dry lands north; pastures were turned to maize, often in small plots let to estate residents. Wheat concentrated on irrigated fields, leaving maize to rain-fed uplands. Through the 1770s, harvests grew as periodic years of drought and scarcity shaped New Spain's agrarian capitalism.

Once a decade, repeatedly and predictably, drought cut harvests on all but the irrigated lands reserved for wheat, the staple of the prosperous. Estate operators then sold the maize stored in their granaries—taking profits in times of high prices driven by scarcity to keep desperate people alive. For the estate-dependent majority, free rations of maize from the harvests they had made assured sustenance in times of plenty and scarcity, shielding then from the costs of decanal dearth. Through most of the eighteenth century, commercial maize cropping delivered secure patriarchal sustenance to a rural majority dependent on estate lands across the Bajío, sustaining population growth, silver capitalism, and global trades.[27]

The famine crisis of 1785–86 changed everything. After decades of population growth, two years of extreme drought brought unprecedented dearth and peak prices. Estate operators took profit as the scarcity proved extreme and people died, near 10 percent in some regions of the Bajío. To limit dearth and death, maize was hauled from coastal zones where wetlands kept harvests strong. When the rains returned, prices dropped—but never to prefamine levels. Survivors generated children to remake families. Estates began to plant maize on irrigated fields while taking back rain-fed fields from tenants, all to expand estate harvests and profit from higher prices. Tenants were pressed into uplands, where first harvests might be good, then fell rapidly as marginal lands lost fertility. Population growth resumed while estate operators turned to new predations, seeking profit by undermining the ways of secure patriarchal dependence that had long sustained life and silver capitalism in the Bajío.[28]

The predations that plagued producing families are revealed in detail in the correspondence of don José Sánchez Espinosa.[29] In 1781, he inherited La Griega near Querétaro and Puerto de Nieto east of San Miguel, estates built before 1700 by don Juan Caballero y Ocío and held by don Francisco de Espinosa y Navarijo, a priest, High Court lawyer, and agrarian capitalist based in Mexico City. The new landed patriarch would press predations on amalgamating people at Puerto de Nieto and the Otomí at La Griega. Their responses differed in the near term—and in revolutionary times after 1810.

Predations in Amalgamating Communities: Puerto de Nieto, San Miguel, Dolores, 1780–1808

On taking control of Puerto de Nieto in 1781, Sánchez Espinosa faced a dispute set off by his uncle's drive to impose new lives on estate dependents—and residents' insistence that they would not be moved. To expand cultivation, Espinosa y Navarijo had sent grazing operations north to Bocas. In 1779, he ordered a group of residents, most enslaved, others not, to move north to care for livestock. The priest, lawyer, and capitalist presumed that ownership of enslaved bodies meant control of where they lived and worked. The enslaved, accustomed to lives of everyday mobility at estates where they married free women to forge families set in amalgamating communities, did not share his view.

The group set to move included fifteen enslaved people: five adult men, two mothers, and eight children—gender not noted. Seven free women and children were assigned to join "voluntarily." The group provided little work at Puerto de Nieto; in time, enslaved children might serve at Bocas. The assumption that free mothers and children could be ordered north presumed enslaved men's patriarchy, expecting women who bore their children to obediently join the trek. They did not. The order to move and the adamant refusal by the enslaved and their free kin demonstrated again that the enslaved had stayed at Puerto de Nieto because of ties to family and community. Forced removal was a predation. Facing the attempt, the enslaved ended slavery at Puerto de Nieto.

One older enslaved man just left. In May 1782, two young enslaved women, both married, fled to Mexico City, where they presented themselves to the magistrate's court. They claimed to be free, an assertion disputed by Sánchez Espinosa, now their owner. They refused to return to the estate, arguing that the forced move broke prevailing customs. The court ordered them sold to the highest bidder—and no one bid. The women then vanish from the records, perhaps joining the capital's urban throngs, perhaps returning north to join husbands away from Puerto de Nieto and Bocas.

In September, two enslaved young men also fled to the capital; presenting themselves in court, they challenged Sánchez Espinosa's right to move them and claimed freedom. Again, the court ordered an auction; again, no one bid. The men were in custody in early November when their mother, María Juliana de Aguilar, wrote Sánchez Espinosa in her own hand. She recognized her status as enslaved (de Aguilar indicated marriage to a man named Aguilar, likely free). She excoriated the young patriarch for breaking her family and its ties to the Puerto de Nieto community. Again, the story ends in silence.

In the spring of 1783, Sánchez Espinosa knew that the attempt to move the enslaved had ended slavery at Puerto de Nieto. His only recourse was to sell the few who had not fled, for pittances of 20 to 30 pesos: free men paid to free enslaved wives and children; the manager's wife bought a serving woman. One man freed his children but not their enslaved mother; Sánchez Espinosa saw her as effectively free. Espinosa y Navarijo had aimed to maintain slavery by moving enslaved people and their free kin north. By flight and recalcitrance, they ended slavery at Puerto de Nieto.[30] The young landed patriarch learned the limits of his powers as he faced new life challenges.

Espinosa y Navarijo died in 1781, amid the challenges to bondage. Sánchez Espinosa committed 700 pesos to fund a perpetual flame in his honor.

From July through October 1782, he undertook a tour of his estates, asserting rule and reviewing managers', workers', and tenants' accounts. Back in the capital, he concluded the sales of the few slaves still at Puerto de Nieto. Then, in September 1783, he faced the sudden death of his wife, doña Mariana de la Mora, daughter of the Conde de Peñasco, the San Luis Potosí mine operator and landlord pivotal to the pacifications of 1767. She had died suddenly after an accident, leaving don José with two young sons. His letters note no grief, no perpetual flame.

They do reveal a relationship with doña María Micaela de Arenaza, a widow living in San Miguel. She had modest estates, a son, and ties to don Domingo de Allende, a Spanish immigrant merchant and father of future political insurgent don Ignacio Allende. Her letters reported small business deals and religious concerns before doña Mariana's injury and death. Afterward, doña María Micaela mixed caring concern with hints welcoming a closer personal tie. Sánchez Espinosa resisted—and took Holy Orders early in 1784. He followed don Juan Caballero y Ocío and don Francisco de Espinosa y Navarijo as a priest-patriarch pressing agrarian capitalism in the Bajío and New Spain—with the added benefit of sons to keep power in the family. The eldest, don Mariano Sánchez y Mora, would later inherit the Peñasco title and vast San Luis Potosí estates.[31]

After settling into life as a priest-patriarch, don José turned to reset operations at Puerto de Nieto. He fired the manager who failed to resolve the crisis of slavery while failing to collect rents. He appointed don Juan José Degollado early in 1785, just before the onset of the great drought, frost, and famine. Degollado oversaw the planting of the estate's first commercial maize on irrigated fields in 1786, gaining modest results. Sánchez Espinosa fired him early in 1787—leading his wife, doña María Guadalupe Zuñiga, to write in protest. She insisted that her husband had brought the estate through the most trying of times and forged new ways of production. As rains returned, profit would come. She won the right for her son to continue renting a rancho. Then when the irrigated maize harvest of 1787–88 yielded more than 2,300 fanegas, relieving the scarcity, Sánchez Espinosa credited the new manager, don Vicente Puente, Degollado's former assistant.[32]

Puerto de Nieto increased maize planting on estate account by increasing irrigation and opening rain-fed former pastures (figure 2.1). The 1792 militia census showed a community of established residents integrated by amalgamations among indigenous people, often Otomí, and others of African ancestry. Without hard ethnic lines, it divided into two segments: one tied by kinship to administrator Puente and his assistant overseeing irrigated

Figure 2.1 Irrigated fields at Puerto de Nieto, San Miguel. Author photo.

cultivation, don José Toribio Rico. Nearly 20 percent of the population was favored with links to the managers. They surely gained benefits in steady labor and access to tenancies. The majority lacked such connections and turned to household cloth making and other craft work to reinforce patriarchal household economies.[33]

Through the 1790s, Puerto de Nieto continued to expand commercial planting, cut worker pay, and take back tenancies. Times of good rains and ample harvests followed by years of scarce rains and high prices kept profits strong. Then, in 1802, Sánchez Espinosa looked to accelerate the shift to commercial cropping. He ordered Rico to complete an inventory of all land let to tenants, current rents, their commercial value, and potential higher rents. Then the estate announced rent increases and ordered the eviction of many who could not pay. In response, the group Rico labeled las muchachas—the girls—invaded the main house, insisting they would not leave unless their families kept their lands. In time, the girls left and the estate increased commercial planting by 20 percent that spring. Ongoing pressures on producing families threatened working patriarchs, their families, and the community. Only "the girls" took action—to limited effect.[34]

The lives faced by the displaced are revealed in accounts from Charco de Araujo, north along the road from San Miguel to Dolores. Long a grazing property, in 1797 it turned to maize, keeping the best lands for estate planting, allocating uplands to tenants. To plant estate fields, it hired *sirvientes*—holding salaries at a new low standard of 3 pesos monthly, a 25 percent cut from earlier times. Only managers gained advances. Others sharecropped on dry uplands, with some families mixing roles to diversify chances of survival. Over three years, yields on estate fields dropped 35 percent; on sharecropped plots they plummeted 55 percent. Families who came to Charco de Araujo did not find viable lives as low salaries, the end of advances, and falling yields drove deepening insecurities.[35]

Facing such predations, two groups of estate residents north of Dolores tried to claim lands for family production. Communities at Santa Bárbara in 1802 and Tequisquiapan in 1804 went to court claiming *indio* status and rights to found landed republics. They sought council rule and community lands, clearly aware of the indigenous republics that shaped life around Mexico City—and at Otomí Querétaro. Landlords resisted. The courts accepted the petitioners' status as *indios*, though many were of mixed ancestry, and their right to republics—if numbers were sufficient and lands available.

Both suits dragged on. The landlord at Santa Bárbara claimed insufficient land and argued that much would have to be taken from nearby holdings of the rich Mariscal de Castilla, seeking the latter's support in opposition. Petitioners at Tequisquiapan gained support from Hidalgo, who sent a vicar to back parishioners' claims. Both suits continued into 1808 without resolution.[36]

Profit-seeking predations challenged patriarchal provision around San Miguel and Dolores. Girls invaded the manager's home at Puerto de Nieto seeking to block evictions—and failed. Men went to court seeking rights as landed communities—and failed. Predations persisted, as did the goal of family production. In 1810, Dolores and San Miguel became crucibles of popular insurgency.

Predations and Otomí Communities:
La Griega and Querétaro, 1790–1808

Parallel predations led to differing responses in the culturally bifurcated Spanish-Otomí world around Querétaro. Early in 1792, Sánchez Espinosa pressed evictions at La Griega, east of the city. A blight had devastated the wheat crop while sparse rains cut the maize harvest, driving prices higher. Manager don José Regalado Franco demanded that leading tenants, most Hispanic, vacate large ranchos. Three responses are known. Don Melchor asked compensation for improvements and permission to store crops until prices peaked; Franco agreed. Aguilar turned to a Querétaro landlord for protection; he failed and vacated.

The greatest resistance came from doña Gertrudis Villaseñor, a widow. She wrote to Sánchez Espinosa complaining that Franco had raised the rent on her rancho at La Venta to a level she could not pay, making it impossible to sustain a family with many children (figure 2.2). Franco offered other lands, but they were not a rancho; they did not include a house, water, cultivable fields, and grazing lands. Don José ordered Franco to offer her the first open rancho, but the eviction must stand. Doña Gertrudis took the case to court; it confirmed the proprietor's right to evict. Still, the judge ordered the estate to pay the costs of the crop in the field and improvements she had made. Sánchez Espinosa offered the price of seed—to be charged against back rents still owed. She demanded the price of seed and the cost of labor, both paid immediately in cash; she would pay back rents when she could. Doña Gertrudis won on both questions, then vacated—with no sign she ever gained a rancho or paid back rents.[37]

In the decade that followed, La Griega expanded planting on estate accounts. At La Venta, it increased four times over. Production shifted from tenants to reliance on *sirvientes* and seasonal hands while the estate pressed earnings down. Salaries, historically above 4 pesos monthly before 1785, fell to 3, with maize rations also cut. The removal of Hispanic tenants shifted production to depend on Otomí *sirvientes*. Annual distributions of goods accounted as advances against salaries persisted. Every year, Franco sent Sánchez Espinosa a list of common and fine cloths, and other goods he believed would keep men at work. The shipment came with don José on an annual Easter visit, before plowing and planting began; he oversaw distribution—with wives and families present. He said Mass and heard confessions, backing his economic power with sacramental sanction and confessional intrusions. Production boomed and profit held as cultivation on estate account consolidated patriarchal dependencies into the early nineteenth century—while tenant production waned and *sirviente* pay and rations fell.[38]

Historically, advances were common across the Bajío—and rarely repaid. They recruited and held *sirvientes* at estates in times of scarce producers. To drive earnings down, advances had to end or be repaid in cash or labor. The Casas estate, south of Querétaro, tried to enforce just that in 1801. In

Figure 2.2 Rancho de la Venta, La Griega, Querétaro. Author photo.

response, Otomí brothers Julián Santos, Andrés Martín, and José María sued owner don Fernando Romero Martínez—Querétaro kin of the Conde de Regla, New Spain's richest mining and landed oligarch. The young men reported that after their father died a year earlier, they took work at Casas. The estate claimed that they owed 40 pesos for goods received by their father and never repaid in labor. They insisted that debts were not heritable and limited by law to 5 pesos. Romero pressed a small debt to make a large point, taking the suit to the High Court in Mexico City, at a cost far more than 40 pesos. Cutting through endless labeling and legalism, the landlord saw that if advances were not enforced, labor costs would not fall. The court ruled that the men must work off the debt.[39] Did they stay on and pay in labor? In times of population pressure, could they find other work?

The Otomí men of La Griega found another way to challenge power. The harvest set to begin in December 1805 promised to be one of the estate's best, more than 11,000 fanegas. Otomí *sirvientes* and their wage-working sons would soon cut, haul, and store the rich yield, to be held until scarcity promised profit. Then disease hit on the eve of the harvest. Many were ill and could not labor; others refused—insisting on the need to care for kin. The Otomí had forged an informal ethnic community. A captain who organized labor and the *fiscal* who led religious life told manager Franco that none would work until the estate funded devotions honoring San Agustín, the community's protector.

Franco wrote to Sánchez Espinosa, insisting that no amount of money would draw the men to work. He asked the priest-patriarch to sanction the festival, fund it, and come to lead its ceremony. Franco knew Sánchez Espinosa would hesitate and that the festival had to happen. The priest-patriarch favored sacramental worship and devotion to Guadalupe. The Otomí community looked to San Agustín and ritual drinking that brought them closer to the divine. Franco argued that if Sánchez Espinosa came, he might legitimate his power and curb excess—read independence. Knowing the festival was inevitable, the manager ordered a barrel of *aguardiente* (cane brandy) from La Teja, Sánchez Espinosa's estate near the capital. The priest-patriarch paid for the drink but did not go to La Griega; the festival went forward and the Otomí completed the harvest.

After the expulsions of the early 1790s, La Griega became more dependent on Otomí workers. With no formal republican rights, the community chose its own labor and religious leaders. In a time when disease might limit the estate harvest, they called a strike—making a larger point while focusing on curing and religious life. They won, disease passed, and Otomí men took salaries and wages in the harvest. Sánchez Espinosa paid a bit more to gain future profits. Otomí men led the resistance, yet in his report to Sánchez Espinosa, Franco labeled them not *los Otomies,* not *los indios*—but *la indiada,* a community feminized. Otomí men resisting power were maligned as women.[40] However maligned, they negotiated to reinforce patriarchy, family, and community in 1805, solidarities that held to 1810 and through the years of insurgency that followed.

Crisis in the Capital of Silver Capitalism, 1808

Mounting predations did not lead directly to insurgencies. Two years of imperial challenges in times of drought began in 1808, shaking regime power while social predations deepened. It all began when Napoleon invaded Spain—an ally. In May, French armies took Madrid and captured Carlos IV and prince Fernando, decapitating Spain's empire. Why? The Haitian Revolution had left France without revenues from America. Defeat at Trafalgar in 1805 left France and Spain without navies to contend for Atlantic power or protect trade. Desperate, the French emperor won the Spanish Bourbons' permission to cross the Pyrenees, aiming to take Lisbon in 1807. When a British fleet took Portugal's monarch to Rio de Janeiro, locking Brazil's gold and sugar to British power, Napoleon turned on Madrid. His goal was New Spain's silver, flowing at historic peaks. Without naval forces, gaining it was improbable. In the attempt, Napoleon broke Spain's empire at the center.[41]

When Madrid fell in May 1808, the Spanish Bourbons accepted a rich exile in Bayonne. The people of Madrid protested (see Goya's *Third of May*) while juntas rose across Spain's diverse regions to contest French rule. Following the Spanish tradition of the sovereignty of the pueblos, in the absence of a monarch cities with councils claimed autonomy and mobilized guerrillas to fight French armies. In Mexico City, the news set off a summer of mobilizations. People took to the streets demanding rights, while the viceroy, oligarchs, and professionals debated whether to call a junta to rule New Spain, aiming to safeguard the silver capitalism still pivotal to the empire and global trade.

Power holders and everyday people debated rights and participations. Classic Spanish doctrine favored the sovereignty of the pueblos, towns with councils. Other voices looked to the sovereignty of "el pueblo," the abstract people, an Anglo-American abstraction. Still others imagined a sovereign *nation*, reflecting French revolutionary innovations. The tradition of sovereign pueblos focused on calls for juntas, councils to defend and preserve the monarchy. A junta of New Spain might serve the power of the oligarchs who ruled silver capitalism as bullion flows held at historic heights.[42]

A junta in Seville, claiming supreme authority in Spain, feared that autonomy in New Spain would cut the silver flowing to fight Napoleon. It sent military men to Mexico City seeking recognition and funding—with instructions to overthrow Viceroy don José de Iturrigaray if a Mexico City junta appeared imminent. When such a junta was called, on the night of September 16 a military coup arrested the viceroy and proclaimed loyalty to Seville—in the name of "*el pueblo*," the people.

The public face of the coup was don Gabriel de Yermo, a struggling merchant and aspiring landlord who had lost sugar estates south of the capital to the Consolidation. He led militia forces to topple a viceroy he resented. He was never the prime author of the coup. Military men from Spain planned it in concert with judges on the Mexico City High Court. Forces drawn from across New Spain occupied the capital, including troops from San Luis

Potosí led by don Félix Calleja and militias from Michoacán commanded by don Agustín de Iturbide, men soon anathema to Bajío revolutionaries.[43]

The coup removed a legitimate viceroy to impose allegiance to the Seville junta. Its military leaders claimed legitimacy based on the sovereignty of the people, an abstraction reflecting the vision of the junta's British allies, not the political pueblos of Spanish tradition. They ended the rule by judicial mediation that had stabilized New Spain and silver capitalism for centuries. Administrative power backed by military force marked a new regime. With no legitimate monarch in Madrid and militarized powers in Mexico City, legitimacy became uncertain in New Spain.[44]

The oligarchs and officials who had moved toward a junta, de facto autonomy, and time to await world developments acquiesced in the coup. Were they awed by the force of the coup? Perhaps. More likely, they knew that a challenge would bring conflicts and disrupt silver capitalism—and its preservation and promotion was their first interest and primary goal. They would wait and watch.

A few imagined more radical responses grounded in the dreams of autonomy and popular sovereignty that had captured the capital in the summer of ferment before the coup. They failed, but one plot is noteworthy. The day after the coup, don Mariano Sánchez y Mora, Sánchez Espinosa's elder son, Conde de Peñasco by his maternal grandfather, owner of rich estates in San Luis Potosí, yet still living under his powerful father's oversight, met with a neighborhood silversmith. They discussed the coup and a plan to reverse it. They aimed to draw in the Conde de Valenciana, another young oligarch whose family held Guanajuato's richest mines, along with the governors of Mexico City's two indigenous republics, San Juan Tenochtitlan and Santiago Tlatelolco, polities including more than thirty thousand people. The dream: mobilize the indigenous city, oust the coup leaders, and proclaim an indigenous king. It proved a fantasy. An indigenous governor reported the plot. The silversmith and his wife faced arrest. Peñasco and Valenciana were taken in for questioning.

Peñasco's testimony on September 20 is revealing. He insisted that he went to the shop only to buy a medallion, then reported a conversation that showed a sharp understanding of the coup and a plan for resistance. He emphasized that once the military had turned to coercion to topple legitimate authorities, only armed resistance could right the wrong. As the right to act belonged to the pueblos, political towns, resistance should be led by the capital's indigenous republics, with one of their governors crowned king. Peñasco's insight that armed power could only be countered by armed resistance proved prescient. His dream that indigenous republics might lead the resistance revealed a limited grasp of the historic ties binding the republics to Spain's imperial regime.

The native governors remained loyal. The silversmith and his wife were held for months. The young oligarchs were questioned and freed. Both were of clans so powerful that officials had to tread lightly—as long as no rising came. Sánchez Espinosa, convinced his son had strayed, stripped him of all roles in family affairs and exiled him to the San Pedro estate near Otumba, sending the seditious young conde to live behind the pyramids of Teotihuacan, a relic of indigenous kingship long past.[45]

Challenges also came to Querétaro in the summer of 1808. On July 27, the indigenous republic there, still overseer of the Otomí majority grounded in rich *huertas*, proclaimed its readiness to lead ten thousand men "to shed our last drop of blood in defense of God and Our Catholic King."[46] That bold stance weighed on the men who ruled Spanish Querétaro. On September 17, the day after the coup (as young Peñasco dreamed of revolution), Corregidor Domínguez, not yet aware of the coup, signed a council document calling for a Cortes or Congress of New Spain. It would gather delegates from *ciudades y villas* (Spanish cities and towns), cathedral chapters, and High Court judges. Provincials excluded in the plans made in the capital would join; indigenous republics would not. Domínguez did argue that a Cortes/Congress was essential to address the *indigencia y miseria* of the *ínfimo pueblo*—the poverty and misery of the poorest people. Only "legitimate powers" could prevent popular acts that would be "hard and bloody."[47] While in the capital, people powerful and poor debated New Spain's role in the empire, Domínguez called for provincial participations, aiming to counter rising popular discontent. He was too late. The coup demobilized New Spain—for a time.

Ecological Crisis, Capitalist Predations, and Mediating Responses: Querétaro, 1808–1810

Regimes and political debates do not live in economic, ecological, or social vacuums. As news arrived of Napoleon taking the Spanish monarchy, the rains of 1808 came late and stayed scarce through the summer of debate; by the September coup, it was clear that maize would be scarce as prices rose from the heartland through the Bajío. Domínguez and the Querétaro Council saw violence simmering in a desperate populace. Their imagined junta sought social pacification.

Oligarchs remained oligarchs. Sánchez Espinosa took reports all summer and fall of withering crops and rising prices. He held ample stocks in storage—including the maize harvested after the Otomí strike and festival at La Griega in 1805. As the coup deposed the viceroy and young Peñasco dreamed of revolution, the priest-patriarch halted maize sales at his Bajío estates, aiming to drive prices higher. By late October, they had doubled and he began sales to profit from hunger.[48]

Before 1808 ended, a rich landed widow took a different tack. Doña María Josefa Vergara turned to instruct the men who presumed to rule Querétaro on ways to regenerate life in predatory times. She lived in a city mansion, keeping four fine coaches while served by a large staff. She owned La Esperanza, Hope, a large and valuable property east of La Griega. In 1807, it included the largest Otomí estate community in the region: 300 adult men, thus at least 1,000 people. With its Hispanic minority, nearly 1,500 people lived and worked at La Esperanza.

She began to write a will in December 1808, aware of the summer events in Mexico City, facing the drought destroying the maize in her fields, knowing that rising prices promised soaring profits and angry people. She also knew the fears of violence that had focused council conversations and Domínguez' September plan. She wrote to instruct the council, offering her estate and its profits to fund a vision of how legitimate power could reform a society at the edge of a crisis laced with violence. Like Domínguez, her goal was reform to preserve property and the prevailing order.

She opened by insisting that neither she nor her late husband, don José Luis Frías, brought wealth or property to their union. They had operated an estate on leasehold, then bought La Esperanza without mortgage. Claiming self-made success, doña María Josefa said nothing about the source of wealth that enabled the purchase and development of La Esperanza. Perhaps a merchant financier in textiles, Frías followed the proven path of investing in land, first by leasehold, then by buying La Esperanza. Set east beyond La Griega, it had been a grazing property. Joining the ongoing regional transformation, Frías and Vergara expanded cultivation, likely drawing families displaced by evictions closer to market centers. Her will offers no hint of the mix of estate cultivation and tenant cropping, only a clear sense of a large population, profitable production—and a powerful urge to "improve" the lives of those who made her profits.

With no children, she left cash bequests to a variety of kin and dependents, some who served, others orphans she raised. She pressed men to more independent lives, women to devout service. She freed the few enslaved women who served her. She gave large bequests to support convent women, emphasizing sacramental worship and charitable service. Our Lady of Pueblito had no place in doña María Josefa's utopia. She funded a school for boys and one for girls at La Esperanza, and four more for girls in Querétaro to teach literacy, sewing, and embroidery. Education and devotion might pacify.

In a second part written just before Christmas 1808, she left La Esperanza to the Querétaro Council, naming Corregidor Domínguez and first magistrate don Pedro de Septién, a powerful merchant-financier and landlord, as executors. The estate must remain intact to fund her vision of Querétaro's future. It would pay the annual tributes of its resident Otomí men, relieving a small burden; it would pay teacher salaries and student meals at convent schools in Querétaro, enabling religious lives.

Then she addressed the poverty and insecurity deepening all around. She founded a Casa de Hospicio, a poor house to shelter disabled and destitute men, removing them from the streets—where she saw too many begging to avoid work. Women also needed work, and the tobacco factory did not accommodate all in need. Vergara founded a House of Refuge, where women would live by spinning, sewing, and embroidering. As patriarchal households dissolved, the refuge would set women to work. To contain crime on city streets, she funded lighting and patrols. With dearth all around, she founded a *pósito*, where officials would oversee supplies and sales of maize in the city. It would not control prices but might shield landed producers (like Vergara and Sánchez Espinosa) from blame for the profit taking that deepened popular desperations. Finally, she turned to aid artisans and shopkeepers: 100,000 pesos would fund a Monte de Piedad, a pawn broker and lender to provide fair credit.

Facing dearth in times of polarization, doña María Josefa Vergara instructed the Querétaro Council on how to preserve profit seeking while cushioning the challenges afflicting so many. She would not limit landed capitalists' ability to profit from scarcity, the foundation of her wealth. Women might gain work; artisans would find credit; men who did not work would be constrained—and fed.

As 1809 began, she saw more to do. Recalling that waves of disease visited in times of dearth, she amended her will so that when disease came, funding would shift to care for the ill. In final mandates, in July 1809, as a second summer of drought turned scarcity into famine, she directed that all her wealth go to feed the city, paying the prices of dearth to deliver La Esperanza's maize to the city. Her charity would feed people while sustaining her profits—a last hope.[49]

Doña María Josefa Vergara saw social predations corroding families and communities. She helped keep people and profit taking alive through the famine of 1809–10. She did not live to see the conflicts that ravaged Guanajuato after 1810—while people in and around Querétaro stayed at home and at work. The most powerful woman at Querétaro cushioned predations.

Silver Peaks, Empire Dissolves, 1809–1810

Contradictions peaked across New Spain in 1809. Total silver production hit 26 million pesos; output at Guanajuato rose above 5.2 million pesos. Still, regional commerce fell.[50] The drought that began in 1808 intensified to drive maize prices and estate profits higher while hunger, poverty, and insecurity stalked people across the Bajío and in the heartland around the capital.

In the summer and fall of 1809, oligarchs sold maize at prices four times higher than in years of good harvests. Sánchez Espinosa's managers only sold at estate granaries, keeping quantities small and forcing transport costs onto consumers. All could see who profited from dearth and who paid in desperation. Landed capitalists told themselves that storing grain to sell in times of dearth was a Christian charity—a very profitable charity. Those who paid dearly to survive surely saw differently.[51]

While silver soared and hunger became desperation across New Spain, Spain's war against Napoleon carried on. In the wake of the 1808 coup, the Mexico City Mining Tribunal pressed Seville to deliver the mercury necessary to refine silver while negotiating with Mexico City merchants to fund production with advances against silver to come.[52] They succeeded. Through 1809 and into 1810, silver flowed at unprecedented levels, crossing the Atlantic in Spanish vessels protected by British escorts. The Anglo-Seville alliance against Napoleon gained funding; how much sustained Spanish resistance and how much served British power is unclear. Record flows of British cloth to New Spain, more than 5 million pesos in 1808 and more than 8 million in 1809, showed that British industry gained amply as New Spain's cloth makers lost markets and income, another predation in time of war and hunger.[53]

Through the fall of 1808 and into 1809, the Spanish fight against Napoleon proved a corrosive and costly stalemate. In New Spain, the military commanders and High Court judges who planned the 1808 coup had named Field Marshall don Pedro Garibay viceroy, a statement of militarizing goals. To legitimize power, in January 1809, the Seville Junta proclaimed that the American empire remained "an essential and integral part of the Spanish monarchy" and called for nine delegates to speak for all of Spain's Americas. It was representation—a radical underrepresentation as Spain retained thirty-six seats for a smaller population. In February, the Seville Junta replaced Marshall Garibay with Mexico City archbishop don Francisco Javier de Lizana y Beaumont, in the long tradition of archbishops serving as interim viceroys—setting a clerical face at the front of the newly militarized regime.[54]

As drought and scarcity deepened, in the spring of 1809, the city council at Valladolid (now Morelia, Michoacán) met to select its delegate to the gathering that would choose New Spain's one delegate to the junta in Seville. Americans argued again for autonomies; immigrants from Spain backed Seville and the fight against Napoleon. Debates spread to public squares, taverns, and beyond in a provincial replay of the Mexico City summer of 1808. The backers of Seville won. The debates revealed political fractures enduring into times of popular desperation.[55]

In the fall, the American faction began unsanctioned meetings in Valladolid. Landlords and professionals, officials and militia leaders called for a "sovereign junta" of Michoacán. They included local indigenous notables, parallel to the inclusion of Mexico City's indigenous governors in the debates of 1808. Valladolid leaders reached out to men in the Bajío, including landlord and militia commander don Ignacio Allende at San Miguel. The goal was an American alliance: landlords and professionals, mixed and indigenous peoples uniting against the immigrant Spanish few maligned as *gachupines* and blamed for the 1808 coup. There was talk of mobilizing militias, not of raising native throngs. Still, immigrant Spanish merchants and officials opposed the call.[56] Surrounded by an angry populace, no rising came. In December, the leaders were detained, taken to the capital, questioned, warned, and released by Lizana y Beaumont in a last act of conciliating mediation.

Soon after the Valladolid movement broke, in November 1809 news arrived in New Spain of the battle at Ocaña, near Toledo. French forces routed Spanish resistance and began a steady march to Seville. As 1810 began, it was clear that vast expenditures of New Spain's silver had not stopped Napoleon in Spain. In February, French troops took Seville. The junta dissolved, naming a regency to carry on at the port of Cádiz—clinging to Spanish soil. The regency deposed Lizana y Beaumont, displeased with his conciliation of autonomists. News of the fall of Seville reached Mexico City in April; the decree removing Lizana y Beaumont came in May, with no replacement named.

In the summer of 1810, no junta ruled Spain, no viceroy led New Spain—while millions of pesos made at the cost of deepening social predations had gone to a failed fight to preserve Bourbon rule. With no legitimate regime and people facing starvation, revolution soon came—debated in Querétaro, made in Guanajuato.

PART II

Breaking Silver Capitalism, 1810–1820

The Hidalgo Revolt

Four Months That Shook New Spain

The revolt that began at Dolores the morning of September 16, 1810, is forever identified with don Miguel Hidalgo y Costilla—and honored as the birth of Mexico. Neither emphasis is ultimately wrong. Still, Hidalgo struggled to lead a revolt laden with contradictions: he and key allies demanded political rights; the majority of insurgents fought for food and families. Militias loyal to the regime crushed the rising after four turbulent months. Hidalgo and other leaders were captured, tried, and executed. A Mexican nation would only begin in 1821. In the interim, popular insurgents made a revolution.

Hidalgo did not plan the conflagration that exploded in the fall of 1810. The political rights he dreamed of did not come. The popular redistributions he feared did, propelled by risings that polarized New Spain as defenders of property faced angry popular insurgents. He tried to mediate for a time and failed. He turned to defend property—and saw his revolt fail. The four months of insurgency he provoked proved a destructive whirlwind that began the Bajío revolution.

Hidalgo mattered. He took the risk of calling a rising most political reformers feared. He struggled to manage its contradictory furies. He knew the powerful yet had never joined their world. He lived among the people yet never shared their struggles and goals. Hidalgo lived between power and the people in a society torn by political polarities and social predations. He rode a storm of violence until insurgents he could not control dispersed in the face of forces mobilized to defend property.

His revolt began as a political challenge to the powers set in Mexico City by the 1808 coup. After the mediating regime broke and military powers prevailed, provincial leaders faced political exclusions while Bajío communities faced grinding social predations. When Hidalgo and his allies rose to claim political autonomies, people struggling to survive took arms to take maize and land to make it. The revolt accelerated the militarization of power, rattled silver production, and stimulated wider popular movements. It changed everything—and resolved nothing.

Querétaro Prelude: Political Dreams and Epigmenio González' Vision

The summer of 1810 brought new political debates. On June 20, New Spain's Mining Tribunal wrote a memo recognizing the collapse of the Seville Junta, the promise of a regency, and the hope that an effective sovereign and the rule of law would soon return. Sitting in Mexico City, the men of the tribunal proclaimed loyalty to vacant powers in times of uncertainty.[1] Among the signatories was the Marqués de San Juan de Rayas, leader of a Guanajuato mining family, supporter of the proposed junta of New Spain in August 1808, then a promoter of mining to fund the fight against Napoleon. Now he faced new challenges.

Among his correspondents was don Ignacio Allende. The San Miguel estate operator and militia commander kept ties with those dreaming of juntas and sovereignty in Querétaro. Built on Otomí foundations, the city had risen to become the gateway to the Bajío, its leading center of commerce, cloth making, and tobacco manufacturing. In the summer of 1808, its Otomí council had proclaimed readiness to fight to the death against French usurpers; in September, don Miguel Domínguez and the Spanish Council called for a junta to remake sovereignty and contain popular discontent. The call came too late, as the coup in the capital militarized power, ended talk of autonomy, and locked New Spain to the Seville Junta and the fight against Napoleon.

Now, in 1810, with Spain's monarchs still imprisoned, the Seville Junta gone, a regency only beginning to imagine new ways of rule at Cádiz, and no viceroy in Mexico City, everything seemed uncertain—again. As silver flowed strong and summer rains promised the first good harvest in two years, new conversations about sovereignty began in Querétaro. There was no formal organization, no planned "conspiracy," and no consensus vision. Discussions and debates emerged at dinners, dances, and literary gatherings among the privileged and prosperous—and in everyday market encounters.

The prominent joined in: Domínguez, the corregidor who had argued against the consolidation in 1805 and in favor of a Cortes of New Spain in 1808, was a constant presence. Discussions came at soirees hosted by him and his wife, doña Josefa Ortiz, who in time proved the more radical of the pair. Don Pedro de Septién, councilman and leading merchant, financier, and landlord, was a presence too. Had doña María Josefa Vergara lived, she surely would have joined, ready to instruct Domínguez, Septién, and the council on needed reforms. Lawyers, clerics, and middling traders were there too. There is no sign that the men of Querétaro's Otomí republic joined, yet it is hard to imagine they were unaware.

Allende was pivotal to linking debates in Querétaro to provincials in outlying towns. He had inherited estates and held a militia command, yet lived in the shadows of the Canal family oligarchs who ruled San Miguel. Allende knew the conversations at Valladolid in 1809. Now he engaged others in San Miguel and nearby, including Hidalgo, the pastor at Dolores who had backed rural men's claims to community rights while losing his own financially struggling estate to the Consolidation.

Among those focused on power and prosperity, discontent focused on the dreams and losses of the summer of 1808: the chance at participation in sovereignty and the losses imposed by the coup that blocked calls for a junta, broke rule by mediation, imposed militarized power, and left a regime of doubtful legitimacy. In the two years since, legitimacy held uncertain, silver boomed, while landed oligarchs profiteered from scarcity—spreading outrage across the Bajío and around Mexico City.[2]

Many in Querétaro's political class imagined a revolt to claim political participations. Most hesitated, fearing that a rising would energize people struggling to survive. The question was how to call a rising, mobilize support, and contain redistributions. Those working toward a revolt, including Allende and doña Josefa Ortiz, reached out to Epigmenio González, a storekeeper in contact with people across the city and from the nearby countryside. His life, writings, and later testimonies reveal the contradictions of the summer of 1810.

González was born in 1781 to parents who claimed Spanish status, without the honor of don or doña. His only godparent was a woman of similar status. They lived near the tobacco factory, then a bastion of male labor. His parents' economic roles are not known; the witnesses to their marriage

Figure 3.1 Epigmenio González' view: Querétaro plaza and Franciscan church. Author photo.

and his baptism labored in the tobacco factory, suggesting ties to that enterprise. His mother died in 1785, his father in 1786, leaving him orphaned in years of famine. He was raised by a grandfather, who died in 1797 amid smallpox. The next year, González found work clerking in the store of doña María Josefa Covarrubias on the square across from the San Francisco church and convent (figure 3.1). There, Epigmenio dealt daily with people buying life necessities in the center of the Bajío's second city. In 1801, he married María Anastasia Juárez, an *india* of unknown parents, an orphan serving Spanish householders. They had three children; none survived in a city marked by infant death.

González lived at the edge of Spanish Querétaro. When doña María Josefa Covarrubias died in 1807, she left Epigmenio a house; her executors enabled him to take over the store with his brother Emeterio. María Anastasia died the next year, leaving Epigmenio a widower. He shared the pains of popular life while attuned to the everyday challenges that escalated from 1808 to 1810.[3]

Late in life, after years of imprisonment and a long exile in Manila, in 1853 he wrote an account of his role in Querétaro's debates of the summer of 1810.[4] He emphasized the leadership of "Capitán Don Ignacio de Allende" and two goals: to break with Spain and benefit "every *mexicano*"—a term common in 1853, barely imagined in 1810. González credited Allende for including "Don Miguel Hidalgo y Costilla and Doña Josefa Ortíz de Domínguez, who did important services, greater than many others who held wealth and power and whose defections caused incalculable harm."[5]

Doña Josefa Ortiz introduced González to Allende in August. Epigmenio, Emeterio, and a few allies began collecting weapons and making ammunition. Meanwhile, Allende and his ally don Juan Aldama sought support among the powerful, beginning with the Marqués de Jaral at his hacienda north of the Bajío, then passing to Salvatierra, Celaya, and Querétaro, where the journey ended on the twenty-fourth.[6]

At Celaya, a militia commander asked Allende what government he aimed to create. Allende answered, according to González, that the decision was not his and he would consult the person who knew best. Allende then invited Hidalgo to Querétaro, where "the venerable Elder" presided over a meeting and stated: "We will make a revolution to improve the kingdom. The goal is to remove *gachupines* from power; they are the cause of all our problems. Everything else should remain as is, awaiting reforms designed by enlightened men." Hidalgo foreshadowed much to come: blame *gachupines*, immigrant Spaniards, for New Spain's troubles; preserve the status quo while awaiting reforms offered by the political men who led the rising. Allende concurred. The American landowner and commander called for risings to begin at Querétaro, San Miguel, and Dolores on September 22.[7]

Allende sent funds to don Joaquín Arias, a militia captain at Celaya chosen to lead the rising at Querétaro. Did Allende lack confidence in Querétaro's men of property? He sent letters to Mexico City, aiming to recruit the

Marqués de Rayas—who replied that it was too late, the project should end, and he would not join.

On September 14, a note from the capital told González that a new viceroy would soon arrive in Mexico City. The shopkeeper sent a letter to alert Allende at San Miguel. The same day, another participant in the planning, jailed on murder charges, revealed the plan.[8] Midnight brought a knock at González' door; there stood Corregidor Domínguez, Brigadier don Ignacio García Rebello, and twenty-five men of the Celaya regiment. They found hundreds of lances and 2,600 cartridges but no firearms. They arrested the González brothers, a servant and a cook, a carpenter's apprentice, and two orphans.

The next day, the commander and the corregidor interrogated Epigmenio. He said nothing of Domínguez' role in the plotting. Epigmenio took responsibility for the arms. Asked the goal of the planning, he said it was to stop the French threat. Told that was the regime's role, he replied that as Spaniards had delivered the kingdom to the French, "the people" had to defend the empire. The same day, doña Josefa Ortiz sent a message to San Miguel warning Allende of the arrests at Querétaro.[9]

González waited all day on the fifteenth for a rising he dreamed would come. The next day, he saw that don Joaquín Arias, the Celaya militia captain Allende funded to lead the revolt at Querétaro, had turned on his allies and joined the roundup. On the sixteenth, learning of risings at Dolores and San Miguel, Commander García Rebollo demanded that the Querétaro Council deliver funds from doña María Josefa Vergara's bequest to pay for defense and loyal troops.[10] Riches the widow had designated to serve the common good would fund armed defense of the established order.

In the following days, authorities searched González home and store to find a "bundle of papers written by my hand," including a detailed plan to transform New Spain.[11] It directly countered Hidalgo's goal of holding the established order with limited reforms. There is no evidence the plan circulated among the men seeking a political movement. Did he share it with doña Josefa Ortiz? In his store on the plaza, González daily engaged people struggling to survive in times of predations deepened by scarcity and profiteering. His plan captured their desperations and dreams.[12]

New Spain would throw off Spanish rule to become Anahuac, the Nahua name for the Mesoamerican heartland. "Prince Electors" would name an emperor. There was no loyalty, feigned or real, to the captive Fernando VII. To restore judicial mediation, every province would have a High Court of two judges. Boards of Preservation would oversee agriculture, commerce and industry, aqueducts and highways. The focus on cultivation and industry, water and trade reflected Querétaro's interests. The absence of a mining board suggests resentment of the power of Guanajuato and its silver. Everywhere, magistrates would mobilize the "unemployed, the inebriated, and those devoted to gambling" in labor gangs to build and maintain roads, fields, and hydraulic works to expand irrigation. Marginal men would serve the common good through public works.

Turning to agriculture, the plan became more radical. The estates of *gachupines* would be expropriated, the land distributed to native families. American landlords loyal to Anahuac would retain estates—while required to turn over the land to tenant growers at rents set by the emperor. The plan would reverse the evictions at the heart of decades of rural predations. Landlords would be rentiers; family growers would rule cultivation in a social inversion within established property relations.

González aimed to prohibit external trade, blocking imports of cloth and clothing. Recent floods of British textiles would end; family cloth makers might find new prosperity. Of course, an end to external trade would also break silver mining. González offered a radical vision, ending silver capitalism, turning cultivation and cloth making over to families, leaving merchants and landlords to profit as they might. He knew his customers' dreams of a world set in family production.

The plan also promised tax reforms: the tributes paid by indigenous and mulatto men would end, replaced by a one-peso contribution paid by all individuals ages twenty through fifty. The residents of convents sustained by alms and active military men and their wives were exempt. The exclusion of military wives confirmed the intent to include most adult women, recognizing and taxing their essential economic roles in the tobacco factory, in textile workshops, and in household economies everywhere. Aiming to boost regional trade, taxes on commerce would fall to 1 percent, down from the 4 to 8 percent taken by historic *alcabalas*. There is no mention of taxes on silver; the end of external trade would cripple silver and its fiscal value. Anahuac would live on family production and internal revenues. González knew producers' struggles; he would turn the Bajío upside down.[13] Insurgencies soon revealed that thousands shared his goals.

When Allende learned of the arrests at Querétaro, he rode to Dolores to meet Hidalgo. Should they flee to the United States, now as close as Louisiana? Or should they raise what allies they could in Dolores and San Miguel, start a revolt, and learn what might come? On the morning of September 16, 2010, they chose insurgency. While Hidalgo and Allende called for political rights, throngs rose to press for redistributions in town and across the countryside all around. Occupied by loyalist troops, Querétaro held back. Goals that Epigmenio González had discovered in his store on the square in Querétaro drove angry insurgencies among estate residents across Guanajuato.

Don Miguel Hidalgo: A Life Between

Don Miguel Hidalgo y Costilla came late to the movement he is famous for leading. He personified the rebellion's contradictions. Arguably, only he could have led a rising that aimed to harness the popular energies grasped by González to serve the drive for political autonomy imagined by Allende. Hidalgo was essential to the explosion of insurgency in September 1810—and pivotal to its demise early in 1811. Four months of violence made it clear that the goals of political autonomy in service of the propertied were incompatible with popular demands for redistribution. In proving that, Hidalgo's revolt shook New Spain—and began a revolution.

Hidalgo lived between the powerful few and the producing many, between the established church and enlightened innovators, between devotees of sacramental worship and people seeking assistance and compassion in devotions to virgins and saints. He was born in 1753, son of the manager of the Corralejo estate, near Pénjamo. His father's family lived as managers and tenants; his mother's family generated clergy. Don Miguel merged traditions of landed and religious mediation.[14]

Corralejo was a modest estate by Bajío standards, valued near 175,000 pesos. Manager don Cristóbal Hidalgo held personal property valued at 7,800 pesos in 1764, including a house in Pénjamo and five slaves. When his mother died in childbirth in 1763, Miguel was barely ten. The eldest son, Manuel, had already left for studies that would lead to roles as a lawyer serving the High Court and the Inquisition in Mexico City—a life of judicial and theological mediation.[15] In 1765, the next two Hidalgo brothers, José Joaquín and Miguel, took a similar path, moving to Valladolid to study at the Jesuit Colegio. They saw the expulsion of their teachers in 1767, then continued at the San Nicolás Seminary. In 1770, they gained bachelor's degrees awarded in Mexico City, experiencing the largest and richest city in the Americas. Don Miguel returned to Valladolid to study, teach, and earn certification in Otomí, showing an interest in indigenous communities. A deacon in 1776, he gained a chair in Latin in 1777. Ordained in 1778, he won a chair in philosophy and theology in 1784.[16]

In 1787, just after the great drought and famine of 1785–86, don Miguel became treasurer of the Cathedral Chapter, overseeing Church finances in Michoacán and across the Bajío. He negotiated a loan of 20,000 pesos to his father, repurposed in 1791 to fund don Miguel and don Manuel's purchase of three small properties at Taximaroa, between the Bajío, Valladolid, and the capital. At the possession ceremony, leaders of the republic of Taximaroa came to "contradict the possession," as it included community lands. Objections noted, the Hidalgo brothers gained title. Soon after, holdings gained for 20,000 pesos were valued at 50,000 as don Miguel took another 7,000-peso loan.[17]

Named rector of San Nicolás in 1790, don Miguel Hidalgo y Costilla seemed poised to thrive in Church administration and financial affairs, in intellectual and theological life, and in training new clergy—while dreaming of prosperity on the land. Then, in 1792, he left Valladolid to serve as interim pastor at Colima, a Spanish parish in the hot country to the south. It was a sudden fall from grace. There were rumors of parties, women, and children—likely true, but not new. Hidalgo famously engaged in enlightened thinking, favoring French authors while joining debates at the intersection of science and penitential religion. Still, such debates marked life among favored clergy and powerful laymen at San Miguel without leading to sanctions. The reasons for Hidalgo's exile remain debated.[18]

In 1793, he won appointment as pastor at San Felipe, at the northern edge of the Bajío. The next year, his brother don Joaquín became pastor at Dolores, a more prosperous parish an uncle had led in the previous decade.[19] Removed from Valladolid, the Hidalgo brothers remade ecclesiastical power north of Guanajuato—while social transformations and predations rattled the countryside.

At San Felipe, don Miguel oversaw church finances and sacramental life. He read texts from France. He sponsored musical and theatrical events. He brought the debates of the eighteenth century to the parish just as the French Revolution challenged monarchical rule, clerical power, and Catholic orthodoxy—and as the enslaved in Saint-Domingue rose to claim freedom and break plantation capitalism. San Felipe became a home for French culture, a *Francia chiquita*—not revolutionary, but free thinking.[20]

In 1800, a friar denounced Hidalgo to the Inquisition. They had met at Taximaroa, where Hidalgo visited regularly to oversee his estates. Talk turned theological and the friar concluded that Hidalgo held heretical views: he questioned the efficacy of God's punishments in the world; he doubted the sanctity of the Church's founding fathers; he read questionable French authors; he defended the Koran. Inquisition judges took testimony: men who knew Hidalgo saw him as a committed theologian and dedicated priest; those who knew his reputation told of disputes, festivals, and fandangos. The Inquisitors concluded that all was hearsay, all disputed. They left the file open and sent Hidalgo back to San Felipe.[21] Did brother don Manuel's role in the Inquisition help that outcome?

Younger brother don Joaquín remained pastor at Dolores while joining in debates and social life at San Felipe. His death, in September 1803, brought don Miguel grief and a new opportunity.[22] In October, the bishop named him pastor at Dolores, seeking spiritual continuity. Don Miguel remained central to the life of the church in the northern Bajío while his new parishioners faced predatory challenges.

In 1804, the cathedral canceled the 20,000-peso loan that had enabled don Manuel and don Miguel to buy the estates at Taximaroa.[23] In 1805, don Miguel sent an assistant to support the suit by residents of Tequisquiapan seeking rights to land and self-rule as a republic. They failed, and soon, so would Hidalgo as an estate operator. He still owed the 7,000 pesos taken to renovate the Taximaroa properties in 1787; in 1807, the Royal Consolidation called in the debt. He could not pay and the regime embargoed the estates, ending his dream of landed prosperity.[24]

Focusing on parish life at Dolores, Hidalgo promoted sodalities to support a lively ritual life. He used parish lands to raise grapes, olives, and silkworms, with an eye to making wine, oil, and fine cloth. He opened workshops for pottery, carpentry, and leather goods in parish buildings. He began brick works too. The goal was to make goods for local markets, bring a bit of income to Hidalgo and the parish, and create employment for growing numbers of men (and some women) facing marginality in an economy of profit and predation. Dreams of scaling the heights of Church power gone, the chance at landed prosperity lost, Hidalgo turned to parish-based crafts and commerce to sustain his parishioners in efforts anticipating doña María Josefa Vergara's Querétaro charities.[25]

Meanwhile, Hidalgo turned to women for hope and solace. After losing his estates to the Consolidation, he spent his "saint's day" with "the Mothers of Teresa" in Querétaro. They gave him an image of Guadalupe embroidered in silk. He wore it on his chest, under his cassock. After years debating the virtues and limits of penitential and sacramental worship and enlightened science, Hidalgo turned to Guadalupe for protection and compassion. He was a late convert. The regime had called Guadalupe to protect New Spain when French Jacobins assaulted Church wealth in 1792 and beheaded Louis XVI in 1793. Hidalgo found her in 1807, just before Napoleon invaded Spain.[26]

When news of Napoleon's 1808 invasion, Mexico City's summer of ferment, and the September coup that ended it came to Dolores, Church authorities at Valladolid sent an edict to be posted across the Michoacán diocese. It called for contributions to defend "religion, the Church, our sovereign, the glory of the nation, and the happiness of the country."[27] Doña María Micaela Rodríguez de Outon, a rich Otomí widow who lived next to Hidalgo's rectory, offered a plan to fund a convent to house devout women, Spanish and indigenous. In times of deepening crisis, prosperous women proposed reforms: Rodríguez de Outon at Dolores, doña María Josefa Vergara at Querétaro.[28]

When news of the fall of the Seville Junta arrived in April 1810, the Mexico City Inquisition sent another proclamation to be posted in churches across New Spain. Hidalgo again complied. It accused Joseph Bonaparte of imposing "the greatest betrayal and horrific anarchy on the faithful people of Spanish America." While "a few Spaniards without honor or religion" served the tyrant, the Inquisitors insisted that "the Supreme Junta and the heroic Spaniards called insurgents" earn the allegiance of New Spain's people. Never announcing that the junta had fallen, the churchmen threatened excommunication to anyone offering "seductive and seditious proposals, whether calling for independence or allegiance to the imposter king José Napoleón."[29] They rejected Napoleonic Spain—and an independent New Spain.

Demanding loyalty to authorities in Mexico City, the Inquisitors announced the reality of anarchy, the honor of insurgency, and the goal of independence—for Spain. Hidalgo soon joined political conversations drawing those themes to focus on New Spain. He later claimed that he talked of independence with Allende as "pure discourse," even as he believed "independence would be useful to the kingdom." Allende drew Hidalgo to Querétaro, where he met "two or three men of little character" who "claimed a following of two hundred plebes."[30] Hidalgo was open to independence and opposed to raising an angry populace. Epigmenio González and Hidalgo reported the same meeting. González noted Hidalgo's insistence on order; the pastor saw González as a man without character.

Days later, Hidalgo received a letter from Allende claiming support from the Marqués de San Juan de Rayas, merchant financiers in the capital including a member of the Fagoaga family, and more. Allende added: "many are ready to join in Querétaro and at haciendas." The report imagined eminent men ready to lead people ready to fight. Only the latter proved true.

Hidalgo turned to making lances at Dolores, joined by "the Gutiérrez" at the Santa Bárbara estate. They "know what we are about and are recruiting people."[31] Hidalgo was ready to call men to arms.

A Last Mediating Dream: Ciriaco García in San Miguel

On September 7, 1810, with planning underway and debates mounting among men seeking rights of governance, Ciriaco García, Gobernador de Naturales at San Miguel, sent a manifesto to Mexico City. San Miguel did not have an indigenous republic with a council and dominion over lands. Still, local natives maintained an Otomí governor to represent them to the Spanish council. Privy to conversations swirling about him, García wrote to an unnamed viceroy about to land.[32] He demanded that the new leader restore just rule by calling a "national junta"—reversing the coup of 1808 and calling for political participations linked to demands for social justice.

He honored "devotion to loyalty and patriotism" while lamenting the "unforgivable crimes of the Mercantile Government now dying." The powers collapsing in Spain imposed "lies, deceptions, and felonies . . . that crush justice. The sacred natural rights and royal laws granted to Americans to reward their virtues have been undermined by the ignominious contempt of despotic usurpers who have stolen sovereignty." García honored the long-established regime and denounced those who imposed despotic ways in search of profit. He went on: "We see the natives of our kingdom downtrodden like slaves, disdained, drowning in hunger, naked like the wandering barbarians of the deserts, without prospects, without gains and waiting to be delivered to the enemies of our holy Catholic religion—the British who will sacrifice us on the altar of commerce." The Otomí governor blamed the powers imposed in 1808 and their British allies for crushing New Spain's people.

García then honored the unnamed new viceroy: "God has sent Your Excellency to set the kingdom in order by installing a national junta that will understand our miseries, and provide cures that reward merit and punish the insolent attackers who took down our legitimate leaders. With that, we will remain at peace." The Otomí leader at San Miguel backed the demands for political participation driving Allende and his allies. He also saw the rising tide of popular outrage that informed González' call for a radical social inversion, aiming to link them in a plan for peace.

It was an improbable dream. Would a new viceroy turn against the flailing few who sent him from Cádiz and the entrenched powers who welcomed him in Mexico City? Would a new junta of officials, oligarchs, and provincial elites turn to seek justice for the many? Viceroy don Francisco Javier Venegas landed on September 14, 1810; the Bajío was in revolt on September 16. Before reaching the capital, Venegas faced a burgeoning revolt in the richest region of New Spain.

Insurgency Explodes: Dolores to Guanajuato

The rising began when Allende and don Juan Aldama rode to Dolores on the evening of Saturday, September 15, to warn Hidalgo of the arrests in Querétaro. The three could flee—or act. They chose to act, assembling a dozen allies, emptying the jail, rounding up local *gachupines* in an overnight sweep. Sunday morning, as people arrived for Mass, Hidalgo was not in church. A crowd went to his door—and he stepped out to call for revolt.[33]

What Hidalgo proclaimed in the *grito de Dolores*, celebrated as Mexico's founding moment, remains debated. Did he shout hatred for Napoleon and the French, death to *gachupines*, and honor to Fernando VII? Did he call for independence and devotion to Guadalupe?[34] Most directly, the revolt challenged the powers set in Mexico City in 1808 by Spanish emissaries aiming to block a local junta and fund resistance to French rule. That fight had failed. Napoleon remained reviled, and *gachupines* were blamed for delivering the realm to military powers, sending vast flows of silver to Seville while failing to secure Spain. Fernando did not reign. Guadalupe was revered. What independence might mean was uncertain.

After the *grito*, "the *indios* and rancheros coming to Sunday mass joined" Hidalgo. They might carry a "club, slingshot, lance, or machete" as tools of work became weapons of rebellion and "*indios* filled sacks with rocks." Best prepared were the two hundred mounted men who came with don Luis Gutiérrez from the Santa Bárbara estate—where residents had earlier gone to court seeking lands and self-rule.[35] Pedro García, an early ally, emphasized: "The pastor possessed a great talent; well educated he had a way of making himself loved. His easy ways, sweet treatment, and power with words gained him many friends and partisans. Native people enjoyed his attention and affection."[36]

Hidalgo, Allende, and the rebel mass marched south toward San Miguel, Allende's hometown. Along the way, they passed Charco de Araujo, Tequisquiapan, Santa Bárbara, and other estates where families had struggled since the 1790s and now lived in desperation: "at every step . . . people along the road and in nearby settlements joined."[37]

At Atotonilco, just north of San Miguel, Hidalgo made a pivotal choice. The sanctuary was the center of penitential worship in the Bajío, devotions Hidalgo had challenged with enlightened science. When a ranchero found a banner with Guadalupe's image in the basement, Hidalgo took her as the emblem of his rising: "Stopping at Atotonilco, I took a canvas image of Guadalupe and set her at the head of the people marching with me; from then on rebel regiments [and] bands of plebes all took the image of Guadalupe."[38] The devotion Hidalgo took to his heart in 1807 shaped his insurgency in 1810.

At San Miguel, fractures surfaced. While Hidalgo and other leaders rounded up immigrant Spaniards and Allende and Aldama recruited local militias, rebel throngs sacked don José Landeta's store. Don Narciso de la Canal, regiment commander and leader of San Miguel's landed-textile oligarchy, held back.[39] Only after insurgent militias stopped the sacking did Canal negotiate a peaceful occupation. A new council loyal to Allende was set; funds taken from the regime and church treasuries provided 80,000 pesos to insurgents soon driving south toward Celaya.[40]

Near Chamacuero, they proclaimed new goals: "The criollos of Dolores and San Miguel" demand "holy liberty. . . . We have imprisoned the *gachupines* who . . . have held us in ignominious slavery for three hundred years, and now are determined to deliver this Christian kingdom to the heretic King of England, causing us to lose our Catholic faith and legitimate king Fernando VII, driving us to a deeper and harder enslavement."

American Spaniards, now labeled criollos, proclaimed immigrant Spaniards, now maligned as *gachupines*, the primary enemy—driving a wedge among people long linked in families and silver capitalism as *españoles*. The *gachupín* offense was tying New Spain and its silver to British protestants. The goal: deflect an angry populace from attacking the power and property of the American Spaniards who had long ruled mining and the land—and recently pressed devastating social predations. Political anger came framed in a religious dream: "Our cause is most holy, and we are ready to offer our lives. *Viva* our holy Catholic faith, *viva* our sovereign lord Fernando VII, and *vivan* the rights that God and nature have given us."[41]

Returning to hard politics, on September 18, Hidalgo and Allende sent a message to authorities at Celaya, stating that they held seventy-eight European Spaniards captured at Dolores and San Miguel, and that all would be executed if Celaya resisted. Celaya's *europeos* fled to Querétaro, aided by local clergy. The City Council and much of the populace then welcomed the rebels, who entered without opposition on September 20.[42] Pedro García saw "disorder and sacking that was quickly corrected."[43] Rebels took another

150,000 pesos from local coffers, convents, and leading families. Hidalgo was proclaimed "Captain General" and "Protector of the Nation," Allende "Lieutenant General," and Aldama "Marshall." Allende later complained that after agreeing to share rule, Hidalgo began to act "for himself alone."[44]

Having occupied Dolores, San Miguel, and Celaya in a matter of days, taking hostages to stymie the powerful, working to contain popular redistributions, and claiming ample funds, Hidalgo and Allende faced a decision. They could turn west to Querétaro, where plotting had begun. But many Querétaro allies were in custody, while others had proclaimed loyalty and backed the loyal militias concentrating there. What the urban Otomí and diverse rural peoples might do was unknown.[45]

The rebels decided to march on Guanajuato, the engine driving silver capitalism. Whatever might come, the mining center was pivotal. On September 21, Hidalgo sent a message to don José Antonio de Riaño, the Intendant who had managed the surge of silver since the 1790s; they knew each other from social encounters. The rebel priest insisted that he aimed to avoid a bloody conflict but that the rising was unstoppable; starting at Dolores with fifteen men, "I am now surrounded by more than 4,000 who have proclaimed me their Captain General. At the head of these forces and following their will, we seek to be independent and govern ourselves. Three hundred years of dependence on the peninsula has been humiliating, shameful, and a great injustice."[46]

Now asserting the goal of independence, Hidalgo reported that he was guarding the "*peninsulares*" taken at Dolores, San Miguel, and Celaya and that a peaceful capitulation of Guanajuato would prevent bloodshed. Riaño should open the city of silver and save many, including himself. The rebel priest added: "We aim to reclaim holy rights . . . usurped by cruel, illegitimate, and unjust conquerors, who aided by the ignorance of the natives usurped their property and customs, vilely converting free men into degraded slaves."[47]

He blamed early conquerors for New Spain's plight, an ideology laden with contradictions. The powerful in Mexico City and the Bajío, most American born, had built New Spain's silver capitalism after 1550 and remained its primary beneficiaries. Hidalgo blamed native peoples for submitting—due to ignorance. He warned Riaño: "The national movement gains strength daily; it is threatening and it is not my place to contain it."[48] If Riaño did not deliver Guanajuato, an angry populace would destroy the city. Hidalgo blamed *gachupines*, denigrated natives, and threatened Riaño with popular ire.

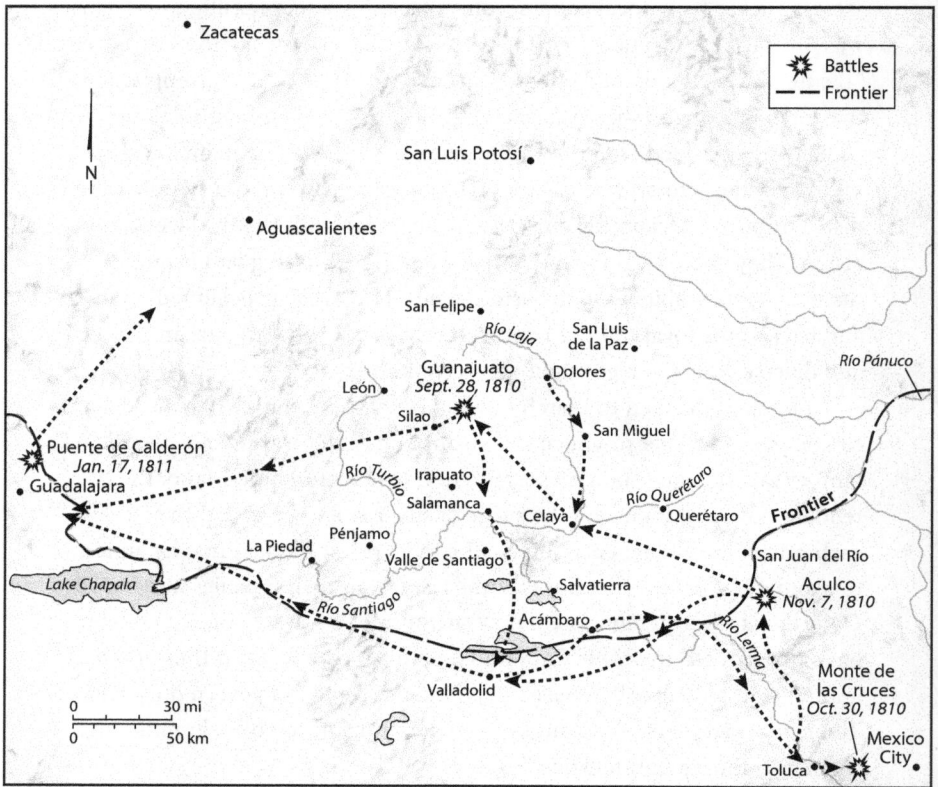

Map 3.1 The route of Hidalgo's revolt.

He sent a different manifesto to Otomí leaders at Querétaro. He lamented that don Miguel Domínguez and others had been jailed by "Europeans" and called the Otomí to free them: "First, so we are not sold to heretics; second, to reclaim the lands of the kingdom; and third, to liberate countrymen at risk of losing their lives for trying to do good." Hidalgo added: "You have nothing to fear, as Our Lady of Guadalupe protects us."[49] Now honoring indigenous leaders, the missive showed ignorance of life and culture in Querétaro: the Otomí council retained dominion over rich *huertas*, Guadalupe had come late to Querétaro, while Our Lady of Pueblito protected people in the city and all around. The council delivered Hidalgo's letter to regime officials.

Having tried to entice Riaño with threats and to recruit Otomí Querétaro with ignorance, Hidalgo marched to the mines. The first stop was Salamanca, a town surrounded by rich lands cultivated by ethnically mixed estate dependents. Most had faced predations and Salamanca rose in apparent unity to welcome the insurgents. Hidalgo designated brothers Albino and Pedro García as local leaders, took 60,000 pesos from the Augustinian convent, and headed to Guanajuato.[50] When the rebels passed through Irapuato and Silao, people joined in throngs.[51] Hidalgo wrote to Riaño claiming fifty thousand insurgents.[52] Pedro García reported that "the growing number of rebels led to food shortages," while he counted twenty thousand rebels, far fewer than imagined by Hidalgo to threaten Riaño. Only six hundred carried firearms, three hundred had lances, while a few had swords. Most wielded machetes as rebel numbers "increased in every rancho and village as we passed."[53]

On September 27, insurgents surged into the canyon below Guanajuato, stopping at the Burras estate owned by the Marqués de San Juan de Rayas. They learned that Riaño had barricaded himself, four hundred troops, and two hundred armed civilians, along with 3 million pesos and the city's maize supply, in the Alhóndiga de Granaditos, the city's fortress-granary. The manager of the Valenciana mine brought news of popular support, details on Riaño's preparations, and two thousand mine workers ready to fight.[54]

A flurry of notes passed between Hidalgo and Riaño, but no words could prevent the conflict to come.[55] The battle for Guanajuato became a siege of the Alhóndiga on September 28 (figure 3.2). Insurgents had superior numbers as the city rose in support. Workers who made the silver that had funded Spain's failed fight against Napoleon felt exploited and maligned. They always faced danger; now production came with scarce and costly staples. They had taken silver to a historic peak—for what gain?

Hidalgo came at the head of an angry rural mob. A manager charged with keeping men at labor in the mines descended from above, backed by irate workers. Riaño and the men who expected to rule and profit took refuge in the Alhóndiga, locking themselves in with a treasure in silver and the maize needed to feed the city. An 1813 report offered a mine operators' perspective: after Riaño took "royal funds" and "the silver" to the fortress granary, "on learning that great treasures were locked inside, the city pleb joined a multitude of *indios* and *castas* in attacking the Alhóndiga fortress with greater fury."[56]

The assault proved brief and deadly. In three hours, three hundred of the powerful and the privileged died, including Riaño. Thousands died among the attacking throngs. Then, with victory at the price of mass casualties, insurgents liberated the silver and maize held in the Alhóndiga, while uncounted numbers sacked the city. Looting lasted the night of the twenty-eighth, all

Figure 3.2 The Alhóndiga, Guanajuato.

day on the twenty-ninth, and into the thirtieth—when Hidalgo, having gathered as much silver as he could for the insurgent treasury, called for a return to order. The mining city pivotal to silver capitalism faced ruin.[57]

The siege in Guanajuato was a turning point. The contradictions inherent in a rising led by men seeking a political nation yet dependent on throngs driven by social outrage became clear for all to see: dreams of rights for the few came tied to redistributions taken by the many. Epigmenio González expected it. Hidalgo feared it. Ciriaco García imagined a compromise. Before the assault on the Alhóndiga, contradictions had played out in threats. In Guanajuato, they became deadly. There was no return for power holders, for the political men who aimed to replace them, or for desperate people who dreamed of justice and sustenance—and were done waiting for their betters to deliver.

After the deadly triumph at Guanajuato, Hidalgo returned to Dolores with a guard of "rancheros from the jurisdiction." He sent a letter to don Narciso de la Canal at San Miguel, calling him to join a "revolution" that aimed to "set the foundations of our liberty and independence."[58] There was no mention of Fernando, no call to Guadalupe. Hidalgo focused on independence, which he hoped would draw a man of power. The reference to revolution surely focused Canal on the death and redistribution at Guanajuato. He stood aside.

Returning to Guanajuato on October 7, Hidalgo sought allies to rule the mining city. Many demurred, claiming oaths to serve the king of Spain. Hidalgo's reply: "Fernando VII . . . does not exist." The Regimento del Príncipe did join the rising, as did two infantry units, one of Valenciana workers, the other drawn from the larger community.[59] Men who made silver joined Hidalgo's throngs.

All was not insurgent victory. On October 6, troops sent north by Viceroy Venegas to protect Querétaro faced an insurgent force at Puente de Caroza, north of the city. Officials reported that indigenous masses headed by a leader under Hidalgo were crushed by loyal troops that pursued them to their village, where they imposed devastating losses. Days later, don José Toribio Rico, manager at Puerto de Nieto just over the pass from Puente de Caroza, wrote to Sánchez Espinosa, reporting that Allende had led an armed detachment against loyalist troops, to face a defeat that left five hundred insurgents dead. After the fight, loyal troops camped at Puerto de Nieto before moving on to Celaya.[60]

Aiming to avoid the troops coming toward him, Hidalgo turned toward Valladolid, seat of the intendancy and diocese of Michoacán, and where he had lived as a student and rising Church leader. News that doña María Catalina Gómez de Larronda had mobilized the manager and residents of her San Antonio estate near Acámbaro to capture don Manuel Merino as he traveled to take office as Intendant of Michoacán cleared the way. The flight of bishop don Miguel Abad y Queipo to Mexico City and of many *europeos* to the low country left Valladolid open.[61] On the march, the insurgents gathered more adherents and funds, arriving on October 16, "welcomed by *indios*, creoles, and churchmen." Hidalgo took another 1 million pesos from royal coffers.[62]

Backed by wide support, rich funds, and new recruits, Hidalgo joined the city council to decree freedom for the enslaved, abolish tributes, and end taxes on native production of pulque. He added: "If the people do not end the sacking, they will be hung immediately on the four gallows we have in the plaza."[63] Hidalgo promised limited reforms—and deadly force against rebels taking redistributions.

At Valladolid, militia regiments from outlying Zitácuaro and Pátzcuaro joined, along with uncounted popular adherents. Don José María

Morelos, a priest who had studied under Hidalgo and served a low-country parish, joined too. Meanwhile, loyal forces concentrated at Querétaro: don Félix Calleja led militias from San Luis Potosí while don Manuel de Flon came north from the capital. Epigmenio González saw the assembling forces from his prison cell.[64]

Toward the Capital: Bajío Insurgents in the Mesoamerican Heartland

Having taken Guanajuato and its silver, Hidalgo and Allende headed toward the capital.[65] At Acámbaro, a command council met to organize irregular forces. Regiments of one thousand men would be led by colonels earning 3 pesos daily. Men with mounts and arms would gain one peso per day, those on foot 4 reales—half a peso. Funds taken across the Bajío allowed Allende to imagine a paid army. He tried to remove Hidalgo from command, but the *cura*'s supporters blocked the attempt.[66] Early on, Allende had let Hidalgo lead, seeing that only he drew mass support. Now, fearing redistributions, he tried to depose Hidalgo and impose military discipline. The council knew that without him, there would be few forces to lead. They again acclaimed Hidalgo as "*generalísmo*." He took a new uniform that layered command onto a foundation of priestly care: "a blue cassock . . . embroidered with gold and silver, with a medallion of the Virgin of Guadalupe around his neck." Hidalgo and still inchoate throngs pressed on toward the capital.[67]

On October 23 at Tlalpujahua, lawyer and miner don Ignacio López Rayón joined. He, too, had known Hidalgo during student days in Valladolid. The teacher tapped Rayón to write a new statement of goals insisting that all *europeos* deliver themselves and their property to the insurgents. Any who had joined them in "commerce, companies, and accounts" must make amends. To promote popular welfare, Rayón's plan again ended tributes and slavery and cut the *alcabala* on internal commerce to 3 percent, leaving 6 percent on imported goods. To appeal to the majority in the Mesoamerican heartland just ahead, "the nation declares all Americans as equal, with no distinctions of category." Hidalgo and Rayón soon learned that legal equality was not native peoples' first goal.[68]

The insurgents arrived at Toluca on October 27, entering without opposition—and without the acclamations they had gained across the Bajío and in Valladolid. As they marched to Santiago Tianguistengo and then Lerma, responses were muted. Allende promised to be in the capital in a few days. Loyal troops, including forces led by don Agustín Iturbide from Valladolid, followed the march.[69] All saw that people around Toluca, most living in indigenous republics, remained at home and at work. The insurgency had entered a different world.

In the high basin west of Mexico City, the towering Nevada de Toluca volcano sent streams to form the headwaters of the Lerma River that flowed north to become the Santiago that irrigated the Bajío bottomlands. The insurgents had followed that hydraulic connection to enter the heartland of Spanish Mesoamerica. There, an indigenous majority lived in republics ruled by native councils with dominion over lands that sustained local families, councils, and religious life. As populations grew in the eighteenth century, community lands provided ever less sustenance, while local leaders sent seasonal work gangs to nearby estates, enabling men to sustain families. Estates and communities locked in symbiotic exploitations that sustained patriarchal ways of provision: estates profited from villagers' seasonal labor to raise crops to feed Mexico City; village men gained wages to sustain families and communities.[70]

Community negotiations limited other predations too. During the drought and scarcity of 1808 to 1810, heartland communities gained suspensions of tributes while men took wages in estate fields, enabling them to buy maize. Scarcity entrenched patriarchy. When Hidalgo's throngs came to the Valley of Toluca, an ample harvest was about to begin. With work and maize on the horizon, few joined the rising.[71] Ultimately, Bajío insurgents fought to gain what most families in heartland republics retained: patriarchal family sustenance. Hidalgo's throngs arrived as invasive outsiders, taking maize local people had made. In the Toluca basin, villagers stood back.

Far from home and without local backing, Hidalgo, Allende, and the Bajío insurgents faced the sierras that separated Toluca from the capital. On October 30 at Monte de las Cruces, rebel regiments from Celaya and Valladolid and battalions from Guanajuato led ten thousand massed rebels. They attacked two thousand better-armed and trained loyal troops backed by artillery. Throngs from the productive core of silver capitalism attacked organized defenders of its financial, commercial, and regime capital.

Insurgents charged, shouting, "*Viva* America and Our Lady of Guadalupe; death to *gachupines* and bad government." Goals were vague, the battle deadly. More than two thousand insurgents died, as did nearly as many defenders. The battle proved a bloody stalemate. Loyalist survivors retreated to the capital; rebels struggled "to meet the necessities of so many people," taking meat, maize, and more "in ranchos and small pueblos."[72]

Hidalgo and Allende sent emissaries to the viceroy, offering terms of surrender. Venegas rejected them.[73] Insurgents might press on—to face a city of more than 100,000, surrounded by water, and showing no sign of welcoming their cause. Recognizing reality and the base of the movement in the Bajío, they turned toward home. Pedro García lamented: "This army, two days earlier so daring and enthusiastic, now marched downcast, silent, and dejected."[74]

Survivors headed north, aiming to block Calleja and Flon from consolidating power in the Bajío. Loyalists had occupied Dolores on October 24 with seven thousand troops, combining Calleja's San Luis Potosí militias and forces Flon led north from the capital. After the carnage at Monte de las Cruces, Calleja marched south.[75] He attacked demoralized insurgents on November 7 at Aculco, in uplands between the heartland and the Bajío.[76] Calleja's forces took few casualties, while one hundred insurgents died, five hundred were wounded, and six hundred were captured. Survivors dispersed to find ways home.[77]

Still, the battle at Aculco proved important. Its violent commotion sent news of insurgency across the Mezquital basin just east—the driest region of the heartland. People there also lived in indigenous republics, but aridity left growing populations to face greater difficulties. Estates long focused on grazing had turned to planting maguey to make pulque for taverns in the capital and the mines at Real del Monte. The fermented drink brought soaring profits to estate operators, led by the Conde de Regla, also the lead mine operator at Real del Monte. It offered little to villagers. After transplanting maguey shoots, pulque required little labor as fields matured for five years and plants were tapped for fifteen more. Otomí villagers across the Mezquital faced aridity, land shortages, and scarce chances to labor.

Without stabilizing symbiotic exploitations, the drought of 1808–10 made life unsustainable; land and labor conflicts escalated in the Mezquital.[78] On learning of the battle at Aculco, Otomí men began raiding Mezquital estates to claim sustenance in raids that cut estate production and in time mining at Real del Monte. The Mezquital risings were never linked to Hidalgo or Allende, never directed by political aspirants. Still, they began amid Hidalgo's retreat and carried on to rattle a key region of silver capitalism just north of the capital into 1815.[79]

After Aculco, Hidalgo retreated to Valladolid while Allende returned to Guanajuato. Hidalgo's proclamations became defensive. On November 13, he insisted that Monte de las Cruces and Aculco led to strategic retreats.[80] In a "Manifesto to the People," he rejected excommunication, declaring himself a devout Catholic, if open to debates within its spacious culture;

his movement carried Guadalupe's banner, while Spain's French foes and British allies were not true Christians. His entire life was devoted to "holy religion" and "the supernatural faith I received in baptism."

New Spain's problems, he insisted again, were caused by "European Spaniards in whose oppressive hands our fate has fallen. . . . They are not Catholics, except for political gain: their God is money." He insisted that "*gachupines*, unnatural men, have broken ties of blood, estranged from nature, fathers, brothers, wives and children."[81] Insurgency was a crusade against *gachupines*, men without religion, without social commitments, who came to America to make money, their only God.

Facing defeat, Hidalgo hardened the myth of *gachupín* power, aiming to turn popular ire away from entrenched oligarchs. It was an uncertain gambit: those who lived the predations of agrarian capitalism after 1790 knew that the landlords who profited from their misery were nearly always American Spaniards. Popular insurgents sacked *gachupines'* stores—and the fields and granaries of Americans' estates. They took what they needed to sustain families, ignoring the myth proclaimed by Hidalgo who hoped to deflect responsibility for social devastations onto a despised few.

Beyond blaming *gachupines*, the manifesto offered a dream of broad participation and shared prosperity: "We will establish a congress representing all the cities and towns of the kingdom, with the goal of maintaining our holy religion, making laws that are gentle, beneficial, and appropriate to the circumstances of every community: we will govern with the compassion of fathers, treating all as brothers while we exile poverty, limit the devastating extractions of money, promote the arts, and fuel industry, making free use of the rich products of our bountiful land."[82]

Hidalgo recognized the desperations that had driven so many of his followers to take arms—and maize. He proposed a congress that would entrust governance to the leading men of cities and towns, excluding the indigenous republics that organized life at Querétaro and across the heartland. Rulers' proclaimed fathers would treat men as brothers in a commitment to patriarchy, while ending poverty and limiting predations. Wealth would no longer be squandered on the failed fight against Napoleon. Arts and industries would be promoted, honoring Hidalgo's successes at Dolores. Still, there was no hint of delivering production to families, the core of Epigmenio González' vision and the dream of many insurgents. Hidalgo offered a caring regime, without popular participations or redistributions.

Popular expropriations continued. In mid-November, don José Toribio Rico was taken captive as men sacked Puerto de Nieto. His report was vague. Had residents rebelled? Had outsiders invaded? Rico implied the latter, while reporting that he escaped unscathed.[83] While Hidalgo promised care, popular rebels claimed their own gains from American-owned and -managed properties.

With Hidalgo dreaming at Valladolid, Allende returned to Guanajuato, the engine of silver capitalism and site of his one military victory. He knew that control of the mining center was pivotal. He wrote Hidalgo, asking him to come to Guanajuato to recruit and restrain popular forces. Meanwhile, Calleja left Querétaro to occupy Celaya, where leaders now welcomed loyalist troops—honoring their victories and fearing popular risings.[84]

Hidalgo stayed in Valladolid, leaving Allende to face Calleja with the men and resources he could muster. As Calleja approached, Allende worked to fortify the canyon city while crowds emptied shops and stores: "Allende took no part in atrocious acts that came from angry people . . . agitated by evil men who led them to cruelty and vengeance." Amid that chaos, Allende could not defend the city. He fled as sackings continued. "Calleja entered without opposition" on November 25.[85]

The loyal commander claimed victory, appointed a new Intendant, and killed as many "insurgents" as he could. After three days, he offered an amnesty, learning that hard repression only provoked more resistance. The second battle of Guanajuato was less Calleja's triumph and more a result of Allende's inability to control an irate populace. Calleja stayed two weeks, setting a semblance of pacification and a mirage of regime power. He announced the opening of the Cádiz Cortes and its promise of a participatory imperial regime—a distant dream in days of violent uncertainty.[86]

Dreams and Devastations at Guadalajara

Hidalgo moved to Guadalajara on November 24; along the way "all the pueblos of the province contributed contingents of men."[87] Soon joined by Allende, they conceded Querétaro, Celaya, and Guanajuato to the regime. Ten weeks of conflict had exposed divisions among rebel leaders and an abyss between leaders' goals and popular demands. Calleja took two weeks to pacify Guanajuato and two more to mobilize forces to confront the insurgents assembling at Guadalajara.[88]

Meanwhile, rebel leaders dreamed and jostled. In late November, Hidalgo issued a proclamation again making the goal of independence clear—while taking a sharp turn to imagine Anglophone support. He offered George Washington and the United States as shining examples. He declared

Spain impotent under French occupation and added that France could never restore Spain's empire. He saw England committed to American independence. Still, "we trust equally in the protection of our Holy Mother Guadalupe."[89] Shifting global powers and Guadalupe's protection made independence inevitable. Did the United States and England hear his call? If they did, they did not respond.

On the twenty-ninth, Hidalgo again abolished tributes, outlawed slavery, cut *alcabalas*, and lifted all limits on indigenous production.[90] On December 1, he prohibited all taking of "crops and forage" from the properties of "beloved Americans."[91] As popular expropriations continued, Hidalgo had only words to contain them. On the fifth, he ordered an end to rentals of indigenous community lands to outsiders. Current rents would support insurgent forces; then land would return to "the natives for cultivation."[92] The reform might benefit community-based people in Michoacán and south of Guadalajara. It offered nothing to estate residents. The next day, Hidalgo again ended tributes and slavery.[93] Repetitions revealed that promises were not calming a populace taking immediate sustenance and retributions.

December 20 saw the first issue of *El Despertador Americano*—The American Awakening. It called "*europeos* . . . captives of high treason . . . frenchified men" who put Americans in chains, while "the generous English" were "incomparably just."[94] The dream of independence backed by Britain and sustained by "our Holy Mother Guadalupe" persisted.[95] It also rang of desperation.

As December ended and Calleja approached, Hidalgo pleaded to men of property: "If you seek public peace, security for your families and haciendas, and prosperity for the kingdom; if you hope that these risings do not degenerate into a revolution in which Americans kill each other, desert the Europeans and unite with us."[96] As American Spaniards mobilized to defend the regime, Hidalgo promised to protect property—and threatened revolution. To Europeans, he offered: "Our goal is to remove you from rule, without hurting your persons or properties."[97] About to face Calleja's troops, Hidalgo again promised to defend property.

On January 14, Hidalgo turned to malign his own base. He condemned "the delinquent conduct of some, who posing as patriots seek nothing but their own sustenance by reprehensible and shameful means." He added: "The transport of women to include them in military camps is shameful and harmful; we order that none may accompany us without express license."[98] In contrast, Pedro García saw "souls consumed with ideas of Liberty; the women of the people, so gracious and seductive, inspiring the people to fight for their rights. Oh, what women! . . . full of passion, mixing with the combatants, seeking a part in our glorious combat. Everything was inspiration."[99] Hidalgo dreamed of independence, defended property, condemned popular expropriations, and maligned insurgent women. García saw women mobilized to inspire and sustain fighting men—the revolution to come.

On January 17, 1811, at Puente de Calderón outside Guadalajara, Hidalgo and Allende sent massed insurgents with minimal training and few arms to battle Calleja's well-organized and armed troops. The fight was no contest: 1,200 insurgents died. Communities in arms again proved no match against trained soldiers. The insurgency of contradictions dissolved.

Hidalgo, Allende, and Aldama fled north, perhaps to seek refuge in the United States. They were soon captured, tried, and executed. Morelos and Rayón started north, then turned south to carry on isolated political fights. The throngs that had remained with Hidalgo returned to home communities, some to indigenous republics around Guadalajara and Valladolid, many to estates across the Bajío. Calleja waited days for insurgents to disperse, then entered Guadalajara on January 20. He offered a general pardon, set new officials in power, and returned to San Luis Potosí to consolidate rule at home.[100] Few imagined that revolution had just begun.

Hidalgo's Final Reflections

As defeated leaders fled north, Allende and his allies stripped Hidalgo of command, blaming him for the defeat of a rising impossible without his inspiration—a rising so laden with contradictions that none could harness its power or limit its destructions. At Saltillo, they were captured, then taken to Chihuahua to be tried and interrogated before certain executions. In May 1811, Hidalgo gave a series of depositions, sharing his final reflections on a life of contradictions.

He stated first that he was "Catholic," "a parish priest," and "a Spaniard."[101] He did not reflect on the many Catholicisms he had grasped in a life of debate. Rejecting excommunication, he remained a priest. And he called himself a Spaniard, the label long shared by people of European descent across New Spain, whatever their place of birth.[102] The posturing to malign *europeos* as *gachupines* and promote alliances among *americanos* as *criollos* had been a ploy seeking to force oppositions and forge alliances. In the end, Hidalgo was an *español*—ready to denigrate the people he had mobilized.

He admitted that "I raised the image of Guadalupe to draw the people."[103] He blamed the destructions of insurgency on the people he and Guadalupe had recruited: "*Indios* and the vilest scoundrels drove the horrors." He blamed "*indios*" for the killings that marked the insurgency from the Bajío, through Valladolid, to Guadalajara.[104] Still, as his confession continued, he blamed the larger insurgent enterprise—and took personal responsibility.

The rising "was unjust and impolitic, . . . it forced incalculable sorrows on religion, custom, and life in our America."[105] A Spaniard who identified with America, he regretted the revolt he led. In a final prison manifesto of May 11, 1811, he stated: "I see the destruction I unleashed, the fortunes lost, the countless widows and orphans left behind, the blood shed with profusion, and what I cannot say without shaking, the countless souls lost because they followed me."[106]

Hidalgo blamed himself for calling people to arms. He did not see that their violence was not customary but the outcome of lives recently subject to predations worsened by profiteering amid famine. He lamented losses of capital—and would not see that much of that capital had been gained by predations upon the producing poor, taking profit from people facing desperate hunger. He lamented that so many who followed him faced eternal damnation. He said nothing about the souls of those who had driven silver capitalism to the destructive extremes that set so many to killing in order to eat.

He did not blame Guadalupe. He had turned to her late in life, taking her image to wear against his chest in 1807, seeking her protection and compassion at a time of economic loss. He raised her banner in September 1810, to call people to insurgency. At the end, he saw that "the image of Guadalupe that all wore in their hats at the beginning, few kept at the end. I do not know why."[107] As defeats and deaths proliferated, did many see her protection as uncertain? In the end, large numbers surely returned to seek compassion from saints and virgins long honored in home communities.

Hidalgo did not abandon Guadalupe. After a ritual stripped him of priesthood, "they found on his chest the sovereign image of Our Lady of Guadalupe, of silk embroidered on parchment, which he took from his chest and said: 'This lady, Mother of God, was carried on my flag and marched ahead of my armies at Aculco and Guanajuato. It is my wish that she returns to the convent of Teresitas in Querétaro where she was made by the revered mothers who gave her to me on my saint's day in 1807.'"[108] Hidalgo kept Guadalupe close to his heart to the end, then had her image returned to the religious women who gave her to him. He lamented the insurgency; he held hope for Guadalupe and the women who sustained her.

The End and a Beginning

Hidalgo's revolt—if it ever was truly his—proved a transforming failure. Provincial leaders failed to gain a congress to reset New Spain in a changing world. Political independence did not come. Regime power held in Mexico City while France ruled Spain—but for Cádiz. Bajío insurgents did gain maize and more in months of retribution and redistribution, in the effort facing uncounted casualties. After the deadly defeats at Monte de las Cruces, Aculco, and Puente de Calderón, they dispersed, most returning to rebuild lives on estate lands. After the provincial political men who called them to arms had fallen to powerful forces backing a Spanish regime more imagined than real, angry people would regroup to seek new routes to sustenance and justice. In a decade of fighting, they made a revolution.

4.

Insurgent Guanajuato

Claiming Maize, Making Community,
Breaking Silver Capitalism, Rattling Patriarchy

After the defeat of Hidalgo's revolt, popular guerrillas carried on for a decade, making a revolution that transformed local lives, the regional economy, and global capitalism. They took control of estate lands, turning them to feed families and sustain guerrilla bands across the rich lands surrounding Guanajuato's mines. While men fought to reclaim patriarchal powers, women took new roles making maize in insurgent communities. Rebel bands periodically invaded the mining city, while insurgent communities controlled essential supplies, together breaking silver capitalism and the global trades it fueled. Infrastructure investment ended, leaving independent mine workers to take what ore they could, selling to refiners desperate for mercury to keep silver flowing.

Pacification only came from 1818 to 1820 when exhausted loyalist commanders sanctioned family rights to make maize on estate lands—and to keep arms to protect hard-won gains. At the end of the decade of revolution, silver mining faced collapse, maize-making communities held strong on the land, and women kept new roles in cultivating families. Insurgents remade the Bajío and forced the world to change in unimagined ways: Asian powers and trades collapsed while England and the United States gained new markets for industries sustained by enslaved producers.

After the fiasco at Puente de Calderón, political resistance fragmented: don Ignacio López Rayón proclaimed a Junta Soberana Nacional Americana at Zitácuaro in uplands south of the Bajío in August 1811, while guerrilla forces led by José María Morelos settled in Pacific lowlands.[1] Dispersed political movements kept dreams of a nation alive, claiming the attention of Viceroy Venegas and General Calleja as they fought to keep New Spain loyal to the Cortes meeting in Cádiz and working to resist Napoleon. Morelos, Rayón, and others pursued alliances of Americans in search of political sovereignty, opposed to despised *gachupines* and thus to Cádiz, and always defending property.[2] Meanwhile, popular insurgents in the Bajío, the Mezquital, and beyond attacked properties held by American and immigrant Spaniards. Political and popular insurgents remained separate and opposed yet proved mutually sustaining as regime forces faced distinct and dispersed challenges.

The Cádiz Constitution of 1812 changed the political field, offering new political rights tied to liberal powers in Spain. As popular risings persisted, support for political independence waned in New Spain. Morelos' 1814 Constitution of Apatzingán proved a last gasp. Written as French forces exited and Fernando reclaimed power in Spain, it proclaimed American sovereignty, defended property, and gained few adherents. Morelos faced capture and execution in 1815.[3]

The empire solidified as Mezquital insurgencies ended the same year. Otomí republics gained pacifications that kept communities strong and armed as "patriotic militias." The regional economy and the mines at Real del Monte began to revive with new respect for community rights and needs, while Bajío insurgents carried on the fight for family rights to make maize on estate lands, keeping mining at Guanajuato in distress.[4]

When Spanish liberal Francisco Javier Mina came to the Bajío with US filibusterers in 1817, he failed to claim the mines while drawing regime forces to attack insurgent fortresses. After Mina's capture and execution, popular insurgents still ruled the basin and nearby uplands. Pacification finally came after 1818 when military forces confirmed estate property rights while delivering the land to tenant families. In an outcome that mirrored Epigmenio González' dream, insurgent communities kept control of production—and arms to defend it.

In the summer of 1820, as pacifications entrenched communities of tenants on the land, the Valenciana mines flooded. The Bajío revolution broke silver capitalism while family maize makers ruled the basin's rich lands. The wealth and power of New Spain were gone, undermining Spain's power before don Agustín Iturbide proclaimed a Mexican empire in 1821. As power seekers struggled to build a nation, family growers held strong on the land across Guanajuato.

1811: Popular Power, Political Projects, Conflictive Chaos

On January 30, 1811, two weeks after Puente de Calderón, don José Toribio Rico reported that a "gang of men" attacked Puerto de Nieto, took him to a mountain camp, sacked the estate, then released him. The marauders rode east toward the Sierra Gorda, taking cloth, tools, and livestock from estates along the way. No one was hurt as raiders took supplies to sustain a guerrilla movement.[5] A week later, a loyalist who fled Celaya for safety at Querétaro wrote authorities in Mexico City to report a dire situation: "The city of Celaya is abandoned and facing anarchy; the Europeans who were a major part of the community have gone." The cause was clear: "With the dispersal of insurgents after the battle at Puente de Calderón, the city is surrounded by growing bands of bad men." The result: "Leading families have fled to refuge in Querétaro, abandoning homes, businesses, and estates."[6]

By May, Rico had fled Puerto de Nieto for safety at Querétaro. He compiled a list of seventy-five men he named as "estate insurgents," including "tenants, squatters, and employees." They had earlier taken him captive and sacked the estate. They destroyed the account books that recorded crops and sales, labor and pay, challenging property and commercial production. Camped in nearby uplands, they threatened daily. Rico also reported that the planting was done, and granaries were full from the past harvest. Still, neither property nor production were secure—and managers were no longer safe.[7]

While anonymous insurgents took control around Celaya and San Miguel, Albino García led risings across the bottomlands around Valle de Santiago and Salamanca. Born at the Cerro Blanco estate near Salamanca and classed an *indio*, García was a skilled horseman known for dealing in contraband tobacco and gunpowder. In 1810, he served as a foreman at an estate near Valle de Santiago. An agile rider, a dealer outside the law, and a leader of working men, he had joined Hidalgo in September 1810 as insurgents headed to the mines of Guanajuato. Later, when Hidalgo moved to Guadalajara, García consolidated power in his homeland. In January 1811, as insurgent political leaders dispersed, he led one of many Bajío guerrilla bands. They sacked the tax office and the homes of leading citizens at Salamanca, destroying the jail and local archives—attacking the means and records of power. In February, a "troop of base insurgents" sacked Irapuato, burning the homes of leading citizens, imposing new officials "sympathetic to the people."[8]

Into May, towns across the bottomlands from Irapuato through Salamanca, Valle de Santiago, and Celaya were regularly invaded, as was San Miguel to the north. Often held for a time, they were always surrounded

Map 4.1 Insurgent Guanajuato.

by insurgents. García and his band drew loyalist attacks—and repeatedly escaped. Loyalist commander don Antonio Gómez de Linares reported insurgent casualties—and growing insurgent numbers.[9]

By summer, life in the Bajío faced a new normal shaped by persistent popular insurgencies. In June, a loyal commander at Irapuato learned of cannon fire at Salamanca. Presuming an attack, he led troops to the scene. He found a "religious fiesta" that included "insurgents and local families," all in the presence of a "loyal" militia. The commander disarmed the few he could and left. In July, a militia leader at León reported Salamanca lost to the regime.[10] Calleja then called don Diego García Conde from San Luis Potosí to pacify "the cradle of revolution." He was to end "the rebel gatherings forming again around Dolores, San Luis de la Paz, and even San Miguel." The loyalists attacked and dispersed four thousand rebels led by don José de la Luz Gutiérrez, an original Dolores insurgent. Then Calleja sent García Conde north to defend the Zacatecas mines, leaving don Francisco Guisarnótegui, an aging yet energetic captain from Spain, to patrol San Miguel as conflicts expanded into the fall.[11]

Meanwhile, Albino García pressed west toward Pénjamo, where don José María Hidalgo y Costilla, brother of the executed insurgent leader, struggled as district magistrate. Calleja sent troops to expel García, pacify Pénjamo, and create a loyal militia. On August 19, they faced 1,500 insurgents. Calleja claimed victory with uncounted rebels killed and key leaders captured. García escaped—and Calleja's troops fled the scene of victory: "Our troops could not remain without lodging and forage for the cavalry, as the bandits [insurgents] flooded in and destroyed the land." Loyal troops could win battles; they could not hold rebel communities.[12]

The loyal Hidalgo reported that only a few "leading citizens" and "native residents" remained in town. He called those who fled to return and join militias; he wrote to estate managers seeking men, mounts, and arms. García soon returned to sack the homes of the prosperous, beating captives, including Magistrate Hidalgo, who wrote: "Pénjamo was left a miserable skeleton; residents are leaving for lands where they can live in peace. . . . The rebels arrested me, sacked my home, and pressed me to flee, as they planned to replace me as Magistrate."[13] Even a loyal Hidalgo was not safe.

While popular insurgents ruled and rattled rural Guanajuato, don Ignacio Rayón, don José Sixto Verduzco, and don José María Liceaga met in the uplands south at Zitácuaro to form a Supreme National American Junta. On August 21, they promised to defend Fernando VII, "our holy religion," and "the liberty of our oppressed patria [fatherland]." They demanded "a fair political and economic order." Defending religion and king, they would "shed our last drops of blood to defend liberty and property."[14] Rayón's junta proclaimed liberty in defense of Fernando and property.

Popular insurgents fought on. On August 31, Albino García attacked Lagos at the northwest edge of the Bajío. Hundreds entered from all sides. Church bells called the town to resist—to no avail. The magistrate and leading citizens were captured, beaten, and paraded all but naked through the streets. Stores and homes of the prosperous were sacked. García named a new magistrate, then left.[15]

Surrounded by insurgents, could mining revive at Guanajuato? Without silver, there was no New Spain—nothing valuable to defend for Spain, nothing to sustain the fight against insurgents, political or popular. The report written in September 1813 detailed the damages to mining inflicted by the invasions of 1810: "Financiers, mine operators, and refinery owners, left without funds to pay weekly costs," shut down. "Even the great Valenciana had to end essential drainage works." Cata, Mellado, and Rayas closed too, though the latter continued drainage. Insurgents took the mules that powered refineries, stopping work there. The mercury essential to refining disappeared, along with the silver needed to pay for everything.[16]

After the insurgents left, Rayas and Mellado reopened on limited scales; Cata resumed in January 1811. Eventually "the opulent Valenciana, the richest of all mines, began to operate again in April, but with *buscones*—who worked for shares of ore." Mining resumed by turning operations over to workers, a redistribution forced by producer risings. Meanwhile, "agricultural produce" was scarce as rural families fed themselves and guerrillas first. "Wealthy residents," fearing new incursions, fled. Lacking funds for drainage, to buy supplies, or to pay workers, without mercury and mules to refine ores, and with the cost of food and all else rising, mining limped forward in the summer of 1811.[17]

Calleja arrived in July to find "decadence, little production, and drainage suspended . . . all at great cost to mine operators and the Royal Treasury." Refineries were idle, leaving "many people without work." The commander feared that "workers facing need will join the insurgents, as among them they live free and without fear of punishment." All knew the value of Guanajuato: "The suspension of work at these most important of mines will compromise life and welfare across the province. When the mines operate, other towns are markets for the fruits of agriculture and industry; should the mines close," the consequences would be fatal.[18]

In August, the Intendant and the City Council joined mine owners to call for a mint at Guanajuato. It might solve the problem of shipping bullion to Mexico City while insurgents ruled the roads. Venegas declined, fearing provincial power and insurgent capture of minted pesos.[19]

Calleja believed that production had reached a level that silver could be shipped to Mexico City and on to Spain, protected by armed convoys. The Guanajuato Council argued that silver must remain to fund operations, pay workers, and stimulate the local economy.[20] Days later, Calleja called for new taxes to pay troops to protect Guanajuato and its mines. He wanted a higher levy on silver; the council preferred taxes on maize.[21] Owners feared levies that would drain capital; Calleja knew that taxes on staples fell on the workers who made silver. No resolution came—nor did mining revive.

In late September, Calleja turned to denounce the Zitácuaro Junta: Rayón and his allies "aim to seduce ignorant and innocent people to continue the robberies, sackings, and atrocities that benefit only the attackers." Heirs to Hidalgo and Allende, they were "strongmen who have forced this barbaric, impolitic, and unjust revolution that is devouring the kingdom."[22] Calleja knew the junta defended property. Still, he blamed political rebels for assaults on property, a myth aiming to hold the propertied loyal to the regime.

The greater challenge facing Calleja, loyal commanders, and Bajío capitalists in the fall of 1811 was to contain popular insurgents. During October and November, while García ruled the bottomlands, pastor don Francisco Uraga and Colonel Guisarnótegui worked to raise militias at San Miguel. Their efforts were stimulated and inhibited by repeated assaults by insurgent bands numbering two hundred to five hundred each, often mounted, variously armed, and entrenched in uplands. Guerrillas fed by rural communities raided San Miguel and Dolores. At times assembling up to two thousand men, they faced loyalist patrols, took losses, escaped, and survived. Loyalists held San Miguel; insurgents ruled the land.[23]

On November 18, popular insurgents returned to Guanajuato. The canyon city faced "bandits beyond count; more than 500 came . . . most mounted and all armed, though few had firearms." Two hundred men defended the square; two were killed. Insurgent deaths were not known. Calleja saw the city's "powerful men, Europeans and Americans," acquit themselves well—except for the Conde de Pérez Gálvez: "the troops from the mine came very late." The Marfil militia stayed home to defend the refineries, while "Silao and León refused to help, facing local insurgents all around."[24]

Calleja set the heads of Allende and Hidalgo in public squares to discourage "insubordination." The city lived "in total misery, with 70,000 beggars whose needs drive them to become insurgents." The solution: invest in mines, stimulate the economy, create jobs, and raise revenues. But that required peace, and in the fall of 1811 "the rich province of Guanajuato, left to newly recruited royalists, must fight endlessly against Gárcia and other multitudes of guerrillas, who with no goal beyond robbery, unite when they see the chance to fall upon important towns."[25]

Then, Calleja left the city to march toward Zitácuaro and the junta. He had reached Acámbaro when García led a larger assault on Guanajuato. Don Francisco Pérez Marañón remained in the city. He saw the earlier assault as "a test for the stronger invasion to come." While Calleja claimed victory, insurgents had gathered all around. Loyal "patriots" again mobilized; calls for assistance went to "commanders at León, Silao, and Irapuato." The latter again refused, insisting on the need to defend homes and towns. Calleja then left with his best troops, feigning a turn on Zitácuaro to avoid blame for another sacking of Guanajuato. The day after the battle, Calleja wrote to Venegas from Acámbaro as if ignorant of the sacking. Surrounded by rural insurgents, he begged for troops and arms.[26] He never moved toward Zitácuaro. The commander had fled to avoid blame for a crushing defeat.

Pérez Marañón detailed the assault. At dawn on November 26, "traitor" Albino García led attacks on the city's lowland gates and from heights all around. Cannon shot rained down on streets and plazas in narrow city canyons: "Fear rose among the people who because of sex, age, or lack of arms could not join in the defense; they took refuge in churches and convents, believing themselves victims of the diabolical furor of enemies whose numbers grew infinitely as the greatest part of people of the city, its mines, and refineries turned against us aiming to take the riches of the powerful—and end their lives." The people joined another sacking of the center and upland at Valenciana. Homes and businesses of the wealthy were set afire. Battles raged from 8:30 in the morning until 1:30 in the afternoon, when the attackers paused to reposition their cannon. A counterattack captured the artillery, setting rebels in flight and drawing cheers from "the few people who defend good order."

A troop from Silao arrived after the battle ended; dragoons from San Luis Potosí came the next day. They helped pacify locals who had joined in expropriations. Pérez Marañón credited urban defense forces with saving the city from García's insurgents and its own people. He reported 14,000 attackers, perhaps the largest rebel force assembled in the Bajío after Hidalgo's rising. Only 200 had rifles; 1,500 fought with pistols, sabers, and lances, "plus the endless throngs of the poor carrying machetes, knives, and clubs." Insurgents were many, arms still few.

Once García's cannon were captured, his men fled, and loyal forces turned on local people: "killing great numbers and taking many prisoners sent to the jail, where after brief trials they faced the punishments they deserved, examples to terrify wicked villainous throngs."[27] Loyalist terror quieted the city of mines. Still, the four assaults and sackings of the mining city, two led by Hidalgo and Allende in the fall of 1810, the two driven by García in November 1811, confirmed the fall of silver capitalism. The global trades it drove dissolved in 1812—and never revived.

While silver fell, popular rebels pressed on. Soon after García's invasion and the sacking of Guanajuato, more than two thousand insurgents camped above Puerto de Nieto, threatening the estate and blocking the pass that led from San Miguel to Querétaro. Guisarnótegui came with troops and raised local loyalists, including don José Toribio Rico who had come from Querétaro to prepare the harvest. Earlier, residents had taken pay and rations to plant maize on irrigated fields. With the harvest soon to begin, the manager aimed to keep the maize to sell for profit. Insurgent residents had other plans.

More than four hundred rebels, including many "estate employees and tenants," died in an assault on the highland fortress. Rico returned to rest in the house once occupied by the muchachas, to learn "no one would speak to me." The battle won, rebels dislodged, and hundreds killed, the estate community was fully alienated. Production defined by Sánchez Espinosa's property, Rico's management, residents' labor, and the sale of crops for profit ended that late November day—destroyed by a deadly loyalist victory. The next morning, the manager and his assistant took the "case of ornaments" and the image of the "Virgin of Sorrows" from the chapel and fled. If residents would not honor property and labor for estate profit, they would lose the cherished images that focused community worship.

From safety in Querétaro, Rico wrote that the city was secure while nearby estates faced sporadic attacks. At San Miguel, Dolores, and San Luis de la Paz, "with the king's troops so far away, the haciendas are facing killings, sacking, and destruction."[28] Puerto de Nieto belonged to the community. Men had taken pay to plant the fields; the community controlled the two thousand to four thousand fanegas harvested. With ten fanegas a year's sustenance, the liberated harvest would feed two hundred to four hundred families in the coming year. Insurgents would rule the estate for years to come.

On December 10, insurgents invaded Dolores, killing magistrate don Ramón Montemayor, sacking the town, and taking several cannons. News reaching San Miguel reported that Captain don José Mariano Ferrer and other militia leaders were captured, then ransomed for more than 2,000 pesos by "the widow of the insurgent chief Abasolo."[29] She had continued estate production; now popular rebels took her profits. As 1811 ended, insurgents ruled all around Dolores and San Miguel while Albino García held the bottomlands around Valle de Santiago and Salamanca. Loyalists held Guanajuato and key towns while rebels repeatedly invaded to rattle power and enable popular redistributions.

The Zitácuaro Junta aimed to join the fray when "Brigadier Commander Friar Laureano Saavedra" set a base at Salvatierra. He railed against García:

"Oh cursed maimed Albino? Atila of this northland, servant of hell, horrible monster of blasphemies, your infamies, your unfathomable infamies, your incalculable destructions have forced so many faithful patriots to move to places held by our tyrannical royalist enemies despite the repugnant violence in their hearts."

Knowing he could not attack García at Salamanca and Valle de Santiago, Saavedra aimed to occupy Celaya with 1,500 "riflemen, lancers, and *macheteros*" backed by six "valiant cannon": "I aim to enter the city in peace, respecting every American and firing only on despotic Europeans. . . . Together we will join arms in defense of our holy religion, our sweet patria, and our virtuous liberty."[30] The junta in arms opposed European despotism and aimed to fight García's destructive insurgents.

As Saavedra entered the Bajío, Pérez Marañón reported that García roamed freely. Mining languished as a convoy arrived with "much tobacco, mercury, and powder, but without funds, food, and other necessities."[31] Days later, Commander Guisarnótegui added: "Insurgents have entered San Miguel without opposition, stealing what little remained while inflicting damage at the haciendas."[32]

Amid chaos that favored García, Saavedra failed. Guisarnótegui reported that "the insurgent Dominican" twice threatened Celaya, claiming ample and well-armed forces. The commander sought 300 to 400 soldiers "to engage them."[33] Then a troop of 150 surprised the rebel friar in his "still warm bed" on December 27. Saavedra fled with eight "lesser chiefs." Loyalists took his cannon, firearms, and horses, ending the junta's attempt to become a third force in the Bajío.[34]

Only then did Calleja move to take Zitácuaro, proclaiming victory on January 2, 1812. He feigned a move north to San Felipe, then drove south toward Zitácuaro while Guisarnótegui ousted Saavedra from Salvatierra. The assaults came in Christmas season, as popular insurgents focused on family and festivals. Loyalists struck political insurgents; popular insurgents stayed home. In the face of Calleja's attack, Rayón, Liceaga, and Verduzco fled south toward Taxco.[35]

In January, Calleja detailed his repression at Zitácuaro. He called Rayón and his allies "sad partisans of the cruel and barbaric revolution of the cura Hidalgo, . . . miserable bandit chiefs who now, after losing the power to pursue their goals, fled as cowards in the face of danger." Aiming to promote peace, he limited executions, sent a few to exile, and pardoned those who pledged loyalty. He struck harder at Zitácuaro's indigenous republics, denying rights to self-rule and community lands, punishment for feeding Rayón's junta.[36]

In the year after Hidalgo's defeat, the Bajío lived chaotic and conflictive times. Popular guerrillas invaded towns, threatening power and enabling redistributions. Estate residents took maize and land for family cropping. Rayón's junta proclaimed a national project in defense of property. Albino García attacked Guanajuato, opening the city to sackings that broke mining and silver capitalism. Then Calleja expelled the junta, exiling political insurgency from the basin where it began. Popular insurgents fought on.

Consolidating Popular Insurgency, 1812–1814

A structure of conflict ruled into the new year: "At San Miguel, our enemies come and go without difficulty. . . . Across the Bajío, estates face endless raids that have taken all their livestock and grains." The harvests that would provide for the coming year were taken by insurgents and the communities that sustained them. Albino García held Valle de Santiago "recruiting people." In Guanajuato, "there is nothing new"—as García attacked again in January, took what he pleased, and left after suffering few casualties.[37] In February, Calleja reported that García ruled the basin while three thousand to four thousand insurgents held the heights above San Miguel.[38]

Through April and May, don Diego García Conde and his lieutenant don Agustín Iturbide chased García. Loyalists saw a "war on bandits" as Guanajuato struggled to defend mining.[39] The Celaya Council reported "a fight pressed by tenacious enemies in the towns of Salamanca, Valle de Santiago, Salvatierra, Acámbaro, and others nearby." Then García hit a convoy, capturing loyalist soldiers, arms and mounts, mercury and blasting powder, and "more than 100,000 pesos," all intended to revive mining at Guanajuato, now claimed to sustain insurgency.[40] Mining could not revive.

On May 5, 1812, Albino García invaded Celaya with five thousand rebels, sacked the town, then left as Guisarnótegui's troops arrived. García declared "an open war to take the fields, sacking grains and stealing livestock, persecuting leaseholders, managers and overseers."[41] As at Puerto de Nieto, insurgents expelled managers, delivering land, livestock, and crops to working families. As May ended, Guisarnótegui's "loyal" troops, unpaid, also sacked Celaya.[42]

Then loyalists and landlords received what seemed the best of news: in early June, Iturbide captured Albino García; taken to Celaya, he faced quick execution.[43] Loyal commanders and desperate proprietors presumed that García made popular insurgency successful. They soon learned that rebel communities generated and sustained guerrillas. Little changed after García's death. In July, Celaya remained a city under siege, its economy in shambles, with no funds to pay loyal troops.[44]

Early in September, desperate and on the run, Rayón's junta offered Constitutional Elements proclaiming "Catholicism the only religion"; that "America is free and independent of all other nations"; and that "sovereignty emanates from the people" yet "resides in the person of don Fernando VII, to be exercised by the Supreme American National Congress." The Elements proposed an independence still linked to Spain's monarchs, overseen by an American congress, and committed to protecting property.[45] The people might be sovereign; they would not be served.

The promised constitution never came. On September 19, 1812, while political insurgents struggled and popular forces ruled rural Guanajuato, Viceroy Venegas published the liberal constitution completed at Cádiz in March. Loyal to the captive Fernando, it offered political rights and limited representation to Americans and promised to protect property. It aimed to hold the empire together to fight Napoleon in Spain and insurgents, political and popular, in New Spain. The space for a politics between regime defenders and insurgents attacking property closed. Political men had to choose.

A few turned to the rebel populace. In November, a patrol outside Celaya found papers written by don José María Liceaga, a member of Rayón's junta. Days later, captured rebels said they reported to Liceaga. A junta leader had turned to join insurgent communities in the battle for control of land and maize.[46] Meanwhile, Doctor don José María Cos found a base at Dolores. A priest and compadre of don José Sánchez Espinosa, in 1810 Cos was the pastor at San Cosme in the city of Guanajuato. After the battle for the Alhóndiga and Allende's November return, Cos was accused of insurgent sympathies. Sánchez Espinosa worried he might join those attacking property. Now, he lived among insurgents, attacking convoys shipping supplies to Guanajuato and San Luis Potosí and silver back to Mexico City. He began to circulate insurgent pesos—revealing access to silver and thinking like a state.[47] As 1813 began, Liceaga and Cos had joined popular guerrillas.

Few political men followed them as the Cádiz Constitution became known. It offered political rights to European and American Spanish men, indigenous and mestizo men (but not men of African origins, a concession to Cuban slave owners). It defended personal property as sacrosanct. Indigenous republics became municipalities open to all citizens. Their corporate lands faced privatization, but amid social and political conflicts, loyalists in New Spain refrained.[48] Offering new political rights while defending property, Cádiz held the powerful and the propertied, American and immigrant Spaniards, to the regime while popular insurgents ruled the Guanajuato countryside.[49]

Then the summer of 1813 brought deadly typhus, killing many, demobilizing more. Stalemate entrenched.[50] In May, Cádiz authorities named Calleja viceroy. In September, he named Iturbide commander in the Bajío, a reward for capturing Albino García. Don Francisco Orrantía succeeded Guisarnótegui in pursuits of popular insurgents.[51]

As regime power solidified, José María Morelos, the one political insurgent with effective military forces, proposed full independence. On September 14, 1813, at Chilpancingo far south of the Bajío, he offered "Sentiments of the Nation." Article 1 stated: "America is free and independent of Spain"— with no mention of Fernando VII. Article 2 repeated: "Catholicism is the only religion." Article 5 stated that "Sovereignty emanates directly from the people," then added "who deposit it with their representatives." The people would not exercise sovereignty; representatives would act in their stead. The Sentiments abolished slavery, breaking with Cádiz' protection of Cuban slave owners. It ended all legal privileges and distinctions, except between Americans and Europeans, breaking with Cádiz' assertion that Spaniards and Americans formed one nation. Defending property, Article 17 stated: "Everyone will preserve their properties and their homes will be respected as sacred asylums."[52] Cádiz called an alliance of the powerful to defend the empire and property. Morelos would divide the powerful to break with the empire—still promising to defend property.

Little changed in the Bajío. On September 21, Guanajuato mine owners documented the destructive impacts of the insurgent incursions since 1810. Through the spring and summer of 1813, no convoy had delivered supplies from the capital. One came in September, without funds to sustain production, consumption, and troops. Still, local forces backed by "the Virgin Most Holy" kept "large and fearsome insurgent forces" at bay, funded by new taxes on maize. Workers and city consumers prayed and paid to protect the limited mining that carried on.

The mine operators complained that the Mexico City mint took a third of all bullion to fund counterinsurgency, up from the fifth standard before 1810. Financiers took "exorbitant profits" to send supplies that rarely came. Mining continued by "destroying the mines" as workers "broke" the works, taking ores from the pillars that supported tunnels. Workers were "mining the pillars, or better said, destroying the mines." As workers ruled: "Only God knows when the mines will be restored."

The operators demanded lower taxes, less costly mercury, armed convoys to protect bullion shipments, and a Guanajuato mint. They held out a dream and a nightmare: "with pacification and public order," and new funding for mining and refining, cultivation would revive and trade would flourish; but now, without ample and affordable mercury, mining in New Spain held near 5 to 6 million pesos yearly, far from the 20 million pesos standard before 1810. Begging for help, the mine operators detailed the impossibility of reviving silver in times of popular insurgency.[53]

Meanwhile, a new insurgent economy set in. On November 22, sixty men attacked the Morales estate, near Celaya, claiming more than fifty teams of oxen. The manager and a small troop gave chase and "ransomed" seven teams, paying to maintain limited cultivation. The rest went to Tequisquiapan, north of San Miguel and Atotonilco, where Rafael Rayas lived with four hundred insurgents. In the chase, the troop discovered that insurgents ruled the estate where in 1804 residents had sued for land as an indigenous republic—with Hidalgo's support. And they saw that Atotonilco, once home to penitential devotions favored by the powerful of San Miguel and where Hidalgo had raised Guadalupe's banner, was now home to an insurgent-ruled regional market.[54]

As 1813 became 1814, Fernando reclaimed his throne; in May 1814, he abrogated the Cádiz Constitution—restoring monarchical rights as the silver capitalism that sustained imperial power remained collapsed. Political insurgents led by Morelos held on in the Pacific hot country while Calleja and Iturbide fought to defend Fernando, property, and Spanish rule. Popular insurgents ruled rural Guanajuato and the Mezquital—strangling mining at Guanajuato and Real del Monte.

In that time of contested change, on October 22, 1814, Morelos offered the Constitution of Apatzingán.[55] Formally a "Constitutional Decree to Liberate Mexican America," it opened by insisting that "apostolic Roman Catholicism is the only religion." Again, "sovereignty resides originally in the people," to be exercised by deputies elected by adult men of all ancestries. Elections staged in levels allowed all men to vote, while the few would rule. Apatzingán addressed maligned *gachupines* in Article 16, granting citizenship to foreign residents who were Catholic and accepted "national liberty."

Then the charter turned to property: Article 17 guaranteed that foreigners would see their "persons and properties" secure. Article 24 stated: "The happiness of the people and every citizen comes from equality, security, property, and liberty." Setting security and property before liberty sent a clear message. Morelos' political nation aimed to attract and protect the propertied and prosperous among Americans now proclaimed Mexicans.

Lest there be doubt, the emphasis was repeated—and repeated. Article 32 asserted again that "the home of every citizen is an inviolable asylum." Article 34 promised that "every individual in society has the right to acquire properties and dispose of them as they choose." Article 35 emphasized that "no one may be deprived of what they possess"—but for public necessity, and then only with just compensation. Article 41 insisted that "citizen's obligations" begin with "complete submission to the laws; an absolute obedience to the authorities." Finally, Article 165 insisted again that the regime would maintain rights to "liberty, property, equality, and security." Morelos proclaimed a Mexican nation in defense of property. No surge of support came.

Iturbide captured Morelos in November 1815. Execution came in December, ending any lingering political threat to the restored regime of Fernando VII. Going forward, the fight was about power and property—both challenged by popular insurgents across Guanajuato.

Popular Insurgents Rule, 1815–1817

With Morelos on the run far to the south, 1815 began with guerrilla forces and insurgent communities entrenched from Dolores, through San Miguel, to Celaya. Don Francisco Orrantía, based in Querétaro, aimed to patrol the routes that led to San Miguel and Dolores, Guanajuato and San Luis Potosí, guarding convoys carrying supplies to the mines and bullion to Mexico City—with little success. On January 14, he assembled five hundred loyalists from Querétaro and San Luis Potosí to hold northern Guanajuato against "the bands of the Ortiz, Rosas, Serapio, Rosales and Moreno."[56] Guerrilla leaders began to have names, indicating enduring power. Reporting "actions" on January 22 and February 7 against "Ortiz and Rosas," Orrantía called for "garrisons in Dolores, San Felipe, and San Luis de la Paz; otherwise we will never pacify those areas." Troops might deny horses to mobile rebels and force "rancheros to live in towns or at estates . . . more open to oversight."[57] Pacification required garrisons to constrain guerrillas and concentrate growers now called rancheros to allow surveillance. It could not be done.

Orrantía reported a July action at Rincón de Ortega against "the rebel chiefs Fernando de Rosas, Encarnación Ortiz, Victor Rosales and Pedro Moreno," the same guerillas he hoped to defeat in January. They now amassed more than 1,200 mounted men backed by cannon. Orrantía killed more than 300, captured another 20, along with 190 firearms, 200 horses, and a few lances and machetes, allowing a convoy from San Luis Potosí to deliver 400 bars of silver, 1,000 mules, and 120,000 sheep to the capital—while estates near San Miguel lost 20,000 sheep to other rebels.[58]

On October 12, he wrote from San Miguel lamenting Calleja's orders to move on: "This jurisdiction along with San Luis de la Paz, Dolores, and San Felipe are moving toward good order." If he stayed, he could bring them to "perfect order"; his departure would return them to insurgent rule.[59] A week later, he reported from Silao that Fernando Rosas had appointed rebel treasury officials "taking revenues from estates around Dolores with great tyranny; those who do not pay face loss of oxen and essential tools." Orrantía's troops gone, insurgents asserted state powers.[60]

In January 1816, he was in Celaya: "The towns face a sad poverty that deepens every day . . . due to the lack of cultivation." Still, "rebels allow essential grains like maize and frijol to supply Guanajuato and Silao, charging one real per carga."[61] Basic staples were not scarce; they were harvested in insurgent communities where families ate first, sustained guerrillas, and sold surplus in towns and mines—paying small taxes to rebel leaders.

On the twentieth, Orrantía returned to San Miguel to guard another convoy, joined by 200 men from San Luis Potosí. They attacked "the rebel Padre Mariano Carmona, Commander General of all bands in the jurisdictions of Dolores and San Felipe." He led 900 rebels camped at La Noria. Orrantía dispersed Carmona's force, then chased Encarnación Ortiz and his 400 men to Xichú at the edge of the Sierra Gorda. Returning to La Noria, Orrantía executed 8 rebels while the convoy passed with 324 bars of silver and 6,000 sheep.[62]

From Querétaro, Orrantía reported difficulties collecting fees to sustain troops and protect convoys while Dolores, San Felipe, and San Luis de la Paz still needed garrisons if there was to be any hope of returning northern Guanajuato to royal rule.[63] Progress proved slow. In June, Dolores had 27 cavalry and 116 infantry, 26 rifles, 40 carbines, and 14 machetes. San Felipe and San Luis de la Paz remained "destroyed by the rebels." He called for 150 men to reclaim them.[64] Through the spring, he captured 40 insurgents, executing 31, sentencing the rest to presidio service. Near San Miguel, he found 2 cannons plus a supply of powder, 27 rifles, and 11 bayonets. Meanwhile, he protected a convoy from Guanajuato to Mexico City with 523 bars of silver and 60,000 sheep.[65]

In August 1816, Orrantía led 1,561 cavalry, backed by 1,726 infantry—3,287 troops to assert regime power and reclaim property across the Bajío between

Guanajuato and Querétaro, San Felipe and Acámbaro.[66] Facing an impossible task, he held the stalemate and guarded convoys.[67]

Meanwhile, insurgent power extended west of the mines. In 1815, managers around León began to report losses of draft animals to insurgents, forcing them to turn production over to tenants. They wrote as if they were forced by outside "insurgents."[68] More likely, residents claimed work teams, took over production, and let managers remain if they acquiesced. Collecting few rents, they reported the change as forced to absentee owners. Their deflections, and perhaps defections, shielded new insurgents' powers.

While insurgents consolidated on the land just west at León, Guanajuato and its mines faced a year of misery in 1816. Foodstuffs and essential supplies were scarce and expensive. In August, insurgents invaded again, again enabling locals in looting, then fleeing in the face of loyal troops.[69] In September, a commander at nearby Silao wrote of "a fatal situation in which I lack the ability to support myself and my family, because rebels do not permit agriculture, the business that sustains me, nor any other activity, bringing commerce and crafts down to levels once unimaginable."[70]

North and west of Guanajuato and León, insurgents turned to new ways to hold power and protect communities. In August, Col. don José de la Cruz ordered forces from Guanajuato, Guadalajara, and Zacatecas to "destroy the rebel Moreno fortified at Cerro del Sombrero, 6 leagues north of León." The rebel was Pedro Moreno, born to a family of American Spaniards who were modest landowners at Lagos (now de Moreno), northwest of León. He had studied in Guadalajara, then returned home to operate a store and family lands. He held back through the first years of insurgency, until trade collapsed and contacts in Valladolid drew him to rebel networks in 1813.[71] He built the fortress at Cerro de Sombrero, where loyalist forces began a long siege in September 1816.[72]

By mid-October, Orrantía, now general commander of the Army of the North, saw a larger insurgent strategy. He wrote to don Juan Ruíz de Apodaca, who had replaced Calleja as viceroy, that three fortified bastions focused power and protected insurgent production: Moreno held Cerro de Sombreros, north of León; Padre Carmona and the Ortizes were building a fortress at Mesa de los Caballos near San Felipe; and Padre José Antonio Torres set a "fortress" at Los Remedios near Pénjamo: "the goal: to monopolize all the maize of the coming harvest."[73] The fortresses would protect family growers, end landed power, and cripple mining.

Orrantía gained detailed intelligence on Padre Torres's fortress: he had 500 men and 600 rifles (no longer scarce among insurgents); he held 6,000 fanegas of maize (enough to feed 600 families for a year), 200 cargas of wheat, and other staples. Camped above a cave with a spring, rebels built a winch lift to draw water to protected heights. "More than 2,000 men worked on the fort," a labor force larger than at any Bajío hacienda, equal to many at Guanajuato mines. Orrantía maligned Torres rebels as an "Yndiada"—othering the ethnically mixed, culturally Hispanic peoples who had long sustained silver capitalism and now mobilized to assault it. He added a list of leaders: beyond Padres Torres and Liceaga (once part of Rayón's junta) there were two priests, a lawyer, and three others labeled "cabecillas"—little chiefs, diminished as Orrantía feared their power.[74]

While insurgents fortified north and west of Guanajuato, popular production still ruled around San Miguel. In August 1816, don José Toribio Rico returned to Puerto de Nieto for the first time in five years. He wrote don José Sánchez Espinosa, dreaming that with a garrison of troops, he could restore estate production and help pacify the region.[75] In early November, a convoy traveling from Querétaro to San Miguel and Dolores faced constant harassment.[76] At Atotonilco, the once penitential shrine still flourished as an insurgent market. Loyalists might attack, but the market carried on.[77]

In late November, Orrantía wrote to Sánchez Espinosa backing Rico's plan. Retaking Puerto de Nieto might limit insurgent threats to supply lines from Querétaro to San Miguel and beyond. He offered to send sixty to seventy men to force "the residents to meet their obligations."[78] In 1811, residents had taken wages to plant maize, then rose to claim the crop. Now, insurgents had planted and Rico aimed to make them deliver the harvest to estate control. Instead, Orrantía sent his troops west to attack the new fortresses. The harvest of 1816 at Puerto de Nieto stayed with the families that planted it as Rico again retreated to Querétaro.

Orrantía turned on Mesa de los Caballos. The fortress near San Felipe preyed on convoys from Querétaro to San Miguel, Guanajuato, and San Luis Potosí. Since the fortress occupied a high plateau about eight kilometers around, and well supplied with wood and water, assault was difficult. The rebels proved obstinate, but regime arms and artillery prevailed at the cost of one hundred casualties. The loyalist revenge: "everyone we found on the mesa, of every category and sex, had their throats cut. Only a few freed themselves by leaping off the mesa to survive."[79]

The brutal victory polarized ongoing conflicts. The strongholds at Sombrero and Remedios held insurgent power west of the mines. Guerrilla bands roamed everywhere. Still, with the fortress nearest San Miguel broken,

Orrantía and Rico again imagined sending troops to Puerto de Nieto to control residents, assert property, and claim the next harvest.

In March 1817, Orrantía wrote again to Sánchez Espinosa. The viceroy had approved a plan to garrison estates, placing fifteen to twenty men at Puerto de Nieto. They would arrive before planting, making the next harvest estate property. Orrantía reported the main house "destroyed." Nearby lands were "deserted" as residents lived at scattered ranchos. A "reunion" concentrating families around the main house restored to serve as a garrison would enable surveillance. Some residents might become "patriots." He asked Sánchez Espinosa to supply arms.[80]

In May, two hundred soldiers dispersed to estates around San Miguel, with thirty sent to Puerto de Nieto. Rico came from Querétaro to join them, hoping for "the total extermination of the rebels"—apparently inspired by the devastation at Mesa de los Caballos. He also worried that "just south of the estate a few guerrilla bands remain"—a first sign of the highland fortress at Xalpa. Many residents took wages to plant fields at Puerto de Nieto; none agreed to arm as patriots.[81]

The planting done and wages gained, the plan dissolved in June. Spanish liberal don Francisco Javier Mina, seeking to disrupt Fernando VII's rule, had traveled to the United States, recruited privateers, landed on the coast east of the Bajío, and marched to join Pedro Moreno at Cerro de Sombrero. Orrantía sent the troops patrolling San Miguel to face the new threat. Rico retreated to Querétaro—again.[82] Residents sacked the great house—again. Rico added: "Surely things are worse than before, as the residents have become boldly insolent."[83] For a third time, the estate paid residents to plant, then saw them claim the harvest as their own. Puerto de Nieto carried on as an insurgent community.

The Mina Incursion, 1817

Mina was a young man of middling origins and some education from the mountains of Navarre in northern Spain. He took to insurgency to fight Napoleon's invasion of 1808, became a local commander in 1810, then was captured and imprisoned in France. Released in 1814, he saw Fernando's abrogation of the Cádiz Constitution as a betrayal. Unable to spark resistance in an exhausted Spain, Mina dreamed of breaking Fernando's power in the empire.[84]

He headed to London in April 1815. After decades of war and trade disruptions, and then victory over Napoleon, it was full of refugees, dreamers, and speculators looking for the next chance in a changing world. There, Mina met don Servando Teresa de Mier, a liberal friar exiled from New Spain and looking for allies. There, too, in February 1816, Mina met Winfield Scott, already a general for his efforts in the War of 1812, now serving the US government in London. He assured Mina that he would find welcome, funding, and recruits in the young nation emerging from war with England. Mina also met don José Francisco de Fagoaga, once among Mexico City's leading merchant financiers, still an estate owner, now exiled in London and dreaming of reviving the silver capitalism his family once led. He promised to back loans Mina raised in London. With famous friends and few funds, Mina sailed from Liverpool in May, landing at Norfolk, Virginia, on July 1, 1816.

He learned that money, supplies, and supporters required visits to Washington, Baltimore, Philadelphia, and New York—where he again met General Scott, who made contacts and helped solicit funds. Having gained what he could, Mina sailed from Annapolis on September 28. Landing in Port-au-Prince, Haiti, on October 12, he met Simón Bolívar, then enjoying Alexandre Petién's protection as he dreamed of liberating Caracas. They spoke of common projects, then went separate ways. Mina spent much of the fall between New Orleans and Galveston, seeking money and men ready to risk an invasion. He sent letters to Guadalupe Victoria, one of a few surviving political insurgents then hiding in the mountains of Veracruz. Mina imagined joining him, to learn that loyalists held nearby ports.

In Galveston on February 22, 1817, Mina proclaimed Fernando VII a traitor for abrogating the Constitution of 1812. The restored empire only benefited the king and monopolists. On Spanish soil, Mina called for the liberation of the Americas. After a return to New Orleans to seek more men, he stopped at the mouth of the Rio Grande to proclaim "liberty and independence for Mexico." He did not come to conquer but to join local liberators. He promised "respect to religion, people, and property."[85] It was a vision shared with Hidalgo and Allende, Rayón, Morelos, and other political insurgents now defeated in New Spain. Could Mina find allies among the Bajío's popular insurgents?

He landed on April 1, 1817, at Soto la Marina, a small port north of Tampico. After weeks of local learning, Mina headed inland in June. Facing skirmishes along the way, he took Ciudad del Maíz and Rio Verde, passed San Luis Potosí and Sierra de Pinos, to arrive at Moreno's Cerro del Sombrero on the twenty-fifth.[86] The troop included 309 men, 109 mounted. Most were from the United States, many from New Orleans; perhaps two dozen had joined in Haiti.[87]

Adding Mina's troop to Moreno's forces and those of Sebastián González and Encarnación Ortiz gave the Cerro's defenders more than 700 armed men. With the men who worked on the fortress, the women who sustained everything, and children, too, the population exceeded 1,200. Orrantía brought forces to mount a siege as the community faced shortages of food and water (which had to be carried from streams below). On the last day of July, 4,000 loyalists surrounded the Cerro and tightened a circle. Mina and a small group broke out, leaving Moreno, local insurgents, and most of Mina's band to face the siege. Mina claimed he aimed to return with munitions and supplies. Orrantía offered to allow women and children to depart; they refused (recalling the slaughter at Caballos).

At night on August 19, desperate defenders attempted to break out. Women and children went first, to be quickly discovered. Royalists fired wildly in the dark, creating mass confusion. "The cries of women and children, the pleas of the wounded," filled the night. Moreno, along with John Bradburn, Mina's lieutenant from New Orleans, and about fifty others escaped in dense fog. Entering the fortress, Orrantía's troops captured Sebastián González, his wife and children, and Moreno's family. Many sick and wounded were found in a hospital and shot. Others were taken prisoner, including 150 men said to be workers, not fighters. They worked for three days demolishing the fort they had built; then the loyalists shot them. This time women and children were pardoned.[88]

Mina and his small troop left the area around Sombrero before the final siege. He passed León and Silao, defeating a small cavalry squadron. On August 17, he joined Padre Torres at Remedios. Born at Cocupao near Lake Pátzcuaro and educated as a priest, Torres was serving a parish near Lake Cuitzeo when insurgency began. He joined Albino García until he died in 1812, stood back for a time, then in 1814 returned to the fray. He built the fortress near Pénjamo, naming the site Los Remedios, honoring one powerful virgin; he labeled its key bulwark Tepeyac, honoring Guadalupe.

When Mina arrived, he found 1,500 insurgents in fortified uplands. Springs and wells provided water drawn by whims from below. There was a hospital, a foundry, an armory, and craft shops: "The insurgents saw the fort at Los Remedios as the bastion of Independence." Loyalist forces began a siege on August 31, amassing 6,000 troops. Torres and Mina tried a dual plan: Torres would hold the fort; Mina would take a mobile troop of 900, harass towns across Bajío, seek reinforcements, and return to confront loyalists from outside the circle of siege. Did Torres suspect that after Mina's desertion at Sombrero, the Spaniard would not stay to face a siege?

Mina recruited Encarnación Ortiz and others still strong north of Guanajuato. He drove east to attack San Luis de la Paz, at the edge of the Sierra Gorda, claiming victory and blocking convoy traffic for a time. He returned to San Miguel, taking a workshop on the plaza near the Oratorio de San Felipe Neri until a seven-hour firefight expelled the invaders.[89] Mina then marched to Valle de Santiago, a hotbed of insurgency since the days of Albino García. In 1817, most lived in straw huts: "The people gave Mina sustenance and funds . . . but did not help with men and arms."[90]

Mina proclaimed his own importance: "Commanders in the province of Guanajuato and my beloved companions in arms: as soon as our enemies learned of my honored arrival in these lands, they mobilized all their resources and troops, abandoning other areas and diverting divisions from other provinces." On that, he was not wrong. He then offered a fictional account of the disaster at Sombreros: "They attacked me at the Sombrero fortress." Mina claimed to have killed more than a thousand loyalists, before "we had to escape due to the lack of water and food." Then, when "the enemy" took the hill, "the troop, the families, and our weapons . . . were all saved with little loss." Could lies erase Mina's desertion and the devastation at Sombrero?

Now it was time to protect and defend Remedios, held by "General don José Antonio Torres with ample forces and abundant food supplies." Mina claimed triumphs at Vizcocho and San Luis de la Paz and argued he would have achieved the same at San Miguel until a thousand loyalists came, admitting defeat and the limits of his forces. As Torres faced siege at Remedios, Mina declared, "Come my noble companions in arms, let us liberate our General and weaken our enemy's forces; with victory we can destroy their plans, paralyze their weak forces, and move toward liberty for all of America."[91] Erasing his own desertion, claiming defeats as victories, Mina called all to relieve to the siege at Remedios.

Then he turned to the mines at Guanajuato, surely the prime interest of his backers in London and the United States. He camped near Irapuato with a force near 1,100 men sustained by women and children. As Mina waited in fields of ripening maize, Orrantía attacked with 800 troops, blocking the way to the mines.[92] Mina then drove west toward Remedios, skirmished with loyalists, to return toward Guanajuato. Joined by Encarnación Ortiz and 300 more guerrillas, Mina prepared to assault the mining city with 1,400 men. Orrantía marched his men for twelve hours to again block the way, setting Mina in flight. He was captured on October 17, executed on November 11.[93]

The siege at Los Remedios continued to the end of the year. Finally, conditions deteriorated to the point that Torres, his troops, and "the countrymen, women, and children" attempted to break out late at night on January 1, 1818. Loyalists sounded the alarm and took arms to prevent the escape. Torres and a few others got away. The men who came with Mina and remained in the fortress all died. Torres's sisters and the wives and children of other leaders were captured, "while common women were shorn of their hair, and left in liberty." The women who sustained life in the fortress were left bald to announce the defeat. Loyalist commanders gained honors and promotions, including don Anastasio Bustamante, whose government Lucas Alamán would lead in the early 1830s.[94]

Mina dreamed of liberating the Americas, backed by commercial interests seeking silver and trade. When he arrived, the fortresses of the western Bajío protected insurgents entrenched in family production and blocking any revival of mining at Guanajuato. Into that crucible of conflict Mina drew loyalist forces from all around, as he proudly proclaimed. They killed him and destroyed the insurgent fortresses while guerrillas fought on, mining struggled—and insurgent families ruled the land.

San Miguel Besieged, 1817–1819

Popular insurgency held strong around San Miguel through 1819. A week after Mina's failed attempt to claim the once rich textile town in September 1817, commander don Ignacio del Corral reported that guerrilla leaders Encarnación Ortiz, Lucas Flores, and "el Pío"—the pious one—had gathered at Los Reyes near San Felipe, while Sebastián González, Montes, and other rebels were "entrenched" at the mountain massif at Xalpa, a highland fortress south of Puerto de Nieto.[95]

Two months later, with Mina dead and Remedios besieged, Corral wrote to Viceroy Apodaca. Unable to pay his troops, he had asked commanders at Querétaro for 1,000 pesos. They sent ten cases of cigars, an insult. Locally, he had collected 4,541 pesos in four months. Townspeople paid one real per fanega of maize and would bear no more: "Collections from the ranchos are the only resource left, but collection requires forces I do not have."[96] Rancheros made maize, recognized no property rights, and paid no taxes.

Without funds, he could not "clean out the bands that control the delivery of foodstuffs." While Querétaro forces aimed to attack the Xalpa fortress south of Puerto de Nieto, Corral could only "operate minimally" near San Miguel. He sent men to "Atotonilco with the goal of blocking the scandalous market the rebels hold there to sustain themselves." The insurgent market flourished, limiting provisioning to San Miguel.[97] Corral's small troop chased guerrillas, claiming mounts and arms, and took what funds they could. They dispersed small bands, captured and killed a few men, and claimed a bit of support for struggling counterinsurgent efforts.[98]

To fight guerrillas, loyalists became guerrillas: "We have learned from experience that when bands of traitors face royal troops in constant movement, they will disperse and not remain to fight." A mobile patrol had killed the "cabecilla Gervasio Vargas," creating a leadership vacuum at Xalpa.[99] "The late Vargas" had become "the idol of all who gathered there, always obeyed. . . . Now there is discord . . . over the succession of command." Corral pleaded for "a mobile division to chase the rebels and open communications between Dolores and San Miguel, San Luis Potosí and Querétaro." Without mobile forces, the insurgent siege of San Miguel would hold.[100]

It continued into 1818. Corral sent patrols into the countryside "to obtain sustenance and finish the rebels." What he paid to gain the former, he did not say. Querétaro troops again attacked Xalpa and gained nothing: "a result of the limited intelligence and knowledge of the commanders." Corral's plan was to "fortify Puerto de Nieto as a base for provisions, destroy the rebels, clear the roads, and protect commerce."[101] The estate sat below Xalpa, where the highway climbed to the pass that led to Santa Rosa and Querétaro. Corral dreamed. Insurgents held Puerto de Nieto until 1820.

On February 28, 1818, Magistrate don José Luis de Pereya and the San Miguel Council reported the town's struggles "since the outbreak of the rebellion." They lamented "the setbacks, losses, and departure of the most prosperous citizens." They honored "those who have remained . . . in the face of the greatest personal and financial losses, the deadly blows they have suffered. . . . The rebellion ruined the leading, richest citizens as destructions and sackings continued into 1814." The once eminent lived "without capital, cultivation, or commerce."

From August 1814 to April 1817, the citizens of San Miguel had loaned 19,000 pesos to support local troops. Then, due to "the new insurrection brought by the detestable Mina, grave destructions have continued as the rebels who surround us have become ever more insolent, especially the swarm of pests at Xalpa." Without means to pay troops, a town once rich in "commerce, capital, and crafts" saw guerrillas block everything. Desperate residents lodged and fed troops in their homes.

With commercial cultivation and trade broken, San Miguel "is a town of artisans" who are leaving in fear of "robberies in their workshops and homes." The council asked for funds to maintain garrisons at Dolores and San Miguel.[102] Commander Corral pleaded for funds to face "the powerful bands at Xalpa led by Sebastián González and the Pachones." With only 95 light cavalry and 31 urban patrolmen, plus "60 royalists without arms and training," he could not stop the Pachones from taking 100 horses sent to supply San Miguel's troop.[103]

At the end of April, Pereya and the council wrote again, now backed by pastor don Francisco Uraga. They insisted that "the few citizens of commerce and estate operators who remain" are "left in misery," causing "the complete suspension of cultivation and trade, . . . while artisans cannot travel to sell their wares due to dangers on the roads." Trade and crafts were locked in town.[104]

The siege continued into September 1818, when Orrantía won a victory over Xalpa-based guerrillas.[105] The *cabecilla* Borja had left the fortress with a band "heading toward Salvatierra. . . . They were defeated on the plains at Apaseo while attacking a convoy." Guerrillas rooted in rugged uplands descended to strike a convoy carrying silver, and were crushed. Corral added, "The same night Camilo [another Xalpa chief] led a great festival celebrating his wife's delivery of a child. What a shame they were not delivered to the Devil!"[106] Xalpa rebels faced defeat, and life went on. In the heat, or the hate, of the moment, the San Miguel commander wished death and damnation upon a mother and her newborn child. The siege of San Miguel held through 1818.[107]

In April 1819, Corral reported that while "absolute ruin" still reigned, loyal forces had captured the "rebel *cabecilla* Camilo Sánchez," who had celebrated his child's birth six months before (when Corral wished father, mother, and infant dead and damned). Sánchez was captured along with 12 men, 8 rifles, and 162 horses.[108] Hoping to calm a conflict nearly a decade old, loyalists began to capture rather than execute insurgents.

The calming took the rest of the year. On December 23, Orrantía wrote from Dolores that a patrol had engaged the "Pachón's band," killing four, taking three carbines and eighteen horses, while amnestying most to settle in "across the Bajío."[109] The same day, another troop killed seven "rebels of Santiago González' band."[110] After Christmas, Orrantía captured six men "caught robbing unfortunate people traveling from place to place; having found neither arms nor horses, I delivered them to the Magistrate."[111] These were desperate men, not feared guerrillas.

On December 30, Orrantía wrote from the Hacienda de la Venta, near Dolores: "I left a detachment to fortify the estate. Now free of insurgent incursions, the rancheros pledged to defend their properties. With that done, I will implement the same settlement at other estates."[112] Long-insurgent estate residents became rancheros in control of production. They had sustained guerrillas for a decade. Now, Orrantía set loyal garrisons at estates to defend family production.[113] The regime began to protect the social inversions taken in revolution.

Amnesty and the Amnestied: San Miguel and Dolores, 1819–1820

From late 1819 into 1820, military and civil authorities at Dolores and San Miguel delivered amnesty to guerrillas. Surviving lists report more than 160 men granted amnesty and settled across the region. Despite the roles of women sustaining insurgent families, communities, and guerrilla bands, none gained formal amnesties: the myth—or dream—of patriarchy persisted.

Also revealing, no amnestied insurgent gained an ethno-racial label: there were no *indios*, mulattoes, or mestizos; no Spaniards, American or European; no criollos or *gachupines*. The rulers of New Spain, American and European, had promoted labels to divide subordinate producers in the interests of power and profit-seeking silver capitalism, labels long defied by amalgamating peoples across Guanajuato. From 1808, political men seeking coalitions against Spanish rule pressed new oppositions: Americans should despise *gachupines*—with Americans including people of European, indigenous, African, and mixed ancestry. Meanwhile, those fighting to defend property repeatedly maligned popular insurgents as *indios*, ignoring amalgamations to mark rebels as lesser beings.

Now, after a decade of social war in which the regime defended property and diverse men and women fought for land and justice, men who fought for power saw men who fought for families and land as men. The rigors of battle and the need for peace refocused visions. Divisive labels faded as defenders of property drew insurgents to accept amnesties in a Bajío remade in revolution.

The lists do provide revealing detail about guerrilla fighters. A first list reported ten men of the Ortiz band (not including *cabecilla* Encarnación), amnestied at La Quemada, an estate between Dolores and San Felipe. They ranged in age from twenty-two to thirty-one, six married, four single. One had lived in rebellion for four years, two for three, one for two, six for one or less. All were young adults, most recently recruited to insurgency. Longest in rebellion was a muleteer, classic preparation for guerrilla life. A small trader had resisted for three years. A potter had joined for a year. The remaining seven were "labradores"—cultivators. Many of their fathers had struggled as dependents on estate lands; sons had taken arms to defend family independence on the land. The muleteer and two labradores (perhaps kin?) remained at La Quemada. The trader, captured at nearby Paso de González, settled there with three labradores (also kin?). The remaining three stayed at the sites of their capture.[114] All had fought with the feared Encarnación Ortiz; he stayed at large while they settled on lands they had occupied.

On January 1, 1820, San Miguel authorities compiled a list of thirty-five men amnestied during November and December. Most came from different guerrilla bands, surrendering singly to be dispersed across the countryside. A group of fourteen came as "Muñoz and his band," with nothing reported about their settlement.[115] Did they remain together as a necessity of their pacification?

A list from Dolores on February 5 reported thirty more men amnestied since late October. Two had been in arms for four years, three for three, eight for two, fifteen for one or less. Again, we see insurgents recruited into recent conflicts, fighting to protect families on the land. Two men are notable: José Jacinto de la Cañada was listed as the "manager" of a rancho who joined residents claiming independence on the land. The last man listed, Francisco Romero of rancho Montelongo, was "an original insurgent, now a collector of transit passes." He had risen with Hidalgo in 1810, to later help control travel. Now he claimed amnesty.[116]

We know less about twenty men amnestied at San Miguel from January 1 to February 4: Four were noted as band captains, two as alferez—patrol leaders. The rest were linked to diverse bands: six from the Borja band supposedly defeated in the fight near Apaseo; three, including a captain, from the guerrilla of El Cabezón; another linked to Camilo Sánchez. All took amnesty and dispersed.[117]

Two weeks later, Orrantía reported a major development. After an exchange of letters with don José Felipe Vázquez, the new Cura de Dolores, Encarnación Ortiz accepted amnesty. Orrantía presumed that military pressure led Ortiz to capitulate and that the elusive guerrilla must be watched: "If the right conditions recur, I will not be surprised if he returns to rebellion."[118] A list of ten men amnestied at Dolores at the end of February included three more from Ortiz' band. Another, José Antonio Hurtado Mendoza, had risen with Hidalgo. Again, all were dispersed.[119]

The same day, Orrantía sent a second list of fifty-four men amnestied at Dolores during February. It included more detail on bands, roles, and time in insurgency. While twenty-two had carried arms for a year or less, and twelve for one to two years, again revealing late recruitments, another twelve had been in rebellion for three years, six during four to five years, and two for six years. Hardened rebels were coming in, including leaders and fighters from key bands. A captain of the Borja band, supposedly crushed months earlier, took amnesty along with two officers and five men. Another officer and nine fighters came from the Ortiz band. All were dispersed to live across the countryside.[120]

The amnesty lists reveal much about insurgency and insurgents. Men took arms in waves, most in two- to three-year periods after 1811. Those amnestied in 1819–20 reveal the strength of the third wave around Dolores and San Miguel. The prevalence of small bands is clear, as is their grounding in the communities they protected. In the cases noting economic roles, *labrador* described the majority: men fought to protect families on the land. That they were married more often than not confirms ties between guerrillas, landed production, and family life—in insurgency and amnesty.

Pacifications Across the Bajío, 1818–1820

Parallel pacifications contained guerrillas across the Bajío from 1818 into 1820. Don Antonio Linares led the efforts in the regions cleared of guerrilla bands after the fall of the fortresses west of Guanajuato. In March 1818, five hundred cultivators at the Zurumuato estate, near Pénjamo, refused to pay rents. Linares troops resettled them along the main road, and still they did not pay. He then recruited five lead leaseholders to oversee subtenant families paying 4 pesos each to plant a fanega of maize yearly. With 10 pesos per fanega standard before the insurgency, the landlord saw gains favoring insurgent residents. He demanded 12 pesos, plus 2 reales to pay a troop to enforce the deal.[121] Linares knew that bargain rents were essential to pacification. The outcome is not reported.

The records of the embargoed estates of the Marqués de San Juan de Rayas during 1818 reveal a broad consolidation of tenant family cropping across the bottomlands. Head of a Guanajuato mining family and a member of New Spain's Mining Tribunal, Rayas had backed calls for a junta of New Spain in 1808, then acquiesced in the coup that tied New Spain to the Seville Junta and the fight against Napoleon. He worked to sustain silver flows at historic peaks into 1810, when French armies took all of Spain but Cádiz. Seeing his efforts and so much silver wasted, Rayas joined Allende in imagining a new junta in the summer of 1810—until it became clear that a rising would bring popular mobilization and threaten property. Rayas stepped back before Hidalgo's revolt began.

Still, in 1816 the regime detained Rayas for rebel sympathies and embargoed his properties. Their operation during 1818 documents the rule of ranchero-*labradores* across lands stretching from Irapuato south toward Michoacán. One major tenant paid 500 pesos; two claimed modest prosperity for 110 and 76 pesos. A group of 12 comfortable rancheros paid from 20 to 50 pesos—averaging less than 40 pesos each. The great majority, 264 labradores, paid less than 20 pesos each, averaging less than 6 pesos. Most lived by planting one fanega on ranchos that included gardens and land to pasture a few animals. Given yields approaching 100 to 1 on rich Bajío soils, they would harvest 80 to 100 fanegas (when rains were good), more than enough to sustain a family with 10 to 12 fanegas, hold supplies for the years of drought sure to come, and sell surpluses in towns or the mining city. Another 92 tenants paid half rents of two pesos or less to plant one fanega, without lands to make ranchos. Owing but a quarter of the rent charged before 1810, they harvested enough maize to sustain households and sell a bit of surplus, while providing seasonal hands in the fields of their more prosperous neighbors.[122]

Nearly 400 tenants paid small rents to live as growers at the Rayas estates, suggesting a population approaching 2,000 dispersed in several communities. These were not egalitarian utopias: a few were favored; a few more were comfortable; more than 70 percent gained solid sustenance; nearly 25 percent raised basic maize and took wages at neighbors' ranchos. Still, no one was desperate, inequities were limited, with predations left in the past. Rents recognized estate property—and proved that producers owned the crops that fed families, communities, and consumers beyond. Families won a social inversion within capitalism: property held while families ruled production.

In the summer of 1820, Colonel don Anastasio Bustamante still worked to pacify the bottomlands around Valle de Santiago, a center of adamant insurgency since Albino García's rising in 1810. To back proprietor rights to rents, Bustamante fortified sixty-two positions: loyalist troops held four towns, seven estates, and three ranchos; patriot guards, former insurgents amnestied and armed to defend the regime and property rights, rent collection and family production, patrolled eighteen haciendas and thirty "rancherías"—informal settlements. Bustamante moved many to live where they could be pressed to pay while former insurgents kept arms to guarantee rights to cultivate in exchange for limited rents.[123] Cultivation and crops belonged to families. Proprietors kept land rights—with no control of production or marketing. Armed ex-insurgents, now tenant family growers, ruled maize making across the bottomlands.

North of San Miguel, in February 1820 Orrantía reported that the hacienda La Quemada near San Felipe, with a population of 1,402 (plus uncounted others at outlying *rancherías*), was settled with a "company of 40 royalists."[124] As March began, he praised pacification "across the north of the province. . . . Among those who remained partisans in rebellion, some died in their obstinacy, others, freed of illusions, came forward to receive the Royal Grace of Amnesty." Communities that had sustained guerrillas "are leaving dispersed settlements, now committed to the good cause [royal order]."[125] He left patrols at three haciendas and at the sanctuary-market at Atotonilco: "Today, their only role is to keep order among the residents. . . . Soon there will be no need for troops of the line."[126]

In March, Orrantía saw pacification with cautious realism. He had sent thirteen "detachments to ensure security in the larger settlements that include most rancheros; . . . in scattered *rancherías* with 30 to 100 families each, I have named a Caudillo [chief] to oversee rancheros who are behaving perfectly well."[127] The commander who fought to destroy guerrillas sustained by insurgent communities now saw the latter as loyal rancheros protected by loyal patrols. The regime guaranteed what insurgents had made: maize-making family ranchos.

Entrenched on the Land: Rancheros and Rancheras at Puerto de Nieto, 1820

The 1820 pacification at Puerto de Nieto provides unique detail about a community remade during insurgency and its persistence as loyalist forces reasserted estate property rights. On March 1, don José Toribio Rico, the long-displaced manager of Puerto de Nieto, wrote to don José Sánchez Espinosa. He had recruited twenty armed men from La Griega, east of Querétaro, to back a return to the estate still ruled by insurgents, aiming to enforce property and collect rents.[128] While his attempts to return in 1816 and 1817 aimed to restore commercial planting, Rico now saw the necessity of family production. Never reporting the negotiations that led to tenant settlements, he kept accounts detailing consolidations of family production—often led by women.[129]

As spring planting began, eighty-two established families were joined by sixty newcomers. Half the community present before 1810 remained; newcomers only began to replace the dead and departed. The heads of households who remained and paid rents are named; newcomers are not. Established families were more prosperous—and more stratified. Ten paid more than 50 pesos in rent as modest commercial growers; nineteen paid from 31 to 50 pesos, as comfortable rancheros; thirty-eight, the core of the community, paid 11 to 30 pesos (most more than 20)—all solid family growers; thirteen paid 10 pesos or less. All held land for maize and more. During insurgency, they had claimed ranchos of diverse size and potential with no manager present, no proprietor paid. They planted according to their needs and productive potential. All made basic sustenance; most a bit more; a few might claim modest profits.

Among the eighty-two established households, fifty shared surnames with residents listed in the 1792 census, likely descendants of families at the estate for decades. Of the thirty-two more recent arrivals, we cannot know how many came between 1792 and 1810, how many found refuge during insurgency, how many had married into established families. The older families were prosperous, dominant among those paying the highest rents; only four paid 10 pesos or less. Still, the largest numbers among those with families present in 1792 and those arriving later were middling rancheros paying 31 to 50 pesos. The established majority made maize and more to live in solid comfort.

The great change was the ascent of women. In 1792, women headed 4 percent of households at Puerto de Nieto, most widows holding a tenancy awaiting a son's adulthood. At pacification in 1820, women were 15 percent of those contracted to pay rents. Seven paid 31 to 50 pesos in rent—a third of the tenants in that favored group. Doña Hermenegilda López was the leading tenant, paying 90 pesos. There were only three women among the tenants arriving after 1792, all paying 11 to 31 pesos—less prosperous, but far from poor. Women had claimed new roles in production and community life as men joined guerrilla forces, and some surely died. Doña Cayetana Montes was the only remaining tenant from a family of mestizos present in 1792 (none then honored as don or doña); in 1820, she paid 50 pesos in rent. Rooted in a less favored clan, she emerged from insurgency among the most prosperous and honored as doña.

Notably, prosperous women led families that included lesser male tenants: Victoriana and Trinidad Aguado paid 25 pesos each, Miguel Aguado only 15. Maria del Pilar Vargas paid 40 pesos, Manuel Vargas 25. Benita Guerrero paid 50 pesos, Pedro Guerrero just 20. And doña Hermenegilda López paid 90 pesos while Francisco Gerardo and Teodoro López paid 40 pesos, Juan Manuel 30, Mateo Leonardo only 10. Nearby, doña Petra, doña Lorenza, and doña María de Jesús Licea paid 50 pesos each while Juan María Licea paid only 22.

The roles claimed by women during years of insurgency should not surprise. Historically, at Bajío estates patriarchy was orchestrated by managerial power. When predations assaulted patriarchy and family welfare from the 1790s, women were among the first to protest—including the girls at Puerto de Nieto. When insurgency broke commercial cropping and managerial power, women took new roles in production. Predatory assaults on men's ability to provide sent many to take the risks of insurgency while women took new roles leading family production—limiting men's patriarchy.

Two decades of predations followed by insurgent-driven transformations remade the Puerto de Nieto community. In 1792, it was built around great clans of six to nine patriarchal households; by 1820, the largest clans linked four or five households that were much less patriarchal. The 1792 census revealed two large sub-communities—one tied by kinship to Rico; the other of families facing his rule. The manager's kin had lived primarily by cultivating estate lands, mixing roles as *sirvientes* and modest tenants; the less favored turned to textiles to supplement estate work and earnings.[130]

When Rico imposed evictions and salary cuts and evicted tenants after 1792, he surely worked to spare his kin. When he returned in 1820, he had no kin among the residents who remade life during the insurgency. Many surely fled with him in 1811; others faced exclusion in the insurgent community. At pacification, Rico rented a modest rancho for 45 pesos. He later hired a son as an assistant; soon removed for "several failures," he kept a small rancho for 15 pesos. Insurgency broke managerial patriarchy to entrench family production. In the effort, women claimed new roles.

A decade of popular insurgency remade Guanajuato, breaking silver capitalism by 1812 while guerrillas fought on to claim and hold the land for family growers. In 1818, regime commanders saw that the only way to pacification was to grant insurgents rights to plant on estate lands. They preserved property while delivering production to family growers who paid small rents. By 1820, Epigmenio González' vision ruled rural Guanajuato.

Then, in 1821, don Agustín Iturbide—who backed the 1808 coup, captured and executed Albino García in 1812, chased insurgents across the Bajío, and defeated Morelos in 1815—mobilized military force to declare Mexico an independent empire. Could silver capitalism revive? Could the imagined Mexico thrive? To understand the challenges and prospects of the Mexico that rose in the wake of the Bajío revolution, we must first explore how agrarian capitalism survived to sustain counterinsurgency in Querétaro after 1810 and how larger fights preserved property across New Spain. They kept the revolution made in Guanajuato within capitalism.

Counterinsurgency Capitalism in Querétaro

Production, Patriarchy,
and the End of Profit at La Griega

In the summer of 1810, the debates imagining new sovereignties in a collapsing Spanish empire focused in Querétaro. There too, Epigmenio González heard his customers' dreams of family cultivation. And there, political men seeking power were paralyzed by fears of popular risings. In September, the Hidalgo revolt erupted in Dolores while Querétaro held as a bastion of loyalist power.[1] To understand the Bajío revolution, we have engaged the lives and actions, goals and gains of those who drove its transforming conflicts across Guanajuato. It is equally important to explore the lives of those who stayed at home and at work during the decade of deadly conflict. Their decisions and adaptations illuminate the limits of the revolution in the near term—and the transforming impacts that followed.

On learning of Hidalgo's rising, Corregidor don Miguel Domínguez, merchant proprietor don Pedro de Septién, and others who dreamed of political sovereignty at Querétaro turned to defend the regime of property. Epigmenio González faced prison, then exile in Manila—his voice silenced. Doña Josefa Ortiz, Dominguez' wife, remained a beacon of radical politics—to face prison in 1816. The inchoate force of Hidalgo's insurgency never came to Querétaro, allowing loyal troops to concentrate there, first to fight Hidalgo, then to chase guerrillas and defend property through years of insurgency. The city carried on: the tobacco factory struggled; large *obrajes* closed while artisan families pressed on; the Otomí Council held loyal while Otomí families kept rich *huertas* that fed city markets.

Across the countryside, estate production carried on too. Dependent families had faced predations parallel to those that struck rural Guanajuato before 1810, yet they rarely turned to insurgency. Querétaro's quick consolidation as a bastion of loyal power is part of the answer. Still, after Hidalgo's fall, insurgent forces scoured Amazcala basin estates early in 1811. Had residents risen to join, they might have broken Querétaro as a fortress of counterinsurgency. They did not.

While Guanajuato and Querétaro shared the profit-seeking ways of silver capitalism, they lived them in contrasting sociocultural ways. Across Guanajuato, peoples of diverse Mesoamerican origins—Mexica, Otomí, and Tarascan—had mixed with the descendants of enslaved Africans to forge amalgamating communities. In Querétaro, Otomí majorities, urban and rural, kept strong cultural cohesions that set producing communities apart from Hispanic neighbors in the city and at estates. As the nineteenth century began, the Otomí lived as subordinates—with a separate republic, rich *huertas*, and Our Lady of Pueblito's protection in the city—while informal ethnic communities negotiated with landlords and managers to hold viable lives at estates like La Griega.

The Otomí City Council had proclaimed staunch support for Fernando VII and Spanish rule after Napoleon's 1808 incursion. The regime, after all, sustained council powers and corporate rights to family *huertas*. By September, with political debates shaking Mexico City and drought spreading across the land, Corregidor Domínguez led the Spanish Council in calling for a congress to address political concerns—and rising social tensions. As the year ended, doña María Josefa Vergara began to write the will dedicating her wealth to charitable service in the city and at her Esperanza estate. Did all that limit predations and calm desperations at Querétaro? Perhaps.

By the summer of 1810, with Napoleon entrenched in Spain, political debates returned to Querétaro—while Epigmenio González heard the distress that led to his plan for tenant family production. Fearing popular action, political men did not rise, González was jailed, and insurgency began with Hidalgo at Dolores to spread across Guanajuato.

Staying at home and at work, the people of rural Querétaro sustained the regime that protected property while families took control of production across Guanajuato. From 1811, Querétaro producers, most Otomí, gained higher earnings and rations, and access to land for family planting. They reversed the predations that provoked insurgencies just west. And by negotiating to claim those gains as estate property held, the men of Querétaro, Hispanic and Otomí, solidified patriarchy.

Still, maintaining capitalism to contain revolution proved costly to capitalists. As pacification came to Guanajuato in 1820, profit collapsed across Querétaro. The gains claimed by producing men also vanished while patriarchy held strong. We must know counterrevolutionary Querétaro to see the complex ties linking capitalism and patriarchy, ethno-racial divisions and social stability—ultimately to understand the roots and gains, limits and impacts of the Bajío revolution from 1810 to 1820.

The accounts of don José Sánchez Espinosa's continuing operations at La Griega provide a close, often personal view of production, work, and family in a divided Hispanic-Otomí estate community. They reveal predations to 1810, then detail adaptations that preserved patriarchal production in years of insurgency. With pacification in 1820, estate profit collapsed, still-dependent families faced new uncertainties—and patriarchy held. Who thrived? The men in-between who served the priest-patriarch by managing counterinsurgency capitalism and negotiating to keep men at work in uncertain times.

Production and Predation Before 1810

La Griega sits at the southern end of the Amazcala basin, where the river turns west to fall through the canyon, pass San Pedro, then water the Otomí *huertas* of urban Querétaro. A rich, irrigated property, its ethnically divided community faced predations from the 1790s. In 1791, 62 Hispanic men (Otomí were excluded in the militia census) headed families with 322 members, an average of more than five each; 54 patriarchs asserted Spanish status, joined by 5 mestizos and 3 mulattoes. Most were tenant growers; the rest were *sirvientes*, salaried employees paid three pesos monthly, plus yearly maize rations of 10 fanegas, enough to feed a small household. Spanish men were endogamous; only three had married mestizas.[2] The next year, manager don José Regalado Franco began the shift from tenancies to estate production that led to doña Gertrudis Villaseñor's protest and many departures.

Plantings of maize and frijol on estate accounts doubled during the next decade while the number of tenants shrank. Holding crops from years of good rains and ample yields to sell when prices peaked in times of drought and scarcity brought good profit. In the spring of 1805, Franco planted 48 fanegas of maize at San Agustín, La Griega's traditional fields, and another 48 at La Venta, the rancho taken from doña Gertrudis. After Franco addressed

Otomí community concerns with disease by funding a festival, the harvest totaled 10,800 fanegas (a yield of 116 to 1). the stocks held awaiting the profits of drought that came in 1808–10. At 40 reales (5 pesos) per fanega, Sánchez Espinosa gained nearly 50,000 pesos from that crop alone—as desperate people faced famine.

The tribute census of 1807 reported 214 Otomí men at La Griega: 191 married, 23 single: 101 lived as *sirvientes* gaining salaries and rations to sustain basic securities; 94 rented small plots; 19 lacked regular employment, laboring seasonally as *alquilados* in estate fields. Notably, unmarried adult men were few: only 11 percent among the Otomí at La Griega, compared with 16 percent across the Amascala basin, and 24 percent across Querétaro's jurisdiction. Failing chances at La Griega sent young Otomí men away, perhaps to find places at outlying estates like doña María Josefa Vergara's La Esperanza, often in urban workshops, where unmarried Otomí men were 40 percent of workers. Many surely visited Epigmenio González' store on the plaza, sharing tales of displacement that led him to imagine a world of tenant growers cultivating estate lands.

While pressing predatory dislocations, Franco kept production and profit strong by favoring Hispanic households, many his kin. When drought threatened, he organized penitential devotions favored by the priest-patriarch and the Hispanic community. When disease threatened, the Otomí abandoned the fields until Franco funded propitiatory devotions to their patron, San Agustín—despite Sánchez Espinosa's objection. The harvest required Otomí hands.[3]

The first year of accounts detail production and work from July 1811 through June 1812, as popular insurgency took hold west across Guanajuato. They document the predations imposed on La Griega producers since 1792.[4] Only 15 leaseholders remained, paying an average of 70 pesos each. Most were prosperous and Hispanic, with just one woman and one Otomí. Eleven announced Spanish status with the prefix don; three others had Spanish surnames. Francisco Lorenzo, the lone Otomí on the list, paid only 16 pesos. Had the 97 Otomí tenants reported in the 1807 tribute count gone? Most lived as subtenants under Spanish leaseholders, paying small rents, raising crops to feed families, and laboring as wage hands in seasons of peak demands. It was an estate-based variant of the symbiotic exploitations that sustained families and kept the peace across most of the heartland to the south. It sustained peace and production at La Griega too.

Meanwhile, the estate employed 139 men as *sirvientes*, paid monthly stipends plus maize rations—both recently cut. Before predations, most *sirvientes* worked year-round to earn 3 pesos monthly, plus 10 fanegas of maize. By 1811, salaries had fallen to 2 pesos; rations to 3 fanegas. And work had become irregular: 59 men served fewer than 6 months to gain 10 pesos or less; 52 worked 6 to 10 months to earn 11 to 20 pesos; only 37 served the full year to gain 24 or more pesos. Rations of 3 fanegas yearly did not feed a family. How did they survive? Sixty-one boys, often sons of struggling *sirvientes*, took pay as *alquilados*. Wages ranged around 1 real daily for the youngest, 1.5 for teens, and 2 for a few nearing adulthood. *Alquilados*—rented hands—worked seasonally: half worked less than 30 days; the rest 30 to 60 days. Fewer than half of *sirvientes* had sons laboring at the estate to help sustain families. Youths who went to the city surely contributed as they could.

While 58 Hispanic and 81 Otomí *sirvientes* faced similar struggles, they did not face them equally: 70 percent of Hispanics gained more than 10 pesos in annual pay; 50 percent of the Otomí got less. Among *alquilados*, Hispanic youths worked more days for higher wages, while Otomí boys labored fewer days for lower pay. After decades of predations, times were hard for all who labored at La Griega; they were hardest on the Otomí majority.

In 1791, most of the Spanish community had lived as tenants. In 1811, a few remained leaseholders served by Otomí subtenants while a large majority worked as *sirvientes* for small salaries and rations. Facing such decline, many had moved on. Of 41 Spanish surnames in the census of 1791, only 12 remained in 1811 (there was greater continuity among insurgents at Puerto de Nieto). The Otomí at La Griega faced greater challenges: still a majority, about half sublet from Spanish leaseholders; the rest gained ever less secure employment and radically reduced rations as sons left to seek work off the estate. Exploitations remained, ever less symbiotic, ever more exploitative. In the aftermath of evictions, the families that remained at La Griega, Hispanic and Otomí, separate and unequal, faced deepening poverty laced with new insecurities.[5]

Facing Insurgency

When insurgency exploded across Guanajuato in the fall of 1810, it did not approach Querétaro or La Griega. In October, manager don José Regalado Franco sent horses to supply loyal troops. In November, he reported an estate in production, untouched by insurgency.[6] Then, in January 1811, as Hidalgo faced defeat at Puente de Calderón and rebels dispersed back across Guanajuato, insurgents began to threaten rural Querétaro.

While workers took pay to harvest the first good maize crop in two years, rebels came out of uplands to the north. Franco's son don José Manuel Franco managed Charcas, near Xichú at the edge of the rugged Sierra Gorda. In mid-January, he reported insurgents all around, attacking nearby estates, taking livestock, recruiting rebels. At month's end, they struck Charcas, bound don José Manuel, and emptied the store of food, salt, cloth, and candles while taking horses and mules, bridles and saddles.[7] The manager was not injured, but the lesson was clear: insurgency was spreading, supplying guerrilla forces by relieving estates of maize, mounts, and more.

Later in the spring, as planting approached, insurgents drove into the Amazcala basin. They struck first at Chichimequillas, a large estate owned by Querétaro's Carmelite convent.[8] They emptied the store and captured and released the manager, padre don José San Román, who fled to the city. Soon rebels hit La Griega, capturing manager Franco and his son don Vicente, looting the store and taking livestock before heading east to La Esperanza, the Francos still held hostage. Unimpressed by the late doña María Josefa Vergara's charities, insurgents took all they could and shot the manager dead. Three days later, the Francos escaped "by a miracle"—likely paying a ransom not reported to Sánchez Espinosa. Don José Regalado Franco took his family to safety in Querétaro, sending another son, don Ysidoro, to check periodically on operations at La Griega.[9] In the spring of 1811, insurgents attacked the three largest, most productive estates east of Querétaro, faced no opposition, took what they would, and escaped. Yet few estate residents joined.

Protecting Property: Hispanic Troopers at La Griega

Despite having faced predations, the people at La Griega and across the Amascala basin stayed at home and at work when insurgents came in 1811. After the rebels passed without provoking local risings, in the summer of 1811 Sánchez Espinosa charged Franco with founding a troop to defend estate property. He spent 18,521 pesos to recruit, arm, and mount the force. The estate paid 8,235 pesos; the priest at San Pedro de la Cañada, the Pame town just east in the canyon on the road to Querétaro, contributed 2,265 pesos.[10] The remaining 8,000 pesos came from neighboring estates. Based at La Griega, the troop would patrol the Amascala basin.

A first list of militiamen from 1813–14 shows 34 troopers, all Hispanic, 13 traceable to families in the 1791 census—11 classed as Spaniards, 1 mestizo, and 1 mulatto. They earned more than 200 pesos for a year's service, five times more than a family with a father and son working as *sirvientes* when insurgency began. Don José Regalado Franco held command; three other Francos rode as troopers. Among Franco kin: two Ontiveros served, including Sergeant don Ysidro; three Aguilar men joined along with two Vertiz.[11] Franco armed a core of men from La Griega's Spanish minority, many his kin, all favored with unprecedented pay.

After its founding, the troop cost 8,000 pesos yearly, paid by La Griega to the end of insurgency. Troopers were the highest paid, most secure employees at the estate. In 1813–14, the first year of full troop accounts, they earned 212 pesos, six times more than the best-paid *sirviente*. From 1813 to 1818, Franco cut the troop to 24 men, 16–20 full time, others recruited for short periods. The troop reinforced managers' power and held a Spanish minority in lives of favored dependence. Still, two dozen armed men could not keep the peace at La Griega and across the Amascala basin. To sustain production, Sánchez Espinosa and the managerial Francos turned estate planting and marketing to deliver secure sustenance to the people of Querétaro and the loyalists based among them, while adapting social relations of production to keep the estate community at work.

The Rise and Fall of Counterinsurgency Capitalism

From 1810, Sánchez Espinosa and the Francos aimed to sustain property, production, and profit in support of counterinsurgency. Through the decade, La Griega focused on maize, first on estate fields, then via leaseholds and subtenants. Into 1817, maize kept families at work and gained limited profits for Sánchez Espinosa. Then, from 1818, drought cut maize harvests—leaving the estate without stocks to sell. It turned to chile, frijol, and wheat to profit for a few more years. Then in 1820, as pacification entrenched family growers on the land across Guanajuato, profit collapsed at La Griega.

Maize brought steady earnings from 1811 through 1817—a sign of transforming change. Before 1810, La Griega stored the rich harvests gained in years of good rains, awaiting peak prices in times of drought. Profit was irregular, yet massive when it came. Profiteering peaked in the drought and famine of 1785–86, turning estate operations to unprecedented predations; it peaked again in the drought and famine of 1808–10, setting off the risings of 1810. Such predations could not continue in the face of insurgency, while counterinsurgency required costly outlays to keep producers at work, changing the dynamics of agrarian capitalism.

At La Griega, the harvest of January 1812 yielded nearly 10,000 fanegas. With insurgency all around, prices rose to 17 reales. Franco sold 9,000 fanegas to earn 19,000 pesos—enough to found the troop. In April 1813, the estate reduced planting to 78 fanegas while allocating more land to tenants. Entering the summer with 7,000 fanegas stored from previous harvests, regular rains and flourishing fields dropped prices to 14.5 reales. Normally, no Bajío agrarian capitalist would sell at that low price, but that fall, La Griega sold 6,500 fanegas to earn more than 11,000 pesos. Harvesting more than 10,000 fanegas in January 1814, another ample harvest again brought down prices, promising little profit. The estate cut commercial planting and began to let more land to tenants, while from 1815 to 1819 good harvests kept prices low. Still, the estate sold as profits waned, its operations sustained by rent payments and sporadic earnings from chile, wheat, and frijol.

During the first years of insurgency, facing the high costs of maintaining the troop and keeping residents at work, La Griega flooded markets with maize while taking historically small gains. Seeing that way of production unsustainable, the estate turned to tenant cropping—keeping the peace and maintaining production by replicating what insurgents were imposing across Guanajuato.

The business of maize went into sharp decline from 1814. Good harvests kept prices low, sustaining people and production while profits waned. The estate entered 1817–18 with only 1,000 fanegas in its granaries. Sparse rains brought the price to 15 reales in the fall of 1817; the estate sold all it had before the harvest, gaining less than 2,000 pesos from the highest price in five years. Thanks to chile and other crops, 1817–18 brought a final year of profit, but the market for maize was gone. La Griega planted only 30 fanegas in spring 1818. With only 500 fanegas in storage, prospects were limited as scarce rains drove the price to 24 reales. The estate sold 424 fanegas to gain less than 1,250 pesos, a historic low that yielded an operating loss of 3,400 pesos.

With rising prices, the estate increased planting to 52 fanegas in the spring of 1819, still half the level of 1810. Another season of sporadic rains drove prices to 40 reales—a historic peak earlier reached only in the famine crises of 1785–86 and 1809–10. But La Griega had little to sell—before or after the harvest of January 1820. Earning 4,000 pesos from 800 fanegas cut the annual loss to 200 pesos for 1819–20. Dreaming of revival, Franco then planted 74 fanegas in the spring of 1821—as New Spain collapsed around him. Good rains promised a good harvest. In the interim, prices held near 39 reales, so he sold the 200 fanegas he had to take 1,000 pesos. Taking so little from such high prices marked the end of agrarian capitalism.

During the decade of insurgency, La Griega maintained maize production to supply loyalist forces and keep estate families at home and at work—relinquishing profits to keep the peace. In 1811 and 1812, the estate returned the pay of *sirvientes* and *alquilados* to pre-predation levels. While the number of *sirvientes* fell from 139 to 124 (as a core of the Spanish became troopers), salaries rose to average 31 pesos and rations returned to 10 fanegas. Sustenance with security returned, essential to keep men at work. Meanwhile, the number of *alquilados* rose from 61 to 86, and while some still labored for 1 real daily, most gained 2. Mean earnings for wage hands rose from 6 to 11 pesos, solid supplements to a *sirviente* father's 30-plus-peso salary and 10 fanegas of maize. To maintain production in the first years of insurgency, Sánchez Espinosa and manager don José Regalado Franco returned lives of patriarchal security to estate residents, Spanish and Otomí.

Then, in 1813, as popular insurgencies entrenched across Guanajuato while typhus threatened life across New Spain, La Griega turned to a new regime of production. It began with the death of manager-commander Franco in 1813 and the ascent of his son don Miguel Trinidad to the dual roles. He gained pay that tripled to 1,000 pesos yearly plus a ration of 52 fanegas, enough maize for the entire Franco clan. The new manager saw that huge harvests sold at low prices would never bring sustained profit. He reduced estate planting to 78 fanegas in the spring of 1813, then to 50 fanegas in May 1814—half the level before 1810. To plant 50 fanegas yearly on irrigated lands, along with fields of chile, frijol, and wheat, Franco kept a shrinking core of Hispanic *sirvientes*: 123 in 1813–14, 89 in 1814–15, 50 in 1816. Pay held at 35 pesos as rations rose to 13 fanegas, sustaining incomes for the few who remained. Hispanic *alquilados* fell from 200 to 140, with the top wage cut to 2 reales. Lives of secure service gave way to dependence on seasonal wage work among Hispanic families.

Also in 1813–14, Franco raised the number of leaseholders from 16 to 50, a level held through 1817. Total lease payments rose to near 2,000 pesos, an average of 40 per tenant. A core of favored Spanish leaseholders paid more and remained key intermediaries. Others took on less, and came and went. A few owed 20 pesos or less. Most of La Griega's Otomí became subtenants, working small plots to make maize for sustenance and small sales. Planting half a fanega would yield 40 to 60 in years of good rains. Families might consume 10, set aside another 10 for dearth to come, and still have 20 to sell for other needs. Meanwhile, in 1814–15 the number of Otomí *alquilado* youth earning 1 to 2 reales daily rose from 86 to 102, while 100 Otomí men began to labor as wage hands for 2.5 reales daily—without maize rations. Otomí families raised maize on subtenant plots while men and boys worked estate fields as wage hands. La Griega revived estate-based symbiotic exploitations to sustain families, patriarchy, and production in times of insurgency.

Such lives were sustaining—if maize harvests were solid and wage work held strong. The estate kept no record of family crop yields, but as subtenant planting continued, the number of Otomí *alquilados* held at 140 in 1815–16, then fell to 101 by 1817–18. Those who worked, worked more days to limit income declines. A few labored more days than the year allowed. "This resulted from working day and night irrigating wheat and chile—with nights accounted as additional days."[12] To sustain a remnant of commercial production and maintain social peace, La Griega offered lives of dependent security to a shrinking Spanish minority, most paid solid salaries and maize rations. Spanish leaseholders were set to oversee Otomí subtenants who planted maize for sustenance, while Hispanic and Otomí men and boys competed to labor as wage hands in estate fields.

Patriarchy held. Only men appear as leaseholders, *sirvientes*, and *alquilados* in the accounts—with one revealing exception: Doña María Dolores González leased Las Navajas for 56 pesos in 1814, then 80 pesos through subsequent years, while her son served in the militia. Her role as a powerful woman was exceptional—explained by the marriage of her daughter doña Justa González to don José Ysidoro Franco.

Negotiating to remain at peace and in production, from 1811 to 1818 the Spanish and Otomí families of La Griega escaped the predations imposed before 1810. New ways of life mixed secure labor service for a Hispanic few, tenant cropping and wage work for the Otomí majority. With that, don Miguel Trinidad saw less need for coercion and reduced the troop to 24 men at arms, 16–20 full time, others recruited for short periods. Pay fell to 165 pesos in 1814–15, then to 125 pesos from 1815 to 1817. Again, he cut costs by reducing the numbers gaining security in La Griega's Hispanic community.

In 1818, as pacification began in Guanajuato, drought returned to La Griega—keeping its historic decanal schedule. Having sold ample maize and delivered solid rations in years of plenty, the estate held only 500 fanegas in storage. That spring, it planted only 30, a historic low. By fall, the price rose to 24 pesos, but the estate could sell only 424 fanegas to earn 1,250 pesos—also historic lows. The number of secure *sirvientes* dropped to 52, mean earnings to 26 pesos, while rations held at 12 fanegas. In the spring of 1819, Franco increased estate planting to 52 fanegas, taking back land from Spanish leaseholders and Otomí subtenants. Drought deepened, the harvest failed, and prices rose to 40 reales. With but 800 fanegas to sell, La Griega gained 4,000 pesos, not enough to break even. In 1820, planting rose to 72 fanegas, taking back more lands from leaseholders and subtenants. Drought held too, leaving the estate to sell but 200 fanegas to gain 1,000 pesos in the summer of pacification.

As ways of production remade to counter insurgency collapsed after 1818 in times of drought without profit, the Spanish few favored with secure salaries and rations held on. Trooper pay fell to 110 pesos yearly, half the level of 1813 when insurgents reigned all around—yet still three times a *sirviente*'s pay. Franco raised the number of sirvientes to 57 in 1819–20, then 66 in 1820–21, while mean salaries fell to 25 pesos, rations to 10 fanegas. Earnings declined, but basic security held among Spanish working families.

The Otomí struggled. Uncounted numbers lost subtenant plots as La Griega returned to commercial planting while harvests on remaining milpa plots fell in times of drought. As many faced hunger, Franco raised the number of alquilados hired in 1818–19 to 154 while reducing their days at work—cutting mean earnings by half to 19 pesos. At prevailing prices, basic family sustenance of 10 fanegas cost 40 pesos, leaving most alquilados with income to buy but half. In 1820–21, the estate hired 168 day-workers as earnings of 20 pesos again bought only half a family's maize supply. As insurgency ended across Guanajuato, at La Griega property held, profit vanished, Spanish dependents held on, and the Otomí majority faced lives of insecurity laced with hunger—again.

Life in the Time of Insurgency: Three Family Histories

Through the decade of insurgency, changing social relations sustained peace, production, and patriarchy at La Griega while agrarian capitalism dissolved. Don José Sánchez Espinosa took profit into 1818. The Otomí majority gained solid earnings while the estate focused on commercial maize from 1811 to 1814. Into 1818, Otomí families found autonomy as subtenants cultivating for sustenance while men and boys earned solid day wages in estate fields. Then as insurgency waned, the estate aimed to revive commercial cropping. Otomí families lost access to milpas as men and boys faced wage cuts. Insecurities returned as the gains claimed by the Otomí during insurgency vanished.

Work trajectories and family ties among La Griega's Hispanic minority can be reconstructed in greater detail.[13] Among the least favored were the men of the Juárez clan, whose lives reveal ongoing struggles to sustain patriarchal ways of sustenance. Five Juárez men worked as sirvientes in 1811–12 as insurgency began. None gained the don, suggesting mixed roots. No Juárez appeared in the 1791 census, indicating that the family came to

La Griega during the times of predation that followed. No Juárez joined the troop. From 1811, Juárez men labored as sirvientes and alquilados, finding gains, then taking losses, to face deep insecurities in 1820—like their Otomí neighbors.

The five Juárez men employed in 1811 gained mean salaries of 22 pesos and rations near 5 fanegas—all historically low; all above estate averages. During the next two years, one more Juárez became a sirviente while another was first in the clan to labor as an alquilado. Earnings held steady while rations soared to 80 fanegas for the clan, an average of 13 per household, more than ample for sustenance as the estate offered solid salaries and ample maize to keep men at peace and at work.

In 1814–15, the Juárez men's gains began to fade. While favored Spaniards gained leaseholds and the Otomí settled as subtenants, the estate turned away from sirvientes to rely on alquilados paid wages without rations. Only four Juárezes remained sirvientes; their cash incomes below the levels of 1811–12. In 1815–16 only one remained, as three shifted to day labor, and four worked as alquilados. With eight men and boys working, total earnings held near 180 pesos—while access to rations plummeted. The clan relied on cash to buy maize; fortunately, for the moment prices held low.

The last Juárez sirviente became an alquilado in 1816–17, after taking a ration of 6 fanegas—half a year's sustenance. Six Juárez alquilados labored for long periods in 1816–17 and 1817–18, gaining total cash incomes of 262 pesos the first year, 267 the next. There were short-term costs: the estate took back 80 pesos in 1816–17, 68 more in 1817–18 to cover past advances in pay never repaid in labor (revealing that advances had continued into insurgency). Still, after covering the debts, clan income held at 181 pesos, 30 per worker, in 1816–17; then rose to 197 pesos, 33 per worker in 1817–18. The gains in cash were real—at the cost of increased labor and new insecurities.

The Juárez remained alquilados to the end of insurgency. Six gained a total of 170 pesos in 1817–18, averaging 28 pesos each. From 1819 into 1821, only five continued to labor. They worked many more days each to gain a total of 236 pesos in 1819–20, then 256 pesos in 1820–21. Mean incomes rose to 47 and then 50 pesos per worker. It might appear a triumph—until the end of rations and soaring maize prices enter the equation. The 12 fanegas needed to sustain a family of four or five, cost 35 pesos in 1818–19—more than the Juárez mean household income of 28. The essential staples cost 60 pesos in 1819–20, far above incomes that peaked at 47 pesos. In 1820–21, the cost of a full maize supply fell to 52 pesos while Juárez family earnings rose to average 50. The balance deceives, as families did not live by maize alone. Poverty laced with insecurity plagued a Juárez clan relegated to day labor at La Griega as insurgency ended and the search for an imagined Mexico began.

The Abendaño clan lived a more favored trajectory, prospering as leaseholders overseeing Otomí subtenants. The family history is uniquely visible as the records of leasing from 1811 are complemented by the will of family patriarch, don José Antonio, written in Querétaro early in 1823.[14] He was born and raised on the Rancho del Derramadero at La Griega, likely around 1770. In 1788, he married doña María Josefa Ontiveros. There were two Abendaño households, both Spanish, in the 1791 census at La Griega, but no Ontiveros. As doña María Josefa brought an ox to the union, she likely came from a tenant family at a nearby estate. Don José Antonio brought livestock worth 500 pesos to the union. The couple had four children. After doña Maria Josefa died in 1800, don José Antonio moved to Querétaro and married doña María Dolores Ontiveros, his late wife's sister or cousin. The move is not explained. But after the expulsion of leading rancheros in the 1790s, leaseholders primarily collected rents from Otomí subtenants. There was little to inhibit living in the city, linking kin at the estate to life in town. They likely knew storekeeper Epigmenio González.

All the Abendaños in the 1811–12 accounts gained the don and lived primarily by leasing ranchos. Don José Antonio, still in Querétaro, paid 110 pesos to lease the Rancho de las Cabezas. Don Jesús and don Miguel Abendaño paid 16 and 15 pesos to plant small ranchos. Two youths labored as alquilados at the top wage of 1.5 reales per day, one working 42 days to earn 8 pesos, the other 49 days to gain 9 pesos. Seasonal labor brought cash incomes to supplement leasehold rents and small rancho production. The next year, the Abendaño leaseholds remained, while no youths labored for wages. In 1813–14, the Abendaños gained from La Griega's rapid turn to leaseholds—while don Ysidro Ontiveros served as sergeant in the estate militia, backed by trooper don Pedro Ontiveros. Cousins reinforced family power as leading tenants and troopers.

Don Francisco del Ángel Abendaño replaced his uncle don José Antonio as lead leaseholder paying 110 pesos to rent Las Cabezas. Did the Francos seek a resident to oversee Otomí subtenants in times of insurgency? Don Francisco paid another 32 pesos to lease added croplands. Don Miguel upped his leasehold to 25 pesos. Don José de Jesús continued at 16 pesos while don Atanacio and young don José, who had earlier labored as alquilados, took on lands for 10 pesos each. Five family tenants combined to pay 203 pesos, mixing subtenant oversight and direct production.

The next year, Abendaño leaseholds consolidated: the new patriarch, don Francisco, paid 180 pesos; don José de Jesús paid 50—taking the family total to 230, while no youths leased separately or worked for wages. In 1815–16, don Miguel and don Atanacio again took modest rentals, paying 20 and 25 pesos, bringing the family total near 300 pesos. Afterwards only the two lead leaseholders continued, paying 225 pesos total in 1816–17, 220 pesos in 1817–18 in a notable decline.

In 1819–20, don Francisco del Angel delivered the rancho de las Cabezas to his widowed mother, doña Rosa de Mendoza, who paid the standard 110 pesos. He kept a smaller leasehold paying 50 pesos. Meanwhile, don José de Jesús took on three holdings to pay 65 pesos, while don Miguel paid 38 pesos, and don Atanacio and don José Antonio paid 24 each. In times of change and challenge, under the widow's oversight, Avendaño leaseholds revived to over 300 pesos while two boys returned to work as alquilados, one for 24 days to gain 4.5 pesos, the other for 36 days and nearly 7 pesos.

In 1820–21, as pacification set in, the troop disbanded (after helping pacify Puerto de Nieto), and political change loomed, doña Rosa stepped back: Don Francisco increased his lease to 92 pesos, don José de Jesús to 118, don Miguel to 90 pesos. They held nearly equal leaseholds to bring the family total to 300 pesos—ample if subtenants paid. Two boys labored, one for only six days and just over a peso, the other for 43 days to gain 8 pesos to supplement family earnings. The Abendaños and their Otomí subtenants held on as scarce rains limited harvests while high maize prices marked insurgency's end. They faced uncertain futures together and unequally: Abendaños might prosper if Otomí subtenants paid rents; the latter surely preferred to eat first.

The Olvera family lived another trajectory mediating between propertied power and Otomí production. Three Olvera men, all Spaniards honored as dons, were listed in the census of 1791. One remained in 1811–12, don Vicente who leased a rancho for 70 pesos. Prosperous, he did not approach the leasehold operations of the Abendaños. He held the same rancho at the same rent to 1813–14, when he was joined by don Basilio, who paid 35 pesos to lease a modest holding. The next year, don Vicente increased his leasehold to 100 pesos (perhaps incorporating don Basilio's rancho) while don Ramón took on another for 20. In 1815–16, don Vicente carried on at 100 pesos as don Ramón increased his to 60. A year later, don Vicente continued, don Ramón paid 110 pesos, while don José Estéban began to lease for 20. Olvera leaseholders paid 237 pesos that year, joining the Abendaños as leading leaseholders in La Griega's new regime of Spanish tenants and Otomí subtenants.

Then 1816–17 brought new power to the Olveras. Don Vicente Olvera carried on as a leading leaseholder, still paying 100 pesos; other kin continued, keeping family leaseholds at 237 pesos. Meanwhile, don Vicente's son—Vicente, without the don—gained a new role in estate management. Don Miguel Trinidad Franco appointed him "Capitán de alquilados"—captain of field hands. As leaseholds peaked while the estate maintained commercial cultivation by employing seasonal alquilados, day laborers denied maize rations, a new overseer was pivotal.

Vicente Olvera lacked the don, suggesting his mother was Otomí. Son of a prosperous Spanish leaseholder while linked to the Otomí community, Vicente brought skills of cross-cultural mediation. Had he facilitated Olvera lease holding by negotiating with Otomí subtenants? Did he speak their language? When manager Franco recruited Vicente to oversee the labor of Otomí alquilados, was he honored among the Otomi, or resented for replacing the labor captains long chosen by the community?

As labor captain, young Vicente earned 2 reales daily for 198 days' work overseeing day-laboring alquilados, gaining 50 pesos plus 8 fanegas of maize. He was the only person paid a daily wage to earn a ration, gaining security to oversee the insecure. While most day hands were Otomí drawn from subtenant families, Vicente also managed Olvera kinsmen in the fields: don Ramón labored 62 days for the standard wage of 1.5 reales to earn almost 12 pesos; don José worked 10 days to gain 2 pesos. The two Vicentes, leaseholder and labor captain, kept the Olvera clan prosperous.

They held their roles to the end of insurgency and after—ever more dependent on Vicente's earnings. In 1817–18, don Vicente still leased for 110 pesos, don Ramón for 20, as leaseholds declined. Vicente earned nearly 75 pesos, plus 8 fanegas maize, for 299 days of labor supervision. The next year he cut back to 225 days, bringing 56 pesos plus a ration increased to 13 fanegas, valuable as maize prices rose. In 1819–20, only don Vicente retained his 110 pesos leasehold, still contracting to collect rents, while don Atanacio labored 50 days for 10 pesos under Vicente's oversight.

In 1820–21, the year of transit from insurgency to independence, don Vicente saw his leasehold cut to 100 pesos, while Vicente's captain service rose back to 290 days, gaining 74 pesos and 13 fanegas. Don Vicente hung on, struggling to collect subtenant rents. Vicente reigned strong over the insecure alquilados, Hispanic and Otomí, who labored as La Griega aimed to revive estate planting amid uncertain prospects for profit.

The three family histories reveal differing struggles and adaptations through the decade of insurgency. The Juárezes, always dependent workers, first gained greater employment, better salaries, and solid rations, to face a shift to day labor—without rations. At first, wages rose as enticements to new insecurities, then fell along with the availability of work. At the end, drought made maize scarce as prices peaked, leaving insecure family earnings unable to cover basic sustenance. The Juárezes lived no better in 1820 than they had in 1810—in that, sharing struggles with their Otomí neighbors.

The Abendaños prospered as modest leaseholders early in the decade, then flourished as lead leaseholders favored by ties to the armed Ontiveros when La Griega turned to focus on Otomí subtenant production from 1813 to 1818. When that regime shook in the face of drought, scarcity, and high prices, a widowed matriarch stepped in to calm competition among family leaseholders, enabling the Abendaños to hold prosperous to the end of insurgency. The Olveras also began as comfortable leaseholders in 1811. Their holdings expanded to 1816, when patriarch don Vicente saw his mestizo son take on oversight of La Griega's growing numbers of day laborers—most Otomí. He earned the highest daily wage plus an ample ration. By the end of the decade, only Don Vicente remained a solid leaseholder while Vicente earned top pay and a large ration to oversee the growing numbers of day workers, Hispanic and Otomí, paid falling wages to labor without rations, buying maize at the price the market imposed. As insurgency ended a few prospered while many struggled—notably the Otomí.

Managing to Profit: The Franco Clan

Counterinsurgency capitalism rose and fell at La Griega under Franco family oversight. In 1811 longtime manager don José Regalado Franco faced an insurgent invasion, paid a ransom to stay alive, returned to complete the spring planting, then built an estate troop while he negotiated increased pay and rations to keep sirvientes, Spanish and Otomí, in the fields into 1813. After his death, don Miguel Trinidad Franco claimed a salary more than tripled to manage the estate and command the troop while turning a to new regime of production focused on Spanish leaseholders and Otomí subtenants. He maintained production and gained small profits into 1818, when drought and scarcity returned to bring the new regime down. Still, don Miguel Trinidad and the managerial Francos continued to thrive.

Don José Regalado Franco began to lead La Griega in 1788, just after the great drought and scarcity of 1785–86. He raised rents, forced evictions, and cut salaries, wages, and rations to take profit for the priest-patriarch.

In 1791, Franco led a clan of four Spanish households, linked by marriage to four more.[15] He proved effective at taking profit by imposing poverty and insecurity onto struggling workers—and knowing when to negotiate with the Otomí to keep them at work.

When insurgents struck La Griega early in 1811, Franco learned to survive and maintain production in new times. As he built the estate troop in 1811–12, manager-commander Franco earned 300 pesos, plus a ration of 52 fanegas of maize—sustenance and much more. He was assisted by mayordomo don Ysidoro Franco, who earned 64 pesos and another 52 fanegas of maize. Another son, don Jose Vicente paid 90 pesos to lease the Rancho de la Campaña, collecting rents from Otomí subtenants. The Francos gained from all aspects of La Griega's counterinsurgency capitalism.

Don José Regalado managed and commanded into 1812–13, when he became ill and died. He was credited the full 300 pesos for the year, while mayordomo don José Ysidoro took over, paid an additional 300 pesos and 52 fanegas while taking on a leasehold for 60 pesos. Don José Vicente increased his leasehold to 116 pesos and young don Ramón Franco took on a small holding for 10. As La Griega turned to leasehold and subtenant production, the Franco's kept managerial control for ample pay and rations, while taking on leaseholds to oversee Otomí family production.

In 1813–14, another of don José Regalado's sons, don Miguel Trinidad Franco, became permanent manager and commander, gaining pay more than tripled to 1,000 pesos, plus a ration of 52 fanegas. Not in the accounts before taking charge, don Miguel Trinidad likely managed a nearby estate. Don José Ysidoro returned serve as mayordomo, his pay set at 182 pesos plus 52 fanegas, well above his earnings before the transition, while his leasehold fell to 20 pesos. Don Vicente saw his leasehold rise to 176 pesos, a lead collector of subtenant rents, while three Franco troopers earned a combined 570 pesos and two boys labored for a few days each to gain 4 pesos. Together, six Franco men and two boys gained 1,754 pesos and over 100 fanegas of maize, while leasing lands for just under 200 pesos—notable earnings in a year Sánchez Espinosa took only 2,800 pesos in profit.

The next year, don Miguel Trinidad continued as manager and troop commander for 1,000 pesos plus 52 fanegas. Don José Ysidoro, departed to manage the smaller Amascala estate nearby, keeping a 40 peso leasehold at La Griega.[16] Don José Vicente Franco increased his leasehold to 270 pesos, don Ramón to 30. The Franco family total reached 320 pesos, nearly a quarter of all leaseholds at la Griega. Four Francos remained troopers, combining to earn 440 pesos. And joining the turn to alquilado labor, young don Ygnacio Franco worked 217 days at 2 reales to earn 68 pesos. Franco earnings held over 1,500 pesos in 1814–15, plus ample rations and collections from subtenants.

Did Sánchez Espinosa think they gained too much? In 1815–16, don Miguel Trinidad remained manager-commander at 1,000 pesos plus rations, while don Vicente's leaseholds fell to 150 pesos. Four troopers still earned over 400 pesos and two Francos labored as alquilados: Ygnacio for 163 days at 2 reales to earn 41 pesos; young Nicolás for 194 days at only 1 real, to claim 24 pesos. Family income fell below 1,500 pesos while leaseholds dropped precipitously.

The Francos soon recovered. In 1816–17, don Miguel Trinidad continued as manager-commander for the same 1,000-peso salary while his ration rose to 156 fanegas. Don José Vicente's leaseholds rose back to 370 pesos. There is no list of troopers that year, but at least three Franco men continued, their pay falling to 100 pesos each the next year. And as Vicente Olvera became Capitán de alquilados, Ygnacio Franco saw his wages cut to 1.5 reales, leading him to work 315 days to earn 60 pesos. Young Nicolas held at 1 real and increased his work to 276 days to gain 35. If the youngest Francos lived challenges faced by many at La Griega, they knew their future prospects were better.

An exchange in the spring of 1817 reveals much about proprietor power, managerial goals, and patriarchy in times insurgency. Sánchez Espinosa's son, don José Mariano, the Conde de Peñasco who had toyed with insurgency in 1808, offered don José Ysidoro Franco the chance to manage the Peñasco properties in San Luis Potosí. His move to Amazcala had paid off. He wrote the young conde saying that he, his wife, and children were honored, but his wife was ill and the idea of moving brought tears to their children's eyes. The conde saw a negotiation. Noting that San Luis Potosí was pacified, while insurgency raged near the Amascala basin, he promised a higher salary and pay for the move. Playing on patriarchy, the conde asked don José Ysidoro if his wife ran his life.[17]

A deal seemed near in May. Don José Ysidoro wrote that if the conde would send 1,000 pesos in silver (a year's salary in advance) and allow time to sell livestock and other goods, despite his wife's illness he would take the role. He presumed management would include a troop command and insisted on bringing "four or six useful men to serve." He demanded what don Miguel Trinidad had at La Griega. Then he inquired about Mina's landing with an imagined 18,000 (not 300) followers.[18] The deal collapsed. In July 1817, amid Mina's intrusion, a manager from one of Sánchez Espinosa's

San Luis estates took over at Peñasco.[19] Local knowledge seemed best in newly uncertain times.

The Francos solidified power at La Griega in 1817–18, the last year Sánchez Espinosa took profit there. Don Miguel Trinidad remained manager and troop commander, his pay the same, his ration cut to 104 fanegas—still ample. Don José Vicente increased his leasehold to 460 pesos while don José Ysidoro took on another for 80 pesos. Francos now held 40 percent of leaseholds (by rental value) at La Griega, ruling subtenant production. Three Francos remained troopers, paid 100 pesos each. Ygnacio and Nicolas continued as alquilados, earning 60 and 35 pesos, while Secundino began the year as an alquilado at 1 real, laboring 154 days to earn 20 pesos—until he joined the troop in April 1818, gaining a raise to 2 reales and a total annual income of 48 pesos. With family earnings of 1,450 pesos, ample rations, and leaseholds totaling 540 pesos, the Francos held strong.

The absence of lists of leaseholders and troopers for 1818–19 allows only confirmation that don Miguel Trinidad remained in charge, still paid 1,000 pesos, his ration back up to 156 fanegas. In a year the estate had but 424 fanegas to sell as prices hit 40 reales, the manager's ration was worth 780 pesos. Ygnacio and Nicolás remained alquilados, joined by young Salvador, who worked 46 days at 1 real. Sánchez Espinosa faced heavy losses while the Francos prospered.

As 1819–20 brought pacification to regions west and scarcity drove maize prices to peak, the Francos ruled in changing times. Don Miguel Trinidad remained in charge, still paid 1,000 pesos and 156 fanegas—still worth 780 pesos, nearly doubling his salary. His son don Ysidoro Trinidad held leaseholds worth 90 pesos while don José Vicente cut back to 210. As the leasehold regime dissolved, the Francos stepped back. Ygnacio and Nicolas carried on as alquilados. The managerial clan prospered as Sánchez Espinosa took more losses. In March 1820, don Miguel Trinidad and don José Vicente Franco led 20 troopers from La Griega to pacify Puerto de Nieto. Then the troop disbanded.

As pacification turned to political transformation, 1820–21 saw the Francos face family losses while consolidating managerial power and solid prosperity. In November 1820, don José Ysidoro's wife, doña Justa González, ill since 1817, passed away. Weeks later, the late manager don José Regalado Franco's widowed wife, called "madrecita" by manager don Miguel Trinidad, also passed on.[20] Then don Miguel Trinidad died as 1821 began. Before his passing, he earned 500 pesos plus 81 fanegas ration (worth 400 pesos). His son don Ysidoro Trinidad, who began the year leasing lands for 200 pesos, took over as manager to gain 322 pesos and 57 fanegas for his service—a third less than his father's remuneration. Don José Vicente continued to lease lands worth 200 pesos.

With the troop disbanded, younger Francos were left to labor as alquilados, to live like Juárezes. Secundino Franco, the last to join the troop, returned to the fields to labor 18 days for 1 real, gaining but 2 pesos. Five other Francos earned 1.5 reales, laboring from 26 to 273 days to earn from 5 to more than 50 pesos. We can only imagine the reactions of troopers who had gained ample earnings to protect property, now set to work the fields for day wages alongside Otomí men and boys.

Still, a newly stratified Franco clan gained 964 pesos in cash, 138 fanegas of maize worth 673 pesos, while leasing lands for a total of 400 pesos. When the troop disbanded, the Francos kept the largest leaseholds at La Griega—asserting direct oversight of surviving Otomí subtenants. While the community faced maize scarcities, high prices, and falling incomes, and the Francos lived personal losses, the managerial clan held economically strong. As Sánchez Espinosa faced losses totaling 4,500 pesos at La Griega from 1818 through 1821, the Francos kept local power and solid prosperity.

Then in May 1821, news came that 1,300 "hombres independientes," political rebels backing Iturbide's imagined empire, had attacked the Colorado estate north of Querétaro, taking livestock and cutting the road to San Luis Potosí.[21] Military men who had fought for a decade to defend property and Spanish rule across the Bájio, now rode to take power in Mexico City. Who knew what might follow?

Property, Production, and Patriarchy—as Agrarian Capitalism Collapsed

From afar, it might appear that life at La Griega carried on through the decade after 1810. Francos managed while production continued; the Hispanic minority remained favored; the Otomí majority faced prejudice. A closer look reveals complex changes: a new troop militarized power; commercial expansion at the cost of risings incomes and rations held the peace at first. Then a turn to leaseholds held by favored Spaniards and worked by Otomí subtenants forged a hierarchy of family growers not unlike the changes forced by insurgents across Guanajuato—while confirming patriarchy.

Complex negotiations of counterinsurgency delayed the fall of agrarian capitalism. While insurgency held strong across Guanajuato through 1817,

Francos prospered and took small profits for Sanchez Espinosa. From 1818, the priest-patriarch faced losses, the Francos prospered, while the resident community, Hispanic minority and Otomí majority, faced lives of deepening insecurity still ruled by patriarchy. Profiteering from scarce maize, the essence of agrarian capitalism in New Spain, was gone, broken by insurgency in Guanajauto, by counterinsurgency in Querétaro.

Silver capitalism gone and global trades broken, Sánchez Espinosa and other oligarchs struggled to keep property without profit across the Bajío. They also faced popular challenges beyond the Bajío, difficulties that reveal the expanding ramifications of revolution across New Spain.

6.

New Spain in the Time of Revolution

Arming Power, Defending Property, Conceding Family Production

The revolution that remade New Spain focused in the Bajío, the exceptionally rich, well-watered basin where mining, manufacturing, and commercial cultivation mixed to drive silver capitalism before 1810. Insurgents ruled the countryside surrounding the Guanajuato mines, breaking silver mining and the global trades it drove while commercial cultivation fell to family growers. Querétaro remained a bastion of regime power where commercial estates carried on in support of counterinsurgency, selling maize at low prices while making costly concessions to producing families—undermining agrarian capitalism there too.

The ten years of revolutionary conflict in the Bajío rattled New Spain's integrated, multiregional silver capitalism: Finance, trade, and administration focused in Mexico City. Mines reached from Taxco and Real del Monte near the capital, through Guanajuato, to San Luis Potosí, Zacatecas, and regions beyond. Bajío estates sustained local mines, textiles towns, and more, while feeding arid zones north, and Mexico City when crops failed nearby. The dry country stretching north grazed sheep that sent wool to Bajío workshops and mutton to cities there and the capital. While insurgency wracked the Bajío, regions from the heartland to San Luis Potosí and beyond faced reverberations that rattled power and production, compounding the challenges that remade New Spain.

North of the Bajío, San Luis Potosí first mobilized as a base of counter-revolution, sending troops to fight in the Bajío and beyond. North of Mexico City, the Mezquital saw Otomí risings that rattled power between the capital and the Real del Monte mines. Both were arid regions with major mines, a contrast with the rich, well-watered lands of the Bajío. Facing distinct markets, they lived contrasting ways of agrarian production. San Luis Potosí was ruled by estates with large resident communities of amalgamating peoples, an arid northern extension of Guanajuato. The dry Mezquital was home to Otomí people living in indigenous republics—the northern zone of the heartland. Both began as grazing regions within early silver capitalism. Mezquital sheep supplied wool, mutton, and more to Mexico City. San Luis Potosí provided the same to the Bajío—and in time to the capital.

Their economies diverged in the eighteenth century when Mezquital landlords drove sheep to regions north, turning estates to make pulque, the indigenous fermented drink, to supply the capital and the mines. Oligarchs took profit from a product that required minimal labor—while the growing numbers in Otomí republics faced shortages of land. Men with declining access to arid lands lacked regular access to wage labor. With symbiotic exploitation impossible, patriarchal provision corroded, to break after 1808. Community-based risings began in the wake of Hidalgo's revolt and endured to 1815—separate from the risings in Guanajuato, while reinforcing the larger challenge to the power of silver capitalism.[1]

In contrast, as sheep and people came north to San Luis Potosí, estates there supplied wool, mutton, and more to the Bajío, the capital, and the heartland in trades that flourished to 1810. To sustain those trades, estate operators, including don José Sánchez Espinosa, sent ample maize north from the Bajío, guaranteeing patriarchal provision before 1810—and into the years of insurgency that followed. There were limited local risings while San Luis Potosí held as a region of estate production mobilized in service of counterinsurgency through the decade of revolution.[2]

Otomí communities across the Mezquital reinforced the insurgencies that remade Guanajuato; amalgamating estate communities in San Luis Potosí stayed at work, joining Querétaro's Otomí in sustaining counterinsurgency. Two regions of aridity, adjacent to the Bajío, lived different routes through revolution. Yet by 1820 both had lived transformations that limited agropastoral capitalism and favored autonomies among families on the land. Their contrasting trajectories must be engaged separately; their parallel transformations reveal the widening reverberations of the Bajío revolution.

The two regions could not have been more different in their responses to the Hidalgo revolt. In San Luis Potosí, commander don Félix Calleja mobilized militias based in estate communities to combat and defeat the original Bajio insurgency so laden with contradictions. Far to the south, on learning of the November 1810 battle at Aculco, a crushing defeat for Hidalgo's insurgent masses, men in Otomí communities across the Mezquital took arms to challenge local estates, claiming maize to feed desperate families, beginning years of insurgency that rattled mining at Real del Monte. After his January 1811 victory at Puente de Calderón, Calleja returned to San Luis Potosí to solidify power and hold production there, while community-based insurgencies spread across the Mezquital. Mezquital insurgents and San Luis Potosí producers shaped the decade of revolution in contrasting ways—yet in the end, they claimed parallel gains that limited agrarian capitalism and corroded oligarchic powers.

Counterrevolution in San Luis Potosí:
Don Juan Nepomuceno de Oviedo

San Luis Potosí began as an arid northern extension of the Bajío. In the eighteenth century, a complex history linked don José Sánchez Espinosa, the powerful landed oligarch with lands reaching from the outskirts of Mexico, through the Bajío, to San Luis Potosí, to the Peñasco family that took wealth from local mines to become the leading landed clan in San Luis Potosí, and don Félix Calleja, military commander there before 1810. They built alliances and negotiated conflicts as they competed for regional power—then allied to fight insurgents when revolution threatened power, property, and profit in the Bajío and beyond.

When insurgency began in the Bajío, Calleja mobilized San Luis Potosí for counterinsurgency. Troops based at Sánchez Espinosa's Bocas estates led by manager-commander don Juan Nepomuceno de Oviedo joined, soon famous as unstoppable Tamarindos. In November 1810, Oviedo was in Celaya, reclaiming the town and chasing guerrillas.[3] He helped Calleja retake Guanajuato after the second insurgent invasion and sacking. Shocked by the destruction there, he learned that insurgents had camped at Bocas and Peñasco on the way to attack the mines at Catorce, just north. Oviedo worried that while he fought in the Bajío, insurgency might overwhelm San Luis Potosí.[4]

As December ended, he learned of "restless souls" at Bocas and worried that residents might turn to insurgency. He cancelled the year-end roundup at outlying Huizache, "as those lands have revolted." Also troubling, the native community at nearby Divina Pastora was in insurrection; its governor called home the "indios" working to expand irrigation at Peñasco. Oviedo worried that "we can't count on the people" of San Luis Potosí.[5] Yet despite rumors and worries, residents at Bocas, Cruces, and Peñasco stayed at work while indigenous peoples in basins east challenged power. Oviedo's troop joined the battle at Puente de Calderón.[6]

Loyalists won, Hidalgo's forces dispersed, and nothing was resolved in the Bajío. Sánchez Espinosa tried to contain insurgents at Puerto de Nieto and failed. By funding a troop and making concessions to residents, he kept peace and production at La Griega. And he backed Oviedo as a key leader in the larger counterinsurgency war. The life and letters of don Juan Nepomuceno de Oviedo offer a window on power and production in San Luis Potosí before 1810 and the mobilization to fight insurgents in the Bajío and beyond into 1812—when he gave his life defending power and property.

Born in the Bajío in 1747, Oviedo moved north as a boy when his father became manager at Bocas, then an undeveloped grazing property. He joined the first Conde de Peñasco in repressing the San Luis Potosí riots of 1767. He became Bocas' manager before Sánchez Espinosa inherited the estate in 1780. The young proprietor depended on Oviedo for knowledge of San Luis Potosí and northern estate operations. Together, they built dams and canals to expand irrigation and draw families to Bocas' dry lands.[7] Like most managers, Oviedo worked to gain profit for Sánchez Espinosa—and build power for himself. He owned a nearby property and leased a large rancho at Bocas. When the irrigation system was ready, it watered estate crops and his own. He placed nephews and cousins as stewards at outlying units. He leased ranchos to sisters and their husbands.[8] A nephew managed the Labor de Ahualulco, expanding cultivation and sending workers to build another dam at Bocas. When he disputed 100 pesos with his uncle, he was gone.[9]

In 1798, Oviedo faced accusations of favoring his family. He swore loyalty to the priest-patriarch: "my crime is serving you." Yes, two sisters leased ranchos and paid rents. A brother served as a steward and would be replaced if he did not serve effectively. Other Oviedos lived in San Luis Potosí and Catorce, taking nothing from Bocas. Oviedo insisted: "until death I will serve you." He remained manager.[10] In 1802, the dam and irrigation system complete, rumors returned: Oviedo took too much water for his own fields, limiting irrigation at Bocas. He defended himself: he used forty-two days of water, paying a peso daily; his sisters gained five days each—and paid. And the dam yielded an additional 500 fanegas of maize on estate fields, easily covering its cost.[11] He remained.

While serving Sánchez Espinosa, Oviedo became a leading man in San Luis Potosí. In 1783, he was named one of four captains in the Legion of San Carlos; the others were all leading landowners. The command recognized Oviedo's service to Sánchez Espinosa, whose regional power was matched only by the commanding Condes de Peñasco, the founder and then his son who inherited the title, vast lands, and command in 1788. After 1800, Oviedo remained a captain in the Legion while he leased another estate, led the local tobacco monopoly, and oversaw elections in the indigenous republic of San Miguel Mezquitic, outside the city of San Luis Potosí.[12] He lived as a provincial patriarch.

In 1802, he sent three sons to study in Mexico City, assisted by Sánchez Espinosa. Oviedo dreamed of clerical careers, the path followed decades earlier by the Hidalgo brothers, sons of a Bajío estate manager. The eldest showed "little talent, little effort, and is not inclined to serve the Church." Oviedo mused that he might return north to trade.[13] He stayed with his brothers while Oviedo pestered Sánchez Espinosa for clerical appointments. None came. In 1808, as imperial crisis mounted, Oviedo lamented the effort.[14] He might live like a provincial patriarch; he remained a dependent manager.

For decades, Oviedo served Sánchez Espinosa while dealing with the Peñascos and Calleja. The balance proved difficult. After the founding Conde de Peñasco's death in 1788, the priest-patriarch offered to facilitate the second conde's economic affairs. With mines dormant and estates limited to the region, the heir struggled. In 1798, creditors accepted Sánchez Espinosa's offer to operate the Peñasco properties in their interest; the Peñascos believed he had forced the bankruptcy. They went to economic war—and learned the power of the Mexico City oligarch. By 1800, the second conde held a title and militia command while Sánchez Espinosa ruled his own Bocas estates and the Peñasco properties, the most powerful man on the land in San Luis Potosí.[15]

When the second conde died in 1805, the priest-patriarch's son don Mariano Sánchez y Mora inherited the Peñasco title and estates. He asked to command the provincial militia, to be rebuffed as Calleja gained the role. The widow Peñasco asked to keep her jewels and operate non-entailed estates on leasehold. Sánchez Espinosa and the creditor's council refused. Confirmed as third conde, don José Mariano set out in December to claim his properties. He went first to Bocas to meet with Oviedo. The elder manager called him "My Lord the young Conde." When don José Mariano went to town for Christmas, the pastor and council greeted him cordially; the local establishment snubbed him—a rejection organized, he believed, by the widow Peñasco and her ally Calleja.

Spending the holidays in isolation, in January 1806 the new conde set out to take legal possession of the hacienda Peñasco on the dry plateau and La Angostura in a fertile basin east. For months, he faced the ire and obstructions of the widow and her allies as costs rose to 6,000 pesos. He called his days in the province "the most hateful time in my life." Oviedo struggled to live between the men he served and the provincials who shaped his daily life.[16] Calleja ordered him to mobilize his troop and head to the Gulf ahead of an imagined British invasion. Back home in April, Oviedo loaned the young conde 1,600 pesos to cover final expenses.[17] In July 1807, Oviedo denied rumors he might leave Sánchez Espinosa's service: "I have lived this miserable life for 61 years, and death will soon come; until it does, I have no wish but to serve you."[18] The manager's regional power ultimately depended on the priest-patriarch—a man of multiregional power based in the capital.

That fall, the priest-patriarch and the young conde set off on a long inspection of their northern properties. As they traveled together, no letters report the details. It must have gone well, for in April 1808, Sánchez Espinosa gave control of the Obra Pía estates (La Griega, Puerto de Nieto, and Bocas) to his titled son, merging operations of their northern properties. Aiming to retire, the priest-patriarch did not imagine the trials to come when Napoleon's armies occupied Madrid a month later.

Learning of the ferment of summer of 1808 in Mexico City, in late September Oviedo wrote to Peñasco. On news of the capture of Spain's sovereigns, people in San Luis Potosí had shouted: "Viva Fernando VII. We will die for God, King, and country." After reading the young conde's letter reporting the promise of a junta backed by the viceroy, then Yermo's coup, Oviedo insisted, "We Americas are free"—sharing Peñasco's disgust with the coup. Did Oviedo know Calleja was in the capital to back the coup? Had Peñasco reported his own seditious conversations the day after? Whatever he knew, Oviedo responded with bravado: half blind, he was ready to lead the men under his command to defend New Spain. By the time Peñasco read Oviedo's letter, the conde had been grilled by viceregal authorities, stripped of landed power by his father, and sent to exile beyond the pyramids.[19]

Political bravado disappeared as drought soon struck San Luis Potosí and focused Oviedo's reports, now sent to Sánchez Espinosa. In the fall of 1809, a second harvest had withered and "hunger and want" led to "fevers everywhere." People were dying at Bocas, nearby estates, and the Catorce mines.[20] The priest-patriarch responded. The herds at Bocas and beyond were pivotal to his profits, as were the people who cared for them. He sent 2,340 fanegas of maize from La Griega to Bocas to guarantee maize rations— while many in the Bajío starved and he profited from their hunger.[21]

In June 1810, Oviedo, again writing to Peñasco, mixed ecological and political concerns. He noted that rains had come to Bocas and thanked Guadalupe for her blessing. The same favor had not come to Angostura. Oviedo added a cryptic note suggesting political unrest: "so many bad Christians have forgotten God, the King, and the land that protect them. . . . Justice suffers as men conspire."[22] Had Oviedo caught wind of conversations at Querétaro? Was something afoot in San Luis Potosí? He wrote to learn Peñasco's knowledge and interest with no hint of sedition.

In late July, he wrote to Sánchez Espinosa, lamenting that rains had ended. With irrigation, Bocas would harvest some maize; across the region, drought was so devastating it would take years of good rains to recover. Oviedo added that Calleja was requisitioning horses for a mobilization to come.[23] Had the northern commander learned of the conversations at Querétaro? Oviedo's last letter before the outbreak of Hidalgo's revolt was written on August 17. Extreme drought still plagued San Luis Potosí; he feared ruin.[24]

It soon came—south in the Bajío. As two years of scarcity ended there, Hidalgo provoked an insurgency sustained by maize standing in the fields awaiting harvest. Calleja and Oviedo raised militias in San Luis Potosí, marching to contain insurgency in a region regaining sustenance, leaving behind a province still facing drought and desperation. Risings came in indigenous Huizache, Divina Pastora, and San Miguel Mezquitic, while Sánchez Espinosa, Peñasco, and others delivered maize to feed estate dependents across dry uplands. Sustenance kept the peace in San Luis Potosí estate communities.[25]

Despite the spats that had set the Mexico City oligarchs against Calleja and the original Peñascos, with Oviedo caught in the middle, Hidalgo's threat to New Spain and silver capitalism forged a reunion of the powerful to fight rebels attacking the regime and landed property. Oviedo and the Tamarindos fought across the Bajío to defeat Hidalgo and contain popular insurgents. Then the troop based at Bocas chased José María Morelos' guerrilla forces, culminating in the 1812 siege of Cuautla in rich lowlands just south of the capital. People in nearby indigenous republics stood back, refraining from joining the political rebel.[26] While leading an assault on

February 19, Oviedo was wounded and died three days later.[27] He gave his life to ensure that political insurgents would never threaten Mexico City. He served Sánchez Espinosa, the regime, and silver capitalism to his end.

Lucas Alamán saw a hero: "Manager of the hacienda de Bocas near San Luis, nearly all the soldiers of the battalion of patriots called the Tamarindos were his dependents; he lived as a patriarch among them, loved and obeyed as a master more than a boss; they knew him as master Oviedo."[28] To Alamán, Oviedo represented the best of New Spain, a manager so beloved by the men who served him that they followed him into battles to defend the regime. Alamán did not see that while Sánchez Espinosa pressed the predatory profiteering that provoked insurgency in the Bajío, he had delivered maize to sustain lives of secure patriarchal dependence at Bocas, maintaining Oviedo as a powerful manager and respected military commander—ready to lead the Tamarindos as loyal counterinsurgents.

The Limits of Oligarchic Power

While Oviedo fought insurgents, Sánchez Espinosa and Peñasco stayed in the capital. Insurgents and counterinsurgents mobilized armed forces to assault and defend property and power, setting the militarized power imposed by the coup of 1808 at the center of fights to preserve property and silver capitalism. With Hidalgo defeated and depending on Oviedo for armed defense, early in 1811 Sánchez Espinosa donated 1,500 pesos to the Congregation of Guadalupe in Querétaro, calling her to counterinsurgency.[29] Facing pleas for financial help from kin and strangers, he resisted, often angrily.[30]

After Oviedo's death and Morelos' defeat at Cuautla in 1812, life in the capital found a semblance of calm. The priest-patriarch attended *tertulias* where oligarchs and officials faced the issues of the day. Short of cash, he claimed insolvency to keep creditors at bay. He worried about strangers, turning away an old friend who came with an unknown companion in days of too many robberies.[31]

The young Conde de Peñasco held in the background. Authorities knew his 1808 dalliance with an indigenous rising, never challenging property but aiming to topple the coup-imposed regime. Under interrogation, he had testified that with power militarized, only armed power could resist its impositions. His savvy father exiled him, denying him power in family affairs. In 1810, when insurgents challenged the regime and property, Peñasco stayed invisible while Oviedo took arms to defend the family and the regime. Then, in 1813, with Oviedo dead, Peñasco emerged to proclaim allegiance to a regime reshaped by Cádiz liberalism. Taking a command in defense of property, in July he was in Toluca as "Commander of the Light Battalion of San Luis Potosí." In September, he was at Sultepec, south of Toluca; in November in Puebla—all far from the deadly conflicts in the Bajío.[32]

Sánchez Espinosa focused on estate operations. He shared his wayward son's view of the centrality of armed power when he founded the troop at La Griega, defending counterinsurgency capitalism while accepting costs that cut profit. Late in 1814, after the return of Fernando and the abrogation of Cádiz, the *Gaceta de México* announced that to honor the king, "the priest don José Sánchez Espinosa" had endowed dowries of 300 pesos for twenty-four orphaned daughters of "Spaniards"—American or peninsular—who died fighting for his majesty.[33] The funds came from the Obra Oía properties, while profits held at La Griega and Bocas.[34] The priest-patriarch would support daughters of the king's martyred defenders. He was less charitable with others. In 1814 and 1815, he began to call in old debts—setting off tense negotiations while gaining little.[35]

Peñasco began to imagine personal independence. In early 1815, he lived with his family in Mexico City—outside his father's household. He tried and failed to gain a stall to trade in the Parián, the great market in the plaza fronting the cathedral and the viceregal palace.[36] He considered leasing out the Peñasco properties, hoping for secure income in times of disruption. Failing, in 1816 he moved to San Luis Potosí to claim direct oversight of estate operations and military power as "Comandante de Cazadores."[37] When Fernando VII confirmed his title in 1817, Peñasco retired from command, asking to keep his uniform and *fuero*—separate justice for military men. He would remain in the north into 1821, proud of his title, military honors, and exemptions.[38] He left others to fight while he struggled to keep power on the land as estate residents pressed to control production.

One notable man did gain wealth from the fusion of military power and counterinsurgency capitalism in New Spain. Don Félix Calleja, the lead field commander fighting political and popular insurgents from 1810 through 1812, then viceroy from 1813 into 1816, returned to Spain with the honor to gain title as Conde de Calderón and the silver to buy lands that made him a leading proprietor on the rich irrigated plains of Valencia. Perhaps the last immigrant Spaniard to extract enough silver to become a landed oligarch, he saw the collapse of agrarian capitalism in New Spain and took his cache of pesos to purchase fertile lands in post-Napoleonic Spain.[39]

Negotiating Production to Keep the Peace:
San Luis Potosí, 1812–1820

With Puerto de Nieto lost to insurgent residents in Guanajuato and La Griega focused on counterinsurgency in Querétaro, Sánchez Espinosa and Peñasco looked to San Luis Potosí to find profit after 1812. They remained the dominant landowners in the region. Early on, the priest-patriarch ruled while the conde faced exile from power and then joined the fight against political insurgents. After moving north in 1816, Peñasco consulted regularly with his father. Seeking independence, he depended on the priest-patriarch's knowledge, contacts, and experience as both struggled in the face of producing families' assertions.

Accounts of operations at Bocas show Sánchez Espinosa taking profits that rose to 1815, held to 1818, then fell to 1820.[40] Peñasco struggled while his operations carried on. The great herds of sheep that yielded mutton, tallow, and wool kept earnings steady while maize and other crops were always uncertain in the arid north. By the end of the decade, the oligarchs were trying new products: cane brandy, mezcal, wine, and cotton. Property held. But profits declined after 1817 as estate residents took new control of production. Epigmenio González' world came north.

Sheep grazing defined pastoral capitalism in San Luis Potosí. Great herds provided mutton to consumers in the Bajío and Mexico City, wool to *obrajes* and artisan shops in Querétaro, San Miguel, and other towns. Tallow sold everywhere to make the candles essential to mining, worship, and nightly light. With the outbreak of insurgency, demand for mutton collapsed in Guanajuato and San Miguel while it rose in Querétaro and Mexico City, centers of refuge and counterinsurgency. Demand for tallow fell in the mines, held strong in devotions, and perhaps rose to illuminate more dangerous nights. Demand for wool fell as Spain's British allies sent cloth to New Spain.

Sales of sheep for slaughter kept northern estates strong. For all the concern over safe passage on the road between insurgent strongholds in Guanajuato and the Sierra Gorda, herds got through (paying tolls to rebels when necessary). At Bocas, sales and prices climbed from 1812 to 1815, when Sánchez Espinosa sold 5,000 head to claim 25,000 pesos. Prices then fell under 4 pesos and sales declined from 1816 to 1819, generating steady but modest earnings. Then, in 1819–20, pacification brought a glut, dropping prices to 2 pesos. Sánchez Espinosa never would have sold for such a price before insurgency; now, in need of income, he sold more than 6,700 head for 13,000 pesos. When prices rose back above 4 pesos in 1820–21, he sold

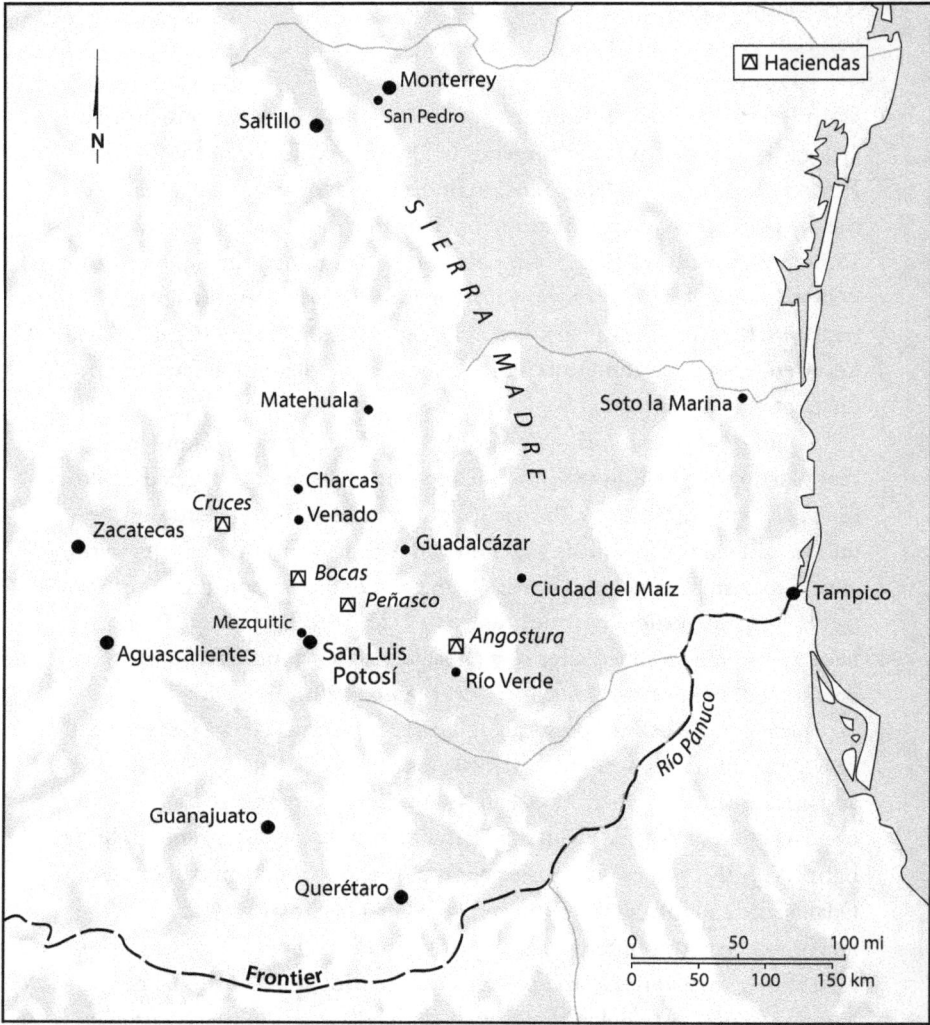

Map 6.1 San Luis Potosí, ca. 1820.

another 5,000 head to take 20,000 pesos. Tallow sales paralleled and rein-forced earnings from sheep sold for mutton; wool sales peaked in 1812–13, then collapsed as New Spain's cloth makers struggled. The maize harvested at Bocas fed residents; never a source of profit, it kept families at work. Land rentals and rents increased to 1817, helping keep the peace; then collections fell as family growers entrenched on the land.

Throughout, production and profit required negotiating with producers. Estate residents pressed for secure sustenance and control of production while oligarchs and managers struggled to defend propertied power. As 1813 ended, the manager at Peñasco reported shortages of workers and the means to pay them, slowing work to repair a dam essential to irrigation. He worried about finding workers for the coming roundup and slaughter. The maize in storage would not cover rations. Rents from small tenants only paid a chaplain. He explained, "Day after day the *sirvientes* complain of necessity." The poorest lived by scavenging maguey and nopal cactus. A convoy was short of men to take on the journey south.[41] Who would risk facing insurgents with families hungry at home?

In March 1814, the slaughter was done but work on the dam had stopped. Two thousand hides sold locally generated 1,200 pesos to pay "*alquilados* working the harvest" and men clearing fields and extending irrigation for new cotton planting. The good news: the irrigated maize harvest exceeded 9,000 fanegas and cotton planting would soon begin. The bad: insurgents had attacked nearby.[42]

The conde considered leasing out Peñasco in 1815. An offer of only 2,000 pesos kept operations on his account.[43] Seeking profit in regional markets, in 1816 the estate sold honey and cheese to earn 3,000 pesos. Production of aguardiente, cane brandy, began with the first ten barrels expected to sell for 25 pesos each. A troop of seven men was guarding the estate in November when a "band of insurgents" struck to steal horses. The troop captain was killed while two rebels died and one was captured. The rest escaped with a horse, two saddles, two rifles, and a machete. Then the provincial commander sent twenty dragoons to defend Peñasco.[44] Production carried on while insurgents rattled the peace.

In 1816, Sánchez Espinosa took solid profits from sales of Bocas' sheep, tallow, and wool and began to finance nearby mines, hoping for silver to fund estate operations. Four bars came in March 2017; more awaited transit south in July and again in January 1818. Eleven came in November.[45] News of prosperity brought collectors seeking past taxes. Managers negotiated settlements.[46] Meanwhile, the priest-patriarch innovated: a "mezcal factory" aimed to tap the maguey ubiquitous across arid plateau lands to supply local taverns.

Residents protested. They had long tapped cactus freely, using juice for beverages and fiber for rough cloth. They feared competing with the estate selling mezcal. When the *fábrica* was ready, the priest-patriarch ordered all nearby maguey reserved for estate production. Residents might tap plants for use but not for "business." Tenant "ranchos making alcoholic drink" were restricted to lands far from the estate factory.[47] Could that be enforced as life was contested across vast spaces? A foreman accused of stealing a mule led the patriarch to reflect on "the lack of loyalty among these people."[48]

Insurgent threats kept troops at northern properties—and armed men disrupted social peace. A May 1817 wedding at far northern Cruces brought a confrontation. The groom and godfather planned a fandango. The steward agreed. During the celebration, a corporal of the guard got drunk and disruptive. The steward jailed him; the troop forced his release. The hierarchy of managerial power broken, the steward sent half the guard south to Bocas—and hoped for peace.[49]

In contested times, providing maize to estate residents remained key to peace and production—and a constant challenge. Insurgency ended the practice of supplying Bocas from Puerto de Nieto—breaking a pillar of agrarian capitalism. Bocas built irrigation, but on dry uplands, scarcities recurred: in 1817, 266 fanegas went to dependent *sirvientes*; 305 went to *peones*, a new label for *alquilados* who now gained rations. Another 514 were sold to "poor residents," likely squatters. The sales brought no profit but were a "charity" to desperate families, essential to sustain life and production.[50]

In June 1817, the Conde de Peñasco ordered a census of his San Luis Potosí estates. He learned of many "squatters" neither employed as *sirvientes* nor contracted to pay rents. They used estate lands for huts, gardens, and more and worked as day laborers. The conde aimed to evict some and charge rents to the rest.[51] Knowing that raised rents and evictions led to insurgency at Puerto de Nieto in 1810, his father counseled restraint: "We cannot evict the squatters at Peñasco now; it is necessary to suffer their presence as turbulence continues to grow. Nothing is more important than to keep the people content, even at the cost of losses." Coercion did not work; guards were "a problem without remedy"—second only to an insurgent takeover.[52]

The advice from the patriarch to his noble son came as Franciso Javier Mina rode through San Luis Potosí. A new manager at Bocas, signing only as Nájera, wrote that Mina led a mounted force of 400 that crossed the estate from June 15 to 18. Nájera hoped the 2,000-man Extremadura regiment would stop them.[53] The troop held back, allowing Mina to join Pedro Moreno at Sombreros.

In July, a group of Mina's men hit the Jaral estates that stretched across the border between Guanajuato and San Luis Potosí. The Conde de Jaral fled. An employee was killed as invaders took cash, jewels, silverware, grain, livestock, and cartloads of hay. Rumors reported losses at 30,000 to 70,000 pesos.[54] Mina's roaming rattled power and production. The Extremadura troop took 200 of Bocas' best horses to "chase" Mina, while a herd of sheep about to head south lacked guards.[55] Peñasco feared disruption by the defenders of the regime more than the threat of Mina's invaders.[56] From Bocas, Nájera wrote that troopers had allowed four of Mina's men taken prisoner to escape, then gave chase with no success. He saw collusion, an alliance of armed men against the estate community.[57]

Once Mina passed, managers looked to resume profitable operations. A new grape harvest yielded just two barrels of wine. The estate had provided supplies and paid 3 pesos per barrel to a vintner now blamed for the small yield. Mezcal did better. Meanwhile, struggles to send sheep south continued. News of a convoy came the day it left, too late to send Bocas' herd.[58]

Maize remained a perpetual challenge. Shipments from irrigated fields at Bocas fed families at Peñasco in the summer of 1817; as supplies became short, father and son debated who should gain the last 300 fanegas.[59] In August, the conde learned of independence in a key segment of the estate community. A weekly cart took tamales to the scattered men who kept estate flocks, returning with 30 or more dead lambs sent by herdsmen to their families. Some became family meals; others were sold at a *tianguis*, a market run by shepherds' wives. Seeing others profit from his property, 1,500 lambs in the course of a year, Peñasco ordered a halt. An overseer reported that herdsmen had always served for salaries and the meat of animals that died in their care. If Peñasco did not concede, they would leave. The nobleman ordered the "proud" overseer to appear—to learn that his knowledge of land and work was essential. He could not be replaced for any amount of money. The meat market carried on.[60]

As families at Peñasco kept their 50 sheep per year, in October Sánchez Espinosa wrote to far northern Cruces, to learn that a regular "tortilla wagon" returned with meat for herdsmen's families there, too. The priest-patriarch saw robbery. Yet the problem required "prudence" to ensure that "the shepherds don't desert us." Ending sheep sharing would undermine estate production.[61] Across San Luis Potosí, property held while families shaped production and kept product.

Experiments and struggles persisted. New cotton harvests enabled cloth making at Peñasco as 1817 ended; the estate supplied fiber to women who spun at home and men who wove in a workshop.[62] Guerrilla attacks still threatened shipments of silver, sheep, and tallow heading south to Mexico City.[63] The February 1818 shearing saw workers take animals for family feasts.[64] Production diversified, commercial links held fragile, and families presumed that much of what they made was theirs.

As 1820 began and insurgents pacified in exchange for family production at Puerto de Nieto and across rural Guanajuato, parallel settlements eased conflicts in San Luis Potosí. When planting began at Bocas in May, rains were promising—and sharecroppers planted all the estate's maize, including on irrigated lands. Sánchez Espinosa conceded northern cultivation to producers, claiming a share of harvests they controlled. His manager blamed the shift on a general "infidelity among *sirvientes.*" They would only work for salaries and solid rations: "a vice these people are born with, and by which they live and die." Now, with silver flows down and profit scarce, the priest-patriarch lacked funds to pay salaries. The turn to sharecropping left the costs of production (beyond seed) to family growers; the estate would gain half the harvest, or what family growers reported as half. Then in June, the rains ended, drought set in, livestock suffered, and crops withered. The January 1821 harvest brought the estate only 425 fanegas from sharecroppers.[65] If forty families had sharecropped, the 10 fanegas each retained was a year's sustenance. If there were more families, hunger loomed. The manager did not report on that; the priest-patriarch did not ask.

Bocas was one of the largest, richest, most populous estates north of the Bajío. In 1810, lives of secure dependence had kept the majority at work while its troop backed Oviedo to protect power and property in the Bajío and beyond. By 1820, a decade of contesting insurgency had enabled community insubordination. To hold production, Sánchez Espinosa's managers turned cultivation to sharecroppers while herdsmen took sheep shares for sustenance and sales. Property held as commercial capitalism waned— sustained by mutton and tallow sales, limited by herdsmen's share taking. What insurgents took across Guanajuato and counterinsurgency mandated at La Griega, families claimed as the price of production at Bocas and across San Luis Potosí—where aridity kept insecurity on the horizon.

Insurgency in the Mezquital: Otomí Communities Challenge Pulque Oligarchs

Just north of the capital, the Mezquital was the driest of the heartland basins surrounding Mexico City. Its Otomí communities turned to insurgency late in 1810 as Hidalgo's throngs passed to the west, escaping the deadly stalemate at Monte de las Cruces to face defeat at Aculco. Hidalgo did not provoke or promote the risings in the Mezquital; the exodus of his retreating throngs

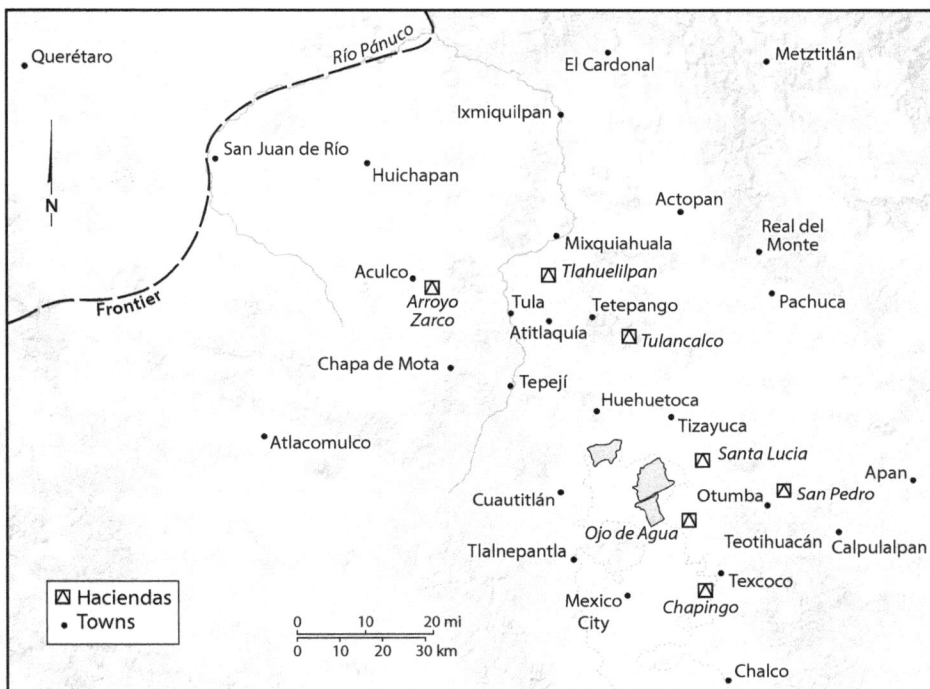

Map 6.2 The Mezquital and the pulque zone, ca. 1820.

announced that popular forces had risen, that political men had divided in response, and that power was rattled. While Calleja and Oviedo raised forces based in estate communities in San Luis Potosí to fight insurgents, men in Otomí republics across the Mezquital turned to raiding estates, taking maize and more. Facing predations made devastating in recent times of drought, Mezquital insurgents multiplied the challenges faced by New Spain's powerholders after 1810.

Like their neighbors across the heartland, Otomí survivors of the sixteenth-century population collapse gained rights as indigenous republics, cultivating dry lands as rains allowed. In the vacated arid spaces, estates grazed sheep.[66] In the eighteenth century, mining surged at Real del Monte while Mezquital communities faced growing populations. Seeing new ways to profit, landlords sent livestock north and turned pastures to fields of maguey, making pulque to supply mine workers and Mexico City taverns. Don Antonio Rodríguez de Pedroso led the transition, honored for his efforts as Conde de San Bartolomé de Jala. The Jesuits followed on lands

Figure 6.1 The Mezquital, pulque country. Author photo.

that sustained colleges in the capital until their expulsion in 1867. When don Pedro Romero de Terreros, soon Conde de Regla, took capital made in trade at Querétaro to claim a bonanza in silver at Real del Monte, he bought the richest Jesuit pulque properties and married his first son to Rodriguez de Pedroso's daughter and primary heir. The merger built a pulque empire stretching from the northern Valley of Mexico through the Mezquital, dominating supplies to Mexico City taverns. Others joined: the Condes de Santiago, New Spain's oldest landed oligarchs, made pulque at Tulancalco; don José Sánchez Espinosa tried the business at San Pedro near Otumba.[67]

From the 1780s, the boom in silver capitalism drove soaring demand for pulque at the mines and in the capital—while growing populations left Otomí families in Mezquital republics short of land. Yet beyond the periodic transplanting of maguey shoots, pulque estates offered little labor during the five years the cactus matured and the fifteen when teams of two to three Otomí men tapped plants and fermented pulque. Poverty laced with insecurity plagued families left with dry plots ever less able to feed growing numbers—with no regular access to wage work that might tie communities to estates in symbiotic exploitations. The drought of 1808 to 1810 sent maize prices soaring, making life more insecure and death common. While oligarchs delivered maize to the San Luis Potosí estate residents essential to rich mutton, tallow, and wool trades, they saw Mezquital villagers as expendable. When Hidalgo's throngs passed nearby, news of insurgency led to risings in angry Mezquital communities.

Again, we know of the Otomí risings though reports by managers serving oligarchs struggling to preserve agrarian capitalism. Don Manuel Olguín managed Tulancalco in the southern Mezquital for doña María Josefa de Velasco y Ovando, first while she oversaw all the Santiago family properties for her sister the condesa in the 1790s, then after 1800 as she ran the pulque estate on leasehold. Olguín never took arms against insurgents, instead negotiating to keep Tulancalco in production in the face of assaults by neighboring villagers during 1811 and 1812. He reported raids invading Tulancalco and nearby estates to take maize and livestock, while pulque production struggled to carry on.

Don Vicente Fernández managed Tlahuelilpan near Tula in the heart of the Mezquital for the Conde de la Cortina. Cortina funded and Fernández led a troop defending property across the Mezquital from 1811 into 1816. Throughout, the manager-commander reported endless chases that dispersed rebels yet rarely broke them—until amnesty and rights to retain arms in home communities brought pacification in 1814 and 1815. During five years, the Mezquital insurgency cut commercial production of maize and pulque in half while adding costs that broke estate profits as mining struggled to carry on at Real del Monte. The amnesty confirmed community rights to land and autonomy, setting a heartland precedent for Bajío pacifications that came five years later.[68]

The early intensity of the Mezquital insurgency led to extensions south into dry pulque zones in the Valley of Mexico. At Sánchez Espinosa's San Pedro near Otumba, pulque flowed into January 1812, when insurgents took control.[69] Accounts from the estates of the Marquesa de Vivanco reveal the impacts of insurgency closer to the capital: Chapingo was a leading cereal grower (now the National Agricultural College) near Texcoco; Ojo de Agua made pulque on dry lands just north on the road to the Mezquital. Both turned ample profits in the decade before 1810: Chapingo followed the classic ways of agrarian capitalism, holding maize to profit from hunger in years of scarcity, taking annual gains ranging from 3 to 14 percent, for a solid mean of 8. Ojo de Agua shipped pulque weekly to Mexico City taverns, claiming regular profits of 6 to 8 percent. The steady profits of pulque balanced the irregular earnings of maize.

After 1810, Chapingo continued maize cropping in a region of symbiotic exploitations, drawing seasonal hands from nearby villages to take profits ranging from 8 to 21 percent, an annual mean of 14 that doubled prior gains. Feeding the capital was good business in times of insurgency. Meanwhile, Ojo de Agua's profits fell in 1810 and 1811 while rebels roamed just north; then earnings and profit vanished while insurgents held the estate from 1812 through 1815.

Don José Sánchez Espinosa faced a parallel divergence in his heartland operations. La Teja, just west of the capital, was an estate of chinampas built in the lake bed and yielding fruits, vegetables, and more to supply city markets year-round. He collected rents from family producers who supplied urban markets strong in times of insurgency.[70] Thanks to rich plots, men's production, and women's marketing, the people of La Teja lived what others pressed to gain in times of revolution.

In the dry pulque zone beyond the pyramids, Sánchez Espinosa gained nothing from San Pedro while local insurgents ruled the estate from 1812 into 1816. While pulque capitalism collapsed, pulque drinking did not. Around Otumba, Otomí villagers tapped maguey they had transplanted for small wages before 1812, to make pulque and send it to the capital in trades the authorities could not block if peace was to hold in city barrios. When Sánchez Espinosa regained access to San Pedro in 1816, his attempts to revive profit revealed much about years of insurgent operations—and challenges that remained.

In August, he sent a new manager, don Juan Estéban Umaña, to the pulque estates. His first report revealed that during years of insurgent rule, maize had been planted and harvested by unknown (or unnamed) locals. Amid the growing season, Sánchez Espinosa aimed to reclaim lands and crops by turning them over to leaseholders—without success. Who would risk taking maize from people recently armed as insurgents? Pulque remained the key to profit. At Hueyapan, the main house, the orchard, the chapel with its images and ornaments, and the *tinacal* (a shed with vats to ferment pulque) were intact. At San Pedro, the chapel and part of the house stood, but the *tinacales* were destroyed, along with the whim that drew water from the well. At outlying ranchos, small houses survived, but the *tinacales* had been burned. Maguey fields remained, flourishing at San Pedro, "reasonable" elsewhere.[71]

With property denied and managers gone, the people of Otumba and nearby villages took maize lands for family production, broke the machinery of pulque capitalism, while preserving fields of maguey for household production to supply families, local markets, and Mexico City taverns. The attempt to revive pulque for profit in 1816 did not prove easy. With the exception of Hueyapan, the machinery of fermentation was broken—or gone. Fields of maguey remained. Had communities transplanted at San Pedro? Elsewhere, transplanting would have to resume, requiring hands and pesos to pay them. A group of local residents accosted Umaña, asking by what right he resumed estate production. He might have answered: by Sánchez Espinosa's right to property. He stated instead that he acted by order of the commander at Tepeapulco: only coercion might restore pulque capitalism.

Sánchez Espinosa and Umaña worked to transplant fields and rebuild *tinacales*. As costs rose, the priest-patriarch sent a still to make mescal, hoping the distilled beverage might fund the revival of the fermented pulque favored by the native majority.[72] In July 1817, Church authorities demanded tithe payments.[73] The priest-patriarch had not paid since January 1812, when insurgents took control. As a religious foundation, his Obra Pía estates were exempt; as free holdings, the pulque estates were not—even with Sánchez Espinosa's priestly status. Lacking funds, he dodged payment.

In the summer of 1818, as production began to rise, the muleteers who had delivered pulque to the capital for rebel producers demanded 25 percent higher rates. Sánchez Espinosa saw the demand as unconscionable, but pulque spoiled if not delivered to city taverns in twenty-four hours, so he paid—sharing earnings with men who had made themselves essential commercial intermediaries during years of insurgency. They, too, faced risks as armed "robbers" plagued the region, taking livestock at San Pedro, harassing shipments to the capital. A commander at Zinguilucan chased attackers with little success as contests over production and marketing continued around Otumba.[74] Facing long-insurgent and still recalcitrant villagers, pulque capitalism proved slow to revive.

Oligarchs in Distress

Don José Sánchez Espinosa remained in the capital as insurgency waned and agrarian capitalism dissolved from 1818 to 1820. He collected rents from families who ruled cultivation and marketing at La Teja. Around Otumba, he left cultivation to tenants while struggling to profit in pulque. La Griega returned to planting on estate account—and profit disappeared. When Puerto de Nieto pacified in 1820, long-insurgent families, many led by strong women, ruled production, paying small rents as tenants. At Bocas and beyond, sharecroppers ruled maize planting, herdsmen shared in the products of sheep grazing, while the priest-patriarch looked to profit in local markets for alcoholic drink. His titled son the Conde de Peñasco lived in San Luis Potosí, adapting to sharecropping and shared grazing while joining the new economy of alcohol. Could oligarchs prosper as families ruled maize making everywhere and took new gains from grazing and pulque production?

The earnings of Sánchez Espinosa's Obra Pía estates, including his Bajío and San Luis Potosí properties, offer a fair index of landed prospects and challenges: they held near 30,000 pesos in 1807–8, before the regime break and the last years of predatory profit taking, when profits surely peaked.[75] They fell to 15,000 pesos in 1811–12 as insurgency set in; returned to 30,000 as counterinsurgency solidified; then fell back to 15,000 in 1820—half the level of prerevolutionary times as peace returned while family production entrenched across regions that once sustained a now devastated silver capitalism. Sánchez Espinosa and Peñasco remained great proprietors while profits plummeted and their prospects as landed capitalists were uncertain, at best.

Parallel challenges faced the Condes de Regla, New Spain's richest mining and landed clan when insurgencies began. The second conde ruled mines at Real del Monte, vast pulque estates nearby, cereal lands in the Bajío, and grazing lands beyond. When he died in 1809, he was propertied beyond his oligarchic peers, yet unlike Sánchez Espinosa, he faced rising debts in times of trade disruption and imperial revenue demands.[76] To limit the decline, his wife, Condesa de Jala and owner of great pulque estates in her own right, took over management of the Regla estates before he died.[77] She ruled through the decade of insurgency, even after her son, don Pedro Josê, third Conde de Regla, gained legal majority, inherited vast properties, and won a seat on the Mexico City Council in 1814. Carrying the clan through times of challenge, she struggled to operate mines at Real del Monte and estates near the capital, through the Mezquital, into the Bajío, and extending north. Her letters are revealing.

In August 1812, she wrote to don Pedro Sierra, general manager of Regla enterprises at Real del Monte and across the Mezquital, lamenting that mines and estates near Zimapán in the northern Mezquital were lost to insurgents. She worried that limited mining at Real del Monte and the estates still working in the southern Mezquital did not make enough to sustain the family and to pay the forces needed to repel Otomí insurgents ransacking properties. She thanked Sierra for setting a troop at the Ajuchitlán estate near San Juan del Río yet insisted it could not be paid on Regla account.

Attuned to the debates of the day, she excoriated the manager for preferring immigrant Spaniards over Americans in managerial roles. Her family power came in Euro-American fusions: her immigrant grandfather had traded, profited, and pioneered pulque capitalism on the land; her American father negotiated to marry her to the American son of an immigrant father who traded, took riches in mines, then bought rich Jesuit lands. The Regla–Jala union merged Euro-American capital to forge a clan ruling New Spain's silver capitalism. To the condesa, favoring *gachupines* in times of insurgency would alienate oligarchs and fuel insurgents' divisive rhetoric. She also reprimanded Sierra for maligning American managers (like don Manuel Olguín at Tulancalco) who deflected insurgents while negotiating to preserve production. Her message (like Olguín's): guard scarce funds, negotiate to keep property, survive—and hope to rebuild.[78]

Letters to kin and allies in Europe reveal deepening pessimism. To her brother-in-law don José, Marques de San Cristóbal, living in London while she oversaw his estates, the condesa reported disruptions of his northern holdings and few earnings. He would accept the stipend she sent.[79] To her friend doña Ines de Jaúregui, wife of José de Iturrigaray, the viceroy deposed in 1808, she lamented the travails of "la casa de mi hijo," the third conde. In March 1813, as insurgents ruled between Real del Monte and the capital, she worried about production, transport, and communication. An October note to her agent in Madrid saw insurgency devouring "this beautiful country" while "disease" plagued "a sad and unhappy people."

Early in 1814, the condesa lamented a life she saw as impoverished: "It costs great difficulty to find a peso, when before one gained thousands with little effort." A year later, she congratulated Iturrigaray on his vindication by the restored Fernando while lamenting that New Spain continued to die in a "fiesta of blood." To his wife, she wrote: "Popular risings are like the waves of the sea; when they land on the sand of the beach, everything dies." As 1816 began, she simply noted that war and poverty persisted, finding no optimism in the calming across the Mezquital.[80]

Still, through years of disruption and despair, the condesa kept the Casa de Regla whole. In October 1817, the young third conde, now a captain in the Royal Cavalry, gained possession of the Marquesado de San Cristóbal. His uncle don José had died in Europe of self-administered drug experiments. When an illegitimate son claimed his title and properties, the condesa ensured that both came to the third conde, whose affairs she ruled. The San Cristóbal estates, including Xalpa in the pulque zone and La Gavia west of

Toluca, remained in family hands. When the third conde could not pay 3,000 pesos to confirm possession, she did, setting a mortgage on his properties.[81]

While the condesa was alive she defended her son's interests and kept creditors at bay. After her death, in November 1819, they forced the High Court of Mexico City to open an auction of non-entailed estates valued at 800,000 pesos, including Ajuchitlán near San Juan del Río, San Francisco near Huichapan, and pulque properties in the northern Mezquital—all recently rattled by insurgency. Although they were offered below their historic values, no one bid. The young conde kept properties as debts mounted.[82]

In 1820, the Spanish monarchy still reigned and don Pedro José Romero de Terreros held four titles of nobility. He was "Gentleman of the Order of his Majesty Fernando VII, . . . Knight of the Order Carlos Tercero," and Familiar of the Inquisition, while also captain of the Viceregal Guard in Mexico City.[83] Rich in honors and lands, after a decade of revolutionary insurgencies and their widening reverberations, the third Conde de Regla was drowning in debt.

Meanwhile, in Guanajauto, silver mining drowned in flood at Valenciana while pacifications protected property by conceding production to family growers. In Querétaro, counterinsurgency capitalism broke profit while oligarchs conceded production on shares across San Luis Potosí. In pulque zones near the capital, resistant villagers kept profits scarce. A decade of revolution broke silver capitalism, undermined the agrarian capitalisms that sustained it, and rattled patriarchy as women took new powers in families on the land and in oligarchic clans. Armed force was everywhere, defending property, taking redistributions, protecting new lives on the land. When forces led by don Agustín Iturbide declared a Mexican empire in 1821 silver capitalism was gone, the future most uncertain.

PART III

Seeking Mexico,
1820–1830

As the World Turned

Imperial Dreams, Capital Failures,
National Challenges

In 1821, don Agustín Iturbide led a coalition of men who had fought to block political independence, then to contain the Bajío revolution—and now turned to proclaim Mexico an independent empire. They faced daunting challenges after the conflicts of 1808 to 1820 had rattled Spain's empire and broken silver capitalism. Napoleon's 1808 occupation of Madrid left a monarchy without monarchs. The regime of judicial mediation that kept social peace in a kingdom of economic dynamism and deep inequities fell in the military coup of 1808. Hidalgo's 1810 political revolt challenged rule by a broken empire, opening the way to mass risings that attacked property to redress social predations.

In the decade of conflict that followed his defeat, support for political independence proved limited while popular insurgents fought hard in pursuit of sustainable family lives making maize on the land. Their efforts strangled the mining that had made New Spain the richest society in the Americas, cutting the trades linking Europe, Asia, and the Americas that powered global commercial capitalism.

In 1812, with military power locked in and silver capitalism gone, the Cádiz Constitution promised new rights and participations aimed to back military efforts to reclaim Spain and preserve the empire. A new liberal order claimed legitimacy by promising (almost) universal (male) rights. In New Spain, political resistance waned while Guanajuato insurgents fought on. They turned once profitable estates into communities of family growers, breaking the agrarian capitalism long at the foundation of silver capitalism in the Bajío. When Fernando VII reclaimed his throne in 1814 and abrogated the liberal constitution, the regime held while popular insurgencies carried on in New Spain.

In 1820, mining remained in collapse while the loyalist military orchestrated pacification settlements across Guanajuato: insurgent communities entrenched on the land recognized estate property and agreed to pay modest rents backed by amnestied guerrillas now sanctioned as "patriotic militias." There would be no return to commercial cultivation, no resumption of profiteering from dearth. Family growers, including many women, ruled rural life across Guanajuato, eating well and supplying local markets, while agrarian capitalism broke in neighboring Querétaro, families claimed new control of production on estates north in San Luis Potosí, and villagers pressed independence in the Mezquital and the world of pulque between the capital and the Real del Monte mines.

The primary beneficiaries of the Bajío revolution were families gaining control of production on the land. Beyond New Spain, the lead beneficiary was industrial England. When the collapse of silver broke long pivotal global trades in Chinese silks and Indian cottons after 1812, markets opened for the emerging industrial textiles of Lancashire, driving the expansion of plantation slavery across the US South. As peace came to New Spain in 1820, a new Anglo-American economy of industry and slavery rose to make a new global capitalism.

Then, in 1821, Spanish military men forced a return to Cádiz liberalism as the price of sailing to defend the empire in the Americas. In New Spain, Iturbide opposed the return and mobilized armed forces to proclaim the Plan de Iguala. Backed by struggling oligarchs and churchmen worried by liberal anticlericalism, Iturbide dreamed of a Mexican empire sustained by a restoration of silver capitalism. Silver proved slow to revive and his empire soon fell, leaving Mexico to face a decade of political uncertainty and commercial depression while families flourished on the land.

Iturbide's Impossible Empire

As the forces that had fought for a decade to preserve regime power and property rights in New Spain appeared to triumph in 1820, officials and commanders, bankrupt mine operators and struggling oligarchs, newly entrenched rancheros and persistent communities turned to restoring order after years of conflict and disruption. It was not to be. The same year, forces assembling to sail to South America refused to embark unless Fernando revived the Cádiz Constitution. He had little choice. Power in Spain had been contested by armed force since 1808. The liberal charter of 1812, written to sustain Fernando's rights to rule Spain and the empire, helped him reclaim the throne in 1814. When he abrogated the Constitution, men fighting for power in New Spain acquiesced to focus on fighting insurgents. When officers led by Colonel Rafael Riego demanded reinstatement, pressing armed power to reclaim liberal rights in 1820, Fernando acquiesced. He knew the military bases of his rule.[1]

New Spain's oligarchs, officials, and church leaders had accepted the liberal charter in 1812, limiting its radical provisions to maintain the fight against political and popular insurgents. Still, neither the powers set in Mexico City nor the political insurgents who fought for independence had committed to the Cádiz charter—written in Spain, with Iberian interests the first concern. Now, in 1820, political insurgents were marginalized and popular insurgents had pacified, while Spanish liberalism had become more anticlerical and threatening to oligarchs facing demise in New Spain.[2]

Soon after the news of Riego's coup and the liberal restoration arrived, the viceroy ordered Iturbide to capture Vicente Guerrero, a political ally of Morelos still in rebellion in the Pacific hot country. Instead, Iturbide raised a coalition of the military men, oligarchs, and church leaders to proclaim the Plan de Iguala early in 1821, drawing Guerrero in too.[3] The plan was complex and often contradictory. Addressed to the viceroy of New Spain, it called a Supreme Junta of North America to protect Catholicism and found a Mexican empire—to be ruled by Fernando VII.

The mobilizations and militarizations begun in 1808 focused Iturbide's mind. Through August and into September of that pivotal year, Viceroy Iturrigaray and key Mexico City oligarchs had moved toward calling a Junta of New Spain. The Junta of Seville, declaring itself Supreme, sent emissaries that organized the coup, toppled the viceroy, and imposed military rule—with Iturbide among the forces occupying the capital. Now, in 1821, he raised military power to call a Supreme Junta of North America to found an empire proclaimed Mexican, named for the city stymied in 1808.[4] Iguala locked in the militarization of power begun by the coup of 1808—while aiming to reverse its imposition of rule set in Spain.

In 1808, military power blocked a junta backed by Mexico City oligarchs. In 1821, Iguala mobilized military power in service of oligarchs rattled by a decade of revolution.[5] The plan offered rhetorical conciliation to defeated political insurgents: the call for a Supreme Junta of *North America* honored Morelos' 1814 declaration of North American independence at Apatzingán. Iturbide named the new empire Mexican, honoring the city of Mexico and the financial, commercial, and landed oligarchs concentrated there. Then, knowing that a Mexican empire ruling North America was an uncertain innovation, the first three articles addressed New Spain, the kingdom that the men of Iguala (except Guerrero) had fought to protect and sustain.

The first article followed Spanish imperial tradition and the Cádiz Constitution in asserting the religious monopoly of Catholicism and the Church. The second proclaimed that "New Spain is independent of the Old, and all other powers." The third promised a monarchy, "moderated" by a "Constitution written for the Kingdom"—New Spain. The empire to be built in New Spain was then complicated by Article 4, calling Fernando to accept the Mexican crown. If he did not come, a Mexican Cortes would invite another member of the "Reigning House" to sit as emperor. Independence would come with a dynasty shared with Spain.

Was the call to Fernando a nod to tradition, a continuation of the recognition of *el deseado* by political actors in Spain and New Spain from 1808 to 1814? Did Iturbide expect Fernando to come? Perhaps. João II still ruled the Portuguese empire from Rio de Janeiro in 1821. Might the first global empires carry on based in their richest new-world kingdoms? This intriguing possibility might have led to a very different nineteenth-century world. Still, everyone knew the fall of silver: Iturbide, Mexico City oligarchs, and Fernando, too. Why take his throne to a kingdom in economic collapse, to be constrained by local military powers? Why trade Riego's army for Iturbide's? The call to Fernando offered a mirage of legitimacy for a Mexican empire set in military power—and uncertain in all else.

In the Iguala plan, the army set mandates prior to knowing who would reign or the constitution to come. First: "All the inhabitants of New Spain, without distinction among Europeans, Africans, and Indios are citizens of the Monarchy." The inclusion of Europeans countered the anti-Spanish rhetoric that had fueled political insurgency; the inclusion of people of African ancestry reversed Cádiz in a nod to Guerrero, a political insurgent of African roots leading mulatto guerrillas.

Next, the plan guaranteed the persons and properties of all citizens. The defense of property affirmed the Iguala coalition's rejection of popular insurgencies. The defense of individual rights left in question the corporate rights to land and self-rule that defined indigenous republics and long sustained social peace and silver capitalism in the heartland. The Cádiz charter had challenged those rights. Calleja had blocked implementation, fearing resistance. Iturbide and Iguala demurred.

Third, the plan confirmed the separate judicial rights (*fueros*) of the clergy while saying nothing about Church capital and property, points of contention since the Consolidation of 1805–8. Left unresolved, the questions of indigenous and ecclesiastical rights and properties would define Mexico's nineteenth century—often in conflictive ways.

The plan then designated the army as the "Military Protector . . . of the Three Guarantees." The first guarantee promised, again, to enforce the institutional and religious monopoly of the Catholic church, with the status of its properties left uncertain. The second defended independence—after offering the throne to Fernando. The third guaranteed "the intimate union of Americans and Europeans," again defying the anti-European passions of defeated political insurgents.

The union of Spaniards spoke to Mexico City oligarchs. For centuries their power was made and reinforced by immigrant men from Spain who built wealth in mining and trade, then married American landed heiresses, fusing capital and land to consolidate enduring wealth. Generations of "intimate unions" forged oligarchic power and sustained silver capitalism.[6] The political conflicts that exploded in 1808 had unleashed resentments of *gachupines*, immigrants favored in trade and high office. Political insurgents enflamed those resentments after 1810, aiming to deflect popular ire from American landlords whose properties faced assault by rural insurgents. In 1821, if a Mexican empire was to revive silver capitalism, unity among European and American Spaniards must hold. Iguala's third guarantee defended the oligarchy that had built silver capitalism.

The rest of the plan focused on military power—asserted in the coup of 1808, intensified in wars among political insurgents, popular guerrillas, and loyalist armies from 1810 to 1820. It was an entrenched outcome of years of revolutionary assertions and regime defense. By August 1821, military power backed by worried churchmen and struggling oligarchs enabled Iturbide to occupy New Spain's key cities. In the Treaty of Córdoba, signed on August 24, Spanish emissary Juan O'Donoju accepted Iguala, awaiting a decision by Fernando.

When Fernando rejected the Mexican crown and declared New Spain in rebellion, Iturbide claimed the throne and proclaimed himself emperor of Mexico. Fernando's refusal marked the definitive break with Spain. Others dreamed of great beginnings, shared in a flourishing press.[7] Nothing was resolved. Power was uncertain and profit remained scarce while communities and families focused on making local lives. Mexico was a dream. Emperor and empire soon fell, toppled by republicans who mobilized armed forces led by Antonio López de Santa Anna.[8]

In 1824, Mexico was re-founded as a federal republic. Still, silver did not revive, armed forces neither demobilized nor depoliticized, ideological and political conflicts persisted—while communities held strong on the land. Contemporary observers saw that foundational challenge. Men struggling to build a new state in Guanajuato knew that without silver they had little to rule. Dreams of reviving mining focused their attention.[9] Lucas Alamán knew too. A son of Guanajuato's mining elite, he had traveled in Europe during years of insurgency, then returned to see pure destruction. He pressed for a revival of mining while honoring Spain's political and cultural traditions.[10]

Clear recognition of the fall of silver, the constraints on national prospects, and the obstacles to revival came from Anglophone emissaries who aimed to open Mexico as a place of investment and trade for the industrial powers rising in the wake of the Bajío revolution. Joel Robert Poinsett, a Congressman from South Carolina, traversed Mexico in 1822 as Iturbide struggled to retain power, detailing the early empire's daunting challenges.[11] Henry Ward joined the first British delegation to Mexico in late 1823 after Iturbide's fall, as London bankers negotiated to fund an uncertain federal republic. He returned as chargé d'affaires from 1825 into 1827, while British investors aimed to revive silver and British manufacturers promoted textile exports, dreaming of trade that would accelerate England's rise. In time, Ward came to understand why British capital could not revive Mexican mines and London loans could not save Mexico's republic.[12] Poinsett and Ward illuminate the challenges left by the decade of revolution and Mexico's early struggles to revive silver and make a nation.

Poinsett's Report: Mexico in Crisis, 1822

When Joel Robert Poinsett landed at Veracruz in October 1822, Spanish forces still held the San Juan de Ulloa fortress, Antonio López de Santa Anna commanded the port, yellow fever threatened life, Iturbide struggled to rule, and "the state of commerce [was] deplorable."[13] Passing through the once prosperous textile city of Puebla, Poinsett saw great churches, palatial homes, and desperate poverty. Ignoring the impact of cloth imports on the local economy, he blamed indigence on "a mild climate and a fertile soil, yielding abundantly to moderate exertions. . . . The people rarely possess habits of industry."[14] It was a revealing bias from a newcomer from South Carolina, where production depended on enslaved hands.

When he arrived in Mexico City, a tour revealed a mix of grandeur and poverty—and rich markets stocked with produce raised, delivered, and sold by native people from Xochimilco and Chalco. Poinsett visited the Conde de Regla, known for "his great possessions, his rich mines, and vast landed estates." He was greeted by a new condesa, "very beautiful and amiable," a young mother who turned to politics. Poinsett "found her very intelligent, and decidedly opposed to the present order of things, which she assures me are contrary to the wishes of the nation, and in opposition to all that is virtuous and enlightened in the country." After avoiding politics and debates with his wife, "the Count took us to see his stables."[15]

As October ended, Poinsett got to the business of his mission—silver. He visited the Casa de Apartado, where gold was separated from silver before the latter was minted to make the pesos that had long shaped New Spain's economy and driven global trades. He visited the mint standing in the shadow of the great cathedral that blessed the power and wealth drawn to New Spain's capital (figure 7.1). He reported Humboldt's figures showing the mint had processed more than 20 million pesos yearly in the 1790s, peaked at 26 million in 1809—to collapse to 4.5 million in 1812, slowly climb to 12 million in 1819, then fall back under 6 million in 1821. Economic collapse was unmistakable. Poinsett returned to his lodgings to learn that Iturbide had dissolved a congress that would not bend to his will. The fusion of economic dissolution and political fragility was clear.[16]

On December 3, Poinsett met Iturbide. He saw a cruel usurper "distinguished for his immorality, . . . his exercise of power arbitrary and tyrannical." Coached by the new Condesa de Regla, Poinsett saw "a government not founded on public opinion, but established and supported by corruption and violence." It "cannot exist without ample means to pay the soldiery. . . . Aware of the state of his funds, . . . he is making great exertions to negotiate loans in England." Mexico required "the support of a great manufacturing and commercial people. We shall gain something, . . . the harvest will be for the British."[17]

Poinsett then reported on the state of commerce. Using Humboldt's figures for 1803, he saw that textile manufacturing, once worth 8 million pesos yearly, had fallen to 4 million. He offered no explanation, while noting that "the coarse cotton cloths of the United States are in great demand." He attributed the fall of mining to "the late revolution," as "the seat of war lay between the principal mines and the capital." He went on: "The water gains upon the

Figure 7.1 The mint, National Palace, and cathedral, Mexico City. Author photo.

mines daily; the roads have become more insecure; the public confidence in the good faith of the government is shaken; and the miner cannot, as formerly, receive immediately the value of the silver he deposits at the mint—the fund destined for that purpose having been used for the exigencies of the state. In the present state of the country, the mines must remain comparatively unproductive. To work them advantageously requires a large capital."[18]

Regime revenues held scarce. Iturbide had recognized 61 million pesos in debts—36 million owed by viceregal authorities, 25 million taken as new loans.[19] With debt ten times current annual silver flows, Iturbide sought new loans in England to pay the military forces that sustained his power. Poinsett noted that in 1804 New Spain's military forces had totaled just over 32,000, two-thirds militias. At the proclamation of Iturbide's empire in 1821, they had risen to 68,000, including 38,000 troops of the line.[20] The contradictions of the moment were clear: military power ruled—and the collapse of silver capitalism left Iturbide without revenues to pay the military and sustain his imagined empire.

Amid his dismally accurate view of Mexico's prospects for mining, manufacturing, and regime stability, Poinsett saw—but did not understand—the agrarian inversions forced by Bajío insurgents. In his narrative of collapse and calamity, he noted: "The agriculture of the kingdom certainly suffered during the wars of the revolution. The most fertile provinces were the theater of all the revolutionary movements. A great deal of capital employed in agriculture was destroyed during that period: but, although the buildings are in ruins, the country appears to be cultivated as extensively and as carefully as ever."[21] The visitor from South Carolina's slave society saw the rich harvests brought by the family production set by the Bajío revolution. He could not explain it—but he began to lose his vision of lazy, unproductive people. He learned more in a later visit to the Bajío.

Ward's First Vision: Urban Desolation, Rural Resilience, and Possibilities—for England, 1823

Henry Ward came to Mexico twice, briefly in 1823 and 1824 after Iturbide's fall, then from 1825 to 1827 as British capital came to revive mines. He kept detailed notes of his encounters and perceptions and on return wrote *Mexico in 1827*, a two-volume work providing a perceptive if often prejudiced vision of Mexico.[22] He began by promoting a Mexican revival in service of industrial Britain. In the end, he reported failures of British capital, a Mexican regime awash in debt, and mines making little silver and less profit. He came to understand how the transformations left by New Spain's decade of revolution created the demand for British capital, limited its chances, and led to its failures.

Landing at Veracruz in December 1823, he found Guadalupe Victoria the governor and commander still facing Spanish siege in the harbor. Ward saw desolation in the port, ragged people in poverty, and Victoria's joy on seeing England ready to engage Mexico's new republic. Heading inland to escape conflict and the tropical climate, Ward found "provisions in abundance" as he passed through inland villages.[23] Ward detoured north of Puebla on reports of riots there. He crossed the plains of Apan, stopping for breakfast at the hacienda San Nicolás, where the Conde de Santiago greeted him graciously—no political conversations noted. He passed flourishing fields of maguey, learned about pulque, and saw Otumba still scarred by years of insurgency. He passed the pyramids at Teotihuacan, slept in their shadows at San Juan, then rode to Guadalupe—greeted there by Foreign Minister Lucas Alamán in an elegant coach made for the deposed Iturbide.[24]

As Ward entered from the north, the capital seemed dismal—until the Alameda and the homes on Calle San Francisco revealed their former opulence. The next day, the cathedral, National Palace, and surrounding streets convinced Ward that "amongst the Capitals of Europe, there were few that could support with any advantage a comparison with Mexico." Visiting the Parián market facing the palace, he "found many articles of domestic manufacture . . . with cotton and woolen cloths from Puebla and Querétaro—a great variety of coloured blankets called *mangas*, used as a cloak while riding by most people, and as a substitute for every other kind of clothing by the lower orders." Noting "a slew of silversmiths" and "cumbrous furniture," Ward saw that "all the other contents of the shops appear to be European, but the supply was scanty, and the price enormous."[25]

In contrast, Ward was struck by the plentiful fruits, vegetables, and flowers in Mexico City's markets and by the hardy people who made and sold them. He offered a long list of tropical fruits and others from northern climes. He was transfixed by the rich chinampas of Xochimilco and life on the canals that delivered their produce to city markets. He saw two classes of canoes, large ones capable of carrying three families and their produce to market and mostly worked by men; small ones worked by women who paddled their own wares and children to market. He noted "the gesticulation of these ladies, when animated by a little pulque on their return home, their extreme volubility, and the energy they display in their quarrels with the tribes of children which they carry about with them." Awed by the strength and agility of the men and women of the chinampa communities that fed the city, Ward saw Mexico's larger challenges.[26] He documented that "a civil war carried on with unexampled cruelty on both sides, had desolated the country for thirteen years." The break with Spain done and Iturbide gone, "the form of government . . . was not definitely decided," while "the population bespoke poverty and distress."[27]

Ward explained, "Trade was in an absolute state of stagnation; for most of the old Spanish capitalists had withdrawn . . . and no new channel of communication had been opened to supply their place. . . . The mines were in like manner abandoned, and all the numberless individuals who depended on these two great sources of national prosperity for subsistence, were reduced to absolute want." He continued, "The effects of such a state of things were felt by every class of society, for a great depreciation in the value of agricultural produce was the consequence of the general distress; and many landed proprietors, whose incomes in better times exceeded fifty and sixty thousand dollars [pesos], were compelled to reside entirely upon their estates, from the impossibility of keeping up an establishment in the capital."[28]

Ward saw the plenty delivered by the people of Xochimilco and the distress of landlords in the capital; he did not see that low agricultural prices reflected the plenty that filled markets, plenty that served cultivators and consumers—and broke oligarchs' profits. Before leaving the capital, Ward experienced one of the city's enduring challenges: at four in the morning on January 14, 1824, an earthquake jolted him awake. Startled, he learned from neighbors that it was a minor shock that did little damage, one more quake in a city that had survived for centuries.[29]

A quick ride to Veracruz led to a delayed departure due to northerly gales. Stuck in the tropical port in the cold winter months, Ward inquired into the causes and deadly impacts of the *vómito negro*, yellow fever. He learned that while people born on the coast, often of African ancestry, seemed immune, those from temperate climes, whether Europe, North America, or the Mexican plateau, were susceptible and rarely survived. His message: come in winter and go inland quickly. Economies can revive, quakes can be survived, but the vomit kills.[30] Ward sailed home in February 1824.

Ward's Second Take, 1825–1827: Seeking British Gain in Capital-Starved Mexico

In 1825, Ward returned as part of a team sent to negotiate a treaty of recognition. Landing at Veracruz in March, the delegation was greeted with joy based on expectations of "the definitive recognition of Mexican independence." Equally good news, Victoria was now president. Spain still held the castle in Veracruz harbor, but the cannon fire had stopped; and "at the anchorage ground, there were more merchant vessels of different countries assembled than had entered the ports of Mexico in the whole year of 1823." The trade of Ward's dreams had begun.[31]

Heading inland, he "lodged at the house of Madame Santa Ana" in Jalapa. Moving on, Ward spent a day in Puebla, noting its great cathedral, a population of 50,000, and "extensive manufactures of cotton, earthenware, and wool." He attributed Puebla's historic wealth to "a country that has produced during the last two centuries, nearly two-thirds of the whole of the silver raised annually in the world." He lamented a population scattered on the streets, ragged native women among them, as large as the underclass in Mexico City.[32] Ward saw Puebla, once rich and prosperous, devastated by the fall of silver—and the collapse of cloth making as British imports flooded in.

As he approached the capital a second time, he reflected on his travels as if he had not seen the desperation plaguing Puebla: "From the moment that I landed, I had been struck with the progress which, in one year, the country had made. There was everywhere an appearance of more settled habits, more subordination amongst the military, and more respect for the civil authorities. . . . The long files of mules we continually passed on their way from the Coast to the Capital afforded evident proofs of an increase of activity in trade."[33] Political peace and open trade defined progress.

In January 1826, the treaty done, Ward returned to Puebla. The governor and state Congress, "chiefly landed proprietors," had passed

> a law by which every Lépero found naked or begging in the streets was condemned to labour at works . . . undertaken by the government for the improvement of the town for the term of one month; at the end . . . he was set at liberty and provided with decent dress, with the offer of employment if he chose to work, and . . . a double penalty if he relapsed. This law, which was most rigorously enforced at first, produced a wonderful effect; as it was accompanied by the introduction of an excellent night police, it soon freed Puebla from the swarms of vagrants, by which it had been previously infested; and it substituted order and decency for the disgusting license which prevailed amongst the lower orders at the period of my first and second visits.[34]

Free trade needed coercion to constrain people displaced by British cottons made of slave-grown fiber.

Ward ended his reflections on Puebla in 1826 by noting plentiful harvests of "wheat, barley, maize, chile, and frijoles, as well as the fruits of almost every climate. With these the market at Puebla is supplied in the greatest abundance; but agriculture in general is in a very depressed state, there being no mines to create a home market."[35] Mining had collapsed; profit-seeking cultivation was depressed, while markets filled with affordable sustenance provided by plentiful harvests made by families strong on the land. Life in Puebla reflected the Bajío revolution.

Finally, Ward stated bluntly that the cloth makers of Puebla would pay a price due to new floods of imported cloth: "The capital [Puebla] can hardly expect under the present system of free intercourse with Europe, to regain its former importance, which depended, principally, upon the native manu-factures of wool and cotton." Among Puebla's 50,000 people, "a large por-tion of these will, probably, be compelled to have recourse to agricultural labors for support. . . . As there is a general complaint of a want of hands amongst landed proprietors, the general interests of the State will gain by the suppression of a branch of industry in the towns."[36] In Ward's dream, silver would revive and the Republic thrive. Agriculture would return as a source of profit for the landed few. Mexican cloth makers would be sacri-ficed on the altar of British profits.

New Spain, Revolution, and the Challenges of Making Mexico

Arriving with a dark vision of Mexico and hopes for British capital, Ward struggled early to understand Mexico's challenges and the failures of British capital.[37] In a preface, he recalled his early optimism: "Viewed through the medium of delusive hope, Spanish America presented nothing but pros-pects of unalloyed advantage. . . . Capital alone was . . . wanting."[38] Later reflections saw that "the Revolution has affected not only their political, but their commercial relations with the rest of the world; its influence has extended to their agriculture and mines, . . . threatening them with total an-nihilation."[39] He came to understand the depth of the revolution—labeled as such—that had broken New Spain's silver capitalism, undermining the potential to generate wealth in an emerging Mexico.

Facing British capital's failures, Ward turned to classic deflections: "lib-erty can alone repair the evils which the struggle for liberty has caused."[40] Yet silver capitalism was not taken down by men seeking political liberty but by victims of capitalist predations fighting for sustenance and survival. The regime of judicial mediation was broken not by seekers of liberty but by military men fighting to preserve silver for the Spanish fight against Na-poleon. The two fights fused to break silver capitalism, opening the world to new Anglo-American industrial ways grounded in slavery. Ward saw all that obliquely. He could not address the ways England's rise constrained Mexico, so he blamed an imagined political culture, a deflecting construct that still marks Anglophone and liberal visions of Mexico.

Ward then shared fundamental British premises: "Mexico cannot, during the present century, be a manufacturing country, and, probably, will not at-tempt it. Her mines, and her agriculture, will enable her, with only common industry, to enjoy all the advantages of the Transatlantic arts."[41] Nor could

Mexico control its trade. That would fall to the United States and England, the former due to proximity and maritime traditions, the latter as the leading producer of industrial textiles.[42] He recognized the new industrial world as an Anglo-American alliance: he knew that people enslaved in the United States raised essential cotton, that British workers tended machines to make cloth, and that US planters and British industrialists profited, as did merchants of both nations. Mexicans would make silver, feed themselves, and buy cloth—if mines would revive and a government stabilize.

Seeking historical perspective, Ward portrayed New Spain as "a long period of misrule," followed by a revolution that brought "the dissolution of all social ties."[43] His general description of Spain's imperial system and the origins of "the Revolution in Mexico" are primers on British prejudices about everything Spanish: autocracy and imposition, closure and Catholicism.[44] Yet his narrative of the conflicts of 1810 to 1821 began noting that "many of the causes of disaffection . . . existing generally across the Spanish colonies did not extend to Mexico."

He grudgingly recognized that New Spain was different: "Her superior population gave her importance, while her mineral treasures, and her proximity to the Peninsula ensured to her a constant supply of European manufactures. The very process too, by which these treasures were drawn from the bosom of the earth, gave great value to the landed property of the interior, from the intimate connection that must always subsist between mining and agriculture; and this concurrence of favorable circumstances diffused a degree of prosperity throughout the country, which few colonies have ever attained, none, certainly exceeded."[45] Ward learned the power and prosperity of New Spain and its silver capitalism. He could not credit Spain, Spanish Americans, or New Spain's diverse peoples. So he honored "favorable circumstances"—just what the Bajío revolution's breaking of Asian trades delivered to England, enabling its rise to industrial power.

His version of "the Revolution" of 1810 to 1820 emphasized insurgent destructions, political conflicts, and the rapid rise and fall of Iturbide's empire. Blind to the predations that drove popular ire and the militarization of power that broke the stabilizing judicial regime, he saw key outcomes clearly: the collapse of silver, the end of agricultural profit, the persistence of militarized politics, the impossibility of a regime facing rising debts without revenues.

Ward also recognized another pivotal transformation of 1808 to 1821: before 1810, New Spain generated the capital that funded its silver economy and trades with Europe, Asia, and beyond, creating revenues that sustained the viceroyalty, Spain, and the empire. No capital came from Spain or Europe to fund silver capitalism; no funds came from Spain to sustain New Spain's regime. The coming of British capital in the 1820s was a radical reversal of historic flows—another inversion set by the Bajío revolution. In 1823, Ward imagined British capital reviving Mexico to serve England's industrial power. By 1827, he was working to explain Britain's capital failures in Mexico.[46]

British Capital as Regime Revenue: A New Predation

Facing costs doubled by military outlays and revenues halved by the collapse of mining, the search for a Mexican regime began in bankruptcy.[47] From late 1822 into 1824, while military men and political actors brought down Iturbide's empire and looked to found a federal republic, interim officials and informal representatives negotiated with the London firm of Goldschmidt and Company to float bonds with a value of 3.2 million pounds sterling. They sold at 58 percent of face value, bringing in only 1.85 million pounds; Goldschmidt took 750,000 pounds in commissions and fees, delivering just 1.1 million pounds to the emerging Federal Republic—which faced an obligation to pay all 3.2 million pounds over thirty years at 5 percent interest. A rough conversion indicates that the new regime gained 5.5 million pesos in essential immediate revenues and obligations to pay 14.5 million pesos—an impossible burden.

Early 1825 saw the negotiation of a second loan, now with Barclays and Company. The republic in place, President Guadalupe Victoria faced huge deficits. Barclays sold bonds to gain another 3.2 million pounds, again at a discount; after taking its cut, it delivered 1.3 million pounds to Mexico—a slight improvement. Mexico received about 6 million pesos, linked to another obligation to pay 14.5 million pesos.[48]

The Goldschmidt and Barclays loans enabled President Victoria to survive his term. But the funds came with obligations that proved unpayable as silver did not revive and military costs held high. The regime faced constant deficits, unable to pay national expenses or London bondholders. Ward knew little of the London bond negotiations during his visit to Mexico in 1823 and 1824. His return in 1825 came amid mounting challenges and complaints. He returned home in 1827 as London faced a bond market collapse blamed on Mexico—deflecting blame from British bankers.

He reported that New Spain's annual revenues held near 20 million pesos from 1790 to 1810: 10 million covered internal expenses, 12 million flowed out—3 million to other regions of Spain's America, 9 million to Spain. Ward emphasized that before "the Revolution of 1810, Mexico had no public debt."[49] He added that "the deficit in the Revenue, which the Revolution occasioned," came from "the loss of the Mining duties and the Monopoly of Tobacco, both of which were reduced to a mere fraction of their former importance." Wartime taxes and 4 to 5 million pesos in forced loans funded loyal forces while deficits soared. Dreaming of support among struggling financiers and oligarchs, Iturbide recognized wartime obligations; hoping to pacify producing people he cut wartime levies. Mining broken and revenues halved, military costs and regime debts continued to rise, leading to new forced loans, higher taxes, and rising political and social discontent.[50]

The discontent helped bring down Iturbide and fuel the drive toward the Federal Republic, which set a new division of revenues. The tribute, the head tax on indigenous and mulatto men and families, was gone, and no one dared set new levies targeting those who took down silver capitalism. The federal government retained the tobacco monopoly, valuable if it could revive, along with import taxes—valuable if Ward's new world of trade would rise. Mining revenues went to newly sovereign states—valuable if silver revived.[51] In the 1820s, silver held strong only in Zacatecas.

Its tax base constrained, the Federal Republic depended on British loans to pay ongoing expenses.[52] The Goldschmidt loan offered 3.2 million pounds sterling to London and European investors; discounted sales delivered 1.6 million pounds, 420,000 taken as a commission and interest in advance—a nice gain for the bankers. The Mexican regime gained short-term funding at the cost of huge obligations. Said Ward, "The terms . . . are usurious enough." The Barclays loan seemed more promising. Offering another 3.2 million pounds, it brought in 2.8 million pounds. The bank again kept a commission and advanced interest totaling more than 450,000 pounds. But nearly 700,000 pounds paid off Goldschmidt borrowers. Less than 1.4 million pounds, or 6.8 million pesos, came to Mexico's treasury. The second loan delayed default on the first.[53] Then Ward noted that Barclays failed to make good on a promised 300,000 pounds, reducing deliveries to Mexico below 1.1 million pounds, or just over 5 million pesos. From what Ward could learn, the two London loans paid more than 2 million pesos in debts, more than 900,000 pesos paid to the military, and 400,000 went to California. Little remained to fund government costs.[54]

Ward searched for optimism: The end of tributes cost 1.3 million pesos yearly; the shift of silver revenues to the states cost another 5.5 million pesos to federal authorities. He was confident, however, that tariffs on trade were rising toward 7 million pesos—thanks to trade with Britain. He argued that "with time and tranquility . . . to repair the devastation caused by the late struggles, and even if the mines prosper in no ordinary degree in the ensuing years, I should think that 1835 would be the earliest period at which it may reasonably be expected that the receipts of the Mexican Treasury can again equal those of 1803."[55] The London loans, usurious and in default in 1827, raised the debts of the Mexican government and set off anger among British bondholders. Ward knew that bondholders would not be paid until Mexican silver drove rising British trades.

British Trade for British Advantage

Again and again, Ward emphasized that Britain's first interest in Mexico was textile trade: "the declaration of the Army in favor of Independence" brought a political emancipation that was also commercial. Spanish merchants lost preference, replaced by Britons, North Americans, and others. He lamented that early on, US merchants ruled imports through northern Gulf ports, with San Luis Potosí an early entrepôt. A last surge of trade in Spanish ships came in 1820–21. Then, after years of transition and turmoil, trade revived from 1824 with US and British ships carrying mostly British goods.[56]

Ward saw triumph: "Native manufactures . . . have fallen gradually into disuse, as Mexicans have discovered that much better things will be obtained at much lower cost." Local manufactures "will soon disappear altogether. . . . The cotton-spinners at Puebla, and in other towns of the interior, have been compelled to turn their industry into some other channel." He added that "a few of the towns, indeed, may suffer by the change at first, but the general interests of the country will be promoted, as well as those of the foreign manufacturer who . . . must see the demand for European productions increase, exactly in proportion to the decrease in the value of the home-made cotton and woolen manufactures, which averaged, before the Revolution, ten millions of dollars [pesos] annually."[57]

Ward was blunt: Mexicans who lived by making cloth, men and women, indigenous and mixed, would pay for the profits of British merchants and manufactures and those of slave-owning US planters. Profit would flow to a few in England, where thousands spent long hours tending machines, and a few more in the US South, where hundreds of thousands were bound to labor. In Mexico, tens of thousands would be displaced.

Ward's dream faced daunting challenges: Mexico's coinage of silver in the mid-1820s held near 8 million pesos yearly, far from the sum needed to import the "advantageous" 10 million pesos of British cloth.[58] Mexican trade would not reach its potential "until the amount of Silver raised again equals the average annual amount . . . before the Revolution: twenty-four millions of dollars [pesos]."[59] Only then would Mexico serve Britain's advantage. He added a key point: Indian cottons must gain no tariff advantage in Mexico.[60] Ward finally recognized—obliquely—that the rise of British cottons depended on displacing artisan-crafted South Asian wares.

He proclaimed: "Happy indeed will Mexico be when the Congress discovers that the interests of the Government . . . are those of the established merchant, . . . that commerce and the revenue must stand or fall together. Then, and only then, will Mexico attain that station which she seems destined to hold hereafter amongst the great communities of the world; for then, and then only, can the wonderful capabilities of her soil, and the not less wonderful abundance of her mineral treasures, be turned to full account."[61] For a rising industrial Britain, everything turned on textiles and trade; for a Mexico coming out of revolution, everything depended on silver. Ward dreamed that British capital could revive Mexican mines to forge a new union of profit—to England's advantage.

British Capital and Mexican Mines: A Failed Revival

If there was one consensus among Mexican power seekers, it was that silver was the key to commercial prosperity and regime revenues. The British interests served by Ward agreed, emphasizing that Mexican silver should buy British industrial cloth. Together they invited British capitalists to fund silver's revival. Yet writing in 1828, Ward recognized that British capital had failed, not because mines could not revive but because British capital did not adapt to the ways and needs of Mexican mining.

Prior to 1810, New Spain's mines yielded an average of 24 million pesos yearly, exporting more than 22 million pesos. "Since the Revolution," production had fallen to average 11 million pesos while exports had risen to 13 million pesos, more than halving output while exports drained capital. Ward added: "In almost all the Mining Districts, although the towns have been ruined by the emigration of the wealthy inhabitants, whose capitals were formally invested in Mining operations, the lower classes have, throughout the Revolution, found means to draw their subsistence from the mines."[62] Mining had turned to sustain workers and local markets, not capitalists and global trade.

Little improved with British capital. Coinage had dropped to 5 million pesos in 1821 and only risen to 7 million in 1826 (the last data available to Ward), below the average since 1810. He struggled to explain: "This is not to be regarded as . . . a failure on the part of the Companies, but . . . that the capital introduced by them had not proved an equivalent for the capital previously withdrawn; or . . . that time had not been allowed to repair the ruinous consequences of the sudden extraction of that capital, and the suspension of all mining."[63] Ward clung to hope.

He added that "before the Revolution . . . almost all classes of the community were interested in the success of the mines. . . . The vast floating capital invested in them . . . gave an impulse to Mining operations altogether unprecedented in the history of the world. . . . If public tranquility had continued undisturbed, the mining produce of Mexico, at the present day, would have exceeded, by at least one-third, the utmost of the richest years before the Revolution."[64] He saw the power of silver capitalism and the destructions of the Bajío revolution—still blind to the capitalist predations that provoked it.

Ward did praise the "fluidity" of the "floating" capital generated by the Mexico City merchant-financiers who for centuries funded silver mines and global trades. They financed multiple mines over long years to counter inherent risks, in time claiming profits and fueling rising silver flows.

> The Civil War entirely destroyed . . . communication between the highest and lowest classes of mining speculators. In many districts, the haciendas of the rescatadores [independent refiners] who bought and processed worker shares and scavengers' finds were ruined, as were the machinery and works of the mines themselves. In others, water was allowed to accumulate to an immense extent, in consequence of the suspension of all the usual labours; while in all, the merchants who had before supplied funds for carrying on the different operations, withdrew their capitals, as soon as the intercourse between the seat of Government and the provinces was interrupted.

He continued:

> In the years 1811 and 1812, the agricultural produce of the country likewise decreased so rapidly, that it became difficult to procure the means of subsistence. The mining towns were surrounded by Insurgent parties, which occupied the whole of the open country, which made it impossible either to receive supplies, or to make remittances, without the protection of a large escort; while the exactions of the officers, by whom these escorts were commanded, (exactions which were reduced to a system, and in which the Viceroy himself [Calleja]

largely participated), doubled the price of quicksilver, and every other article consumed in the mines.

All this "reduced the value of silver."

Still, "the real evil of the Revolution . . . was not the destruction of the *matériel* of the mines . . . that could have prevented them from recovering as soon as the first fury of the Civil War had subsided." It was "the want of confidence, and the constant risk to which capitals were exposed, which . . . led to the dissolution of a system, which had required three centuries to bring to the state of perfection in which it existed at the start of the War of Independence."[65]

Ward now saw New Spain's silver economy as a "state of perfection," high praise for silver capitalism—without the name: "I do not believe that I am guilty of any exaggeration in stating, that there never was a greater spirit of enterprise, more liberality, or . . . better faith, displayed in any part of the world, than amongst the miners of Mexico before the year 1810." The fall came "after the great convulsions of 1810, 1811, and 1812," when "nothing remained to denote, amidst the general wreck, the epoch of splendor which had so immediately preceded it."[66]

Ward exalted the profitable productivity of New Spain's silver capitalism. He would not see the predations that drove rural people across Guanajuato to rise in 1810 to claim food and the land to make it—sustaining families first, rattling local trade, bringing down mining and the global trades it drove. He would never report that the fall of Asian trades had enabled Britain's industrial rise.

British capital was the only remedy he could imagine, a solution not aimed at reviving silver capitalism but at funding British industry and trade. He listed the joint ventures linking Mexican mine owners and British investors in 1827: the Real del Monte Company tied the Regla family mines to British operators led by Captain Vetch; the Anglo-American Company linked Valenciana and Mellado at Guanajuato to mines at San Luis Potosí under the direction of Mr. Williamson; the United Mexican Company operated the Rayas and Cata mines at Guanajuato, along with Quebradillo and others on the Veta Grande at Zacatecas, all managed by Lucas Alamán, Mr. Glennie, and Mr. Agassis.

The Real del Monte Company had invested 400,000 pounds (2 million pesos). Of a promised 1 million pounds, the Anglo-American Company had delivered 800,000 pounds (4 million pesos). United Mexican Company promised 1.2 million pounds and invested 800,000 (another 4 million pesos). Smaller British, US, and German projects brought total investment to 2.75 million pounds (nearly 14 million pesos).[67]

Ward then offered an explanation of limited outcomes. He focused first on the depth of destructions and the accompanying floods, costing great investment and endless labors. British industrial pumps found some success at Real del Monte but generally foundered on the costs of carrying such heavy equipment into the Mexican highlands, only to face scarcities of timber (after centuries of mining) and the absence of coal. Ward concluded that except at Real del Monte, traditional ways of drainage by mule-driven whims and adits (tunnels driven to drain water from below working veins) were most cost effective. Attempts to recruit Cornish and other British miners failed too (again, except at Real del Monte). Ward came to appreciate the skilled efforts of Mexican mine workers when fairly remunerated for the risks inherent in dangerous labors.

With slow learning, joint ventures carried on. But except at Zacatecas (where insurgency was limited), few saw rising production or profits for Mexican mine owners, joint companies, or British investors.[68] Ward repeatedly described the underlying problem: to gain concessions to operate mines, companies committed to annual payments to the Reglas and other owners. To recruit capital in England, they promised regular dividends to investors. Yet such commitments were incompatible with the inherent risks of Mexican mining; they had never marked funding by New Spain's merchant financiers. Silver mining was by definition costly and risky—deep underground, chasing veins of ore that came and went, facing floods and collapse. Such challenges were constant in boom times; they deepened when insurgency destroyed mines, refineries, and established ways of operation.

In the eighteenth century, capital accumulation and investment in Mexico City built on flexible (Ward called it fluid) financing to surmount risks, fund mining and trade, profit the most fortunate, and sustain an industry of dynamic inequities. Merchant financiers joined Atlantic and Asian trades to gain capital to invest in mining. They contracted with multiple mine operators, often in several centers, to advance cash, supplies, and mercury in exchange for receipt of the first silver flows from the mines. As long as many mines continued to produce, operators and financiers carried on. When mines failed, as many did, operators faced bankruptcy while financiers carried on funding multiple operations. When mines boomed, as they did rarely, but spectacularly at Regla's Real del Monte and at Rayas and Valenciana at Guanajuato, operators gained fame and fortune—and invested in the security of commercial estates. Merchant financiers gained ample rewards too, continued in finance and trade, and in time also invested in landed operations.

Notably, there was never a date set for mine operator profits or investor dividends. In a world of great risk and greater potential gain, everyone—operators and refiners, traders and financiers, and workers, too—carried on until a few became rich and powerful, more prospered, many saw failure, and too many faced maiming injuries, even death. It was a raw, competitive, and risky capitalism that drove New Spain and global trades to 1810.[69]

With the collapse of silver flows and Asian trades after 1810 to 1812, the chance to make capital in Mexico City ended. Established financiers did not leave the business of silver; popular insurgents ended the business of making silver at Guanajuato and capital in Mexico City. After 1821, with silver mines drowned and Asian trades broken, British capital appeared the only source of financing. But Mexican mine owners, facing collapse while holding landed wealth mired in debt, demanded annual payment for rights to work their mines. British investors demanded regular dividends. But the expectation of regular payments from mines that might produce nothing for years while risks of collapse, physical and financial, remained, limited chances of success. Ward reported that payments made cut the funds available for infrastructure; payments not made led to debts that limited future investment. British capital lacked the flexibility, the fluidity, that marked silver capitalism before 1810, undermining chances of revival.

It was not just mining that had collapsed but the larger integrated complex of silver capitalism. Insurgencies led to flooded and collapsed mines and a sharp downturn in silver flows. The fall of mining broke the global trades tied to silver, ending the capital accumulation that drove everything. The larger integrated system could not revive as British industrial textiles claimed global markets, blocking the Asian trades and capital accumulations that had fueled silver capitalism. British capitalists might dream of reviving Mexican mines. They would never fund Asian cloth trades, enable capital accumulation by Mexico City merchant financiers, or support a renewal of Mexican cloth making. They aimed to restore Mexican mining—while blocking any revival of silver capitalism.

When British investors demanded scheduled payments, they inhibited the revival of mines defined by uncertainties and risks. They did not know the structure of fluid capital that had built and sustained a risky yet dynamically profitable silver capitalism. Ward learned of those realities after years in Mexico. Surely, Lucas Alamán, son of the Guanajuato mining elite, knew them, as did the Conde de Regla, grandson of the greatest of New Spain's silver capitalists. Mexican mine owners knew the challenges of reviving their mines. They, too, demanded regular payments, joining British financiers and managers in shifting risks to British bondholders—as had the London bankers who funded a desperate Mexican regime in 1823 and 1824. They colluded in parallel failures ultimately grounded in the transformations forced by Bajío revolutionaries—as Ward had also learned.

By 1827, London bonds faced default. Mexican mines yielded little silver and less profit. British brokers gained; British investors got little. The Mexican regime and Mexican mining limped on while Mexico's promise in London capital markets collapsed while British cloth flooded into Mexico.

Mexico After Silver Capitalism—the Politics of Impossibility

With London loans leading to default and deficits, with British trade destroying Mexican cloth making, and with British capital unable to revive Mexican mines, a stable national state remained an impossible dream marked by militarized politics. Revenues held near half the levels normal before 1810. Military men and their troops ruled politics and had to be paid—costs absent before 1810 that doubled regime outlays after 1820, ensuring endless deficits. Families entrenched on the land blocked revivals of agrarian capitalism in the Bajío and beyond, while heartland communities retrenched on their lands to claim higher wages for seasonal labor, leaving commercial cultivation without profit around the capital too.[70]

Through the 1820s, those seeking a national regime faced endless frustrations. This is not the place to sort out the morass of early Mexican politics. The end of judicial mediation, the militarization of politics, and the fall of silver capitalism explain almost everything. The political details are confounding, mostly revealing the flailing of men seeking power. Still, key conflicts reveal more.

With the collapse of Iturbide's empire, political and military men turned to found a federal republic. The preference for a republic, pressed by military men led by Antonio López de Santa Anna, reflected discontent with Iturbide's imperial impositions.[71] The turn to federalism, sovereign states linked in a national republic, has been less emphasized.[72] The Preamble to the 1824 Constitution emphasized why Mexico's diverse regions needed distinct laws. Lorenzo de Zavala, president of the Constituent Congress, wrote: "What rules of convergence and uniformity can be shared between the hot lands of Veracruz and the icy mountains of New Mexico? How could the same institutions rule the people of California and Sonora and those of Yucatán and Tamaulipas?"

The challenge was how to deliver laws appropriate to such diversity in a political world remade by liberal visions. New Spain had mobilized its diversity to generate and sustain power, prosperity, and stability thanks to diverse laws for diverse peoples, notably for indigenous republics, and to judicial mediations that aimed to balance conflicting claims. The decade of conflict just passed entrenched distinct regional ways of production and power, social relations and culture—while the Cádiz Constitution convinced liberals like Zavala that every polity needed universal laws and common ways of justice.

Federalism appeared to be the solution: universal laws designed for diverse regions. The Preamble continued: "Here are the advantages of a federal system: to give every people laws appropriate to their customs, locality, and other circumstances," enabling all "to dedicate themselves without constraints to the creation and betterment of every way of prosperity; setting at the head of administration men who love their homeland and have the knowledge to develop it with skill." Mexico needed states and laws adapted to its regional diversities.

While the dream might appear inclusive and liberating, Zavala added that the states of Mexico's republic must "create the courts necessary for the quick punishment of delinquents, the protection of property, and the security of their inhabitants."[73] Mexico's republicans would make multiple states with laws appropriate to their diversity, universally enforced to protect property—without mediations to accommodate diverse local interests, ways of life, and cultures.

The distribution of revenues remained a challenge. The tributes paid by indigenous and mulatto men had ended, a necessity of pacification. Mining revenues went to the states, accepted by national authorities in times of mining collapse. Had silver revived, states from Mexico (the heartland and more) to Guanajuato, San Luis Potosí and Zacatecas, Durango and Chihuahua might have flourished. With mining strong only at Zacatecas, that state became pivotally important and powerful in the 1820s and 1830s.[74] The collapse of textiles spread poverty and made revenues scarce in states across the interior highlands; the fall of cotton production in Pacific lowlands struck growers and revenues there.

With tariffs and other levies on international trade kept low by a national regime dependent on British capital and trade, revenues could never cover costs kept high by military expenditures. Federalism might forge laws appropriate to Mexico's diverse regions and peoples, but the fall of mining rattled commercial ways everywhere and the collapse of textiles left people in diverse regions without viable lives. London loans sustained the presidency of Guadalupe Victoria from 1824 to 1828—while political uncertainties and divisions escalated.

In a society long grounded in Catholicism and committed to it by Cádiz liberalism and Iturbide's Iguala, early republican factions focused on two Masonic rites. The Scottish Rite came from Spain and appealed to conservative interests dreaming of restoring New Spain and the power of Mexico City. The York Rite came with Poinsett when he returned as US ambassador in 1825. It appealed to liberal and provincial interests. With no solutions to mining collapse and revenue deficits in sight, Yorkinos pressed a vocal anti-Spanish, anti-*gachupín* campaign. Reviving the mantra Hidalgo and Allende had used to try to unite political rebels and stop popular raiding of American Spaniards' estates, Yorkinos aimed to blame the new nation's problems on Spanish immigrants—not British predations.

Spanish immigrants had been key participants in the commercial-financial world that financed mining and invested in commercial estates during silver capitalism's decades of dynamism.[75] The revolution that broke silver capitalism also broke its leading financiers. Many had returned to Spain. Few who came in the 1820s were wealthy or powerful. Those who remained were often aging bureaucrats or provincial traders. Why mobilize to expel them? Yorkinos inflamed passions in campaigns of deflection, promoting provincial and reforming interests while mining failed to revive, debts rose, and British imports corroded textile communities. The expulsion law of 1827 led to few departures.[76] The anti-Spanish campaign did fuel the rise of Vicente Guerrero as an alternative to those who had backed Guadalupe Victoria and hoped to hold power after 1828.

Guerrero, the mulatto former muleteer and political heir to Morelos, had joined Iturbide in Iguala, then worked toward a more popular politics, notably by defending cotton growers in Pacific lowlands, his home region, and artisan cloth makers struggling everywhere in the face of British imports. In December 1828, after an indirect election in which Guerrero came in second, people in Mexico City sacked the Parián—the market facing the cathedral and the National Palace. A center of sales of imported cloths, it symbolized the import economy destroying the lives of urban artisans and rural cotton growers. Amid anti-Spanish noise, Guerrero turned to cut British imports and revive Mexican textiles, supporting mulatto growers along Gulf and Pacific coasts and reviving artisan production to complement entrenched family cultivation for sustenance.[77]

In politics too complex to detail here, Guerrero claimed the presidency early in 1829. He set key policies that impacted Mexico's future, working to block textile imports to protect Mexican producers while abolishing the remnants of slavery. He was deposed later that year (and killed in 1831), replaced by conservative vice president General Anastasio Bustamante, who had long fought and then pacified Bajío revolutionaries. Bustamante ceded governance to Lucas Alamán, who despised Bajío revolutionaries and dreamed of reviving silver to make Mexico industrial.[78] Guerrero and Alamán both opposed British hegemony in the wake of its debt-ridden failures: Guerrero aimed to favored artisan families and coastal cotton growers; Alamán would turn to promote capital intensive national industries.

Still Looking North: Slavery and the Dilemma of Mexican Texas

The Bajío revolution, the fall of silver, and the political morass of the 1820s merged to stall the centuries-long northward drive of silver capitalism. Commercial life waned from Texas to California, enabling reassertions of independent indigenous powers while energizing Anglo-American westward expansion. As US cotton planters looked to work Texas lands with enslaved hands, the new capitalism of industry and slavery constrained Mexico as it struggled to forge a new regime and find new prosperity. A Texas opened to cotton and slavery might bring commercial gains to Mexico by reviving ways of bondage long fading in New Spain. Guerrero's 1829 abolition stood in the way.

Silver capitalism had driven north from the late sixteenth century, setting its northern outpost among people relabeled Pueblos in a region renamed New Mexico (figure 7.2). After the Pueblo revolt and frontier recession of the late seventeenth century, Spanish settlement returned to Santa Fe and drove to San Antonio, Texas, in the early eighteenth century. Then, from the 1760s, presidios and missions engaged native peoples along the California coast, setting a capital in Monterey in 1770, reaching San Francisco in 1776. To 1810, Spanish towns and presidios, native pueblos and mission settlements, shaped a northern frontier where trade drew independent people from far beyond to engage Spanish North America.[79]

The Bajío revolution broke that northward thrust. Presidio troops withdrew from Texas and New Mexico to face insurgents in regions south. The dearth of silver undermined trades that had kept contested peace with Comanches, Apaches, and nations beyond.[80] In 1821, Iturbide dreamed of reviv-

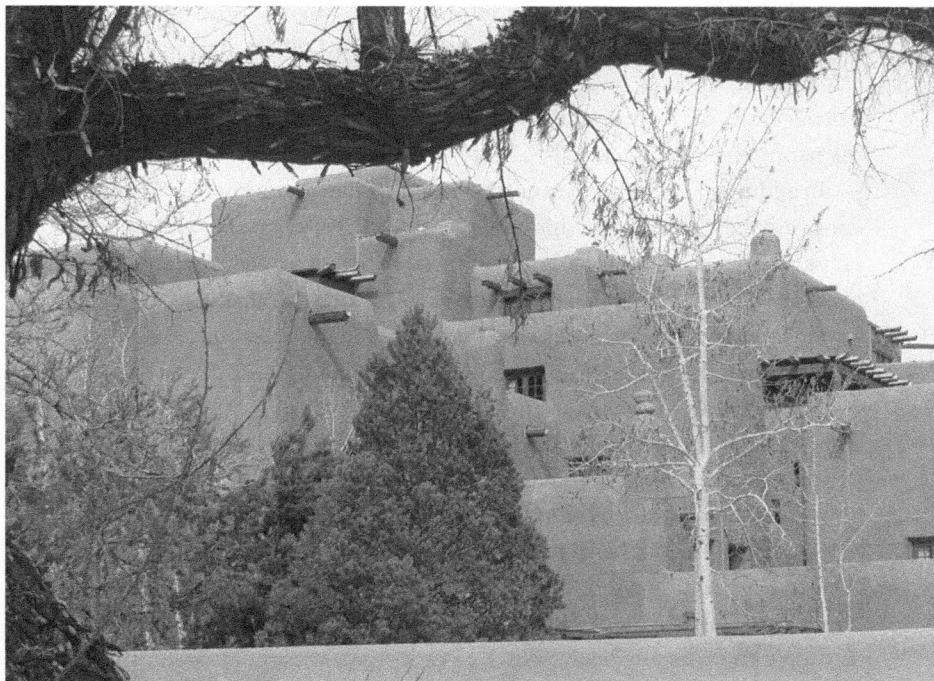

Figure 7.2 Adobe Power in Santa Fe, New Mexico. Author photo.

ing silver capitalism, pacifying the frontier, re-energizing trade with native peoples, and renewing the drive into a North America becoming Mexican.

Iturbide named General Anastasio Bustamante, a leader in pacifying the Bajío, as Captain General of the Northern Provinces. In Mexico City, Francisco de Azcárate, a famed participant in the autonomy movement of 1808, led regime discussions. In March 1822, after talks with Bustamante in San Antonio, a Comanche council met to consider proposals for a treaty of peace and trade. The council—a junta in the Mexican text—agreed to send a delegation to Mexico City led by Chief Guonique. He met with Azcárate to write a pact signed in December and approved by Iturbide in January 1823.

The treaty offered "perpetual peace and friendship between the two nations," beginning with a mutual return of prisoners. "The Comanche nation" would defend the frontiers of Texas, Coahuila, Nuevo León, and Nuevo Santander, "from the incursions of the barbarous nations." Mexicans and Comanches would also join against any Spanish or other European incursion, with Mexico supplying "munitions of war." Then the pact turned to trade: "The Comanche will trade only in Béjar [San Antonio]." Mexican merchants will supply "every class of silks, woolens, cottons, . . . the tools of arts and crafts, horses, mules, bulls, sheep, and goats." The Comanche would deliver "hides of bison, donkey, deer, bear, beaver, otter," plus foodstuffs and the natural fruits of the land"—all free of taxes.

In addition, "Every four years, the emperor will welcome twelve Comanche youth to be educated in this capital to study the sciences and arts. When prepared, they will return to their nation to share their civilization and education."[81] A new missionary engagement might draw Comanches to more settled lives and Christian culture. The treaty sought peace, territorial defense, and commercial exchange, setting Mexico and the Comanche as dual powers in Texas. Mexicans would focus in San Antonio, with settlements along the coast and northeast to Nacodoches; Comanches would rule from San Antonio to Santa Fe. The deal might protect Comanche and Mexican independence—if Mexico could sustain armed forces and supply trade goods.

The dream crashed as political conflicts and budget deficits prevented Mexico from setting a solid administrative and military presence in Texas. The scarcity of silver kept Mexican traders in San Antonio without goods to supply the Comanche and others. Peace never took hold. Meanwhile, Anglo-American traders tied to Louisiana and St. Louis supplied guns to Comanches, Apaches, and others in exchange for livestock taken from Mexican settlers in raids that pressed south into Mexico.

While Mexican trade and expansion were stymied, settlers came from the United States. The Austin family gained legal grants to settle lands along the coastal plain, aiming to open cotton production with enslaved hands; others came to take what they could in unsettled times. In the northeast around Nacodoches, Cherokee and other native people displaced by the expansion of cotton and slavery across the US South came west in search of refuge, often joined by Anglo-American traders and speculators ready to take any advantage they could. Squeezed between Mexicans unable to sustain power and trade and newcomers driving west to plant on native lands, Comanches, Apaches, and others raided each other and Mexican settlements across Texas and in regions south.

A chance at stabilization came in 1828 when Stephen Austin allied with Cherokees seeking refuge and Mexican authorities clinging to power, all aiming to constrain the Comanche. Mexican power in Texas turned from Comanche alliance to dependence on US cotton and slaveholding interests. Complications deepened when Guerrero ended slavery in Mexico in 1829 while Anglo-Americans continued to drag enslaved workers into Texas.[82]

While pursuits of silver and industry energized by Alamán helped revive Mexican capitalism in the 1830s, questions of settlement and slavery drove conflicts in Texas. While the Bajío led Mexico toward a new silver-industrial capitalism fed by family growers, Anglo-Texans led a rising US imperialism that promoted the expansion of slavery.

To understand the North America remade after 1830, we must first understand the complex ramifications of the Bajío revolution in Mexico during the 1820s. Families consolidated lives on the land across Guanajuato, claimed parallel ways across Querétaro, and pressed for autonomies far beyond— bringing down once-powerful landed oligarchs. Maize making families and communities held strong, ensuring that the silver-industrial capitalism that rose after 1830 depended on their productive ways.

8 .

Independent Guanajuato

Strong Communities,
Strong Women, Independent Cultures

Guanajuato insurgents fought for a decade after 1810 to build new communities on the land, in the effort breaking silver capitalism. In the 1820s, British capital failed to revive silver and a Mexican nation remained a dream. Meanwhile, Guanajuato communities held strong on the land. Estate property remained, but families ruled production, paying limited rents. Women took new roles in production, marketing, and religious culture. Men who dreamed of power in the new state complained while families made new lives in post-revolutionary communities. Power seekers had to adapt.[1]

When Guanajuato became a state of the Federal Republic in 1824, its mines remained broken. While Mexican silver output held near 50 percent of the level that enabled New Spain to drive global capitalism before 1810, Guanajuato, wracked by the decade of insurgency, saw flows that averaged 5.2 million pesos yearly before 1810, hold below 500,000 from 1822 to 1825, then rise to 1.6 million in 1830. British investment brought Guanajuato silver from 10 percent to 30 percent of prerevolutionary levels—survival, but far from revival.[2]

Meanwhile, families at Puerto de Nieto and beyond built new lives on the land. Joel Poinsett, Henry Ward, and don Carlos Montes de Oca, first governor of Guanajuato, all saw ample and widely shared sustenance while lamenting the loss of agrarian capitalism. They blamed economic travails on popular destructions, revolutionary transformations, insubordinate women, and barbaric Indians. With limited visions and prejudiced eyes, they were not wrong. Together, they document the enduring gains taken by the insurgent men and producing women who made new communities to sustain families first.

Poinsett's Guanajuato: A Traveler's Tale

After recording his impressions of Mexico City as Iturbide's empire collapsed, Poinsett headed north to see Guanajuato's famed mines, also in collapse. Leaving Querétaro, he passed through "a fertile land and well cultivated country, and over a smooth road. The hills on both sides of the valley are in a state of cultivation, and we saw some large haciendas. I find, on inquiry, that land here is in the hands of wealthy proprietors." Property held. "At 11 o'clock we halted at a *Rancho*, a collection of huts, where travelers who pass this road generally stop to refresh themselves. We found in them, as usual, ample provisions of mutton, fowls, and eggs. The road is much better supplied with provisions than that of Veracruz. . . . The traveler who cannot relish corn cakes [tortillas], nor drink pulque, has only to carry with him bread and wine from town to town, and he will fare sumptuously on this route." Family growers made plenty on the land.

"Leaving Apaseo, we entered that rich tract of country called the Bajío, . . . the finest portion of the kingdom." Monarchy held in 1822.

> It merits all its reputation. It is rich and fertile, and highly cultivated, producing all the fruits of Europe and many of those of the tropics. This plain extends from Celaya to Leon, and is covered with small towns, villages, and farms. We passed the river Laxa on a handsome stone bridge of five arches. . . . In summer, the Laxa is a deep and rapid torrent, and frequently overflows its bounds, inundating the country for a considerable distance round. These inundations fertilize the soil. A farmer boasted to us that his land on the spot yielded one hundred and eighty to one [for maize]. Another assured me that seventy-five to one was not uncommon.[3]

At Celaya, "The terrace of the church commands an extensive view of the valley . . . which is carefully cultivated and very thickly settled. Within every three or four leagues, there are small villages with churches and spires, and the whole valley is spotted with *Ranchos*."[4] Poinsett then reflected: "The plains of the Bajío, . . . are perhaps the most productive in Mexico."[5] The next day, he crossed the bottomlands: "We were off at the dawn. . . . The soil is a rich vegetable loam, and laid out in this manner like our finest rice fields. . . . The river Santiago, which in the length of its course equals that of the Rhine or the Elbe, fertilizes the whole of this valley. The lands of Celaya, Salamanca, Irapuato, and León are irrigated by its waters."[6] "We leave the small towns of Salamanca and Irapuato unseen"; still, finding so many towns "near together . . . proves the great fertility and abundance of this tract of country."

> At noon, we stopped at a rancho of huts that surrounded the ruins of a hacienda. As usual we found the people civil and engaging, and they supplied us abundantly with fowls, eggs, and milk. These hovels are small and too dirty to eat in, and we generally breakfast in the open air, and in the presence of a curious multitude. The people that surrounded us this morning were every shade of color between black and white. . . . This hacienda was burnt in the first year of the revolution and not far off we saw another in ruins. In our progress from San Juan del Rio, we have seen a great many in ruins.

Poinsett saw people of mixed ancestry who had destroyed the symbols of estate power, kept rough huts on land they did not own, and harvested rich crops they were happy to share with the curious traveler.

He added: "These haciendas are generally spacious buildings, with two court yards: the first contains the dwelling—the rooms opening onto the court; the second offices; and some of them have a third court, with stabling for two or three hundred mules, and granaries of ample dimensions, oil mills, and great stores of farming utensils; and they all have a chapel annexed to the house. . . . The loss of such buildings is ruinous to the farmer [owner], and no attempt has yet been made to repair them."[7] Later, "we reached an hacienda . . . in so ruinous a state that there was not a habitable room in it, not even an enclosure for our mules. We were compelled to urge on our tired cattle for another weary league, to an hacienda where we have been kindly received and plentifully supplied with provisions."[8]

The next day, "anxious to arrive at Guanajuato at an early hour, we . . . continued our ride through a fertile, thickly settled, and well cultivated valley, interspersed with orchards and gardens. As we approached the mountains, the land became rugged and broken, but still cultivated, principally in Indian corn. Labourers were employed cutting down the corn stalks with a reaping hook, and stacking them, blades and all, for fodder."[9] From Querétaro to Guanajuato, Poinsett saw vibrant towns, richly cultivated land, tables of plenty amply shared—and estates in ruin. Agrarian capitalism was gone while families and communities took rich harvests from lands they had once worked for others' profit. The visitor from South Carolina documented in detail the outcomes of revolution on the Bajío bottomlands.

When he entered the canyon city of Guanajuato, he saw its historic power and plenty gone: "The principal mines . . . are now nearly filled with water, and are but partially worked. . . . The town of Valenciana which formerly contained a population of twenty-two thousand souls, is now in ruins, and the population reduced to four thousand. . . . There are about one thousand workers at present employed."[10] The greatest of the mines, flooded as insurgency waned, barely survived.

Production fallen and capital scarce, "the mine is now worked by halves—the workers receiving half of the profits and the owner of the mine the other half." Poinsett detailed a system of shared production and marketing: workers organized in teams of five, a lead pickman backed by four haulers; they kept half the ore, selling to refiners who competed to buy in open markets: "There are two such days in the week, Wednesday and Saturday, and the market sales amount to between five and six thousand dollars."[11] A thousand workers would gain five to six pesos twice weekly, claiming 500 pesos yearly for hard risk-laden work. Two hundred skilled pickmen gained more—perhaps 1,000 pesos yearly. Haulers earned 200 to 300 pesos to carry heavy sacks of ore up long ladders, still ample pay for the times. Mines were in crisis; surviving workers prospered in a world of shared production.

The Valenciana refinery processed the owners' half of the ore and what it could buy in bidding from its workers. Women still sorted and graded ores, honored for their skill and dexterity—surely still paid less than men. Men and mules still waded through mixtures of ore and mercury, absorbing poison to turn ore into bullion.[12] Risk still defined work in the mines and refineries; shared production now delivered more to those who took the greatest risks.

Poinsett reported a census taken in May 1822. In a total population of 35,733 (down from 50,000 before 1810), 15,377 lived in the canyon city. Around the upland mines, Valenciana reported 3,778; Mellado 1,100; San Juan de Rayas 451. Valenciana had fallen; other mines had fallen more. The lowland refining center of Marfil retained 2,851 people; Burras, mixing refining, grazing, and cultivation, reported 4,854—access to land retained population. Unmarried adults and children formed a large majority of 20,244: 9,038 men and 11,206 women. Married couples totaled 11,963. There were 1,406 widowers, outnumbered by 2,121 widows.[13] Women exceeded men by nearly 3,000 in the once great mining center. They ruled markets in plazas and kept taverns Poinsett saw as centers of dissipation.

He concluded: "The state of the mines is deplorable. . . . It will require large capital to establish forcing pumps to extract water. In many instances it will be impossible to employ steam as the moving power, from the scarcity of fuel."[14] The envoy called for free mercury, lower taxes, and a government that inspired confidence—meaning the end of Iturbide's monarchy and a turn to republican rule.[15] Poinsett honored rural prosperity and dreamed of a silver revival—without understanding their links.

Leaving Guanajuato for regions north, he headed to San Felipe, once Hidalgo's parish. There Poinsett saw a town in ruins while he honored "muleteers . . . a patient, hardy race of men—sober, attentive to their mules, and careful of the goods committed to their charge. They are remarkably honest, always cheerful and ready to serve their employer."[16] The South Carolinian praised free men of African roots. North at Jaral, he praised tenant growers' rich harvests; on the road to San Luis Potosí, he saw productive fields among estate ruins. Markets were richly supplied with meats, fruits, and vegetables; peddlers were everywhere selling everything.[17] The economy made in revolution flourished.

Turning north to the mines at San Pedro and Catorce, Poinsett again saw closures caused by flooding. At Catorce, the Obregón family (also owners of Valenciana) had ceded half ownership to British investors promising steam pumps, then stuck in nearby mountains.[18] Like Guanajuato, in 1822 San Luis Potosí was defined by broken mines surrounded by family growers on the land.

Heading toward the Gulf, Poinsett stopped at a rancho. With men away tending sheep, women wove shawls, using wool from family flocks and cotton from nearby lowlands: "They did not use a loom, but had the warp so adjusted, that one end was fastened to a pin in the wall, and the other passed around the waist. These shawls are two and a half yards long, and three quarters wide. It is two months' work to make one and the price is eight dollars. They might be manufactured in our country for less than two."[19] While raising children, making daily meals, and tending gardens, the women of the rancho might earn 48 pesos a year making shawls in a family economy. Poinsett was quick to propose they be displaced by machine-made cloth.[20]

Lamenting the fall of silver, Poinsett recorded the consolidation of family production on estate lands across Bajío bottomlands, on dry plateaus from San Felipe to San Luis Potosí, and in the valleys east. He detailed the triumph of Bajío revolutionaries—without understanding.

Puerto de Nieto: Consolidating a Ranchero Community

What Poinsett described in brief encounters across a wide countryside, the people of Puerto de Nieto lived daily east of San Miguel. Adamant insurgents from 1810 to 1820, they consolidated lives on the land in the 1820s. Formally recognizing estate property and paying rents, if irregularly, they held strong as ranchero growers to 1826 (when accounts end). What they claimed in insurgency, they kept and consolidated in times of independence—family production with new roles for women.[21]

Agrarian capitalism was gone. No crops were planted on estate account, no workers paid to harvest estate fields in the 1820s. Don José Toribio Rico returned as manager, reduced to collecting rents—which proved a challenge. From 1820 to 1826, families that forged ranchos during insurgency increased their rentals and production; newcomers joined, increasing production and expanding the community. As we saw, eighty tenants remained at pacification in 1820—many from families long at the estate. Others had left or died in the decade of insurgency. Among the survivors, a few paid more than 50 pesos as commercial growers, most (more than 70 percent) paid 10 to 50 pesos as modest rancheros; a few paid 10 pesos or less for small plots (10 pesos paid to plant one fanega; at 50 to 1, enough to sustain a family, pay rent, and little more; multiples of 10 enable rough calculations of family welfare).

To increase production, in 1820 Rico recruited sixty new tenants paying 10 pesos each, an underclass of outsiders set to live among more prosperous insurgent-ranchero tenants. Were they displaced by insurgency and searching for new lives? They joined a community of tenant family production—at the bottom of a new hierarchy of inequality.

In 1821, many newcomers took on larger holdings. While the number of tenants held at 142, those paying 10 pesos or less dropped from 74 to 55—less than 40 percent. The modest rancheros paying 10 to 50 pesos rose from 59 to 73—a stronger core of the community. The prosperous paying more than 50 pesos rose from 9 to 14—a growing leading sector. Total rents jumped from 3,000 to 4,000 pesos—evidence of increasing production and a solid income for José Sánchez Espinosa. The pattern held into 1823. Poor tenants increased by one, modest rancheros by two, while prosperous commercial growers rose from 14 to 18, solidifying the top of the community.

The first season of drought since pacification came in 1823–24. Total tenants jumped from 149 to 170, with nearly all the newcomers poor maize tenants. Rico sought increased rents, newcomers a chance to plant. Many established ranchero-tenants, facing lost harvests, refused to pay rent— culminating a trend. In 1820–21, 97 percent of rents were paid. In 1821–22, payment fell to 92 percent; in 1822–23, it dropped to 79 percent. Then, with drought cutting yields, payment fell to 63 percent in 1823–24—and no one was evicted. Puerto de Nieto's rancheros recognized estate property by promising to pay rents. They paid when they could, withheld when crops failed—and remained to plant in a consolidating community.

In 1824–25, Rico again settled new, mostly poor tenants, bringing the total to 180—again making the poor nearly half the community. With good rains, most paid and some covered arrears. Still, accumulated unpaid rents totaled more than 2,000 pesos. In 1825–26, the last year of accounts, Rico recruited more new tenants, about half poor, half more prosperous. Among 197 tenants, total rents exceeded 4,000 pesos, with the mean over 20. Compliance neared 100 percent. Still, 2,000 pesos of arrears remained, likely never paid.

Rico shared little of that negotiation with Sánchez Espinosa. In March 1822, as withholding passed 20 percent, the manager wrote only that most rents had been paid. In September 1823, as withholding approached 40 percent, he reported nothing new or notable. In December 1824, after the recruitment of new tenants and a good harvest, Rico stated: "I have no particular news," then added: "I am demanding that the tenants pay their rents for this year and what they owe from the past."[22]

A bit of flavor comes from an 1825 letter to Sánchez Espinosa from José Lázaro Arteaga. The muleteer was kin to don Miguel Arteaga, an established tenant then increasing his rental from 20 to 45 pesos—a sign of prosperity. José pleaded for a rancho at Puerto de Nieto, claiming a current tenant was "very insolvent," owed two years' back rent, and had neither cash nor goods to pay. The muleteer bypassed Rico, implying the manager was easy on tenants. Arteaga did not gain a rancho. Rico's last letter to Sánchez Espinosa noted only that "tenants are slowly paying their rents, mostly in partial installments."[23] A stratified community of tenant rancheros paid when they could—or would.

Before 1810, Sánchez Espinosa took peak profit in time of drought, stimulating the insurgency that broke silver capitalism. In the 1820s, Rico ceded rents when rains failed, denying details to the aging priest-patriarch, keeping peace on the land. Rents paid brought income while once insurgent families and newcomers, too, gained sustenance and more.

Remaking Families on the Land

Most of the rancheros present at pacification in 1820 had lived through insurgency, some men as guerrillas, many women and men sustaining rebel forces. Of the 80 tenants named in 1820, more than 60 percent had kin listed in the census of 1792: 8 clans with 14 tenants counted as Spaniards; 9 clans with 17 tenants descended from families mixing Spaniards and mestizos; another 9 clans with 16 tenants mixed mulattoes and *indios*. Spanish tenants often lacked kin in the post-insurgency community. Amalgamating families always had kin: one Spanish-mestizo clan included 6 tenants. In contrast, the families arriving after 1792 had few kin in the community in 1820.

The 26 clans present since the 1790s ruled Puerto de Nieto to 1826, expanding to include 69 tenant households—35 percent of the community, and by far the most prosperous rancheros. Eight Spanish clans grew to 23 tenant households, with lead tenants paying more than 60 pesos in rent. The 9 Spanish-mestizo clans grew to include 24 tenants, their lead tenants paying more than 60 pesos. The 9 mulatto-*indio* clans also included 24 households in 1826, their lead rents only 45 pesos. Those present in 1820 but without roots in the 1790s fared less well. Of 34 households, 17 remained without kin in 1826. Lead rents rose only from 20 to 26 pesos. Inequities were real; dire poverty rare. The 49 clans present at pacification in 1820 led the community with 101 tenant households in 1826.

The newcomers recruited in 1820 and after remained poor and marginal. Rico settled 10 in 1821; 7 in 1822; 3 in 1823; 6 in 1824; 5 in 1826. All arrived without kin. Most paid minimal rents. They got by—and likely provided labor services to more prosperous neighbors, a source of income not recorded in estate accounts. A few latecomers came from clans at the estate in the 1790s: one Spanish-mestizo returned in 1821 to pay 22 pesos; a Spaniard arrived in 1824 and paid 35. Had they gone off in insurgency, to return seeking land from Rico? The rest were poor and gained marginal lands for small rents, perhaps displaced from other estates. Established families grounded in long residence and entrenched in years of insurgency held the center of the community. Newcomers got by.

Women Disrupting Patriarchy

Into the 1820s, a core of women solidified the new roles they had claimed in times of insurgency. In 1792, as the predations of silver capitalism accelerated, only 6 women, all widows, headed families in a community of 146 households, 4 percent. At pacification in 1820, 80 households remained, with 12 led by women—now 15 percent and among the most prosperous. In the years that followed, women expanded production and kin networks to keep leading roles at Puerto de Nieto.

Doña Hermenegilda López was the leading ranchera at Puerto de Nieto in 1820. Of Spanish roots, she leased a large holding for 90 pesos, withholding payment in 1823–24, then covering the debt and paying regularly through 1826. She was the dominant tenant in the largest clan in the community. In 1820, four López men paid 10 to 40 pesos each, none with a rancho half as valuable as hers. A fifth male began to rent in 1821; one died in 1822; another rented with his son in 1823 Throughout, doña Hermenegilda overshadowed her male kin. Only she earned the title doña. From 1820 through 1826, doña Hermenegilda López ruled Puerto de Nieto's leading clan.

In contrast, doña Cayetana Montes, from a family listed as mestizo in 1792, had no kin nearby in 1820 when she rented a prosperous rancho for 50 pesos. She paid in full in the drought year of 1823–24, to gain a rancho valued at 75 pesos from 1824 on. A year later, her son became a joint tenant. Likely a widow as insurgency ended, she shared power as her son neared adulthood.

Other women prospered while overshadowing male kin. María del Pilar Vargas, of Spanish-mestizo ancestry, rented a rancho for 40 pesos from 1820 through 1826. She paid only 25 pesos in 1822–23, nothing in 1824—and never covered the arrears. Kinsman Manuel Vargas paid 25 pesos faithfully, while by María del Pilar, who rented a more valuable rancho, paid less regularly and escaped meaningful rents. He complied while she resisted. The Guerreros, descended from a large mestizo clan present in 1792, lived a parallel course: Benita rented for 50 pesos, paid nothing in 1822–23 and 1823–24—and successfully evaded 40 pesos when accounts ended in 1826. Pedro paid 20 pesos every year; Vicente began renting for 30 pesos in 1821, paid 4 in 1822–23, nothing in 1823–24—then brought his account to full compliance by 1826. Matriarchs evaded; men complied.

The Aguados descended from a clan of Spaniards at the estate in 1792. In 1820, Victoriana paid 20 pesos, as did Trinidad, while Miguel rented for 15. A year later, in 1821, Santos Aguado took on a rancho for 100 pesos— asserting patriarchy. Had he fled to join or evade insurgency? Whatever the reality, Rico welcomed him in 1821 to claim patriarchal leadership. The Aguado men paid rents in full. Victoriana, perhaps honored in the insurgent community, paid half in 1823–24 and evaded 10 pesos in the final accounting of 1826. Less eminent in the clan, she asserted independence from the estate.

The Licea women stand out. Descended from a large Spanish clan present in 1792, doña Petra paid 50 pesos regularly from 1820, to gain lands that increased her rental to 62 pesos from 1824. Doña Lorenza began at the same 50 pesos—but took a different path. She paid only 25 pesos the first year, nothing from 1821 through 1825, then only 28 pesos in 1825–26. She owed nearly 250 pesos as accounts ended—and never faced eviction. In 1824–25, she began to rent jointly with don Juan Licea and still did not pay. Doña Lorenza Licea remained a prosperous ranchera, refusing to pay rent—refusing to recognize estate property. We can only imagine the role in the community during and after insurgency that enabled her assertive independence.

María de Jesús Licea, not a doña, also rented for 50 pesos in 1820. She paid faithfully for three years, inconsistently for three more, ending accounts owing 12 pesos. Gerardo López, likely her son, became a joint tenant in 1824–25. Marriage apparently linked the Liceas to the López clan headed by the powerful doña Hermenegilda, forging an extended family headed by four feisty women while men struggled in their shadows. Juan María Licea owed 22 pesos from 1820, paid nothing for four years—then caught up fully from 1824 to 1826. Guadalupe took on a rancho for 40 pesos in 1821, paid for two years, withheld in 1823–24, to end accounts still owing 40 pesos. The name could indicate a man or woman; withholding rent was common to women. If Guadalupe was a woman, the Liceas were an exceptionally powerful clan led by five women taking different paths to family independence.

There were also poor women tenants at Puerto de Nieto. Few had roots in the community of the 1790s; few had kin in the 1820s. They appear to have been widowed or otherwise uprooted. Among those present at pacification in 1820, doña Mariana Montemayor, likely Spanish by her noble prefix, rented for 20 pesos yearly from 1820 to 1826. She joined the more powerful rancheras in withholding rents in 1822–23 and 1823–24, then paid the arrears and full rents from 1824 to 1826. Without the kin networks of her powerful ranchera neighbors, she could negotiate rents but eventually paid. Salvadora Moreno rented for 15 pesos from 1820 to 1826, paying every year but 1823–24, still owing 10 pesos when accounts ended. Ysidra Castañeda paid 12 pesos yearly from 1820 to 1823, withheld in 1823–24—to take on lands worth 16 pesos and pay all rents and arrears by 1826. Anastasia Córdova was the poorest woman tenant at pacification. Of Spanish-mulatto roots, her kinsman Lucas rented for 18 pesos from 1820 to 1826 while she paid only 5. Both paid in full every year. Being poor and mixed led to compliance.

Five more women took on tenancies after 1820, none rooted in the 1790s community. All were poor and part of small clans struggling to get by. José Valerio Galván paid 5 pesos yearly from 1820 to 1826; Marcela Galván joined him in 1821, paying 10 pesos, withholding in 1823–24, then covering the arrears. Starting a year after pacification, she tripled limited family cultivation. Carlos and Antonio Marcial Chaves rented for 25 and 10 pesos, respectively, in 1820, paying regularly, enabling Carlos to increase his rental to 35 pesos in 1822. María de los Reyes Chaves began in 1821, paying 17 pesos faithfully every year—middle tenant in a middling family.

María Josefa Bárcenas arrived in 1822 without kin, taking on a rancho for 20 pesos. She paid nothing for two years, only 6 and 7 pesos in the next two, ending the accounts owing 67 pesos, most of the rent for four years. María Josefa took a rancho, rarely paid, and did not leave. Did she have powerful allies in the community? The last two women to become tenants were marginal members of poor patriarchal families. Ramón Santana paid 14 pesos every year beginning in 1821. Micaela Santana joined him in 1824, taking a plot for 5 pesos. The next year, Ramón increased his rental to 24 pesos, Micaela paid 6, and Anastacio took a rancho for 16. Micaela remained the poorest tenant in a struggling clan. Most marginal of all was María Juliana Beltrán. She arrived with Ygnacio Beltrán in 1824—both paying 6 pesos in rent. The next year, Manuel Beltrán paid 15 pesos for a less marginal holding, displacing María Juliana in a struggling patriarchal clan.

Muchachas Hold Strong

After 1820, women carried on as leading members of leading families at Puerto de Nieto, keeping and expanding roles claimed in insurgency. Their rise was a long time coming. In 1802, Rico reported that muchachas had taken over his house to protest his plan to evict families in a pursuit of higher rents and expanded commercial production. Presuming the girls were ten to fifteen years old in 1802, they approached adulthood as insurgency began and entered their thirties in post-insurgency times. The leading tenant rancheras of the 1820s came from families in the estate community since the 1790s. Many were present in 1802, and some surely joined the protest. When fathers and brothers turned to insurgency after 1810, muchachas, now young women, took control of production. They continued as ranchera tenants in the 1820s as Rico adapted to their long assertions.

The Limits of Labor in the Ranchero Community

In the same years, with production dispersed among nearly two hundred tenant growers, labor in service of estate profit all but vanished at Puerto de Nieto. After employing hundreds as *sirvientes* and *alquilados* before 1810, the estate paid only three employees in 1820: the manager Rico and two assistants, all reduced to collecting rents. In 1823, the estate took on five woodsmen and stock herders, increased to six in 1824. Most worked for a few months while part of tenant families. To keep five to seven workers from 1823 to 1826, the estate engaged seventeen men, most briefly.

Estate employment supplemented maize cropping for a few men in poor tenant families. Chrisanto Nava was a poor tenant paying 12 pesos in rent since 1820. He became a foreman overseeing the few herdsmen in the fall of 1823. Lucas Córdova, of mulatto roots, had been one of the poorest, most isolated tenants since 1820. He took work as a woodsman in 1823 before becoming a manager's assistant in 1824. The cowherds and woodsmen taken on in 1823 came from similar backgrounds. While Miguel de Santiago Álvarez rented for 8 pesos, Magdaleno Álvarez worked as a woodsman for less than four months and Pantaleón Álvarez herded cattle less than two. While José María Telles rented for 15 pesos, Vicente Telles worked almost two years herding cattle from 1823 to 1825. More typical, José Guadalupe Telles was a woodsman for twenty-six days. Justo Rodríguez came from a more prosperous ranchero clan. While kin paid up to 80 pesos to rent, Justo held a 15-peso rancho and served as a woodsman for eight months in 1823–24.

A few employees were not linked to named tenant families. Pedro Tobar was a woodsman for five months in 1823–24, the drought year. Santiago Martínez cared for horses for five weeks in 1824–25. Agustín Quintero labored as a woodsman from March 1824 until accounts ended in 1826—another rare case of long employment. Were they among the poor residents who rented plots for 10 pesos and remained unnamed? Their marginality is clear.

Managers' aides earned 60 pesos yearly, plus 26 fanegas of maize, lower salaries but higher rations than before insurgency. Woodsmen and herders, had they worked full years, might earn 40 pesos and 13 fanegas, levels common before predations hit. Few took the roles for long in the 1820s. No man from a clan including eminent rancheras took pay from the estate after 1820. Did strong women oppose employment by male kin, knowing such roles reinforced estate power? Families ruled by leading women produced enough to spare men the need to labor. Women's rise challenged patriarchy as a social relation of production.

Indios in the Ranchero Community

The ranchero community built at Puerto de Nieto during and after insurgency included families of Spanish and mixed ancestries while opening new leadership roles for women. An *indio* minority, almost invisible, struggled to join. All eighty tenants named at pacification in 1820, most prosperous rancheros, showed Spanish patronyms—a sign of Hispanic culture. Were there Otomí or other indigenous people among the sixty unnamed maize tenants Rico recruited to plant for 10 pesos or less? Probably. Yet among the nearly thirty maize tenants given ranchero status in 1821, only one, Manuel Claudio, appears indigenous—and he paid for a small holding at 5 pesos. Many natives likely remained among the thirty to forty tenants still unnamed as they planted plots for 10 pesos to the end of accounts. *Indio* or not, they formed an underclass in the Hispanic ranchero community. Utopia is rare.

Three indigenous men took employment, at least briefly. Francisco *el cochero* received 15 pesos plus 5 fanegas of maize in 1824–25. José Tomas served as a *semanero*, a weekly worker, from October 1823 to February 1824, when José Anacleto took over. No pay is recorded; rations were a third of those allotted the poorest Hispanic workers. How did they live? Unrecorded in the estate accounts, new labor relations surely emerged within the stratified community. Prosperous tenants, including rancheras, who paid 30 pesos or more yearly, planted crops needing more hands than a family could provide at harvest time. Marginal tenants, including unnamed *indios*, planted crops barely sufficient to sustenance; men and boys surely labored in the fields of their ranchero neighbors to gain maize, pesos, or both. After insurgency, hierarchies of tenant family production ended agrarian capitalism, remade gender relations, and reset labor relations at Puerto de Nieto.

Independent Religious Communities

Communities pressing autonomies on the land also pursued religious independence. As insurgency ended, some clergy resisted that independence. Demanding compliant worship and higher fees, they provoked conflicts with parishioners. Other communities, including Puerto de Nieto, built relationships with clerics ready to foster integrating devotions.

Don Francisco Uraga, already pastor at San Miguel in 1810, refrained from joining Hidalgo. He returned in 1817 to rebuild clerical oversight in the town and across surrounding regions radically changed during years of insurgency. In detailed correspondence with Church officials in Valladolid, he reported concerns and adaptations from times of pacification through the years of ranchero consolidation.

In 1817, he worried about clergy and communities in the long-insurgent Sierra Gorda. San Luis de la Paz, an indigenous community under Jesuit oversight before 1767, was a center of insurgency after 1810. Pastor don Francisco Primo had fled. Uraga lamented, "No clergy dare to go there and those lands are more roiled than ever." Primo joined royalist patrols, dressed too well, and spent too much money: "He is young and corruption is everywhere." A "Padre Yndio" struggled to serve the parish while the pastor fought insurgents and took profit. Uraga insisted that the Sierra needed clerics who spoke native tongues: "there are confessions in twenty languages, . . . in addition a tribe of Pames whose only Christianity is baptism, as no one knows their language."

Pozos was a small, more Hispanic mining center south of San Luis de la Paz. Its pastor, don Luis Correa, "a good man, now tired and very ill," had retreated to Querétaro, leaving sacraments to Uraga and his assistants at San Miguel. Health restored, Correa returned as insurgency waned. Still, "nothing goes well." Where the Bajío met the Sierra, Hispanic and indigenous communities saw little clerical engagement in times of insurgency and pacification.[24]

Parallel challenges came in the southern Bajío as insurgents pacified. Late in 1818, Padre don José Antonio Montes wrote from Cuitzeo complaining of poor health, exhaustion, and problems that began with insurgency. The pastor was also an estate owner who lamented that early in insurgency, "soon after I gained the property it was taken by rebels. . . . They took me prisoner and devoured the grains and livestock, leaving the property stripped of everything." Montes fled. Five years later, he returned to face "the miseries left by the rebels' burning of the town, my house, and hacienda, leaving the parish without resources even for my sustenance."[25] The community had expelled the priest, leaving families to pursue their own religious ways. Montes' return was not welcomed.

Conflicts between clergy and communities revived after Iturbide's fall. In May 1823, "The Magistrate and Republic of the native community of San Juan de Ysla" near Celaya wrote: "Pastor D. Juan Zavala does not meet his obligatory duties; he only says Sunday Mass if we pay him twelve reales; if not, there is no Mass. . . . He leaves us alone in the Pueblo, and many die without divine blessing; . . . many babies are born, and whether they are healthy and strong or ill, we must travel to receive Baptismal waters; and when by chance he is here to baptize a newborn, he demands ten reales, far more than the customary five."

An investigation confirmed that Zavala spent weekdays in Querétaro, weekends in the parish, while he raised fees. Still, his clerical superiors found him "of good conduct," insisting that "it is publicly known that the *indios* of the Pueblo de Ysla are the worst behaved of all in the Bajío—in every way." The condemnation confirmed the villagers' earlier insurgency. The bishop ordered Zavala to live in the community, visiting Querétaro only in "grave necessity."[26] Zavala responded, insisting that burials without the sacrament were due to "his parishioners' little zeal in caring for the souls of the sick." As to baptism, he argued, "as I regularly live in Querétaro, they always bring newborns to me for baptism." Zavala expected villagers to come to him and pay double fees.[27]

Conflict divided pastor and parishioners at Salvatierra, south of Celaya, in the same month. Pastor Don Basilio Peralta y Quesada complained: "Maliciously and without cause . . . they do not pay parish fees, expecting their priests to live on tithes." He blamed "the impious and scandalous paper published in the capital by El Pensador Mexicano under the title 'The New Revolution the Nation Awaits.'" Peralta saw his parishioners as "simple," misled by José Joaquín Fernández de Lizardi, an anticlerical republican who wrote as El Pensador. Refusing clerical fees, they cause "damage to priests and religion." Peralta added that with "this torrent of evils . . . I cannot serve in the poorest indigenous chapel; . . . they refuse to pay for burials."[28] Two years later, Peralta wrote of "slander" attacking the clergy: "We are targets of terrible sarcasms." Now "they have sent a complaint to the state government portraying me as profaning the church and taking its ornaments."[29] Religious conflict raged at Salvatierra.

Meanwhile, don Francisco Uraga remained at San Miguel, reporting challenges to church finances in a city facing enduring economic difficulties. Insurgency had made it impossible to pay San Miguel's "diocesan contributions" from 1810 to 1819. In 1824, "war, disease, and the emigration of useful people . . . in the face of military drafts have reduced the parish by half, with only poor people remaining." As a result, "the tithe, the barometer of population and production, brings less than a third of the revenue it yielded in 1809."[30]

In 1825, Uraga reported serving 28,790 people: 13,605 men, 15,185 women. Parish and sacristy gained 5,000 pesos yearly to support the pastor, a *teniente*, and three vicars, along with services, festivals, and functions. Eighteen other clerics lived in the parish, funded by chaplaincies or convents with endowment totaling 223,818 pesos. At the standard 5 percent, they should yield more than 11,000 pesos in annual income. Amid the post-insurgency

Figure 8.1 Parish church and Allende House on the plaza in San Miguel. Author photo.

commercial decline, little came.[31] At Atotonilco, once rich as the site of penitential retreats for the powerful, after Hidalgo took the banner of Guadalupe from the basement the sanctuary grounds became an insurgent market. In May 1824, Uraga noted the decline of "annual exercises at Atotonilco."[32] In 1825, two priests lived on 600 pesos in annual income from rented lands and 12,000 pesos in pilgrim alms. Did they come to do penance, or to honor the Virgin and the insurgents she had led? Uraga did not say.

Meanwhile, heterodoxies challenged life at San Miguel (figure 8.1). In 1817, "on my return from Mexico [City], I saw my parish threatened by errors and false doctrines pressed by Libertarians, Masons, and Materialists seeking followers." Uraga's early response: "I educated the people in my sermons with some effect; I might have tried judicial efforts, but as there was no government then, things would have gotten worse; it was necessary to await more opportune times." He could preach but not press. Now, in May 1824, heterodoxies were less public yet still reported in confessions.[33]

Then, in July, Uraga received formal complaints "against Mucio Maycote, Ygnacio Taboada and José Ygnacio Ontiveros, denounced for spreading attacks on religion." Uraga hesitated: "It would be unfair to reveal the complainants to the miscreants, given the vengeance they might unleash. The delinquents remain free, and Maycote, a pharmacist with poisons at hand, might use them silently to ruin lives: A terrible escess! Yet not remote."[34] Again, Uraga chose caution.

The Ranchero Priest of San Miguel—and Puerto de Nieto

While politicized religious conflicts focused in cities and towns, a new religious independence set in across the countryside around San Miguel. In March 1824, Uraga heard charges against "my vicar Salas." The complaint: "the indecent clothes he wears in constant travels and his excess taking of masses that he could not say in many years." How did "indecent" dress lead to excess Mass offerings? Why was that a problem? Salas' "ranchero" appeal brought him fees other vicars coveted.

Bachiller don Cayetano Salas explained: "In the church I always wear a cassock; . . . to hear outlying confessions on frequent long rides, I wear a shirt, boots, and country hat, as they are more comfortable and protect me from the wind, rains, and other weather." Riding across the country, Salas dressed "a lo ranchero"—country garb that gave comfort and protection— and announced his union with communities on the land.

Uraga's sacristan, responsible for distributing masses and fees among the vicars, added: "It is true that Father Salas receives more than all others; but not by my hand, but from the Yndios who seek him out for counsel and blessings." Salas rode and preached "as a ranchero." The sacristan in town saw "Yndios" in the countryside. Salas breached an urban-rural divide and took pay for 123 masses in six months, declining 100 more. Uraga grasped the importance of Salas' ministry and brushed aside the other vicars' complaints: "There is no grave problem. . . . He is humble, docile, selfless, and tireless in his work, worth three vicars. Without him, many would have died without the sacraments."[35] Salas delivered baptism, mass, confession, and last rites to families and communities on the land.

The ranchero families of Puerto de Nieto valued the ranchero priest. In 1822, before complaints began, Salas began to lease a rancho for 20 pesos. The obligation fell to 12 pesos the next year and continued to the end of accounts in 1826. After the first year, nothing was paid. The accounts closed with Salas owing 48 pesos. Perhaps he rented to seek a bit of income. Yet the ranchero priest was well paid and constantly riding circuit across rural San Miguel. Surely, the community rented the rancho with Salas' approval and in his name, cultivating it communally to sustain local devotions and festivals.

Did the women of Puerto de Nieto take a leading role in the ties linking the community and the ranchero priest? Probably. Their lead in withholding rents surely enabled Salas and the community to escape payment for the rancho that sustained local devotions. Rico would not dare evict the priest who served the community that produced everything, paid rents irregularly, and would resist any attempt to disrupt religious life. Religious independence marked the community entrenched on the land.

Before 1808, Sánchez Espinosa had used inspection visits during Easter seasons to require residents to say annual confessions to him—an intrusive use of religion to sanctify estate power. When Rico fled Puerto de Nieto in 1811 as insurgents took control, he absconded with key religious images, chalices, and more from the chapel. A decade later, the community that emerged from insurgency ruled production and took control of religious life, backed by a ranchero priest and funded by a rancho they worked without paying rent—making Sánchez Espinosa fund their preferred devotions.

Independent Guanajuato: A Governor's Lament

Don Carlos Montes de Oca served as the first governor of Guanajuato, a sovereign state of the Federal Republic founded in 1824. His *Memorias* reporting on 1825 and 1826 record his frustrations as he struggled to lead in the face of commercial collapse and popular power on the land. He proclaimed the sovereignty of the people, yet politics after independence were mostly affairs of towns and leading men.[36] The *Memorias* show that the governor rejected everything the people had built in times of insurgency. He knew the collapse of mining. Unable to change that, he focused his ire on the rural majority, indigenous people, and women. All resisted dependence in times of independence. Liberty was for men of education and wealth. The majority required constraints.

In detailing his frustrations and imagined solutions, Montes de Oca revealed much about the society that frustrated him: "This land is among the most fertile in the world" yet "is all but deserted on its plains, leaving much land uncultivated." Yet reporting on 1825, he saw "maize, wheat, frijol, chile, chick peas, barley, peas, and more harvested in abundance."[37] Uncultivated plains yielded abundant foodstuffs? According to Montes de Oca, "The state's agriculture still suffers from the recent revolution in which men dropped their plows to take arms in defense of their rights" while "the animals necessary to cultivation vanished. Estates were burned, *labradores* moved to fortified towns or fled to the highlands to survive."

The governor's *labradores* were agrarian capitalists: "The capital that gave life to cultivation lost, the land became an uninhabitable desert; impoverished estate owners have not been able to revive once established ways." Capitalists made cultivation flourish—meaning profitable. The revolution had destroyed them, leaving the land a "desert." Cultivation without capital was of no value "but to feed people."[38] Montes de Oca saw family cultivation feeding people without profit—a calamity in his eyes.

The governor returned to the same themes in his *Memoria* reporting on 1826, again blaming the destructions of insurgency. He lamented losses of capital and the persistence of debts. Then he turned to the heart of the matter: "No one can attempt large plantings, which alone maintain the price of grains and stimulate agricultural growth." The governor lamented the collapse of the capitalist cultivation that had kept staples prices high, a system he insisted served the interest "of the public which depended on commercial crops in years of dearth." He offered the classic legitimation of agrarian capitalism: oligarchic growers took ample harvests, held them until years of drought and dearth, to take peak profits sustaining desperate families.

Yet no desperate scarcity had hit Guanajuato since 1820. The 1823–24 drought led to rent withholding, not hunger, at Puerto de Nieto. In times of ranchero cultivation scarcity cut landlord earnings. Montes de Oca insisted a return to capitalist cultivation would serve small growers too: "Poor growers barely bring in the harvest when they sell at low prices, . . . never escaping miserable poverty."[39] Still, rancheros resisted any return to agrarian capitalism.

The rancheros and tenants of independent Guanajuato sought sustenance first, income second, and bits of profit when possible. Into the 1820s, few starved while prices held low. Montes de Oca saw crisis: landed proprietors could not profit, pay debts and taxes, and fuel a commercial economy—a collapse demanding solution. With mining reviving only slowly, the governor proposed reforestation: "Forests are perpetual conductors of the moisture that revives fields sterilized by drought and burned by the sun's rays. Their refuse fertilizes broken lands; their fruits feed us; with their trunks we build houses, churches, and tools of work; their leaves, branches, and more become life essentials."

Montes de Oca saw ecological and economic gains: "the state mining council" promoted reforestation to gain timber essential to mining—a long-term project that in time would create capital. Meanwhile, "uncultivated land would bear fruit; animals would find fresh grass for pasture; forests would capture the sun's blazing rays, draw new rains, and bring sure harvests."[40] Unstated, reforestation would require landlords to take back lands from tenants planting crops and grazing livestock on hillsides. Proprietors would lose rents; family cultivation would decline—as would common access to wood and grazing lands, key supplements to ranchero production and family sustenance. The governor dreamed. When he wrote in 1826, rancheros ruled and miners adapted.

When Montes de Oca worried about public health, he again blamed the people. A "terrible measles epidemic" ravaged communities late in 1825. In his *Memoria*, he focused on Salvatierra: "The desolation has been great, because the people will not subject themselves to the cures prescribed by the educated, while still following local curers and healers whose ignorance and stupidity holds their confidence. The scarcity of doctors, surgeons, and pharmacists is extreme, so the government aims to provide them—paid by pueblo funds."[41] The governor saw poverty, ignorance, and stupidity; the state must take community funds and impose "scientific" cures.

Yet the demographic counts in the same *Memoria* challenged the governor's claims. He reported birth and death totals for about half of Guanajuato's jurisdiction for 1825, the measles year. Both birth and death rates were near 78 per thousand, the former indicating good fertility, the latter documenting epidemic deaths. Yet death rates were highest in the most Hispanic jurisdictions: urban Guanajuato and nearby Silao and León; they were lowest in the most rural, most ranchero, and most indigenous zones.[42] Rural dispersal remained the best defense against the spread of disease, and folk cures were at least as effective as the "modern" medicine of the 1820s. In his second *Memoria*, Montes de Oca reported 1826 birth and death rates for the entire state, after the epidemic and in a year of good harvests. The birth rate held high at 70 per thousand; the death rate fell to 30 per thousand as population increase approached 4 percent.[43] Ranchero communities made ample sustenance, ate well, and sold surpluses at low prices. Mining struggled, commerce held limited, and the majority gained solid nutrition. The governor lamented—blind to his own censuses.

Blaming Barbaric *Yndios*

The governor criticized the rancheros who ruled Guanajuato's new economy only obliquely. He attacked native minorities directly, lamenting "indigenous privileges." In July 1824, his first address to the state Congress emphasized "how prejudicial to *indios* were the ancient privileges granted machiaveli-cally by the kings of Spain." Montes de Oca then insisted his goal was "the growth of their pueblos, . . . the promotion and advance of enlightenment," adding: "none of this can succeed until we uproot the unseemly privileges granted to maintain the ignorance and degradation of the natives." He asked: "Are not those called *indios* also citizens?"[44]

The liberal governor attacked the separate legal and judicial rights and the corporate lands that sustained indigenous republics along Guanajuato's southern margins and in the Sierra Gorda. In a state committed to univer-sal law and justice, such indigenous "privilege" must end. He emphasized: "The government believes that it will serve *indios* . . . to divide among them their community lands."

Then the "beneficiaries" should "pay primary schoolteachers . . . and doc-tors."[45] Their lands privatized, community members would pay outsiders to (re)educate their children and replace local curers. The lands that sustained native families would cease to be inalienable, opened to sale and loss for debt. Children would be pressed to learn Spanish and accept liberal tenets. There is no sign that the Otomí and Tarascan communities along Guana-juato's southern margins welcomed such change. The long independent and recently insurgent peoples of the Sierra Gorda surely would not accept them.

Montes de Oca offered liberal impositions to fix problems that commu-nities did not see as problems. Corporate landholding and self-government were their strength, the base of a historic independence now being repli-cated in the insurgent-ranchero communities that ruled the core of rural Guanajuato.

In 1826, the governor continued maligning indigenous citizens: "What can we say about the peoples long called *indios*? Ah! Sad people drowned by a tyrannical regime in barbarism and degrading humiliation and misery." To the governor and other liberals, Spain's regime granting rights of land, self-rule, and mediating justice kept native communities in barbarism. He then turned on the native peoples who lived without republics in the Si-erra Gorda: "In much of the state, they live dispersed in *rancherías* where they know no civilization, ruled by capricious ignorance and superstition." Other natives "live at the edge of towns . . . where they keep old customs and languages, and rarely gain spiritual aid, as few know Otomí." Montes de Oca saw barbarism in indigenous republics, free people in the Sierra, and natives struggling to live at the edge of towns too.

The cure was education. The state needed "schools in every settlement of natives, requiring that parents send their children." The governor knew that "they are set to work very young." Schooling was essential so that "in twenty or thirty years, we will hear no language but that shared across the [national] republic." Forced education would make Spanish-speaking citizens, "facilitating religious and civic knowledge" and making "men capable of knowing the benefits of our independence and ready to forget forever the subversive ways some have pursued and proposed to others."[46]

The problem with indigenous peoples, whether in landed republics, free settlements, at the edge of towns, or in ranchero communities, was legal, linguistic, and cultural separation, an independence that fueled subversion and resistance. A governor devoted to personal freedom and popular sovereignty pressed forced cultural change: "This plan must mobilize parish priests and other clergy, who by their own obligations and interests must take part, along with estate owners and managers."[47] The liberal governor saw native peoples as "barbaric" and in need of forced liberation from the "privileges" of self-rule and community landholding.[48] In the 1820s and long after, rural communities, ranchero and indigenous, saw little gain in liberal dreams.

The Impossible Solution: (Re)Subordinating Independent Women

After demanding the reeducation of indigenous peoples, the governor turned on women:

> No less important are schools for women. . . . Few in the common classes having even a limited education, many are not the good mothers and wives they should be: the former teach their tender children only absurdities and follies, . . . the latter, without instruction in household management, domestic care of children, and daily care for husbands, sadly cause annoyances that lead to discomfort, conflict, faulty upbringing, and ruined families. And women who do not marry . . . cannot protect themselves or resist the ambushes of their pursuers, leading many to the horrors of prostitution, . . . fatal outcomes bringing grave damage to society—in which no one doubts the influence of women and the great benefit of their being intelligent, discrete, and virtuous.[49]

Women—badly educated; disobedient to husbands; sexually independent—were the root of the problems plaguing post-insurgency Guanajuato. In the governor's vision, they had to be educated to obedience, educate their children to patriarchal ways, marry and obey without objection or discord, and remain chaste outside of marriage. Montes de Oca and his liberal allies could not revive mining; they could not rule rural production; they could not shape religious life; and they could not make women obey. He blamed native peoples and women for the popular independence that carried on as mining failed to revive, agrarian capitalism vanished, and state revenues held low. He was not wrong.

Guanajuato in Henry Ward's Eyes, 1826–1827

In November 1826, freed of pressing business in the capital, Ward headed to the Guanajuato remade by insurgents and lamented by Montes de Oca. Arriving at Celaya on the tenth, He noted a "really fine" plaza, cathedral, and center, with outlying barrios "poor and miserable." The Bajío was "celebrated in Mexico . . . as the seat of the great agricultural riches of the country, and the scene of the most cruel ravages of the Civil War," a basin "thrown out of cultivation since the Revolution, when the failure of the mines at Guanajuato deprived the farmers of their markets." He presumed that the collapse of mining had broken agrarian capitalism—blind to the predations of agrarian capitalism that drove insurgents to end commercial cropping, in the effort crushing silver capitalism.[50]

Entering the mining center on the twelfth, Ward was met by Mr. Williamson and Mr. Jones of the Anglo-Mexican Mining Association. They offered lodging and orientation to an industry struggling to revive. Ward detailed the current mix of high costs and constant obstacles, adding dreams of revival and profits to come. The system of *buscones* that kept mining going during the years of insurgency and ruled when Poinsett visited in 1822 continued in 1826: workers still delivered half the ores they cut to operators and sold the other half to "rescatadores," independent refiners. "Pepenadores, men and women," then broke the ore with hammers, separating three classes by mineral content.

Ward reported the failure of British steam technology and the success of Mexican ways of drainage.[51] He lamented the coming Cornish miners: "There were some good and useful men amongst them, . . . but the generality of the Cornish left behind them a character for ignorance, low debauchery, insubordination, and insolence." Finally, "the Directors in England were fortunately induced to abandon the system, and to employ natives in all the operative parts of the principal undertakings. The management alone is now European, . . . having shown a proper disposition to conciliate the natives by acquiring their language."[52] Local workers proved essential; British managers adapted.

Figure 8.2 Valenciana Mine complex, high above Guanajuato. Author photo.

A visit to Valenciana documented the depth of postrevolutionary challenges (figure 8.2). "When the Company took possession" there were "four hundred and fifty varas [yards] to drain, and this not merely perpendicular in depth, but disseminated throughout the whole of the workings, most of which had been so long under water that the communications were destroyed, the timbering falling to pieces, and many of the lower levels filled up by masses of rock."

Ward detailed: "Drainage commenced on the 1st of February 1825. Steam engines were not employed upon it, on account of the scarcity of fuel; but eight Malacates (horse-whims) of the largest kind were erected around the Tiro General, and kept at work day and night for twenty-one months, in which time they lowered the water 185 varas"—less than 40 percent of the flooded depth, at a cost of 672,264 pesos. Profits were nowhere in sight when Ward entered the mine. Easy steps led 60 *varas* down to a chapel, where "a prayer is usually recited by the chief miner before a large picture the Virgin." Risk required protection. Descending farther, Ward learned that during the drainage, "ores were raised which produced at times silver enough to nearly cover the weekly expenses of the mine"—6,000 pesos to pay uncounted workers and sustain three hundred horses required for the drainage.[53] Prospects for profit remained uncertain.

After eight days exploring mines, Ward concluded: "The town of Guanajuato . . . contains many splendid memorials of the former wealth of its inhabitants. . . . A great part of the landed property in Guanajuato . . . belongs to mining families. . . . From the Governor, don Carlos Montes de Oca, a man of liberal and enlightened views, the Foreign Companies have received every encouragement." Still, "the quantity of silver raised in 1825 [was] very small."[54]

Ward's last reflection: "Guanajuato may be called either a Mining or an Agricultural State, for the prosperity of the two branches is so closely connected that one can hardly flourish without the other. The importance of the great Haciendas of the Baxío ceased at the same moment with that of the mines, and is reviving at present in proportion as the capitals invested in them create anew a demand for agricultural produce." Still blind to the predations that provoked the revolution, and to the popular insurgents who broke silver capitalism, Ward saw nothing of the entrenched rancheros who ruled cultivation to serve families and communities first. Revival would prove harder than he imagined.

Finally, he returned to what mattered most to England: "Manufactures of wool and cotton abounded formerly in the towns of Leon, Irapuato, Silao, San Miguel, and Salamanca . . . but the 'Mantas,' 'Rebozos,' 'Pañetes,' and 'Gergetillas,' for which they were famous, have already been replaced by similar articles from Europe and the United States." Honoring gains for British industry, Ward cared little for Guanajuato artisans. He lamented the fall of mining and commercial cropping. Cloth makers drowning in imports gained no sympathy.

Berlandier's Perspective, 1827

Jean Louis Berlandier, a French naturalist traveling to meet native peoples on Mexico's northern frontiers, visited Guanajuato in late November 1827, a year after Ward. Passing Puerto de Nieto, Berlandier reported "fields covered with fruits of the land raised by hard-working indigenous people." He saw the rich productivity of small growers he presumed indigenous. Arriving in San Miguel, "one of the most beautiful sights a traveler could see," he reported "industrious people" plagued by "the constant emigration of working people who turn to mining or agriculture due to scarce employment in the city." In good times, population might reach ten or eleven thousand, making "blankets, quilts, shawls, and all kinds of iron goods." When the cloth imports Ward celebrated came, people fled in search of work, leaving only seven to eight thousand. Berlandier saw a once rich and still beautiful textile town pummeled by industrial imports.[55]

Arriving in Guanajuato days later, Berlandier saw less beauty and deeper challenges. Entering via Marfil, "one sees ruined and abandoned refineries, where in other times thousands had worked constantly." He saw the Alhóndiga as the mining city's most notable structure: built by Intendant Riaño to store grain to sustain mining, he died there at the hands of insurgents. Berlandier added, "from the first shout for liberty . . . the mines faced ruin and workers left to find work elsewhere." Population plummeted. In 1805, the center had 41,000 people, the surrounding mines another 29,600. The 1826 census showed only 33,488 total inhabitants, risen to 34,611 in 1827—still down by half.

On mining, Berlandier reported that "Valenciana, run today by the Anglo-Mexican Company, requires immense labors to drain its principal tunnels; yet we know with certainty that while the veins yield nothing, the costs are covered by destroying the pillars that in times of bonanza were left to protect the workers."[56] Still drowned and little productive, Valenciana saw its Anglo-Mexican operators pay for revival by taking down the silver-laden columns that sustained the works and protected workers. The Anglo-Mexican Company joined insurgents and *buscones* in destroying the structural pillars that sustained mining. No bonanza would come soon.

Berlandier saw the radical disruptions of working lives at Guanajuato and San Miguel caused by the collapse of mining and the flood of British textiles. He also saw the productive strength of the rancheros and rancheras of Puerto de Nieto. He could not foresee that only when Mexican capital reclaimed the mines, Mexican industries displaced British cloth, and both adapted to families making maize on the land would capitalism revive in the Bajío—the ultimate triumph of the Bajío revolution.

The world envisioned by Epigmenio González in 1810 ruled rural Guanajuato through the 1820s. And while British capital failed to revive flooded mines, and British cloth pummeled Mexican cloth makers, family cultivation spread across Querétaro—consolidating the Bajío revolution.

9.

Querétaro After Insurgency

Agrarian Capitalism Falls,
Families Claim Maize—and More

While Guanajuato insurgents broke silver capitalism and claimed family control of production after 1810, Querétaro remained a bastion of counterinsurgency. Early on, La Griega continued commercial cropping in support of counterinsurgency. Then, as insurgency held strong, don José Sánchez Espinosa delivered half of estate planting to tenant growers, holding men at work by granting gains parallel to those imposed by insurgents across Guanajuato. With pacification in 1820, La Griega resumed commercial cropping as profit vanished. Sánchez Espinosa dreamed of reviving agrarian capitalism in the 1820s, but the collapse of silver and the widening consolidation of family production challenged commercial cropping across Querétaro. Estate profits vanished while tenant family production took hold across the state—in time remaking life at La Griega too.

Meanwhile, Querétaro's historic textile economy struggled. By 1820, most large *obrajes* had failed in the face of British imports. Household workshops carried on, still making cloth for local markets as imports drove prices down. They survived while maize prices held low. As agrarian capitalism failed and estates turned to tenant cropping, rural Querétaro came to mirror the Guanajuato forged in insurgency—except that the negotiated turn to family production held Querétaro women in traditional roles: raising children, keeping gardens, grinding maize, making cloth and clothing. Where men took arms to fight for land and patriarchy, they claimed land while women took roles that challenged patriarchy. Where men stayed at work and gained land in postrevolutionary negotiations, patriarchy held stronger. Still, by 1830 Epigmenio González' world came home as ranchero and tenant family production entrenched across Querétaro. In time women asserted new roles as estate operators, Church funders, and rancheras ruling family purse strings.

Querétaro in 1822: Don Pedro Telmo Worries

Don Pedro Telmo was a Spaniard who came to Mexico before 1810, fought with Iturbide to defend Spanish rule and landed property, then settled in Querétaro to operate a landed estate. Aiming to hold American and European Spaniards united in Iturbide's Mexican empire, he merged military command, active politics, and pursuit of landed power. Early in 1822, Iturbide, not yet emperor, asked Telmo to report on Querétaro.[1] He relayed Querétaro's support for Iturbide: "Independence is seen generally as just, useful, and beneficial; the current government as good."[2]

Still, Telmo saw rising difficulties. Attempts to build a militia had begun well, recruiting three hundred men, most urban artisans. But with few arms and no pay, they skipped Sunday drills. In April, the regular regiment stationed at Querétaro, also short on pay, threatened to sack the city. The council paid and the troop returned to barracks, demonstrating again where power lay in times of uncertainty. The same day: "the people rioted, . . . with more than 600 threatening a sacking."[3] Military ire and popular riots did not portend an easy transition of power.

Telmo offered a list of difficulties. Regime revenues had collapsed. A once prosperous tobacco monopoly faced trafficking in public markets while its officials dealt in stolen product. It was a "scandal" that a monopoly that generated 45,000 pesos monthly before 1810 and still raised 16,000 to 18,000 pesos monthly in 1819 and 1820 now brought only 4,000 to 5,000 pesos per month. Meanwhile, commerce collapsed and alcabala sales tax revenues had fallen from 10,000 to 16,000 pesos monthly in 1818 to 1820 to less than 2,000 pesos in 1822. Without revenues, no state could survive.[4]

Ultimately, the problem was the fall of Querétaro's textile economy. Open ports flooded Mexico with imports, cutting local production. The regime must protect "crafts, industry, cultivation, and trade." If "imports keep filling markets, . . . they will ruin national workshops." What Ward celebrated, Telmo condemned. He called for "the promotion of national production" to stimulate commerce and revenues: "If manufacturing and trade are not protected and promoted, *labradores* cannot cultivate." Worse: "the owners of large estates . . . will not be able to pay *sirvientes*." With planting for profit impossible, estates could not employ workers.

Telmo concluded: "Agriculture feeds humanity and increases its numbers; it increases wealth, limiting need and social dissolution; it brings joy to states and promotes business, sustaining the power of empires. The key questions are: what will be the consequences of not protecting this leading sector? What will that mean for trade? And without cultivation and trade, will poverty and robbery dissolve society and general tranquility?"[5] For Telmo, the collapse of cloth making was breaking commercial cultivation, leaving a society without order, profit, revenue, or state power. With a revival of silver beyond imagination in 1822, the protection of textiles might promote commercial life and reverse the decline of commercial cultivation. Family goals were not his concern.

Querétaro in 1822: Joel Poinsett's Vision

Joel Poinsett passed through Querétaro in the fall of 1822, bringing an outsider's vision. He traversed a rich countryside to find the textile city facing an uncertain future. As he arrived from the south, the heights above San Juan del Río opened a view of "the whole valley, which is the most fertile and the best cultivated we have seen in this country." Continuing north, he observed that "nothing can exceed the beauty of the country . . . in a high state of cultivation. The principal culture is Indian corn." Deep wells used whims to draw water to the surface; streams flowed "with the fullness and rapidity of torrents."[6]

Travelling north, "At noon we stopped opposite a large hacienda at a small collection of hovels, constructed with stones and mud, and thatched with straw. We found in these miserable habitations . . . the greatest abundance of the necessities of life. At the door of one of them, there were two sheep hanging that had been lately killed; and the women offered for sale, turkeys, fowls, mutton, corn, onions, and a great variety of fruits, vegetables, and herbs."[7] The hacienda was not a ruin; the huts were rough and sustenance was ample—sold by women who ruled marketing and the provisioning of travelers.

Soon Poinsett was "cheered by the sight of Querétaro, and the rich and fertile valley in which it was situated. A lofty aqueduct on sixty arches, traverses a part of the valley and carries the water to the town. . . . Fountains are seen in every street; in the principal square, opposite our meson, there is a very large one overflowing with excellent water."[8] The city's hydraulic works awed the visitor: "Querétaro is a large and well-built town containing no less than thirty thousand inhabitants. . . . We saw a great many handsome public and private edifices. We found, as usual in this country, an unnecessary number of churches and convents. That of San Francisco is very spacious, ornamented with an extensive garden." Carrying Anglo-protestant prejudices, Poinsett was impressed by the great San Francisco that had long dominated Querétaro.[9]

Turning to the economy, he wrote: "The manufactures of this place have suffered in common with every branch of industry in Mexico; they are still carried on, particularly those of woolen and cotton stuffs, but on a reduced scale." He noted "upwards of eleven thousand Indians in Querétaro" yet never visited the rich *huertas* that sustained Otomí families and city markets.[10]

Poinsett did see vibrant markets: "We have been amused for some time with the motley assembly on the square," a crowd surely including people of Spanish, Otomí, and mixed descent—a gathering unlikely in Poinsett's slave South.

> It is Saturday, and on the evening of this day there is a market or rather a fair held. They begin to assemble about a half-hour before sun-down, so as to display their wares to advantage, the business now going on by candlelight. We saw a poor peddler carefully spreading out on the pavement odd pieces of old iron, spurs, bridle-bits, nails, and screws; the manufacturer hanging up his cotton and woolen goods; and the jockey dashing about on a gallant steed, loudly calling on by-standers to admire its rare qualities and to purchase.[11]

The problem in Poinsett's eyes:

> The mass of the people here will not for many years consume foreign manufactures. Their dress is simple and they are accustomed to wear cloth made in the country, and in many instances to manufacture it themselves. . . . Cotton is raised in the country, and their flocks furnish an abundance of wool of tolerably good quality. Their cloths are dyed of various colors, which they understand how to fix, and to render bright and durable. Their manufactures are either on a very small scale, in towns, or are domestic as in the country, where families make what little they require.

Poinsett lamented: "The machinery is very defective, and the cotton is separated from the seed by hand. . . . Everything in this country is done by manual labor."[12]

Of course, manual labor, mostly enslaved, drove Poinsett's South. The problem in post-insurgency Mexico: manual work served to sustain families, not to profit industrialists and planters. Poinsett heard stories of the earlier presence of enslaved Africans in Querétaro *obrajes*. They had mixed with native people to become "mestizos," freeing children to live as free workers.[13]

Poinsett did not pause to contemplate such liberating amalgamations. He did begin to admire Querétaro's social and cultural integrations: "In the morning our muleteers went to mass. I accompanied them to the church of San Francisco, which was crowded with people of all classes. I like the equality on which all people worship the Deity in a catholic church. There are no pews nor seats for the rich. The house of God is open to all, and all without distinction stand or kneel before the altar."[14]

Telmo sought protections to revive textiles—and hopefully to stimulate profitable commercial cultivation. Poinsett saw vibrant markets and cultural integrations while seeking the decline of the textile production that had long sustained Querétaro's vibrant city life. Textiles would not soon revive, while families took control of production across the countryside, eating well and filling markets while profit stayed scarce and state powers struggled without revenues.

Agrarian Capitalism Falls: La Griega, 1820–1826

Meanwhile, don José Sánchez Espinosa aimed to revive agrarian capitalism at La Griega. While Puerto de Nieto's residents claimed the estate and its lands for insurgency and family production from 1811 to 1820, the priest-patriarch had kept the peace and commercial production at La Griega, first by raising the pay and rations of workers, then mixing commercial planting and tenant family cropping. When pacification at Puerto de Nieto required a full turn to tenant family production, he tried to restore commercial cropping at La Griega. He failed. His attempt to carry on as the last agrarian capitalist in the Bajío reveals much about life in rural Querétaro in the wake of revolution.

The fall of 1820 proved a time of sorrows for the managerial Francos who had kept the peace and overseen production through the decade of insurgency. In November, the family matriarch, widow of don José Regalado Franco and "*madrecita*" to current manager don Miguel Trinidad, passed away. In early 1821, the manager followed his mother to the grave.[15] In May, don José Vicente Franco, long La Griega's lead leaseholder and leader of the troop that pacified Puerto de Nieto, became permanent manager. He gained the 1,000 pesos and 156 fanegas of maize that had rewarded his late brother to manage the estate, even as the troop disbanded. He continued to lease a rancho paying 200 pesos annual rent.[16] Could he return commercial gain to an estate that had not seen a profit in three years?

In the face of insurgency, La Griega had cut annual estate maize planting from near 100 fanegas to under 50, turning half the estate fields to leasehold-ers who let to Otomí subtenants. Peace, production, and patriarchy held. In 1820, after two years of poor harvests and peak prices brought the estate no profit as it held no maize in storage, the new manager took back land and in-creased commercial planting to 74 fanegas. Rentals to large leaseholders and Otomí subtenants held steady; lesser tenants, often Otomí, fell from 40 in 1819–20, to 20 in 1820–21, then to 10 or fewer until accounts ended in 1826. Could direct cultivation complemented by Spanish leaseholders and Otomí subtenants—a post-insurgency compromise—revive agrarian capitalism?

As he increased estate planting, Franco complained of shortages of plow teams, resistant ex-tenants, and recalcitrant workers.[17] Worse, the return to large-scale maize planting did not bring profits. The 74 fanegas planted in the spring of 1820, favored with good rains, yielded 5,644 fanegas—nearly 80 to 1. The price collapsed, falling below 9 reales. Desperate for income, the estate sold more than 2,000 fanegas—limiting losses that still exceeded 1,000 pesos.

During the next three years, modest rains brought limited harvests, yet prices rose only to 16 reales in 1822–23. La Griega then sold 3,000 fanegas held in storage to earn more than 6,000 pesos—its only profit of the post-insurgency years. In 1823–24, yields improved, prices fell to 12 reales per fanega, and losses returned. The harvests of 1825 and 1826 proved ample, dropping prices back to historic lows near 9 reales. Desperate for cash, La Griega sold nearly 5,000 fanegas to limit losses. The agrarian capitalism that profited from scarcity to sustain silver capitalism before 1810 was gone. After 1820, commercial cropping faced family growers flooding markets across the Bajío. People ate well and affordably while estate profits collapsed—an inversion imposed by Guanajuato revolutionaries.

Other crops proved less profitable. Ample rains and irrigation brought a good wheat crop in 1820–21. Regional prices peaked at 9 pesos (of 8 reales) per carga (2 fanegas); La Griega earned nearly 2,400 pesos to help limit losses. Then wheat fell to hold near 3 to 4 pesos per carga to 1826, leaving income from wheat to average just 260 pesos yearly. Chile earned La Griega more than 1,000 pesos in 1822–23 when the price hit 5 pesos per fanega. Then it fell and the estate gained less than 100 pesos yearly to 1826. Frijol brought nearly 700 pesos yearly from 1821 to 1823, to earn only 283 pesos in 1824–25 and a mere 53 in 1825–26. Staples prices fell after 1821, as ranchero and tenant growers flooded Bajío markets. La Griega revived commercial cropping to see profit vanish.[18]

Constraining Tenant Production; Negotiating Labor, 1820–1826

Meanwhile, the number of tenants on La Griega's accounts dropped from 53 to 37 in 1820–21. The leading leaseholders displaying the don remained. Poorer tenants, often Otomí, lost holdings to more prosperous Hispanic neighbors. Total rents fell only from 2,212 to 2,115 pesos—suggesting not a turn from tenant production but a return to Otomí subtenants paying Spanish leaseholders. The next year, in 1821–22, the number of leaseholders fell to 22, total rents to 1,765 pesos. A core of twelve dons remained—as did two Otomí. At the end of the accounts in 1826, only 14 leaseholders remained, owing a total of 1,385 pesos, a mean of nearly 100 pesos each. A few Spanish leaseholders held strong—overseeing a shrinking community of Otomí subtenants. La Griega's rental income had fallen by nearly half while estate harvests brought losses that kept the estate in deficit.

Tenant rancheras were few. Doña María Dolores González came from a Spanish family at the estate in the 1790s. Linked by marriage to the Francos, she leased the Rancho de las Navajas from the beginning of accounts in 1811 until 1823. She paid 56 pesos yearly to 1813, then 80 pesos to 1823 (when she ceased to rent, likely having died). In 1823–24, doña Francisca González took on the Rancho de las Sepulturas for 100 pesos and held it until the end of accounts in 1826. She paid only 40 pesos in 1823–24 and again in 1824–25, and covered no arrears before accounts ended, a ranchera able to evade rent and eviction at La Griega—thanks to ties to the Franco clan.

The other prosperous ranchera was doña Dolores Aguilar. She gained a rancho in 1823 for 80 pesos and held it through 1826. Rooted in the Hispanic community since the 1790s, four Aguilar men had tried lease holding for brief terms between 1812 and 1818, none paying more than 60 pesos in rent. None continued into the 1820s. Doña Dolores appears to be the surviving matriarch of a long-serving Hispanic clan. She kept Otomí subtenants in production and collected enough rent to cover her lease obligations—

while many men lost leaseholds. The few women leaseholders at La Griega were notable, but not a transforming presence like the rancheras who held strong at Puerto de Nieto.

A revival of estate cropping required workers; profit in times of low prices required reduced labor costs. The balance proved elusive at La Griega after 1820. Employment and earnings had peaked in 1819–20, keeping men at work as pacification set in to the west: 57 *sirvientes* gained mean salaries of 37 pesos, plus rations of 12 fanegas of maize (worth 60 pesos at the prevailing price), peak earnings during the years from 1811 to 1826. The same year, 154 men and boys labored as *alquilados*, most gaining 1.5 reales daily to work 90 days or less. Many labored far more, bringing mean earnings to 19 pesos. The year insurgency ended at Puerto de Nieto, La Griega paid 8,455 pesos in money and maize to workers, a historic gain for workers that blocked profit.

In 1820–21, the number of secure *sirvientes* rose from 57 to 66; mean salaries fell to 25 pesos, as many of the newly hired worked only part of the year. Mean rations fell to 11 fanegas, still ample for family sustenance (their cash value falling to near 50 pesos). The same year, the number of *alquilados* rose to 168 and mean earnings hit 20 pesos, bringing total wage earnings to 3,391 pesos—another historic peak. Total value to workers fell slightly due to falling maize prices but held above 8,000 pesos. Even with militia costs cut to 500 pesos, the estate lost 900 pesos. Workers gained while the estate struggled.

For Sánchez Espinosa, ever the agrarian capitalist, costs had to fall. In 1821–22, the year of independence, La Griega increased the number of *sirvientes* from 66 to 87 while mean salaries fell to 23 pesos. Mean rations fell to 10 fanegas; as the price dropped to 9 reales, their cost to the estate plummeted. The number of *alquilados* dropped from 168 to 111; those who remained worked more days, raising mean earnings to 26 pesos. The militia cost only 133 pesos as it disbanded. Still, losses rose to 1,134 pesos. Cutting wage-earning day workers did not bring back profits.

A brief revival occurred in 1823–24. Two good harvests had allowed the estate to accumulate maize, while a historically poor crop yielded 19 to 1, the worst in fifteen years of accounts. Yet in post-insurgency times, the price rose only to 16 reales per fanega—far below the 40 of 1819–20. Sales of more than 3,000 fanegas brought 6,000 pesos. The same year, the number of *sirvientes* returned to 87 with mean salaries of 27 pesos. Mean rations held near 10 fanegas, worth 20 pesos at the new price. *Alquilados* rose to

130, still far below the number at pacification, while mean earnings fell to 21 pesos. Total cash payments to workers rose above 5,000 pesos—more than covered by the 6,000 pesos earned by the maize they raised. Adding lease-holder rents and earnings from other crops, La Griega took nearly 3,500 pesos in profit—while total remunerations to producers approached 7,000 pesos. As Mexico's empire became a republic, La Griega took profit while producers gained solid earnings.

That year proved an exception—and a turning point. In 1824–25, the estate gained a better maize yield, still well below historic norms. The price fell to 12 reales while the estate had little to sell. The number of *sirvientes* jumped to 114. Many newcomers worked only part of the year, cutting mean salaries to 22 pesos, rations to 8.5 fanegas. The number of *alquilados* dropped to 114 as mean earnings rose to 24 pesos. Total remunerations fell to 5,000 pesos while estate losses returned.

From 1824 into 1826, strong maize harvests kept prices low, holding near 9 reales per fanega. La Griega cut the number of *sirvientes* from 114 to 105 in 1824–25 to hold at 106 in 1825–26. Mean cash earnings rose to hold at 25 pesos per year, with rations near 10 fanegas, below the levels of 1820. Remunerations to *alquilados* fell radically. Numbers dropped to 94 in 1824–25, then rose to 120 in 1825–26, but mean earnings fell by half to hold near 11 pesos both years. At the end of estate accounts and don José Sánchez Espinosa's life as a landed capitalist, *sirvientes* faced reduced salaries and rations; *alquilados* faced reduced wages without rations—and profit remained a memory.

The Decline of the Otomí at La Griega

The remunerations that blocked profits after 1820 mostly benefited Hispanic men. In 1819–20, as pacification set in, only 57 secure *sirvientes* labored at La Griega, their numbers fallen by half—with Hispanics a majority of 37. The number of *alquilados* had risen from 61 to 164, nearly tripling—and Hispanics now outnumbered Otomí as wage workers 92 to 72. When struggles to find profit brought the number of secure *sirvientes* back to 106 in 1826, 72 were Hispanic, only 34 Otomí—down from 81 in 1811. When day laboring *alquilados* fell back to 120, two-thirds were Hispanic. At the end of estate accounts, 1 Otomí tenant remained, along with 34 *sirvientes* and 40 *alquilados*. Uncounted Otomí subtenants still planted on the lands of 14 Spanish lease-holders; a few found wage work in estate fields to supplement small plantings. A disadvantaged majority in 1811, the Otomí sustained La Griega through years of counterinsurgency—to face disposession and evictions by 1826.

Three Families at La Griega, 1820–1826

The three Hispanic families whose lives illuminated the challenges of work and life at La Griega in times of insurgency carried on into the 1820s. The Juárez remained laboring men; the Abendaños mixed leaseholds and labor; the Olveras merged leaseholds and labor oversight. Their divergent routes through post-insurgency times reveal much about the last years of agrarian capitalism.

In 1811–12, five Juárez men had labored as *sirvientes*; none gained the don, suggesting mixed origins. Working into times of insurgency, salaries held steady while rations rose. Then, from 1815, as La Griega turned to leasehold and subtenant production, the Juárez men lived by day labor without rations as demand for *alquilados* rose and cash earnings soared. They lived well while maize remained plentiful and inexpensive. Then, when drought drove maize prices to 5 pesos per fanega from 1818 to 1820, earnings per Juárez worker hit 47 pesos in 1819–20 and 51 pesos in 1820–21. They learned the liability of waged insecurity as 50-peso incomes barely bought a basic family ration of 10 fanegas.

Facing that, Jesús de Juárez led a return to lives as secure *sirvientes*. In 1820–21, he had labored 264 days to earn 50 pesos. The next year, he began as an *alquilado*, then gained *sirviente* employment. His earnings fell while he gained a weekly maize ration at no cost. The outcome was clear in 1822–23. He earned only 12 pesos, plus 12 fanegas of maize. His household would eat—and get by. The same year, Bartolo Juárez, family patriarch, joined the shift. He stepped back from 55 pesos in cash earnings as an *alquilado* to take 22 pesos plus 12 fanegas of maize. The sustenance of life, maize became the prime currency of work, pay, and trade after insurgency. Two Juárez men carried on as *alquilados*, laboring more than 300 days each: Nicolás gained the top wage of 1.5 reales; Ysidro took the youth wage of 1 real. The clan balanced secure sustenance and cash income. Meanwhile, Mariano Juárez faced decline and departure. He had worked 300 days for the top wage in 1820–21. As two kin became *sirvientes* and two others remained fully employed *alquilados*, he worked only 113 days in 1821–22, a mere 24 in 1822–23, and then left. Mariano's loss of work and departure reminded all that estate interests ruled.

That became clear in the following years. In 1823–24, Bartolo and Jesús remained *sirvientes*, gaining more than 25 pesos and 9 fanegas each. Meanwhile, the estate ended the option of men working 300 days at 1.5 reales, shifting Nicolás to *sirviente* employment as plentiful and cheap maize made rations the estate's preferred remuneration. Anselmo Juárez labored 121 days for 1.5 reales, to be terminated in March 1824; Santiago worked just 70 days, then faced the same fate. Only young Ysidoro, likely son of the patriarch Bartolo, labored more than 300 days—for 1 real. His cash earnings exceeded his father's—while the patriarch's rations guaranteed family sustenance.

In 1824–25, the Juárez clan seemed settled in post-pacification laboring lives. Bartolo, Jesús, and Nicolás remained *sirvientes*, earning near 20 pesos and 9 fanegas each. Young Ysidoro continued as the only family *alquilado*, working 283 days to gain 35 pesos. Into 1825–26, the three Juárez men continued as *sirvientes*, with salaries more than 25 pesos and rations holding near 9 fanegas. Then, in the spring of 1826, Jesús Juárez left. At the end of accounts, only Bartolo and Nicolás remained *sirvientes*; Ysidoro was the only Juárez *alquilado*, working near 300 days for 1 real.

After laboring to sustain production through years of insurgency and post-pacification attempts to restore commercial cultivation, the Juárez family that had seen as many as eight men and boys employed found itself with only two men and a boy paid at La Griega. By 1826, the rewards of loyal labor service were gone, as were many once loyal workers—Juárez and others, including most Otomí.

The Abendaño men appear more favored. Of Spanish status and honored as dons, they lived as leaseholders before, during, and after insurgency. Still, they faced a trajectory of rise and decline not unlike the less-favored Juárez clan. When insurgency began, family patriarch don José Antonio Abendaño lived in Querétaro while leasing a rancho for 110 pesos—the largest leasehold then at La Griega. Two sons, don Jesús and don Miguel, rented small holdings for 15 pesos while three youths labored for 40 to 60 days each at 1.5 reales. The family mixed leaseholds and labor to prosper.

The Abendaños, aided by ties to the Ontiveros men in the estate troop, increased leasehold operations during the years of counterinsurgency. They also faced internal tensions likely linked to the absence of the patriarch. In 1813, don Francisco Abendaño replaced the absent don José Antonio as lead tenant, his lease up to 180 pesos. Then, in 1819–20, as militia power ended and the Ontiveros left, don Francisco ceded more than half his operations to the widow doña Rosa Mendoza. She split the family leaseholds into three parallel units and stepped back. Abendaño leaseholds peaked in 1820–21, as insurgency waned and political conflicts rose. Don Francisco leased for 92 pesos, don Jesús for 118, and don Miguel for 90 as they worked to collect rents from Otomí subtenants in times of scarcity. Two youths labored for 1.5 reales daily, one working 43 days, the other only 6, to gain small cash earnings. If subtenants paid, the Abendaños gained.

Then, as La Griega turned to revive estate cropping, the Abendaños and others lost leaseholds. In 1821–22, don Francisco rented for only 50 pesos, don Jesús for 40. Don Atanacio, an irregular tenant, gained a large leasehold for 100 pesos. Three youths labored 3, 6, and 11 days each. The next year, family leaseholds hit a low: don Francisco paid 40 pesos, don Jesús 40, and don Atanacio was gone. The clan leased less than when insurgency began—no reward for leasing through insurgency in service of power, property, and profit.

In January 1823, the elder patriarch don José Antonio Abendaño wrote a will in Querétaro. He had lived at the estate in the boom times of silver capitalism, moved to the city as predations escalated, kept a large leasehold in the early years of insurgency, then watched kin carry on through times of conflict and pacification. Twice marrying Ontiveros women, he cemented links to a clan strong in the estate militia after 1811. He lamented that city life brought only difficulties: "The little I gained paid for family sustenance, expenses, and medicines." He owned only his house—to be sold to pay a debt to a daughter-in-law. He left nothing to his heirs at La Griega. Strong in Spanish Catholic culture, he asked for burial in a habit of San Francisco at the Santiago parish. He would not return to La Griega, even in death.[19]

After the elder's death, the Abendaños consolidated a limited prosperity. In 1823–24, don Francisco and don Jesús continued to rent for 50 and 40 pesos; doña Josefa Abendaño, the late patriarch's daughter by his second wife, took on a rancho for 20 pesos, a small concession to honor family services. No Abendaño labored—and with crops lost to drought, no Abendaño paid rent. The next year, all three kept their leaseholds, paying arrears and current rents, while two youths went to the fields, laboring 20 and 40 days for 1.5 reales to gain cash.

The final year of accounts saw doña Josefa Abendaño's two-year tenancy end. The men carried on, don Francisco leasing again for 50 pesos, don Jesús for 40. Three youths labored for 32, 33, and 39 days each. At 1.5 reales, they gained 6 to 7 pesos each. After years of sustaining La Griega as lead leaseholders overseeing Otomí subtenants, the Abendaños got by. Patriarchy held: two women had claimed brief participations, to be edged aside by male kin. Futures were uncertain.

The Olvera family history proved less complex, yet equally revealing of life at La Griega after 1820. In 1811–12, don Vicente, of a Spanish family long at the estate, rented an ample rancho for 70 pesos. He increased his holdings to pay 100 pesos in 1814–15, contracting for that or more until accounts ended in 1826. Several kin joined as modest tenants between 1813 and 1818; then all but the patriarch ended their rentals as the estate returned to commercial cropping. The turn to production with *alquilados* gaining wages without rations brought new power and income to the Olveras. In 1816–17, Vicente Olvera, never honored as don, likely don Vicente's son by an Otomí mother, became Capitán de Alquilados, overseer of the day workers ever more pivotal to estate production.

At pacification in 1819–20, three Vicentes led Olvera power and prosperity at La Griega. Don Vicente still rented his rancho for 100 pesos; Vicente earned 2 reales daily for 297 days as *capitán*, claiming more than 74 pesos and 13 fanegas of maize (the only *alquilado* to earn a ration, gaining security to manage the insecure). The third Vicente, no don, and likely the *capitán*'s son or nephew, rented a small plot for 10 pesos while laboring for 24 days at the standard 1.5 reales wage to earn nearly 5 pesos. Anastacio Olvera added five days' work for the same wage. At pacification, the Olveras mixed leaseholds, labor oversight, and wage work in estate fields.

Change began in 1820–21. Don Vicente retained his 100-peso rancho. Vicente remained *capitán*, working 290 days to gain 74 pesos and 13 fanegas. The younger Vicente lost his lease and labored just 15 days. Anastacio either left the estate or was left without work. Change accelerated in 1821–22. Don Vicente carried on. Vicente began the year as *capitán* at the usual wage and ration. Through March 1822, he worked 199 days to earn nearly 50 pesos and 7 fanegas. Then, as Otomí *alquilados* became less pivotal to estate production, the position of *capitán* ended. Vicente was named an *ayudante*, aide to manager don José Vicente Franco. A monthly salary brought 35 pesos for the rest of the year; his ration delivered 9 more fanegas of maize. No other Olvera leased or labored.

The new arrangement served the Olveras and the estate well. Don Vicente continued to rent for 100 pesos to the end of accounts in 1826. Like many, he did not pay in 1823–24, held arrears through 1824–25, to pay in full by 1826—pressing Otomí subtenants in the process. The mestizo Vicente carried on as *ayudante*, his salary up to 102 pesos in 1823–24, back to 91 pesos in 1824–25, to peak at 128 pesos in 1825–26. Throughout, he gained at least 26 fanegas of maize yearly. The Olveras would eat, whatever the state of the harvest or the price of maize. When the youngest Vicente returned to labor for 14 days in 1824–25, then 44 days in 1825 alongside José María Olvera (likely a brother), the youths gained spending money. The family did not need their earnings.

When Sánchez Espinosa tried to revive agrarian capitalism at La Griega after 1820, Otomí families faced exclusions while favored Hispanic families struggled. The Juárez saw labor and remunerations rise and then fall; the Abendaños saw access to leaseholds rise and fall. Only the Olveras kept solid prosperity, thanks to a rich leasehold and a managerial role mediating between landed power and wage workers in times of insecurity.

Keeping Power and Prosperity at La Griega: The Managerial Francos, 1820–1826

From 1820 to 1826, Franco men continued to manage La Griega. While producers struggled and don José Sánchez Espinosa saw profit vanish, the Francos kept local power and took ample earnings. In 1819–20, the year of regional pacification, don Miguel Franco remained manager, still earning 1,000 pesos plus a ration that had risen to 156 fanegas—sustenance for 12 to 15 households and worth 780 pesos at then high prices. Don José Vicente remained a leading leaseholder, paying 220 pesos to collect subtenant rents. Don José Ysidoro returned to rent for 120 pesos. Two young Francos labored as *alquilados*: Ygnacio for 290 days at 1.5 reales to gain 55 pesos; young Nicolás for 264 days at 1 real to earn 33 pesos. With total salaries and wages near 1,100 pesos, rations of 156 fanegas, and leases totaling 340 pesos, the Francos prospered in times of uncertain transition.

Don Miguel, the manager, died as 1821 began. Don José Ysidoro, who had increased his leasehold to 200 pesos, gained 322 pesos and 57 fanegas in maize for four months' interim service. Don José Vicente, still leasing for 200 pesos, became permanent manager in May. Meanwhile, six Francos labored as *alquilados*, five at the top wage of 1.5 reales: Ygnacio worked 273 days to gain 51 pesos, Nicolás 202 days for 38 pesos, Agustín 199 days for 37 pesos, Gregorio 94 days for 18 pesos, Felipe 26 days for 5 pesos, and young Secundino 18 days at 1 real to earn 2 pesos. The family held strong.

In the summer of 1821, as Iturbide's drive for a Mexican empire passed nearby, the Francos held a solid mix of managerial power, leasehold production, and labor participation. Don José Vicente continued to lease for 200 pesos while managing the estate for 1,000 pesos plus 156 fanegas of maize. Don José Ysidoro leased for 180 pesos while serving as mayordomo, the manager's assistant, for 90 pesos and 52 fanegas. The two lead Francos mixed management with oversight of Otomí subtenants. Nicolás and Ygnacio continued to labor for the top wage, Nicolás gaining 59 pesos, Ygnacio 54. Agustín quit day labor to rent a small plot for 10 pesos. Gregorio left and Manuel Franco came on midyear as a *sirviente*, paid 14 pesos and 6 fanegas in the remaining months of the account.

Little changed in 1822–23, except that don José Ysidoro's pay as mayordomo jumped to 242 pesos and a newcomer, Tomás Franco, labored to earn 35 pesos. The Francos kept power, leaseholds, and earnings as Sánchez Espinosa's profits stayed scarce.

The administrative settlement of 1821 collapsed in 1823–24, the year of scarce maize and unpaid leases. Don José Vicente continued to manage and lease through April 1824. When he did not pay his 200-peso rent, Sánchez Espinosa removed him as manager but not leaseholder. Don José Ysidoro lost his leasehold worth 200 pesos—and became manager. The priest-patriarch separated management of commercial cultivation from lease holding and subtenant oversight. And the Francos prospered. The new manager continued to gain 1,000 pesos and 156 fanegas to the end of accounts in 1826. Don José Vicente continued to lease for 200 pesos—owing for 1823–24, paying only 50 pesos in 1824–25, then paying the current rent and 200 pesos arrears in 1825–26—still owing 150 pesos.

With the new managerial structure, the Francos drew kin to changing roles. Nicolás became a *sirviente* in 1824–25, earning 29 pesos and 7 fanegas—and then left. Ygnacio, already a *sirviente*, became a *capitán* overseeing now mostly Hispanic *sirvientes*, his earnings up to 53 pesos and 13 fanegas. Agustín, previously a small tenant and *sirviente* for brief terms, became a vaquero (cattle herder) in 1824–25, gaining 27 pesos and 13 fanegas through the end of accounts in 1826. Gregorio returned as a *sirviente* for nine weeks of 1824–25, earning 6 pesos and 1.5 fanegas—then left again. Secundino Franco came on as La Griega's *caballerango*, horse wrangler, in the spring of 1826, earning 6 pesos and 2 fanegas before accounts ended. Franco power and earnings held strong.

The shuffling of roles suggests uncertainty as news spread of the priest-patriarch's declining health and the Francos prepared for new challenges and opportunities. As 1825 began, don José Vicente, still holding the large 200-peso lease at La Griega, managed the Atongo estate in nearby uplands. In January, he signed a nine-year lease to operate Santa Cruz and Dolores on the Amazcala plain for 2,000 pesos annual rent, pledging two houses in Querétaro as surety.[20] He had mixed management and leaseholds at La Griega, to buy two city properties without lien. Now managing Atongo and leasing Santa Cruz and Dolores, he might prosper in a world without Sánchez Espinosa.

When the La Griega accounts ended in June 1826, profit was gone—as were many Otomí families. The managerial Francos prospered. The Olveras, who mixed leasing with labor oversight, hung on; the Abendaños, who leased and labored, and the Juárez, who only labored, faced decline. A failed search for profit pressed new predations on producing families as agrarian capitalism collapsed.

Beyond La Griega: Landlords Face Debt
and Flee Risk, 1821–1826

While don José Sánchez Espinosa, among the most propertied and prosperous landed capitalists in New Spain in 1810, struggled to maintain commercial operations at La Griega after 1820, most proprietors in the new state
of Querétaro lived deeper challenges. Facing the fall of silver, the collapse
of textiles, and the end of profits, they turned early to leasing estates, deflecting production, risks, and losses onto others—who turned to rely on
subtenant family growers. Notarial records document proprietors' struggles and emerging ways of production in which landlords aimed to gain
rents, leaseholders took on risks, and families made maize for sustenance
and local markets.

From 1821 through 1825, notary Domingo Vallejo recorded 20 leases of
rural properties and one small sale. Few saw gain in estate purchases; fewer
had funds to buy. Leased properties ranged from ranchos claiming 200 pesos
in annual rent to estates gaining more than 2,000 pesos. Proprietors facing
debts leased, seeking steady incomes. Lead tenants took on leases, dreaming of gain in uncertain times. The historic dynamics of agrarian capitalism inverted: before 1810, while silver flourished, proprietors took risks to
gain profits; after the fall of silver, landlords pursued fixed incomes, passing risks onto leaseholders who left production to subtenant families. Few
profited; many ate well.

The first lease recorded in January 1821 is revealing. Doña Ysabel and
doña María Ygnacia de Austri, widowed sisters, leased the hacienda Labor
del Jaguey, just outside Querétaro, to don José Duró, Teniente Coronel Sar-
gento Mayor of the Plaza de Querétaro. The contract was for nine years, with
an option for two more. The rent would be 1,000 pesos the first three years,
1,200 the next three, 1,400 the final three—and 1,600 if the two-year option
was taken. The early rent was reduced "as there are no walls or fences, no
dam, no livestock of any kind, not even granaries, as those that existed are
ruined—without roofs or doors."[21] The decade of insurgency left the property a ruin: had it been attacked, neglected, or taken over by residents who
cultivated with little concern for the structures that supported commercial
operations? Structural deterioration made the military officer's power and
salary keys to reconstruction. The Austri sisters hoped for rising returns.

The lease introduced enduring patterns. Among those who leased out
estates claiming rents of 1,000 pesos or more through 1825, five were let
by women, three by convents, only two by men. Among those letting out

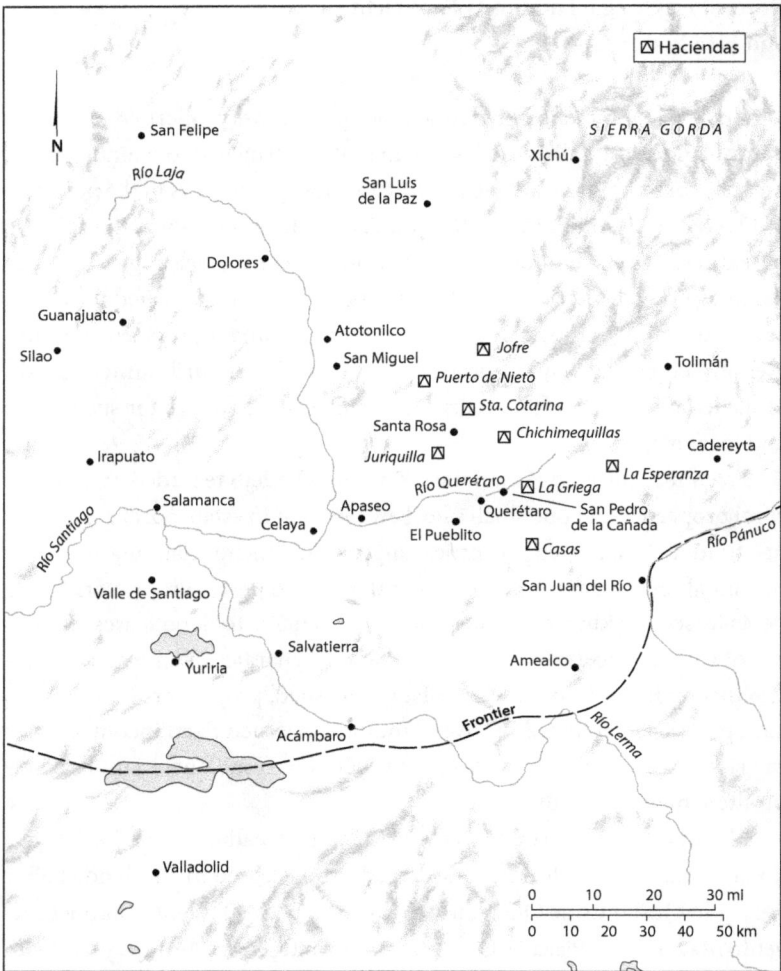

Map 9.1 Querétaro after insurgency.

smaller properties, two were women, one a convent, and seven were men—
four priests and three laymen. Only men took on lead leases. Patriarchy held
in direct estate operations.

A look at the men who took on leases is more revealing. When retired Lt.
Col. don Francisco Crespo Gil, a Querétaro merchant, leased out the small
Silva property near Celaya for 500 pesos in February 1821, he chose as tenant
don Romualdo Nágera, "a roaming trader living in Querétaro."[22] He was likely
Crespo's commercial dependent, trading in the new economy of ranchero

and tenant production. He had income, ties to rural people, and, hopefully, loyalty to the proprietor. When retired Lt. Col. don Agustin Frías leased out the small Rancho de Olveras for 220 pesos in November 1822, he chose don Manuel Soria, a transporter hauling goods around Querétaro and Celaya.[23] Men with rural contacts and knowledge were needed to revive small estates.

Leasing larger estates required financial assets often backed by military power. In December 1823, retired Lt. don Francisco Soberón leased the Molino de San José, a mill with adjacent lands at San Pedro de la Cañada between Querétaro and La Griega, to Captain don Juan Salazar—active in the military and regional director of the National Tobacco Monopoly.[24] He would bring military power and solid income to the tasks ahead. In February 1824, don Juan Manuel Septién, son of a leading Querétaro family, leased out the Juriquilla, San Ysidro, and La Solana estates he recently inherited from his grandmother, doña Felipa de Villanueva. The properties lay north of Querétaro, near the town of Santa Rosa, Juriquilla with irrigated fields, San Ysidro and La Solano in uplands. As tenant, Septién chose don José María Yañez, a merchant and magistrate in Santa Rosa.[25] Local knowledge, political and/or military engagement, and financial resources all mattered in leasing larger properties.

As in the Austri sisters' lease, provisions for repairs were common in early contracts, especially for estates west and north of Querétaro that had been exposed to insurgent incursions. The March 1821 lease of Coyotes, near Salvatierra in the heart of insurgent country, required the opening of irrigation ditches and new roofing for the granary. At Vegil, west of Querétaro, the January 1822 lease mandated 1,000 pesos in repairs, to be deducted from 2,500 pesos in rent. Damage and decay were less a concern east of La Cañada, where militias like the La Griega troop had kept insurgents at bay.[26]

In 1824, don Antonio Agustín Guerrero y Ocío, heir to an illustrious family, holder of vast Guerrero family estates, and Querétaro's deputy in the Congress writing Mexico's new constitution, leased out two properties. In January, he let the Rancho del Mayorazgo, southeast of San Juan del Río in uplands near Huichapan, where insurgent activity had been intense. He charged 450 pesos yearly—plus 500 pesos in repairs. Guerrero emphasized larger concerns: the owner and leaseholder would split costs of "reclaiming the lands usurped by neighbors," while the new operator "will not allow the building of a chapel at the place they claim as a pueblo." Local people had occupied rancho lands and planned a chapel to assert pueblo rights. The locally based leaseholder would use "his intimate knowledge of those lands" to defend the property.[27]

In November, Guerrero leased out Capulín, a vast property north of Querétaro in Guanajuato, at the edge of the Sierra Gorda. The rent of 5,375 pesos was the highest recorded in the post-insurgency decade; repair deductions were limited to 250 pesos yearly, to total 1,650 pesos during the seven-year term; and there was no escape for revolution, "no rebate for draught or flood." The leaseholder explicitly gained rights to sublet ranchos, pastures, woodlands, and charcoal works, while insisting he watch neighbors closely.[28] By delivering production to tenant families, the lease limited concerns that uprisings might cut production and end the leaseholder's ability to pay.

While questions of repairs and defense of property reflected years of insurgency, leases also addressed new concerns tied to state building. Taxes came first: the contract for a modest rancho in 1822 simply stated that taxes and any other government charges would be paid half by the owner, half by the leaseholder. From the fall of 1823 through 1824, as Iturbide's empire collapsed and a republican future held uncertain, leases for large properties—Santa Cruz and Dolores, Juriquilla, San Ysidro, and La Solana, and the great Capulín—also split tax payments between owners and lessees.[29]

Times of political uncertainty also brought worries about destructive violence. The Vegil lease of January 1822 offered the leaseholder no relief for "floods, fire, sterility, robbery, sacking—nor anything imagined or un-imagined." In August 1823, as Iturbide's rule crumbled, doña María Luisa Servín leased Santa Cruz and Dolores, north of La Griega, to don Juan Bringas. Key provisions recognized uncertain times: "If years of the lease prove abundant, he will pay 2,000 pesos, plus 500 more." But "if sackings, fires, or things like those that ruined estates in recent years should come, he is not responsible."[30]

Following that precedent, every lease of a large property from 1823 through 1825 included insurgency-risk clauses. In the 1823 lease of Comunidad and Texedo, doña Felipa Arias stated: "if (may God forbid) another revolution comes, and results in the destruction or burning of houses and granaries, and the theft of goods and livestock by rebels too numerous to repel," the owner would suffer the costs.[31] When don José Manuel Septién leased his Santa Rosa basin properties to Magistrate don José María Yañez, the insurgency provision was simple and direct: "in the unexpected case of a disastrous revolution like that of the year ten, may God forbid, the lease-holder may leave the estates, owing only the rent due to the day of the break." Fear of insurrection led to escape clauses.[32]

By January 1825, doña María Luisa Servín's lease of Santa Cruz and Dolores to don Juan Bringas had ended. She cut the cost to 2,000 pesos and leased to don José Vicente Franco, once the manager and still a leaseholder at La Griega, and now manager at Atongo. If anyone could revive production, it was Franco. Still, the lease offered an escape: if "riotous people" destroyed buildings or stole livestock, don Vicente faced no charges. And "disgracefully . . . if there is another revolution or uprising that blocks estate operations, the rent ends that day, with the leaseholder free to choose to continue or not."[33] In February, the lease of Aguacaliente, near Apaseo, noted that in the case of "revolution," the tenant owed two months' notice to leave or renegotiate the lease. In April, the lease for nearby Santa Rosa de la Galera left the tenant free of all risks should a rising like 1810 recur.[34]

More of the same came in 1826—along with new developments. In February, the Congregation of Guadalupe let the Vegil estate near the city for seven years at 2,000 pesos to Vicente Camacho, citizen of Querétaro—backed by Colonel José María Baca. The congregation would pay for repairs and property taxes, Camacho for improvements and sales taxes. Should the tenant fail to pay, the lease would end.[35] A clerical institution sought a local tenant backed by a military man to revive estate income.

Don Nicolás María de Berazaluce, vice governor of Querétaro, managed the property of his wife, doña María de Sandiel y Torres. In March, he leased the Amazcala estate, just north of La Griega, to don José Luis Lamas for seven years, the rent of 3,000 pesos to be paid in thirds in advance. If not paid, the lease would end. Grain in storage would be replaced by the tenant at the end of the lease; wheat standing in the fields would also be returned at the end. Amazcala had shifted in part to tenant cropping, the only way to pay in advance. To gain maize to hold in storage, the estate had turned to sharecropping; wheat was sown on estate account. Camacho paid for improvements; the owner paid taxes. There would be no relief for flood, drought, plague, or assaults.[36] A political man leased out his wife's inheritance, shifting risks to a leaseholder while sharecroppers made maize and took wages in wheat fields.

In 1826, Vallejo began recording leases and sales of *huertas*, always for cash. In January, the Congregation of Guadalupe leased three *huertas* and one "plot," all in the city, for one year—with an option for five more. Don José González would pay 500 pesos in cash rent, plus costs to plant new trees.[37] In April, Ciudadano José María Gómez, as guardian of his nine-year-old son Antonio, sold a "piece of land" along the river above the dam leading to the aqueduct in la Cañada, to doña Manuela López de Ecala, widow of "Republican" don Tomás Rodríguez. She paid 185 pesos in cash—no stipulations; no worries.[38] Continued sales for cash showed the strength of the *huerta* economy.[39]

Meanwhile, 1826 brought evidence of new ways forward in uncertain times—for a few. Doña María Trinidad Fernández de Herrera, "associate of her husband don Joaquín de Haller," *vecinos* of Querétaro, received 3,000 pesos "in cash" from doña Mariana Fernández de Herrera, her sister and "legitimate spouse of don José María Frias, First Justice of the Peace and Jefe Político" of Querétaro. The funds came from the estate of don Francisco Antonio Hernández de Herrera, late father of the two sisters. They were set as a lien on the Hacienda de Barajas held by doña María Trinidad and Haller. The latter signed as don Joaquín de Haller y Puch, a European immigrant trading in the city.[40] A new social fusion pursued power: two sisters of an old landed family saw one marry a European merchant, the other a political man. Investing jointly in the estate, they helped fund Haller's dealings. A landed, commercial, political clan found solid prosperity—a rarity in challenging times.

Populations Grow, 1822–1826

While leading landowners struggled and family growers delivered plentiful maize harvests at low prices, Querétaro's population grew. Birth-baptismal and death-burial records from 1822 through 1826 show births averaging 77 per thousand, deaths 46 per thousand, a growth of 3 percent per year over five years.[41] A healthy, well-nourished population grew in parallel to the rate suggested by the figures reported for Guanajuato in 1825 and 1826. Dispersed production and ample sustenance, claimed by insurgents in Guanajuato, negotiated as agrarian capitalism dissolved across Querétaro, brought sustaining nutrition.

Regional variations across Querétaro suggest more. The jurisdiction including the city of Querétaro and nearby basins including Amazcala and Santa Rosa reported a high birth rate of 82 per thousand and a high death rate of 55 per thousand, indicating growth of 2.7 percent. San Juan del Río, more rural with a diverse hinterland, reported births at 68 per thousand and deaths at 48, leaving growth near 2 percent. The two jurisdictions with the largest towns and richest basin lands included 70 percent of the state population and reported growth of 2 to 3 percent. Less populated uplands stretching east and north of the city reported 4 to 5 percent growth rates from 1822 to 1826. Long settled by dispersed indigenous peoples, they kept solid autonomies, ample nutrition, good health, and strong growth in the 1820s. A series of local censuses from 1826 reveal more.

Pame Persistence: *Labradores* and *Hortelanos*
at San Pedro de la Cañada, 1826

Set in the canyon west of La Griega, where the Amazcala River descends to water the city and its *huertas*, San Pedro was a historic Pame community. Family growers worked irrigated *huertas* in en enduring indigenous republic. Living between the loyal city of Querétaro and La Griega, its people neither joined nor faced disruptive insurgencies after 1810. In 1826, the town included 1,117 residents: 549 men and 568 women. Men were few among thirteen to twenty-five years old, as youths and unmarried men left to work in the city (or evade militia service). More than 40 percent of men were thirty or older while only 22 percent of women attained such age. The childbearing that brought population growth came with deadly results for too many mothers.

The census details the productive roles of 348 men, youths and adults, listing another 37 as *vagos*, vagrants. More than 85 percent worked the land: 22 were *labradores* working ranchos they owned or leased; 276 were *hortelanos* working *huertas* held as community domain to sustain families and send produce to Querétaro markets. Two grain millers, 2 hog raisers, 2 cane millers, and 1 woodsman joined an economy of shared prosperity integrated by 4 merchants, a notary, a sacristan (did the priest live in Querétaro?), and a constable. A carpenter, a bricklayer, and 8 masons attended to construction. Four tailors made clothing. And 7 musicians and 11 distillers of cane brandy kept taverns that offered diversions drawing city people to rest and respite in the canyon.[42]

Women's roles are not listed. Still, we know that they produced and raised children, worked *huertas*, marketed produce, made cloth and clothing—and labored endlessly to turn maize into tortillas to sustain families. San Pedro flourished as a community of family growers comfortable on the land. No landed proprietor took rent from their land or sought profit from their work. They lived lives of autonomy on community lands.

Communities on Estate Lands: *Labradores*
and *Gañanes* in the Santa Rosa Basin, 1826

On lands long ruled by large estates, the fall of agrarian capitalism opened the way to communities of tenant family growers that adapted to diverse ecologies while negotiating complex ethno-cultural relations. That independence and diversity are detailed in the censuses for the town of Santa Rosa and the six estate communities that occupied the basin that stretches northwest from Querétaro, on the road to San Luis Potosí.

Separated by a ridge from Puerto de Nieto and the guerrilla bastion at Xalpa, Santa Rosa estates were rarely occupied but often rattled by insurgents after 1810. Into the 1820s, the fall of Guanajuato's mines and the decline of Querétaro textiles cut markets for estate produce while family growers at Puerto de Nieto and beyond made maize plentiful and cheap. The 1826 censuses show commercial cropping gone, while lease holding and subtenant family planting entrenched across the Santa Rosa basin.

The town of Santa Rosa sits on a low ridge on the road leading north, along the stream that waters the basin. Never an indigenous republic, it held no community lands. The 1826 census reported 49 men's roles: 16 were merchants, all Hispanic, only 2 honored as don. There was a notary, a barber (and healer), a blacksmith, and 2 muleteers. In addition, 23 cultivators, 6 *labradores*, and 17 *gañanes* (small growers) lived in town while working land at nearby estates.[43] The town was a place of trade and crafts, serving people at outlying estate communities.

The six basin estates remained property of two landed clans: the Septiéns and the Velascos. None reported a manager or overseer as large-scale commercial cropping was gone. The census counted 261 *labradores* and 1,095 *gañanes* across the basin.[44] *Labrador* was a long-established label for men operating rural properties. A great landowner like don José Sánchez Espinosa might call himself a *labrador*, honoring his oversight of production and marketing. Owner-operators and lead leaseholders of modest haciendas and ranchos also claimed the label. In 1826, most *labradores* around Santa Rosa were leaseholders claiming distinction from the small growers labeled *gañanes*.

The latter term is revealing. Rare in the Bajío before 1810, it was common across basins near Mexico City in the seventeenth and eighteenth centuries, where it labeled indigenous people living on estate lands. They gained rights to build huts, keep gardens, and cultivate maize plots while providing seasonal labor in estate fields.[45] Across Santa Rosa after 1820, *labrador* and *gañan* labeled both Hispanic and indigenous men. *Labradores* leased large holdings; *gañanes* held rights to live on estate lands, planting maize for sustenance while paying rent, delivering crop shares, and/or providing seasonal labor to a leasehold *labrador*. In 1826, of 261 *labradores*, 175 were Hispanic, 86 Otomí. Among *gañanes*, 533 were Hispanic, 562 indigenous. Santa Rosa estate communities were internally stratified yet not ethnically exclusionary.

Thanks to the militia census reporting Hispanic residents in 1791, tribute counts of indigenous men in 1807, and the state census of 1826, we can explore how diverse residents had mixed and moved before, during, and after insurgency to forge locally distinct communities of maize-making families across a rich basin where Querétaro met Guanajuato.

In 1824, the Septién clan leased the Juriquilla complex to don José María Yañez, a merchant-magistrate at Santa Rosa. The properties included rich basin lands at Juriquilla south of town, along with uplands just west at San Ysidro and San Miguelito. The censuses reveal communities in reconstruction.[46] At the core bottomland property of Juriquilla, the 1791 militia census reported 33 Hispanic households with 142 people. Four managers were Spanish, as was the blacksmith. Ethnic separation was evident in 12 Spanish-mestizo households and 19 mulatto-indigenous households: 11 secure *sirvientes* split between Spaniards and mulattoes; 13 tenants were mulatto, with only 1 Spanish. Three of 4 muleteers were mulattoes. Juriquilla planted estate fields with favored Spanish-mestizo *sirvientes*—and indigenous workers uncounted in the militia lists. Mulattoes lived as tenants generating rents and muleteers attending to transport.

The 1807 tribute census reported 66 married indigenous men at Juriquilla and 24 still single—including established residents and recent arrivals. At upland San Ysidro, there were 43 married adults, only 2 still single, indicating departures—perhaps to Juriquilla, perhaps to the city. On the eve of insurgency, Juriquilla and San Ysidro combined to retain a favored Spanish-mestizo minority, falling numbers of mulattoes, and a large yet dependent indigenous majority: 30 Hispanic households included 120 people, far exceeded by more than 100 indigenous households with 400 people.

By 1826, Juriquilla had changed. At the lowland center, 22 Hispanic households were barely outnumbered by 29 indigenous neighbors. Six *labradores* included 3 Hispanic and 3 indigenous men. Among *gañanes*, 19 Hispanics shared the role with 26 Otomí households. In a community reduced to 200 residents, Hispanic and indigenous families lived as neighbors and shared roles. Did they mix? We do not know. The same 1826 census reported upland peoples at San Miguelito rather than nearby San Ysidro. There, Hispanic *labradores* outnumbered the indigenous 13 to 1; among *gañanes*, Hispanics led 41 to 22. Hispanic families seeking new lives on the land had moved to Juriquilla's western uplands, settling at San Miguelito and marginalizing San Ysidro's indigenous families, many of whom had moved on. By 1826, Juriquilla and its uplands were remade in two communities of tenant growers: ethnically balanced on fertile lowlands, mostly Hispanic in nearby uplands.

La Solana, in uplands east of Santa Rosa, was also a Septién estate. In the 1791 count, 21 Hispanic households included 121 people, split between Spaniards and mestizos—no mulattoes present.[47] The 15 *sirvientes* split evenly between Spaniards and mestizos; among tenants, Spaniards outnumbered mestizos 11 to 7. In a Spanish-mestizo community, roles were more shared than stratified. The 1807 tribute count reported 68 married men and 33 single—a total native population near 240, double the Hispanic population reported in 1791. Again, Hispanic residents had been pressed out and many Otomí were newcomers in 1807 as La Solana remained a segregated community.

In 1826, La Solana reported no *labradores*. Production fell to 30 Hispanic and 21 indigenous *gañanes*, a new Hispanic majority in a population fallen to near 200 as Otomí families left or were forced away. A pattern emerges at the Septién estates: populations shrank; few *labradores* remained while a multicultural majority of *gañanes* produced for sustenance.

North of town, Velasco family estates ruled the land. Santa Catarina was the most fertile and best irrigated. In the uplands east, Monte del Negro paralleled nearby La Solana with a limited yet diverse population. North of Santa Catarina, Buenavista included bottomlands and uplands, ruling the entrance to the pass that led west to Puerto de Nieto. Each estate had lived a different transformation.

The change at Santa Catarina was striking.[48] The 1791 militia census recorded only 13 Hispanic households, 8 mulatto, 5 Spanish-mestizo, with a total population of 55. Spaniards led among 4 managers; mulattoes were a majority among 9 *sirvientes* and 5 stock herders. The 1807 tribute count revealed a native majority: 47 men laboring for the estate (28 married men likely *sirvientes*; 19 single and surely *alquilados*), along with 43 tenants and "squatters." An indigenous population near 300 dwarfed a Hispanic population nearer 50 as 1810 approached.

In 1826, while indigenous numbers had fallen at nearby estates, they more than doubled at Santa Catarina. The census counted 17 Hispanic men: 16 *labradores* and 1 *gañan* outnumbered by 150 indigenous men—48 favored as *labradores*, 102 living as *gañanes*. Population had soared past 650, with 70 Hispanic and nearly 600 indigenous. While Otomí families left nearby estates (and La Griega), large numbers settled at Santa Catarina. Had its well-watered lands been remade as *huertas*, requiring the intense labors long practiced by Otomí families along the river just north of the Querétaro city center?

In the uplands east, Monte del Negro followed a different trajectory.[49] In 1791, it reported just 8 Hispanic households, 5 recorded as mulatto, likely descendants of settlers who gave the site its name. The total Hispanic population held near 35. The 1807 tribute count revealed another indigenous majority, 48 men living as laboring dependents, 15 as tenants and squatters in a total population around 250. A small Hispanic, mostly mulatto minority ruled a large native majority. By 1826, population numbers had inverted as social relations changed radically. There were 32 Hispanic *labradores* and 78 Hispanic *gañanes*, far outnumbering 14 native *labradores* and 42 native *gañanes*. At Monte del Negro, the Hispanic population surged while indigenous numbers held steady and became a minority.

The last Velasco estate, Buenavista, ruled the route to Puerto de Nieto and San Miguel. It included the northern end of the irrigable basin lands, along with ample uplands.[50] In 1791, it included 33 non-indigenous households: 16 Spanish, 13 mestizo, 2 mulatto—a total Hispanic population of 152; 23 tenant cultivators included 13 Spaniards, 8 mestizos, and the 2 mulattoes, while among dependent workers, 4 were Spanish, 6 mestizo, 4 mulatto, often youths living in their fathers' households. In 1807, Buenavista reported the largest indigenous population at the Septién and Velasco estates: 47 men, 33 married and 14 single, labored—the former mostly *sirvientes*, the latter primarily *alquilados*; another 76, 57 married and 19 single, lived as tenants and squatters. An Otomí population near 500 far outnumbered the Hispanic population at Buenavista before 1810. There, too, ethnic segregation inhibited insurgency—as it exploded just west over the ridge at Puerto de Nieto.

By 1826, Buenavista, too, had changed radically. Eighty-nine Hispanic households far outnumbered 43 Otomí. Hispanics dominated among *labradores* 42 to 6; they outnumbered native *gañanes*, 47 to 37. During insurgency and after, Hispanic cultivators came to rule at Buenavista, outnumbering a shrunken indigenous population 360 to 170. Had the Otomí majority at Buenavista in 1807 moved south to more fertile lands at Santa Catarina? Had the Hispanic community at Buenavista solidified by trading with the insurgent community at Puerto de Nieto? How did men at Buenavista see the assertive *rancheras* just west?

The six Santa Rosa estates had shared broad similarities with La Griega before 1810: favored Hispanic minorities and solid Otomí majorities mixed tenant cropping with labor in estate fields (with local diversities everywhere). Segregations limited insurgency. By 1826, while La Griega struggled to maintain commercial cropping and limit tenant production, Santa Rosa estates saw hierarchies of tenant production entrenched. Hispanic and Otomí residents held parallel roles even as new segregations set in. And while Otomí families faced exclusion at La Griega, many found new lives as *gañanes* around Santa Rosa, notably on the fertile lands of Santa Catarina.

Jofre in 1826: Estate Planting Wanes,
Family Cropping Gains

North of the Santa Rosa basin, the plains give way to a series of valleys and uplands on the road to San Luis Potosí. There, Jofre was a large and complex estate community. Long a Guerrero family property, it was held in the 1820s by don Antonio Guerrero y Ocío, a leader in Querétaro and federal politics. He had leased out Capulín, just north in Guanajuato, in 1824. Still, operating Jofre in 1826, he saw growing Hispanic and indigenous populations expand tenant production.

The 1791 militia census listed 186 Hispanic households with a total population of 835—the largest number in Querétaro estate counts.[51] Spaniards led with 98; mestizos 62; mulattoes 22; caciques 2. With 80 percent born at the estate, Jofre was an established community. Its Hispanic population was both diverse and endogamous: Spaniards married Spaniards, mestizos married mestizos, mulattoes married mulattoes. Spaniards and mulattoes often began as dependent workers in estate fields, shifting to tenancies in uplands as they became older, providing Jofre with equal numbers in both roles. Mestizos showed similar life trajectories—with many more tenants than workers. The estate then maintained a balance between commercial planting and tenant cropping. Life trajectories suggest that men preferred lives as tenant growers. Small but growing numbers of newcomers in the uplands suggest that families displaced by predations and evictions on more fertile basin lands came to settle.

The 1807 tribute count shows a large indigenous population with similar preferences: 43 married men and 27 still single labored; 89 married and 39 single lived as tenants and squatters, the married likely tenants, many of the unmarried squatters. The 198 indigenous households with a population near 700 gave Jofre the largest native population then counted at a Querétaro estate. A total population near 1,500 in 1810, 800 Hispanic, 700 indigenous, made Jofre the largest, most diverse, yet still ethnically segregated estate in Querétaro.

The 1826 census reveals a Hispanic population risen to 335 households and likely 1,350 people—a near 40 percent increase. The indigenous population rose to 359 households, now a majority nearing 1,500 residents—double the numbers before 1810. Small growers prevailed: *labradores* were only 68; *gañanes* a great majority at 626. And while Hispanics were favored as *labradores*, 53 to 15, 282 Hispanic households lived as *gañanes* surrounded by 344 indigenous families holding parallel lives. Hispanic and indigenous families flooded to Jofre during and after the years of insurgency, taking up lives as tenants focused on family sustenance.

One Estate, Many Communities: Chichimequillas in 1826

Chichimequillas lay at the end of the Amascala basin, north of La Griega, south of Jofre. A uniquely detailed census of 1826 confirms both the primary trends and local complexities of rural Querétaro's post-insurgency reconstructions. Long owned and operated by Querétaro's Carmelite Convent, it included irrigated fields and rugged uplands. Already in 1791, it was more than a cultivating community. It included 75 Hispanic households, with near 400 residents, more than half Spanish and deeply endogamous, the rest mestizo, mulatto, and mixing. They included 20 tenants and 29 workers, split nearly evenly between Spaniards and mixing men. Eleven attended to livestock and transport. And there were craftsmen—3 blacksmiths, a baker, a tailor, 3 hatmakers, along with a cloth-making community of 20: 10 weavers, 5 spinners, 4 carders, and a finisher in a community of social and productive diversity (in that parallel to Puerto de Nieto).

In 1807, the estate reported 200 indigenous men, 167 married, 33 single, spread as workers and tenants across multiple settlements. In 1810, Chichimequillas included a Hispanic population near 400, an Otomí population over 700, thus an estate total over 1,000.[52] Ethnically divided like La Griega, insurgents had attacked in 1811, then moved on as the community did not rise—again like La Griega.

In 1826, the population had fallen to 906, still the second largest at a Querétaro estate, with 343 families scattered across its lands. *Labradores* were the leading producers, with 69 Hispanics and 42 indigenous across 8 settlements. Notably, the census reported just 1 *gañan*, with 88 men counted as *sin oficio*. Those recorded as *sin oficio*, second in number only to *labradores*, lived without formal ties to the estate. Most lived among *labradores*, with informal roles parallel to the *gañanes* around Santa Rosa just west. Others squatted in uplands and had not faced removal as they labored seasonally for *labradores*. Independent, often informal lives on the land were strong at Chichimequillas in 1826.

Still, the 111 *labradores* and the 50 *sin oficio* working the land were less than half of the 343 men heading families at Chichimequillas. Others lived in communities forging new complexities. The *casco* was the historic center of commercial operations, home to managers, assistants, chaplains, and more. In 1826, a mayordomo and three assistants still lived there, along with one *labrador*. They were surrounded by 48 *sirvientes*, a cowherd, 2 shepherds, and a woodsman. Estate production with paid workers persisted—as it did on a larger scale, with 106 *sirvientes* at La Griega. At Chichimequillas, however, commercial cropping carried on while tenant production expanded. And its *sirvientes* were young and indigenous: three-fourths under thirty; two-thirds Otomí. Had some come from La Griega?

Near the *casco*, the settlement called the *cuadrilla* was once home to those, mostly Otomí, who provided seasonal labor to complement the work of *sirvientes* in estate fields. In 1826, the name persisted but the community had changed. It was young, 77 percent under thirty, and 85 percent Hispanic, including five *labradores*, a shepherd, and a hen keeper, plus twelve *sin oficio*—squatters likely planting a bit and surely working in fields planted by the estate and the *labradores*.

The cloth-making community carried on, too. In 1826, there were 8 households headed by weavers, 12 by spinners, 1 by a carder—all men, and except for 4 spinners, all Hispanic. Half the weavers were over thirty; the carder and the spinners were young, except for two widowers. The one merchant at Chichimequillas lived among the cloth makers. Don Agustín Herrera was thirty and single, living in a household with his sixty-year-old widowed mother and two sisters, also single. They were the only people honored as don and doña at the estate. Had they come from the city, aiming to link the textile community to wider markets? Nearby were a school-master, a blacksmith, a brick mason, and two muleteers. Chichimequillas remained a complex community.

Just south of the *casco* were two settlements, one small, one large, that shared ways common around Santa Rosa. Jiquen had 43 residents, its producing men split between 7 *labradores*, 7 *sin oficio*, and a *pulquero*. A shoemaker and a weaver added to estate artisanry. And Jiquen was mostly Hispanic: only one *labrador*, one *sin oficio*, and the *pulquero* were indigenous.

Santa María lay farther south. It reported 225 residents, a fourth of the estate and ethnically mixed. There were 24 Hispanic *labradores* and 11 indigenous, joined by 11 Hispanics *sin oficio* and 8 indigenous. The one man labeled a *gañan* showed that the enumerator knew the difference between a formal link to the land and informal lives. On the main Amazcala road, Santa María also included 6 muleteers plus a spinner, a carder, and 2 shoemakers. Hispanics predominated, while indigenous men found parallel roles. Notably, 60 percent of the population was twenty or younger, with many single men between sixteen and twenty seeking new lives. Among *labradores*, fifteen were over thirty, perhaps the core of a surviving community; twenty were younger, including many newcomers. The Otomí were nearly a third of both cohorts. Had exiles come from La Griega?

Baño lay north of the *casco*, where the Amazcala River left the mountains to water the plains. There were nine *labradores*, 5 Hispanic and 4 indigenous, heading large, often multigeneration households totaling 61 people. On rich lands away from roads and centers of trade, established family cultivators kept large and growing families without *sin oficios* to labor. Nearby Solano was similar—yet different. A small upland settlement on marginal lands, it included 18 *labradores* (16 indigenous), with only 34 total residents. Many were unmarried; few couples had children. The estate welcomed young Otomí men and families in search of new lives. More exiles from La Griega?

Northwest of the *casco*, along the upland route that led to Buenavista and Puerto de Nieto, lay Tierra Blanca, a majority Hispanic community. It included 22 *labradores*, 19 Hispanic, 3 indigenous, in a population totaling 55 (2.5 per household). Young Hispanic families and single newcomers built a new settlement—again without *sin oficios*. Further upland, Lajitas included 18 *labradores*, 11 Hispanic and 7 indigenous, in a population of 59, thus 3 per household in a more mixed community. Adults were older and single new-comers few in a settlement with most adults twenty or older, most children under ten. Lajitas appears to have been a small settlement of couples who had fled insurgency to find modest prosperity.

Chichimequillas offered refuge to families, Hispanic and Otomí, some displaced by the early impacts of insurgencies, others seeking new lives as estates like La Griega pressed people off the land in post-insurgency times (figure 9.1). The Carmelites welcomed the new diversity, including many squatters. The estate's diverse communities appeared to prosper.

Finally, there was Zuriel, one of the largest communities at Chichime-quillas, radically different, and a revelation. There were 63 household heads, nearly all Hispanic, in a population of 185—again 3 per household. There were 11 *labradores*, only 2 indigenous, plus an indigenous carpenter, a Hispanic tailor, and a winemaker. Far more numerous were the 46 men, most married Hispanic heads of households, listed as *sin oficio*. Four *labradores* were under thirty. Thirty of the *sin oficio* were heads of household, eleven over forty. Did elder men labor in service of young and struggling *labradores*?

Zuriel seems a mystery—until three heads of household appear listed as *ladrones*, robbers. The settlement sat in heights overlooking the road from Querétaro to San Luis Potosí, near the turn west to Puerto de Nieto and San

Figure 9.1 Main house at Chichimequillas, Querétaro. Author photo.

Miguel. The *ladrones* and *sin oficio* householders of Zuriel were petty capitalists in a post-insurgency Bajío, preying on passing traders and muleteers.
Another inversion emerges: insurgencies set off by predations pressed by
capitalists squeezing profit from the people who made their wealth had led
to independent predators taking profit from the prosperous in uncertain
times. We may presume that in the style of Robin Hood—or the bandit-hero
Chucho el Roto, long resident and still honored in Querétaro—Zuriel "entrepreneurs" did not prey upon their neighbors and shared a bit of their gains.

Querétaro's Carmelites kept a core of commercial production and a
cloth-making community, welcomed tenant *labradores*, and watched while
diverse others—Hispanic and Otomí, tenants, squatters, and thieves—settled
at Chichimequillas. There and across the state, no primary post-insurgency
adaptation ruled; ethnic relations and social stratifications differed everywhere. Still, by 1826 an overarching pattern had set in: landed property held
while agrarian capitalism had dissolved, ceding cultivation to leaseholders
and subtenants, *labradores*, *gañanes*, and squatters. Epigmenio González'
dream had come to define rural Querétaro.

Querétaro Transformed: Henry Ward's 1826 Encounter

Ward passed through Querétaro in 1826, just as the census confirmed the rule of family cropping. He lamented the fall of agrarian capitalism, reported the plenty all around—while struck by the persistence of cloth making in the face of imports. At San Juan del Río, he reported that "the vicinity of the town abounds in gardens and fruit trees, which gave a cheerful air to the scene." Heading north, "we breakfasted at the Hacienda de Saus . . . where all the abundance of the Baxío seemed to commence. We found in a poor little Rancho, provisions of all kinds: milk and eggs, excellent bread, tortillas of course, with chile for those who liked it, and large plates of frijoles." Ward met the new Bajío, rich in produce and ready to share: "From Saus . . . cultivation increased rapidly: we saw vast plains of maize at each turn."[53]

Approaching Querétaro from the heights to the south, "the first appearance of the aqueduct, by which the town is supplied water from a spring in the mountains . . . is very picturesque. Its arches are lofty, bright, and bold, and its vast extent gives it an air of great magnificence as it stretches across the plain." Ward praised the church of Guadalupe and the Convent of San Francisco that dominated the main plaza. The Santa Clara convent, west of the center, housed "two hundred and fifty females, composed of seventy nuns and as many young ladies sent there for their education with lay-sisters and attendants."[54] The monuments to Querétaro's glories stood.

Ward explains, "We were much struck with the busy look of Querétaro, which has quite the air of a manufacturing district. More than half the houses contain shops and the whole population is engaged either in small trades, or in the wool manufactories, which are still very numerous, . . . Coarse Tapalos and Mangas of different patterns are manufactured, part of which are retailed upon the spot in the great plaza, where a market is held every evening by torchlight, and part sent to the Capital or other great towns." Ward added that "the demand for these manufactures has decreased very much since the ports were opened to European imports"—a success in his eyes.[55]

Finally, he reported the triumph of family production: "The crop of maize had been lost in consequence of the extreme dryness of the season, and the price of maize had risen. . . . There were, however, no apprehensions of a scarcity, as 300,000 fanegas were known to be on hand within the territories of the state."[56] One dry summer did not make dearth in the new Querétaro. Family growers fed everyone.

Landlords, Leaseholders, and Subtenants: Greater Querétaro, 1827–1830

Landlord struggles, leasehold operation, and family production continued to define rural Querétaro to 1830. In March 1827, doña María Pando, widow of Col. don Fernando Romero Martínez, leased the Casas estate, south of Querétaro, to Lt. Col. don José María Baca for 1,800 pesos. The estate had been the focus of the suit filed in 1801 by youths resisting attempts to make them work off their fathers' debts. In light of that history, the 1827 lease is revealing: the rich family linked to the Condes de Regla no longer profited. The new lease required that leaseholder and subtenant debts be recognized— with no expectation of payment. With maize no longer a source of profit, pulque shaped operations at Casas. The lessee must preserve fields of maguey, supply Querétaro taverns, and pay rent monthly.[57] Family growers ruled maize; the Romero widow and Baca hoped to gain from pulque.

In another revealing lease signed in August 1827, doña María Ygnacia Landeta, of one of the families that had ruled textiles, trade, and landed power at San Miguel before 1810 and now a widow living in Querétaro, leased the Santa Barbara estate north of San Felipe to a nephew, don Luis Gonzaga de la Canal, a son of San Miguel's once-dominant clan. They had operated the estate in joint company; now she leased to the young patriarch, leaving him to face risks and costs of repairs while she claimed 100 pesos monthly, 300 more at year's end, plus 100 to sustain "the Sisters at [San Miguel] de Allende."[58]

While landed women and men leased out estates, only men took on leases. Most taking on large properties still came with military and/or administrative roles in the new national order. Lt. Col. don José María Baca leased Casas. Don Crecensio Mena, a Querétaro councilman, leased Tlacote el Alto northwest of the city, backed by don Pablo Gutiérrez, a local merchant. Don José María Sánchez de Arriola, a judge on the High Court of Michoacán, leased San Nicolás and Morales near Chamacuero south of San Miguel in Guanajuato—in partnership with an estate manager. Men with state power and salaries backed by merchants and managers took on risks to enter an uncertain landed economy.[59]

Concerns with insurgency past, repairs and taxes now fell to leaseholders as proprietors aimed for income without obligations. Political worries revived when the Republic faced the contested transition of 1828–29 that brought Vicente Guerrero to power. The 1829 lease of San Nicolás and Morales stated: "if during the nine years of the lease, political convulsions . . .

should block the free use and cultivations of the estates, at that moment, the lease will cease."[60]

The leases of 1827 through 1830 also document the new ways of production. Except at Casas in 1827 and La Griega in 1830, the work and pay of *sirvientes* vanished as concerns. Tenant cropping ruled: the 1828 contract for Tlacote el Alto gave the leaseholder the right to "give out lands on shares, for rents, or any means chosen." The outgoing tenant and all subtenants kept rights to pasture livestock and store crops into the coming year. An 1829 contract for San Nicolás and Morales near Chamacuero delivered rights to "sublet lands and ranchos." The 1830 lease of Santa Barbara del Sabino, near Apaseo, confirmed sharecropper rights to harvests and stock grazing.[61]

La Griega returned to view in an 1830 lease. When Sánchez Espinosa died in 1827, control passed to his son don Mariano Sánchez y Mora, ex-Conde de Peñasco. The 1830 contract was said to be written in Mexico City between don Mariano Francisco de Lara, counselor of the State of Querétaro, and don José Mariano Sánchez Espinosa. Did Vallejo and Lara mis-record the name of the new proprietor? Or was the lease a forgery, said to be signed by a proprietor they did not know?

What is clear is that Sánchez y Mora's power was vanishing in a morass of debt. Lara, a man of Querétaro's state government, already leased the Ranchos del Coyme and del Coyotillas, half of the estate's best arable land. The new contract gave him the right to sublease Coyme to *ciudadano* Lázaro Barrón, a resident at La Griega. The politically connected provincial aimed to deliver half his leasehold to a man on the land for 400 pesos paid annually for five years. Neither would allow livestock or *sirvientes* to use the *montes*, suggesting residents or outsiders were edging into estate uplands.

Barrón gained Coyme's main house. *Sirvientes* and livestock now there would join Lara at Coyotillos. If some wished to stay at Coyme, they could pay debts to Lara and remain. Lara's maize could remain in both *trojes* through 1831; Barrón would gain the granary at Coyme before the harvest of January 1832. Lara could pasture sheep at Coyme into the same year. Barrón could plant irrigated wheat but not disturb "the crops planted by the sharecroppers." Lara's maize, part planted by *sirvientes*, part by sharecroppers, awaited harvest and would remain his—and theirs. The stubble would go to Barrón, not Lara's *medieros*. A final revelation: Barrón could not sign.[62]

After Sánchez Espinosa's death, Sánchez y Mora had leased half of La Griega's operations to Lara, a local state official. Lara failed to profit, and, unable to pay his rent, turned half his leasehold over to Barrón, less educated but grounded in the community on the land. Did the notary and official record the deal without the new proprietor's consent? They likely expected that Sánchez y Mora would not notice if the sublease led to regular rent payment. That remained uncertain in 1830; with agrarian capitalism gone, fragmenting leaseholds delivered the lands of La Griega to families making maize.

Selling Out—and Buying In: Querétaro Landlords in 1829

After 1820, few estates were sold around Querétaro, as few could or would buy in a collapsed economy.[63] Sales resumed in 1829, when the owners of five small estates found buyers to relieve them of debts. On March 14, doña Felipa Josefa and doña Ana Francisca Arias, sisters, single, and over twenty-five, sold Tejeda and Comunidad, near the city, to don Salvador Frías for 35,000 pesos. Their father bought the estates in 1787; they sustained the family for decades, passing to the sisters before 1822—when they leased them for 2,100 pesos yearly, a rent cut to 2,000 pesos in 1823, suggesting a value of 40,000 pesos. The 1829 sale showed further decline.[64] Frías paid cash as the sisters looked to a safer investment.

Four days later, don Juan María Marquez of Querétaro sold Ojozarco, a small property on irrigated bottomlands near Celaya, for 18,500 pesos. The buyer, Lic. Don Ramón Estévan Martínez del Río, was a lawyer living in Querétaro. He paid 3,000 pesos in cash, promised 5,000 more in a year, and recognized 10,500 pesos to creditors.[65] Marquez escaped debts; Martínez del Río hoped his law practice would buy entry into the community of landed proprietors.

A week later, doña Josefa Dolores de Castillo y Alvarez sold San Pablo, south near Jerécuaro, for 20,000 pesos. Bought by her grandfather in 1770, its arable plus grazing lands had sustained the family through insurgency. The buyer, don Ygnacio Argomaniz, led the National Postal Service at Querétaro. He paid nothing down, recognized 3,800 pesos owed the ex-Marqués de Salvatierra, and promised the rest in 1,000-peso yearly installments at 3 percent. It was a lease to own, propelled by doña Josefa Dolores' arrival in Bordeaux, fleeing Mexico's political turmoil and collapsing economy. She left a Querétaro ally to find a buyer, which he did on terms little favorable to the seller.[66]

Meanwhile, siblings don Tomás Fermín and doña Manuela López de Ecala, the latter a widow, bought neighboring estates a week apart. On March 24, don Tomás bought Jurica el Grande for 59,907 pesos, a 25 percent discount from an inventory of 1821. It, too, included cropland, plus a grazing site. He recognized 5,000 pesos to support clergy and 16,514 pesos to the

Arias sisters (who invested half the capital they had gained ten days earlier). At 5 percent interest, they would collect 825 pesos yearly to sustain comfortable lives in Querétaro. Don Tomás Fermín paid the remaining 33,393 pesos at signing, a large sum in trying times.[67] The source of his funds is not noted, but in the 1790s he ran a large *obraje* making woolen cloth.[68] Had he become a merchant-financier linking family cloth makers to wool suppliers and city markets? Did he aim to set up textile operations at Jurica?

Then, on April 1, 1829, doña Manuela López de Ecala bought San Pedro Martir for 33,000 pesos. Its sloping lands just west of Jurica added less fertile and less valuable yet still cultivable lands to the family holdings. She paid 13,000 pesos down and recognized 3,000 pesos to Querétaro's Merced hospital, 2,666 to sustain one cleric, and 10,000 to another. She pledged 1,000 a year over five years to clear the remaining 4,333 pesos.[69] Why take on the adjacent estate for continuing obligations? San Pedro Martir included populations of *labradores* and *gañanes* on rain-dependent lands. Their rents might pay to complete the purchase and the annual interest to the three creditors. Family growers might also support her brother's textile economy. A mix of tenant production and rural cloth making would bring the ways of Chichimequillas to lands nearer the city.

After a decade of negotiations and adaptations, diverse hierarchies of tenant production ruled estates across Querétaro. Landlords juggled operations mixing limited direct operation, large leaseholds, planting by tenants and subtenants, cloth making, and robbery. Few proprietors profited, men with military power and state roles took on leases dreaming of gains that rarely came, while family growers made ample affordable maize, feeding themselves and city consumers. The gains taken by insurgents in Guanajuato after 1810 came to rule Querétaro in the 1820s. Agrarian capitalism was a memory in the Bajío.

Mexico in the Wake
of Revolution

Oligarchs Fall, Women Press On,
Families Make Maize—and More

Through the 1820s, while mining held low and industrial imports challenged cloth makers, family growers held strong in Guanajuato and consolidated on the land across Querétaro. Given the historic role of the Bajío in New Spain and the world, the revolution made there rattled power and production across the larger domains long linked in the dynamism of silver capitalism. As Iturbide's imagined empire rose and fell, then the federal regime grappled with scarce revenues and an uncertain future, struggling landed oligarchs faced rising debts, lost properties, and vanishing powers as family growers claimed control of maize and more across wider regions. And as leading men failed to sustain landed power, women stepped forward to limit the fall of once powerful clans.

New Spain's landed oligarchs faced an economic battering during the decade of insurgency. Their trials continued through the 1820s and extended beyond the Bajío. Without silver to stimulate markets and while family growers kept maize plentiful and prices low, profit vanished from estate operations across widening regions. The once great landed families concentrated in Mexico City saw power crumble. The struggles of the Condes de Santiago, eminent since the sixteenth century, and of the Conde de Regla, heir to the greatest mining and landed fortune of the eighteenth, tell much. The fall of the Conde de Peñasco reveals more, thanks to records that detail popular pressures, personal failures, and two wives' efforts to break the family fall.

Insurgency broke agrarian capitalism in Guanajuato before 1820. It ended across Querétaro in the 1820s. And long popular struggles broke commercial production across San Luis Potosí from the 1820s into the 1840s while communities constrained pulque capitalism near Mexico City. Frances "Fanny" Calderón de la Barca, Scottish wife of Spain's first ambassador to Mexico, joined the world of falling oligarchs as the 1830s ended. She shared city life and rural encounters with women working to keep eminence alive. Few succeeded as producing families and communities consolidated on the land.

Oligarchs in the Age of Iguala

In 1821, Iturbide proclaimed the Plan de Iguala, mobilizing military commanders backed by high churchmen and struggling oligarchs dreaming of restoring wealth and power in New Spain. They learned that armed power could topple a regime but could not revive silver capitalism or the revenues essential to the empire they imagined. And in that world remade in revolution, Mexico City oligarchs could not restore landed power while family growers ruled production, ate well, and made maize plentiful.

In 1820, the Teruel family struggled to keep properties from the southeastern Bajío around San Juan del Río, where their Tequisquiapan was the largest in the jurisdiction, to the Valley of Toluca, where they held two estates, to Chalco, where they owned three more. Mounting debts forced auctions while buyers proved scarce as agrarian capitalism collapsed. They kept their property but power and profit were gone—the mark of oligarchic life in the wake of the Bajío revolution.[1]

Don José Antonio González Alonso, Marqués de Santa Cruz de Inguanzo, once First Magistrate of the Mexico City Council and long owner of the Casasano sugar estate near Cuernavaca, died in 1816 deep in debt. In 1820, the Auditor de Guerra charged with funding the military ordered an auction seeking 300,000 pesos.[2] The same year, don Gabriel de Yturbe y Iraeta, once a leading merchant and captain in Mexico City's commercial regiment, saw creditors force an auction of two fine houses in the capital along with the San Diego del Ojo estate in Durango, the latter valued at nearly 500,000 pesos.[3] Again, buyers proved scarce, leaving debts to plague a once powerful clan.

Don Pedro Ygnacio de Valdivieso, Marqués de San Miguel de Aguayo, held vast lands in northern Coahuila. On his death in 1820, creditors forced an auction to lease the family holdings at Parras, west of Saltillo. Young don José María gained the title and rights to inalienable entailed properties. He won appointment to Iturbide's Sovereign Junta of the Mexican Empire. But the new marqués had no economic power as his scarce earnings flowed to creditors.[4]

After insurgency and the fall of silver capitalism, the entails that had protected oligarchic family properties became problematic. They kept key properties from division, sale, and loss to creditors, passing them intact to favored heirs, preferably male. In 1821, Iturbide and his allies faced a dilemma: if entails persisted, oligarchs would keep property while facing debts that made profit impossible; if entail ended, they would lose property—with no clear route to revive profit.

In 1823, a wobbling regime found a compromise. Current holders could sell up to half their entailed properties (by value). The rest would remain inalienable by sale or seizure until they passed to the next heir. Selling half might pay creditors and gain capital to revive operations on what remained.[5] Oligarchs might carry on as less landed proprietors, the best they could imagine as agrarian capitalism dissolved. The opening slowed but did not halt oligarchs' demise. Many retained land, modest wealth, and memories of titled eminence. Most lost effective landed power, sooner or later. Without silver, the capital that funded commercial cultivation vanished while family growers flooded markets with ample and affordable maize. Oligarchs kept land and memories of nobility. Power vanished.

The fall of the young Marqués de San Miguel de Aguayo is illuminating. Facing mounting debts he could not pay, in 1825 he sold disentailed northern properties to English investors led by Baring Brothers. While some dreamed that British capital could revive mining, the Barings imagined profit in a revival of agrarian capitalism. They failed together. Estates that were valued at more than a million pesos at their purchase in 1825 sold for just over 200,000 pesos in 1840 to the Sánchez Navarro family, northern provincials who struggled to keep landed eminence into the late 1860s. Neither silver capitalism nor agrarian capitalism could be restored by British capital after 1820.[6]

Condes de Santiago Fall, 1820–1835

Aguayo was not the greatest to fall. The Condes de Santiago Calimaya were the oldest of New Spain's landed oligarchs. Their wealth built on powers wielded by Viceroys don Luis de Velasco I (New Spain, 1550–64) and II (New Spain, 1590–95; Peru, 1596–1604; New Spain, 1607–11)—both pivotal to the foundation of silver capitalism, both linked to leading miners and estate builders, all accumulating titles and entailed estates. In the middle of the eighteenth century, multiple titles and entails concentrated in the hands of don Juan Lorenzo Gutiérrez Altamirano y Velasco. He held the Atengo estates that ruled the Valley of Toluca west of the capital; Molino de Flores, a rich grain and milling property near Texcoco; Tulancalco, the pulque estate between the capital and the Real del Monte mines; and properties on rich Bajío bottomlands near Salvatierra.[7] After his death, Santiago family power held strong through the 1790s—led by women.

The conde had four daughters. He had arranged for the eldest to marry a High Court judge, aiming to fuse landed and judicial power. When she died before her father, her sister Doña María Isabel Velasco y Ovando inherited the titles and entails. Never married, she set her youngest sister, doña María Josefa, also single, to manage the family enterprises across the heartland and beyond. Together they claimed steady profits. When the condesa died in 1802, titles, entails, and landed operations went to a third sister, who had married don Leonel Gómez de Cervantes. Patriarchy restored, he ruled until 1810, when two sons deposed the father to take maternal inheritances: don José María Cervantes y Velasco, Conde de Santiago and Marqués de Salinas, gained the Toluca valley estates; don Miguel Cervantes y Velasco, Marqués de Salvatierra, got Molino de Flores, Tulancalco, and Bajío properties. They expected to remain landed, rich, and powerful.

They soon faced challenges in times of insurgency. The Toluca basin communities that rejected Hidalgo kept sending workers to don José María's Atengo properties, supplying the capital and sustaining counterinsurgency. Don Miguel faced greater challenges. While Molina de Flores still operated, Otomí insurgents cut production and ended profits at Tulancalco, while insurgent residents occupied his lands at Salvatierra. Both brothers took commands to defend power. In 1821, both the Conde de Santiago and the Marqués de Salvatierra gained appointment to Iturbide's Junta Soberano del Imperio along with the young Marques de Aguayo and the third Conde de Regla. All held titles and entailed patrimonies; all struggled to hold the wealth their entails presumed to deliver.[8]

Don José María, ex-Conde de Santiago Calimaya, soon faced greater challenges in the new nation. The indigenous republics that surrounded Atengo had disputed estate labor relations and landholdings in local spats and judicial claims in the late eighteenth century. The Santiago matriarchs, aided by their brother-in-law the judge, fended off the threats. Living in self-governing republics, planting limited lands, and taking wages in Atengo fields, Valley of Toluca villagers stayed home as Hidalgo passed by and worked to sustain the capital through the decade of insurgency that followed.

Then, as the Federal Republic began in 1824, State of Mexico governor don Lorenzo de Zavala, a staunch liberal foe of Iturbide and oligarchy, backed long simmering suits that challenged Atengo's lands. Community victories cut estate operations and profits as villagers gained new lands to make maize, feed families, and supply markets—keeping prices low.[9] In the new republic, the Conde de Santiago lost land and profit while community-based family growers gained new autonomies.

His brother don Miguel, Marqués de Salvatierra, faced greater challenges. From 1811 through 1815, Tulancalco was rattled by insurgents, generating losses and destructions.[10] His Salvatierra properties were beyond reach until the Bajío pacified after 1818. He turned to trade, to face mounting debts only cleared by the end of entail. Beginning in 1825, he sold properties to pay creditors, reducing the family patrimony to revive production on what remained—to the chagrin of his son and heir.[11]

Into the 1830s, don Miguel Gómez de Cervantes retained Molino de Flores, its wheat fields and mill; Tulancalco, the pulque property between the capital and Real del Monte; small Salvatierra estates; plus lands near Apatzingán. The Bajío properties yielded small rents. He operated Tulancalco directly, selling maize and pulque in Real del Monte, Pachuca, and Mexico City for little gain. He gave management of Molino de Flores to his son, who complained of paltry earnings.[12] The Cervantes y Velasco brothers, ex-Conde de Santiago and ex-Marqués de Salvatierra, heirs to landed oligarchy, remained honored men in conservative circles. Their wealth and power paled before those of their grandfather and aunt, the last conde and condesa to hold unified properties. Agrarian capitalism gone, Santiago men struggled.

The Conde de Regla Falls, 1820–1846

Don Pedro Romero de Terreros had claimed the greatest accumulation of wealth and landed power gained under eighteenth-century silver capitalism, ennobled as Conde de Regla. At his death in 1782, he left an estate valued at 6.5 million pesos—formally divided among six heirs. The second conde kept mines in operation and family estates strong to his death in 1809. The widowed second condesa kept merged Regla and Jala family properties intact through the challenges of insurgency.[13]

When don Pedro José Romero de Terreros gained his majority, title as third Conde de Regla, and a seat on the Mexico City Council in 1814, he remained under his mother's rule. She kept creditors at bay to her death in 1819. Soon after, they forced an auction of non-entailed properties valued near 800,000 pesos.[14] In an economy broken by insurgency, no one could buy. The fall of silver capitalism broke Regla family wealth and sustained its properties—for a time. In April 1820, don Pedro José held four titles, two from his father, two from his mother, all tied to landed entails. Honored by Fernando VII in Spain and viceregal powers in New Spain, he was eminent, landed—and drowning in debt.[15]

In October 1821, he gained appointment to Iturbide's Junta Soberano del Imperio.[16] In March 1822, while the emperor struggled to rule, creditors advertised Regla properties valued at 820,000 pesos. Again, buyers proved scarce, preserving Regla's lands and debts.[17] In August 1823, after the law opened entails and as Iturbide's empire collapsed, the struggling conde announced his intent to disentail properties tied to three of his four titles.[18] In 1824, as the empire's opponents founded the Federal Republic, he transferred operating control of the mines and refineries at Real del Monte to British investors, hoping their capital and pumps could revive production. Silver began to flow in the late 1820s, rose through the 1830s, to hold steady in the 1840s. Yet production never met costs and neither Regla or his British partners profited. On his death in 1846, he owed 4 million pesos to bankrupt British investors and creditors.[19]

While the British Company managed the mines, Regla struggled on the land. The Jala pulque properties around Otumba, valued at 230,000 pesos when he inherited them, were worth only 170,500 pesos in 1836—a 25 percent decline from a post-insurgency low.[20] Things were worse at nearby Cuautengo. Valued at 153,400 pesos in 1819, it was worth just 55,603 pesos in 1836.[21] Without funds for transplanting and facing recalcitrant communities, profit plummeted.

The small San José Gasave and Coatepec estates lay near Zempoala in the northern valley of Mexico. Together valued at 29,979 pesos in 1819, in 1827 the struggling conde leased them to don José Meneses, a local resident. Landlord and tenant joined in a revealing deal: the conde agreed to sell the properties to Meneses when disentailment was done, at the price an inventory then showed. In return, the tenant loaned 20,000 pesos to Regla. The ex-conde owed 1,000 pesos in annual interest, but would not pay.[22] The provincial Meneses delivered 20,000 pesos to the indebted ex-nobleman in exchange for rent-free operation of pulque estates. Meneses kept production strong. When disentailment came in 1836, the properties held their value at 28,761 pesos.[23]

Facing endless difficulties, in 1834 the ex-Conde de Regla turned to lease Santa Lucía, long the pride of Jesuit and Regla family holdings. Colonel don

José Pérez Tejada of nearby Tepotzotlán agreed to pay 3,000 pesos yearly, suggesting a value of 60,000 pesos, a collapse from pre-insurgency times. It took Pérez two years to pay the first year's rent; then the conde deferred all payments until 1840.[24] Cash poor and burdened with debts, the ex-Conde de Regla remained rich in property when he finally disentailed key patrimonies in 1836. The Condado de Regla, including Santa Lucía and other estates, the refineries at Real del Monte, but not the mines (subsoil rights could not be entailed), was valued at the "enorme suma de" 2,296,934 pesos, an inflation reflecting earlier times of silver capitalism—or perhaps the value offered to British investors to draw their capital. The San Cristóbal holdings, long patrimony of his wayward uncle don José, included estates from the northern heartland to the Bajío, now overvalued at 1,226,062 pesos. The properties of his mother's Condado de Jala were valued at only 199,222 pesos—a collapse reflecting current realities.[25]

Struggles did not end. Don José Meneses, the provincial who had leased to purchase Gasave and Coatepec in 1827, died in 1838. His heirs canceled the contract, leaving the ex-conde owing 20,000 pesos and desperate for a buyer.[26] Ajuchitlán near San Juan del Río had been offered for sale by creditors in 1819. No buyer appeared, and in 1839 debts still plagued its operation.[27] In 1840, Regla sold La Gavia, a vast undeveloped estate west of Toluca, to don Francisco Echeverría, a Veracruz merchant and former treasury minister—among the few with capital to buy.[28]

The third Conde de Regla died in April 1846 as US forces mobilized to invade Mexico. His father had died in time to escape the insurgencies that broke New Spain; the struggling son left the world before the war that took Mexico's north into the United States. By then, Regla power was gone.

The Conde de Peñasco Falls, 1820–1845

When don Mariano Sánchez y Mora, ex-Conde de Peñasco, inherited his father's properties in 1827, the combined landholdings approached those of the Santiagos and Regla. He struggled to keep estates and revive profits into the 1840s. His letters reveal in unique detail the endless pressures from below that drove Peñasco's oligarchic demise—while two wives attempted to slow the family fall.

From 1780 to 1810, don José Sánchez Espinosa profited by operating estates from La Teja at the edge of the capital and San Pedro making pulque near Otumba, through La Griega and Puerto de Nieto in the Bajío, to the vast Bocas estates in San Luis Potosí. His marriage brought the Peñasco title and San Luis Potosí estates to his son in 1805. Young Peñasco's dalliance with rebellion in 1808 proved brief. When residents took Puerto de Nieto for insurgency in 1811, father and son turned to resist the revolution that broke silver capitalism—with limited success.

When Sánchez Espinosa reclaimed Puerto de Nieto in 1820, he gained solid rents from tenant growers entrenched in a ranchero community. He maintained commercial production at La Griega to his death in 1827, reaping losses. Northern grazing operations kept profit alive while he struggled to revive pulque near the capital. Young Peñasco had long flailed in his father's powerful shadow. After the priest-patriarch's death, Peñasco struggled to hold and take profit from family properties stretching from the heartland, through the Bajío, and across San Luis Potosí.

In 1820, as pacification delivered production to tenant family growers at Puerto de Nieto and Sánchez Espinosa dreamed of reviving agrarian capitalism at La Griega, the conde struggled to profit in San Luis Potosí. Like many in his generation, he turned to politics. Early in 1821, he aimed to serve as San Luis Potosí's deputy in the new liberal Cortes soon to meet in Spain. He came second, named *suplente*. In April, as Iturbide's Iguala movement gained momentum, Peñasco resigned his role in liberal Spain yet did not gain a seat on Iturbide's Junta Soberana beside the young Regla, Santiago, and Aguayo patriarchs.[29] Did Iturbide remember Peñasco's dream of an indigenous rising in 1808? Did Peñasco's recent dalliance with Spanish liberalism disqualify him?

In the fall of 1821, as Iturbide occupied the capital, the conde left for his northern estates. He complained that only ten armed men remained to protect property and chase *ladrones* across San Luis Potosí. General don José Antonio Echavarri blamed lack of enlistments in the new national militia. In December, Peñasco faced a demand for 2,000 pesos as a forced loan to the imperial treasury.[30] The military-oligarchic alliance seeking power was short of recruits and funds.

In January 1822, Peñasco's brother-in-law, don Cosme Flores Alatorre, wrote from the capital about the politics of a new city council. He saw three factions: Jacobins (adamant liberals); Catholics (committed to the old order, clearly the correspondents' choice); and adherents of don José María Fagoaga (a rare oligarch who had backed independence after 1810). Flores Alatorre feared that Fagoaga had locked up the Catholic party, eliminating any role for Peñasco.[31]

Political winds could shift quickly. In March, news came that Spain's Cortes had rejected the Treaty of Córdoba, blocking any union of Spain and Mexico under a shared monarch. On March 18, 1822, a military *pronunciamiento* declared Iturbide emperor; the next day, Congress voted what the military pronounced. Peñasco sat as one of three representatives of the nobility in Iturbide's first Constituent Congress, where rival Fagoaga represented hacendados. Peñasco joined those affirming Iturbide's empire; Fagoaga led a group of sixty who opposed. By August, Fagoaga was in jail while Peñasco represented San Luis Potosí on the Junta Instituyente charged with making the Mexican empire constitutional.[32]

His political ascent proved brief. Early 1823 brought the Plan de Casa Mata, backed by don Antonio López de Santa Anna and provincial republican forces. Iturbide resigned in March and left Mexico; by October Peñasco was back in San Luis Potosí reading letters from his father, still in the capital, still apolitical, still ruling family affairs. He instructed his titled son, exiled again, on the necessities of estate operations, finance, and transportation.[33] Through 1823 and 1824, Peñasco remained in the north trying to revive estate profits. Seeking a role in government, he wrote don Miguel Rámos Arizpe, the voice of northern republicanism. Nothing came.[34]

Political aspirations blocked, Peñasco faced his powerful father's failing health. In November 1824, don Gabriel de Armijo, military commander at San Luis Potosí, spread news of the priest-patriarch's illness.[35] In April 1825, Peñasco, "your son the Conde," wrote to "my beloved father, with all my appreciation and respect" lamenting a judicial order set by the patriarch limiting the funds available to the ex-conde as his father's health waned and economic challenges mounted. Family survival focused their correspondence until the priest-patriarch died in August 1827.[36]

The power long in the hands of the priest-patriarch faced a reckoning. Sánchez Espinosa had adapted to insurgent-imposed family production at Puerto de Nieto, taking rents when he could. He had continued commercial operations at La Griega, gaining profit just once after 1820. Accounts show one source of steady earnings in the early Mexican years: sheep grazing at northern properties. From 1820 to 1826, annual receipts from sales of mutton, hides, and tallow in the capital approached 20,000 pesos, with expenses under 10,000.[37] Those earnings had to cover costs and losses at estates from the heartland, through the Bajío, and across San Luis Potosí. Funds were perpetually scarce.

In 1827, soon after his father's death, Peñasco lost control of Puerto de Nieto and La Griega to creditors. In 1828, Br. don Felipe Ochoa, treasurer of the Congregation of Guadalupe in Querétaro, demanded payment on a 51,000-peso lien set on the core Bajío estates since 1708. Sánchez Espinosa had stopped paying and Ochoa had covered the arrears for the honored—

or feared—priest-patriarch.[38] Peñasco insisted he could not pay due to "the great losses taken by all the haciendas across the north due to two years of terrible drought. . . . We have no money."[39]

Historically, when northern grazing estates lost livestock and income in years of drought, losses were balanced by profit taking at cereal estates like La Griega and Puerto de Nieto. Now, drought brought rent withholding at Puerto de Nieto while markets flooded with maize cut prices and profits at La Griega. The mix of ecologies, products, and markets that sustained agrarian capitalism had ended. Peñasco, rich in land, was broke. He struggled for years to pay the congregation.[40]

In 1830, he still held claim to La Griega—without active oversight. Former manager don José Ysidoro Franco leased half the property; don Mariano Francisco de Lara, an official in Querétaro state government, leased the rest—both paying their rents to creditors. The contract filed in Querétaro by Lara that year likely was forged. He had leased two major ranchos since 1829 and failed to profit; now he sublet half his operation to an estate resident, Lorenzo Barrón, to open greater subleasing. Family production ruled at La Griega—all subject to approval by an unnamed creditors' agent.[41]

In 1837, don Francisco Fagoaga, heir to powers built in silver banking and mining finance, commerce and landholding, and kin to the ex-conde's political nemesis don José María, bought La Griega in an auction forced by creditors. In 1839, Fagoaga leased the estate to don Juan Crisóstomo Couto of Querétaro, who sublet Coyme and Coyotillos to doña María Francesca de Lara, widow of the tenant of 1830. Hierarchies of leasing and subleasing still ruled at La Griega.[42]

Once rich Bajío properties lost, Peñasco remained vastly landed and cash deprived. In San Luis Potosí, he retained Bocas and Cruces, Peñasco and Angostura. Near Mexico City, he held La Teja and the pulque estates at Otumba. In the early 1830s, he lived in the capital, welcomed by the conservative regime of General Anastasio Bustamante and Lucas Alamán. He focused on La Teja, hoping to live on rents from the estate of rich chinampas—lake bed plots, endlessly productive of fruits, vegetables, and more. Set at the edge of the city, La Teja rarely appeared in family letters. Now, a local parish demanded payments past due on a mortgage; 1832 brought laments of buildings needing repair, uncertain irrigation, and conflicts with tenants; in 1834, Peñasco sought a leaseholder to deal with tenant family growers—without success.[43]

Challenges at La Teja unresolved, in 1833 he set out to inspect his San Luis Potosí estates—and escape a liberal government taking power. His wife, doña María Antonia Flores Alatorre, stayed in the capital, attended to business—and challenged Peñasco's rule of estate operations. She addressed the "Conde de Peñasco," followed by "My Beloved *Hijito* (Little Son), with all my affection." A decade after the end of titles, the ex-conde clung to the pretense of nobility. Doña María Antonia's infantilization of her husband might be taken as affection but for her repeated insults to his managerial skills. She complained of health concerns, liberal attacks on religious institutions, and Peñasco's incompetence.[44]

She insisted he personally supervise the annual roundup and branding at Angostura. If he did not, livestock would be lost to managers and tenants. When he did not, she excoriated him: "As long as you do not go to Angostura, your trip is worthless; you will not remedy the estate's enormous problems."[45] A month later, she pressed him again to go to Angostura, now to oversee the *matanza*, the annual slaughter. She goaded him to challenge manager don José José María Pastor, insisting that her husband "must fix endless problems." Two weeks later, the slaughter done without his presences, the tallow en route to Mexico City, she again pleaded with Peñasco to go to Angostura. She insisted that Pastor lied in accounts and reports, running the property for his own gain.[46]

In March, she complained of failing health—and that the tallow arrived late, cutting earnings. The hides had not arrived, causing more losses. Meanwhile, family growers leasing chinampas at La Teja refused to pay rents. She tried again to find a leaseholder—and failed. Meanwhile, income from the pulque estates near Otumba barely covered expenses. In the early 1830s, Peñasco's wife treated him as his father had—a distracted dependent not to be trusted with economic decisions.[47]

Her last letter in 1834 saw doom. She lamented her husband's inability to fix "the problems at the haciendas." She backed his order to halt the clearing of woodlands to expand cultivation; new cropping would only lower prices and estate profits. Still, she doubted tenants would respect his mandate. She closed by reporting her joy at his coming return, continued problems selling pulque, and a "strong earthquake" that had shaken life in the capital.[48] Peñasco struggled to play patriarch, squeezed between assertive tenants, controlling managers, and a wife who would not abide his incompetence.

He remained the leading landholder in San Luis Potosí while he returned to live in the capital. In 1837, he aimed to reform operations at Bocas and prepare his son don José María Sánchez y Flores to succeed as patriarch. Peñasco enlisted don José Ysidoro Franco, last of his father's managers at La Griega and a lead tenant there during years of creditor oversight. Now, with the Fagoaga takeover, Peñasco hired him to manage Bocas and introduce Sánchez y Flores to its problems and possibilities.[49] Franco's letters reveal a world where producers still challenged propertied power.

In June, he was at Bocas with "my patron . . . his wife and their wonderful children." Franco's first report was mixed: while "furious drought" raged north at Cruces, at Bocas rains had begun and irrigation allowed planting in fields too dry to sow earlier. With crops "average," Franco aimed to expand irrigation. In early July, he reported failing rains, "a bit of maize and some frijol" on estate fields, while "the sharecroppers" who worked non-irrigated land "have had to replant seed lost to drought." Sharecroppers ruled maize; their losses were also estate losses. Franco proposed a new dam "in the highest place possible" to increase irrigated planting on estate accounts. But a dam and canals required capital and labor while the tithe collector at San Luis Potosí demanded three years of past-due payments. Funds for a capital project were scarce.[50]

In August, Franco defended his management at Bocas. He blamed drought and insisted that he was a "manager of fields," not "accounts."[51] Franco had managed fields and accounts at La Griega in the 1820s—when he gained more than Sánchez Espinosa. Perhaps fearing a repeat, Peñasco removed him early in 1838. Don José María Bruno Duque took over, to report: "I have been careful dealing with tenants, . . . trying to avoid the losses that come to the estate when they refuse to pay rents they see as too high; they avoid paying, offering any excuse they can invent."[52] When Peñasco proposed a return to cropping with hired *sirvientes*, Bruno replied that workers demanded advances, creating debts never repaid. With no cash to pay workers and prices kept low by tenant production, as planting began in May 1838, Bruno lamented: "It would be good to have no tenants, as they cause so many problems; but there are now so many it is impossible to remove them."[53]

In June 1839, Bruno reported late and limited rains at Bocas, yet "the price of maize has not risen despite the drought; we must sell what we can."[54] Scarce rains six months after the harvest had not raised prices to profitable levels while tenant growers fed themselves. In February 1840, after sharecroppers harvested the drought-threatened maize, Bruno lamented that he could not sell the half he received, except to day laborers working on estate projects. As March began, he returned to blaming "drought, snow, and hail," threats that historically drove profits.[55] In June, Bruno pivoted to support the sharecroppers who ruled production at Bocas: "As many have seen worms invade their fields, I have given them seed to replant." Without their crops, there was no production and no estate share.[56]

As the 1840s began, the ex-Conde de Peñasco kept vast lands across San Luis Potosí yet gained no profit as managers, tenants, and sharecroppers ruled production mixing grazing and maize cropping. He remained in the capital, where doña María Antonio died in 1840. He quickly took a new wife, and turned to focus on the family pulque estates at San Pedro near Otumba. His father had let them to tenants after insurgents shook the region. Peñasco reclaimed them for direct operations in 1841 and struggled to profit in the face of resistant communities—as his second wife challenged his power.

Deliveries to capital taverns rose from 70 cargas weekly in 1841, to 73 through 1842, 75 in 1843, to 80 from January to April 1844.[57] But prices never covered costs kept high by demanding workers and defiant villagers. In January 1841, workers were scarce and "badly disposed."[58] In May, as village-based *peones* planted maize and tapped maguey, Peñasco complained that San Pedro drew too much cash. His manager replied curtly that he could return to "leasing these lands"—the only way to operate without a steady cash flow.[59] In July, the estate still struggled to find workers to transplant maguey. In October, scarce muleteers cut shipments to the capital while villagers refused to work without maize rations—which the estate could not provide even as the staple sold for a historic low price of 6.5 reales per fanega.[60]

Complaints faded in 1842. The January harvest provided maize for rations while the ex-conde sent 70 pesos weekly to fund operations. A neighboring landlord, don Luis Rodríguez, challenged San Pedro's right to three *caballerias* of land (120 ha. or 200 acres) and won in court. It seemed a small problem. Land was the least important factor of production; the need was for workers, and for the moment San Pedro had cash and maize to pay them.

Pulque held strong into 1843, despite January hail and February floods.[61] In April, manager don Justo Hermosillo wrote to doña Vicentita Yrolo de Sánchez y Mora, addressing her as "My Lady, with respect."[62] The ex-conde had married a new wife early in 1841; in 1843, she took control of his pulque business—the last enterprise standing. She learned of difficulties hiring muleteers. She demanded specifics on maize plantings and an explanation for why the manager aimed to buy 100 fanegas from neighboring San José Acolman as a May hailstorm brought rising prices. She demanded accounts of villagers' work and wages. She called for action when muleteers mistreated mules. In July, as the estate transplanted new fields of maguey, she sent funds to pay workers.[63] The ex-conde got vague reports while she read the details of transplanting, labor, weather, shipments, and financing.[64]

Then, in October, a letter came from Francisco Segueyro addressed to don Mariano Sánchez de Espinosa. The message: "The pulque business has been decadent for years for reasons we all know. . . . Several people have proposed solutions, recently seeking government protection; having not achieved that . . . every day goes from bad to worse, with losses falling on proprietors." Segueyro claimed to know "the way to fix the business, . . . ending bankruptcies and gaining more from prevailing prices." He called a meeting of "producers" to benefit "the public."[65]

The pulque business was in crisis. Labor costs and shipping were beyond grower control. Producers should meet to limit production, allocate market shares, and raise prices. Nothing came of the proposal. Through the fall of 1843 and into 1844, production at San Pedro held high. So did costs as workers remained recalcitrant.[66] Pulque production without profit persisted under doña Vicentita.

In September, a new manager, the fourth in three years, wrote a desperate letter to the ex-conde detailing how resistant, threatening, and expropriating villagers blocked profitable operations: "Problems come from the people of Tlanoapa; their animals graze on estate pastures, and they steal *aguamiel* [the sap fermented to make pulque]; armed, they steal with impunity, and now they have threatened my life—and any who serve your interests." The villagers attacked "a *tlachiquero* [maguey tapper] who defended our *aguamiel*; wounding him gravely."

A judge at Tlanolapa claimed illness and did nothing; the court at Tepeapulco stayed silent: "My Lord, I have tried to punish the riotous mobs attacking your respected affairs, and to avoid the death they have promised me. Now a crowd has come to the gate, furious men and women hurling stones, and one *indio* named Blas Yslas with an open knife promising to cut my throat. To avoid dishonor to your estate and affairs, I prudently hid."[67] Village men and women attacked. The manager hid.

While doña Vicentita struggled to profit and landed men dreamed of a cartel, villagers at Tlanolapa grazed livestock on estate lands, stole *tlachique* to make pulque, wounded a native worker who served the estate, and, when a new manager sought redress in local courts, took to the fields to threaten his life. Pulque capitalism was gone. Through the fall of 1844 and into 1845, doña Vicentita continued to oversee San Pedro and the pulque business, while the ex-conde read letters from San Luis Potosí detailing a final settling of accounts with managers and tenants as he lost Bocas, the last of the northern properties that had sustained his father's wealth and economic eminence.[68] On the eve of the War for North America, Peñasco kept his namesake northern holdings, La Teja at the edge of the capital, and San Pedro. He took limited rents at Peñasco and from chinampas that fed the capital. Doña Vicentita ran pulque operations in search of profit that did not come. Landed oligarchy lay dying.

Fanny Calderón's Mexico: Falling Oligarchs, Jostling Throngs, Women Rising to Carry On

Frances "Fanny" Calderón de la Barca came to Mexico as the 1830s ended. Born Frances Inglis in Scotland, she migrated in 1831 with her family to the United States, where she met Ángel Calderón de la Barca. Born in Buenos Aires, he had fought against Napoleon in Spain, then rose in Spain's diplomatic service, to be named its first emissary to the United States. Fanny converted to Catholicism, married the diplomat in 1838, and joined him when he became Spain's first ambassador to Mexico late in 1839.[69]

She found a welcome among women in struggling oligarchic clans. Access began with the Conde de la Cortina, a friend of the ambassador since years of exile and education in Madrid. Fanny's first impression: "with a very rich mother, himself very extravagant . . . I hear him called *inconsequente* and capricious." She later included the conde in a list of distinguished Mexicans, emphasizing scholarship, literary ambitions, and devotion to the arts.[70] There was no mention of economic power—nor of his father's mobilization of troops to defend pulque estates from Otomí rebels in the Mezquital after 1810.

His mother earned more attention: "The old countess, immensely rich and once very handsome, retains some *beaux restes* (beautiful remains), but rather a hard expression—a very distinguished woman, of great natural talent, one of the true ladies of the old school of whom not many specimens now remain in Mexico." A visit to her home revealed an impressive structure: walls were painted with religious images; the sitting room housed "the finest of Broadwood's grand pianos, which no one ever touches." Amid remnants of luxury, the visitor found the matriarch and her family "in a little ill-furnished miserable room, with two candles—the countess in an old rebozo and a pair of diamond earrings, Paulita [Cortina's wife] bundled up in shawls and fur, and curling Joaquina's hair—everything looking poor, dirty, and uncomfortable."[71] Oligarchy past, proud women pressed on.

Through the Cortinas, the ambassador and his wife met the Adalids. Cortinas and Adalids were cousins, heirs to patrimonies built in commerce and invested in pulque estates during the boom years of silver capitalism.[72] In January 1840, they introduced the Calderóns to what remained of elite society in Mexico City. To Fanny, the theater was "disgusting," "dirty," and "unworthy of this fine city." The opening of Congress brought a first encounter with Our Lady of Guadalupe, her portrait facing the presidential chair. Soon after, the Cortinas and Adalids took the Calderóns to visit Guadalupe's temple north of the capital: "As usual we were accompanied by four armed riders," and along the way "we met nothing but arrieros, peasants, léperos [urban rabble], and soldiers" while passing through "miserable suburbs, dirty, with a commingling of odours." A trip to the shrine that historically united the people of the heartland revealed social chasms—and armed men everywhere. Two days later, they were off to a bullfight, where declining elites sat above a disrespectful populace they feared.[73]

Holy Week brought the Calderóns deeper into the capital's religious culture. On Thursday, they joined the Condesa de Santiago in her private balcony in the great San Francisco convent church. The Scotswoman saw the scene as "splendid," drawn by a sculpture portraying the Last Supper. Then visiting "innumerable churches," she lamented that "the number of léperos in rags was astonishing, greatly exceeding that of well-dressed people." Along the Calle San Francisco, long lined with the palaces of oligarchic privilege, Fanny saw only "beaux restes of former days."[74]

A procession showed "the Virgin, the saints, the Holy Trinity, the Savior in different passages of life, imprisonment, and crucifixion, represented by figures magnificently dressed, placed on lofty scaffoldings of immense weight, supported by different bodies of men. One is carried by coachmen, another by the *aguadores* (water carriers), a third by *cargadores* (porters), a Herculean race."[75] Elites on balconies and people in the streets watched simultaneously, but not together, as working men carried heavy images of suffering and redemption.

Good Friday took the Calderóns back to the Condesa de Santiago's balcony at San Francisco, where "the Adoration and Procession of the Cross" were "very fine." Later they strolled to join friends on a balcony of the national (once viceregal) palace, overlooking "the most beautiful and original scene . . . presented towards sunset on the great square." She found the Zócalo "noble" but for an unsightly Parian market. People of all classes filled the plaza: men and women; Spanish, mestizo, and native; English and German. Again, the Calderóns and their once noble friends gazed from above.[76]

Later they crossed the plaza, entering the cathedral for a performance of *Le Miserere*, a musical call for God's mercy. Inside, "the crowd was so intolerable" they considered leaving until priests escorted them to a private viewing area "near the Virgin." Later, Fanny was happy to leave: "It was now eleven o'clock and the pulquerías were open for the refreshment of the faithful; though order had prevailed, it was not likely to endure." The Calderóns walked home in fear, passing pulquerías filled with léperos they saw as ever more drunk, ever more threatening.[77] Pulque was not scarce.

Later they traveled with the Adalids to see "life on the great pulque haciendas." The historic beverage "is said to be the most wholesome drink in the world, and remarkably agreeable when one has overcome the first shock occasioned by its rancid odour. . . . The maguey is [was] a source of unfailing profit, the consumption being enormous, so that many of the richest families in the capital owe their fortune entirely to the produce of their maguey." Now, however, the Adalids "frequently sell their plants to the Indians. A maguey which costs a real when first planted, will when ready to be cut sell for twelve or eighteen dollars (pesos)—a tolerable profit when considering that it grows in almost any soil, requires little manure, and . . . no very special care."[78]

Sharecropping—or share-tapping—had come to pulque. Adalid owned the land and paid to transplant fields of maguey. After the five-year wait for maturity, he sold rights to tap to villagers—who made pulque and sold it to muleteers to deliver to city taverns. Independent *tlachiqueros* and muleteers ruled pulque production while Adalid collected what he could.

A visit to the Soapayuca estate east of Otumba revealed the darker, conflictive, and dangerous side of the business. The property was run by "an administrator, to whom Adalid pays a large annual sum, and whose place is by no means a sinecure, as he lives in perpetual danger from robbers. He is captain of a troop of soldiers, and, as his life has been spent in 'persecuting robbers,' he is an object of intense hatred. . . . He gave us a terrible account of these night attacks."[79]

Villagers in the pulque zone carried on as productive insurgents. The estate troop might punish a few but could not stop independent tapping. Thanks to formal share-tapping and villager theft, pulque was plentiful and cheap. Estate owners paid for transplanting and found profit scarce; managers faced attack and estate-contracted tappers risked assault, even maiming, to gain steady earnings. Night tappers took what they could, claiming income to sustain families facing dry lands while periodic transplanting brought only limited and irregular wages. Earlier in the face of such challenges, villagers had turned to insurgency, claiming control of production after 1810. Facing proprietors' attempts to revive profit in the 1840s, they mixed limited formal wage work with "independent" tapping to supply city taverns. Proprietors struggled to profit while villagers carried on—enabling city tavern goers to drown the insecurities of life.

Back in the capital, in July 1841 Calderón met a woman she saw as the immoral face of women's rise in oligarchic circles: "I was lately at a marriage feast given to celebrate the wedding of the sister of the lady of Don Lucas Alamán with a Spaniard. The fête was given at the hacienda of the Conde de Peñasco, celebrated for his love of beaux arts, his gallery, &c." The feast was at his La Teja property, just west of the Alameda, the first country house at the edge of the capital.

> [Peñasco's] first wife having died some time ago he has recently married a young lady—very handsome—of low birth and doubtful reputation. This new countess was looking very splendid, dressed in rose colour, with a profusion of diamonds. After dinner we adjourned to another room, where I admired the beauty of a little child who was playing about on the floor, "Yes, she is pretty, I have a little girl just about that age," said the countess, "and a boy a year older."
>
> "Indeed," said I, rather astonished, seeing that she had been married about six months.
>
> "Yes," said she, "my little girl is very pretty, quite French—not in the least Mexican—and indeed I myself am much more Spanish in my feeling than Mexican."

The new condesa longed for the days when Mexico City oligarchs were Spanish—wherever they were born. Calderón wondered if she had met a young widow, now remarried. Asking a nearby guest, she learned: "'Oh no!' said she, 'she was never married before. She alludes to children she had before the count became acquainted with her!'"

"Amiable naiveté! And yet Mme. Alamán, one of the most prudish women in Mexico, was actually faisant la cour to this woman, and loading her with attentions and caresses. Don Lucas was aux petits with her. Ainsi, va le monde au Mexique. I must say, however, that this was a singular instance."[80] The ex-conde faced a collapse of oligarchic power common among his peers. He gained just enough to sustain his love of the arts and to keep a new wife in gowns and diamonds. Doña Vicentita soon proved more than a social climber. Seeing the violent popular pressures that blocked profit in pulque, she pressed Peñasco aside, aiming to manage the dark world where pulque makers contested pulque property. She kept pulque and limited income flowing for a time.

In the fall of 1841, the Scotswoman met women more ably sustaining landed eminence. To escape political conflicts in the capital, the Calderóns spent a month at San Xavier, an estate developed by the Jesuits, long held by the Reglas, and now owned by the "Señoras de Fagoaga . . . millionaires, being rich in haciendas and silver mines; very religious, very charitable, and what is less common here, very learned."[81] She honored their rural world:

> The country is extremely pretty, being a corn and not a maguey district. . . . There is a large reservoir of water, and the garden, which covers a great space of ground, is kept in good order. There are beautiful walks in the neighborhood, leading to Indian villages, old churches, and farms; and all the lanes are bordered with fruit trees. All along the lanes are small Indian huts, with their usual mud floor, small altar, earthen vessels, and a collection of daubs on the walls (especially of the virgin of Guadalupe). . . . When the men are at work, [the huts are occupied] by the Indian woman [and] her scantily-clad progeny.

The Calderóns walked the district without fear.[82]

Toward the end of the month, they joined a manager and one of the sister's husbands, not named, on a ride across the Lechería estate to Molino Viejo in nearby hills. They passed churches, villages, and "countless" estates. Only a manager lived at Lechería, with no garden or orchard: "It is surrounded by fertile and profitable fields of corn [wheat] and maize."[83] In 1841, profit earned notice. The sisters likely planted wheat on estate account with seasonal workers drawn from villages. They surely drew tenants or sharecroppers to make maize. The Fagoaga sisters' San Xavier estates made maize and profit while villagers carried on in peace, notable and uncommon in the 1840s.[84]

Calderón knew that Fagoaga men had joined in politics since the wars for independence while retaining mines and estates.[85] Don José María competed with the Conde de Peñasco in the Iturbide era. Don Francisco took control of La Griega in the late 1830s. Now the sisters held former Regla estates. The Fagoagas were a rarity: an oligarchic clan that survived insurgencies and political wars after 1810 to keep property, gain more, and maintain profitable operations into the 1840s. Was that success the sisters' doing? Calderón suggests that, and more. Shortly after returning from San Xavier, one of the sisters took Fanny to tour "every hospital, jail, college, and madhouse in Mexico City."[86] Charitable service helped maintain women's oligarchic eminence.

Exceptional women in times of oligarchic decline, the Fagoaga sisters oversaw prosperous estates on cereal lands north of the capital while attending to urban social challenges. They lived socially conscious ways of agrarian capitalism parallel to doña María Josefa Vergara's dreams for Querétaro in 1809. The Fagoaga sisters were rare oligarchs with the wealth to fund charities in the 1840s and the vision to know the necessity of such work in times of social contest.

Despite women's efforts, the fall of oligarchic power proved an enduring legacy of the Bajío revolution. The Fagoagas might survive, led by powerful and socially conscious sisters. Still, no landed class would ground an oligarchic tradition, blocking Lucas Alamán's dream of a conservative regime. When silver revived and industry began in the 1830s, sustenance came from families making maize, pulque, and more—in the Bajío and regions north, and across the heartland surrounding the capital.[87]

PART IV

Making Silver-Industrial Capitalism, 1830–1860

11.

A New Bajío, 1830–1845

Silver Revives, Industry Rises,
Landlords Struggle—and Family Growers
Carry Everything

Into the 1830s, the Bajío revolution appeared a triumph for families on the land, a calamity for Mexican capitalists and the state, and an enduring opportunity for rising Anglo-American industrial powers. Still, post-revolutionary transformations were not done. The settlements that gave families control of production across the Bajío and beyond had preserved property rights. Silver remained valuable in the world. After Guanajuato mines returned to Mexican operators in the 1830s, production soared to heights unseen before 1810; when national leaders turned to blunt British power by promoting national industries, textile mills rose in the Bajío and beyond—all sustained by family growers from the heartland, through the Bajío, and across San Luis Potosí. A new silver-industrial capitalism fed by family maize makers opened new horizons for regime builders, profit seekers, and families strong on the land—while assertive women appeared everywhere.

The 1830s brought the beginnings of a new Bajío. Silver revived as local capital and capitalists regained control of mining in Guanajuato. Mechanized industry came to Querétaro, also under local control. Meanwhile, rancheros and other family growers ruled production on the land, keeping maize and other foods plentiful and affordable while landlords grappled with endless debts that blocked any revival of oligarchic power. A new silver-industrial capitalism sustained by family growers opened a world of new possibilities in the wake of the Bajío revolution.

Economic gains began as political instabilities set in. As President Guadalupe Victoria completed his term in 1828, the national regime faced debilitating debts to London bondholders. In a contested election, Vicente Guerrero, the mulatto political insurgent who had outlived Morelos and backed Iturbide, claimed the presidency and turned to block textile imports, aiming to protect artisan families and coastal cotton growers. In 1829, a conservative coalition ousted Guerrero, installing a government led by General Anastasio Bustamante and Lucas Alamán. From 1830, they worked to revive mining with less reliance on British capital and to block British imports by promoting industrial textiles. In times of political uncertainty, Guanajuato silver revived while work began on the Hércules cotton mill east of Querétaro. The early 1840s saw mining boom at La Luz, high above Guanajuato, while Hércules flourished in Querétaro. A new capitalism led by silver, stimulated by industry, and fed by ranchero growers and family maize makers remade the Bajío.

Guanajuato Silver Revives

For decades before 1810, New Spain's silver output had averaged more than 22 million pesos yearly, more than 5 million at Guanajuato. After 1810, production fell by half, averaging only 11.5 million pesos to 1820, sustained by Zacatecas and regions north where insurgency was limited.[1] Guanajuato's Valenciana, long the city's leading mine yielding more than 1.4 million pesos yearly before 1809, fell below 300,000 from 1811 to 1815. Facing production without investment, it yielded only 180,000 pesos yearly from 1816 to 1819— and when the works flooded in 1820, production fell to 80,000 pesos, a level held with fluctuations from 1821 to 1825.[2]

In the early 1820s, national production fell to 8 million pesos yearly, while total Guanajuato silver (now with its own mint) held near 500,000 pesos, 6 percent of a fallen national total. The coming of British capital began a slow revival. Output across Mexico rose to nearly 11 million pesos yearly from 1826 to 1830, still half the level of the decades before 1810. Guanajuato flows rose from 500,000 to 2.5 million pesos in the 1820s, nearly a quarter of a still-depressed national output in 1830.[3]

The revival of Guanajuato silver to half of pre-insurgency levels drew workers to mining and began to stimulate markets. Still, profits held scarce.

Figures for Valenciana under the Anglo-Mexican Company show a loss in 1828, small profits from 1829 to 1833, then losses that led to English withdrawal in 1836. For British investors, the experiment proved a catastrophe.[4] For Guanajuato and the Bajío, gains were limited but real. Investment brought workers back to drainage, extraction, and refining. Mines bought livestock and paid salaries stimulating markets for food, drink, and more. A British-funded revival without profit began to drag Guanajuato mines out of depression.

When Valenciana returned to operation by the Pérez Gálvez family, led by don Juan de Dios and his widowed sister doña Francisca de Paula, it reported a loss of 23,000 pesos in 1837, then profits averaging 61,300 pesos from 1838 through 1843. With family financing and management, costs averaging 120,000 pesos yearly generated silver valued over 180,000—a limited investment and output. Valenciana was but a small part of a Guanajuato silver revival that rose to 3 million pesos yearly during the same years, as national output held near 12 million, still half of flows before 1810.[5]

Then came the light: La Luz. The jump of silver output at Guanajuato to more than 4 million pesos in 1844 came at new mines opened at La Luz, high above Valenciana (figure 11.1). Sudden bonanzas take time, investment, and luck. The Pérez Gálvez siblings began to work the upland mine in 1832 "with limited success," while the British still operated Valenciana. In 1835, they linked La Luz to a new *socabón*, a deep drainage tunnel. In 1838, don Marcelino Rocha, a Guanajuato merchant, joined to contribute financing. The 1844 bonanza cleared debts to Rocha, setting the stage for boom under Pérez Gálvez rule.[6]

In 1843, La Luz reported a profit of 45,000 pesos, distributed in 12 shares. How many the Pérez Gálvez and Rocha held is not clear. In 1844, profits soared past 700,000 pesos, with dividends paid to holders of 55 shares worth 12,700 pesos each—an uncounted many held by don Juan de Dios and doña Francisca de Paula. Profits dipped to 560,000 pesos in 1845 while the family consolidated control by reducing shareholders to 45—keeping each dividend worth 12,400 pesos.[7] A locally financed shareholding capitalism drove the boom at La Luz in the 1840s.

The British had tried to revive mining by investing in old and long-productive mines while mandating regular dividends to distant investors. Costs were high in drainage and reconstructions laden with deep uncertainty. The bonanza at La Luz came at new mines in nearby geological

Figure 11.1 Mineral de la Luz, high above Guanajuato.

formations. Risks were real there, too, but the Pérez Gálvez covered
them first by tapping limited silver at Valenciana, then drawing on local
financiers—with all waiting for returns until silver flowed strong. Success
in the early 1840s revealed the power of local capital invested for the long
term, the benefits of local knowledge, the skills of local mine workers, and
a strong global demand for silver.

Textiles: Challenges and Industrial Beginnings

Spanish regional alliances with England against France had opened New Spain to British cloth in 1808. Then after 1810, the collapse of New Spain's silver broke cloth making and exports in China and India, opening global markets to British industrial cottons while insurgency rattled textiles across the Bajío. British cloth flowed in during years of war that continued in Spain to 1814, in New Spain to 1820. From 1821 into 1823, Iturbide aimed to block imports and revive Mexican cloth making. His fall gave power to liberal republicans who welcomed British imports to gain financing and investment.

Imports held strong while British capital funded Mexico's national regime and mining in the 1820s.[8] Reporting the collapse of Mexican cloth making, Joel Poinsett saw it as inevitable; Henry Ward insisted it was good for Mexico and Mexicans. When Guerrero gained power in 1828, he turned to prohibit cloth imports, aiming to protect Mexican artisans and cotton growers, most small planters along Gulf and Pacific Coasts, the latter his home region and political base.[9]

When Anastasio Bustamante ousted Guerrero, he built a cabinet led by Lucas Alamán. Alamán had joined British capital in trying to revive mining at Guanajuato and beyond, gaining production without profit. He had no interest in Ward's goal of producing silver to buy British cloth. To counter that vision, in 1830 Alamán founded the Banco de Avío, aiming to tax imports to finance Mexican industries.[10] The bank's first board included don José Mariano Sánchez y Mora, ex-Conde de Peñasco, a leading sheep grazer flailing to profit at estates across San Luis Potosí. He provided an aristocratic face to back Alamán's endeavors. The board quickly sought reports on cloth making and crafts across Mexico. The responses from the Bajío are revealing. Ward had reported collapse—his dream. The surveys showed that large workshops had fallen, while household producers struggled on.

The first report came in January 1831 from Acámbaro. Francisco Zambrano wrote: "Before 1810 this town owed its wealth to making woolen cloth on 150 looms making goods worth more than 200,000 pesos, in addition to the cloth made on countless small looms worked by poor family household." Now only one large shop carried on while small weavers struggled. The problem was lack of capital, markets, and machinery to compete with foreign imports—the latter sure to claim the bank's attention. Beyond capital and machinery, the key was renewed ties to the northern estates that had historically supplied wool and bought cloth for sale to residents and nearby communities.[11]

The report from Salvatierra, just beyond on the rich bottomlands, stated simply: "A few workshops make ordinary cloth; one weaves better quality material; output is very limited because sales are only local and producers face extreme poverty."[12] West at Yuriria, on the lake of the same name, an indigenous community made cotton goods: 200,000 rebozos and 2,000 to 3,000 mantas for regional markets.[13] At Valle de Santiago, northwest along the river, people made cotton cloth sold nearby. As to woolens, small herds of sheep provided wool turned to cloth by "poor artisans" whose output "cannot be confirmed." The cloth was "ordinary, as the poor artisans cannot make fine cloth."[14]

The report from Silao, near the mines, is revealing in other ways. Cotton was not grown locally, leaving weavers to buy fiber from "the coasts at Acapulco and Colima." They made "shawls and blankets" to 1826, while mining held limited. The report concluded, "Today they don't make half, as imported cloth becomes abundant." The beginning of revival at the mines stimulated imports—Ward's dream.[15]

In the western basin, Pénjamo, home of the Hidalgo family, reported: "Across most of this land," water is just below the surface; "at only three to five yards depth, there is ample water to irrigate a *huerta* with one well." Small growers have planted cotton "since time immemorial," though harvests are "small, as families only plant on the side, not as a business." They made "ordinary cloth called manta, . . . along with shawls, with strong local markets supplying everyday cloth."

"Before the year 10, more than 200,000 head of sheep" grazed on local estate lands. "They disappeared during the times" when guerrillas and communities took sheep for food. Now "they are returning, numbering thirty to forty thousand," only 15 to 20 percent of the former flocks. The wool supplied "many woolen workshops" making "the rough cloth they call *mangas*; the ordinary weave they call *guerguetilla*; and others called *frazada*—the last made in quantity for everyday clothing."[16] Pénjamo families raised maize and cotton, and grazed sheep, too, feeding families and making cloth for local markets. Despite the reporter's denigrating vision, at Pénjamo as across Guanajuato, household cloth making carried on.

Querétaro had faced a greater fall, given the centrality of textiles in the local economy. Before 1810, its *obrajes* and household artisans supplied the Bajío and regions north. In May 1831, José Antonio del Raso began by reporting that in 1800, "woolen manufacturing" had occupied 20 large *obrajes* and 250 smaller shops, employing 6,000 workers. While insurgency spared Querétaro, the decade of war cut cloth production: "Before the insurrection, our cloth mostly supplied the residents of northern estates." Since 1810, the northerners had built "workshops" supplying residents and local markets "at lower prices." In Querétaro, "profits" fell; with fewer than 50 wide looms now operating, "they barely employ a thousand workers." Raso added: "Our *obrajes* will never return to the way they were before the insurrection, unless we raise the quality of our cloth so that it will sell in markets across the republic." Commercial revival "requires capital, machines, and protection."[17] Raso preached to Alamán.

Interest soon turned to action. In August 1831, Governor don Manuel López de Ecala, with roots in textiles, founded the Compañia Industrial de Querétaro. In February 1832, its junta, including Raso, now a deputy in the state Congress, contracted to buy Molino Colorado, a grain mill on the river that flowed through the canyon at San Pedro. The purchase came with the water rights needed to power a textile mill. The price was 74,000 pesos, but the junta paid only 20,000, recognizing 34,000 owed to Captain don José Fernández Murillo and 20,000 to his sister doña Manuela, the former owners.[18]

A week later, the Banco de Avío approved a loan of 30,000 pesos to the Querétaro company, bringing its debt to 85,000 pesos. In November 1830, the bank had ordered machinery from France for a woolen mill at Aguascalientes, near Zacatecas. The project had collapsed and Alamán looked to Querétaro. The machinery landed at Veracruz, along with technicians recruited to install it and teach operations. Challenges of transport across the sierras stalled delivery. The October 1832 fall of the Bustamante–Alamán regime to liberal free traders led by Santa Anna and Valentín Gómez Farías ended the Molino Grande project, stalling the rise of industry in Querétaro.[19]

Hércules Rising

Then, late in the 1830s, don Cayetano Rubio found a way. Born in 1791 to a Cádiz merchant family, as Napoleon's armies drove south in 1809, he joined two brothers in flight to Veracruz, carrying a rich inheritance. During the decade of insurgency, he thrived by funding war and trade. By 1818, he was in Querétaro, where he married doña María Manuela Primo, daughter of Spanish military officer don Manuel Telmo Primo. Rubio sat on the city council that backed Iturbide in 1821, part of the support Telmo trumpeted in 1822. Later, Rubio moved north to trade in San Luis Potosí.[20]

The route from San Luis Potosí to Tampico was a major avenue for silver exports in the late 1820s. In 1826, of 10.25 million pesos minted in Mexico, 3.9

million came from Zacatecas and 1.1 million from San Luis Potosí—nearly half. In 1827, 3.2 million silver pesos exited through Tampico, a third of national exports of 9.7 million; in 1828, 4.5 million of 12.4 million departed there, more than a third of a rising total.[21] San Luis Potosí became a pivot of silver transit and trade enabling Rubio to profit. He avoided expulsion as a Spaniard in the political heat of 1828, then funded the fight to block a Spanish landing at Tampico in 1829, proving his loyalty to Mexico—and to profit.[22]

He returned to Querétaro in the late 1830s. Silver was rising at Guanajuato; at more than 3 million pesos yearly it exceeded a quarter of Mexico's total.[23] In 1837, he joined a brother in a contract to manage Querétaro's tobacco factory. Turning to industry, in 1838 he bought Molino Colorado from the Murillos, taking on the obligation for 54,000 pesos to make the siblings partners in the project.[24] Was the debt to the Banco de Avío canceled? If so, that was its only contribution to Rubio's project. He renamed the mill Hércules and bought German machinery to spin and weave cotton goods.

In 1839, lobbying the Querétaro Council for greater water rights, he honored his dream: "Molino Colorado, a factory focused on making thread, cloth, and printed cottons, will employ multitudes of workers, recently vagrants and now hard working and useful." With construction underway, workers "now earning more than 6,000 pesos monthly, are animating the languid commerce of our city." Soon, "the mill will employ larger numbers, including more than 400 families, now without means to survive, stimulating commerce even more." Rubio argued that additional waters "are absolutely necessary, both to maintain the new community forming around the mill and to drive machines, notably for printing cloth." The industrialist pleaded the needs of working people and the need for more water for production. The council granted the new flow, with the proviso that Rubio maintain a public fountain twenty-four hours a day.[25]

In 1844, as the mill began production, the Rubios asked the council for the right to hold all river water for nine hours every day, "compensating the owners of lands along the river below." The council should "see a work of public interest." The council agreed to an eight-hour monopoly, subject to a public overseer and a promise that users downstream would not be deprived. Rubio promised 4,000 pesos to fund a local theater.[26]

A year later, the council worried that "citizens working *huertas* face water shortages, because Molino Colorado is taking clean water and destroying it." The mill was taking more than the allotted water, and what passed on was "full of filth," polluting what flowed to the *huertas* that sustained Otomí families and city markets. The council's response: ask the Justice of

Figure 11.2 Hércules rising in the canyon east of Querétaro.

the Peace at the mill community, Juan José Garfias, to monitor use.[27] Was he independent of Rubio? With Hércules in operation, Querétaro became industrial—with new productivity and new pollutions (figure 11.2).

Querétaro Manufacturing: Raso's 1845 Report

In 1845, José del Raso, an early promoter of industry at Querétaro, published *Notas Estadísticas* on the state's new economy, offering glowing praise for the social benefits of Hércules. He honored a total investment of 800,000 pesos that led to 4,200 working mechanized spindles, while 1,000 were "paralyzed" as spinning capacity exceeded the needs of 212 power looms making manta and 100 hand looms weaving varied cloths. Other machines stamped cloth "European style." During its first year of operation, Hércules consumed 6,073 quintales (more than 600,000 kilograms) of cleaned cotton to make 55,000 "pieces of manta." Spending 3,000 pesos weekly on materials and labor, the mill employed 584 women in preparation and spinning, a labor-saving mechanization of women's work, and 292 men in weaving, long a male role. And construction continued, employing 400 men and spending 1,200 pesos weekly on labor and materials. Overall, Raso reported that the mill sustained

1,276 families, injecting more than 200,000 pesos into the Querétaro economy. How much it paid the mill's working men and women, he did not say.[28]

The present mill was only a beginning: "When the construction underway is completed and all the machinery is activated, . . . production and population will increase, new income will relieve misery and improve customs. Popular idleness will end, promoting virtuous lives. Morality is tied to work, with great gains flowing from enterprises that promote work." The gospel of work, promising moral benefit to those who labored at machines, came to Catholic Querétaro.

On women, Raso wrote: "A workshop full of women presents an interesting spectacle to the eyes of a thoughtful and sensible man. A group of robust youth, very clean and honestly dressed, their attention focused on the thread they make, the shuttle that runs, and the spool that fills, opens serious reflections. The tranquil and peaceful appearance of these creatures reveals the inner peace brought by their innocent work. Observing them brings the most pleasant emotions."[29] Raso saw the mill disciplining women. He did not state the obvious: disciplined women labored to benefit profit takers in an industrializing city. Mill women, young, dependent, and disciplined, were the antitheses of the rancheras of Puerto de Nieto—mature, independent, and assertive. Hércules might solve two problems: scarce profit and independent women.

Hércules did not monopolize cotton production at Querétaro: 75 household shops still worked 182 looms, occupying 232 family members in traditional gendered roles. Artisans and the new mill drew fiber from Gulf coast lowlands. Households there continued to plant and clean, spin and weave for use and local markets. New mills like Hércules stimulated increased coastal planting, with commercial gins cleaning seed from fiber, making transport inland and upland less costly.[30]

Querétaro's historical woolens hung on.[31] In 1844, nine *obrajes* employed more than a thousand workers (mostly men) to weave woolens, often putting out spinning to women at home. Raso also reported 195 family shops making finer woolens. With 265 looms, they employed 416 producers, including spinning women and weaving men.

Hércules concentrated profit and paid workers double what they might earn in family shops, more than double the wages paid in *obrajes*. Yet the combined earnings of a husband and wife in a family shop equaled those of a man at Hércules, while artisans retained day-to-day independence in times of market revival. Beyond Querétaro city, cotton and woolen workshops held on in even numbers at San Juan del Río, cottons far exceeded woolens at upland Cadereita, and cottons monopolized production in the

Sierra around Tolimán, where indigenous men worked small plots while women made cloth and more. Family economies with relative autonomies held on as industry came to Querétaro.

Cloth was not the state's only industry. The tobacco factory had revived and remained the largest employer. Raso reported that in 1843, it produced 6,250,000 cartons of cigarettes, 4,125,000 of cigars, with a total value of nearly 650,000 pesos. Nearly 30 percent sold in Querétaro; the rest were sent to Guanajuato and Michoacán, Durango and Chihuahua—all stimulated by silver revival. It employed 400 men and 1,200 women for a total payroll of 116,000 pesos—an average of more than 70 pesos each, with men surely making more than women. In 1844, another 400 workers were added, bringing women to 1,500, less than half the numbers of 1809, more than double the number now at Hércules.[32]

Raso's report on urban crafts beyond textiles and tobacco reveals more about the mix of industrial innovation, commercial revival, and enduring autonomies in the new Querétaro.[33] Purveyors of commercial sustenance were few. Yes, bakers were everywhere, making and selling bread for prosperous Hispanic households. At Querétaro and San Juan del Río, they were far outnumbered by *hortelanos*, Otomí family growers raising fruits and vegetables for use and sale to neighbors. No tortilla sellers are listed. In 1844, for the majority, urban sustenance remained a family affair, ruled by women who labored long and hard to feed families, factories, and workshops.

Commercial craftsmen, mostly men, still made men's clothing, hats, and shoes across the state. Bricklayers, woodworkers, and blacksmiths and other metal workers were everywhere, building Hércules and a reviving commercial city. Muleteers were everywhere, too, carrying goods in trade. Sellers of alcoholic beverages nearly equaled muleteers as sociable drink shaped city life. The silversmiths numerous in Querétaro and San Juan del Río, plus three in Cadereita, show that a few found prosperity.

Hércules led a commercial revival at Querétaro. Still, employment in woolens only reached 1,750—far below the pre-insurgency 6,000 earlier reported by Raso. And 725 household cotton makers plus the 876 at Hércules kept the total of textile workers in 1844 at 3,350, just over half those engaged in woolens alone in 1800. The 1,600 in the tobacco factory in 1844 remained well below the 2,500 mostly women working there in 1809.[34] Manufacturing had risen from the depths of collapse, yet held far short of the employment it provided during the boom times of silver capitalism. Of course, that was the goal of industrialization: maximum production and profit with minimum employment and pay.

As silver revived, imports still shaped and limited a mixed industrial-artisan economy. National imports peaked at more than 11 million pesos in 1843, including nearly 4 million in cottons and 800,000 in woolens. In 1844, the total dropped to 7.6 million pesos as cottons fell to 1.85 million pesos, a drop linked to the opening of Hércules and other Mexican mills, while woolen imports rose to just over 900,000 pesos. The trend held into 1845: total national imports fell below 7 million pesos as cottons dropped to 1.45 million pesos and woolens fell under 750,000 pesos.[35]

Reports from the Bajío reveal more. Querétaro kept trade records for 1842 and 1843. Its total imports held near 267,000 pesos both years, a minor share of a national flow over 11 million in 1843.[36] Before Hércules, Querétaro lacked wealth to buy imports; with Hércules, the factory met local demand. Guanajuato did not report until 1846, as war with the United States began. Its silver output then exceeded 4 million pesos while state imports reached 1.175 million pesos—more than 10 percent of the national total reported a year earlier. And Guanajuato's imports included 220,000 pesos of cottons, 142,000 pesos of woolens, 177,000 pesos of linens, and 115,000 pesos of silks, bringing cloth to total 668,000 pesos.[37] Rising silver flows kept imports accessible for those seeking luxury or novelty. In the city of silver, mining wealth drew luxury imports; in the manufacturing center of Querétaro, industry and artisans supplied local markets. Both were fed by family growers on the land.

Lives on the Land: Landlords Lease, Families Produce

As mines revived and industry began, landed proprietors continued to struggle while family growers held strong across the Bajío. Landlord challenges and grower persistence are reported in notarial registers that recorded transactions all around Querétaro and across nearby Guanajuato from Celaya to San Miguel and San Felipe. They reveal the diverse ways that Bajío landlords, like Mexico City oligarchs, struggled to limit losses of property, wealth, and power while family growers ruled production.

While landlords from the most propertied to the marginal faced challenges, they responded in diverse ways that changed over time—while never breaking their fall or limiting family growers' rule of sustenance in the new silver-industrial capitalism. Few proprietors profited. Two cases illustrate histories of enduring proprietor trials and eventual leaseholder successes.

Don Antonio Guerrero y Ocío remained a Mexico City oligarch and leading Bajío proprietor. Through the 1820s, he had continued to operate

Jofre, turning its lands over to rising numbers of tenant families. In 1824, he leased the vast Capulín estate, north of Jofre in Guanajuato, for the ample rent of 5,375 pesos yearly, sanctioning subleasing while charging the new operator with defending the property from invasive neighbors.[38] In May 1831, Guerrero y Ocío appeared as *ciudadano* Antonio Ocío, eschewing the honor of the *don*. He leased Jofre to *ciudadanos* Juan Goycochea and Ygnacio Dolores Retana, the former a deputy in Querétaro's congress, the latter a local merchant. Ocío aimed to limit risks and gain income by leasing for seven years for 4,500 pesos yearly. The leaseholders would collect rents due to Ocío first and defend estate lands and borders, confirming residents' independence and neighbors' incursions. Ocío could keep grain in the *trojes* until a "buen precio" came—if it did. If the first year's rent was not paid, the contract would end.[39]

The seven-year lease lasted four. In September 1835, Ocío again leased Jofre for seven years, the rent cut to 4,000 pesos. The first year was paid at signing: 3,000 pesos *fuertes* (silver), 1,000 in copper—another discount. Lic. D. Ramón Estévan Martínez, a lawyer before the federal courts, took on challenges. Maize from previous harvests remained in the *trojes*, with more in the chapel—all now sold to don Joaquin Haller. Martínez would oversee the coming maize harvest, valued at only 10 reales per fanega, and store it until prices rose. He would continue to collect rents due to Ocío from before 1830 and pay for losses of livestock and damage to buildings, whether from "revolution or sacking." In the mid-1830s, estate cropping did not pay, subtenants still withheld rents, and profit remained scarce. Ocío cut the rent and shifted risks to a new lawyer tenant.[40]

The 1835 lease held as the regional economy began to revive. Jofre next appears in May 1845, when don Manuel Guerrero y Ocío, don Antonio's son, living in Querétaro, leased the property to don Antonio Benavente for five years at a rent raised to 4,500 pesos. The tenant was a manager at Jaral, skilled in dealing with ranchero and tenant growers at the vast estate north of Guanajuato.[41] The Guerrero y Ocío clan kept property and gained rent while rancheros and tenants still ruled production.

A second sequence of leases reveals parallel challenges at Chichimequillas, the large and diverse Carmelite property south of Jofre. The convent had overseen operations through the 1820s, welcoming family growers and squatters. In 1831, don Joaquin de Haller y Puch leased the estate. A European immigrant, he had come to trade, married doña María Trinidad Fernández de Herrera of a local landed family, and became a new kind of maize merchant. Early in 1831 he had advanced 1,360 pesos to La Esperanza, still held by the city of Querétaro, to pay for the costs of the January maize harvest. In March, the manager conveyed 1,450 fanegas of maize cut two harvests earlier to cover the advance plus 150 pesos in interest. Valued at 8 reales per fanega, the grain would remain at the estate. Another 466 fanegas, recently cut and valued at 6 reales, were also delivered to Haller.[42] Haller financed maize, took the crop as payment, and stored it in others' granaries in times of scarce capital, ample maize, and low prices. He did the same at Jofre in 1835.

In August 1831, Haller leased Chichimequillas for nine years at 4,000 pesos. He would pay in thirds and in advance, gaining control of cultivation on estate accounts, rents from subtenants, and oversight of a store, inn, and baths. As surety, he pledged the Hacienda de Vicario and its ranchos, along with several urban properties. Any increase in estate herds belonged to Haller, though the Carmelites might buy if they wished. At the end of the lease, Haller could store crops at the estate for up to a year. After years of informal operation, the estate needed rebuilding: land needed to be cleared and leveled; walls, drainage ditches, and irrigation channels needed repair; buildings required reconstruction. Costs estimated at 4,000 to 5,000 pesos, equal to another year's rent, fell to Haller.

He was not responsible for "thefts or any other damage caused by a war." Any litigation fell to the convent, along with "government obligations." Carmelites might come for vacations; when they traveled, they could take estate mounts and men to assist them. Haller might buy staples now in storage or hold them to sell for the order, "except for the maize held on account of the leaseholder at 12 reales per fanega." Grain Haller had funded could stay in storage awaiting a higher price. Shifting from financing maize to full estate operation, Haller expected to succeed. The estate would not be sold during the lease, unless to him. Should the lease be extended, Haller would pay the same rent.[43]

A year later, in August 1832, the Querétaro congress expelled Haller from the state. Had the immigrant fallen from grace for political reasons? Late in 1833, the exile still in force, the convent transferred the lease to doña María Trinidad, at the same rent, time, and terms—and paid her 10,000 pesos for improvements made by Haller.[44] The original lease made Haller responsible for repairs; the large payment now paid aimed to encourage doña María Trinidad to take on a lease the fathers found beneficial.

The new deal worked. Haller carried on as a maize merchant while doña María Trinidad kept the lease at Chichimequillas. In 1841, now Haller's widow, she leased for another nine years, the rent raised to 4,300 pesos. All repairs and improvements remained paid by the tenant; the Carmelites still paid for litigation. Taxes were split—a new cost to doña María Trinidad, who remained free of responsibility for damages of war or insurgency. If the Carmelites aimed to sell, she held first option. And at the end of the lease, she could store crops for a year, awaiting rising prices.[45] Convent proprietor and woman leaseholder moved forward, with doña María Trinidad paying a slightly higher rent, sharing tax burdens, and dealing in maize mostly raised by sharecroppers.

In April 1842, the entrepreneurial widow also dealt in maize beyond Chichimequillas. Don Marcos Herrera (a kinsman?) sold her the maize stored at Calamanda, south of La Griega. He held 2,000 fanegas harvested in January 1841 and valued at 14 reales, and another 2,000 from January 1842 valued at 18 reales. Prices were rising—without knowing what the rains of 1842 might bring. Needing cash to fund another season of planting, Herrera sold the crops to doña María Trinidad for 3,500 pesos, 1,800 on delivery to the Querétaro *alhóndiga*, 1,700 to be paid by September. The seller paid for delivery and the sales tax.[46] She bought at a large discount—paying only 7 reales per fanega for 2,000 fanegas valued at 14 and another 2,000 valued at 18. Buying cheaply, she could profit. The cash-strapped grower could carry on for another season.

In September 1843, doña María Trinidad, profiting as a leaseholder and maize speculator, sold the Vicario estate near Apaseo that had served as collateral for the first Chichimequillas lease. Don Pablo González del Cosío of Querétaro paid 36,500 pesos, no cash down, recognizing 27,000 as a lien that would pay 1,350 pesos yearly to her capital funds, leaving 9,500 to be paid by 1848.[47] The entrepreneurial woman sold a modest estate to a man who took on risks of production and marketing, while she gained a stream of cash to fund her dealings in maize—now based not on scarcity but on endless low prices. Doña María Trinidad Fernández de Herrera, widow of Haller y Puch, led a new way of agrarian capitalism at Querétaro in the 1840s.

Few men or women found parallel success. Through the 1830s, numerous landlords leased estates for 800 to 2,000 pesos yearly, their income often reduced as rents paid obligations to clerical creditors. Meanwhile, rancheros, tenants, and sharecroppers fed families and supplied markets.[48]

An October 1833 contract reveals ongoing struggles to profit. Don Juan de Cajiga of Mexico City leased San Ysidro de Lira, north of San Juan del Río, to Mariano Arana, a Querétaro merchant, for seven years at 3,500 pesos. The leaseholder gained 2,000 fanegas of maize from the last harvest, plus 100 fanegas of frijol and wheat for the next planting. Arana would thresh recently harvested wheat, then send the grain to Cajiga to sell in Mexico City. Cajiga's managers would oversee the coming harvest of maize and frijol sown by the estate and its "medieros"—sharecroppers. Arana would guard livestock, make repairs, maintain irrigation, and defend uplands, "keeping on the young men hired to do that." Cajiga paid taxes; losses to "armed factions" were shared.

Then the contract addressed ongoing difficulties: "Arana will also take on the debts owed by current *sirvientes*, sharecroppers, and tenants." Proprietor and leaseholder would collect "diligently." Recognizing persistent uncertainties, debts at the end should not exceed those at the start.[49] The estate mixed wheat planting with paid *sirvientes*, sharecropping of maize, and production by tenant rancheros. *Sirvientes* took advances never repaid; sharecroppers failed to deliver crop shares; rancheros paid in good years, withheld in bad. Debts to the estate mounted. With no expectation of collection, the lease dreamed that producers' unpaid obligations would not increase. Family growers held strong.

A series of leases for San José de Vegil, west of Querétaro on the road to Pueblito, details challenges solved by sharing risks and costs. The estate was part of an *obra pía* supporting Querétaro's Congregation of Guadalupe. During insurgency and after, leases brought little gain.[50] In 1826, the congregation leased Vegil to Vicente Camacho of Querétaro for seven years, the rent cut to 2,000 pesos. Repairs fell to Camacho; the congregation paid taxes.[51] In 1833, they renewed at the same rent for nine years, with the congregation paying 150 pesos to repair the *troje*, Camacho restoring boundary walls and increasing the herd.[52] Again the lease held, leading to a contract in 1843 for nine years at 2,000 pesos, now with doña Maria Leonides Salazar, Camacho's widow.[53] Shared risk at low rent served the convent proprietor and another widowed leasehold operator.

Women Carrying Landed Clans and Clerical Corporations

Two women, doña María Trinidad Fernández de Herrera at Chichimequillas and doña Maria Leonides Salazar at Vegil, proved effective leasehold operators of estates owned by Querétaro clerical corporations in the 1830s and 1840s. Most convents and congregations depended on liens set on others' estates, constantly struggling to collect the interest to fund their religious activities. In the 1830s, Santo Domingo, San Francisco, Santa Theresa, Santa Rosa Yterbo, Santa Clara, and Guadalupe all joined in contracts leasing out others' debt-burdened estates, seeking rents ranging from 30 to 600 pesos from small properties valued from 600 to 12,000 pesos.[54]

In the same years, leading women in landed clans in Querétaro and nearby towns worked to hold family properties while sustaining clerics and church institutions. Notable women with modest properties ranging from 15,000 to 45,000 pesos tied uncertain estate operations to ways of funding struggling clergy and clerical institutions. In November 1833, the widow doña Estefana Plaza bought the Ojozarco estate near Celaya from lawyer don Ramón Martínez de los Rios. She paid 15,000 pesos—it was "not worth more"—by recognizing a 5,000-peso chaplaincy to sustain a priest in Mexico City, another 3,000 pesos owed a Querétaro cleric, and 2,500 pesos invested in doña María Trinidad Fernández de Herrera's leasehold operation at Chichimequillas. Doña Estafana paid 4,500 pesos in cash to buy an estate to sustain herself, support two clerics, and fund an entrepreneurial woman.[55]

Two years later, in 1835, doña Petra de la Canal, executor of the estate of doña María Ignacia Landeta, both heirs to landed oligarchs once entrenched at San Miguel, turned to sustain religious institutions. Doña Petra funded pious endowments set as liens on Santa Barbara and other estates around San Miguel: 3,400 pesos would serve the San Miguel parish church; 4,700 pesos would fund the Canal-founded Convento de Monjas; another 2,500 pesos served Our Lady of Loreto; and 1,000 pesos went to Querétaro's San Francisco convent.[56]

Then, in 1839, she sold Santa Barbara in a contract that aimed to relieve her of risks while funding religious obligations more than doubled from 11,600 to nearly 25,000 pesos. Beyond the original bequests, she added chaplaincies for several priests. The contract revealed ongoing challenges. Santa Barbara's grazing lands held. But of 38 *caballerías* of arable land (about 1,500 hectares), 11 had been claimed by the town of San Felipe, another 7 by María Gertrudis and José María Ortiz. Such losses might cut the estate's arable land by half. Did that explain the sale to don Manuel Ortíz of San Felipe—likely the "ennobled" kinsman of the challengers, perhaps able to settle their claims? The price was 45,000 pesos, including 25,000 in religious endowments, the interest to be paid annually by the buyer. Ortíz delivered only 6,000 pesos to doña Petra, leaving nearly 15,000 pesos to be paid after resolution of the land claims.[57] Doña Petra gained limited cash, sustained clerical activities, and escaped risks.

Another Canal woman aimed to escape risk and attend to family wealth, less attentive to clerical needs. In 1836, Dona Catalina de la Canal y Jauregui, widow of don Manuel de Samaniego del Castillo, lived in Mexico City. She leased the Ortega estate near San Luis de la Paz to don Juan Nepomuceno and don José María Vázquez, residents of the town at the edge of the Sierra.

They would pay 1,750 pesos "in silver" for seven years. With 750 fanegas of maize in the granary valued at less than 8 reales, the crop in the fields went to the new tenants. Doña Catalina shifted risks to brothers who knew San Luis de la Paz and were backed by their mother, doña Guadalupe Zuñiga de Vázquez.[58]

Late in 1837, doña Catalina aimed to escape risk at a different Santa Barbara estate near Apaseo. Don José Pérez Arce of Querétaro took a seven-year lease at 650 pesos, promising to repair granaries; preserve buildings, woodlands, plow teams, and tools; and seek no compensation for "locusts, epidemics, sterile years, or other things beyond control."[59]

When the Ortega lease ended in 1842, doña Catalina sold the property to the Vázquez brothers in a contract that revealed more about the heiress's challenges. The estate included 5 *sitios de ganado mayor*, about 25,000 hectares, mixing limited arable land with rugged uplands near lands of the "*indios* of San Luis de la Paz." The property was valued at 29,300 pesos and sold for 26,600. The buyers took on 14,000 pesos mortgaged to Querétaro's Santa Clara Convent and 8,600 pesos owed to a Señor Oteyza. Doña Catalina gained 4,000 pesos in cash to escape obligations.[60] The convent expected 700 pesos in yearly income. The Vázquez family gained property and a chance at provincial prosperity.

The women of once eminent Bajío families negotiated to sustain declining clans, struggling clerical institutions, and religious men and women. Profit remained a dream.

Santa Rosa Estates: Fragmentation and Reaggregation

Strategic leasing kept a few large properties intact through years of scarce profits. Others less valuable were sold to escape risk. Meanwhile, the Santa Rosa basin estates delivered to *labradores* and *gañanes* in the 1820s saw ownership and operation, meaning rent collection, fragment in the 1830s. Proprietors struggling to collect rents sold off once large estates in shares— while family growers carried on.

In September 1833, *ciudadano* Manuel Velasco y Cauto, rooted in Querétaro, served as prefect at Amoles deep in the Sierra Gorda. He leased "the section of the hacienda de Monte de Negro he holds, . . . with its tenants, offices, and house" for five years at 480 pesos to sisters doña Gertrudis, doña Agustina, and doña María de Jesús Peña, all of Querétaro. The women paid 300 pesos in advance; Velasco and his co-heirs would pay for irrigation rights every September.[61] Velasco family ownership had divided among many heirs while production relied on tenant growers. Living at distant Amoles, Velasco could not collect rents, so he leased to the Peña sisters. Ownership, rent collection, and production all fragmented. In 1836, another Velasco heir leased "a piece of a share of the land at the Hacienda de Santa Catarina," to Br. D. Manuel Borja y Gonzalez for five years at 325 pesos. Borja gained "the benefit of water, tenants, products" in another contract to lease a section of estate lands, gain water rights, and collect subtenant rents.[62]

Then, in 1841, three members of the Velasco family leased "the section of land they hold at Monte de Negro" for nine years at 300 pesos to don Benito Nicohi, a local official in Querétaro. The proprietors were heirs to fragmented ownership. Nicohi, by his name and role, was an heir to Otomí nobility. Recruited to collect rents for a landed woman and her children, Nicohi might be effective dealing with Otomí tenants. The share in question included two houses, one *caballería* (40 hectares) of arable land, and a "serviceable granary," but no livestock or equipment. The contract added: "neighbors have moved in, usurping lands; . . . the leaseholder, if he wishes, may reclaim them."[63] Sharecroppers ruled maize, delivering estate shares to a granary. Nicohi would collect rents, store maize until sale, and pay 300 pesos to the proprietors. Expelling squatters was an uncertain option.

Then, in 1843, as mining rose at Guanajuato and Hércules neared production, the fragmented shares of Monte del Negro began reconsolidating. On February 10, doña María de Jesus Martinez leased her *suerte* to don Joaquín Pina, a Querétaro merchant, for seven years at 400 pesos, payable as 20 pesos monthly, plus 160 at the end of each year. The rentier-shareholder would gain a monthly stipend, plus a sum for annual expenses. On the twenty-second, don Sabás Antonio Domínguez, president of the Junta Departmental (governor under central rule), acting as *apoderado* of Doña Dolores Ruiz, widow and executor of don Manuel Velasco, rented a second share to the merchant Pina for nine years at 485 pesos—40 monthly, plus 5 to repair the granary. The same day, as executor for don José Longino Zendeja, Domínguez leased a third "section of land" at Monte de Negro to Pina for 325 pesos, 27 paid monthly.[64] Pina accumulated estate shares by leasehold, paying still struggling proprietor-rentiers.

He also leased two sections at Santa Catarina, on the river north of Santa Rosa. On February 3, via don Vicente Domínguez, departmental deputy and likely an ally and kinsmen of don Sabás Antonio, Pina took on this "parcel of land" for nine years at 325 pesos, split in three installments yearly. Then, on the twenty-seventh, Pina leased a second "section of land" at Santa Catarina for five years at 360 pesos—paid at 30 pesos per month.[65] The department president, his political allies, and the merchant Pina merged three shares of Monte de Negro and two at Santa Catarina in lease operations, paying more than 1,650 pesos yearly, a substantial rent. Were commercial prospects improving as silver rose just west at Guanajuato?

A March 1843 contract suggests optimism and realism. Don Ygnacio Trejo leased San Miguelito, west of Juriquilla, for seven years at 1,100 pesos to don Antonio Anieves. Woodlands were sparse, to be used only for estate needs. Grain in storage was enough only for the next planting: 25 fanegas of maize, 11 of frijol—and 6 cargas of trigo. Two fields for wheat needed cleaning, to be done by the tenant. Maize was planted by sharecroppers who gained seed from the estate, then kept half the harvest. There were 42 oxen, 60 milk cows, and 16 bulls, along with 274 goats, and 438 sheep raised for wool sold to nearby household cloth makers. The estate was diversifying. The granary was recently rebuilt with 100 beams, a ceramic roof, and metal doors; three stone dams were free of mud buildup. The estate seemed poised to profit—grounded in sharecropping.

An image of Our Lady of Sorrows marked the main house. Saint Michael reigned in the chapel along with "several images set there by the *indios*."[66] The estate had protectors; Otomí sharecroppers kept theirs, too—surely including our Lady at Pueblito, so close by. The owner and leaseholder at San Miguelito aimed to profit by mixing commercial planting of wheat, small livestock operations, maize made by sharecroppers—and cultural respect for Otomí maize makers.

The possibilities and limits of commercial revival emerge in a contract to lease San Ysidro in August 1844, amid the summer growing season. Part of the Juriquilla complex, the estate was owned by doña María Dolores Septién; her husband, Squadron Commander don Timoteo Fernández de Jauregui, arranged the lease. The couple represented financial power long past, landed power hanging on, and an active military role. The lease revealed difficulties. The rent was 400 pesos for seven years—with an escape clause for the tenant after three. The lessee, Br. don Guadalupe Perrusquia, pastor at Santa Rosa, must guard the uplands and build fences, splitting costs with the owners. He gained use of the "water from the dam" and "pastures and croplands." The priest-tenant could sublet as he chose.[67] An attempt to plant on estate accounts had failed. Struggling oligarchs hoped a local priest might oversee a return to prosperity with maize sown by tenants and sharecroppers.

Selling Out and Buying In: Estate Sales, 1839–1843

Beginning in 1839, small estates valued under 25,000 pesos began to sell. Most lay west of Querétaro, from Pueblito to greater Celaya, where markets stimulated by mining were more accessible. A few were east near San Pedro de la Cañada, where construction at Hércules promised opportunity. Still, cash was scarce and most sales were debt transfers as sellers escaped obligations and buyers took them on, hoping rising markets might bring relief.

In January 1839, a creditors council led by Querétaro merchant don Juan José Borja sold four estates clustered around La Capilla, west of the city along the river, to don Cresencio Mena for 54,000 pesos. He paid nothing down, gaining ownership by recognizing the debts that forced the sale.[68] Borja orchestrated the sale and served as guarantor. Well-watered properties offered hope of profit; no one was ready to invest cash. Two days later, doña Sabás Diez de la Madrid of Querétaro, with her husband's consent, sold the Hacienda San Juan, near Chamacuero north of Celaya on the road to San Miguel. The estate, valued at 7,807 pesos, was purchased by don Pedro Llaca of Querétaro for 746 pesos down; he recognized 3,000 pesos along with 1,761 past-due interest to a Chamacuero sodality and promised the remaining 3,740 pesos over seven years.[69] Another purchase relieved an owner of debts.

In February, a small estate at the edge of Querétaro, San Cayetano Bolaños, faced auction for a second time in two years. Don Ygnacio Fernández de Jauregui had gained the property in 1837 for 9,400 pesos. Now he sold to don Pedro Gutiérrez, who recognized 2,000 pesos owed to the Carmelites, 500 owed to a sodality at Querétaro's Santiago Parish, and 1,600 owed to doña Dolores Dávila.[70]

In April, don Ygnacio Argomaniz, Querétaro postal administrator, sold San Pablo, south of Celaya, for 23,900 pesos. The buyer, don Policarpo Gómez Muñoz of Querétaro, recognized 15,000 pesos at the low rate of 2.5 percent yearly: 3,500 to don Miguel de Cervantes, ex-Marqués de Salvatierra; the rest to religious lenders, including 2,000 to Santa Clara and 2,000 to San Francisco in Querétaro. Lienholders accepted half the standard return to gain something. Gómez Muñoz promised to pay the remaining 8,550 pesos in eight annual installments of 1,000 pesos at 5 percent.[71] As mining revived, the owner escaped debts, creditors took returns cut in half, and the buyer hoped for profit.

Later, in 1839, doña Sabás Diez de la Madrid sold two more properties. In October, don Juan Goichea bought San Luis Obispo near Chamacuero. An estate valued near 26,000 pesos, brought just over 1,000 pesos at signing while Goichea took on obligations to religious institutions totaling 16,500 pesos—enough to convince doña Sabás to sell at a 30 percent discount.[72] Her last sale is most revealing: In December, she sold La Cantera, an estate west of Querétaro on the road to Pueblito, for 12,037 pesos to doña Justa Roja, a widow living at Alfajayuca, east of the city beyond La Griega. After recognizing 4,253 pesos owed to four religious institutions in Celaya, doña Justa paid 1,000 down by a *libranza* (letter of credit), promised 2,000 more by May 1840, another 780 by December 1840, and the remaining 4,000 in two later payments.[73] Doña Sabás escaped debts in return for promises; doña Justa delivered a 1,000-peso credit and took on nearly 7,000 pesos in cash obligations—hoping to profit in a commercial revival.

The new decade brought more bargain purchases. In February 1840, agents for several church creditors sold Picacho, near Chamacuero, for 22,300 pesos to don Gervasio Antonio de Fraga, Senior Justice on the Querétaro Superior Court. He paid nothing down while recognizing existing liens.[74] In March, heirs to Allende and Fernández de Jauregui properties sold estates near Celaya to don Manuel Zimabilla of Querétaro for 25,000 pesos. The sellers canceled 10,000 pesos owed by the buyer; he recognized the rest to Celaya clerical institutions—and gained 500 pesos in cash to seal the deal.[75]

Then, in April 1841, executors for postal director Argomaniz sold Fresno Alto, near Jerécuaro, to the governor of Querétaro, Lt. Col. don Jose Francisco Figueroa. He paid nothing down, recognized more than 20,000 pesos owed to church institutions from Morelia to Querétaro, and took on a 7,300 debt to the Argomaniz estate.[76] Another military-political man gained properties and obligations, hoping to profit.

With Hércules under construction, estate sales began east of Querétaro, too. In December 1839, don Francisco de Paula Mesa, a member of the state governing council, took control of properties at La Cañada inherited by his wife and her brothers. They included two ranchos, four houses, two *huertas*, and a still to make aguardiente (cane brandy)—together valued at 36,000 pesos. To gain the full inheritance, Mesa took on a 7,000-peso debt to his brothers-in-law, 4,000 pesos in obligations to religious institutions, and 3,000 more to a pharmacy professor.[77]

Early in 1842, don Marcos Herrera and don Julian de San Fuente contracted to buy half shares of Calamanda, east of La Cañada, for 16,000 pesos. They promised 2,000 pesos in March, another 2,000 in June, while recognizing 6,000 pesos to Querétaro's Franciscans and the same to the Sodality of Jesus of Nazareth.[78] In November 1843, Malchorra near La Cañada changed hands. Seven members of the Diez Marina family held shares valued from 7,000 to 1,000 pesos, with 1,000 pesos owed the Carmelites. Lic. don Juan Plata, a Querétaro priest, gained ownership by recognizing 23,000 pesos in obligations.[79]

A final purchase of a small estate saw don Tomás Fermín López de Ecala buy San Bernadino, west of Querétaro, near his other holdings. Late in 1843, he committed to pay 2,600 pesos due to Santa Clara, 2,000 owed to the Santa Ana parish—and to deliver 4,410 divided among "innumerable heirs" led by don Francisco de Paula Mesa.[80] Another estate divided among heirs and deep in debts to clerical lenders sold to a buyer who saw chances of consolidation for gain. López de Ecala held larger nearby properties mixing estate planting, tenant cropping, and cloth making, giving him hope for success.

The sales of small estates that came with the commercial opening of the late 1830s allowed struggling landowners to escape debts, delivering ownership to political men with landed aspirations who took on obligations to sustain rentier families and clerical institutions—and dream of profit.

Proprietors Hanging On: Estate Leasing, 1841–1845

Other landlords still leased, keeping property, seeking steady rents, and avoiding risks. In 1841, Col. don Juan José de la Llata y Barbero, of an old Querétaro family, leased four Celaya ranchos for five years to don Crecencio Mena, already active as a leasehold operator west of Querétaro. The rent was 750 pesos yearly, 100 paid to the cathedral at Morelia, 100 to a Querétaro court, 550 to Llata y Barbero.[81] In September, *ciudadano* Timoteo Fernández de Jauregui, of another old Querétaro clan, leased Labor de la Fuente, Malacate, and Cerrogordo, all at Celaya, to Nicolás Mercado for seven years at 1,700 pesos—no liens noted.[82]

In March 1842, doña Josefa Velasco de la Torre y Teruel, heir to a fusion of Mexico City landed clans, leased five estates around Apaseo to Br. don José María Moreno y Baso, the pastor at Tequisquiapan, near her larger holdings around San Juan del Río. Another landed woman held onto important properties. Early in 1843, don Mariano Fernández de Jauregui of Querétaro joined the clergyman's contract, financing operations and contributing 1,500 pesos to the rent. When Moreno y Baso faced 3,700 in arrears in September 1845, don Domingo de Letona, doña Josefa's husband, took on the lease.[83] She owned, he leased—another inversion of power in world rattling patriarchy.

A series of leases for estates along the river west of Querétaro reveal more about owners, leasehold operators, and ways of production as the economy revived. In January 1842, *ciudadano* Agustín Frías y Tovar, an established landlord, leased the rancho San Ysidro, southwest of the city, to *ciudadano* José María Olvera for five years at 650 pesos. Repairs to a dam and reservoir fell to the owner and a neighboring proprietor. With maize left to sharecroppers, the estate sold pulque to city taverns for a steady income. In 1844, the lease passed to Simón Olvera, still insisting on the importance of sustaining sharecroppers and maintaining fields of maguey.[84]

In January 1844, Captain don Manuel Acevedo, deputy in the departmental assembly, leased Colorado, Durazno, and an inn on the road to Celaya to don Manuel María Vertiz, also a deputy, for 1,550 pesos. In August, doña María Guadalupe Acevedo, wife of a judge who was also a deputy, leased half of her hacienda de la Cueva to her brother, now Lt. Col. don Manuel Acevedo, for nine years at a rent to be set by inventory.[85] Families merging old landholdings, military power, and political roles leased to carry on—and hope for profits.

A final transaction of 1845 reveals a lease culminating in a sale to benefit an old landed clan and a rising agricultural entrepreneur. The hacienda Comunidad and rancho Tejeda had been bought in 1829 by don Salvador Frías from sisters doña Felipa Josefa and doña Ana Francisca Arías. After Frías's death, an 1840 inventory valued the properties inherited by his son don Estevan at 24,800 pesos. In 1841, he had leased to don Cresencio Mena—then aggregating leaseholds. Now, in 1845, General don Estevan Frías sold the properties for 23,500 pesos to now Lt. Col. don Cresencio Mena—who paid 470 pesos in cash while recognizing 23,030 owed to doña Ana Canalizo, widow of don Salvador, and don José María Frías.[86] A landed general facing financial challenges and a Lt. Col. skilled in estate operation made a deal: the old clan would escape debts and hope for income; the leasehold accumulator bought an estate for little cash—and obligations to sustain the Frías family.

The sales and leases of the late 1830s and early 1840s show Querétaro landed families facing debts while finding profit scarce in a world of fragmented ownership, consolidating leaseholds, and entrenched family production. Many lost properties; others retained estates burdened with debts that funded clerics and convents. A few women prospered as leasehold operators of leading estates; more juggled to sustain comfortable lives and religious institutions.

Before 1810, silver gained in mining and commerce had flowed to fund estate operations, at times by purchase as with the Reglas, often by marriage as Sánchez Espinosa linked to a Peñasco daughter. When silver collapsed in times of insurgency and political wars, military and political men turned to the land—with limited financial success.[87] When silver began to revive in the 1830s and 1840s, family growers kept maize plentiful and affordable, inhibiting estate profit while political-military men dreamed of revenue from the land.

In April 1845, a group led by Governor don Sabás Antonio Domínguez met in Querétaro. There were seven Assembly deputies, including Acevedo, Vertiz, and José del Raso. Key military, state, and city officials joined along with men of the Arias, Frías, Jauregui, Samaniego, and Septién clans. A Franco of the clan that once managed La Griega was there, along with Crecensio Mena, the accumulator of leaseholds. Twenty in all, they pledged 30,821 pesos, an average of 1,500 each, to build an elegant theater. Cayetano Rubio promised 4,000 pesos.[88] No landed clan approached the industrialist's wealth.

Smallholdings in the Shadow of Hércules:
Huertas, 1841–1845

While landed proprietors, leaseholders, and rentiers struggled, small growers held strong. The early 1840s saw rising numbers of sales and rentals of small holdings, notably of *huertas* along the river from La Cañada through the northern barrios of the city, "the other bank." Most were cash transactions as water and *huertas* became more valuable while Hércules stimulated markets.

In 1841, Lic. Ramón Martínez de los Ríos, the lawyer who dreamed of landed wealth, owned four large *huertas* with water rights. Rather than plant the traditional Otomí mix of annual vegetables and perennial fruits, he raised maguey and made pulque for nearby taverns, along with alfalfa to feed the livestock that kept city life moving. He leased to Victoriano López for five years at 650 pesos, suggesting rich production and promising markets. A year later, the lawyer, now a don, leased the *huertas* to don José María González for four years at a rent cut to a still ample 440 pesos.[89]

Early in 1842, *ciudadano* Luis Olvera purchased six small plots stretching north from the river in the San Roque barrio, adjacent to lands he already held. Two were sold by María Ygnacia, one by María Gertrudis, both Otomí; another by Antonia Quintero, perhaps mixed. Hispanic men sold two others. Olvera paid 100 pesos for all six, stating that the sale was not legally recorded but witnessed to allow future sales to "trapicheros"—distillers of popular beverages.[90] Long communal Otomí *huertas*, lacking formal titles, required documentation when sold to outsiders seeking profit.

In July 1842, María Merced and María Gervasia Bárcena, sisters at Pueblito, sold a plot inherited from their grandmother to Doña Dolores

Contreras, also of Pueblito, for 40 pesos.[91] In January 1843, don Porfirio Valderas inherited a nearby *nopalera* from his mother, doña Ana María Díaz, who ran a stand selling the native delicacy surrounded by others in the same trade. Young don Porfirio sold the plot for 30 pesos to *ciudadano* Juan Álvarez, who likely carried on the business.[92]

In December 1843, María Anastasia Hermenegilda de Lugo, proclaiming herself an adult "de estado libre"—unmarried—sold a *huerta* on the Calle Santiago in Querétaro to José Antonio Pérez for 30 pesos.[93] In the same barrio, the widow doña Guadalupe Vázquez had contracted to sell a *huerta* to Vicente Hernández for 40 pesos in 1839. Having paid only 29 in 1845, he completed the deal.[94] Market growth drew Hispanic men to plots long held by Otomí women.

In February 1844, Juan León of San Pedro de la Cañada confirmed ownership of a plot measuring only 27 by 39 *varas* (yards) in the barrio del Molino. It was valuable because it bordered the road to Querétaro and the aqueduct that sent water to the city. He brought, as witnesses, don Ygnacio Martínez, 67, a merchant at San Pedro married to doña Guadalupe Vázquez, and don Juan María Moreno, 60, an *hortelano* at San Pedro married to María Martín—likely Indigenous. A Hispanic commercial couple and a mixed pair working a *huerta* were asked to prove ownership as Juan León sold the plot to don José María Garfías, the local magistrate, for 35 pesos cash.[95]

Change was underway in the world of *huertas* along the river from La Cañada, past Hércules, and through Querétaro as the prosperous and the indigenous poor lived commercial revivals. Hispanic men bought as indigenous women sold. Was patriarchy reviving or were Otomí women taking cash and turning to new opportunities in the industrializing city?

Life on the Land: Raso's 1845 Report

Don José Antonio del Raso promoted industry, yet knew that Querétaro remained grounded on the land. In his 1845 report, he honored "well-located estates, beautiful fields, . . . wonderful people, and hydraulic works."[96] Everything was plentiful—but profit.

Raso reported 124 haciendas and 392 ranchos, the former mostly in basin lowlands, the latter spread across rugged uplands. He listed producers to suggest a return to estate production: 2,200 herders kept livestock for salaries and rations; 6,000 "peones" (*sirvientes* relabeled) gained salaries and rations; nearly 3,200 *alquilados* labored seasonally for wages, along with 4,000 muchachos. Yet given the endless references in the leases and sales of basin estates, it seems certain that many of Raso's peons and most *alquilados* were *medieros* (sharecroppers) who also worked seasonally for wages. Read carefully, Raso contradicted his own vision of revived estate production.

He reported that 2,100 men leased to work estate uplands, extracting more than 380,000 pesos worth of wood, charcoal, maguey, and nopal, paying just 77,000 pesos in rents, and marketing more than 300,000 pesos of produce—each taking nearly 145 pesos yearly (surely complemented by maize plots).[97] Family efforts yielded sustenance and more. He buried his report of 2,729 *huertas* with 336,549 "fruit trees" in a note. Families with nearly 125 fruit trees each while planting diverse vegetables plus maize for sustenance barely counted in Raso's eyes.[98] Yet the *hortelanos* of Querétaro and San Juan del Río, most Otomí, sustained families and city markets, keeping industry alive.

Also buried in the text, Raso recognized the struggles of commercial growers: "Leaseholders and owners, lacking capital to fund production, have adopted the system of distributing lands in subrentals among tenants often called rancheros, and *terrazgueros* [resident dependents]—2,610 lesser *labradores* who barely sustain themselves because they sell their crops at low prices year after year. There are estates that do not plant a twelfth of what their tenants sow."[99]

With obvious lament, Raso reported the family production that kept food plentiful and prices low—sustaining growing numbers. He recorded that a state population near 90,000 in 1822 after the disruptions of insurgency had doubled to 180,000 in 1844.[100] Baptismal and burial records (presumed equal to births and deaths) documented slow growth amid disruptions in the 1820s, little gain in the face of disease that culminated in the cholera of 1833, then a steady rise from 1834 to 1844.[101] Growth concentrated in Querétaro and nearby basins, and in Sierra uplands, the former mixing industry and tenant family production, the latter a region of refuge for families seeking independence on the land. *Hortelanos*, rancheros, tenant families, and independent people fed themselves and Querétaro well.

Production and Income in the New Querétaro

Raso's figures for economic activity across Querétaro allow calculations of employment and production in agriculture and industry, artisanry and commerce, and the professions. They reveal a world of shared sustenance, prosperity for a few—and wealth concentrating in Rubio's hands.

Raso reported that agriculture engaged nearly 40 percent of the economically active population, generating nearly 30 percent of total value produced, as each rural producer accounted for nearly 100 pesos. It was an under-report. Raso's figures do not include more than 2,000 *hortelanos* in the parish of San Sebastián, *la otra banda*, with a population approaching 10,000.[102] If they raised produce worth 100 pesos, surely an underestimate of year-round irrigated cropping, they added 200,000 pesos to the state's agricultural sector—bringing it even with urban industrial production.

And most family growers sustained themselves: produce never marketed, never commercially counted. If 10,000 households, half of rural producers, consumed 10 fanegas of maize valued at 1 peso each, and 10 pesos of chile, frijol, tuna, and more, they added another 200,000 pesos of value to agricultural production—bringing it beyond the value of urban commerce and industry. If this estimate of self-sustenance is close to accurate, it shows that production for consumption was fragmented, yet a key part of agriculture in a commercializing society. Family growers fed themselves and kept prices low, subsidizing industry and more across Querétaro.

Turning to industry, Raso saw two sectors. Factories, meaning Hércules, employed only 7 percent of the working population to generate 15 percent of the state's production by value. Nonfactory industry included *obrajes* and family shops making woolens, along with household producers of cotton goods. Their operations engaged more than 30 percent of producers, while generating just 18 percent of product by value. Facing industrial competition, artisan cloth makers also subsidized consumers.

Raso listed artisans separately, including silversmiths, tailors, shoemakers, and bakers who did better than household cloth makers. He dispersed figures showing nearly 600 women laboring at Hércules, 1,500 in the tobacco factory, and 5,500 urban domestics, seemingly aiming to downplay the roles of 7,000 city women who worked for pay in the industrializing city.

Among those who produced little but claimed income, a few lived modestly as rentiers collecting on *censos*, the liens on property recorded in notarial logs. Merchants did better; Raso's estimate of 1,200 pesos income each included a few larger dealers, many middling traders, and large numbers of shopkeepers and peddlers. They claimed more than their share of earnings as Querétaro revived commercially. Lawyers and other professionals were few and also took more than their share. Only the religious gained more, averaging 1,500 pesos to sustain comfortable lives in convents and parishes. The women and others who negotiated obligations to sustain clergy found success. More than 120 public employees averaged nearly 700 pesos, better than any group but clergy and merchants. The government paid its officials well—Raso among them.

His 1845 survey reveals a broad dispersal of production, urban and rural, limited inequality, and great wealth flowing to the Rubios thanks to the industrial concentration at Hércules. Families on urban *huertas*, tenants spread across basin estates, and uncounted others in uplands fed themselves, urban producers, and Hércules's workers. Family artisans held on in cities and towns. Together, they sustained and subsidized Hércules, the harbinger of a new industrial Querétaro.

A new Bajío consolidated in the early 1840s. Silver revived and industry began; landlords struggled while families on the land fed themselves and everyone else. Proprietors leased to escape risk as maize held plentiful and prices low. A few leasehold operators, including notable women, profited. Most owners and leaseholders, men and women, faced endless debts—juggling to live as rentiers while the rural majority made maize plentiful, affordable, and thus unprofitable.

Women were active everywhere—proprietors juggling to maintain city lives and religious allies; leaseholders taking profit in challenging times; rancheras leading rural clans; laborers in the tobacco factory and working machines at Hércules. The majority of women, urban and rural, labored daily, making meals and more to sustain families and communities across a Bajío remade in revolution. With agrarian capitalism gone, women challenged patriarchs and patriarchy in diverse ways as family production sustained reviving mines, rising industries, and growing populations.

12.

A New Capitalism, 1845–1860

Silver Peaks, Industry Expands,
Rancheros Thrive—and Family Growers
Feed Everyone

The United States invaded Mexico in 1846, starting a war to claim lands from Texas to California. In time, the War for North America would turn the course of Mexican, North American, and world history. Yet in the near term, it did not derail the new silver-industrial capitalism grounded in family cultivation that brought economic dynamism and shared prosperity to the Bajío. Guanajuato's silver rose to historic heights in the 1850s, industry consolidated in Querétaro and regions beyond, while family growers fed themselves and everyone else. The new capitalism that came out of the Bajío revolution drove a dynamic new Mexico into the 1860s.

Anglo-Americans had other plans. After seceding to promote cotton and slavery in 1836, the Republic of Texas failed to consolidate a regime or an export economy, in good part due to the fall of cotton prices in the panic of 1837—as the new Bajío economy began to rise. In the early 1840s, British and US industries revived, driving new demand for cotton. In 1845, President James Polk signed a bill annexing Texas, leading the United States to a war to claim Texas for cotton and slavery—and California for gold.[1] In April 1846, US troops crossed the Nueces River to set a new border at the Rio Grande. Formal war came in May. While US land and naval expeditions converged on northern California, US troops crossed the Rio Grande, invading lands everyone recognized as Mexican. They took Monterrey in a deadly battle in September, then broke an armistice to gain Saltillo, gateway to the inland plateau. After a winter of consolidation, they faced an army driven north by Antonio López de Santa Anna at La Angostura, just south, in February 1847. A deadly stalemate set the stage for another year of war.[2]

The war between nations came amid ongoing conflicts with native peoples, Comanches and many others. Multilateral fights disputed rights to vast territories.[3] Seeking to break the stalemate, US forces landed at Veracruz in March, driving inland to take Puebla in May and Mexico City in September. Mexican leaders fled to Querétaro, taking refuge in a center of peace and prosperity, while people in the capital took to rooftops to hurl paving stones at US Marines.[4] Meanwhile, US forces occupied New Mexico and California—all gained along with Texas in the Treaty of Guadalupe Hidalgo, signed at Our Lady's shrine outside Mexico City in February 1848, revised at Querétaro on May 30.

The war rattled Mexico's attempts to consolidate a regime and blocked revival of the northward expansion stalled since 1808.[5] In the Bajío, Querétaro hosted national authorities for nearly a year, gaining access to Guanajuato's soaring silver flows. Bajío mining, industry, and trade continued to grow during the war, still grounded in cultivating communities—while risings in the Sierra Gorda just east provoked instability where basin lands met the mountains north of Querétaro.[6]

After the war, political divides led to a last Santa Anna–Alamán regime in the early 1850s, followed by a mobilization pressing liberal dreams.[7] Taking power in 1855, liberals enacted laws ending the separate legal and land rights of the Church and indigenous communities. Confirmed in the 1857 Constitution, the challenges to clerical powers provoked a political war that rattled the nation until liberals retook power under Benito Juárez in 1860.[8] Still, from the War for North America that began in 1846 through the War of Reform that ended in 1860, Guanajuato mining held strong, Hércules led industrial expansion at Querétaro, while rancheros and family growers made ample maize across the Bajío—until the French invasion of 1863 again rattled the new Bajío.

Silver Peaks at Guanajuato

In 1846, as war began to the north, Guanajauto silver output held at more than 4 million pesos. As US troops took Mexico City in 1847, output jumped past 6 million pesos. In 1848, with peace and the loss of northern territories, it passed 7 million pesos. The boom reflected more than wartime demand as production approached 8 million pesos from the late 1840s into the 1850s.[9]

Guanajuato silver sustained wartime Mexico, then soared to historic heights to drive a postwar boom across the Bajío and beyond.

Pedro Monroy, a mining engineer at Guanajuato in the 1880s, reported: "The bonanza at La Luz benefited many shareholders, and drove a great circulation of money across the region."[10] During the war, the Pérez Gálvez siblings' La Luz led the surge, paying dividends worth a quarter of the total regional output. After the war, yields at La Luz declined while production at adjacent San José de los Muchachos, also run by the Pérez Gálvez, drove regional output to a historic peak, holding above 7.5 million pesos yearly from 1849 to 1852—50 percent more than Guanajuato's historic highs before 1810.[11]

The boom was financed locally. After breaking with British partners, the Pérez Gálvez drew on limited flows from aging Valenciana to fund the excavation, drainage, and labor that led to bonanza at La Luz. Monroy reported that don Juan de Dios Pérez Gálvez earned 3.35 million pesos as the primary financier during the early boom.[12] The British house of Manning and Mackintosh leased the Guanajuato mint and took profit averaging 60,000 pesos yearly before facing bankruptcy in 1850—gaining radically less than the Pérez Gálvez, local financiers, and shareholders.[13]

The postwar years brought different challenges. The bonanza was still rising when don Juan de Dios died in 1848, assaulted on a highway in Querétaro while traveling between Mexico City and San Luis Potosí.[14] Looking back from the 1880s, the engineer Monroy saw "the death of the man who led the manly enterprise" leading to "the decadence . . . of all the Guanajuato mines" under doña Francisca de Paula's rule.[15] His gendered bias is belied by production figures. She brought the boom to its historic peak during the four years after her brother's death, as Guanajuato production held at more than 7.5 million pesos yearly from 1849 through 1852, led by La Luz and San José de los Muchachos, mines she controlled. Dividends from San José peaked at nearly 1.6 million pesos per year, bringing doña Francisca and her investors unprecedented wealth. When flows receded, output held near 5 million pesos yearly from 1853 to 1860—the level attained before 1810.[16] Doña Francisca de Paula Pérez Gálvez was the richest person in Mexico, surely among the richest the world.

The eulogy offered at her 1868 funeral offers revelations, again through a gendered lens. Monsignor Ignacio Montes de Oca, doctor of theology and law and kin to the governor who had railed against independent women in 1826, honored doña Francisca de Paula—obliquely.[17] He began lamenting "the war for independence, with its destructions, horrors, killings, and retaliations," a revolution that "devastated our cities. . . . A long war that ruined countless precious lives and broke a thousand great fortunes." Memories of revolutionary insurgency still burned in a man of the Church serving the powerful in the 1860s: "Mexico was independent but miserable. The country gained its liberty but the patricians who had formed its aristocracy, under the new regime lost . . . their titles, their influence, and their eminence, and were in danger of losing the properties the revolution had not already devoured."

Montes de Oca explained, "Capital exhausted and business paralyzed, the poor had no work as the once rich lacked the resources to employ their former workers, especially in the risky works of our deceptive mines." Doña Francisca de Paula, "rich heiress in a family once opulent," turned to "aid the indigent, delivering work to 3 million unfortunate people that the war had left without bread, and to protect them from abuse by the powerful and avaricious." Obliquely said, she restored mines that provided work and income sustaining half of Mexico's then six million people—without the abuses that had provoked the risings of 1810. Her "business" was "charity."[18] Like the Fagoaga sisters in Mexico City, doña Francisca de Paula merged profit taking with care to serve, or at least pacify, society.

The monsignor never mentioned her late brother, don Juan de Dios. He credited the revival of the Pérez Gálvez mines to doña Francisca de Paula's drive to create work and income for those who lived by labor. While don Juan de Dios traded, financed mines, and invested in northern lands, she stayed in Guanajuato to oversee mining. Doña Francisca de Paula Pérez Gálvez was an active partner before 1848, led the boom of 1849 to 1852, and limited the decline that followed.

After her brother's death, doña Francisca de Paula kept a commercial "Casa de Guanajuato," with branches in Mexico City, Silao, and Acámbaro. She kept the northern properties, including Bocas and Cruces, acquired by her brother in the 1840s as the ex-Conde de Peñasco faced bankruptcy. When residents "built towns on her lands and took others claimed as unoccupied," she found stabilizing responses: in 1849, "tenants displaced" at Bocas claimed 7,000 hectares to found Ahualulco; doña Francisca de Paula turned to "the fragmentation of agricultural property," leasing large units to kin and trusted dependents charged with defending property rights and collecting rents from dispersed tenants and subtenants.[19] The entrepreneurial widow personified the new silver-industrial capitalism, operating the richest of mines while collecting rents from family growers who ruled production on northern estates.

Was Guanajuato the city of wealth and work the pastor saw as doña Francisca de Paula's legacy? Wealth certainly flowed to the Pérez Gálvez and their capitalist allies. Census counts show thousands drawn to the city, its mines, and refineries in times of boom, despite maiming and deadly risks. The city and its mining and refining districts counted 55,000 people in 1792 as production neared the peak of 5 million pesos yearly that held through 1809.[20] During and after insurgency, the population fell to 37,000 in 1822: 16,000 in the city, more than 20,000 at outlying mines. An 1825 count showed further decline to near 33,000. Then, in 1851 (just after the cholera of 1850), with the mines at La Luz in boom, more than 36,000 lived in the center, nearly 27,000 in nearby mines and refineries, plus 24,000 at La Luz. A total of more than 87,000 made Guanajuato larger than any Mexican city but the capital. In 1854, as modest decline set in, a population just under 86,000 was not a sign of collapse.[21] With and without her brother, doña Francisca de Paula Pérez Gálvez led a surge of mining, wealth, and work at Guanajuato.

As the surge peaked in the early 1850s, Guanajuato became a target of political-military forces seeking power and funds to sustain it. Wisely, Governor Octaviano Muñoz Ledo aimed to keep the state out of political turmoil. In 1852, President Mariano Arista invited Muñoz Ledo to join his cabinet; he chose to stay in Guanajuato.[22] He held back from the conflicts that brought Santa Anna and Lucas Alamán to rule in 1853.[23] Asked to join General José López Uraga and an alliance of Querétaro, Michoacán, San Luis Potosí, and Puebla against Arista, Muñoz Ledo declined. Problems began when a September attack on "the mines at La Luz . . . led to disgraceful acts, as the poor were seduced by the rebels."[24] Recalling the insurgent invasions and worker risings that broke mining after 1810, the governor stood back from political conflicts that would impose "great military costs, . . . hateful forced loans, and conscriptions."[25]

While the governor saw that "everything depends on Guanajuato," he knew that "the man who has a fortune to lose, who enjoys a certain social position, who is jealous of his reputation and good name, and can expect no gain from revolution, resists . . . engagements that could result in the loss of so much; . . . Men of comfort and substance are the best guarantors of public order."[26]

The revolt went on without Muñoz Ledo and Guanajuato. When forces from Aguascalientes took the city in December, the governor left as Santa Anna and Alamán took power.[27] According to Muñoz Ledo, "The path of legality lost, . . . my duty was to preserve [Guanajuato] . . . from the contagion of revolution and the plague of anarchy."[28] Popular risings must not recur. Memories of 1810 shaped the 1850s. Muñoz Ledo took credit for saving

Guanajuato: "I have been the only victim of this revolution," taking credit for preserving the wealth, power, and prosperity of the state.[29]

He concluded: "When a state . . . holds within itself the elements of power and greatness, when it flourishes with prosperity in ways that serve public welfare, when it counts on unique ways of prosperity and delivers abundant means of sustenance to the needy while every business flourishes—and the State meets the needs of the people," leaders must not break "the system of governance."[30] Muñoz Ledo spoke of men. Had he consulted doña Francisca de Paula Pérez Gálvez as she ruled mining? Surely they pursued a common goal: keep silver flowing strong in times of peaceful production.

The Silver City in 1860: José Guadalupe Romero's Report

Everyday power, production, and life were more complicated. José Guadalupe Romero's report on life in the mining center as political war ended and liberals reclaimed power in 1860 detailed great riches, wide prosperity, and the deadly challenges still inherent in mining. Born in nearby Silao as insurgency raged in 1814, Romero became a lawyer and a priest who rose to know Guanajuato from long experience.[31] He honored a city center focused on a fine Palacio de Gobierno and an adjacent jail, both facing the main parish church. Power, coercion, and devotion merged. The state Congress and City Council met nearby, sustained by courts and revenue services. The Alhóndiga reminded everyone of the 1810 battle to rule the city, silver, and maize.[32]

The rich city grappled with inequities. For the poor, "Guanajuato has a poor house and a pawnshop." The comfortable are served by "a beautiful house of baths, a carriage center, good hotels, eight inns, a telegraph office, and many water fountains." There were "two printing presses, a post office, a good theater, . . . a bull ring, a mint, and many warehouses and comercial shops."[33] To escape the crowded center, "leading citizens have built beautiful country villas."[34]

For social control: "The city has a police force paid by public funds." For sustenance: "The market is always as well supplied as that in Mexico City, except for fish, which is only found on holy days; the bread and meat are as good as in Europe; the necessities of life and the most superfluous foods are found in abundance; the frozen ices are without match in the republic. . . . The beautiful rustic figures crafted in silver are avidly bought by Europeans who carry them home as curiosities."[35]

"The people of the city are religious, active, and obedient to authorities," while "mine workers turn to drink, gambling, and disorder on festival days, when they spend in a moment what they earned in a week." As in earlier boom times, those who risked life and limb in mines and refineries spent on worldly escapes, knowing health and life might vanish in a moment. Well behaved or rowdy, "most of the people are Spanish or mixed."[36] Marfil, along the river flowing south, remained a center of refining with "thousands of laborers" working 350 grinding mills. Romero noted that Valenciana retained architectural splendor built in times past.[37]

The risks and rewards of mining now concentrated high above at La Luz, "a small plain . . . dominated by the peak at Cubilete." Before the bonanza, it had a "miserable chapel" serving "poor residents." Now, "a decent temple," begun in 1846, remained unfinished. A pastor and three vicars served the boomtown, aided by a "brotherhood of the Vela Perpetua honoring the Holy Sacrament." Did doña Francisca de Paula sponsor the sodality led by Catholic women, aiming to offer spiritual guidance to those who made her wealth?[38] With 18,000 people at upland La Luz, a local council drew 20,000 pesos yearly to support two schools "for children of both sexes" and "a small police force." There was a "cockfighting ring" and a "bull ring," along with four taverns and "a great number of stores and shops." Mining, trade, and recreation thrived.[39]

Still, people faced challenges. La Luz "lacks potable water," though a new dam "provides for necessities," meaning the mines, "and the citizens," meaning the prosperous: "People live by labor in the mines, by petty trade, by muleteering, and some crafts." And while "the climate is generally healthy, . . . epidemic diseases have struck terribly." Romero blamed "the disorders of the mine workers." Still, "the cholera of 1850 claimed more than 2,500 victims"—likely due more to putrid water than to raucus lives. The cleric went on: "Plagues of smallpox, thyphus, and more strike with great force: they too result from the vices of the mine workers and poor ventilation in the mines." Romero blamed workers for the 6,000 people who died at La Luz from 1845 to 1850, even as "poisoned air" prevailed in mines, a malady "that cripples the most robust man in eight months."[40]

In 1860, as mining held strong at La Luz, a few profited, many prospered— and the men who labored to make silver faced maiming and death. Nearly a third of the population died in the peak years of the boom. They came, lived risks, and were replaced because mine work still paid beyond any other. They drank and gambled, knowing the future might never come, paying in death and disability for riches that favored a few and drove commercial life across the Bajío. Doña Francisca de Paula invested for profit and funded social services, keeping the boom alive. Romero knew that mining built power and prosperity on maiming and deadly impositions—and blamed workers. Laden with contradictions, silver fueled the new silver-industrial capitalism that energized life in the Bajío and across Mexico.

Industry, Crafts, and Commerce at Querétaro

Stimulated by Guanajuato's silver, industry grew at Querétaro in the 1840s and 1850s. A few profited, many prospered, and more labored in a city of industry, crafts, and commerce. Hércules expanded rapidly after opening in 1844: mechanical spindles rose from 4,200 to 9,200 by 1854; mechanical looms from 212 to 450; manual looms from 150 to 370, as power looms still could not keep up with spinning machines. The workforce rose from fewer than 900 to more than 2,500, most still women. The workers' share of the value of production fell from 52 to 31 percent, the goal of mechanization.[41] Cayetano Rubio profited.

To raise production, he claimed increased water resources. In June 1848, doña Manuela López de Ecala leased Molino Blanco, on the river below Hércules, to don Agustín de Lastra, vice consul of Spain in Querétaro.[42] He passed the site to Rubio, who built a second mill at La Purísima, sending new polluted flows to the city and *huertas* below.[43] The social costs of industry also grew.

Juan María Balbontín's report on Querétaro economic life in 1854 shows a consolidation of the industrial and commercial ways reported by Raso a decade earlier. Government employment had grown to nearly 2,000, with more than 1,000 working as police, most in and near the capital. With fewer than 200 judicial employees, the shift from judicial rule to a state of coercion is clear. Fewer than 800 lived in service of the Church and religion, while religious devotions flourished among the powerful and the populace. About 70 legal professionals worked to support property rights, while nearly 100 students pursued such roles. More than 130 medical professionals included 14 women midwives.[44]

Commercial life intensified and diversified. Those specializing in trade— from wholesalers, to storekeepers, to peddlers—remained essential. Those making apparel for sale carried on, still led by shoemakers. Commercial purveyors of sustenance and specialty foods were everywhere: there were biscuit bakers, coffee makers, and nearly 200 butchers; 88 cooks plus 28 chocolatiers, and 25 confectioners offering sweets; nearly 200 bread bakers remained, joined by more than 30 cheese makers and nearly 150 pulque vendors. New and notable, Balbontín reported 536 women tortilla vendors.[45]

As industrial work spread, growing numbers lived by wages, purchasing food—and sweets.

As production and labor expanded at Hércules, traditional textiles struggled. Balbontín reported 1,234 "producers" making coarse woolens as the *obraje* sector waned. One held by a family exiled in Spain sold for a mere 500 pesos in 1846; another leased for five years at 100 pesos rent in 1848, suggesting a value near 2,000 pesos; a third sold for under 4,700 pesos in 1849, two-thirds the value indicated by an appraisal the year before.[46] While old *obrajes* carried on and lost value, 1,038 family weavers made woolens as Hércules displaced family cotton makers. They were sustained by uncounted wives, daughters, and other women who spun wool into yarn. Construction and carrying trades held strong, as did household servants—at least numerically.[47]

Balbontín reported growing numbers of women leading commercial lives: 14 midwives and 40 atole vendors, nearly 550 tortilla sellers and 91 seamstresses. He counted 860 women cigar rollers and 1,500 women and girls laboring at Hércules. Add 156 washer women and presume that at least half of 2,000 domestic workers were women, and more than 4,000 worked to live in a city of 25,000—excluding the *otra banda*, where women worked *huertas* and took produce to city markets.[48] As industry expanded, women were drawn to new roles mixing market opportunities and laboring dependence.

A Liberal in the Industrial City: Guillermo Prieto's Querétaro

Guillermo Prieto, a leader rising in national liberal circles, was treasury minister in Mariano Arista's cabinet. When Santa Anna and Alamán took power in 1853, they exiled Prieto to Querétaro. Rooted in Mexico City, Prieto had much to learn. He kept a journal, published as *Viajes de orden suprema* (Travels by order of the dictator), authored by "Fidel," faithful to Mexico and liberalism.[49]

Arriving under guard from Mexico City, Prieto, like every traveler, was struck by "the divine landscape of Querétaro." He saw church towers with soaring crosses, homes and buildings set among tall green trees, crystal waters delivered by the great aqueduct—while women washed clothes on the banks of the river that took water to the *otra banda* and the *huertas*.[50] His mood turned when on arrival he was treated as a criminal by "ferocious police," then turned again when greeted by a kind innkeeper near the Santa Clara Convent. Querétaro proved a city of unexpected encounters, "a consoling exception in times of persecution."[51]

Early on, Prieto joined a *tertulia* at the home of Sr. Frías—which of the many, he did not say. The political exile mixed with the locally prominent and prosperous. From Frías he learned: "he's a doctor, he's a lawyer, he's a printer, he's a ranchero."[52] Later, walking the portals around the plaza, he saw "a life-sized Christ made of cane." As people passed, some nodded in devotion while others looked to other concerns. The liberal exile noted "a kind of devout citizen, without a habit, . . . agile while humble, sharing his efforts and assistance, his support and visits to nuns in an honest life seeking a path to heaven."[53] Prieto saw men seeking prosperity while sustaining the church and devotions. Not liberal, they could be admirable.

He noted devotion to Our Lady of Merced in a chapel east of the center, yet barely saw Our Lady of Pueblito, who reigned just west.[54] The liberal concluded: "Querétaro excels in devotion, with many convents, pious foundations, and devotions while the *indios* of nearby pueblos come to the city to honor their saints; all this draws energy to the city and its churches."[55]

Under the portals near the Christ were "rural growers who complain of weather and plagues, . . . merchants who lament the bad road to Tampico, . . . aging employees who share news and spat with merchants."[56] After his early encounters, Prieto lamented: "Querétaro, for its small population and limited activity, and for its traditional customs, is a city, though . . . beautiful, also sad and without great attraction for a man of Mexico City."[57]

Over time, Prieto came to know Querétaro's vibrant commercial life (figure 12.1). There was no one great market, as markets were everywhere on streets and plazas. The greatest assemblies were on the "lower plaza" facing the towering Franciscan church and convent, with shops all around—once Epigmenio González' plaza:

> People flood in as the day grows, a thousand sellers setting their wares in symetrical rows, creating a homogeneity of goods. . . . They raise racks of serapes and cloths of every color, from a distance creating capricious blends; people come, noise rises, and every stall, every person, appears agitated. Maize is weighed, cloth is measured, trumpets are tried, youngsters hit drums, . . . everything interrupted by the ringing of bells. . . . And the commotion comes in every language: the *yankee* carter spats with the Otomí; the *payo* [ranchero] with the haughty Spaniards who will not abide jesting; the shopkeeper skilled in the language of Moctezuma and struggling with the language of Cortés.[58]

Figure 12.1 José Augustín Arrieta, *La Sorpreza*, 1850. Arrieta painting held by
MNH-INAH.

Commercial Querétaro was a melting pot.

Prieto saw the *otra banda*, the Otomí city, as "poor," yet "the banks of the barrio are very fertile, made of maize plots, *huertas* of fruit trees, with hills crossed by picturesque pathways." He sampled "the famous *atole de leche, y los tamales de la otra banda*."[59] Recognizing that Otomí *huertas* fed the city, he headed to San Pedro de la Cañada, the Pame community in the canyon. The road wound along a "river with crystaline waters, beautiful and picturesque. Between the road and the river are richly planted lands, shadowed by the high arches that lead to the factory [Hércules, unnamed], the visitor's eyes drawn to the women washing clothes and bathing in the river in the shadow of a magnificent cypress."[60] The liberal appreciated clear waters, rich *huertas*, and (again) women washing and bathing. He barely glanced at industrial Hércules and the women and men working there.

At San Pedro he soaked in warm spring baths: "The thermal waters of the bath earn their delicious name for their purity, warmth, and sensuality; they refresh and revive the body and bring joy and clarity to the soul." La

Cañada, with its *huertas*, restaurants, and baths, "is the place to engage and enjoy the best of Querétaro."[61]

Back in the city, an invasion angered Prieto: "The good life shared here . . . was suddenly diminished, vanishing with the simple announcement of a press gang. The sacking of men, the barbarous sacking of men by other men, taking a soldier to serve another, . . . this legal amputation to reinforce the powers of extortion, . . . this cruelty they call military virtue, . . . what sacrilege!" Prieto, perhaps blind to Cádiz liberalism's original military goals, lamented: "I saw them come to devastate like an epidemic, preying on poverty and scouring places of work, spreading tears while pressing atrocious crimes, turning towns into deserts." He honored local leaders who warned of the press gang's coming and shielded those they could from its predations.[62]

Contradictions ruled Prieto's Querétaro: facing "obvious decadence, it held great potential for lives of prosperity." Beautiful homes marked the center; outlying barrios lived in "filth and misery." He went on: "In other times, Querétaro with its mills making serapes, its shops making hats, all surrounded by the noise of a thousand workshops, had an air of fiesta, the breath of people who lived by work." The old order gone, "today, the mills are destroyed, popular industry buried; a few looms for blankets and shawls remain, while the tobacco factory and the spinning mill are the great sources of work. Monopolies!"[63]

Prieto could not see that before 1810, New Spain's silver capitalism stimulated regional trade and manufacturing. He would not see that it was industrial cloth imported from Britain after 1808 that pummeled Querétaro workshops—until Hércules led a revival, bringing profit to Rubio, labor to a strategic few, and displacement to many. Rubio gained as household artisans struggled. Free trade was no solution for the people.

Prieto worried about Querétaro women. He lamented the few who funded the church and its devotions.[64] He blamed "the misery of the poor" on "inattention . . . to the education of women. In Querétaro there are examples of diseases and prostitution sadly precocious among women. The tobacco factory and the great cotton mill have accustomed women to new liberties, and when work is scarce, their only recourse is prostitution."[65] In 1845, Raso had praised industrial work as disciplining women; in 1853, Prieto saw industrial liberation leading to prostitution.

With time, Prieto's views evolved: "The *indio* has long been seen as lazy, yet there are no more active people. . . . They have been portrayed as inert and helpless. Yet without them, who would attend to everyday trade? Who have done more to meet our basic needs? Working the land is an endless source of benefit. . . . Where would we be without *indios*?" Still, "the party of liberty" must end community land rights and reeducate indigenous people to "purify" their religion.[66]

Most of all, the liberal Prieto came to appreciate Querétaro's markets: "The gatherings are immense; . . . they bring together the fisherman from Chapala and the man making chimes in Acámbaro, the weaver of shawls from San Miguel and the man bringing pottery from Cadereyta, the muleteer from Jaral and the horse trainer from Ciénega, the bold mine worker from Guanajuato scattering pesos, . . . *indios* from the uplands and plains." There were "languages so different; a mosaic of dress and human blending that surprises, stupifies and brings fascination with all the sounds, colors, and appearances that mix and confound to make indescribable memories." A world of unfathomable diversity met in Querétaro markets.

Prieto went on: "The market lasts all day with times of rise and calm until evening prayers bring a last surge, and then everything ends. Still, the market, or better trade, stays open as it moves to the shops under the portals and to the streets where it carries on under artificial light. Then the sea of humanity exits the plaza to roam the nearby streets." As market days became evenings, "food vendors line the streets, meeting tastes and filling needs with love in front of stores and shops, illuminating everything from the inside of the shops to the middle of the street with elegant lanterns"— all in contrast with "the somber appearance, grave silence, and dusty loneliness of so many streets in Mexico City."[67] In time, Prieto saw Querétaro outshine the capital.

The markets of Querétaro were the place to meet

> the ranchero, so natural and near perfect, . . . the ranchero without pretense or loneliness, the ranchero with his family, . . . speaking with caution, courteous with the poor and his peers, servile before the eminent, cunning and haughty with strangers, silent while his wife speaks with a merchant, . . . frank, assertive, yet tender, . . . a good husband, strong advocate, and charming lover, independent and never a fool. This is the *payo*, . . . always with his wife in her proper rebozo, a long skirt, and sturdy shoes.

Notably, "the *rancherita* carries the money." Women held the cash and dealt with merchants when ranchero families went to city markets.

To Prieto, "these rancheros, modest stockmen, comfortable tenants and muleteers, dependents of some stature on the haciendas, are the most notable people of Querétaro."[68] The liberal exile honored the rancheros who flourished in the new ways made during and after the Bajío revolution; he praised the markets they fueled, lamented the industry they sustained, and dreamed of transforming the Otomí who made and sustained at least as much in Querétaro's vibrant industrial-commercial world.

Otomí *Huertas* in the Time of Industry

The Otomí families who kept *huertas* at the edge of the city had long sustained themselves and city markets. When Hércules brought industry to the river, new challenges and chances arose from San Pedro, past the great mill, to the *otra banda* as industrial lives simultaneously crowded and depended on indigenous growers working the most fertile of lands. New sales, most for cash and often from Otomí women to Hispanic men, hinted at privatizations of communal lands—a core part of Prieto's liberal dream.[69]

In October 1846, as war loomed, a sodality leased a *huerta* to a layman for 100 pesos yearly, suggesting a value near 2,000—stating that the lease might help defend against privatization. In July 1847, war underway, a priest leased another *huerta* (claimed as personal property) at the same rent for seven years, noting a valuable alfalfa crop. In November, the Congregation of Guadalupe leased two *huerta* complexes to don Mariano Pimentel at 500 pesos for five years. The rent suggests a value near 10,000 pesos for irrigated lands that included more than 300 fruit trees, plus "grain." A week later, Pimentel sublet three *huertas* at La Santísima to don Yndalecio Velasco for 300 pesos yearly.[70]

A sale in December 1846 reveals continuing accumulations. Marcelino Hidalgo bought multiple *huertas* and a *meson* from Ynez Rodríguez for 4,000 pesos. She gained cash; he aimed to profit as war began.[71] Other sales were less rich yet always in cash. Earlier, *huertas* rarely brought 200 pesos, with most sold for less than 100. During 1847, with Hércules in production and national leaders in Querétaro, values regularly approached 400 pesos. All had water rights, a few included solid homes; others had baths or aguardiente distilleries serving a rising recreation economy.[72] In 1845 Mariano Peralto and Navor Barrero had rented a small *huerta* for 15 pesos to build public baths; in 1848, they leased an adjacent *huerta* for 80 pesos, forging a recreational complex valued at 2,000 pesos.[73]

During and after the war, there were more transactions in less valuable *huertas*, most under 100 pesos. At the edge of the industrializing city, small *huertas* sold from women to men, showing women's long importance and men's new assertions. Among 26 sales from 1846 through 1851, 16 saw women sell to men, 8 saw men sell to men, and 2 saw women sell to women. No man sold to a woman.[74] Hispanic men pursued prosperity and patriarchy on historic Otomí *huertas* in the rising industrial city.

Still, women were not simply thrust aside. In April 1847, the widow María Josefa Galván sold a "piece of *huerta*" in San Sebastián, inherited from her sister, to don Juan Nepomuceno de Argomaniz, owner of an adjacent *huerta*, for 40 pesos. She kept a *huerta* near others held by the Congregation of Guadalupe and a sodality devoted to Our Lady of the Rosary.[75] In May, María Justa Landa, single and unmarried, inherited a *huerta* on the river at La Cañada from her mother. She sold in October to María Josefa Sánchez, owner of an adjacent *huerta*.[76] In May 1849, María de Jesús Corona gained 50 pesos cash for a *huerta* at San Sebastián bought decades earlier from her sister. To prove ownership, she presented men making leather goods on adjacent *huertas* worked by wives.[77]

Widow María Martínez Hernández was guardian of a minor daughter who inherited a huerta at La Cañada. Seeking court approval, she pleaded "the need to sell to provide food to the girl, as its small yield does not cover essential expenses." Still, "she has other plots that need repairs that can only be done with cash from the sale." With ownership confirmed by an *hortelano* and wife and a rebozo weaver and wife, the court approved a sale for 58 pesos to Filomeno Cercas.[78]

In September 1850, doña Paula Sánchez, unmarried, owned a *huerta* in the *otra banda* of Querétaro. She presented cousins María Ygnacia and María Tomasa Pérez as witnesses to sell for 30 pesos to María Paula Ramírez, owner of an adjacent *huerta*.[79] In October, a group of six siblings and cousins, men and women, held three *huertas* at La Cañada, an inheritance from their grandmother never formally divided. They joined to sell one that mixed wheat plots, fruit orchards, avocados, and quince. As witnesses, they presented two men from La Cañada, both dons, one an *hortelano*, the other a "money runner." The buyer was *ciudadano* Luz Gonzalez, "citizen at the Hércules factory."[80] A mill employee bought a *huerta*, likely to be worked by his wife and family.

In March 1851, María Teresa de Jesús, unmarried and working at Hércules, took a different tack. She sold a *huerta* inherited from her grandmother, offering two men as witnesses, a widowed basket weaver and a neighboring *hortelano*. Don Juan de la Luz Rosales, owner of an adjacent *huerta*, paid 36 pesos.[81] Without kin to work the *huerta*, María Teresa chose the wages of millwork.

The *huerta* market held strong into the 1850s. In San Sabastián, don Atilano Valenciana bought five from 1844 to 1847, four from women. In 1851, he sold them to don Ygnacio Herrera for 250 pesos cash.[82] A month later, also in San Sebastián, José Gabriel Calzonsi owned a residence and *huerta* with water rights, a legacy from his grandmother; Tiburcio Martínez, 75, a shoemaker who had leased the *huerta*, and José María Barrón, 40, a widowed "wool craftsman," affirmed ownership. Calzonsi sold the house and *huerta* for 20 pesos to don Cresencia Gómez, who owned *huertas* just north and south.[83]

In the 1840s and 1850s, *huerta*-based enterprises mixed family cultivation and diverse crafts to flourish in the industrial-commercial city. Hispanic men bought in while Otomí women carried on sustaining life and recreation—despite waters limited and polluted by Hércules.

The Querétraro Countryside: Proprietors Struggle, Families Produce

Across the wider countryside, rancheros and tenants ruled production through the 1850s, making maize to feed themselves and the city while keeping prices low. In an enduring post-insurgency agrarian economy, proprietors found profit scarce and faced endless rounds of debt and default while family growers made maize and more.

East of Hércules and La Cañada, the Amazcala basin stretched from La Griega north. In May 1846, as war loomed, the rancho Servín sold for under 2,500 pesos, two-thirds its former value. In May 1847, María Manuela Martínez sold a share of the rancho Corrales she inherited from her mother to don Melchor Hernández, a tenant at La Griega, for 150 pesos; in October, her brother sold his share to Mariano Landeros for 158 pesos. The same month, doña Paula Camacho sold part of Saldariego, south of La Griega, for 200 pesos to Don Mariano Vertiz.[84] In November, a struggling landlord leased nearby San Nicolás del Pozo to Trinidad and Agapito Peregrino for 450 pesos yearly. The tenants were to protect uplands from invasive squatters and others who took wood and more.[85] In 1850, the Servín rancho sold again, now for less than 2,300 pesos.[86] Then, in 1852, don Trinidad Peregrino leased San Nicolás del Pozo to his son don Manuel for the same 450 pesos—with mandates to protect uplands, preserve magueys, and make repairs.[87]

Another long episode reveals landed dreams and bankrupt realities. Don Mariano Oyarzábal had served as treasurer of the nation and the State of Querétaro, a deputy in the national congress, and minister of the State

Supreme Court. His 1847 will stated that he had used government salaries to buy the hacienda Agua del Coyote, sections of Amascala and Dolores, and San José del Alto, all in the Amazcala basin. When his estate settled in 1851, he owed large debts to the Santa Clara Convent. His wife, doña María Fernández de Castro, was his sole heir, leading to a settlement in which her brother leased the estates to pay the debts. The widow gained 100 pesos monthly until the convent was paid.[88] A powerful man with government salaries had bought estates from owners seeking to escape debts. His widow learned that haciendas rarely paid in rural Querétaro.

The coming years proved no better for landlords. In 1853, don Ciriaco Hernández, a tenant at La Griega, bought the Rancho de Hernández at the adjacent hacienda Colorado from a city merchant for 2,000 pesos cash. The owner aimed to cover debts; the ranchero leaseholder became a proprietor. The merchant signed; the ranchero could not—but he knew how to prosper on the land.[89]

Meanwhile, landlord struggles continued in the Santa Rosa basin. Ownership remained fragmented while rancheros and tenants ruled production. In October 1846, don Joaquin Pino, once an accumulator of share leases, faced financial challenges. He transferred leases of five shares to a new operator based in Mexico City. A week later, the parish priest at Santa Rosa bought San Miguel for a mere 12,000 pesos, noted as "a just price," recognizing 6,000 owed to Santa Clara and 6,000 to the Congregation of Guadalupe.[90] The priest owned to collect rents to pay clerical lenders.

In April 1848, don Timoteo Fernández de Jaúregui, now owner of the Juriquilla complex, formed a partnership to gain funds from don José Atilano Maldonado, who also leased San Ysidro for 350 pesos yearly.[91] In July 1849, share accumulator Pino died, leaving his widow with lease rights to six "shares" at Santa Rosa estates and obligations for rents never paid. Ex-governor don Sabás Antonio Domínguez, who had sponsored Pino's share accumulation and was now a federal senator, took on the leases to free the widow from impossible obligations, hoping political status and a senator's salary would keep creditors at bay. In 1850, another widow holding debt-burdened shares at Monte de Negro leased to a deputy in the state congress, hoping he might protect her property rights.[92]

By 1854, the Buenavista estate at the north end of the basin was owned by don José Luis Legorreta, a Spaniard living in Querétaro, backed by national Minister of Relations, don Manuel Diez de Bonilla. Facing tenants who did not pay, Legorreta leased four ranchos to lawyer don Vidal Martínez de los Ríos and overseer don José Merced Vázquez. They gained rights to pasture in the uplands bordering Puerto de Nieto, just west. They could use water for their own needs but must not share with "other tenants."[93] Could the new lead tenants claim rents and profit?

Proprietors faced similar challenges all around Querétaro. The Machona hacienda, valued at 23,000 pesos in 1842, inventoried at 18,000 pesos in December 1846 yet sold for 13,000 pesos as dams and other structures needed repair. In 1848, three properties valued over 30,000 pesos sold for 16,000 pesos.[94] Leasing also remained problematic. In 1849, political entrepreneur don Sabás Antonio Domínguez owned the Hacienda de Batán, southwest of the city. He leased out its mill, hoping to gain a secure 600 pesos yearly. In 1850, Lt. Col. Crecensio Mena owned Vargas and Tejada and leased out a rancho to gain 300 pesos yearly. In 1851, doña María Leonidas Salazar's long lease of Vegil ended with 3,000 pesos due. In 1855, she was forced to set the charge as a mortgage on her city home.[95]

In 1855, don José Nicolás Arauz, a Querétaro merchant, bought Santa María de Carrillo from the estate of doña Dolores Murillo. He then leased to don Marcos Saavedra of Celaya at 2,000 pesos for seven years, with a discount for improvements and no relief for "sterile, or even extremely sterile years." The current crop would remain in storage until prices rose.[96] Such deals passed as optimism.

The basin stretching south to San Juan del Río also saw challenges. In April 1847, don Agustin Fernández de Córdoba, one of multiple proprietors of Jaral north of Guanajuato, owned four estates centered at Ajuchitlancito. He leased them to don Lorenzo de Vicente of San Juan del Río at 4,600 pesos for seven years—plus two more on Vicente's option. The lessee accepted all debts owed by *sirvientes* and tenants to the owner—who would accept all owed the lessee at the end.[97] Across Querétaro, estate harvests rarely paid while workers took advances for work not delivered and tenants made maize while withholding rents. Proprietors juggled as debts mounted.[98] Meanwhile, family growers, mostly tenants, fed themselves and everyone else to sustain lives of solid sustenance.

Guillermo Prieto Meets Rural Querétaro

Santa Anna apparently saw Prieto living too comfortably in the city, so he banished him to a deeper exile east of San Juan del Río. There he discovered vibrant lives on the land. He continued to admire rancheros and denigrate indigenous peoples while awed by the plenty they produced as he struggled to understand. Passing by earlier, he had noted: "The valley from San Juan

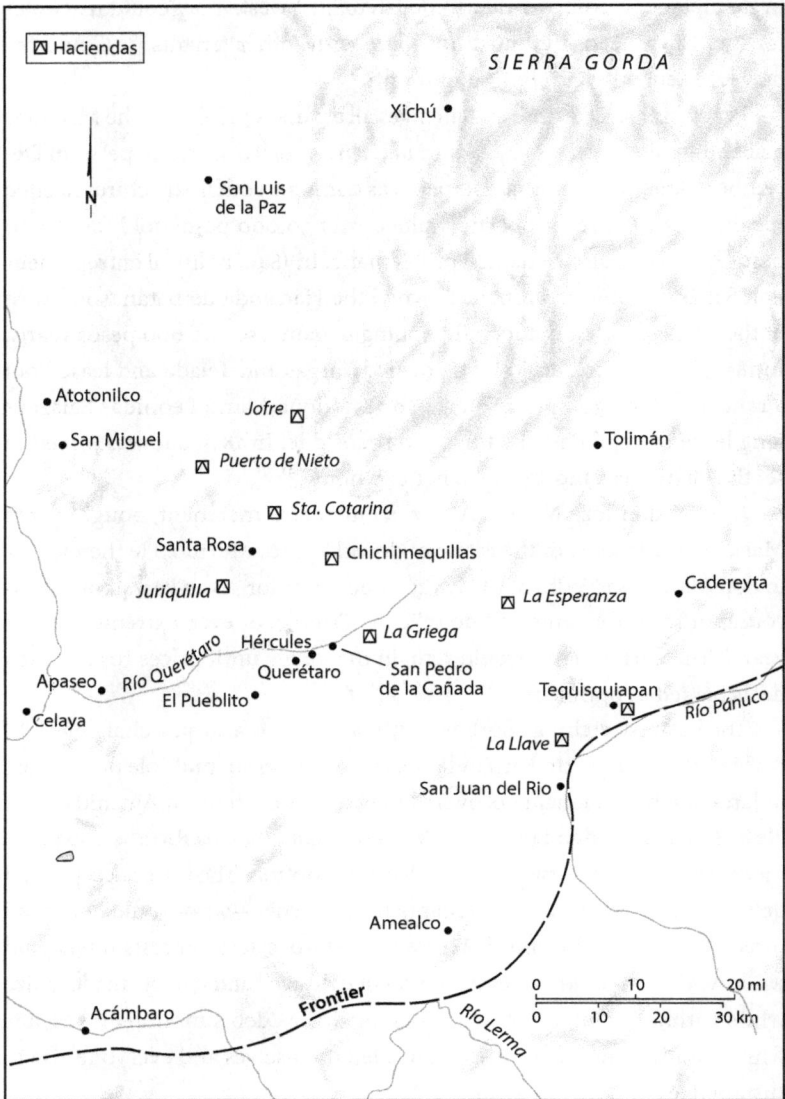

Map 12.1 Guillermo Prieto's Querétaro, 1853.

del Río along the road to Querétaro is the most fertile, picturesque, and pleasant land imaginable. Cultivation has advanced notably, . . . introducing substantial improvements."[99] He saw rich harvests while blind to the people who made them.

On his second visit to San Juan del Río, he saw challenges. Town crafts had declined; the liberal promoter of imports did not say why. *Huertas* were less productive because the Arroyozarco estate, up-river in the State of Mexico, had built a dam and reservoir that cut downstream flows.[100] Still, "the poor live by planting *huertas*, by muleteering, by trading in meats and grains, and other goods and crafts of small value. . . . Lovers of work, *obediente* to authority, no powerful vices prevail among them." He noted devotion to "El Señor de Sacro Monte" and lamented "clerical influence." Still, "the people are good, charitable, and generous."[101]

Visiting the hacienda La Llave north of town, Prieto saw "one of the magnificent properties of the old Mexican aristocracy," still held by "don José María Cervantes, once Conde de Santiago." One manager oversaw La Llave, nearby La Cañada for don Francisco de Iturbe, and his own estates. He was a rent collector. Prieto saw "lands yielding abundant harvests of maize, wheat, frijol, and chickpeas, all of quality." The manager reported an estate valued at 400,000 pesos yielding 40,000 pesos in yearly profit—a rarity if true.[102] Like most Bajío estates in the 1850s, La Llave kept livestock and planted wheat on estate account, with maize, frijol, and chile raised by tenants and sharecroppers. Having lost lands at Atengo south of Toluca, the ex-conde kept a solid prosperity by collecting rents in the southern Bajío.

Prieto's next stop was upland at Tequisquiapan. There, he reported estate operators as arrogant, rancheros as the heart of rural life, while native people faced "misery." The plaza announced plenty: "An endless row of crates filled with bright tuna cactus, the manna of the *indio*, ending with several vendors offering sacks of maguey stalks along with toasted ears of maize. Another row showed fruit, large avocados, and delicious peaches, some good-quality grapes, and fiery pomegranates, . . . ending with a semicircle of onions. . . . Across the way, golden mountains of maize shine as vendors add more golden grain. . . . Women making and selling tortillas" were everywhere. Reporting plenty he characterized as misery, Prieto asked: "Why does the *indio* take refuge, living among the tunas of the wild mountains?"[103] The answer was clear—though the urban liberal would not see it: native people lived free in the wild plenty of the uplands.

Prieto then crossed the river to the hacienda Tequisquiapan, "greeted with generosity by Doña Guadalupe Michaus, owner of the estate, her noble sons, and the wise don Juan Llaca, manager of the business."[104] The Michaus were kin to the Condes de Santiago. Savoring doña Guadalupe's hospitality, the liberal only glanced at the people who made plenty on her lands, mixed with free *indios* in the market, and kept devotions he despised.[105]

Did word reach Mexico City that Prieto also lived too well at Tequis-quiapan? Sent farther north to Cadereita, he met the community at Sunday Mass: "It was not repugnant. . . . These are not the naked decadent *indios* that surround Mexico City, . . . but the svelt ranchero with bowed legs and a slim waist, agile ways and limber arms, upright head and a gaze both intelligent and picaresque." The community honored *La Peregrina*—the Pilgrim Virgin of Bethlehem, "a revered Lady."[106] Then "as Mass ended, the *tianguis* or market began, sellers and buyers merging in a lively crowd. . . . Sellers set up in symetrical rows, forming streets that filled with buyers. . . . One row sold *comales* to grind maize, jugs to carry drinks, rough fabric made of maguey fiber, and hats woven of palm fronds, a row that ended in pyramids of salt, whiter than snow. . . . Another row offered every kind of chile." Everywhere, proprietors and native buyers locked in endless bargaining.

Prieto went on, "Fruit displays marked another row, . . . while women's dress and men's clothing ruled the center of the plaza. . . . Maize lay just beyond, sellers surrounded by avid buyers." He added:

> At the edge of the plaza were . . . rivers of mole, lakes of frijoles, and mysterious dishes beyond description. So live the indigenous people of Cadereyta. . . . On the other side were circles of country-men, friends who met to eat, rancheros from hearby haciendas, families of vendors who brought goods from Tolimán, Boyé, and Santa María, along with rancheros who traveled from Rincón, Santa Bárbara, el Ciervo, even el Doctor, 8 leagues [40 kilometers] away. . . . The throngs talked, spatted, and bargained, energetically supplying themselves with the best possible provisions.[107]

Prieto saw a community where rancheros and *indios* lived, prayed, traded, and ate close together. Then, "between four and five in the afternoon, the crowd dispersed, merchants gathering their wares, leaving a deep silence. . . . The roads to the ranchos and haciendas filled with carts pulled by ragged horses or young colts, carrying proud rancheros and rancheras in wide hats and woven shawls, a tiny rancherita at her side gazing behind."[108] The liberal honored rancheros, diminished the role of rancheras, detested the church, denigrated religion, and maligned the native people who made so much of the plenty he reported in the uplands northeast of San Juan del Río.[109]

In the markets that drew people to the plazas and portals of Querétaro, and those that gathered rancheros and *indios* in uplands above San Juan del Río, Prieto saw—and struggled to understand—the plenty made by family growers and the energetic trade that enlivened deeply personal commercial worlds. Despite the laments of power seekers and fallen oligarchs, the Bajío revolution had not broken cultivation or commerce. It delivered them to the people.

Balbontín's Rural Querétaro

José María Balbontín surveyed production in rural Querétaro in 1854.[110] While 98 haciendas still ruled proprietorship across the basins around Querétaro and San Juan del Río, 226 independent ranchos concentrated in uplands. Production was led by 5,400 *labradores*, the great majority tenants, while the survey recorded 12,000 *jornaleros*, still the deflecting label for subtenants and sharecroppers who produced for sustenance and worked seasonally for wages. Most families on the land cultivated for sustenance and sales, engaged in crafts, and worked for wages. With more than 3,500 *hortelanos* at Querétaro and San Juan del Río, we see a state of landlord struggles while rancheros and tenants, family growers and sharecroppers fed families, communities, and cities.

Balbontín reported average annual maize harvests over 700,000 fanegas. With a family of 4 or 5 requiring 10 to 12 fanegas yearly, Querétaro cultivators fed 70,000 families, at least 280,000 people—in a state with about 160,000 total. Family growers made more than enough to feed themselves and people across the state, to sell out of state, and to hold stores for years of drought. Balbontín noted a prevailing price of 8 reales (1 peso) per fanega. No contract reported a price above 2 pesos, while many lamented prices too low to cover costs. Family growers made ample maize to sustain industrializing Querétaro.

Balbontín noted great strength in the people around Huimilpan, in uplands west of San Juan del Río, where ranchero proprietors ruled. In the early 1850s, eight ranchos sold for prices from 90 to 800 pesos, most from 150 to 400, only one relying on limited credit.[111] Balbontín saw prosperity: "The climate is healthy and epidemic diseases are rare; even cholera never came in the three waves that it struck the Republic. Beyond that, the people reproduce easily and live happily, focusing on cultivating fields, making pottery they take to sell in wide markets, . . . and in exploiting rich forests."[112] In Huimilpan, healthy upland rancheros lived comfortably making maize, crockery, and wood products.

Between Silver Boom and Sierra Insurgency: Rural Guanajuato

Meanwhile, on the lands once ruled by insurgency across eastern Guanajuato, rancheros and family growers carried a dynamic agrarian economy while proprietors still grappled with debts and losses. East of San Miguel, near Puerto de Nieto, in 1842, doña Francisca de Paula Cabrera had ceded the rancho de Cabrera to don Pablo González de Cosío of Querétaro to cover a 7,350-peso debt. In January 1846, don Pablo sold the property, better the debts, to his brother don Vicente, for only 3,500 pesos—300 recognized to the San Francisco Convent in San Miguel, 300 to a sodality there, with the rest to be paid in 500-peso annual installments. The value of the property had halved, and the notary confirmed "it is worth no more."[113] Proprietor struggles persisted on the eve of war.

Xalpa, in uplands south of Puerto de Nieto, was the staunchest of guerrilla fortresses during the decade of insurgency. Afterward it was home to independent residents. In April 1850, the estate was still owned by don Tomás Fernández de Jaúregui, an old landed family tied to Querétaro and San Miguel. As a struggling leaseholder prepared to depart, he leased the estate to don José María Redondo of San Miguel. The previous operator would leave 150 fanegas of maize for the coming spring planting "if he has it." The new lease would be for five to seven years, at Redondo's discretion. The 2,750-peso rent was forgiven so the tenant could rebuild the dam, replace roofs on two granaries, and restore fencing. Jalpa had not operated commercially since insurgency. A community descended from insurgents had ruled production for three decades. Now, in times of silver boom, the owner dreamed of commercial planting. The new tenant had limited funds; a *fianza* guarantee, from a resident of Venado, north of San Luis Potosí, failed. The owner, now prefect at Querétaro, had to back the lease—taking on all the risks he aimed to escape.[114]

Proprietors also struggled to hold estates, gain income, and escape risk on the bottomlands around Celaya. In January 1847, amid wartime uncertainties, don Francisco Berduzco, governor of Querétaro, leased San Francisco Camargo to don Joaquín Guerrero for seven years at 2,200 pesos yearly. The tenant committed to rebuild dams and irrigation works and build a store, aiming to sell to a tenant community. Berduzco had planted grapevines, olive trees, and fruit orchards; Guerrero would maintain them. The wheat about to harvest remained the governor's. He had hoped to find profit in time of economic revival, planting wheat and promoting perennials, while leaving maize to sharecroppers. Now fearing wartime conflicts—"in the event of a revolution, if a belligerent party occupies the estate . . . and causes fires or other destructions"—the owner and leaseholder shared liability.[115] Neither war nor revolution struck locally while the governor and leaseholder shared risks to carry on.

As the war ended and national authorities prepared to leave Querétaro, in August 1848, Br. don Manuel López de Ecala, a priest from a prominent Querétaro clan, leased the Sabanilla estate south of Celaya to don José Fernández Cano, a Spanish citizen trading in the region. The owner had planted wheat and the tenant would continue; maguey fields and orchards promised produce with little labor; sharecroppers planted maize with seed provided by the estate. In addition, "the leaseholder agrees to deliver to the proprietor in Querétaro, the potable water and pulque he customarily receives."[116] Had Hércules so polluted Querétaro's water that the priest had barrels sent from his hacienda? Did he drink pulque or sell it to parishioners?

Then, from 1851 through 1853, the heirs to doña Mariana Fernández de Herrera's estates entered lease deals to preserve property rights while setting others to face the risks of production and marketing around Apaseo. In February 1851, her widowed husband, don José María Frías y Tovar, leased Barajas to don José Camacho at 3,000 pesos for seven years. The tenant would repair the residence, dam, fences, and threshing floor aiming to restore commercial wheat. Two years later, another Frías y Tovar joined to provide financing and gain a third of the rent.[117]

An October 1852 deal set by don Francisco Frías y Herrero revealed landlord worries and ranchero independence. The estate was La Cuevita, also at Apaseo; the tenant was don Nemesio Escoto, an *agrimensor* (rural surveyor). The lease was for seven years, at 1,300 pesos the first year and 1,400 thereafter. If Escoto built a new dam, the lease would extend another four years. The deal included uncounted ranchos and a mandate that tenants could not be evicted despite "the vices that make rancheros unbearable." They were insufferable and essential. The coming maize harvest would deliver 500 fanegas to Escoto for sharecropper planting. Valued at 12 reales per fanega, it could not be profitably sold. The estate sold maize gained in shares, wheat harvests, plus frijol, barley, and chickpeas, and earning less than 1,500 pesos. Only ranchero and subtenant rents led to limited profits.[118]

In July 1853, don Estéban Frías y Tovar leased Belén, also near Apaseo, to kinsman don Antonio Frías y Herrero for seven years at 1,200 pesos, plus four cargas of hay to sustain the owner's city stables and one of frijol to supply his table. The owner kept the ranchos and their rents, leaving the leaseholder to seek profit in estate cropping, a rarity at mid-century.[119] Rancheros may have been insufferable; their rents kept proprietors on the land.

Another lease at Apaseo in 1854 reveals both challenges and hopes. The hacienda Jaúregui had belonged to doña Apolonia Vega, then passed to her minor children. Her widowed husband now leased the property to don Juan Gutiérrez García, another Spaniard trading in Querétaro. He paid cash to clear debts totaling 4,400 pesos and committed to pay 3,500 pesos in rent during nine years. Again, repairs to improve irrigation were mandated; the owners could not cover these expenses, the monied tenant might.[120] As silver peaked, at Guanajuato proprietors around Celaya aimed to restore irrigated wheat cropping. Facing debt and short of capital, they relied on monied leaseholders, tenant rancheros, and family maize growers.

North of Querétaro, where Guanajuato met the Sierra Gorda, landlord power dissolved while ranchero production entrenched. In July 1846, as war loomed, a major turn came at San José Casas Viejas, the town founded in the eighteenth century on Capulín estate lands. Doña María Estefana Plaza had built a commercial empire, including a house and store on the plaza, called El Gigante, and another house and store called La Abundancia by the parish church. She owned an inn near Gigante, an office and corral behind the church, another corral near a pond, plus a third house with stone walls that bounded maguey fields. She also leased the ranchos La Llorona and Padre Macias from Capulín. Now her heirs, two sons and a daughter, leased out the entire complex for five years at 720 pesos, suggesting a value near 14,400. The lessee, don Mariano Mena, lived at Casas Viejas; his brother Col. don Cresencio Mena, long pivotal to politics and property at Querétaro, guaranteed the lease.[121]

In April 1849, with war over but insurgents still roaming just east in the Sierra, a larger lease revealed larger challenges. Don Antonio de Ocío had died and Capulín belonged to his three children: doña Trinidad, doña Dolores, and don Francisco, all minors. Their father had designated don Cayetano Rubio as executor and guardian. He leased Capulín to don Secundino Arbizu of Querétaro for seven years at 5,500 pesos. Expectations were high. But if a "general revolution" blocked operations, the contract would end. Challenge to boundaries would be reported to the owners or Rubio.[122] The Ocíos and Rubios saw potential—and worried about conflicts and land invasions.

Another revelation came in 1853. Doña Trinidad Arauz had inherited Santiago de Agostadero, farther east and upland near Xichú, from her mother. Her husband arranged to lease the property to two local men at 2,000 pesos for seven years. They would replace the house and expand maguey planting for pulque production. "Comandante don Tomás Mejía," a leader in rebellious Sierra politics, backed the contract—by arms more than cash.[123] Otomí, conservative, and a leader of resistant Sierra communities, Mejía was a force in the region—and now backing allies on the land.

The fall of 1854 saw transactions that announced the end of the old order ruled by haciendas like Capulín. Two nuns at Santa Clara, sisters among the heirs to don José Francisco Velasco, had inherited the San Gerónimo estate at Casas Viejas (now renamed San José Iturbide), along with shares in Monte de Negro, Santa Catarina, and Buenavista in the Santa Rita basin. A complex contract ceded all the old shares to creditors, ending years of shareholder struggles, while San Gerónimo split into twelve new "shares." The two nuns inherited one; two other sisters gained one—a twenty-fourth part each. Another went to the lawyers.[124] Proprietorship became shareholding, with shares of little value.

Then, doña Trinidad Arauz leased out the two estates she inherited near Xichú: Santiago del Agostadero and San Diego. The lease of the former, backed by Mejía a year earlier, had failed. A new tenant would pay 2,000 pesos during seven years, mandated to build a still to profit from drink stronger than pulque. The tenant at San Diego would pay 1,500 for two years while transplanting maguey; then 2,000 pesos for seven more, as production of pulque and/or mescal began.[125] Such production required little labor, flourished on dry land, and might bring profit in markets of release and recreation.

In December 1854, don José de Jesús de Jaúregui, heir to an old Querétaro and San Miguel landed clan, owned San Diego de la Trasquila near San José Iturbide. Gained from his mother's legacy in 1841, it came with mortgages: 15,600 pesos owed to five individual lenders, 8,000 due the Convent of Santa Clara, and 1,500 owed the Congregation of Guadalupe. Jaúregui might hold title; he served creditor-shareholders. Now he sold to don José María Sauto, of an old San Miguel textile and landed family, who recognized the 21,400 pesos in old liens, 12,000 pesos as a new mortgage to Santa Clara (thus owing the sisters 20,000 pesos), while paying 13,900 pesos in cash to Jaúregui.[126] The indebted landlord gained cash; the new owner took on burdensome obligations; rancheros and other tenants carried on.

The records of rural property across Querétaro and eastern Guanajuato reveal that landlord struggles persisted into the 1850s. Debts plagued proprietors, leading to sales and leases that aimed to share risks, gaining limited income for owners and paying obligations to lenders and clerical institutions. The mining boom at Guanajuato and the rise of industry at Querétaro did not revive proprietor profits—blocked by the abundance made everywhere by rancheros, subtenants, and sharecroppers.

Struggling landlords despised rancheros yet relied on them to keep estates in production and pay rents. Prieto honored rancheros and, grudgingly, rancheras too, while wishing they focused less on religious devotions. It might seem a morass of contradictions until we see that Prieto surely understood that rancheros and family growers drove the fall of landed oligarchs, opening the way for the rise of liberal rule.

Romero's Guanajuato: Dynamic Production, Catholic Renovation, Intrusive Liberalism

In 1860, José Guadalupe Romero reported lives of production and devotion amid plenty across Guanajuato through sympathetic clerical eyes. Born in Silao in times of insurgency, he gained primary education locally, took legal studies in the mining city as it became state capital in the 1820s, to become rector of the Colegio del Estado in the 1820s. He later pursued religious studies, to be ordained a priest in 1838. After serving as a vicar at Silao, Apaseo, Salamanca, and Guanajuato, he became pastor at Piedra Gorda and then San Felipe. He knew every corner of the state before being named a canon at the Cathedral in Morelia in 1853.[127] While serving there, he toured the diocese that included Guanajuato, generating a detailed survey focused on production, education, and devotions. As communities remade in insurgency engaged the silver boom and sustained a commercial revival, he lamented rebellions past, resented liberal intrusions, and honored popular production and devotions.

Romero began in his hometown of Silao, set where basin lands met the road to the mines. He praised population growth since the 1820s as cultivation dispersed across haciendas and ranchos, sustaining religious constructions, devotions, and service foundations. He credited the coming of the Sisters of Charity in 1846 for "good customs." People lived by cultivation, transport, trade, and work in the mines—all disrupted in August 1860, when Silao faced the battle in which liberal armies defeated General don Miguel Miramón to take Guanajuato and return Benito Juárez to power: "The latest revolution paralyzed trade, blocking the fountains of wealth in Silao."[128]

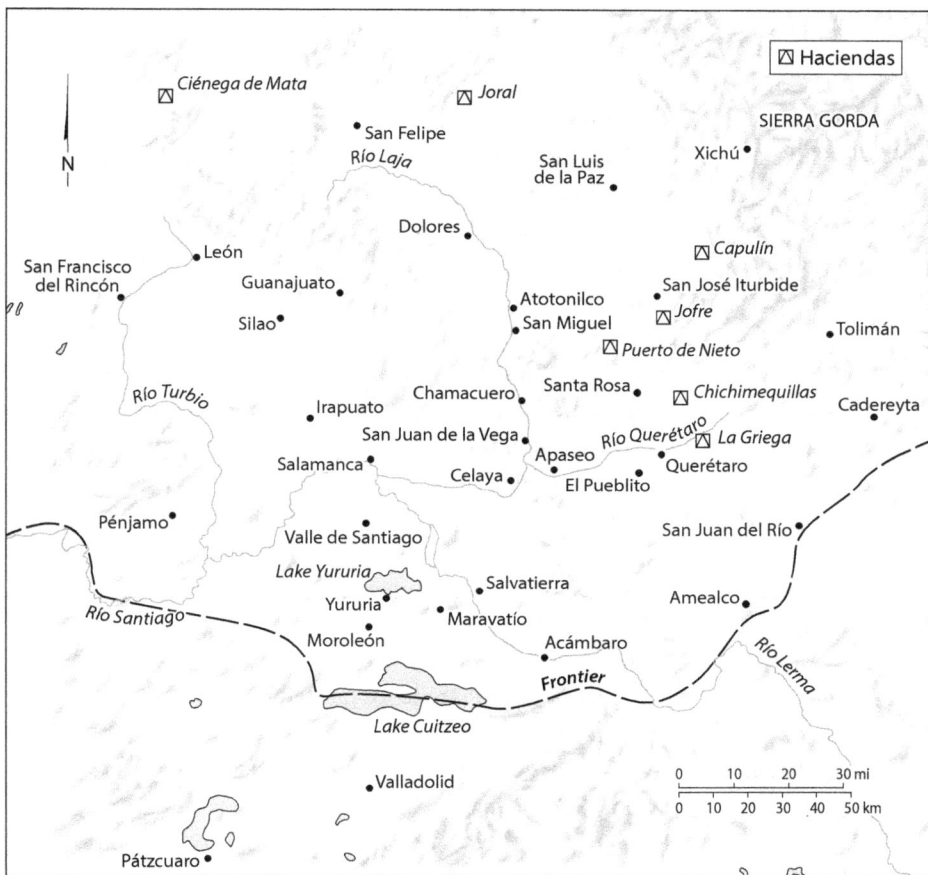

Map 12.2 José Guadalupe Romero's Guanajuato, 1860.

Turning south to Irapuato, he noted an insurgent incursion of 1812, then honored devotions to Guadalupe and a new temple built in 1846. Production dispersed across thirty haciendas and nearly one hundred ranchos, with "notable progress" in population, devotions, and production. There were nine new churches and chapels, new schools, public lighting, "and a great number of stores" with "workshops making cloth and shawls." The community thrived despite recent liberal predations on pious funds.[129]

South on rich bottomlands, Salamanca was mostly Otomí. Romero noted new churches, a new jail with a chapel, but no public lighting or paved roads. Families worked the land; makers of rebozos, sombreros, and zapatos served local markets; a pottery workshop promised new prosperity. With "mal de San Lázaro," elephantiasis, endemic, Romero called "the government to take precautions."[130]

Still farther south, Valle de Santiago was the last of the bottomland towns tied to the mining center. Romero saw a history marked by waves of destruction. Burned in 1810, it was destroyed by Albino García in 1812. The church was rebuilt beginning in 1826, yet the revival of devotions proved limited. When a major estate divided, "the redistribution set off disputes that ruined growers across the area; unrest persists." Despite conflicts, "the land is very fertile; it yields abundant cane for sugar, melons, cucumbers, sweet potatoes, maize, wheat, chickpeas, chile, barley, and all kinds of vegetables; these fields are perhaps the best cultivated in the Bajío." Then came liberal armies en route to Guanajauto: "The horrid sacking unleashed in 1855 by defenders of the [liberal] plan de Ayutla, cut population, trade, and life in the town."[131] On the bottomlands near the mines, Romero saw rich cultivation, family cloth making, and religious revivals. He condemned liberal incursions that shook life and took pious funds as they marched twice to take the mines.

West at León, Romero celebrated the new Bajío. Spared the first insurgencies, it lived popular risings from 1814 to 1818. Production revived early as León's location gave access to both Zacatecas and Guanajuato. By 1860, population had grown to more than 100,000, including 31 haciendas, 230 ranchos, and uncounted *huertas* along the Río Turbío. Growers planted 3,200 fanegas of maize, 850 cargas of wheat, and more. Devotions to San Felipe Neri began in the 1830s; a dedication to Nuestra Señora de la Luz came in the 1840s as mines soared, along with a Franciscan college, fathers of Saint Vincent de Paul, Sisters of Charity, and the Vela Perpetua, the vigil led by devout laywomen honoring the Eucharist.

Romero sang praises: "City commerce is vibrant and the people are industrious and devoted to work. On the plaza, stores sell clothing and groceries, grain and wood products; commercial shops with many entries offer goods from across the country—anything one could want for sustenance, comfort, and display." The "arts, crafts, agriculture, commerce, and transport draw ample capital." The center included a public granary, two barracks for troops, a printing press, and six schools. There was a "magnificent plaza de armas" and twelve other plazas; eighteen inns, two hotels, a stagecoach station, a hospital, and a poorhouse. Diseases remained: typhus, dysentary, and periodic visits of cholera. Yet Romero saw the people of León as the longest lived, healthiest in the Bajío, in part because "the city is surrounded by countless *huertas* and beautiful gardens, . . . sites of delicious retreats and recreation." Querétaro had come to León.

Still, order required a solid jail, a penitentiary under construction, and policing by 60 magistrates, 350 patrolmen, and 400 assistants. Liberals had expelled the fathers of St. Vincent de Paul in 1857. Romero respected policing but preferred clerical integration.[132]

South of León at San Pedro Piedra Gorda, much of the population lived on the lands of another hacienda de Jalpa, centered across the border in Jalisco. The great dam that sustained irrigation had collapsed; the last Marquesa de Jalpa, doña Manuela Monterde, rebuilt it by selling "part of her lands." Another surviving oligarch sold property to keep what she could.[133]

Farther south lay Pénjamo, Miguel Hidalgo's birthplace. To Romero, it neither flourished nor struggled. With 6,000 people in town, there were new devotions (including the Vela Perpetua) and new chapels, along with two schools, public fountains, a plaza and a small alameda, two inns, and "some trade in local goods." Most of the district's 40,000 residents lived at 10 haciendas and more than 70 ranchos.[134] Cuitzeo de las Naranjas (now Abasolo) had separated from Pénjamo to become a town in 1851 and a parish in 1854. Struggling proprietors sold land, long a hacienda held by the Obregón family, to residents who built a town with two schools, an inn, and "some *huertas*"; a small church and Vela Perpetua devotions were coming. The parish included 3 haciendas and 53 ranchos, with 15,000 people engaged in "agriculture, small trade, transport and the mechanical arts and crafts."[135]

Romero then turned east to San Miguel, long fallen from its historic role as a center of cloth making and trade surrounded by rich haciendas like Puerto de Nieto. Recalling glories past, he honored the renovation of the main church from 1840 to 1846 and the arrival of the Vela Perpetua. Clerical presence held strong: 6 priests assigned to the parish, 14 others in residence, plus 2 Franciscan friars. The center had 19,000 residents, 3 public schools, 23 public fountains, a fine plaza and 5 *plazuelas*, along with good lighting, public baths, and 7 *mesones*, plus a coliseum—all legacies of earlier prosperity. A battalion of civic militia remained too. Crafts focused on sarapes and ponchos, bedding and cushions, and pottery. The countryside included 15 haciendas and 80 ranchos with more than 15,000 people, a third Otomí. Romero never glanced toward the basin east of town. Did rancheras hold on at Puerto de Nieto? Had production revived at long insurgent Xalpa?

Just north, he stopped at Atotonilco to offer a misremembered history. He described stark murals and sculptures depicting the passion of Christ, claiming the sanctuary began as a place to correct "criminals." Did he not know it was a center of penitential devotions led by San Miguel oligarchs? Could he not know that Hidalgo had taken Guadalupe's banner there? Was the insurgent market that flourished after 1810 gone? Romero said nothing about any of that or current devotions.[136]

Dolores, where insurgency began, fared little better in Romero's portrayal. He saw a "magnificent parish church," old sodalities, and a new Vela Perpetua. He recalled Hidalgo's promotion of pottery, vineyards, and wine making—and noted their persistence. Of the once insurgent countryside, he saw that half the land remained property of the great La Erre estate, one of 15 haciendas sharing the land with 125 ranchos.[137] He said nothing about the people whose forebears began the revolution that remade the region and the world—and had been amnestied to live as rancheros on the land.

San Felipe, where Hidalgo had served as pastor before insurgency and Romero had followed afterwards, gained closer attention. He reported 47,500 people. The town offered a "pretty plaza" and two *plazuelas*, public fountains, five taverns, two schools, and a jail with a chapel completed in 1855. The Vela Perpetua had come in the 1840s while indigenous families kept separate sodalities. Ample "fertile irrigated lands" included "a great number of *huertas* raising pears and more." Repeated redistributions led to "envy" and conflicts.

Outside town, rural families lived dispersed across 26 haciendas and more than 100 ranchos. Of the parish's 7 curates, 5 lived at haciendas becoming communities. On high plateau lands, wheat was ample and ground at four mills. There were 2 "mezcal distilleries" and a press making olive oil. Estates raised wheat and livestock; tenants made maize.[138] San Diego del Bizcocho, a town of 2,600, was surrounded by 17 haciendas and 32 ranchos sustaining 15,000 people. There were 2 schools, 2 "shabby inns," a "small, ugly, and poor" church with a pastor, 2 curates, and a Vela Perpetua.[139]

Jaral, the vast estate long held by the Condes de Jaral, was also "magnificent." While property rights dispersed among heirs, the hacienda became a community. Long home to a curate linked to San Felipe, in 1855 it became an independent parish. The estate chapel remained, joined by a new church built in the 1830s dedicated to Our Lady of Mercy. A pastor and 2 curates served 6,500 at the estate center, another 3,000 on surrounding lands. There were 2 schools and 3 taverns, a plaza and an alameda, and "pyramid granaries" facing the "main house . . . a true palace."

Romero was most impressed by "the magnificent dam that provided irrigation to fields of chiles." While maize, the staple of everyday sustenance, remained the domain of family growers, Jaral commercialized chiles. Sharecroppers planted 4,800 fanegas of maize; the estate planted 1,130 cargas of wheat and 1,480 fanegas of barley, plus unrecorded chiles; another 1,800 fanegas of frijol, garbanzo, chile, and hortalizas were sown by diverse growers. Jaral kept 40,000 head of cattle and "the best horses in the state."[140] The estate and its community were rich and diverse, energized in the 1820s by mines north at Zacatecas, boosted from the 1840s by the surge at Guanajuato. Shareholding proprietors maintained irrigation and found gain mixing estate crops, grazing, and sharecropped maize. Jaral had revived limited commercial operations while the dispersal of family production kept growing maize-making communities strong on estate lands.

Romero then turned south to Celaya, Guanajuato's largest and most diverse jurisdiction in the 1850s. Set on rich lands between industrial Querétaro and the Guanajuato mines, the district included 190,000 people, near a quarter of the state population. In the city, he honored legacies of earlier times, notably the architecture of don Francisco Tresguerros. Insurgency had halted construction of the great church he designed; Romero honored its completion in the commercial-religious revival of the 1840s.

In 1860, there was a new sanctuary devoted to Guadalupe, sodalities including the Vela Perpetua, and a new Beaterio de Jesús Nazareno that brought women to educate young girls. The city parish included a pastor, sacristan, and three curates, with more serving outlying districts. The city had a council, a court, and the usual two schools—plus public fountains, street lighting, a theater, a printing press, a granary, "prisons," and "a woolen factory that supports a large number of families." Celaya had joined the industrial Bajío, its woolens complementing Hércules' cottons while family shops made "blankets and shawls," all sustaining "active trade with Guanajuato and Mexico [City]."

Romero praised cultivation around Celaya. He saw "owners and tenants on the land" sustaining life with "vast plantings of wheat, maize, and chile." He honored olive orchards that yielded "great quantities of oil capable of competing in taste and color with imports from Spain."[141] Celaya had survived insurgency to revive as a center of industry and crafts surrounded by rich irrigated lands worked by tenants and subtenants—most of the latter maize makers.

Just north of the city, 7 small pueblos, 28 haciendas, and more than 75 ranchos shaped a region politically centered at the Otomí town of San Juan de la Vega, its parish based at nearby Santa Cruz. The former retained 3,000 people; the latter exceeded 15,000 and was noted for "good markets and pleasant *huertas*." El Huaje, once an hacienda, was now a pueblo with a poor church, a school, and "two inns selling food to travelers between Guadalajara, Guanajuato, and Mexico [City]." El Rincón had 2,680 people dedicated to agriculture, a good church linked to an hacienda and its ranchos, "cotton weaving," and "miserable petty trade." Amoles had 6,000 people, a council and 2 schools, and a new church with 2 clerics. At Neutla in uplands west of Chamacuero, Romero reported 2,000 Otomí. The Santa Cruz district planted 2,800 fanegas of maize, 1,000 cargas of wheat, 1,200 fanegas of barley, and 450 of vegetables.[142] Dispersed production prevailed and prospered.

Chamacuero sat north along the Laja on the road to San Miguel, home to 11,000 Otomí "who understand Spanish." The church was "good," though an altar "in the modern style" displeased Romero. A sodality honored Nuestra Señora de los Remedios, but no Vela Perpetua had come to the indigenous town famed as the birthplace of liberal ideologue José María Luis Mora. There were the usual two schools, a plaza, two taverns, a public fountain, and "trade on festival days." With 19 haciendas and 35 ranchos, Chamacuero was "surrounded by a great number of *huertas* that yield exquisite fruits, notably the famous limes that support many families."[143] As Mora's liberal successors aimed to privatize lands, *huertas* sustained indigenous lives and trade at Chamacuero.

Romero then turned south of Celaya to the zones shaped by the great river that began in the Toluca basin west of Mexico City, fell north to enter the Bajío, then renamed the Santiago, flowed west to Lake Chapala and the Pacific. Acámbaro had thrived in the eighteenth century as a center of cultivation and artisan textiles. After insurgency, it shared the religious revivals of the 1840s, rebuilt churches, and founded new devotions and social services. The center was well paved; illuminated shops under portals did brisk business, collecting funds to build a new bridge over the river. There were fountains, baths, and *huertas*. Family maize and household cloth making carried "solid trade" while Romero lamented that "agriculture does not profit." There were 39 haciendas and nearly 100 ranchos with populations of "indios tarascos y otomites . . . europeos y mistos."[144]

North along the river, Salvatierra was a Hispanic-indigenous community of past eminence, recent revival, and limited prosperity. The church designed by Tresguerros was "among the best in the bishopric." There were old and new sodalities, including the Vela Perpetua. Capuchin sisters came to build a chapel and offer social services. The center had a broad plaza and three plazuelas, two schools, four taverns, and a plaza de gallos—and "a great number of *huertas* that yield the fruits of temperate zones, and the hot lands too." Still, the "great commerce" that flourished before 1810 had fallen "almost to nothing" despite "the spinning mill built by don Patricio Valencia." Cultivation carried on at 29 haciendas and 89 ranchos. Seven haciendas kept chapels serving active communities. Industry had come while family crafts carried on; *huertas* and tenant growers held strong.

Why did commercial life fall? "Fevers, dysentaries, and epidemic diseases are entrenched and malignant in the city center: the cholera invasions of 1833 and 1850 took more victims in Salvatierera than anywhere across the Bajío." Romero then added: "The people here suffered greatly from the recent [liberal] revolution."[145] Cholera and liberal incursions rattled a once prosperous town—while maize growers held strong on the land.

The river flowed west past the Agustinians' St. Nicolás hacienda. Yuriria lay farther west, away from the river on the shores of the lake of the same name. Romero noted a healthier climate, lamented Padre Torres' burnings in times of insurgency, and reported that between 1818 and 1830 refugees from Yuriria, Salvatierra, and Valle de Santiago had moved to found La Congregación (now Moroleón) just over the border in Michoacán. With 4,500 inhabitants, a church, six taverns, and "many stores," the new town took trade from Yuriría.

Still, the latter retained 50,000 people, half Spanish and mixed, half indigenous, two schools, two "shabby inns," three plazas, and "some *huertas* with fruit trees." In 1845, 3,000 people had lived by the "weaving" cotton goods. Hércules took their markets, leaving indigenous families to live from the lake. They took "rich yields of fish—catfish so big they weigh up to an arroba [12 kilograms], along with ample whitefish, abjundant sardines and char. . . . The *indios* live by fishing, weaving petates [bed mats] from lakeside reeds, and . . . making pottery with the excellent clays of the same shores."

Agriculture had gained when the Agustinians divided the Santa Mónica estate into 91 ranchos leased at "very modest prices." Then, privatizations pressed by the 1856 Ley Lerdo "have disturbed the recipients, with great prejudice to the poor growers here." Romero saw commerce ruined, even as cultivators planted 2,800 fanegas of maize, 650 cargas of wheat, and 1,200 fanegas of frijoles, chile, fruit, and some "caña de azucar."

Yuriria had survived a postinsurgency exodus. An 1829 attempt by church authorities to remove a revered image provoked riots in defense of local devotions. Hércules broke local cotton workshops in 1845. In the 1850s, liberals pressed privatizations threatening rancheros while taking golden images from the church—an assault on community devotions.[146] Rattled by exodus, industry, and liberalism, Yuriria's people held on, making sustenance on the land and the lake.

Romero completed his tour of Guanajuato in zones near Querétaro. Apaseo was prosperous without gross inequities. It had a council, two schools, a pleasant plaza, three plazuelas, and three taverns. A pastor and three curates served the parish; three sodalities and the Vela Perpetua focused popular devotions. Among 34 haciendas, several included chapels offering Mass on festival days; there were 40 ranchos, fewer than in most Guanajuato regions. Still, property records show Apaseo estate owners struggling with debt, juggling fragmenting sales and leases, while letting cultivation to tenants and subtenants. Romero saw "beautiful *huertas* yielding the most exquisite fruits" sold in Querétaro and Celaya. "Advanced agriculture" yielded "abundant harvests of wheat, maize, chile, beans, barley and chickpeas." Apaseo was the new Bajío: proprietors flailed while family growers made plenty.

Farther north, Romero saw little to honor in the communities still rattled by conflict at the edge of the Sierra Gorda. In San Luis de la Paz, he noted two schools, a solid church, a pastor and four vicars (one bilingual in Otomí), many sodalities, the Vela Perpetua, and a new chapel devoted to Guadalupe. The town had 7,600 residents, the outlying country another 20,000 spread across 10 haciendas and 125 ranchos—implying but not detailing dispersed family production.[147] Just south, with mines in decline, Pozos included 10,000 people, most Otomí living on four haciendas and uncounted ranchos.[148] In the highlands east, Xichú's mines were also dormant. A community of nearly 10,000, most Otomí, worshiped in a solid church served by two clerics, with one sodality and the Vela Perpetua as the population lived dispersed. Romero added: "Here and across the Sierra, property is concentrated; for every one or two proprietors, thousands live as tenants, . . . the root of constant discontent."[149]

Meanwhile, the new Bajío consolidated at Casas Viejas, now San José Iturbide. The town began in the eighteenth century as an informal settlement on Capulín estate lands. When it became a parish in 1777, excavation for the church unearthed a village believed to be a "Chichimeca" site ruined in sixteenth-century wars: thus, the name "Casas Viejas." The new town survived years of insurgency to gain a council in 1821. Rapid growth left a church "unable to hold the parishioners." Later, a pastor rebuilt the altar and brought the Vela Perpetua. In 1860, the center had 600 houses and 3,600 residents, a large plaza, a post office, three taverns, and "*huertas* with fruit trees"; the parish had 18,000 people, the political town included 32,500 spread across Capulín, San Gerónimo (its ownership fragmented), and two other estates.

A long transformation had remade Capulín. Long part of the Guerrereo estates held by don Antonio Ocío, after insurgency, he had passed oversight to leaseholders while production dispersed among rancheros and sharecroppers. The town of Casas Viejas prospered, evidenced by doña María Estefana Plana's trade at El Gigante and La Abundancia tied to leasing ranchos—enterprises that passed to a Mena rooted in Querétaro after her death in 1846. Then, on Ocío's death in 1849, Capulín passed to three minor heirs, as executor Cayetano Rubio leased the property to a Querétaro ally.

The new plan did not hold. Romero reported that during the Santa Anna–Alamán regime of 1853, "hard-working people decided to buy the hacienda Capulín, ending the need to pay four pesos yearly for every homesite, in the process subdividing the property. . . . They bought Capulín and San Gerónimo, dividing the land into great ranchos." Prosperous town residents and ranchero tenants combined to buy Capulín, making the town independent and rancheros landed proprietors. Romero concluded: "The people of this parish are religious, peaceful, and devoted to work."[150] Who could complain? Proprietors facing scarce profits and rising debts sold lands to town merchants and rancheros who sublet to family growers.

Casas Viejas completed the new Bajío: in times of silver revival and industrial rise, local merchants and rancheros came together to buy estates and distribute the land to ensure hierarchies of family production. How ironic that it came in a town renamed to honor Iturbide—the staunchest foe of the Bajío revolutionaries who led the fight that secured family maize making on estate lands.

Romero documented the persistent strength of the silver industrial capitalism sustained by diverse family growers across Guanajuato. Notably, while the family production claimed by insurgents there spread across Querétaro after 1820, the family huertas long pivotal to Otomí life in Querétaro appeared everywhere that waters permitted across Guanajuato by 1860. While silver revived to power Guanajuato and industrial textiles rose to remake Querétaro, a shared base of family production consolidated on the land. Rancheros, tenants, sharecroppers and hortelanos were everywhere.

The Bajío in 1860: Silver-Industrial Capitalism Sustained by Family Growers

In the 1850s, mining peaked at Guanajuato while industry thrived at Querétaro and spread beyond; landed property remained yet had lost economic power and productive primacy to rancheros and family growers. In 1860, perhaps 350 haciendas remained in Guanajuato, another 100 in Querétaro, far outnumbered by near 1,500 independent ranchos in Guanajuato, 225 across Querétaro.[151] Many more ranchos operated as leaseholds on estate lands. Meanwhile, haciendas and ranchos remained home to uncounted subtenants: family growers and sharecroppers. Hierarchies of tenancy shaped the rural Bajío, while thousands of families kept *huertas* in Querétaro and in growing numbers across Guanajuato.

A fair estimate would find nearly 2,000 ranchero owners or leasehold operators across the Bajio, outnumbered by 20,000 tenant-rancheros—suggesting a ranchero population near 100,000. Another 40,000 subtenants and sharecroppers, many also seasonal wage workers, brought the producing population on estate lands to near 300,000. Recognizing the 3,500 Otomí *hortelanos* reported by Balbontín in Querétaro and an equal number to count the many noted by Romero across Guanajuato adds another 7,000 families and 30,000 peoples to family growers across the Bajío. At least 330,000 family growers at the foundation of a flourishing silver-industrial capitalism.

With the combined populations of the states of Querétaro and Guanajuato approaching 800,000, 40 percent lived as maize makers on the land. They fed themselves, the more than 80,000 people at Guanajuato and its mines, the 40,000 each in industry and manufacturing at Querétaro and León, along with the tens of thousands in the other towns dispersed across the region. To 1860, diverse family growers sustained a vibrant silver-industrial capitalism. The rural world remade by Bajío revolutionaries—Epigmenio González' world—held strong.

Another legacy of the era of revolution also held. The militarized power begun in the coup of 1808 had consolidated in the decade of revolution.[152] Militarized politics defined nation building from 1821. They were reinforced in wars against Texas secessionists and US invaders, then mobilized again as liberals fought conservatives in the 1850s. While endless negotiations among landlords and cultivators, women and men, shaped life on the land, Romero and Balbontín reported concentrations of police and prisons in key cities: Guanajuato and La Luz; Querétaro, Celaya, and León; Salamanca and San Felipe. While rural families consolidated lives of shared sustenance, urban mining and industrial centers concentrated wealth built on local lives of laboring dependency and insecurity. Police and prisons, new coercive ways of social control concentrated there to defend power.

Devotions held strong everywhere, honored by the cleric Romero, disliked by the liberal Prieto.[153] Shared worship might reinforce communities of family growers across the land while diverse, even contested devotions often marked cities and towns. The powerful, conservatives in Querétaro, moderate liberals in Guanajuato, turned to coercions to hold peace and production in the raucous and risky world of mining in Guanajuato and domains of industry and manufacturing in Querétaro, Celaya, and León.

In the process, political powers and urban leaders built an ever more Weberian state grounded in concentrations of coercive powers.[154] The mediating ways of New Spain and its vibrant silver capitalism were left in the past. While informal negotiations built and maintained rural lives set in diverse ways family production across the Bajío, the men aiming to rule the new silver-industrial capitalism built states sustained by police and prisons—ways of power lamented by Prieto in 1853, noted as normal by Romero in 1860. A rising industrial economy powered by silver and backed by emerging states depended on family growers for sustenance. A powerful few profited, a few more prospered, while many lived sustaining autonomies. Could that capitalism forged in the wake of revolution carry on as the US drove toward continental power?

Breaking the New Bajío

US Imperialism, Liberal Assertions,
French Invasion—and a Cross of Gold,
1845–1880

From the 1830s, a new silver-industrial capitalism rose in the Bajío, adapting to the ranchero and family growers who ruled cultivation and communities on the land while generating new openings for women. Yet as silver, industry, and family maize makers held strong through the 1840s and 1850s, international and internal conflicts began to constrain Mexicans' futures. The US invasion and land taking of the 1840s set off Mexican political conflicts during the 1850s, leading to French occupation and Hapsburg imperial imposition in the 1860s. Throughout, the Mexico forged by Bajío revolutionaries proved resilient—until England, the US, and Germany imposed a gold standard in 1873. With silver devalued, Mexican capitalism and Mexican lives would never be the same.

Before 1810, the silver capitalism grounded in the Bajío had energized drives into North America, engaging New Mexico from the 1580s, Texas after 1700, coastal California from the late 1760s to reach San Francisco in 1776. After 1810, the revolution that broke silver capitalism also broke its northward dynamism, enabling new assertions of indigenous power and independence from the great plains to the Pacific. The same revolution opened global markets for Anglo-American industrial textiles, driving US cotton and slavery west toward Texas.[1] While silver-industrial capitalism rose in the Bajío in the 1830s, Texas seceded from Mexico aiming to preserve slavery and promote the expansion of cotton. Then, in the 1840s, the War for North America took Texas, New Mexico, and California into the United States, blocking Mexican northward expansion. Still, the silver-industrial capitalism grounded in family cropping held strong in the Bajío.

The financial costs and territorial losses of the war set off escalating national political conflicts. Liberals challenging Church property and cultural primacy and aiming to end indigenous rights to self-rule and community lands took arms to claim power in 1855. Their 1857 Constitution led Conservatives to a three-year War of Reform that brought disruptions but not radical destructions to the Bajío. When Benito Juárez led liberals back to power in 1860, Bajío mines, industries, and maize makers still flourished. Then, national conservatives facing political marginalization invited a French intervention that prolonged disruptive wars, imposed Maximilian of Hapsburg as emperor, preserved liberal programs, and deepened internal divisions. From 1864 through 1867, war focused in the Bajío, disrupting mining and rattling family maize growers.

Still, as war ended in 1867 and liberals reclaimed national rule, silver began to revive in the Bajío and beyond. Simultaneously, Juárez pressed privatizations of indigenous community lands and attacks on religious cultures, provoking popular resistance. Could the silver-industrial capitalism sustained by family maize makers hold strong under liberal rule? We will never know. In 1873, the United States, bolstered by gold mined in California and Colorado lands once Mexican, joined England and Germany on a gold standard. The leading industrial powers ended the long reign of silver as capital in global trade. The Bajío and Mexico would adapt and survive—but never again flourish as they had during the centuries of silver capitalism and the decades of silver-industrial capitalism built after the Bajío revolution. The dynamic link between silver and capitalism, forged by Chinese power in the 1550s, broke in the face of US power in the 1870s.[2]

From Insurrection to Invasion: New Spain,
Mexico, and the United States, 1810–1850

When Hidalgo called for political revolt at Dolores in September 1810, throngs of popular insurgents recently pummeled by predatory exploitations rose to take maize and, in time, land to make it. They were joined by Guanajuato mine workers and their neighbors taking all they could in the richest place in the Americas. Carrying on the fight for autonomies on the land long after Hidalgo's defeat, popular insurgents broke silver capitalism, cutting production and trade of Chinese silks and porcelains and Indian cottons, too. Unplanned and unimagined reverberations of Bajío insurgencies opened global markets to British industries supplied with cotton made by slaves in the US South. India and China faced long struggles to adapt, the former constrained by British imperial power, the latter restrained by British and US incursions—and opium delivered from India by British traders. In time, Britain gained global industrial primacy while the US forged a new economy of industry, cotton, and slavery.[3]

The Bajío revolution broke silver capitalism and the global trades it fueled, opening the world to new industrial powers grounded in plantation slavery. The fall of Asia and the rise of Anglo-American industrial capitalism were underway by 1815, before Mexican independence and before the new silver-industrial capitalism grounded in family maize making rose in the Bajío from the 1830s to energize in the 1840s.

At that pivotal moment, the United States invaded Mexico to claim the lands from Texas to California. The two nations of North America had been on a collision course since the 1820s. As industrial cotton textiles rose in England and then New England, US southern planters looked to Texas's rich coastal plains for expansion.[4] The welcome offered to Stephen Austin to develop cotton and slavery in Texas faced challenge when Vicente Guerrero abolished the remnants of slavery in Mexico in 1829. Attempts to keep bondage alive via states' rights federalism collapsed when Santa Anna turned Mexico to central rule in 1835, leading Texas to secede in 1836 to preserve slavery. Mexico could not defeat the rebels yet would not recognize Texas independence. The new republic struggled, leading the United States to annexation late in 1845—and to a war to claim Texas, New Mexico, and California in 1846.

Setting aside myths of "Manifest Destiny," taking Texas to expand cotton and slavery is all but universally seen as the first goal of the war.[5] Incorporating California appears secondary, its riches in gold a surprise encounter in 1849. That vision is no longer tenable. Robert Wyllie, a representative of British bondholders, published a book in English in London in 1844, then in Spanish in Mexico City in 1845, announcing ample gold "north of Los Angeles" and promoting an Anglo-Mexican project to develop mines, settle California, and block US advances. If US leaders did not already know about California gold, their emissaries in London and Mexico surely learned of it from Wyllie.[6] The United States sent John Fremont overland to California in 1845 and in 1846 ordered naval forces to land the moment war began.[7]

The United States went to war to claim Texas for cotton and slavery and California for gold as money-capital to fund national expansion. Regional political divisions inhibited Mexico's response while US economic advantage set in industry and plantation slavery generated ample revenues to fund military operations.[8] A nation since 1776, the United States had profited in trade during the French and Haitian revolutionary wars, then built a new economy of industry and slavery that energized after Bajío insurgents broke New Spain's silver capitalism in 1812. Mexico emerged from revolution to face independence in 1821 with silver capitalism gone and national revenues scarce. When silver revived and industry rose in the early 1840s, politics remained contested and national revenues held scarce.[9] The timing was perfect for the United States.

The United States also had stronger military capacities. Its war for independence had been an international conflict. The congress that declared independence in 1776 sent formal armies led by George Washington, backed by French navies, and funded by New Spain's pesos to face British forces.[10] After the British ceded at Yorktown in 1781 and conceded US independence in Paris in 1783, Washington depoliticized the military. The young nation founded a military academy in 1802, before it faced a second formal war with England in 1812. Then, as industry and slavery expanded, the US military focused on clearing western lands of native peoples in endless fights between "nations."[11] The United States built a professional officer corps and armed forces, including a navy bolstered in 1845 by the Naval Academy at Annapolis.

In contrast, New Spain had kept formal military forces primarily at ports and northern frontiers, relying on limited militias for internal social control. Attempts to increase military power from the 1760s led to resistance and enduring limits.[12] The regime militarized in the 1808 coup that imposed authorities ready to deliver silver to Spain's fight against Napoleon, an imposition that contributed to the outbreak of revolution in 1810. The decade of insurgency and counterinsurgency focused armed power on internal politics and social control.[13] Insurgents pacified, silver capitalism gone, and the Bajío transformed, the military made Mexico independent in 1821, promising constitutional bases that were long contested. Mexican military commanders were political first, not by long tradition but due to the 1808 Napoleonic incursion and the conflicts of 1810 to 1824.

Contrasting military leadership, more professional in the United States, mostly political in Mexico, mattered. Still, both nations' forces mixed small formal armies with citizen soldiers—volunteers in the United States, National Guards in Mexico. When war came, both belligerents faced the limited numbers and capacities of formal forces and the unruly, often unreliable behavior of volunteers and guards.[14]

Figure C.1 Customs house at Monterey, capital of Spanish and Mexican California, 1770 to 1846. Author photo.

Pivotally decisive, Mexico had no effective navy. The naval power that defended Spanish silver capitalism in the Atlantic was based in Havana; Guayaquil and Manila kept naval forces to protect Pacific trades. Gulf coasts were protected first by yellow fever and malaria. The result was a powerful silver capitalism financially centered in Mexico City, its trade guarded by navies harbored in island ports. After 1821, the Atlantic forces remained Spanish, still based in Havana to guard Cuba's rising sugar and slave economy. When US forces moved to land at Veracruz in 1846, Mexico had no navy to respond. New Spain's strength to maintain silver capitalism with limited internal military capacities, stabilized by a mediating judicial regime, and protected at sea by Spain's navy, became Mexico's weakness when silver collapsed and mediating justice ceded to militarized politics in a nation without a navy.[15]

After the Bajío revolution broke silver capitalism, Mexico had neither economic nor military power in the northern lands that drew US interest.

Map C.1 A nation constrained: Mexico after 1848.

To fight the invasion that began in Texas in 1846, Santa Anna drove forces north to block armies that had crossed the Rio Grande, stalling them around Monterrey and Saltillo. Mexico could not stop the naval landing at Veracruz that set forces ashore to take Mexico City in 1847. Nor could it block the invasions by land and sea that took California from San Diego and Los Angeles in the south to the capital at Monterey (figure C.1), San Francisco, and regions inland in the north. The resistance of formal armies, regional guards, and the people of Mexico City made the United States pay a price for the land and gold it took in a war of aggression. Still, the US victory of 1848 was near inevitable.[16]

The War for North America did not derail the new Bajío. The region's wealth, shielded by forces north of San Luis Potosí, drew national authorities to Querétaro as US marines took Mexico City. Peace signed and land lost in 1848, mining held strong at Guanajuato to peak in the early 1850s, while industry consolidated at Querétaro and spread beyond.[17] Prospects for northward expansion were gone but the silver-industrial capitalism grounded in family maize flourished through the 1850s.

In the Wake of US Imperialism:
Mexican Liberalism Rises

After the war, political conflicts escalated in both the United States and Mexico. In the US, disputes over the expansion of slavery into territories taken from Mexico helped drive the South toward secession and the nation to Civil War.[18] The causes, course, and outcomes of that deadly and destructive conflict are much studied and well recognized.[19] In Mexico, the loss of northern territories led to a politics of blame debating the promise and possibility of conservative and liberal projects as routes forward.[20] Presidents José Joaquín de Herrera and Mariano Arista tried financial reforms to bolster the national regime in the late 1840s and early 1850s. Santa Anna's last coup took the presidency in 1853, calling Lucas Alamán to a final attempt to forge a conservative national regime. His death in June led to the liberal rising of 1854 that ended Santa Anna's rule and political career in 1855.

Before that rising, liberal visions for Mexico had been aspirational. Rooted in the 1812 Cádiz Constitution, liberals offered endless political promises amid struggles to found the nation.[21] They opposed industrialization; they aimed to limit Church wealth and cultural primacy; they railed against indigenous community self-governance and corporate landholding—all with little success before the 1850s.[22]

The 1854 Ayutla rising led by Juan Álvarez turned the dynamic of Mexican politics. Heir to Vicente Guerrero's hegemony along the southwest coast, Álvarez mobilized lowland mulattoes (often cotton growers) and highland indigenous communities (mostly maize makers) in a popular alliance that ousted Santa Anna.[23] Yet on taking power in 1855, Álvarez faced an urban liberal coalition that rejected his rule. Ideological liberals turned hard against

Church power and indigenous communities. The 1855 Ley Juárez ended separate jurisdiction for clergy and military; the 1856 Ley Lerdo denied corporate property rights, the base of the remnant economic power of the Church and of persistent family maize making in indigenous communities.[24] Set in the Constitution of 1857, the attacks on the military, the church, and native communities turned conservatives to a fight for political survival. Facing war, liberals soon led by Benito Juárez, the Zapotec former governor of Oaxaca, turned to nationalizing church properties to fund the War of Reform.[25]

Like Calleja in 1813, midcentury liberals refrained from pressing privatizations of community lands, knowing resistance would come quickly. As most indigenous communities and ranchero maize makers stood aside, three years of political war brought Juárez and the liberals back to power in 1860. Romero's report on life in Guanajuato as the war ended showed that liberal mandates and disruptions had shaken the region, but had not derailed mining nor broken vibrant rural economies grounded in family maize and rich *huertas*. The silver-industrial capitalism forged in the wake of the Bajío revolution held.

Could it thrive under liberal rule after 1860? A world of conflict rattled the attempt. As the reform war ended and liberals reclaimed power in Mexico, US southern states seceded from the Union in a Confederacy that fought to preserve slavery from 1861 to 1865. In the shadow of that war, Mexican conservatives backed a French occupation that began in 1862 and imposed the ill-fated monarchy of Maximilian of Hapsburg from 1864. Then, with the Union restored in 1865, the United States pressured France to exit Mexico, which it did in the face of looming war with Prussia in 1867. When Maximilian chose to stay, he was captured, tried, and executed in 1867 as liberals reclaimed power.[26]

In the United States, postwar times brought Union power, northern industrial renovation, and a southern reconstruction that turned freed people into sharecroppers making cotton while westward expansion drove native peoples off ancestral lands.[27] In Mexico, the return of liberal rule in 1867 under Juárez brought four goals: reviving silver production (a national consensus); opening trade (a liberal commandment); privatizing indigenous community lands (a liberal dream); and ousting the Church from education and public culture (the liberal creed).

Silver did revive, helping Juárez consolidate liberal rule. National output held near 16 million pesos through the years of conflict, then rose to more than 19 million pesos after liberal restoration in 1867.[28] Other goals proved contested and difficult.

Liberals promoted free trade. Long allied with merchant interests, they backed the trade of silver for cloth promoted in the 1820s by Henry Ward.[29] From 1824 through 1827, while British capital funded mines and the national regime, Mexico bought 8 million pesos of cloth yearly, nearly the exact amount of silver minted. Imports fell when Guerrero set tariffs to favor cloth makers in 1829 and then Alamán turned to promote mechanized industry in the 1830s. In 1856, as liberals took power, national silver output reached 18 million pesos, with cloth imports only 7.6 million pesos—just over 40 percent.[30] That was the way of silver-industrial capitalism.

Returning to power in 1867, liberals opened Mexican ports. By 1872, cloth imports rose to 11.4 million pesos, more than 60 percent of the 19 million pesos minted that year. As established industries struggled, workers faced pressures and began to organize. Juárez and his successor, Sebastian Lerdo de Tejada, backed mutual aid societies—and fought unions.[31] The industrial side of silver-industrial capitalism carried on under restored liberalism, shaken but not broken.

Juárez, the Zapotec liberal, believed he knew what was best for indigenous communities. On returning to power in 1867, he turned to enforce the Ley Lerdo and privatize community lands. He quickly learned that many did not share his vision. Communities rose in armed resistance at Chalco, Mexico City's granary where estates and communities made maize, wheat, and more, and in the Mezquital, where community maize and estate maguey competed on dry lands.[32] There were risings in Nayarit northwest of the Bajío and in Chiapas on the Guatemalan border. Other communities, from Purépecha, Michoacán, to the Huasteca of Veracruz, negotiated to limit privatizations.[33] Facing widening resistance, Juárez stood back. Yet regionally, communal holdings were often declared privatized without surveys, leaving new "owners" without titles to document property rights.[34]

In 1867, liberals also revived attacks on Catholic cultural primacy—in public life and social services, education and community devotions. Church property all but gone, liberals turned against devotions in public spaces. They demanded state registration of births, marriages, and deaths, leaving sacramental sanctions as options bearing costs. They promoted state schools to serve middling families in cities and towns. In their efforts, liberals alienated deeply Catholic people in diverse communities. In Michoacán and the southern Bajío, they provoked revolts in defense of religion in ranchero, mulatto, and Indigenous communities.[35]

Given their alienation of so many, how did liberals hold power? Much of the answer lies in the reverberations of the Bajío revolution. While insurgents claimed lands for family production and built local religious cultures, they broke the power of once dominant landed oligarchs, the historic base of conservative power. Thus did Lucas Alamán rail against the "destructions" of the Bajío revolution. When he published his *Historia de Méjico* in 1853, his dreams of a Mexico set in silver and industry were coming true. Yet his political project failed as landed power dissolved.[36] In the 1840s and 1850s, once powerful landed clans struggled to survive while women worked to maintain property, sustain Church institutions, and back religious politics.[37] Despite women's efforts, oligarchs and the Church lacked the property and profits to block the liberals' rise to power in the 1850s and their return in 1860 after victory in the war of reform. The liberal consolidation of power was interrupted in the 1860s by French invasion and the imposition of the short-lived empire of Maximilian of Hapsburg. An examination of those incursions focused on the Bajío reveals much about the enduring strength of silver-industrial capitalism—and its sudden fall.

Liberal Power in the Bajío, 1855–1863

The Bajío was pivotal to the persistence of silver-industrial capitalism through the wars of the 1850s and 1860s—the target of every faction seeking power. Guanajuato was the richest city in Mexico in the aftermath of the War for North America, its silver production holding near 7.5 million pesos yearly from 1848 to 1852 as the California gold rush began. It then fell to near 5 million pesos yearly during the conflicts surrounding the rise of liberal rule from 1853 to 1860. In 1857, as liberals wrote their constitution, one report had Guanajuato minting 4.75 million pesos, another 5 million—with 660,000 in gold bringing total minting to 5.65 million pesos. The Bajío mining center then minted 30 percent of all the bullion coined in Mexico, with Mexico City well back at 22 percent, followed by Zacatecas at 20 percent of a total of 19.3 million pesos. Meanwhile, California gold rose to near 29 million pesos in 1856, to fall back to 20.4 million pesos in 1857—barely higher than Mexican silver output in a still bimetallic world. Mexican and Californian minting held parallel through 1859 as the United States approached Civil War and Liberals fought Conservatives for power in Mexico. Mexican silver held strong to 1863, still led by Guanajuato.[38]

Then, years of battles and disruptions focused in the Bajío, corroding its silver-industrial capitalism. Wars first pressing French-imperial rule and then liberal restoration converged in the Bajío to break silver mining there for a second time. Silver production that had peaked at more than 7.5

million pesos yearly from 1848 to 1852 and held near 5 million from 1856 to 1863, fell to 3 million from 1865 through 1870.[39]

After Governor Octaviano Muñoz Ledo kept Guanajuato neutral in the conflicts that brought Santa Anna and Alamán to power in 1853, the state proved pivotal to the rise of liberal rule. In August 1855, Guanajuato's leading liberal, Manuel Doblado, proclaimed support for Juan Álvarez and the Ayutla movement and named himself state governor. Months of conflict in a national cabinet that included Melchor Ocampo, Benito Juárez, Guillermo Prieto, and Ignacio Comonfort led Doblado to reject Álvarez' rule on December 5. The southern general resigned on December 10—after the Ley Juárez ended clerical and military judicial privileges, before the Ley Lerdo ended Church and community corporate land rights.

Was the hard liberal turn against land rights latter only possible with Álvarez deposed? His power was grounded among mulatto coastal growers and inland indigenous communities—whose rights he respected. With their backing, he led the forces that ousted Santa Anna and claimed national power, only to face months of challenge by more "pure" liberal ideologues. He survived until Doblado and silver-rich Guanajuato rejected his rule—enabling the national liberal turn against indigenous community rights.

Doblado proposed interim rule by a triumvirate to include the president of the Supreme Court (Juárez, Zapotec and anticlerical), the director of the Mining Tribunal, and a representative of Comonfort (military and moderate). Doblado also called for preserving Catholicism as the nation's religious culture.[40] In his liberalism, Guanajuato silver would mediate between liberal factions and protect Catholic culture. When Conservatives rose in war to resist liberal reforms in 1858, Comonfort defected and Juárez became president. He nationalized Church properties to fund liberal survival while stepping back from privatizing community land rights—both essential to the return of liberal rule in 1860.

While thanks to Doblado the turn to liberalism in 1855 was little contested in Guanajuato, it proved divisive and destructive in Querétaro. When Santa Anna left the presidency and Governor Ángel Cabrera called for recognition of Ayutla, troops awaiting pay rioted in the capital. Cabrera fell and instability reigned until Tomás Mejía came down from the Sierra to occupy the city in October 1856—to be forced back to the Sierra by Comonfort. Mejía, the Otomí conservative, would hold strong in the highlands until 1867, contesting the power of Benito Juárez, the Zapotec liberal.[41]

When radical anticlericalism and the privatization of Church properties and community lands were set in the Constitution of 1857, Comonfort turned to join the conservatives in a war to block liberal rule and reforms. Mejía reclaimed Querétaro in October. In January 1858, Juárez fled north, to be welcomed by Doblado in Guanajuato. There, as president of the Supreme Court he formally succeeded Comonfort as president and called for national mobilization to defend the liberal constitution. In February, he set off on a journey that led west to Guadalajara, down the Pacific coast, across Panama, and then to Veracruz, where he settled to lead liberals during the War of Reform. In the port, he controlled revenues from trade, limiting funds to conservatives in the capital while trying to live the liberal dream of free trade.

Holding Querétaro thanks to Mejía, conservatives focused on taking back Guanajuato and its silver. In March 1858, Miguel Miramón defeated Doblado and liberal forces at Salamanca, opening the way to the mines. Conservatives held the silver center while production rose from 4.75 million pesos in 1857 to 5.4 million in 1860, sustaining their forces while conflicts rattled towns and rural growers.[42]

In August 1860, the battle at Silao brought Doblado back to power in Guanajuato. Liberals reclaimed Querétaro in November, with José María Arteaga named governor in February 1861. With the Constitution of 1857 restored, Guanajuato silver, fallen to 4.9 million pesos in 1861, rose back to 5.25 million in 1863. Romero's 1860 survey lamented liberal incursions while reporting a thriving regional economy.[43] The Reform War rattled but did not break the Bajío.

Still, it took a toll. Population reports suggest that Guanajuato lost 7 percent of its population during the years of liberal rise and reform wars.[44] In January 1861, a liberal state Congress lamented: "Everything collapsed in times of invasion and vandalism: revenues, education, roads, industry, rights and more. When the legitimate [liberal] government regained the state capital, it found the ruins left by the pillaging of those who call themselves conservatives, people impoverished, commerce ruined, the sources of public wealth everywhere blocked."[45] The cleric Romero saw less destruction and more promise. Still, the first liberal era and its wars had shaken Guanajuato.

French Power and Imperial Rule, 1862–1867

The wars of the 1850s brought national debts, burdensome since the British fiasco of the 1820s, to new heights. The original London debts had compounded to more than 62 million pesos; British and Spanish conventions added 12 million more. The 600,000 owed to the French brought recognized debts to 75 million pesos in 1861—more than four times annual national revenues and silver production, both then holding between 16 and 17 million pesos. Conservatives contracted another 52 million pesos in foreign debt to fund their failed fight against the liberals, and lenders backed by foreign powers expected to be paid. Claims rose to 130 million pesos, nearly eight times annual silver flows.[46]

Back in power, Juárez saw impossibility and suspended payment in July 1861. France, the least of the creditors, recruited Spain and England to an expedition to land at Veracruz and force a resumption of payments. Juárez brought Doblado to join negotiations that led England and Spain to withdraw early in 1862. French troops remained, marching inland to meet defeat at Puebla on May 5—the famous national triumph of Cinco de Mayo. Undeterred, Napoleon III sent 30,000 more troops, taking Puebla in March 1863, then Mexico City in June.[47] Another Napoleon aimed to solve France's problems by taking New Spain's, now Mexico's, silver.

After four months in the capital, French forces turned to claim Guanajuato in October. The reasons were clear: in 1863, the mint there coined 5.25 million pesos, Zacatecas 4.3 million, Mexico City only 3.1 million (from production at Taxco and Real del Monte), for a national total of 17.8 million pesos. Power and debt payment required silver, and most was mined and minted at Guanajuato and Zacatecas, just beyond. A force of 11,000 headed to the Bajío in two columns, one via Querétaro, the other Acámbaro.

As French and allied Mexican forces approached the mining city, on December 6 Governor Doblado exited, first to León, then north to Saltillo. On the eighth, troops led by Tomás Mejía, having reclaimed Querétaro, took Guanajuato without opposition. French troops came the next day. The locally powerful met in the home of a leading mining financier to name new authorities. The military-political story suggests an easy French-Conservative occupation of the Bajío.[48]

A closer look reveals that French and conservative armies brought impositions and disruptions that constrained mining, took maize from family growers, and provoked social conflicts. The troops left Mexico City in October, to facilitate travel after summer rains ended. Along the march, maize stood ripe in the fields, edible while drying. French and conservative armies "liberated" maize from family growers entrenched across the Bajío. Social challenges followed. From January 1864, the southern and western Bajío saw bandits and guerrilla bands proclaim opposition to French rule while claiming the staples of survival.[49] Then, the summer of 1864 brought extreme drought. Local maize prices rose to 9 pesos per fanega—twice pre-revolutionary peaks.[50]

Dearth plagued the Bajío. Looking back from the first day of 1865, a local journalist lamented: "Never before had public misery reached the horrible extreme that plagued the year 1864. Everything was paralyzed, businesses stalled, mining abandoned, and making everything worse, extortions of funds ended monetary circulations. . . . Businesses closed, suspending payments and ceding property to creditors. The people of Guanajuato feel a general disgust; the decadence is complete."[51] Another writer added: "Guanajuato suffers atrocious disease and dearth. . . . Enormous misery reigns, leaving the mining city in desperation. May God take pity on us!"[52] The invaders having broken sustenance, Guanajuato silver fell from 5.25 million pesos in 1863 to 3.57 million pesos in 1865—a fall of over 30 percent.[53]

Amid dearth, urban desperation, and mining decline, José María Diez de Sollano came home to Guanajuato. Born in San Miguel in 1820 as insurgency ended and ordained a priest just before the War for North America, he rose to serve as pastor at the Sagrario Metropolitano, the parish tied to the Mexico City cathedral. In February 1864, as French troops occupied the state and desperation set in, he came to sit as the first bishop of León, serving all of Guanajuato. His antipathy to liberal programs was known: in 1857, he had publicly rejected limits on clerical justice and privatizations of Church properties.[54] Arriving in León in times of challenge, his first pastoral letter promised stabilizing continuity: "It is our spirit to bring no change to the honorable rules, ways, and customs kept in the lands that form our new diocese." He ordered three Masses said everywhere: one to the Holy Spirit, one to the Sacred Heart of Christ, and one to the "Most Holy Virgin Mother of Light"—de la Luz, the last named "protector of the Bishopric." He honored a trinity culminating with a virgin pivotal to popular devotions, a source of light, and namesake of the mines that had revived Guanajuato silver.[55]

In June, a new pastoral letter turned divisive. He asked Maximilian of Hapsburg—recently arrived, drawn by Mexican Conservatives, and backed by Napoleon III's troops—to block liberal programs in the face of "the misfortunes of the Church and our nation." As the imported emperor "has now entered the capital of the empire and taken the Mexican throne to exuberant acclaim," he must stop "the protestants, and especially the pseudo-philosophers, deists, socialists, and demagogues" that threaten the nation. The solution: "the people must look to our teaching," focusing on "humble, fervent, and endless prayer, especially in public devotions."[56] Clergy would instruct; people would obey.

Liberals, from Guanajuato governor Carlos Montes de Oca in the 1820s to Guillermo Prieto in the 1850s, had long dreamed of reeducating the people to become liberal citizens. Now, in the 1860s, the first bishop of León would make the diverse people and believers of Guanajuato into obedient subjects. Openness to diversity had made New Spain's and México's Catholicisms strong. As Diez de Sollano grew up in San Miguel in the 1820s, pastor Francisco Uraga had honored the ranchero priest who catered to rural community devotions. In 1860, José Guadalupe Romero detailed the diverse ways of worship that energized and integrated life across the state. The descendants of the people who made the Bajío revolution were not likely to obey a bishop who told them to pray obediently.

Then, while scarcity and insecurity reigned, Maximilian came to the Bajío in August 1864. Like the conservatives, liberals, and French commanders who preceded him, he knew where wealth and power were made. He spent six days in Querétaro, two each in Celaya and Salamanca, then paused for two weeks in Irapuato. Facing dearth and desperation all around, he pleaded for charitable solutions. He spent two days in San Miguel, two more in Dolores, then entered Guanajuato to gain honors from the locally eminent and visit mines at Mellado, Cata, and Rayas.

Did doña Francisca de Paula Pérez Gálvez join the welcome? Her rich mines at upland La Luz were not on the emperor's itinerary. He later stopped in León—did he visit the bishop?—and at Corralejo, Hidalgo's birthplace. Having seen Guanajuato's mines in collapse and fields facing dearth, Maximilian called for rural guards to defend property—echoing Hidalgo more than six decades later.[57] His blindness to the ways and needs of the people who made the Bajío revolution and now struggled to survive was blatant. In that, the emperor and the bishop converged.

Maximilian promised peace, capital, infrastructure, and the protection of property—promises he could not keep. Maize prices held at devastating peaks through 1865, imposing costs on mines and life challenges on workers. Meanwhile, mine operators lost capital to forced contributions and loans taken to sustain the empire.[58] Without capital, doña Francisco de Paula Pérez Gálvez returned Valenciana to *buscones*, the independent crews that took ore as they could, then sold to refiners. Production limped forward and infrastructure crumbled—again. In 1865 and 1866, she formed a company including kin in the Rul family to finance refining.[59] Others did the same. In 1864, Demetrio Montes de Oca and Ignacio Rocha formed the Compañia Minera de Guanajuato, selling shares to gain 2,000 pesos to finance mines as violent conflicts cut local silver flows.[60]

Amid conflict and decline, doña Francisca de Paula prepared to turn her mines at Valenciana and La Luz over to Miguel Rul, a nephew and heir to her mining shares and landed properties. She orchestrated his future rule of Guanajuato's once leading mines—Valenciana, La Luz, and more—and estates ranging from his vast Cieneguilla near Aguascalientes to her Bocas and Peñasco in San Luis Potosí, all now worked by leaseholders and subtenants. She had led Guanajuato mining to its historic peak from 1848 to 1852, then limited its decline in the face of political conflicts. Now, in the face of French incursion and mining collapse, she set a young kinsman to carry on as he could.

Meanwhile, imperial rule failed to consolidate. Banditry was rampant across the southern Bajío into 1865. In February, Maximilian confirmed freedom of worship and the nationalization of Church properties—appealing to liberal foes, alienating ecclesiastical allies and many Catholic believers. In May, the French commander at León prohibited all public gatherings, including religious festivals, that did not have his sanction.

Nature conspired too: when rains broke the drought in September, too late to save the harvest, they came in torrents that unleashed devastating floods in Guanajuato, León, Silao, and Irapuato; Celaya and Salamanca; Chamacuero and Dolores. Production and life, urban and rural, took another pummeling. In the wake of those disruptions, imperial authorities removed the military from social patrols, calling the owners of estates and ranchos to contain bandits. The empire turned away from social control in times of ecological challenge, social unrest, and mining collapse in Guanajuato.[61]

Conflict with the Church deepened in 1866. In a pastoral letter, Diez de Sollano rejected Maximilian's confirmation of the "civil registry" that affirmed state recording of births, marriages, and deaths. In public confrontation with the emperor, the bishop saw "spiritual ruin" and insisted there would be no dispensations from sacramental sanction of life's key moments.[62] In June, he bluntly feared that "Protestantism threatens to remove the yoke of Church authority." He rejected the Protestant emphasis on direct encounters with the Bible, insisting that the Church instruct people who "do not understand," adding "it is essential that our public, universal, permanent, supreme, infallible, and unfailing authority" present singular truths.[63] Could a bishop take a more authoritarian stance, fulfilling liberal presumptions while challenging enduring traditions of independent popular devotions?

Amid social and cultural polarizations, war returned to the Bajío. With Union victory in the United States, calls for French withdrawal from Mexico rose. Guerrilla incursions from Michoacán rattled the southern Bajío while Florencio Antillón stepped forward to lead liberals back to power in the Bajío. Born in Guanajuato in 1830, he had joined the military in 1847 to fight the United States; he was at Puebla in 1862, then with Doblado to contest the French drive inland in 1863. While Maximilian ruled, Antillón ran a pharmacy in Guanajuato, then settled south of Celaya. In August 1866, he called liberals to rise against French troops and Maximilian's empire, promising: "I will not punish, burn, or extort."[64]

Early in 1867, as French troops withdrew to face Prussian challenges at home, regional forces faced off in the Bajío. Conservative Tomás Mejía pressed west into Guanajuato; liberal Antillón took León and Silao to block him. Mejía's ally Miguel Miramón briefly took the mining city in January, then retreated north. Antillón set liberal authorities in León and entered Guanajuato on January 26, declaring himself state commander and interim governor. He then raised forces to join the siege of Querétaro from March to mid-May. Destructions earlier focused in Guanajuato moved to the industrial city.[65]

Maximilian came north in February to join Mejía and Miramón. Backed by 12,000 troops, they chose Querétaro for a last stand to defend the monarchy abandoned by the French. The city's convents became barracks; roof beams and church bells became metal to make blades and bullets. Men faced conscription; livestock was taken to feed troops, haul weapons, and more; women were pressed to grind maize, make tortillas, and more. The siege began in March. Life and defense of the city were rattled when republican troops broke an arch of the great aqueduct that brought water to the center. Growing numbers of wounded found care in a hospital at Hércules—east along the river. Defenders fought on: "Despite the frightful misery endured by all, desertions were few until the last days of the siege." A final battle on May 15 brought the capture of Maximilian, Mejía, and Miramón, followed by a trial and their execution on June 19 on the Cerro de las Campanas.[66]

The siege of Querétaro was destructive. We don't know the visions or participations of the Otomí still working *huertas* along the river, nor of the mill workers at Hércules. Lives were surely disrupted as infrastructure was turned to war in the once dynamic center of industry and trade, crafts and cultivation. The lively markets that Prieto admired surely waned. Guanajuato and Querétaro both faced challenges of reconstruction in 1867, Guanajuato favored by silver, Querétaro prejudiced by the animosity of restored liberal rulers.

Liberal Reconstruction in the Bajío, 1867–1876

After the siege and victory at Querétaro, Juárez named Antillón provisional governor of Guanajuato. In his first address, in December 1867, he reported devastation: "families orphaned, fortunes destroyed." Facing less than 5 pesos in the state treasury, he needed 19,000 to sustain 500 cavalry troops still fighting rebels near Irapuato and Pénjamo. Less organized "criminals" also plagued the state, requiring a larger Guardia Nacional to end a "wave of vandalism." He lamented "the fall of public revenues and the social paralysis left by the war." Only "enduring peace can revive the state, bringing guarantees to the ample capital needed to revive circulation and development." National authorities soon ceded 55,000 pesos of silver for state needs, enabling Antillón to turn "the magnificent once Agustinian convent at Salamanca into a penitentiary to contain criminals." In a revealing new meaning of "development," silver would pay to turn a convent into a prison—highlighting liberal commitments to a state grounded in coercive social controls.[67]

Church opposition hardened. In 1870, bishop Diez de Sollano announced Pius IX's Vatican Council confirmation of papal infallibility. In 1872, he denounced liberal support for Freemasonry. In 1873, de decried the dissolution of religious communities dedicated to social service.[68] When pressures to privatize community lands came followed by attacks on church participation in public life, leading to religious wars across Michoacán in 1873, Diez de Sollano hardened his authoritarian line.[69] In an 1874 pastoral letter, he lamented "the near universal derangement of society by decatholicization, . . . deforming it from its heights to its foundations, decatholicizing not only politics, legislation, and family life, but every aspect of education, driving youth to disbelief and materialism." Everything was wrong in liberal Mexico. The solution was church-ruled devotions and education—with no thought of consulting the faithful or adapting to people's diverse ways of devotion.[70]

While liberals dreamed of imposing change and churchmen pressed authoritarian ways, silver remained the key to power and prosperity in the Bajío and across Mexico. If it revived, much was possible; if it did not, decline would rule. After doña Francisca de Paula Pérez Gálvez' death in 1868, Miguel Rul organized La Compañia Restauradora de Valenciana, drawing investors to provide capital to drain and restore the infrastructure of the once great mine, pummeled for a second time by war and scavenging production. New steam pumps requiring less of the region's scarce firewood helped drainage but the price of mercury rose due to a monopoly built by the House of Rothchild. In 1872, Rul employed 2,500 of the 9,000 workers laboring in mines at Guanajuato. Silver began to revive while profits stayed scarce.[71]

When Governor Antillón assessed Guanajuato in September 1873, after six years of liberal rule, he saw limited progress in the mines. Silver production had risen to 4.5 million pesos in 1871–72, then fell back to 4 million in 1872–73, blamed on the Rothchilds' monopoly. The governor did succeed in raising tax revenues. Totaling 794,632 pesos in 1872, only 140,921

(18 percent) came from silver, 334,837 (42 percent) came from sales, and 247,748 (31 percent) came from a head tax on adult men. Revenues from mining were just 3 percent of the value of production, a subsidy to a leading sector struggling to revive.[72] Producing people across the state paid for the mix of education, policing, and jails that liberals saw as essential to the social peace that enabled mining. The governor lauded achievements in education, while building jails and funding police to fill them. The liberal dream of cultural transformation backed by a coercive state held.

Antillón paid little attention to Guanajuato's rural majority, beyond noting that maize was ample and affordable in 1871–72. His silence suggests that peaceful production had revived, still led by ranchero and tenant family growers.[73] Just north, Miguel Rul maintained dispersed production via hierarchies of leaseholds, with rancheros and subtenants remaining primary producers.[74] While liberals and churchmen aimed to remake their lives, rural families held strong on the land.

While silver led a limited economic revival in Guanajuato, Querétaro struggled. After the city was wracked by the siege that ended Maximilian's rule, the liberal victors denigrated the state as a traitorous base of conservative resistance. Seeking a way forward, liberal governor Julio María Cervantes organized councils of leading citizens to restore revenues, commerce, and cultivation, justice, education, and more. Public lighting and urban patrols promised security in the capital and San Juan del Río. A new road to the port of Tampico and a rail link to Mexico City and León were dreams awaiting resources.[75]

The factories that had powered Querétaro's industrial leadership in the 1840s and 1850s struggled after 1867. Cayetano Rubio continued to claim ever more of the water that passed his mills while people working *huertas* along the river below still complained of shortages and pollution. When two mills run by competitors closed, Rubio monopolized industrial employment. He pressed down wages and began to pay in scrip redeemable only at a company store, in time provoking Querétaro's first strike in 1877. More than 300 workers left to work at mills in Tlalpan, south of Mexico City. New president Porfirio Díaz, a liberal open to compromise to solidify power, stopped payment in scrip. The strike ended, production resumed, and industry hung on at Querétaro into the liberal era.[76]

A time of war and political polarization, social predations and economic disruptions, saw population decline across the Bajío. The population of Querétaro, reported near 180,000 in 1855, was counted at 153,286 in 1873, a fall approaching 15 percent.[77] From 1855 to 1868, the population of

Guanajuato reportedly fell from 874,474 to 729,988, more than 16 percent.[78] The decline was likely nearer 10 percent, due to an overestimate in the 1855 Querétaro count and a radical undercount at León in 1868.[79] Still, a fall of 10 percent revealed deep regional dislocations.

The Bajío that saw a dynamic post-revolutionary silver-industrial capitalism drive to new heights in the 1850s became the focus of liberal and French-imperial drives to power from the late 1850s into the 1860s, costing the basin primacy in Mexico. Still, silver-industrial capitalism showed resilient strength in regions less pummeled by the wars of the 1850s and 1860s: While Guanajuato silver fell to half its historic peaks of 1849 to 1852, national flows rose to hold above 19 million pesos yearly from 1868 to 1870, the highest level since 1810. And while industry faded at Querétaro, it expanded from Veracruz through Puebla to regions around Mexico City and Guadalajara.[80]

Centers of silver shifted and industry dispersed, with everything still sustained by family maize makers: rancheros who thrived from the Bajío to the uplands of Jalisco and Michoacán; tenants and sharecroppers in the Bajío and regions north; indigenous families in the heartland and regions south. Despite being pummeled by war in the Bajío, the silver-industrial capitalism fed by family maize growers seemed poised to revive in Mexico after 1867. Producing people everywhere showed remarkable resiliency coming out of midcentury times of polarization, disruption, and predation.

Breaking Mexico on a Cross of Gold

Then, in 1873, the United States delivered a second assault that broke the silver-industrial capitalism that rose in the wake of the Bajío revolution and began to revive after the restoration of liberal rule in 1867. Funded by California and Colorado gold taken by war in the 1840s, the United States joined Britain and Germany on a gold standard, radically devaluing silver in the industrial world. Historically, New Spain's silver had generated the capital to fund dynamism at home and fuel global trades. After the Bajío revolution, silver revived to fund a new silver-industrial capitalism poised to expand and revive historic northward drives. The US invasion of 1846 blocked northward expansion. The industrial powers' turn to gold in 1873 broke the power of silver in global capitalism, ending centuries of capital independence in New Spain and then Mexico.

As the value of silver plummeted. Capital dependency shaped Mexico's future. Silver production still rose in volume and peso value but became ever less valuable in gold-ruled global finance and trade. Output valued near 20 million pesos in 1870 rose to 40 million pesos yearly by 1890, and 60 million pesos by 1900—tripling its value in silver. Its value in gold barely matched Mexico's population growth of 50 percent.[81]

Complex ramifications followed: Mexican industry held on. Factories operating in the 1870s had purchased machinery while silver retained value; in the years that followed, imported cloth became more costly in silver pesos, protecting markets for national textiles.[82] In the 1880s, seeking railroads to integrate the national economy and link Mexico to US markets, the Díaz regime contracted foreign funding in gold; revenues gained in depreciating silver created rising debts.[83] By the 1890s, trunk lines reached from Mexico City, through the Bajío to Laredo and El Paso—with links to St. Louis and Chicago, Denver, Los Angeles, and San Francisco. With the power of silver gone, Mexico built a new industrial-export economy dependent on US capital and tied to US markets. The promise of the Bajío revolution and the silver-industrial capitalism sustained by family growers broke in 1873. Mexicans were left to search for new futures.

Mexico Since 1875

Silver Gone, Families Carry On—Until Globalizing
Capital Claimed Maize

After 1875, power, production, and life changed radically in the Bajío and across Mexico. With the power of silver as capital gone, politics stabilized under Porfirio Diáz' moderate liberal rule while US capital and markets reshaped economic life. Families continued to make maize and more while liberal privatizations and population growth combined to corrode family cultivation before 1910. A second revolution forced land redistributions that brought a revival of family cropping tied to an experiment in national industry from 1910 to 1950. Then population explosion and technological innovations ended autonomies on the land as urbanizing globalization transformed Mexico and the world. A century and a half of transforming changes began with the end of capital independence and concluded with the end of family autonomies.

Mexicans faced political stability unprecedented since 1810, while economic dependencies deepened as global industrial capitalism peaked from 1876 to 1910. They lived a second revolution that brought a new state and an attempt at national capitalism grounded in restored family maize making from 1910 to 1950. Political stability held in a Cold War world as unprecedented population explosions urbanized lives and industrialized maize from 1950 to 1990. Then globalization and North American integration entrenched capital dependencies, driving Mexicans north while capitalist maize making settled in the United States. Mexicans at home and across El Norte live locked in dependent insecurities. The medical and technological marvels that generated such transforming changes benefit a powerful, favored, and prosperous few while growing numbers face insecurities and desperations, fueling violence that increasingly pummels women.[1]

Liberal Consolidation, Capital Dependence, Family Corrosions, 1875–1910

When Porfirio Díaz raised liberal military forces to oust Sebastián Lerdo de Tejada as president in 1876, he led the last armed transfer of national power in Mexico's nineteenth century. After conservative defeats in the wars of the 1850s and their failed collaboration with French imperial forces in the 1860s, liberals ruled. Benito Juárez and Lerdo pressed radical and disruptive anti-indigenous, anti-labor, and anticlerical policies from 1867. Then Díaz moderated his stances while recruiting foreign capital to build a rail network that integrated the Mexican and US economies and brought new export development.[2] He consolidated state power by depoliticizing the military that set him to rule, turning it to social control while regional allies built police and prisons to deal with local conflicts.[3]

After 1873, the Bajío never reclaimed the global power it held as the engine of New Spain's silver capitalism, nor the national leadership built in the wake of the 1810 revolution. Still, its mines, industries, and maize remained important to Mexico and North America. The rail lines heading north from Mexico City in the 1880s passed through Querétaro before one continued on to San Luis Potosí, Monterrey, and Laredo, another turned northwest via León to Zacatecas, Torreón, and El Paso, with a branch west to Guadalajara and the Pacific.

Guanajuato mining continued under Miguel Rul's leadership; production fell in volume and more radically in value in gold.[4] Hard labors continued while regional prosperity waned.[5] Querétaro kept industrial and commercial ways as a center of rail transport.[6] León's leather and shoe industries and craft weaving rose to serve national markets. And the Bajío remained sustained by estates planting wheat while rancheros and tenants, subtenants and sharecroppers made maize and more.[7] Prosperous and well fed, the Bajío no longer led Mexico's economy.

Meanwhile, new export economies rose across Mexico's diverse regions. In the coastal foothills of Veracruz, Oaxaca, and Chiapas, growers turned to coffee, drawing indigenous highlanders to seasonal labor. The latter gained wages to supplement maize made on community lands, sustaining themselves and subsidizing coffee planters. Women regularly trekked to pick while patriarchy solidified in home communities.[8] Elsewhere, indigenous peoples led export economies: Totonacs ruled a vanilla boom at Papantla; in the rainforests of southeast Yucatán, Maya peoples independent since the 1840s "Caste War" ruled production of chicle for export in a new chewing gum economy. In both regions family maize makers sustained everything and patriarchy held strong.[9]

In dry northwest Yucatán, Mayas faced absorption as workers at estates raising henequen to make twine for machines harvesting wheat across the Mississippi basin. Planters ruled, men labored, while women ground maize to make tortillas.[10] In diverse ways, indigenous people across Mesoamerican Mexico joined, sustained, and subsidized new export economies serving global markets.

Mineral exports boomed too. The volume of Mexican silver production rose to new heights as its value in gold waned.[11] New techniques of mining and refining cut costs and labor, a turn led in the 1890s by the Guggenheim's America Smelting and Refining Company. They brought US capital to build massive industrial smelting complexes at Aguascalientes and Monterrey, drawing ore by rail from across the Mexican north, shipping refined silver and profits to the United States.[12] Maize raised by rancheros and tenants sustained the new silver economy and Guggenheim profits too.

When copper rose at Cananea just south of the Arizona border, William Greene brought capital and new technology to mine the metal essential to an electrifying world, while maize makers in Hispanic Chihuahua and Yaqui Sonora sustained his production and profits.[13] When oil was found after 1900 in Gulf lowlands near Tampico, Englishman Weetman Pearson and Californian Edward Doheny imported capital, drills, and the essentials of refining to drive production for export—sustained by local indigenous maize growers.[14] Mexico's new export capitalism was fed by family-made maize.

The rise of Monterrey showed the potential and limits of the new industrial-export economy. Long an outpost of Spanish settlement surrounded by native maize makers and grazing estates, in the eighteenth century its region sent livestock south to the Bajío and people north to Texas. The Bajío revolution and the fall of silver capitalism rattled those links as Comanche and other independent peoples pressed south. When the War for North America set a new border at the Rio Grande, Monterrey began to rise as a commercial-industrial center. A cotton factory came in 1853, part of the new silver-industrial capitalism. During the US Civil War, local merchants, European and Mexican, took raw cotton sent south across the river, labeled it Mexican, and shipped it out at Matamoros, via Havana, to buyers in England and New England—drawing capital to the borderland city.[15]

When rails came in the 1880s, Monterrey capitalists were ready. They imported machines to build the Fundidora, an iron and steel complex making rails for Mexico's national network. Ore and coal came from nearby Coahuila, solving the energy challenges that limited industries in the center and south before the coming of oil after 1900.[16] With textiles established, trunk lines built, and iron ore and coal nearby, Monterrey-made rails carried imported engines and rolling stock across Mexico.

Monterrey capitalists, immigrant and national, soon built a beer industry that also made glass bottles and cardboard boxes, profiting by challenging pulque as the fuel of recreation and release in urban industrial Mexico. And the Guggenheims sent capital and technology to build a new silver refining complex, processing ores drawn from across Mexico's north to send silver to the United States—a profitable extraction that became the base of celebrated philanthropies focused in the United States.[17] Monterrey became a borderlands industrial center integrating the US and Mexican economies, producing for both markets, while dependent on imported capital and technologies in key sectors. The city was fed by maize made by nearby family growers, estates across the northeast, and in years of scarcity by imports from the United States—a harbinger of times to come.

Textile mills also flourished from Veracruz through Puebla to Mexico City, around Guadalajara and beyond.[18] Many drew women to labor, rattling patriarchy to hold men's wages down. And industry everywhere was sustained by maize made by indigenous families, Hispanic rancheros, diverse tenants, and commercial growers. After silver fell, maize fed Mexico's new industrial-export capitalism.

While state powers consolidated, political and social violence stayed local, industry held on and exports rose, renewed population growth pressured ways of sustenance in a national territory halved by losses to the US in 1848. From 9.5 million in 1876, numbers reached 15 million in 1895. The demographic rise indicates solid sustenance, still made mostly by family growers. Yet the average heights that peaked in 1850 as the silver capitalism grounded in family maize making rose, fell to lows after 1900.[19] As population rose, nutrition deteriorated in the face of land privatizations that cut family cropping in indigenous communities while new exports drove profit-seeking land use in coastal zones and the borderlands. Export expansions limited planting for sustenance while offering little labor to those working to survive. Exports boomed while social pressures rose.

Another Revolution: Claiming Maize for Families, Dreaming of National Capitalism, 1910–1950

The Mexico remade after 1873—dependent on US capital and markets, sustaining industry and promoting exports, and fed by Mexican maize makers facing steady corrosions—broke in a second revolution unleashed in 1910. It began amid another regime crisis: the problem of succession as Porfirio Díaz' lifetime liberal-authoritarian rule approached its end. Economic challenges deepened when Mexico adopted the gold standard in 1905, demonetizing already devalued silver. Then the US economy collapsed in the Panic of 1907, bringing challenges deepened by another drought after 1908. With politics shaken, the economy rattled, and rural families struggling, popular risings focused in two key regions from 1910: the heartland south of Mexico City and the northern borderlands.

In the heartland, community-based people whose forbears had stayed home during the Bajío revolution after 1810 rose to drive Emiliano Zapata's revolution after 1910. Historically grounded in self-governing landed republics, they had sustained silver capitalism through the eighteenth century, adapting to population growth by mixing family cultivation with seasonal labor in estate fields. After 1820 they retrenched in community ways as landed oligarchs struggled. Villagers resisted pressures to privatize lands in the 1840s and 1850s, then took arms when Juárez became assertive in the late 1860s—making commitments to community-based family cultivation adamantly clear.[20]

In the face of that resistance, Juárez, Lerdo, and Díaz backed off hard privatizations. The goal remained, often implemented by undocumented transformations that proclaimed privatization without completing surveys or providing titles. When population growth pressed families, plots were divided, sold, and seized for debts. Local merchant-accumulators gained while growing numbers of men lived without land after 1890. Meanwhile, access to labor declined as sugar refineries industrialized around Cuernavaca, upland wheat growers mechanized planting and harvesting, and transport turned from mules to rails. Men struggled to provide while women searched for ways to sustain families. A new generation of men denied the role of "provider" joined Zapata in long fights to restore patriarchal sustenance.[21] A community-based replay of the Bajío revolution powered Zapata's heartland rising after 1910.

The northern risings led by Pancho Villa came out of challenges that struck the regions that became borderlands in 1848 and were energized by rail transport and export economies from the 1880s. For two decades, new economies boomed, drawing people north to work in exports and industries, and on the estates and ranchos that sustained everything. Exports broke after Mexico joined the US on the gold standard in 2005, then the Panic of 2007 saw US capital fall and markets crash. Francisco Madero, son of a leading northern banking, industrial, and landed family, led the political challenge to Díaz in 1910, backed by popular risings led by Villa and others. While corrosive liberal privatizations in times of population growth and rural mechanizations led to community risings in the heartland, the collapse of the industrial-export economy drove political rebellion and popular risings in the north.[22]

In both regions, men fought to restore patriarchal family production on the land: community-based in the heartland; ranchero-focused in the north. In both, women mobilized to sustain insurgents while facing disruptions and violence. In the Zapatista heartland, communities took the land and claimed lives making maize during the decade of revolution. In the north, Villa promised to deliver land to remake ranchero lives after victory—which never came.[23]

While men in pursuit of national power and people on the land in the heartland and the borderlands took arms, most people in the Bajío stayed home and at work during the 1910 revolution. No longer an engine of capitalist dynamism, its family growers faced limited pressures on the land. Still, the basin mattered. Northern liberal Constitutionalists led by Venustiano Carranza and Álvaro Obregón gained power in 1915, first by containing Zapatista guerrillas beyond the mountains south of Mexico City, then fighting at El Ébano to hold the oil fields around Tampico—holding export revenues that peaked during Europe's Great War. Those earnings funded a siege of industrial Monterrey that blocked access to raw materials, energy, markets, and maize to break a Villista–Maderista alliance focused in the city. The fall of Monterrey derailed an agrarian-industrial-religious coalition, everything the Constitutionalists were not.[24] With Zapata contained, oil revenue strong, and Monterrey broken, the final battles to defeat Villa came in the Bajío—at Celaya and then León from April into June 1915. In 1917, the victors assembled in Querétaro to write a constitution laden with contradictions.

The new charter promised land rights to communities, labor rights to workers, and subsoil rights to the nation—all responding to revolutionary demands, all diverging from core Liberal-Constitutionalist dreams. The Bajío revolution of 1810 and the national conflagration of 1910 mixed political fights for power with popular risings seeking autonomies on the land amid global wars and capitalist transformations. When Mexico began in 1821, New Spain's silver capitalism had fallen, Anglo-American industrial capitalism was rising, and Bajío insurgents had claimed new lives on the land, forcing struggling landlords and insecure state makers to adapt. In 1917, armed state makers claimed power in Mexico as Anglo-American allies won a war that preserved industrial capitalism. Liberal-Constitutionalists set pacifying visions of agrarian redistribution in a new constitution, then worked long and hard to delay and deflect implementation.[25]

Zapata had been killed, his movement constrained, when Obregón ousted Carranza in 1920. Seeking Zapatista support to consolidate rule, the general who brought the Constitutionalists to power began to deliver land to heartland communities in the early 1920s, aiming to pacify long-resistant people and tie them to the new regime. More accurately, he aimed to tie men to the regime. After women again mobilized to sustain families, communities, and guerrillas in times of revolution, the reconstruction of the 1920s was set by an armed state that reinforced patriarchy by awarding ejido land only to men.[26]

The rise of family cultivation after 1810 began with Bajío insurgents and spread after 1820 as commercial planters struggled and state powers flailed—enabling local autonomies and opening new roles to women. The restoration of family cultivation after 1920 responded to insurgent demands rooted in the heartland, but was designed and implemented by reviving state powers that resisted local autonomies and restricted women's gains.

The new reform proved reluctant and limited. In the mid-1920s, Obregón's successor, Plutarco Elías Calles, turned against agrarian reform to focus on anticlerical programs, aiming to drive the clergy from public life. His turn to classic liberalism led to Cristero risings across Michoacán, Guanajuato, Jalisco, and regions beyond, again mobilizing fighting men and sustaining women to defend local autonomies, cultural and more. Calles learned again that to recruit fighters loyal to the regime, he had to deliver land to communities. Men seeking to restore maize from Veracruz to San Luis Potosí gained land by defending a regime pressing anticlericalism into ranchero communities in Michoacán, the Bajío, and beyond.

Meanwhile, the world changed. While Obregón, Calles, and their successors fought to rule, global oil shifted operations from Mexico to Venezuela to avoid threats of nationalization as henequen exports fell to global competition.[27] The export economies that sustained the Constitutionalists' liberal dreams became ever less viable while communities still pressed for land and cultural autonomies. When global depression broke industrial capitalism in the 1930s, ending Mexican access to US capital and markets, liberal economic, social, and cultural policies became untenable—even when pressed by "revolutionaries."[28]

Taking power as president in 1934, Lázaro Cárdenas marginalized Calles, sent him into exile, and turned to reconstructions that recognized a changing world and popular demands. He accelerated land reform, enabling a revival of family maize making that brought a national surge in nutrition.[29] He promoted national industry and set labor rights as national policy. He nationalized petroleum in 1938, aiming to forge a new national capitalism led by industry, promising rights to workers, and sustained by family maize growers—all incorporated in a mediating, party-based authoritarian regime.[30] More than a century after the 1808 coup broke New Spain's mediating regime and set military men in power, Cárdenas pulled armed forces back from national politics and returned to state mediations to stabilize a national capitalism he dreamed would be led by oil and industry—and he knew had to be fed by family-made maize.

Liberal legacies endured in national education programs that Cárdenas labeled socialist—perhaps to cover his drive to national capitalism. Few nineteenth-century liberals would have objected to anything but the socialist label—and new openings to women as teachers and students. Many Catholics saw a return to liberal impositions and mobilized in opposition. Yet by delivering land to men in ejido grants and openings to women in education, Cárdenas divided to rule. He built a secular regime promoting national capitalism by restoring mediating governance while reviving Mesoamerican traditions of patriarchal family maize making.[31]

The project held through World War II. In 1942, Cárdenas joined his successor's cabinet as defense minister, focused on supporting the US war effort. He turned Mexico's national industrial-agrarian economy to deliver copper and oil, food and cloth, and bracero workers in an alliance of capitalist neighbors in time of global war. Mexico acquiesced in the drafting of nearly half a million Mexican citizens into the US military, where they faced deadly action. Then, when the war ended, the US recognized Mexico's support by turning to subsidize capital and open markets for allies and foes from Europe to Asia, leaving Mexico and other American nations to fend for themselves in a new Cold War world.[32]

Population Explosion, Urbanization, and "Green Revolution," 1950–1990

In the 1930s, the political Cárdenas understood that he had to deliver land to family maize makers to stabilize his regime. The capitalist Cárdenas worried that land recipients fed families first, delivering limited surpluses to sustain the urban industrial Mexico he saw as the nation's future. Seeking a way forward, at the 1940 inauguration, when Cárdenas handed power to Miguel Ávila Camacho, the promoter of national capitalism stood next to Nelson Rockefeller and US vice president Henry Wallace. Rockefeller came with foundation funding; Wallace brought the expertise of his family's business, Pioneer Seeds. Together they would introduce mechanized cultivation based on hybrid seeds and chemical fertilizers, pesticides, and herbicides to Mexico. The goal was to adapt industrial-chemical agriculture to raise wheat on Mexico's high dry lands, feeding urban consumers. That "green revolution" earned Norman Borlaug a Nobel Prize.

After the war, US pharmaceutical companies came to sell the lifesaving antibiotics developed to keep allied soldiers alive, now offered to save children in families across Mexico.[33] To great joy, growing numbers survived childhood maladies, driving Mexico's population from under 20 million in 1940 to near 50 million by 1970. To feed that soaring population, Mexican leaders turned the green revolution to maize. Production and yields soared, too. But hybrid seeds cannot be kept from the previous harvest, requiring annual purchases along with costly chemical fertilizers, pesticides, and herbicides. Made by machines few families could afford, new harvests yielded maize enough to sustain rapidly growing numbers—while eliminating human work. Family maize making dissolved as industrial-chemical ways of cultivation spread across Mexico after 1950.[34]

Displaced people fled to cities where foreign capital fueled cycles of boom and collapse, industrial machines made more goods with ever fewer workers, and *molinos de nixtamal* liberated women from endless hours of labor grinding maize to make tortillas.[35] In a mechanizing, urbanizing world, men struggled to find work and income while women became less burdened with labors of sustenance—escaping painful work—too often without compensating access to earnings. They struggled to find income to buy maize and more—while Mexico City grew from 2 million people in 1940 to almost 9 million in 1970.[36]

The Mexico forged under Cárdenas in the 1930s and consolidated in ties to a US at war in the 1940s, faced unprecedented challenges when population pressure met "labor-saving" technologies in the 1950s. Deepening inequities laced with insecurities fueled urban and rural challenges to the regime in the 1960s, threats to stability met by violence. Cycles of boom and bust driven by foreign capital led to repeated crashes. Wealth concentrated among a favored few; prosperity spread among middle sectors; favored labor sectors gained solid incomes and benefits—while rural growers were pressed off the land and urban majorities faced deepening insecurities. Student protests in 1968 revealed discontent among frustrated middle-class youth; the government massacre at Tlatelolco announced a return to military repression.[37]

In the 1970s, the regime tried a return to mediations while OPEC (the Organization of the Petroleum Exporting Countries) raised global energy costs and rattled capitalism everywhere. US capital rushed to fund production in deep oil reservoirs recently found by Petróleos Mexicanos (PEMEX), the national oil monopoly founded by Cárdenas. An oil boom revived prosperities unequally shared from 1977 to 1981. Then the surge in Mexican oil joined North Sea flows to break OPEC prices, leaving PEMEX and the regime unable to pay enormous debts to US banks. New York lenders had funded PEMEX, aiming to increase supplies and bring down prices. Could they be surprised that success brought impossible debts and financial collapse to Mexico?[38]

The fall of petro-industrial development grounded in chemical cultivation left Mexicans to face a lost decade—a crash far worse that the earlier depression, when family-made maize cushioned the national crisis. The authoritarian-mediating regime forged by Lázaro Cárdenas in the 1930s lost legitimacy; calls to democratize in pursuit of national welfare were led by his son Cuauhtémoc. Others downplayed the role of US capital and global markets in driving the boom of the late 1970s and the collapse of 1981, calling for global integration in the world of power. In 1986, Mexico joined the General Agreement on Tariffs and Trade (GATT), beginning a global turn. In 1988, the younger Cárdenas "lost" a disputed election to Carlos Salinas de Gortari—who led Mexico into the North American Free Trade Agreement (NAFTA), accelerating globalization in the 1990s.[39]

Globalizing Lives, Entrenched Insecurities, Regime Challenges: 1990–2025

Mexico's population continued to soar, reaching 20 million in the capital metropolis and 100 million across the nation by 2000. Without capital made by silver or petroleum, without sustenance set in family cultivation or secure wages, Mexicans struggled. NAFTA promised open borders for capital and goods, while aiming to lock people in home nations. The goal was to hold Mexicans as low-waged workers for industries invited to locate among them. In the lead-up to the pact, Salinas broke Mexican unions to ensure wages held low.[40] In 1992, he opened the ejido lands long granted as state-protected family holdings to privatization, bringing classic Mexican liberalism to neoliberalization. He hoped to promote sales and commercialization. Many refrained, knowing landlessness would surely follow.[41]

On January 1, 1994, the day NAFTA took effect, middle-class rebels led a rising of Maya peoples in the Chiapas lowlands at Mexico's far southern edge. Many had been driven from highland homes by landlessness, to face new lives in tropics first rattled by petroleum boom in nearby Tabasco, then disrupted by its crash, all while revolutionary conflicts rose across the border in Guatemala. Leaders labeled the movement Zapatista to honor the revolutionary who led heartland rebels after 1910. The rising claimed national and global attention, yet proved brief. Within two weeks, the Mexican military forced a stalemate. Long negotiations generated much rhetoric and little change.[42] A repeat of Zapata's historic revolt proved impossible. After industrial-chemical cropping ended family maize making across Mexico, no third revolution sustained by families on the land would come.[43] Without local maize, no rebellion could endure to restore lives of family autonomy on the land.

Meanwhile, Salinas moved toward late summer elections. When his chosen candidate Luis Donaldo Colosio was assassinated, he turned to Ernesto Zedillo. During the campaign, Salinas kept the value of the peso artificially high, holding economic prosperity. He devalued in December, setting off a crash as Zedillo took office. The first year of NAFTA began with rural insurgency and ended in economic collapse. The former was contained by military force, the latter limited by US financial assistance. Meanwhile, the jobs Salinas hoped to draw to Mexico flowed to China. The promise of NAFTA, built on presumptions of minimally paid work for Mexicans, proved even less than the little advertised.

Mexicans became Mexico's primary export, as millions fled north seeking new chances in lands once Mexican—subsidizing US power and prosperity with minimally paid labors. In an ultimate migration, capitalist cultivation of maize moved north to the United States. Mississippi basin lands and the great plains proved ideal for making mechanized, chemically fueled crops— and profitable thanks to US government subsidies. Mexicans lived dependent on imported maize while global agribusiness turned Mexican lands to fruits and vegetables made with chemicals and seasonal hands, and sold to ready US consumers.[44]

The Bajío found new importance in the world remade by NAFTA. Its rich lands make strawberries, broccoli, and more for US markets, while car makers, plane manufacturers, and others tap local workers to finish industrial goods shipped north. The lands of La Griega are now Querétaro's international airport, serving factories assembling corporate jets for Canada's Bombardier Corporation and its worldwide customers. Capitalists profit and workers get by—employed because they gain less than those in the United States and Canada. In the Bajío and across a heartland now 85 percent urban, north in Aguascalientes, Saltillo, and Hermosillo, and along the border, transnational capital profits in auto and electronics assembly plants. The industrial workers employed there, men and women, are a minority of Mexicans "favored" by wages definitionally low by North American standards. Larger majorities struggle with insecurity and marginality in urban barrios as prosperity holds scarce and sustenance stays uncertain.

Showing historic resilience, Mexicans revived historical migrations north to build new lives across the US, in lands once Mexican and far beyond. They face prejudice as their work profits a powerful few while making food, building cities, and providing services to sustain a prosperous many. Industrial maize made in the USA profits global capitalism while Mexicans struggle to sustain themselves and others by laboring across an urbanizing North America.

Then there is the other economy. In times of NAFTA, a long-developing binational drug economy rose to incalculable yet unquestioned eminence. As capital made in Mexico vanished in legally sanctioned trades, Mexican drug cartels concentrated wealth. While Mexican maize making waned, cultivation of marijuana and opioids rose—until the former became legal and the latter was replaced by chemical fentanyl. Again, profit soared while paying work vanished. Now, as opioids and fentanyl remain illegal, cartels raise armed forces to protect their means of production, transport, and sales, challenging state power by replicating state power.[45]

Powerful interests in the United States ensure that weapons keep flowing to cartels in Mexico and gangs across North America. Sustaining everything, drug demand holds strong across the United States, in cities and towns, among the wealthy, the prosperous, the poor, and the desperate. Lives shaped by pervasive insecurities send too many in search of a fix that can never be a solution—except for cartel capitalists. Drug capitalism concentrates wealth and consolidates dependencies, while endless violence challenges and sustains state rule—maiming struggling bodies, families, and communities.[46]

In our urbanizing globalizing world, with provision set in family maize making gone, community-based revolution impossible, and inequities and dependent insecurities fueling desperations everywhere, violence is pervasive. Most notably, violence by men upon women has become an everyday plague in Mexico and across North America, too.

When men made maize and women made tortillas, linked during relations of family sustenance, they negotiated patriarchal powers and inequities. When predations blocked patriarchal provision while family sustenance of the land remained possible, men turned to revolutions backed by sustaining women to twice reclaim lives making maize on the land—challenging patriarchy in communities built in insurgency after 1810; reinforcing patriarchy in state-made ejidos after 1920. Now, with maize lost to globalizing capitalism, men without ways to provide do violence upon each other and on women in an endless pandemic of destructions.[47]

The End of History

All this marks the end of a macro-cycle in the histories of Mesoamerica, New Spain, and Mexico, North America and global capitalism. Family-made maize fed communities and kingdoms in Mesoamerica as population grew toward 25 million around 1500. The invasion of old-world pathogens cut that population radically, breaking kingdoms, devastating families and communities—and opening land to enable ample maize making by survivors. China's turn to silver in the 1550s brought unprecedented chances for profit to Europeans in New Spain, leading to a new world of silver capitalism fed by maize. Sustenance came in two variants: in the self-governing landed republics rebuilt in the Mesoamerican heartland around Mexico City and in regions south; at profit-seeking commercial estates worked by migrants from Mesoamerica, people bound from Africa, and their amalgamating offspring in the Bajío and regions north.

When the eighteenth century brought silver boom and population revival, people in heartland republics mixed family cultivation with men's seasonal labor at nearby estates to maintain patriarchy, families, and communities. In the Bajío, agrarian capitalists turned predatory in the 1790s, cutting estate residents' earnings and maize rations, raising rents and evicting tenants—predations that became deadly in the drought of 1808 to 1810 as imperial crisis broke mediating rule. In that crucible of challenges, men unable to provide for families across rural Guanajuato took arms to claim their definition of independence: family maize making on the land. In a decade of fighting, they gained land while women took new roles in cultivation and community life. Together they broke Asian trades, opening the world to new Anglo-American industrial ways grounded in expansions of slavery.

Communities remade in and after the Bajío revolution held strong on the land to sustain the new silver-industrial capitalism that rose to flourish from 1830 to 1860. In time, however, the new capitalism grounded in family maize making was rattled by US invasion and Mexican liberal impositions, then pummeled in the Bajío by French imperial predations. Yet it survived, poised to revive across Mexico after 1867, when in 1873 the United States demonetized silver. Centuries of history capitalized by silver and sustained by maize ended.

After the fall of silver, a new export-industrial capitalism rose across Mexico, sustained by family maize makers until agrarian capitalism set new predations upon heartland communities after 1890 and borderlands export capitalism collapsed after 1907. When regime crisis and drought merged again after 1908, men in Zapata's heartland and Villa's borderlands rose in 1910 to drive a new revolution aiming to revive family maize making. They forced an agrarian reconstruction that enabled family growers to feed themselves and sustain a new national-industrial capitalism to 1950. Then, global medical capitalism sent populations soaring, driving urbanizations fed by industrial-chemical maize. Family maize making vanished while new generations faced uncertain, often desperate lives in Mexican cities and across the United States.[48]

Finally, globalizing capitalism took maize north to be made by machines and chemicals in the United States. It sustains Mexico, North America, and much of the world—while Mexicans face near exclusion from production of the staple that fed Mesoamerica, New Spain, and Mexico for millennia.[49]

The United States joined rising industrial hegemons to break the power of silver as capital in the 1870s. US capitalists took control of maize making as the twentieth century ended. A new era marked by globalizing urbanization, family insecurities, and proliferating violence profits global capital, legal and illegal, while plaguing Mexicans and countless others. Is there a way forward to shared prosperity, secure sustenance, gender equity, and lives of hope? If we care about justice or just basic sustenance, we must ask.

ACKNOWLEDGMENTS

The Bajío Revolution culminates more than a half century of learning, research, and writing, aimed at rethinking the history of Mexico from the perspective of people on the land—while in time taking on more complex questions of power and global capitalism. My debts are infinite. Every person and institution acknowledged in my previous work, every scholar cited, every student who made me think in new ways—all earn continuing thanks.

A core earns renewed honor. At Wellesley High School, William Chapman taught me that history mattered and must be relevant to contemporary challenges. Mildred Thelen was a great Spanish teacher. She sent me to the New England Spoken Spanish Contest, where victory earned me a summer in San Miguel de Allende in 1965. There I engaged Mexican history and culture while the historic Bajío town remained a center of art and history—not yet a retreat for the wealthy. I heard Edmundo O'Gorman speak on Mexican history. I joined a friend's visit to an optometrist in Celaya, where on entering the office I faced an aerial photo of the Southbridge, Massachusetts, home of American Optical Company, where my father had worked. While I struggled to process that encounter with global capitalism, a Mexican man I saw as a peasant came in. Opening a chat to pass the time, the young gringo on his way to college learned that the Mexican who worked the land was the most perceptive, philosophical, and worldly person he had ever met. My need to understand Mexicans living on the land began that day.

When I returned to attend Holy Cross College, William Green pressed me to become an analytical scholar writing clear prose. He showed me first that my prose was fuzzy; when my writing improved, he saw my fuzzy thinking and pressed me to analyze more clearly. I am still trying. The honors program led by John Anderson welcomed me as a Fenwick Scholar, the student with the lowest GPA ever to gain that privilege. It allowed me to pursue an independent thesis free of curricular demands in my senior year. I took on the 1910 agrarian revolution in Mexico—to face the midyear publication of John Womack's *Zapata and the Mexican Revolution*, again teaching me how little I knew.

I learned enough to join the doctoral program in Latin American history at the University of Texas at Austin in the fall of 1969. Students warned me to avoid Nettie Lee Benson. Richard Sinkin wisely told me that advice was stupid. Returning in the fall of 1970, I engaged Miss Benson—who told me if I would learn the political history that she found essential, she would welcome my pursuit of social history. I tried and she did. Under her guidance I completed my first study of estates and communities in postindependence Chalco—the beginning of everything I have attempted since. She told the editors of the *Hispanic American Historical Review* to publish the work, and after years of analytical and textual streamlining, they did. What began in San Miguel in the Bajío thanks to Miss Thelen, energized in encounters with Chalco in the heartland thanks to Miss Benson.

Others came on board: James Lockhart taught me local social history; Richard Graham showed me global perspectives on Brazil and Latin America; and Richard Adams drew me to new ways of thinking at the intersection of material power, ways of production, and cultural adaptations. I met Friedrich Katz when he joined weeks of discussions in Adams's seminar on structural theory. In Austin, too, I found a community of student-scholars who have shaped my life and career. Pat Carroll was there when I arrived in the fall of 1969. In the fall of 1971, at a picnic to welcome Lorenzo Meyer as a visiting scholar, my wife, Jane, met Lynore Brown and Carolyn Melosi; they brought Jonathan, Marty, and me together. We still teach and encourage each other more than a half century later.

On landing a joint appointment in Latin American history at St. Olaf and Carleton Colleges in Minnesota beginning in 1977, colleagues encouraged me to teach based on engaging diverse texts while challenging students to think and write independently. Richard Klawiter and Andrew Isenberg at St. Olaf and Sarah Pruett, Laura Tilly, and Sarah Chambers at Carleton made me a better teacher while I worked to become a more analytical scholar. Early in the 70s, Asunción Lavrin challenged me to present a paper on women and power in New Spain's landed elite—leading to my first attempt at gendered history, published in *The Americas*. Soon, Tulio Halperin Donghi invited me to visit at Berkeley and Friedrich Katz called me to join the volume *Riot, Rebellion, and Revolution*—drawing me to new scholarly communities and analytical perspectives. All that made *From Insurrection to Revolution* a more insightful and impactful book.

A move to Boston College in 1988 brought the chance to recruit Karen Spalding, the great social historian of Andean peoples, as a stimulating colleague. Our doctoral student Erin O'Connor reminded me again that gender matters. In the same years, Jack Womack invited me to work with a group of Harvard doctoral students, including Jim Brennan, Emilio Kourí, and Aurora Gómez. They remain a circle of engaged stimulation and support.

Landing at Georgetown in 1993 brought me to a transforming community of scholars and students. John McNeill added global perspectives to the ecological questions I first encountered thanks to Marty Melosi. John also drew me to the links between Spanish American silver and China, radically turning my work. Meanwhile, Jim Collins helped me see that states matter while Judith Tucker, Katie Benton-Cohen, and a stream of doctoral students led me to new gendered visions: Larisa Veloz on women and migration from 1890 to 1965; Rebecca Andrews on the strong market women grounded in the chinampas of Xochimilco from 1700 to 1850.

I gained new perspectives on Mexico working with Theresa Alfaro Velcamp on Arab migration. Gillian McGillivray brought me new understandings of sugar, slavery, and revolutions in Cuba, and sugar without slavery in post-revolutionary Mexico. Luis Fernando Granados taught me about Mexico City from 1800 to 1850; Emilio Coral returned me to the city from 1940 to 1970. I discovered regional complexities with Fernando Pérez Montesino on indigenous Michoacán from 1800 to 1920; Rodolfo Fernández on industrial Monterrey from 1880 to 1920; and Adrienne Kates on Maya peoples' chicle tapping and global trades from 1890 to 1940. Hillar Schwertner plumbed the binational challenges of water and capitalism in Tijuandiego in the nineteenth and twentieth centuries. And now Marcella Hardin is exploring the challenges of migration at the Chiapas–Guatemala border from the 1970s to the 1990s, while Victoria Saeki-Serna engages the complexities of Mexican governance in the face of internal challenges and US power from the student revolt of 1968 to the global crash of the 1980s.

Georgetown undergraduates have also been sources of learning and stimulus: among many, Alejandra Domenzain and Peter Stanton, Cody Williams and Martha Guerrero pursued studies grounded in history yet essential to understand and engage a world calling for change—which all have gone on to promote in their own ways.

Scholars who were not my teachers or colleagues also contributed mightily to my ongoing work. Friedrich Katz and William Taylor served as long-term mentors and inspirations. Early on, Enrique Florescano taught me the importance of maize to Mexican history. More recently, Alfredo Ávila delivered essential understandings of the politics of independence. José Antonio Serrano oriented me to the politics of independence in Guanajuato. And Juan Ortíz opened the role of the military in the wars for independence and then revealed the complexities of Felix Calleja's defense of imperial power while extracting personal wealth in silver.

Two Mexican scholars proved crucial to this book. Carlos Herrejón wrote a book on the enlightenment in Guanajuato, provided a collection of documents on Hidalgo, delivered a magisterial study of his life and revolt, to then write an analysis of Morelos—all essential to understand Hidalgo's political revolt, its defeat, and the revolution that followed. Pivotally, Carlos introduced me to Epigmenio González—the shopkeeper who foresaw the goals and key outcomes of the Bajío revolution.

Carlos Armando Preciado de Alba is a younger scholar. I knew him and his work on Guanajuato after independence, but only came to see the importance of his book on the French intervention after I understood the silver-industrial revival in the Bajío from 1830 to 1860. He graciously sent me a copy, enabling me to understand the challenges that shook the Bajío in the 1860s. I could not have written the conclusion without his essential work.

Throughout, key editors have sustained me. When I finished the manuscript that became *From Insurrection to Revolution*, it concluded in 1820 but for an epilogue looking a century forward. Several leading academic presses declined. Sandy Thatcher at Princeton not only took on the project but, in response to Bill Taylor's suggestion that my epilogue was the most innovative part of the study, offered the opportunity to add part 2, rethinking Mexico from 1820 to 1940. The expansion made the book an academic bestseller.

When I turned to the work that became *Making a New World* and now *The Bajío Revolution*, I again approached leading university presses. Again, all but one stepped back. Valerie Millholland, the editor who built Duke's transforming series on Latin America and global labor, gender, and culture issues, offered a contract. When administrative obligations slowed completion, she told me to take the time to get it right. A first version of *Making a New World* focused on the years after 1760 to argue that a precocious capitalism had begun in the Bajío. Bill Taylor again delivered an evaluation that saw the importance of the work—and noted that few would believe it without a detailed engagement with earlier founding centuries. Valerie offered space to write it. The book doubled in length, she published it, and multiple awards justified the expansion.

The reception of *Making a New World*, mostly positive, revealed that few understood how the Bajío differed from the Mesoamerican regions just south. Seeking a remedy, I turned to write *The Mexican Heartland*. A major press offered a contract, then imposed restrictions that made it impossible. I turned to Princeton, where Brigitta van Rheinberg welcomed the volume, and like Sandy Thatcher before her, offered me time and space to extend the analysis another hundred years, continuing to the end of the twentieth century. The book is much better for the challenge and the opportunity.

While writing *Heartland*, I saw the radical turn of regime power from judicial mediation to military imposition that came in the crisis of 1808. To address that pivotal yet little recognized turn, I wrote *Mexico City, 1808*. University of New Mexico editorial director Clark Whitehead and series editor Kris Lane jumped at the offering—making that publication the smoothest to date. The book they facilitated proved foundational to understanding the Bajío revolution and the Mexico that followed.

The current book remains a sequel to *Making a New World*, at the end guided through evaluations by Gisela Fosado, once Valerie Millholland's assistant, now Duke's editorial director. Valerie's spirit inspires us both as we work together to bring a study simultaneously local and global, social and cultural, gendered and political, to completion. Alejandra Mejía has guided a complex volume into production with grace and efficiency.

Learning and teaching are never separate from family. I met Jane Maloney on St. Patrick's Day 1969 as I gained a mix of acceptances and rejections to doctoral programs. She supported my decision to go to Texas—and gave me Gibson's *Aztecs Under Spanish Rule* as a graduation gift. We became closer as she completed her nursing degree from Massachusetts General and went to work as an RN on the cardiac floor at Boston Children's Hospital while I studied Portuguese at Harvard. At the end of the summer, we decided to marry and kept it to ourselves while I went to Austin and Jane remained at Children's. She visited and gained a welcome to Austin and Mexican Texas thanks to Linda Delgado and Nacho Campos. At Christmas we announced our engagement—and I stayed home to pursue a "conscientious objection" while helping coordinate a department of Spanish-speaking women at Beth Israel Hospital and Jane continued caring for children next door.

We married on May 1, 1970—an international Labor Day darkened by Nixon's bombing of Cambodia. Moving to Austin that fall, I returned to classes while Jane went to work at the Student Health Center along with Donna Carroll and Paulette Gravois—soon honored as the "Florence Nightingales of the Night Shift." We soon met the Browns and the Melosis, who with the Carrolls, Gravois, and Campos-Delgados became an intersecting community of strength and survival. Funded by Fulbright to spend 1973 in Mexico City, I worked in the archives while Jane cared for children in the intensive-care unit at IMAN—the National Children's Hospital. Midyear we traveled to serve as *padrinos* to Andrés Campos Delgado.

Back in Austin, my sister Ann provided a beach retreat in Galveston while I finished my PhD and Jane earned her BA in psychology in 1976. While home in Massachusetts to grieve at Jane's dad's funeral, the University of Rhode Island offered a one-year visit that allowed her to live close to her mother and brothers during a difficult year. Off to St. Olaf in 1977, we welcomed María early in 1979. When I was invited by Tulio Halperin to teach Mexican history at Berkeley in 1981, we met the active world of greater San Francisco—knowing Gabriela would join us back in Minnesota as winter set in. An NEH-funded year in Austin in 1983–84 allowed me to write *From Insurrection to Revolution* while we reconnected with the Melosi, Gravois, Campos, and Delgado clans. Paulette Gravois entertained our girls while Jane and I took an excursion through Zacatecas, Aguascalientes, and Guadalajara, across the Bajío, and back north through San Luis Potosí—a close encounter with regions that focus this work.

Back in Minnesota, Jane became the state's first rural AIDS educator, I finished the expanded *From Insurrection*, and María wondered why as a grown-up I kept going to school. The book opened new possibilities: Boston College offered me a job beginning in 1988, giving our daughters the chance to live near grandparents, aunts, uncles, and cousins. My dad and Gramma Lil moved to Cape Cod to give us a retreat near the beach. When BC denied tenure to Karen Spalding, my presence became untenable. While stewing in my office knowing appeals were exhausted, the phone rang. Arturo Valenzuela wondered if I might move to Georgetown. In 1993, I joined a globalizing history department and an energetic Latin America studies program. María and Gabriela found better schools; Dad and Lil moved back to Virginia Beach to keep us nearby—and near the beach. Jane lamented the move away from her vast family but found meaning attending to the health of Georgetown students, a commitment she took on with her usual caring energy.

The history department called me to be director of graduate studies and then chair through the years after 2000 while I worked to write *Making a New World*. As I left department responsibilities behind, time and the success of that book enabled Jane and me to travel: to Ireland, Jane's ancestral world; to London and Poland for conferences; to Madrid and Seville for research essential to *The Bajío Revolution*; to Barcelona, Salamanca, and back to Madrid for conferences; and repeatedly to Mexico City, Querétaro, and Guanajuato for last bits of research.

Meanwhile, María graduated from the University of Virginia, worked for a time in the Civil Rights Division of the US Justice Department, earned an MA in international affairs at Georgetown, and won a Fulbright to Mexico. There she met Israel Mejía, now her husband. The obstacles to marrying a Mexican offered hard learning about the worst of binational relations in the crisis years of 2008–11. They surmounted and their union brought bicultural strength to our family that included Israel's mother, Pilar, until she left us amid COVID-19 in Mexico City—another sad learning experience.

Gabriela, too, faced diverse life challenges until, inspired by becoming Aunty Gaby to her friend Leanne's daughter Theresa, she completed an education in early childhood development. She serves in a Head Start classroom of mostly Latina/o children seeking their way in a world that does not always welcome them. Gabriela's dedication to the weakest yet most promising has brought a new dimension to our family. Through decades of trial and triumph, Jane, María and Israel, and Gabriela have inspired me. I dedicate this book to the Mexican families who still struggle to make sustainable lives, and to my multicultural family—with a special smile for Gabriela as she helps families and communities become stronger.

APPENDIX A

Querétaro Population, 1778–1854

Table A.1 Querétaro District Population, 1778

Jurisdiction	Spaniards	Mestizos	Mulattoes	Indios	Total
Querétaro City	6,735	4,521	3,009	5,874	20,139
San Sebastián	345	708	509	5,596	7,198
La Cañada	134	100	52	2,909	3,195
San Fran. (Pueblito)	42	33		2,571	2,646
Huimilpan	8			1,091	1,099
Haciendas	1,954	2,359	820	7,195	12,328
Qro. City Total	9,218	7,721	4,430	11,470	46,605
San Juan del Río	1,328	532	520	2,346	4,726
Tequisquiapan	134	150	244	1,978	2,506
Pueblos (4)	67	8		1,242	1,317
Haciendas	1,573	1,639	1,213	6,849	11,274
S. Juan Juris. Total	3,102	2,329	1,977	12,415	19,823
San Pedro Tolimán	273			1,375	1,648
Tolimanejo	350	46	78	1,165	1,639
Pueblos (3)				3,924	3,924
Haciendas	994	163	378	610	2,125
Tolimán Juris. Total	1,617	209	456	7,074	9,356
Qro. District Total	13,937	10,259	6,863	44,725	75,784

Source: José Ignacio Urquiola Permisán, "La región centro-sur de Querétaro," in *Historia de la cuestión agraria mexicana: Estado de Querétaro*, vol. 1, ed. José Ignacio Urquiola Permisán (Juan Pablos, 1989), 158, my calculations.

Table A.2 Querétaro Population, 1790–1822

1790			
Region	City/Town	Rural Jurisdiction	Total
Querétaro	29,702	15,657	45,359
San Juan del Río	6,713	8,191	14,904
Amealco	763	2,165	2,928
Tolimán	2,641	5,876	8,517
Total	38,819	31,889	70,708
1793			
Total			77,660
CA. 1810			
Total			ca. 100,000
1822			
Querétaro			32,469
San Juan del Río			21,653
Amealco			8,457
Cadereita			10,685
Tolimán			10,495
Jalpam			6,561
Total			90,410

Source: Raso, *Notas estadísticas*, 97–99.

Table A.3 Querétaro Population, 1843–1844

	1843	1844	% 1844
QUERÉTARO CITY			
Central Parish			
Santiago	7,485	7,206	
Santa Ana	11,470	11,656	
Divina Pastora	6,380	6,380	
Center Total	25,335	25,242	

La otra banda			
San Sebastián	9,680	10,060	
City Total	35,015	35,302	21%
San Pedro de la Cañada	13,320	13,777	
Pueblito	5,360	5,591	
Santa Rosa	10,800	11,226	
Querétaro Region Total	64,495	65,896	37%
SOUTHERN BASIN			
San Juan del Río	23,480	24,232	
Tequisqiapan	10,260	10,466	
Southern Basin Total	33,740	34,698	19%
SOUTHERN UPLANDS			
Huimilpan	5,800	6,029	
Amealco	11,642	12,072	
Uplands Total	17,442	18,101	10%
THE SIERRAS			
Cadereyta	18,416	19,060	
Palmas	1,500	1,546	
Tolimán	9,291	9,605	
Tolimanejo	10,849	11,284	
Peñamiller	4,351	4,464	
Doctor	2,070	2,094	
Jalpan	8,208	8,476	
Landa	4,426	4,541	
Sierras Total	59,111	61,070	34%
State/Dept. Total	174,988	179,675	

Source: Raso, *Notas estadísticas*, 112.

Table A.4 Querétaro Population, ca. 1854

State of Querétaro

Age Range	Male	Female	Total
Birth–15	28,202	30,040	58,242
16–50	31,682	43,939	75,621
51+	6,236	7,020	13,256
Total	66,120	80,999	147,117
RACES	Europeans: 73		Creole: 2,244
	Mestizo: 70,373		*Indio* and African: 54
	Indio-Otomí: 74,376		

Literate men and women: 8,390

City of Querétaro

Age Range	Male	Female	Total
Birth–15	4,470	5,073	9,543
16–50	5,843	9,269	15,112
51+	1,156	1,645	2,801
Total	11,469	15,987	27,456
RACES	European: 36		Creole: 1,188
	Mestizo: 18,288		*Indio* and African: 15
	Indio: 7,934		

Literate men and women: 3,458

Source: Balbontín, *Estadística del Estado de Querétaro*, 145–46, 154.

Silver and Mining, 1810–1870

Table B.1 Silver Minted Nationally and at Guanajuato, 1822–1845 (in pesos)

Year	National Total	Guanajuato Total	Guanajuato Percent
1822	9,119,570	390,228	
1823	9,455, 991	502,358	
1824	8,759, 460	587,312	
1825	3,166,039	401,673	
Mean (4 yr.)	7,625,265	470,392	6%
1826	11,538,419	540,040	
1827	9,343,744	933,011	
1828	10,569,916	1,404,060	
1829	11,732,338	1,796,876	
1830	11,539,539	2,417,302	
Mean	10,944,872	1,636,907	15%
1831	8,457,030	2,198,250	
1832	12,515,008	2,555,200	
1833	12,276,204	2,995,000	
1834	12,532,147	2,532,500	
1835	11,439,638	2,232,000	
Mean	11,444,005	2,502,606	22%
1836	11,102,692	2,300,500	
1837	11,073,843	2,857,000	

Year	National Total	Guanajuato Total	Guanajuato Percent
1838	12,577,282	2,697,000	
1839	11,906,850	3,029,000	
1840	12,393,270	3,460,500	
Mean	11,810,787	2,876,800	24%
1841	12,750,026	3,296,000	
1842	12,983,423	2,948,500	
1843	11,524,391	2,964,200	
1844	13,065,452	4,219,900	
1845	7,108,532	4,040,500	
Mean	11,486,364	3,493,850	30%

Source: Eduardo Flores Clair, Cuaútehmoc Velasco Ávila, and Elía Ramírez Bautista, *Estadísticas mineras de México en el siglo XIX* (Dirección de Estudios Históricos, INAH, 1985), cuadro 5, 25–28, cuadro 11, 44–46, my calculations.

Table B.2 Silver Minted Nationally and at Guanajuato, 1846–1870 (in pesos)

Year	National Total	Guanajuato Total	Guanajuato Percent
1846	27,534,390	4,025,859	
1847	8,993,974	6,004,500	
1848	18,078,159	7,093,400	
1849	17,960,246	7,773,850	
1850	17,681,237	7,801,300	
Mean	18,057,593	6,535,742	36%
1851	16,251,673	7.011,750	
1852	16,898,703	7,625,650	
1853	15,811,447	6,245,922	
1854	16,284,534	5,029,700	
1855	16,628,534	4,698,800	
Mean	16,374,940	6,122,364	37%

1856	18,208,991	4,306,524	
1857	16,586,760	4,747,300	
1858	15,753,760	4,725,256	
1859	15,985,518	5,046,120	
1860	14,418,696	5,371,271	
Mean	16,189,545	4,829,294	30%
1861	16,267,455	4,887,200	
1862	16,963,933	4,250,844	
1863	17,774,367	5,242,200	
1864	17,012,230	4,113,200	
1865	16,421,072	3,572,000	
Mean	16,887,813	4,413,089	26%
1866	16,772,550	3,673,000	
1867	17,850,945	3,708,000	
1868	19,257,820	3,719,000	
1869	19,960,757	3,551,000	
1870	19,334,867	3,559,000	
Mean	18,635,389	3,642,000	20%

Source: Eduardo Flores Clair, Cuaútehmoc Velasco Ávila, and Elía Ramírez Bautista, *Estadísticas mineras de México en el siglo XIX* (Dirección de Estudios Históricos, INAH, 1985), cuadro 5, 25–28, cuadro 11, 44–46, my calculations.

Table B.3 Production, Costs, and Profits at Valenciana (in pesos), 1788–1825

Year	Production	Costs	Profit	Profit as % Prod.
1788–1809 Total	30,944,400	18,776,828	12,167,589	39%
Per Year	1,406,564	853,492	553,072	
1810	869,068	899,521	-30,553	
1811	323,762	122,687	201,074	
1812	279,600	144,003	135,596	
1813	258,920	238,443	20,477	
1814	305,638	215,519	90,381	
1815	279,346	235,520	73,826	
1811–15 Total	1,447,176	956,172	521,454	9%
Per Year	289,435	191,234	104,291	
1816	178,513	149,081	29.482	
1817	165,987	136,429	29,558	
1818	174,971	142,317	32,654	
1819	202,415	180,743	21,672	
1820	80,184	63,351	16,832	
1816–20 Total	802,070	671,921	130,198	16%
Per Year	160,414	134,384	26,040	
1821	101,139	63,351	28,329	
1822	71,451	60,575	9,875	
1823	36,199	32,045	4,154	
1824	117,145	87,341	29,802	
1825	31,414	11,589	19,825	
1821–25 Total	357,348	254,901	91,985	28%
Per Year	71,470	50,980	18,397	

Source: Monroy, "Las minas de Guanajuato," 69–748, 373–74.

Table B.4 Profit and Loss: Valenciana Under the Compañía Anglo-Mexicana, 1828–1836

Year	Profit	Loss
1828		136,478
1829	248,092	
1830	40,976	
1831	154,145	
1832	21,173	
1833	No report: "el cólera morbus epidemia hizo grandes estragos"	
1834	62,170	
1835		33,187
1836		2,700
Total	526,556	172,365
Total Profit	354,191	
Profit per Year	39,355	

Source: Monroy, "Las minas de Guanajuato," 379–81.

Table B.5 Production, Costs, Profit, and Loss: Valenciana Under Casa Pérez Gálvez (pesos), 1837–1848

Year	Production	Costs	Profit	Loss
1837	137,767	160,805		23,038
1838	179,337	95,635	83,701	
1839	152,131	81,051	71,080	
1840	252,143	101,921	150,224	
1841	223,066	150,376	72,690	
1842	159,165	114,684	48,081	
1843	163,727	137,375	26,352	
1837–43 Total	1,267,367	841,847	452,128	23,038
Per Year	181,052	120,264	61,299 (34%)	

Year	Production	Costs	Profit	Loss
1844	122,172	127,274		4,502
1845	139,174	99,088	39,675	
1846	57,303	63,776		6,473
1847	28,658	38,762		10,104
1848	26,609	29,724		3,115
1844–48 Total	373,916	358,624	39,675	24,194
Per Year	74,783	71,725	15,482 (21%)	

Source: Monroy, "Las minas de Guanajuato," 381.

Table B.6 Dividends Paid (in Pesos): Mina de la Luz, 1843–1856

Year	No. Shares	Total Dividends	Value per Share
1843	12	45,248	3,771
1844	55	701,934	12,762
1845	45	558,228	12,405
1846	51	1,006,752	19,740
1847	53	981,600	18,521
1848	51	1,326,612	26,012
1849	34	596,000	17,529
1850	26	322,500	12,403
1851	29	408,500	14,086
1852	22	720,443	32,747
1853	23	148,353	6,450
1854	52	135,672	2,609
1855	45	55,231	1,227
1856	22	9,766	444

Source: Monroy, "Las minas de Guanajuato," 103, my calculations.

Table B.7 Shares and Dividends (in Pesos): San José de los Muchachos, 1847–1859

Year	No. Shares	Total Dividends	Value per Share
1847	16	844,317	52,770
1848	50	1,087,932	21,759
1849	52	1,906,425	36,662
1850	50	1,523,265	30,465
1851	52	1,648,300	31,698
1852	52	1,356,222	26,081
1853	52	477,412	9,181
1854	52	193,089	3,713
1855	52	282,567	5,434
1856	53	241,385	4,554
1857	52	323,908	6,229
1858	51	162,154	3,179
1859	20	27,466	1,373

Source: Monroy, "Las minas de Guanajuato," 103, my calculations.

Table B.8 Profits and Losses at Mellado (in Pesos), 1831–1860

Year	Profits	Losses
1831	8,247	
1832	42,195	
1833	42,398	
1834	45,073	
1835	58,371	
1836	175,192	
1837	108,800	
1838	121,600	
1839	201,767	

1840	252,348	
1841	134,400	
1842	76,800	
1843	134,400	
1844	128,880	
1845	70,400	
1846	19,200	
1847	16,798	
1848		18.791
1849		28,049
1850		46,673
1851		56,745
1852	47,421	
1853		30,987
1854	14,468	
1855		3,320
1856	3,427	
1857	23,891	
1858	16,261	
1859	2,421	
1860	943	

Source: Monroy, "Las minas de Guanajuato," 391–92.

Table B.9 Guanajuato and Its Mines: Population, 1822–1865

Year	City	Mines/ Refineries	La Luz	Total
1822	15,379	20,354		36,733
1825				33,444
1851	36,311	26,951	24,000	87,342
1854	63,567		22,345	85,912
1865	47,440		10,493	57,933

Source: Monroy, "Las minas de Guanajuato," 419–20.

Production and Population at Querétaro Estates, 1791–1826

Table C.1 Septién–Juriquilla Properties, Santa Rosa, 1791–1826

Juriquilla

1791: NON-INDIGENOUS RESIDENTS: 33 HOUSEHOLDS, 142 PEOPLE
12 Spanish-mestizo households; 19 mulatto-indigenous households
4 managers—mostly Spanish
11 labradores—split Spanish-mulatto
14 arrendatarios—13 mulattoes
4 arrieros—3 mulattoes
1 herrero—Spanish; 1 vaquero—mulatto
19 born at estate—13 mulattoes

1807: INDIGENOUS MEN			
	Married 66	Single 24	Total 90
	Estimated indigenous pop.: 320		
1826:	Labradores	3 Hispanic	3 indigenous	6 total
	Gañanes	19 Hispanic	26 indigenous	45 total
	Total	22 Hispanic	29 indigenous	51 total
	Est. pop.	90 Hispanic	120 indigenous	210 total pop.

San Ysidro

1791: NO NON-INDIGENOUS RESIDENTS LISTED

1807: INDIGENOUS TRIBUTARIES

Married: 43	Single: 2	Total: 45
Est. Indigenous pop.: 200		

San Miguelito

1826

Labradores	13 Hispanic	1 indigenous	14 total
Gañanes	28 Hispanic	21 indigenous	49 total
Total	41 Hispanic	22 indigenous	63 total
Est. pop.	160 Hispanic	80 indigenous	240 total pop.

JURIQUILLA–SAN YSIDRO–SAN MIGUELITO

Estimated total pop. pre-1810: 670; ca. 75 Spanish, ca. 75 mulatto, ca. 520 indigenous

Estimated pop. 1826: 450; ca. 250 Hispanic, 200 indigenous

Sources: 1791: Tutino, *Making a New World*, app. F, tables F.16–F.20; 1807: Tutino, *Making a New World*, app. G, table G.16; 1826: AHQ-P, 1826, Juriquilla, San Miguelito.

Table C.2 Septién–La Solana Property, Santa Rosa, 1791–1826

1791: NON-INDIGENOUS RESIDENTS			
12 Spanish households, 51 people			
11 mestizo households, 60 people			
23 total households; 111 total pop.			
Labradores	8 Spanish; 7 mestizo, 15 total		
Tenants	11 Spanish; 7 mestizo, 18 total		

1807: INDIGENOUS MEN			
68 married; 33 single; 101 total			
	Estimated indigenous pop.: 320		

1826: ESTATE RESIDENTS			
Labradores	None		
Gañanes	30 Hispanic	21 indigenous	51 total
Est. total pop.:	120 Hispanic	80 indigenous	200 total pop.

Sources: 1791: Tutino, *Making a New World*, app. F, tables F.21–F.25; 1807: Tutino, *Making a New World*, App. G, table G.15; 1826: AHQ-P, 1826, La Solana.

Table C.3 The Velasco–Santa Catarina Property, Santa Rosa, 1791–1826

1791: NON-INDIGENOUS HOUSEHOLDS

2 Spanish

2 mestizo

8 mulatto

13 households; total non-indigenous pop. 55

Economic Roles:

4 managers

9 labradores

5 stock herders

1807: INDIGENOUS MEN

At Sta. Catarina:	28 married	19 single	47 total
Tenants & arrimados:	30 married	13 single	43 total
Total	58 married	32 single	90 total
	Est. indigenous pop.: 300		

1826

Labradores	16 Hispanic	48 indigenous	64 total
Gañanes	1 Hispanic	102 indigenous	103 total
Total	17 Hispanic	150 indigenous	167 total
Est. total pop.:	70 Hispanic	600 indigenous	670 total pop.

Sources: 1791: Tutino, *Making a New World*, app. F, tables F.26–F.30; 1807: Tutino, *Making a New World*, app. G, table G.16; 1826: AHQ-P, 1826, Santa Catarina.

Table C.4 Velasco Properties, Monte del Negro, Santa Rosa, 1791–1826

1791: NON-INDIGENOUS HOUSEHOLDS

1 Spanish

2 mestizo

5 mulatto

8 households; total non-indigenous pop. 34

1807: INDIGENOUS MEN

Monte del Negro:	38 married	10 single	48 total
Tenants & arrimados:	10 married	5 single	15 total
Total	48 married	15 single	63 total
	Est. indigenous pop.: 225		

1826

Labradores	32 Hispanic	13 indigenous	45 total
Gañanes	76 Hispanic	42 indigenous	118 total
Total	108 Hispanic	55 indigenous	163 total
Est. total pop.:	400 Hispanic	200 indigenous	600 total pop.

Sources: 1791: Tutino, *Making a New World*, app. G, tables G.31–G.33, p. 591; 1807: Tutino, *Making a New World*, app. G, tables G.31–G.33, p. 615; 1826: AHQ, Padrones 1826, Monte del Negro.

Table C.5 Velasco Properties, Buenavista, Santa Rosa, 1791–1826

1791: NON-INDIGENOUS HOUSEHOLDS

16 Spanish

13 mestizo

2 mulatto

2 indio

33 total; total non-indigenous pop.: 152

Cultivators:

	Dependents: 14 (10; 20 years or younger)
	Tenants: 23 (13: 21–49 years; 7: 41–70 years)
	Spaniards: 13 tenants: 4 dependents: 9
	Mestizos: 8 tenants: 6 dependents: 2
	Mulattoes: 16 tenants: 13 dependents: 3

1807: INDIGENOUS MEN

Buenavista	33 married	14 single	47 total
Tenants & arrimados	64 married	19 single	83 total
Total	97 married	33 single	130 total
	Estimated indigenous pop.: 450		

1826

Labradores	42 Hispanic	6 indigenous	48 total
Gañanes	47 Hispanic	37 indigenous	84 total
Total	89 Hispanic	43 indigenous	132 total
Est. pop.	360 Hispanic	170 indigenous	530 total

Sources: 1791: Tutino, *Making a New World*, app. F, tables F.34–F.39; 1807: Tutino, *Making a New World*, app. F, table F.16; 1826: AHQ-P, 1826, Buenavista.

Table C.6 Guerrero Property, Jofre, 1791–1826

98 Spanish

68 mestizo

22 mulatto

2 cacique

Total non-indigenous households: 186

15 of 186 household heads, 8 percent, were women

Total non-indigenous pop.: 835

Place of Birth	Jofre	Querétaro	Other	Total
Spaniards	83	7	7	97
Mestizos	48	10	1	59
Mulattoes	18			18
Total	149	17	8	174

Marriage Links

Spanish-Spanish	69
Spanish-mestizo	17
Mestizo-mestizo	46
Mulatto-mulatto	16

Cultivators by Age and Ethnicity

Ages	Spanish		Mestizo		Mulatto		Total	
	Tenants	Workers	Tenants	Workers	Tenants	Workers	Tenants	Workers
<20	6	38	3	23	11	11	20	72
21–40	54	50	34	9	6	4	94	63
41+	31	1	25		9	1	65	2
Total	91	89	62	32	17	16	170	137

Total cultivators: 307—Many workers remained dependent in tenant households

1807

Indigenous Men	Married	Single	Total
Jofre	43	27	70
Tenants/Arrimados	89	39	128
Total	132	66	198

Est. indigenous pop.: 600

1826

Labradores	Hispanic 53	indigenous 15	Total	68
Gañanes	Hispanic 282	indigenous 344	Total	626
Total	Hispanic 335	indigenous 359	Total	694

Est. total pop.: 2,800

Sources: 1791: Tutino, *Making a New World*, app. F, tables F.44–F.48 1807: Tutino, *Making a New World*, app. G, table G.16; 1826: AHQ-P, 1826, Jofre.

Table C.7 Carmelite Property, Chichimequillas, 1791–1826

1791: NON-INDIGENOUS HOUSEHOLDS	
75 total	381 total pop.

ETHNICITY OF HOUSEHOLD HEADS	
Spanish	39
Mestizo	17
Mulatto	10
Cacique	2
Total	68

Ethnic Pairing	
Spanish-Spanish	30
Spanish-mestizo	9
Mestizo-mestizo	13
Mulatto-Spanish	5
Mulatto-mestizo	2
Mulatto-mulatto	2
Mulatto-indigenous	1
Cacique-Cacica	1
Cacique-mestiza	1
Total	64

Economic Roles:	Managers:	5 (4 Spanish; 1 mulatto)
Crafts:	Herreros	3 (1 Spanish; 2 mestizo)
	Panadero	1 (Spanish)
	Sastre	1 (Spanish)
	Hatmakers	3 (all Spanish)

Textiles:	Weavers	10 (8 Spanish; 2 mulatto)
	Carders	4 (3 Spanish; 1 mestizo)
	Spinners	5 (2 Spanish; 3 mestizo)
	Dorador	1 (Spanish)
Livestock:	Arriero	1 (mulatto)
	Caporal	3 (2 mestizo; 1 mulatto)
	Vaquero	5 (1 mestizo; 4 mulatto)
	Shepherd	1 (Spanish)
	Forest Guard	1 (Spanish)
Cultivation:	Tenants	20: 11 Spanish; 9 mestizo (18: 30+)
	Workers	29; 11 Spanish; 14 mestizo; 2 mulatto; 2 caciques (15: 30+)

1807

Indigenous Men	Married	Single	Total
Hacienda	67	11	78
Labores (2)	46	2	48
Tenants/Arrimados	54	20	74
Total	167	33	200

Est. indigenous pop.: 700

1826: AN ESTATE OF MANY COMMUNITIES

Total households: 343; total pop. 906

Casco:	Managers	4 (all Hispanic)
	Stock tenders	4 (all Hispanic)
	Labrador	1 (Hispanic)
	Sirvientes	48 (18 Hispanic; 32 indigenous; 36: 30 yrs. or younger)
	Total	55

Cuadrilla:	Shepherd	1 (Hispanic)
	Hen keeper	1 (Hispanic)
	Labradores	5 (4 Hispanic; 1 indigenous)
	Sin oficio	12 (10 Hispanic; 2 indigenous)
	Total	19 (80 percent under 30 yrs.)
Textile Village:	Merchant	1 (Hispanic and don)
	Weavers	8 (all Hispanic)
	Spinners	12 (8 Hispanic; 4 indigenous)
	Carder	1 (Hispanic)
	Total	22
Jiquén:	Weaver	1 (Hispanic)
	Shoemaker	1 (Hispanic)
	Labradores	7 (6 Hispanic; 1 indigenous)
	Sin oficio	7 (6 Hispanic: 1 indigenous)
	Pulquero	1 (indigenous)
	Total	17
Santa María:	Shoemakers	2 (Hispanic)
	Spinner	1 (Hispanic)
	Carder	1 (Hispanic)
	Muleteers	6 (all Hispanic)
	Labradores	35 (24 Hispanic; 11 indigenous)
	Sin Oficio	19 (11 Hispanic; 8 indigenous)
	Gañan	1 (indigenous)
	Total	65 households; 225 pop.: 60% 20 yrs. or younger
Baño:	Labradores	9 (5 Hispanic; 4 indigenous)
	Total	9; total pop. 61: large families in established community

Solano:	Labradores	18 (2 Hispanic; 16 indigenous)
	Total	18; total pop. 34: small families in new community
Tierra Blanca:	Labradores	22 (18 Hispanic; 4 indigenous)
	Total	22; total pop. 55: emerging families in recent community
Lajitas:	Labradores	18 (11 Hispanic; 7 indigenous)
	Total	18; total pop. 59: growing families in recent community
Zuriel:	Carpenter:	1 (indigenous)
	Tailor:	1 (Hispanic)
	Vinatero:	1 (Hispanic)
	Labradores:	11 (9 Hispanic; 2 indigenous)
	Sin oficio:	46 (40 Hispanic; 6 indigenous)
	Ladrones:	3 (all Hispanic)
	Total	**63; total pop. 185: growing families in new community**

127 of 343 households: 37%; 394 of 906 total population: 44%—lived at recently settled outlying communities on Chichimequillas lands

Sources: 1791: Tutino, *Making a New World*, app. F, tables F.11–F.15 1807: Tutino, *Making a New World*, app. G, table G.16; 1826: AHQ-P, 1826, Chichimequillas.

APPENDIX D

Production and Work at Querétaro, 1840–1854

Table D.1 The Querétaro Textile Industry, 1844

Querétaro District

Woolens: 9 *obrajes* work looms, employ 1,017 workers, gaining a total of 70,000 pesos

ca. 70 pesos per worker

195 *trapiches* work 265 looms, employ 416 producers, gaining a total of 37,440 pesos

ca. 90 pesos per producer

Cottons: 75 *trapiches* work 182 looms, employ 232 producers, gaining a total of 19,552 pesos

ca. 84 pesos per producer

Hércules works 312 power looms, employs 876 workers, gaining a total of 156,000 pesos

ca. 180 pesos per worker

San Juan del Río District

Woolens: 141 *trapiches* work 141 looms, employ 282 producers, gaining a total of 23,400 pesos

ca. 83 pesos per producer

Cottons: 146 *trapiches* work 146 looms, employ 292 producers, gaining a total of 4,019 pesos

ca. 14 pesos per producer

Cadereita District

Woolens: 15 *trapiches* work 15 looms, employ 30 producers, gaining a total of 2,340 pesos

ca. 78 pesos per producer

Cottons: 39 *trapiches* work 39 looms, employ 78 producers, gaining a total of 1,200 pesos

ca. 15 pesos per producer

Tolimán District

Cottons: 60 *trapiches* work 60 looms, employ 120 producers, gaining a total of 1,500 pesos

ca. 16 pesos per producer

Source: Raso, *Notas estadísticas*, 67.

Table D.2 Rural Querétaro, 1840–1845

| Property | Jurisdiction | | | | | | |
	Querétaro	San Juan del Río	Amealco	Cadereita	Tolimán	Jalpan	Total
Haciendas	66	29	12	11	5	1	124
Ranchos	12	31	256	64	4	25	392

Maize:	Planted, 1839: 7,811 fanegas	Harvested, 1840: 624,880 fanegas	Yield: 80 to 1
Fanegas per capita, ca. 160,000 pop.: 4	Fanegas per family of 4–5: 18		

Agricultural Producers, ca. 1844	Querétaro Total
Hacienda Owners	124
Rancho Owners	392
Hacienda Leaseholders	23
Estate Administrators	20
Stewards	124
Stock Herders	2,197
Peones with Rations	6,000
Alquilados	3,174
Muchachos	4,000
Colonos and Terrazgueros	2,699
Leñeros, Carboneros, Tuneros, Madereros	2,107
Hortelanos	2,729

Source: Raso, *Notas estadísticas*, 28, 34–38, 44, 49–50.

Table D.3 Work and Production in Querétaro, 1843

Sector	Persons Occupied		Production Value		Value
	No.	%	Pesos	%	Per Person
AGRICULTURE	20,747	39	2,054,075	29	99
INDUSTRY AND URBAN CRAFTS					
Industria Fabril	3,633	7	1,101,952	15	303
Industria Urbana	16,404	31	1,279,590	18	78
Artisans	1,150	2	172,500	2	150
Tobacco (w/o Women)	488	1	142,170	2	291
Mineros	251	.5	17,941	.3	71
Women (Factories & Domestics)	7,174	14	573,920	8	80
Industry/Urban Total	29,100	55	3,295,773	46	113
COMMERCE AND PROFESSIONS					
Censualistas	1,037	2	163,887	2	157
Comercio (estimated)	1,800	3	1,200,000	17	667
Lawyers & Professionals	51	.1	51,000	.7	1,000
Religious	159	.3	256,824	4	1,615
Clerks	128	.2	25,600	.4	200
Employees (State/plus)	121	.2	82,700	1	683
Comm./Prof. Total:	3,296		1,780,011	25	540
Total Economically Active	53,143		7,122,559 GDP		134
Total Population		174, 988	41p. per capita GDP		

Source: Raso, Notas estadísticas, 78, 112, my calculations.

Table D.4 Production and Labor at Hércules, 1844–1854

Year	Spindles		Looms		Workers		Payroll	Pay per Worker
	Active	Idle	Mechanical	Manual	Men	Women	pesos	pesos
1844	4,200	960	212	130	292	584	156,000	178
1853	7,500		500			3,000	250,000	83
1854	9,200		450	370	1,250	1,250	460,000	184

VALUE OF PRODUCTION (PESOS)

Year	Thread	Cloth	Total	Per Worker		Pay %	
				Women	Men	Total	Value
1844			299,361	342	52		
1854	682,500	807,500	1,490,000	546	646	596	31

Sources: 1844: Raso, *Notas estadísticas*, 62–64; 1853: Tutino, *Mexican Heartland*, app., table A.14; 1854: Balbontín, *Estadística*, 178–79, my calculations.

Table D.5 Querétaro Professionals, 1854

Government Linked		
State Officials	196	(8 retired)
Military Personnel	328	(11 retired)
Municipal Employees	156	
Police	1,033	
Judicial	188	
Teachers	69	
Public Works	2	
Total	1,972	(at 4 per family, ca. 7,888; 5% of state population)

Church Linked		
Secular Clergy	63	
Regular Clergy	209	
Monks	10	
Novices	15	
Nuns	126	
Novices	10	
Lay Assistants	211	
Convent Servants	95	
Burial Assistants	22	
Total	761	(at 1 dependent each, ca. 1,522; 1% of state population)

Independent Professionals		
Lawyers	30	
Property Admin.	14	
Notaries	7	
Printers	17	
Students	99	
Musicians	80	
Architect	1	
Total	248	(at 3 dependents each, c. 992; .6% of state population)

Medical Professionals		
Médicos y cirujanos	18	
Boticarios	14	
Barberos	86	
Parteras	14	
Total	132	(at 3 dependents each, ca. 528; .4% of state population)

Source: Balbontín, Estadística, 146–54, my calculations.

Table D.6 Commerce, Consumption, and Clothing: Querétaro, 1854

Commercial Lives	
Merchants	922
Commercial Brokers	14
Business Agents	5
Commercial Dependents	155
Lenders at Interest	5
Resellers	75
Buhoneros (peddlers)	23
Vendedores Ambulantes	90
Total	1,289 (at 4 per household, ca. 5,156 population; ca. 4% of state)

Food Purveyors	
Atoleras	40
Aguadores	91
Bizcocheros	20
Cafeteros	11
Carniceros	196
Cervecereros	8
Cocineros	88
Confiteros	8
Chocolateros	28
Dulceros	25
Fruteros	22
Horneros	31
Neveros	7
Panaderos	183
Pasteleros	6
Pulqueros	141

Queso/Mantequeros	32
Tortilleras Públicas	536
Total	**1,474**
	(at 4 per household, ca. 5,892 population; ca. 4% of state)

Clothing Makers

Bordadores	95
Costureras	91
Modistas	2
Peineteros	10
Sastres	399
Sombreros	91
Zapateros	803
Total	**1,491**
	(at 4 per household, ca. 5,964 population; ca. 4% of state)

Source: Balbontín, *Estadística*, 148–54, my calculations.

Table D.7 Crafts at Querétaro, 1854

Alfareros	167
Alambiqueros	27
Bataneros	20
Bordadores	95
Carpinteros	336
Cereros	18
Cesteros	30
Coheteros	56
Curtidores	195
Encuadernadores	11
Escultores	18

Fabricantes	1,234
Fundidores	10
Herreros	175
Hojalateros	34
Industriales	107
Jaboneros	43
Mecateros	1,037
Plomeros	4
Plateros	94
Reboceros	220
Relojeros	9
Talabarteros	44
Tejedores	1,038
Tintoreros	13
Torcedoras cigarros	860
Torneros	10
Veleros	76
Total	5,981 (at 4 per household, ca. 23,924 population; ca. 16% of state)

Source: Balbontín, *Estadística*, 148–54.

Table D.8 Construction, Carrying, and Labor: Querétaro, 1854

Construction	
Albañiles	427
Caleros	112
Canteros	44
Ladrilleros	87
Pintores	67
Total	737 (at 4 per household, ca. 2,948 population; ca. 2% of state)

Carrying Trades	
Arrieros	1,167
Aguadores	91
Cargadores	31
Carroceros	17
Cocheros	45
Carreteros	31
Total	1,382 (at 4 per household, ca. 5,528 population; ca. 4% of state)

Urban Labor and Domestic Service	
Jornaleros urbanos	872
Lavanderas	156
Sirvientes domésticos	2,022
Total	3,050 (at 1.5 dependents each: 7,627 population; ca. 5% of state)

Source: Balbontín, *Estadística*, 148–54.

Table D.9 Agrarian Querétaro, 1854

Haciendas: 98

Ranchos: 226

Area: 13,465 caballerias (ca. 638,600 hectares): 1,971 ha. per estate

Planted: 898 caballerias (ca. 35,920 hectares)

Value: 4,641,690 pesos; 14,327 pesos per estate

Empleados and jornaleros, latter at 1.5 reales per day: 5,613

Huertas
Area: 85 caballerias (3,400 hectares): ca. 1 hectare per huerta

Valor: 486,433 pesos; 138 pesos per huerta

Empleados and jornaleros: 286

Grazing Properties
Area: 6,595 caballerías (263,800 hectares): 29,311 ha. per estate

Planted: 192 caballerías

Valor: 716,451 pesos

Utilidad anual: 91,734 pesos; 10,192 per estate; 13% of value

Empleados y jornaleros: 662

Annual Planting
Maize: 7,006 fanegas planted; 701,066 harvested (100 to 1); 1 peso per fanega

Frijol: 12 reales (1.5 pesos) per fanega

Chile Bueno: 8 pesos per arroba (ca. 10 kilos)

Wheat: 1,858 fanegas planted; 45,572 fanegas harvested; (25 to 1); value: 129,084 pesos; 2.8 pesos per fanega

Agricultural Census

Hacendados	109
Administradores	36
Mayordomos	56
Agricultores	228
Labradores	5,408
Jornaleros	11,888
Hortelanos	3,514
Ganaderos	80
Vaqueros	162
Carboneros	540
Total	22,019 (at 4 per household, 88,076 = 60% of population)

Source: Balbontín, *Estadística*, 99–102, 148–54, 166, 190–91.

Table D.10 Sustaining Querétaro, 1854: Population and Production

	Sector Population	% at 147,000	% at 170,000
THE PROFESSIONS			
Government	7,518	5	4
Church	1,522	1	0.9
Indep. Professions	890	0.6	0.5
Medical Profs.	578	0.4	0.3
Professional Total	10,558	7	6
COMMERCIAL LIFE			
Commerce	5,156	4	3
Food Purveyors	5,892	4	3
Clothing	5,964	4	4
Commercial Total	17,012	12	10
MANUFACTURING			
Crafts	23,929	16	14
Hércules	7,500	5	4
Manufacturing Total	31,429	21	18
URBAN WORK			
Construction	2,948	2	2
Carrying Trades	5,528	4	3
Labor/Domestic Service	7,627	5	4
Urban Work Total	16,103	11	9
Agriculture	88,076	60	52
Querétaro Total	163,178	111	95

Source: Tables D.4–D.9, my calculations.

Mexican Population, Production, Trade, Revenue, and Debt, ca. 1861

Table E.1 Population, ca. 1861

Region	State Pop.	Capital City Pop.	State Budget (pesos)
GREATER BAJÍO			
BAJÍO			
Guanajuato	896,588	68,986	615,890
Querétaro	148,786	27,492	134,619
Bajío Total	1,145,374 (14% of Mexico)		750,509 (13%)
NEAR NORTH			
Jalisco	815,752	72,918 (Guadalajara)	482,120
San Luis Potosí	398,888	26,841	116,685
Zacatecas	309,962	22,514	684,320
Aguascalientes	92,260	41,974	34,200
Greater Bajío Total	2,762,236 (33% of Mexico)		1,317,325 (23%)
GREATER HEARTLAND			
HEARTLAND			
Mexico State	1,023,856	18,918 (Toluca)	512,872
Federal District	246,456	210,327 (Mexico)	358,132
Heartland Total	1,270,312 (15% of Mexico)		871,004 (15%)
GREATER HEARTLAND			
Puebla	682,110	74,103	452,814
Michoacán	489,800	26,109 (Morelia)	254,614

Greater Heartland Total	2,442,222 (29% of Mexico)	1,578,432 (27%)
Greater Bajío-Heartland Total Pop.	5,204,458 (62% of Mexico)	
Greater Bajío-Heartland Total State Budgets		2,895,757 (51% of State Budgets)
Mexico Total Pop.	8,396,524	Total State Budgets: 5,724,067

Source: José María Pérez Hernández, *Estadística de la República Mexicana* (Tipografía del Gobierno, 1862), 63, 193, my calculations.

Table E.2 Resident Foreigners in Mexico, ca. 1861

Nationality	Number	Percent
Spanish	12,162	46
French	7,218	27
English	2,493	9
United States	1,747	6
German (Alemán)	1,738	6
Italian	760	3
Total	26,975	

Source: Pérez Hernández, *Estadística*, 67, my calculations.

Table E.3 Ethno-Racial Classifications, Mexico, ca. 1861

Classification	Population	Percent
Caucasian-White	2,138,540	25%
Amarilla americana o indio puro	5,121,899	61%
Indios civilizados	4,799,899	57%
Indios bárbaros	322,000	4%
Etiópico puro	35,860	0.5%
Mezcla: Caucasiano-indio	742,010	9%

Caucasiano-etiópico	266,000	3%
Caucasiano-chino	8,200	0.1%
Amarillo-etiópico	124,000	1.5%
Total	8,396,524	

Source: Pérez Hernández, *Estadística*, 74, my percentages.

Table E.4 Primary Occupations, Mexico, ca. 1861

Occupation	Number	Percent
Proprietors: Urban and Rural	262,340	9%
Merchants: Large and Small	146,174	5%
Rural Growers: Large and Small	268,984	9%
Artisans	64,348	2%
Domestic Servants	294,325	10%
Jornaleros*	1,816,766	50%
MILITARY		
Permanent Troops	19,678	
Active Forces	16,300	
Guardias nacionales	22,600	
Military Total	58,578	2%
Total	3,011,766	

* Wage workers; catch-all for majority mixing tenants, sharecroppers, and laborers.
Source: Pérez Hernández, *Estadistica*, 77–78, my percentages.

Table E.5 Rural Property Values, Mexico, ca. 1861

Properties	Number	Total Value	Mean
Haciendas	4,418	397,620,000	90,000
Ranchos	11,550	114,650,000	9,925
Huertas & Quintas	7,512	42,295,741	5.030
Total	23,480	554,565,741	23,619

Source: Pérez Hernández, *Estadística*, 121, my calculations.

Table E.6 Commercial Agricultural and Livestock Production, Mexico, ca. 1861

Crop	Cargas (2 fanegas)	Mean Price	Total Value (pesos)	Percent
Maize	4,144,536	4 pesos	16,578.144	18%
Frijol	2,172,268	9 pesos	19,550,412	21%
Wheat Flour	1,694,415	12 pesos	20,332,980	22%
Pulque/Mezcal			4,064,169	4%
Sugar/ Aguardiente			6,388,380	7%
Tobacco			6,091,631	6%
Cotton			14,661,456	16%
Total Commercial Agriculture (including minor crops)			94,418,061	

Livestock	No. Head	Mean Price	Total Value (pesos)	Percent
Cattle	898,345	14 pesos	12,576,220	18%
Sheep	5,503,610	2 pesos	11,007,220	16%
Hogs	2,513,490	9 pesos	22,621,410	33%
Tallow			13,218,720	19%
Hides			1,591,213	2%
Wool			1,185,320	2%
Total Commercial Livestock (including lesser products)			68,619,952	

Source: Pérez Hernández, *Estadística*, 103–15, 117–18.

Table E.7 Cotton Gins in Mexico, ca. 1861

State	Number	Percent
COASTAL LOWLANDS		
Veracruz	8	
Oaxaca	6	
Guerrero	6	
Colima	4	
Coastal Total	24	73%
NORTHERN LAGUNA		
Chihuahua	4	
Durango	3	
Coahuila	2	
Laguna Total	9	27%
Mexico Total	33	

Source: Pérez Hernández, Estadística, 140.

Table E.8 Gold and Silver Mintage (in Pesos): Mexico, 1857

Mint	Gold Minted	Silver Minted	Total Minted	Percent
Guanajuato	658,300	4,986,816	5,645,116	29%
Mexico City	165,663	4,165,537	4,331,202	22%
Zacatecas	80,246	3,818,420	3,898,660	20%
San Luis Potosí	85,144	2,162,409	2,247,553	12%
Culiacán	164,242	869,786	1,034,028	5%
Durango	74,874	719,276	794,150	4%
Guadalajara	112,468	644,882	757,350	4%
Chihuahua	18,636	575,500	594,130	3%
Total	1,359,573	17,942,628	19,302,201	

Source: Pérez Hernández, Estadística, 130.

Table E.9 Total Mintage, Gold and Silver (in Pesos), California and Mexico, 1855–1859

Year	California	Mexico
1855	21,581,752	19,788,497
1856	28,851,777	19,004,342
1857	20,426,500	19,302,201
1858	18,049,450	19,832,414
1859	17,452,300	18,794,522
Total	106,361,779	97,601,976
Mean	21,272,356	19,590,395

Source: Pérez Hernández, Estadística, 130.

Table E.10 Commercial Activity (in Pesos), Mexico, ca. 1861

Sector	Sales	Percent
Agriculture	104,933,679	26%
Livestock	68,619,452	16%
Agro-Pastoral Total	173,553,631	42%
Artisanry	150,000,000	37%
Factory/ Manufacturing	57,985,424	14%
Artisanal/Factory Total	207,985,424	51%
Mineral	27,256,238	7%
Total	408,795,293	

International Trade	Total Imports	Commercial Exports	Bullion Exports
	30,010,000	7,246,900	ca. 24,000,000

Imports	Origin	Estimated Value in pesos	Percent
	England	13,000,000	43%
	United States	5,000,000	17%
	France	5,000,000	17%
	Germany	2,000,000	7%
	Spain	1,500,000	5%
	Cuba	1,500,000	5%
	China	1,000,000	3%
	Total (including small nations)	30,010,000	

Source: Pérez Hernández, *Estadística*, 152–55, my calculations.

Table E.11 National State Revenues and International Debts, 1861

Revenue Sector	Estimated Receipts	Percent
COMMERCE		
Imports	5,000,000	30%
Exports	600,000	4%
Internal (alcabalas)	3,600,000	21%
Commerce Total:	**9,200,000**	**55%**
MINING		
3% on Production	750,000	5%
Real per Mark	390,000	2%
Minting Tax	200,000	1%
Mining Total	**1,340,000**	**8%**
PERSONAL		
Personal Contribution (head tax)	1,300,000	8%
Total Revenues (with lesser taxes)	**16,837,000**	
FOREIGN DEBT (IN PESOS)		
English Original	62,254,134	
English Conventions	5,641,020	
Spanish Conventions	6,324,899	
French Conventions	580,000	
Original Debt plus Conventions, 1861	**74,803,053**	
Debt contacted under Zuloaga/ Miramón	52,141,000	
Foreign Debt Total, 1861	**126,944,892**	
Internal Debt Total	46,000,000	
Total National Regime Debt	**172,944,892**	
Annual Interest, at 3%	**5,188,346**	

Source: Pérez Hernández, *Estadística*, 202.

APPENDIX F

Population and Production in Guanajuato, 1855–1876

Table F.1 Guanajuato Population, ca. 1855–1868

District	ca. 1855	ca. 1864	1868
GUANAJUATO			
Guanajuato	63,567	43,872	56,012
La Luz		22,345	13,670
Silao	42,020	37,927	46,096
Irapuato	35,009	33,144	46,266
Salamanca	25,379	30,795	(combined 47,109)
Valle de Santiago	25,004	33,594	
Dist. Total	213,324	179,322	209,153
CELAYA			
Celaya	40,621	37,455	29,203
Apaseo	17,513	15,727	7,820
Chamacuero	10,000	10,395	7,884
Santa Cruz	14,000	14,605	11,607
Salvatierra/Yurriria	73,195	71,552	60,700
Jerécuaro	21,580	18,181	10,510
Acámbaro	14,475	11,945	15,671
Dist. Total	191,530	179,860	178,330

ALLENDE			
San Miguel Allende	38,008	36,517	36,911
Dolores Hidalgo	57,014	32,917	44,883
San Diego Bizcocho	21,263	11,780	
San Felipe	40,353	53,726	40,944
San Luis de la Paz	51,675	51,675	23,820
San José Iturbide	20,197	26,197	40,185
Dist. Total	**231,510**	**201,032**	**198,330**
LEÓN			
León	50,012	80,052	78,930
Purísima Rincón	7,785		6,919
S. Fran. Rincón	15,533		16,127
S. Pedro Piedragorda	16,932	24,326	17,404
Pénjamo	47,670	54,173	27,960
Dist. Total	**137,905**	**158,551**	**147,346**
State Total	**774,073**	**718,775**	**729,988**

Sources: García y Cubas, *Atlas geográfico*; Preciado de Alba, *Guanajuato*, cuadro 6, 118; Antillón, *Memoria . . . 1873*, cuadro 4.

Table F.2 Resident Foreigners in Department of Guanajuato, 1865

RESIDENCE

Nationality	Guanajuato	Celaya	León	Silao	Other	Total
Spanish	30	23	10	13	35	111
French	52	7	12	4	5	80
English	19				7	26
German	20	3				23
Portuguese	11					11
Prussian	7					7
United States	4					4
Other	15		1			16
Total	158	30	26	17	47	278
Percent	57%	11%	9%	6%	17%	

Source: Preciado, Guanajuato, Cuadro 7, 119, my calculations.

Table F.3 Silver Production in Guanajuato, 1855 and 1871–1873 (in pesos)

Years	1855	1871–72	1872–73
	4,698,800	4,499,191	4,068,778

MINE WORKERS

Valenciana			1,950
Guanajuato Total			3,900

Sources: Garcia y Cubas, Atlas geográfico; Antillón, Memoria . . . 1873, cuadro 16.

Table F.4 Guanajuato Industry and Manufacturing, ca. 1855

Imdustrial Fábricas
Salamanca, cotton weaving, 12,000 pieces per year: value, 48,000 pesos
Salvatierra, cotton spinning, 13,800 lbs. per year: value, 60,375 pesos
Celaya, woolen cloths (cashmeres; carpets): 4,500 pieces per year: value, 350,500 pesos
Total annual value industrial cloth: 458,875 pesos

Industry and Manufacturing Combined	Value of Production (pesos)	No. of Workers
CLOTH		
Frezadas	428,850	5,156
Mantas	145,500	380
Rebozos	85,800	1,169
Zarapes	200,200	1,270
Textiles Total	860,350	7,975
LEATHER		
Cordobanes	112,750	270
Vaquetas	97,500	185
Gamusas	50,000	185
Pieles curtidas	37,500	200
Leather Total	297,750	850
CONSUMABLES		
Aguardiente	502,200	379
Harina	157,750	49
Consumables Total	659,950	428
APPAREL		
Sombreros	16,875	200
TOTAL		
Total	1,938,283	9,453

Industrial cloth: 53% of textile production by value

24% of total manufacturing by value

Source: García y Cubas, *Atlas geográfico*.

Table F.5 Manufacturing and Trade Businesses in Guanajuato Cities, ca. 1864

Activity	Guanajuato	León	Celaya	Salamanca
INDUSTRY				
Metal	38	41	13	7
Leather	5	118	13	4
Wood	16	23	23	8
Cloth	16	15	9	11
Pottery	8	20		20
ALMACENES (LARGE ENTERPRISES)				
Bread	11	22	5	4
Maize	7		4	2
Meat	18	14	5	2
Rebozos	287	11	70	
Tobacco	85	90	3	7
TIENDAS (SMALL SHOPS)				
Groceries	94	60		
Dry Goods	11	15		
Mixed	15	21	35	13
Wine	16	2		1
Shoes	16	2	1	

Source: Preciado de Alba, Guanajuato, anexo VIII, 187–93, my calculations.

Table F.6 Guanajuato Harvests, ca. 1855

Crop	Quantity	Value in Pesos
Maize	6,975,790 fanegas	6,975,790
Wheat	205,301 cargas	1,231,803
Chile	353,700 cargas	706,600
Fruits		472,346
Barley	287,040 cargas	427,760
Vegetables		134,300
Frijol	8,605 fanegas	120,752
Lumber		111,200
Garbanzo	61,855 fanegas	92,782
Sugar Cane	30,750 cargas	53,956
Total		10,341,035

Source: García y Cubas, *Atlas geográfico*. Two fanegas make one carga.

Table F.7 Guanajuato Urban Consumption, 1871–1872

City	Maize in Fanegas	Wheat Flour in Cargas
Guanajuato	473,900	4,000
León	173,500	4,800
Celaya	154,209	4,500
Abasolo	96,400	
Acámbaro	88,500	
Silao	81,500	
Allende	21,000	2,000
Total	1,404,200	15,300

Source: Antillón, *Memoria . . . 1873*, cuadro 20.

Table F.8 Guanajuato State Revenues, ca. 1855 (in Pesos)

ON SILVER	
3 percent on production	117,246
On circulation	34,957
Total Silver	152,205
Percent of Total Revenues	15%
ON CONSUMPTION	
Internal Sales	256,399
On imports	71,071
Total Consumption	327,470
Percent of Total Revenues	33%
CORREOS	
Total Correos	332,686
Percent of Total Revenues	34%
Total Revenues	983,664

Source: García y Cubas, *Atlas geográfico*, my calculations.

Table F.9 Guanajuato State Revenues, 1872 (in Pesos)

District	Silver	Consumption	Direct Tax	Total	Percent
Capital	137,713	172,925	29,427	356,345	45%
León		49,948	35,236	103,535	13%
Celaya	1,108	30,938	34,906	73,408	9%
Allende	207	15,560	35,907	56,194	7%
Salvatierra	36	15,542	32,477	56,075	7%
Irapuato	76	30,430	46,573	90,162	11%
Silao		10,944	16,952	31,731	4%
San Luis de la Paz	70	9,498	17,167	30,162	4%
State Total	140,921	334,837	247,785	794,632	
Percent	18%	42%	31%		

Source: Antillón, *Memoria . . . 1873*, cuadro 30, my calculations.

The Bajío in Mexico, 1876–1895

Table G.1 The Bajío in Mexico: Population, 1876, 1886, 1895

Region/State	1876		1886		1895	
Pop.	%	Pop.	%	Pop.	%	
BAJÍO						
Guanajuato	900,000	9	968,113	9	1,069,418	8
Querétaro	166,643	2	203,250	2	232,305	2
Bajío Total	1,066,643	11	1,171,363	11	1,301,723	10
NEAR NORTH						
Jalisco	980,000	10	1,145,662	11	1,114,765	9
San Luis Potosí	525,110	6	516,486	5	571,420	5
Zacatecas	414,000	4	465,862	4	456,241	4
Aguascalientes	90,000	1	140,430	1	104,693	1
Near North Total	2,009,110	21	2,268,440	21	2,247,119	18
Bajío/Near North Total	3,075,753	32	3,439,803	32	3,548,842	28
HEARTLAND						
Mexico (state)	663,557	7	710,753	7	842,873	7
Hidalgo	427,340	5	434,091	4	563,824	5
Morelos	150,000	2	141,565	1	159,123	1
Dist. Fed. Mex.	340,000	4	426,804	4	474,860	4
Heartland Total	1,580,897	17	1,713,213	16	2,040,680	16

Puebla	700,000	7	784,470	7	992,426	8
Tlaxcala	122,000	1	138,478	1	168,358	1
Michoacán	628,240	7	784,108	7	898,809	7
Gr. Heartland Total	1,450,240	15	1,706,686	16	2,059,593	16
Heartland/ Gr. Heartland Total	3,031,137	32	3,419,899	32	4,100,273	32

SOUTH

Oaxaca	661,706	7	761,274	7	897,182	7
Guerrero	325,000	3	353,193	3	420,926	3
Yucatán	300,000	3	302,315	3	298,569	2
Campeche	86,000	1	90,413	1	88,144	1
Chiapas	195,000	2	242,029	2	320,694	3
South Total	1,372,706	15	1,749,222	16	2,025,515	16

GULF

Veracruz	520,000	5	582,441	5	863,220	7
Tamaulipas	140,000	2	140,137	1	209,106	2
Tabasco	95,597	1	104,747	1	134,856	1
Gulf Total	755,597	8	827,325	8	1,207,182	10

NORTH

Durango	285,000	3	204,000	2	296,979	2
Chihuahua	190,000	2	225,251	2	265,546	2
Nuevo León	190,000	2	201,732	2	311,365	3
Coahuila	104,137	1	144,594	1	242,021	2
North Total	769,137	8	775,577	7	1,115,911	9

Sinaloa	200,000	2	225,251	2	265,546	2
Sonora	115,000	1	143,924	1	192,721	2
Tepic	(in Jalisco)		131,019	1	168,358	1
Colima	65,827	1	72,591	1	55,718	
Baja Cal.	25,000		30,208		42,875	
Pacific NW Total	405,827	4	603,003	6	725,218	6
National Total	9,495,157		10,791,685		12,700,294	

Sources: 1876: Antonio García Cubas, *The Republic of Mexico in 1876*, trans. George Henderson (La Enseñanza, 1876), 12.; 1886: Antonio García Cubas, *Atlas geográfico y estadístico de los Estados Unidos Mexicanos* (Imprenta de Murguía, 1887), 11–12; 1895: "Primer censo nacional de la República Mexicana," Instituto Nacional de Estadística, Geografía, e Informática.

NOTES

Prologue

1   The origins of the Bajío as a region foundational to global capitalism are detailed in Tutino, *Making a New World*; on the muchachas' protest, see 383–90.

2   The decade of revolution and its aftermath at Puerto de Nieto are the focus of Tutino, "Revolution in Mexican Independence."

3   Flynn and Giraldez, "Born with a Silver Spoon."

4   Crosby, *Columbian Exchange.*

5   See Warman, *Corn and Capitalism*, and the conceptual explorations in Tutino, *Making a New World*, 44–62.

6   For a parallel, different, and perceptive perspective on maize and its role as sustenance in Mexico, focused on women's long labors making tortillas and their recent liberations, see Gómez-Galvariatto, *El pan nuestro.*

7   López Austin and López Luján, *Mexico's Indigenous Past.*

8   For a critique of the notion of conquest—in Cortés' own words—see Cortés, *Relación de 1820.*

9   Tutino, *Mexican Heartland*, pt. 1.

10 Tutino, *Making a New World*, pt. 1.

11 For comparisons, see Tutino, *Mexican Heartland*, chap. 2; Lane, *Potosí*; and Mangan, *Trading Roles.*

12 Tutino, *Mexican Heartland*, chap. 3; on household negotiations of patriarchy, see Stern, *Secret History of Gender.*

13 Detailed in W. Taylor, *Drinking, Homicide, and Rebellion.*

14 Tutino, *Making a New World*, pt. 2.

15 For a larger perspective, see Tutino, "Revolutionary Capacity of Rural Communities."

16 The long global primacy of China is revealed in Pomeranz, *Great Divergence*. The impact of the fall of silver in China is detailed in Lin, *China Upside Down*. On India, see Parthasarathi, *Why Europe Grew Rich and Asia Did Not.*

17   On capitalism and slavery in the United States, see Beckert, *Empire of Cotton*; and Baptist, *Half Has Never Been Told*.

18   The rise of militarized rule in New Spain is the focus of Tutino, *Mexico City, 1808*.

19   This long era of conflict and change is the focus of Tutino, *Mexican Heartland*, pts. 2 and 3.

20   This transformation is explored in Tutino and Melosi, *New World Cities*.

Introduction

1   Since the 1990s I have searched for leaders and manifestos in public debates and diverse archives. I have found none.

2   The essential new study is Carlos Herrejón Peredo's transforming *Hidalgo: Maestro, Párroco, Insurgente*—here after cited: *Hidalgo MPI*.

3   His story was brought to light, and to me, by Herrejón Peredo, *Hidalgo MPI*.

4   Tutino, "Revolution in Mexican Independence."

5   See also Van Young's fine biography, *A Life Together*.

6   Ward, *Mexico in 1827*, 2 vols.

7   See Hale, *Mexican Liberalism*; and Hale, *Transformation of Liberalism*.

8   On the rise of sugar and slavery, the classic study is Verlinden, *Beginnings of Modern Colonization*.

9   Foundations are detailed in Schwartz, "Indian Labor and New World Plantations." On the long history of sugar and slavery in Brazil, see Schwartz, *Sugar Plantations*. For comparative perspectives, see Schwartz, *Tropical Babylon*.

10   The key study of the shift to the Caribbean is Dunn, *Rise of the Planter Class*.

11   All detailed in Burnard and Garrigus, *Plantation Machine*.

12   Recently revealed in E. Cross, *Company Politics*.

13   The classic work on the Haitian Revolution is James, *Black Jacobins*. New scholarship showing slaves as protagonists began with Fick, *Making of Haiti*, followed by Dubois, *Avengers of the New World*, quote on 230. Fick synthesizes the impacts of the conflict in "From Slave Colony to Black Nation."

14   This key point was made first by Fick in *Making of Haiti*, then confirmed by Dubois in *Avengers of the New World*.

15   See B. Stein and S. Stein, *Edge of Crisis*; and B. Stein and S. Stein, *Crisis in an Atlantic Empire*.

16   See Tone, *Fatal Knot*; and Cayuela Fernández and Gallego Palomares, *La Guerra de independencia*.

17   Tutino, *Mexico City, 1808*.

18 This builds on Braudel, *Civilization and Capitalism*; Pomeranz, *Great Divergence*; Findlay and O'Rourke, *Power and Plenty*; and was developed for New Spain in Tutino, *Making a New World*; and Tutino, *Mexican Heartland*.

19 Allen, *British Industrial Revolution*.

20 Lin, *China Upside Down*; Platt, *Imperial Twilight*.

21 This complex hemispheric transformation is explored in Tutino, *New Countries*.

22 On the Atlantic slave trade, see Lovejoy, *Transformations in Slavery*, tables 3.4 and 7.4. On the US internal slave trade, see Baptist, *Half Has Never Been Told*.

23 Trouillot, *Silencing the Past*.

24 This is the integrating theme and goal of Tutino, *Mexican Heartland*.

25 Poinsett, *Notes on Mexico*; Ward, *Mexico in 1827*, 2 vols.

26 Calderón de la Barca, *Life in Mexico*.

27 Prieto, "Fidel"; Romero, *Noticias*.

28 Stites, *The Four Horsemen*.

29 On the fall of autonomies in the world of globalization, see Tutino, "Revolutionary Capacity of Rural Communities"; Tutino, *Mexican Heartland*, pt. 3; and the epilogue in the current volume. On urbanizing dependencies across the Americas, see Tutino and Melosi, *New World Cities*.

Chapter 1. A New World in the Bajío

1 This chapter synthesizes and revises the detailed analysis in Tutino, *Making a New World*.

2 On geography and precontact history, see Tutino, *Making a New World*, 65–71. On Mesoamerica and the arid regions stretching north, see López Austin and López Luján, *Mexico's Indigenous Past*.

3 The classic study of the impact of disease is Crosby, *Columbian Exchange*, building on demographic studies later collected in Cook and Borah, *Essays in Population History*.

4 On Otomí origins, see Tutino, *Making a New World*, 71–77; and Somohano Martínez, *La versión histórica*.

5 On Chinese demand and America silver, see Flynn and Giraldez, "Born with a Silver Spoon."

6 Tutino, *Mexican Heartland*, chap. 1, synthesizes the role of Chinese demand across Spanish America and the emergence of distinct silver societies in the Andes, Mesoamerica, and the Bajío.

7   On the China trade, see Giraldez, *Age of Trade*. On the role of Italians orchestrating the impact of silver across Europe and into Asia, along with silver's role stimulating Italian intellectual, cultural, and artistic leadership, see Braudel, *Out of Italy*.

8   On Chichimeca wars, see Powell, *Soldiers, Indians, and Silver*; and Powell, *Mexico's Miguel Caldero*. On Otomí and other Mesoamerican forces, see Tutino, *Making a New World*, 77–94.

9   This sketch of early Querétaro synthesizes Tutino, *Making a New World*, 94–120.

10   Early labor at Querétaro is explored in Tutino, *Making a New World*, 102–12 and appendix A, analyzing more than four hundred work contracts made before 1610 and published by Urquiola Permisán, in *Trabajadores de campo y ciudad*.

11   On Our Lady of Pueblito, the original narrative is Vilaplana, *Histórico y sagrado novenario*.

12   The origins of Guanajuato are detailed in Tutino, *Making a New World*, chap. 2. It builds on the work of regional scholars, notably Castro Rivas, Rangel López, and Tovar Rangel, *Desarrollo sociodemográfico*; López Lara, *El obispado de Michoacán*; and Torres, *El beneficio de la plata*.

13   See the analysis of ethnic and racial amalgamations in the bottomlands in Tutino, *Making a New World*, 144–55 and tables B.8 to B.29, building on local censuses transcribed and published in Carrillo Cázares, *Partidos y padrones*.

14   See the detailed portrait of the life, properties, and estate operations of de la Cruz in Tutino, *Making a New World*, 140–44 and tables B.1 to B.7, building on materials in Baroni Boissonas, *La formación de la estructura agraria*.

15   This is detailed over time, in Tutino, *Making a New World*, chaps. 2, 3, and 7.

16   On the war, see Kamen, *War of Succession in Spain*.

17   See Tutino, *Making a New World*, 159–64 and table D.1. For a first-person account, see Berthe, *Las nuevas memorias*.

18   The classic is Boxer, *Golden Age of Brazil*; for gender, see Higgins, "Licentious Liberty."

19   That shift was a key emphasis of Lynch's classic *Spain Under the Hapsburgs*, vol. 2, *Spain and America, 1598–1700*.

20   On Brazilian gold, see Boxer, *Golden Age of Brazil*; on Italian financial dealings in Europe, see Braudel, *Out of Italy*.

21   See Parthasarathi, *Why Europe Grew Rich and Asia Did Not*.

22   On African exports, see Lovejoy, *Transformations in Slavery*, tables 3.4 and 3.5.

23   Tutino, *Making a New World*, table D.1.

24   Tutino, *Making a New World*, tables C.24 and C.25.

25   Tutino, *Making a New World*, tables C.1 and C.2.

26   On San Miguel, see Tutino, *Making a New World*, tables C.21 and C.22; on Mexico City, see Tutino, *Mexican Heartland*, table A.2.

27   Tutino, *Making a New World*, table C.37.

28   This synthesizes Tutino, *Making a New World*, 192–209, quote on 204.

29   This synthesizes Tutino, *Making a New World*, 183–91; and Hernández, *La soledad del silencio*.

30   This synthesizes Tutino, *Making a New World*, 171–83.

31   The key study of women's lives and ethnic-racial amalgamation remains Guevara Sanginés, *Guanajuato diverso*.

32   This discussion builds on documents in Rionda Arreguín, *La Compañía de Jesús*, quotes on 179–80 and 182–83. All translations are mine unless otherwise indicated.

33   Rodríguez Frausto, "Universidad de Guanajuato," 72.

34   Ajofrín, *Diario del viaje*, 265, 267, 272, 277.

35   This survey of rural social relations in the Bajío from 1700 to 1750 synthesizes Tutino, *Making a New World*, 164–71.

36   On Caballero y Ocío, see Ferrusca Beltrán, *Querétaro*; the will and inventory are in Rincón Frías, "Testamento de don Juan Caballero y Ocío."

37   The detailed accounts are in Alcaide Águilar, *La hacienda "Ciénega de Mata"*; calculations and interpretations are mine.

38   Throughout Tutino, *Making a New World*, I document how work relations grounded in advanced payments creating obligations to labor were demanded by producers and reluctantly accepted by employers who offered the greatest advances to the most valued employees. I show the inability of debts to hold workers, except in *obrajes* (where they could be locked in). At rural estates, advances favored workers whose mobility was rarely constrained before 1790.

      Shelley Streeby in *American Sensations* documents how the label "debt peonage" was invented by ideologues pressing the US war to invade Mexico and take its northern territories in the 1840s. They promoted the notion of Mexican debt bondage as a coercion equal to or worse than slavery, enabling US forces to invade Mexico as "liberators." Of course, no liberation happened as Texas was taken to expand slavery.

39   For a brief summary, see Tutino, *Making a New World*, 463; I rely on the now classic analyses of Gutiérrez, *When Jesus Came*; and Brooks, *Captives and Cousins*.

40   See Hadley, *Minería y sociedad*.

41   Tutino, *Making a New World*, 209–24; on the Yaqui and the northwest, see Folsom, *Yaquis*; and Radding, *Wandering Peoples*; on Escandón and

the Gulf Coast, see Osante, *Orígenes del Nuevo Santander*; on Texas, see de la Teja, *San Antonio de Béjar*; and Barr, *Peace Came in the Form of a Woman*.

Chapter 2. Shaking the New World

1   This is the key message of Findlay and O'Rourke, *Power and Plenty*.

2   For an analysis focused on Britain and North America, see Anderson, *Crucible of War*.

3   See Tutino, *Making a New World*, chap. 4; Castro Gutiérrez, *Nueva ley y nuevo rey*; and Tutino, *Mexico City, 1808*, chap. 6.

4   Mining production figures are in Tutino, *Making a New World*, table D.1.

5   Calculations of commerce in the Bajío and regions north are in Tutino, *Making a New World*, tables D.2 to D.10.

6   The key analysis is Valle Pavón, *Donativos, préstamos y privilegios*.

7   This era is detailed in S. Stein and B. Stein, *Apogee of Empire*.

8   See Burnard and Garrigus, *Plantation Machine*.

9   E. Cross, *Company Politics*.

10   Dubois, *Avengers of the New World*, sets Haiti in the context of the French Revolution. Granados, *En el espejo haitiano*, shows the impact of Haiti in the Caribbean and New Spain. On the slave trade, see Lovejoy, *Transformations in Slavery*, tables 3.4 and 7.4; and Inikori, "Volume of the British Slave Trade," table II.

11   The essential study of Spain's participation in this era of war is B. Stein and S. Stein, *Edge of Crisis*.

12   See Carlos Marichal's pivotal study, *La bancarrota del virreinato*.

13   This is the focus of Herr, *Rural Change and Royal Finances*.

14   The Corregidor's report is Domínguez, "La representación contra la consolidación, 1805," in Brading, *El ocaso del virreinato*, 229–51, discussed in Tutino, *Making a New World*, 436–42.

15   See Tutino, *Mexico City, 1808*, chap. 8; Wobeser, *Dominación colonial*; and Valle Pavón, *Finanzas piadosas*.

16   See Tutino, *Making a New World*, 302–16, building on Brading, *Miners and Merchants*.

17   The complexities and local variations of textile production are explored in Tutino, *Making a New World*, 316–51.

18   See Tutino, *Making a New World*, 339–41; and Tutino, *Mexico City, 1808*, 87–89, 118–19, building upon Deans-Smith, *Bureaucrats, Planters, and Workers*; and González Gómez, *El tobacco virreinal*.

19   See Tutino, *Making a New World*, 402–24; and Herrejón, *Del sermón al discurso cívico*.

20   See Tutino, *Making a New World*, 416–24.

21   Colombini y Camayori, *Querétaro triunfante*. For excerpts and discussion, see Tutino, *Making a New World*, 424–32.

22   Zeláa, *Glorias de Querétaro*. For discussion, see Tutino, *Making a New World*, 433–36.

23   Tutino, *Making a New World*, appendix C, especially table C.37.

24   The key study is Molina del Villar, *La Nueva España y el matlazahuatl*.

25   The data are in Serrano Contreras, "La ciudad de Santiago de Querétaro," 545–50.

26   Tutino, *Making a New World*, 421, based on data in Castro Rivas and Rangel López, *Relación histórica*, 106–8.

27   The classic study is Florescano, *Precios del maíz*; see also Tutino, *Mexican Heartland*, chap. 3.

28   Production patterns are well known, thanks to Brading, "La estructura de la producción"; Brading, *Haciendas and Ranchos*; Morin, *Michoacán en la Nueva España*; Murphy, *Irrigation in the Bajío*; and Tutino, *Making a New World*, chaps. 4–8.

29   The Sánchez Espinosa correspondence is in the García Collection of Benson Latin American Library, UTB-G. The letters are cited here as JSE, followed by date written.

30   This pivotal episode is detailed in Tutino, *Making a New World*, 355–59.

31   The family transitions are detailed in Tutino, *Making a New World*, 265–70.

32   The managerial struggles during drought are detailed in Tutino, *Making a New World*, 383–85.

33   Tutino, *Making a New World*, appendix F.

34   See Tutino, *Making a New World*, 387–88.

35   I explore these accounts in Tutino, *From Insurrection to Revolution*, 82–90 and appendix B.

36   The two cases are explored in detail in Tutino, *Making a New World*, 390–97.

37   On Villaseñor and the La Griega conflicts of 1992, see Tutino, *Making a New World*, 369–71.

38   Tutino, *Making a New World*, 371–74.

39   The case is detailed in Tutino, *Making a New World*, based on AGN, Tierras, vol. 1351, no. 9, fols. 1–24 (1801).

40   See Tutino, *Making a New World*, 380–82; on ritual alcohol use, see W. Taylor, *Drinking, Homicide, and Rebellion*.

41 The key source on Napoleon's incursion is B. Stein and S. Stein, *Crisis in an Atlantic Empire.*

42 Detailed in Tutino, *Mexico City, 1808*, chap. 9.

43 Detailed in Tutino, *Mexico City, 1808*, chap. 10.

44 This is the core argument of Tutino, *Mexico City, 1808.*

45 The plot is outlined in Tutino, *Mexico City, 1808*, 209–20, based on AHN, Consejo de Indias, vol. 21204, 1809–10.

46 Quoted in Guerra, *Modernidades e independencias*, 153.

47 The core of the text is reproduced and discussed in Herrejón Peredo, *HidalgoMPI*, 250–54.

48 Detailed in Tutino, *Making a New World*, 397–99.

49 Vergara Hernández, *Testimonio*, discussed in detail in Tutino, *Making a New World*, 442–47.

50 Data are in Tutino, *Making a New World*, appendix D, tables D.1 and D.2.

51 On profiteering in staples as "Christian charity," see Tutino, *Making a New World*, 296–99; on profiteering at La Griega and Puerto de Nieto in 1808–10, see 397–402; on parallels around Mexico City, see Tutino, *Mexican Heartland*, 128–31.

52 The negotiations are in AGI, México, vol. 2248, correspondence from Nov. 1808 to Sep. 1809.

53 See Tutino, *Mexico City, 1808*, 236–39.

54 See Guerra, *Modernidades e independencias*, 135; and Tutino, *Mexico City, 1808*, chap. 11.

55 Guerra, *Modernidades e independencies*, 198–202.

56 Terán, "1809"; on mediations, see Tutino, *Mexico City, 1808*, chap. 11.

Chapter 3. The Hidalgo Revolt

1 The memo is in AGI, México, vol. 2248, June 20, 1810.

2 Herrejón Peredo, *HidalgoMPI*, 266–99, provides the best narrative of the Querétaro process.

3 The details of González' life are presented in Agraz García de Alba, *Epigmenio González*, 8–22. Documents are reproduced in the original language; Agraz García de Alba's text is in modern, patriotic Mexican usage. Read carefully, they open new visions.

4 Epigmenio González, "Relación sucinta de los Principios de la Revolución Mexicana de 1810 . . . ," in Agraz García de Alba, *Epigmenio González*, 97–102.

5 González, "Relación," 97.

6   González, "Relación," 97.

7   González, "Relación," 98.

8   González, "Relación," 98.

9   González, "Relación," 99.

10   González, "Relación," 100.

11   González, "Relación," 100.

12   The plan is reproduced in Agraz García de Alba, *Epigmenio González*, 94–95, edited into language of Mexican patriotism. In *HidalgoMPI*, 279–82, Herrejón Peredo offers long excerpts from the plan as he found it in the archives, along with an analysis on 279–87. I follow Herrejón's innovative understanding, adding context from Tutino, *Making a New World*.

13   Agraz García de Alba, *Epigmenio González*, 108–12: testimonios, Querétaro, Nov. 15–16, 1810.

14   Hidalgo's early life is sketched in Herrejón Peredo, *HidalgoMPI*, 25–35. That work is key to understanding the insurgent priest, along with the collection of documents in Herrejón Peredo, *Hidalgo: Razones de la independencia y biografía documental*—hereafter cited *Hidalgo RBD*. The classic study is Hamill, *Hidalgo Revolt*.

15   Herrejón Peredo, *HidalgoRBD*, 76–77, 145.

16   Herrejón Peredo, *HidalgoMPI*, 37–42, 56–66; Herrejón Peredo, *HidalgoRBD*, 46, 50, 67, 76–77.

17   Herrejón Peredo, *HidalgoRBD*, 61–62, 76–82.

18   Herrejón Peredo, *HidalgoMPI*, 105–10.

19   Herrejón Peredo, *HidalgoMPI*, 114–21.

20   Herrejón Peredo, *HidalgoMPI*, 144–64.

21   Herrejón Peredo, *HidalgoRBD*, 106–41; Hamill, *Hidalgo Revolt*, 67–77; Herrejón Peredo, *HidalgoMPI*, 166–201.

22   Herrejón Peredo, *HidalgoMPI*, 202–3.

23   Herrejón Peredo, *HidalgoMPI*, 204–11.

24   Herrejón Peredo, *HidalgoRBD*, 194–96.

25   Herrejón Peredo, *HidalgoMPI*, 234–38; Hamill, *Hidalgo Revolt*, 80–88.

26   Terán, "La Virgen de Guadalupe contra Napoleón Bonaparte."

27   Herrejón Peredo, *HidalgoRBD*, 187.

28   Herrejón Peredo, *HidalgoMPI*, 229–34.

29   Herrejón Peredo, *HidalgoRBD*, 199–204.

30   Herrejón Peredo, *HidalgoRBD*, 300.

31   Herrejón Peredo, *HidalgoRBD*, 301.

32 The text, received in the capital after the insurgency began and quoted in this section, is in AGN, Operaciones de Guerra, vol. 20, fol. 1, Sep. 7, 1810.

33 Herrejón Peredo, *HidalgoRBD*, 310; García, *Con el cura Hidalgo*, 35–36, 43: a sympathetic, first-person account.

34 Hamill, *Hidalgo Revolt*, 118–23; García, *Con el cura Hidalgo*, 43–44.

35 Herrejón Peredo, *HidalgoRBD*, 302–3.

36 García, *Con el cura Hidalgo*, 31.

37 García, *Con el cura Hidalgo*, 46.

38 Herrejón Peredo, *HidalgoRBD*, 310. On Atotonilco, see Hernández, *La soledad del silencio*.

39 García, *Con el cura Hidalgo*, 50.

40 Detailed in Herrejón Peredo, *HidalgoMPI*, 300–314.

41 The text is reproduced in Herrejón Peredo, *HidalgoRBD*, 210.

42 Herrejón Peredo, *HidalgoRBD*, 206.

43 García, *Con el cura Hidalgo*, 51.

44 Herrejón Peredo, *HidalgoMPI*, 320–21.

45 García, *Con el cura Hidalgo*, 52, reports the dilemma; the musings about González are mine.

46 Herrejón Peredo, *HidalgoHBD*, 207.

47 Herrejón Peredo, *HidalgoHBD*, 208.

48 Herrejón Peredo, *HidalgoHBD*, 208.

49 Herrejón Peredo, *HidalgoRBD*, 214.

50 Herrejón Peredo, *HidalgoMPI*, 321.

51 Herrejón Peredo, *HidalgoMPI*, 321–22.

52 Herrejón Peredo, *HidalgoRBD*, 211.

53 García, *Con el cura Hidalgo*, 52, 58, 64.

54 Herrejón Peredo, *HidalgoMPI*, 325–26.

55 Herrejón Peredo, *HidalgoMPI*, 326–34.

56 AGI, México, vol. 2249, Guanajuato miners report of Sep. 21, 1813, copy of Nov. 4, 1814.

57 Garcia, *Con el cura Hidalgo*, 69; Hamill, *Hidalgo Revolt*, 137–41; and Herrejón Peredo, *HidalgoMPI*, 334–38, detail the siege and aftermath.

58 García, *Con el cura Hidalgo*, 69; Herrejón Peredo, *HidalgoRBD*, 215.

59 Herrejón Peredo, *HidalgoMPI*, 335.

60 The formal report is in Herrejón Peredo, *HidalgoMPI*, 340; Rico's report is in JSE, Oct. 10, 1810.

61   Herrejón Peredo, *HidalgoMPI*, 340–43.

62   García, *Con el cura Hidalgo*, 79.

63   Herrejón Peredo, *HidalgoRBD*, 216–17.

64   González, "Relación," 100–101.

65   The larger sequence is in Herrejón Peredo, *HidalgoMPI*, 341–56.

66   Herrejón Peredo, *HidalgoMPI*, 359–60.

67   Herrejón Peredo, *HidalgoMPI*, 362–63.

68   Herrejón Peredo, *HidalgoMPI*, 366–67.

69   Herrejón Peredo, *HidalgoMPI*, 372–81.

70   This synthesizes the analysis in Tutino, *Mexican Heartland*, chaps. 2–3.

71   On drought in the heartland, see Tutino, *Mexican Heartland*, 128–31.

72   García, *Con el cura Hidalgo*, 81–85, quotes on 84, 85; on casualties, see Hamill, *Hidalgo Revolt*, 126; the most detailed narrative is Herrejón Peredo, *HidalgoMPI*, 381–84.

73   Herrejón Peredo, *HidalgoMPI*, 384–85.

74   García, *Con el cura Hidalgo*, 90.

75   Benavides Martínez, *De milicianos a soldados del rey*, 304–5, details Calleja's movements from regime sources.

76   García, *Con el cura Hidalgo*, 92–95; Hamill, *Hidalgo Revolt*, 161.

77   Herrejón Peredo, *HidalgoMPI*, 391–98.

78   See Tutino, *Mexican Heartland*, chaps. 3–4; Melville, *Plague of Sheep*; and Graham, "Environmental, Social, and Political Change."

79   See Tutino, *Mexican Heartland*, chap. 4; Hamnett, *Roots of Insurgency*; and Van Young, *Other Rebellion*.

80   Herrejón Peredo, *HidalgoRBD*, 228–29; Herrejón Peredo, *HidalgoMPI*, 398–99.

81   Herrejón Peredo, *HidalgoRBD*, 230–31.

82   Herrejón Peredo, *HidalgoRBD*, 232–33.

83   JSE, Nov. 18, 1810.

84   Hamill, *Hidalgo Revolt*, 184.

85   García, *Con el cura Hidalgo*, 105–6.

86   Benavides Martínez, *De milicianos a soldados del rey*, 306.

87   García, *Con el cura Hidalgo*, 114.

88   On Guadalajara before insurgency, see Van Young, *Hacienda and Market*; and Ibarra, *Mercado e institución*; on the independence era, see Olveda, *De la insurrección a la independencia*.

89   Herrejón Peredo, *HidalgoRBD*, 245–46.

90   Herrejón Peredo, *HidalgoRBD*, 142.

91   Herrejón Peredo, *HidalgoRBD*, 248.

92   Herrejón Peredo, *HidalgoRBD*, 252.

93   Herrejón Peredo, *HidalgoRBD*, 253.

94   *Despertador*, no. 1 (Dec. 20, 1810): 4–6.

95   *Despertador*, no. 2 (Dec. 27, 1810): 17–18.

96   Herrejón Peredo, *HidalgoRBD*, 264.

97   Herrejón Peredo, *HidalgoRBD*, 265.

98   Herrejón Peredo, *HidalgoRBD*, 287–88.

99   García, *Con el cura Hidalgo*, 116–18.

100   Benavides Martínez, *De milicianos a soldados del rey*, 308–15.

101   Herrejón Peredo, *HidalgoRBD*, 298.

102   This is explored throughout Tutino, *Mexico City, 1808*.

103   Herrejón Peredo, *HidalgoRBD*, 310.

104   Herrejón Peredo, *HidalgoRBD*, 312–13.

105   Herrejón Peredo, *HidalgoRBD*, 324.

106   Herrejón Peredo, *HidalgoRBD*, 326.

107   Herrejón Peredo, *HidalgoRBD*, 310.

108   Herrejón Peredo, *HidalgoRBD*, 346.

Chapter 4. Insurgent Guanajuato

1   On Morelos and his political insurgency, see Herrejón Peredo, *Morelos*.

2   On the decade of political insurgencies, see Van Young, *Other Rebellion*.

3   See Tutino, "De Hidalgo a Apatzingán."

4   See Tutino, *Mexican Heartland*, chap. 4.

5   JSE, Feb. 3, 1811.

6   AGN-OG, vol. 30, fols. 63–64, Feb. 9, 1811.

7   JSE, May 4, 1811.

8   Osorno, *El insurgente Albino García*, 25, 31–32, 41; Ortiz Escamilla, *Guerra y gobierno*, 102.

9   Osorno, *El insurgente Albino García*, 46, 228–30.

10   Ortiz Escamilla, *Guerra y gobierno*, 111.

11   Alamán, *Historia de Méjico*, 2:186–88, 191.

12   Calleja to Venegas, Aug. 28, 1811, in Osorno, *El insurgente Albino García*, 231–33.

13   Hidalgo y Costilla to Calleja, Aug. 22, 1811, in Osorno, *El insurgente Albino García*, 234–35.

14   De la Torre Villar, *La Constitución de Apartzingán*, 207–10, documents no. 12–13, Aug. 21, 1811.

15   Josef Manuel Jauregui to Calleja, Sep. 4, 1811, in Osorno, *El insurgente Albino García*.

16   AGI, México, vol. 2249, copia, Madrid, Nov. 4, 1814, Guanajuato memorial, Sep. 21, 1813.

17   AGI, México, vol. 2249, Guanajuato memorial, Sep. 21, 1813.

18   AGI, México, vol. 2249, Guanajuato memorial, Sep. 21, 1813.

19   AGI, México, vol. 2249, Guanajuato memorial, Sep. 21, 1813.

20   AGN-OG, vol. 30, fols. 105–6, Aug. 14, 1811.

21   AGN-OG, vol. 30, fols. 107–8, Aug. 17, 1811.

22   De la Torre Villar, *La Constitución de Apatzingán*, 212–13, doc. 15, Calleja, Sep. 28, 1811.

23   The conflicts of the autumn of 1811 in and around San Miguel are summarized in Ortiz Escamilla, *Guerra y gobierno*, 103–4; and detailed in AGN-OG, vol. 435, fols., 8–9, 14–15, 16–18, 22–23, 36–40, 44–45, 56–59, Guisarnótegui's reports, dated Oct. 8 to Nov. 11, 1811; and AGN-OG, vol. 195, fols. 182–85, 187–93, 195–96, Calleja's reports, Nov. 11–28, 1811.

24   AGN-OG, vol. 195, fols. 105–6, Nov. 19, 1811.

25   Alamán, *Historia de Méjico*, 2:201, 254.

26   AGN-OG, vol. 195, fols. 122–23, Nov. 27, 1811.

27   Pérez Marañón's report is in AGN-OG, vol. 195, fols. 256–59, Dec. 13, 1811.

28   For Rico's report, see JSE, Dec. 2, 1811; on Puerto de Nieto during and after insurgency, see Tutino, "Revolution in Mexican Independence."

29   AGN-OG, vol. 435, fol. 89, Dec. 26, 1811.

30   AGN-OG, vol. 435, fols. 101–2, Dec. 17, 1811.

31   AGN-OG, vol. 195, fols. 287–88, Dec. 20, 1811.

32   AGN-OG, vol. 435, fols. 90–91, Dec. 26, 1811.

33   AGN-OG, vol. 435, fol. 92, Dec. 26, 1811.

34   AGN-OG, vol. 435, fols. 97–98, Jan. 19, 1812.

35   De la Torre Villar, *La Constitución de Apatzingán*, 216, doc. 17, Calleja to Virrey, Zitácuaro, Jan. 2, 1812.

36   De la Torre Villar, *La Constitución de Apatzingán*, 217–19, doc. 18, Bando to Calleja, Zitácuaro, Dec. 5, 1812.

37 AGN-OG, vol. 435, fol. 100, Jan. 19, 1812.

38 Ortiz Escamilla, *Guerra y gobierno*, 104–6, 111; Alamán, *Historia de Méjico*, 3:111–15.

39 AGN-OG, vol. 30, fols. 161–63, Apr. 1811; Alamán, *Historia de Méjico*, 3:122–23.

40 AGN-OG, vol. 31, fols. 125–30, Apr. 20, 1812.

41 AGN-OG, vol. 435, fols. 115–16, May 8, 1812.

42 AGN-OG, vol. 31, fols. 137–41, May 25, 1812.

43 See Iturbide to García Conde, June 6, 1812, García Conde to Venegas, June 5, 1812, García Conde to Venegas, June 10, 1812, all in Osorno, *El insurgente Albino García*, 292–300.

44 AGN-OG, vol. 435, fols. 184–85, July 15, 1812.

45 De la Torre Villar, *La Constitución de Apatzingán*, 358–61, doc. 74, Elementos Constitucionales, Sep. 4, 1812.

46 AGN-OG, vol. 435, fols. 126–37, Nov. 23, 1812.

47 On Cos and Sánchez Espinosa, see JSE, Dec. 11, 1810; on Cos and Liceaga in the Bajío late in 1812, see Ortiz Escamilla, *Guerra y gobierno*, 131–32; and Alamán, *Historia de Méjico*, 3:230–31.

48 On the Cádiz Constitution, see Breña, *El primer liberalismo español*; on implementation in indigenous republics, see Guarisco, *Los indios del valle de México*.

49 AGN-OG, vol. 435, fols. 141–42, Jan. 10, 1813; AGN-OG, fol. 169, June 14, 1813.

50 See Tutino, *Mexican Heartland*, chap. 5, for a preliminary discussion.

51 Alamán, *Historia de Méjico*, 3:244–45, 316–17.

52 De la Torre Villar, *La Constitución de Apatzingán*, 375–76, doc. 83, Sentimientos de la Nación, Sep. 14, 1814.

53 AGI, México, vol. 2149, Guanajuato memorial, Sep. 21, 1813.

54 AGN-OG, vol. 435, fols. 236–37, Nov. 27, 1813.

55 De la Torre Villar, *La Constitución de Apatzingán*, 381–402, doc. 86, Decreto Constitucional, Oct. 22, 1814.

56 AGN-OG, vol. 619, fol. 8, Jan. 14, 1815.

57 AGN-OG, vol. 619, fols. 11–12, Feb. 25, 1815.

58 AGN-OG, vol. 619, fols. 14–15, Aug. 17, 1815.

59 AGN-OG, vol. 619, fols. 21–22, Oct. 12, 1815.

60 AGN-OG, vol. 619, fols. 28–29, Oct. 21, 1815.

61 AGN-OG, vol. 619, fol. 36, Jan. 18, 1816.

62 AGN-OG, vol. 620, fols. 1–2, Feb. 14, 1816.

63   AGN-OG, vol. 619, fols. 40–41, 48–48, Feb. 16, 1816.

64   AGN-OG, vol. 619, fols. 59–60, June 22, 1816; AGN-OG, fol. 68, June 25, 1816.

65   AGN-OG, vol. 619, fol. 67, June 25, 1816.

66   AGN-OG, vol. 619, fols. 98–99, Aug. 26, 1816.

67   AGN-OG, vol. 619, fol. 102, Sep. 1, 1816.

68   Brading, *Haciendas and Ranchos*, 95–114.

69   Alamán, *Historia de Méjico*, 4:193–96.

70   AGN-OG, vol. 620, fol. 8, Sep. 18, 1816; AGN-OG, fol. 21, Oct. 25, 1816.

71   Pérez Rodríguez, *Xavier Mina*, 257–58.

72   AGN-OG, vol. 619, fols. 185–87, Oct. 2, 1816.

73   AGN-OG, vol. 619, fols. 202–3, Oct. 18, 1816.

74   AGN-OG, vol. 619, fols. 217, Oct. 15, 1816.

75   JSE, Aug. 28, 1816.

76   AGN-OG, vol. 619, fols. 307–10.

77   AGN-OG, vol. 619, fols. 410–13, Nov. 12, 1816.

78   JSE, Nov. 23, 1816.

79   Alamán, *Historia de Méjico*, 4:349.

80   JSE, Mar. 27, 1817.

81   JSE, May 8, 2017.

82   JSE, June 24, 1817; CPP, June 24, 1817; CPP, July 8, 1817.

83   JSE, Aug. 19, 1817; CPP, Sept. 28, 1817; CPP, Sep. 30, 1817.

84   Pérez Rodríguez, *Xavier Mina*, chap. 1.

85   Perez Rodríguez, *Xavier Mina*, quotes on 161; the larger discussion synthesizes chap. 2.

86   Mina's early explorations and march inland are detailed in Pérez Rodríguez, *Xavier Mina*, chap. 3.

87   Pérez Rodríguez, *Xavier Mina*, 256–57.

88   Alamán, *Historia de Méjico*, 4:383–89, quote on 388. I rely on Alamán and his near contemporary local knowledge for understanding Mina and the sieges in the Bajío; Pérez Rodríguez, *Xavier Mina*, chap. 4, offers a political narrative focused on Mina.

89   Alamán, *Historia de Méjico*, 4:390–94. Corral's report on the defense of San Miguel is in AGN-OG, vol. 949, fol. 220, Sep. 11, 1817. Sánchez Espinosa's lament of blocked commerce is in JSE, Sep. 30, 1817. The detail on the siege of the rebozo workshop comes from Corral's later report in AGN-OG, vol. 949, fols. 228–29, Sep. 12, 1818.

90   Alamán, *Historia de Méjico*, 4:394.

91   Mina's manifesto is in AGN-OG, vol. 949, fol. 264, Sep. 14, 1817.

92   Alamán, *Historia de Méjico*, 4:396–97.

93   Alamán, *Historia de Méjico*, 4:397–99.

94   Alamán, *Historia de Méjico*, 4:404–6. On hints of rape as a loyalist tool of
      pacification in the Mezquital, see Tutino, *Mexican Heartland*, chap. 4; on
      Alamán's later service with Bustamante, see Tutino, *Mexican Heartland*,
      chap. 6.

95   AGN-OG, vol. 949, fols. 232–39, Sept. 21, 1817.

96   AGN-OG, vol. 949, fols. 276–80, Nov. 23, 1817.

97   AGN-OG, vol. 949, fols. 276–80, Nov. 23, 1817.

98   AGN-OG, vol. 949, fols. 276–80, Nov. 23, 1817.

99   AGN-OG, vol. 949, fols. 276–80, Nov. 23, 1817.

100   AGN-OG, vol. 949, fols. 276–80, Nov. 23, 1817.

101   AGN-OG, vol. 949, fol. 288, Jan. 6, 1818.

102   AGN-OG, vol. 31, fols. 222–25, Feb. 28, 1818.

103   AGN-OG, vol. 949, fols. 288–89, Mar. 4, 1818.

104   AGN-OG, vol. 31, fols. 226–27, Apr. 19, 1818.

105   AGN-OG, vol. 949, fol. 244, Sep. 27, 1818.

106   AGN-OG, vol. 949, fol. 243, Oct. 26, 1818.

107   AGN-OG, vol. 31, fols. 229–30, Nov. 25, 1818.

108   Corral in AGN-OG, vol. 949, fols. 260–61, June 17, 1819; Orrantía in
      AGN-OG, vol. 949, fol. 262, June 17, 1819.

109   AGN-OG, vol. 620, fol. 42, Dec. 23, 1819.

110   AGN-OG, vol. 620, fol. 49, Dec. 23, 1819.

111   AGN-OG, vol. 620, fol. 54, Dec. 27, 1819.

112   AGN-OG, vol. 620, fol. 56, Dec. 30, 1819.

113   AGN-OG, vol. 620, fols. 58–59, Jan. 9, 2020.

114   AGN-OG, vol. 620, fol. 65, Dec. 30, 1818.

115   AGN-OG, vol. 620, fol. 66, Jan. 1, 1820.

116   AGN-OG, vol. 620, fol. 108, Feb. 5, 1820.

117   AGN-OG, vol. 620, fol. 146, Feb. 6, 1920.

118   AGN-OG, vol. 620, fol. 125, Feb. 19, 1820.

119   AGN-OG, vol. 620, fol. 143, Feb. 29, 1820.

120   AGN-OG, vol. 620, fol. 144, Mar. 1, 1820.

121   See Hamnett, "Royalist Counterinsurgency"; and Hamnett, "Anastasio
      Bustamante."

122 AGN, Infidencias, vol. 91, fols. 142–43, 1818.

123 Hamnett, "Anastasio Bustamante."

124 AGN-OG, vol. 620, fol. 120, Feb. 17, 1820.

125 AGN-OG, vol. 620, fols. 152–53, Mar. 2, 1820.

126 AGN-OG, vol. 620, fol. 155, Mar. 2, 1820.

127 AGN-OG, vol. 620, fols. 160–61, Mar. 13, 1820.

128 JSE, Mar. 1, 2020.

129 AGN-BN, vol. 554, Puerto de Nieto accounts, 1820–21; Tutino, "Revolution in Mexican Independence."

130 Tutino, *Making a New World*, 359–67.

Chapter 5. Counterinsurgency Capitalism in Querétaro

1 I explore politics at Querétaro during the decade of insurgency in Tutino, "Querétaro y los orígenes de la nación."

2 Tutino, *Making a New World*, 362–63.

3 Tutino, *Making a New World*, 379–79.

4 The accounts that focus this chapter are in AGN, vol. 554. They offer detailed tabulations of production and work, rents and sales from 1811–12 to 1825–26, with accounts breaking on June 30. Constant citations would be useless.

5 AGN-BN, vol. 554, La Griega accounts, 1811–12.

6 JSE, Oct. 10, 1810; JSE, 214–122, Nov. 18, 1810.

7 JSE, Jan. 18, 1811; Feb. 3, 1811.

8 See Tutino, *Making a New World*, 363.

9 JSE, 214–130, May 4, 1811.

10 AGN-BN, vol. 554, La Griega, 1811–12.

11 AGN-BN, vol. 554, La Griega, 1813–14.

12 AGN-BN, vol. 554, La Griega, 1814–15.

13 The accounts followed the standard practice of recording Hispanic peoples' surnames and presuming none for the Otomí.

14 AHQ, NV, no. 21, 1823, exp. 13, fols. 30–30v, Jan. 24, 1823.

15 Tutino, *Making a New World*, 368.

16 CPP, Feb. 16, 1817.

17 CPP, Feb. 16, 1817.

18 CPP, May 15, 1817.

19 JSE, July 24, 1817.

20   CPP, 147, Nov. 22, 1820.

21   JSE, May 30, 1821.

Chapter 6. New Spain in the Time of Revolution

1   On the Mezquital, see Tutino, *Mexican Heartland*, chaps. 3–4.

2   On secure sustenance inhibiting insurgency in San Luis Potosí, see Tutino, *From Insurrection to Revolution*, 161–63.

3   JSE, Nov. 18, 1810.

4   JSE, Dec. 11, 1810.

5   CPP, Dec. 29, 1810.

6   JSE, Jan. 18, 1811.

7   JSE, Nov. 25, 1781; JSE, Feb. 18, 1782; Benavides Martínez, *De milicianos a soldados del rey*, 181–82.

8   AGN, Vínculos, vol. 79, no. 2, fol. 1–6; UTB-G, Misc. Folder 27A, Oviedo, Sep. 5, 1791, Mar. 21, 1805; JSE, Sep. 12, 1797; JSE, Dec. 10, 1798; JSE, Dec. 6, 1802.

9   JSE, Sep. 14, 1792; JSE, Nov. 19, 1792.

10   JSE, Dec. 10, 1798.

11   JSE, Dec. 6, 1802.

12   AGN, Tierras, vol. 1363, exp. 1, fol. 13, 1805; JSE, Apr. 1, 1805; JSE, Sep. 30, 1805.

13   JSE, Nov. 8, 1802; JSE, July 18, 1803.

14   JSE, Mar. 25, 1805; JSE, Sep. 8, 1806; Aug. 19, 1806; JSE, Jan. 5, 1807; JSE, July 27, 1807; CPP, Sep. 29, 1808.

15   See Tutino, *Making a New World*, 273–74.

16   Tutino, *Making a New World*, 275–76.

17   JSE, 213–533, Sep. 30, 1805; JSE, 213–535, Oct. 3, 1805; JSE, 213–498, Oct. 21, 1805; JSE, 214–19, Feb. 8, 1806; JSE, 214–36, July 27, 1806.

18   JSE, July 27, 1807.

19   On Oviedo, see CPP, Sep. 29, 1808; on Peñasco in the city, see Tutino, *Mexico City, 1808*, 209–20.

20   JSE, Nov. 30, 1809; JSE, Dec. 25, 1809.

21   JSE, Nov. 24, 1809; JSE, Jan. 3, 1810.

22   CPP, June 21, 1810.

23   JSE, July 26, 1810.

24   CPP, Aug. 17, 1810.

25   On Mezquitic, see Tutino, *From Insurrection to Revolution*, 163–64.

26   On the siege of Cuautla in the heartland conflicts of 1810 to 1820, see Tutino, *Mexican Heartland*, chap. 5.

27   JSE, Feb. 1814.

28   Alamán, *Historia de Méjico*, 2:320.

29   JSE, Jan. 18, 1811; JSE, Feb. 3, 1811.

30   JSE, Jan. 28, 1812.

31   JSE, June 4, 1813; JSE, July 16, 1813; CPP, Sep. 3, 1813; CPP, Nov. 18, 1813.

32   CPP, June 18, 1813; CPP, Sep. 3, 1813; CPP, Nov. 18, 1813.

33   *Gaceta de México*, no. 1313 (Nov. 29, 1814); *Gaceta de México*, no. 1319 (Dec. 1, 1814).

34   See Tutino, *Making a New World*, 296.

35   JSE, Feb. 16, 1814; JSE, Oct. 20, 1815; JSE, Oct. 29, 1815; JSE, Jan. 9, 1818.

36   JSE, Feb. 18, 1815.

37   CPP, June 6, 1815; CPP, Sep. 23, 1816.

38   CPP, Apr. 28, 1817; CPP, Aug. 27, 1817; CPP, Mar. 21, 1821.

39   This is the key finding of Ortiz Escamilla, *Calleja*.

40   AGN-BN, Bocas accounts, 1811–1820.

41   CPP, Dec. 28, 1813.

42   CPP, Mar. 9, 1814.

43   CPP, June 6, 1815.

44   CPP, Nov. 6, 1816.

45   JSE, Mar. 26, 1817; JSE, July 24, 1817; Jan. 9, 1818; JSE, Nov. 6, 1818.

46   JSE, 214–188, 1817.

47   CPP, Apr. 30, 1817.

48   CPP, May 27, 1817.

49   UTB-G, Misc. 27A, José Antonio Oviedo, May 28, 1817; CPP, May 28, 1817.

50   CPP, June 3, 1817; JSE, June 9, 1817.

51   CPP, June 24, 1817.

52   CPP, July 8, 1817.

53   JSE, June 20, 1817.

54   JSE July 23, 1817.

55   JSE, June 14, 1817; JSE, June 17, 1817; JSE, June 20, 1817; JSE, June 24, 1817.

56   JSE, June 24, 1817.

57   CPP, Sep. 30, 1817.

58   CPP, Sep. 30, 1817; CPP, Oct. 10, 1817; CPP, Oct. 13, 1817.

59   CPP, July 22, 1817.

60   JSE, Aug. 19, 1817.

61   CPP, Oct. 29, 1817.

62   CPP, Dec. 8, 1817.

63   JSE, Mar. 9, 1818.

64   CPP, Feb. 11, 1818.

65   JSE, May 15, 1820; JSE, July 19, 1820; JSE, June 6, 1820; JSE, Oct. 3, 1820; JSE, Feb. 10, 1821.

66   See Melville, *Plague of Sheep*; and Graham, "Environmental, Social, and Political Change."

67   This synthesizes materials detailed in Tutino, *Mexican Heartland*, chap. 3; and Tutino, *Mexico City, 1808*, chap. 2.

68   This synthesizes detail in Tutino, *Mexican Heartland*, chap. 4.

69   JSE, Jan. 26, 1813; JSE, Aug. 28, 1816.

70   CPP, July 6, 1818.

71   JSE, Aug. 28, 1816.

72   JSE, Aug. 28, 1816; JSE, Jan. 22, 1817; JSE, July 18, 1817.

73   JSE, July 23, 1817.

74   JSE, June 23, 1818.

75   Tutino, *Making a New World*, 294–95.

76   On the Jala and Regla clans, see Tutino, *Mexican Heartland*, chap. 3; and Tutino, *Mexico City, 1808*, chaps. 2–3.

77   PCRun, Meritos, 1803; PCRun, f.d. 1811.

78   Romero de Terreros, "La condesa escribe," 459–60.

79   Romero de Terreros, "La condesa escribe," 460–61.

80   Romero de Terreros, "La condesa escribe," 461–67.

81   PCRun, Sucesion al Marquesado de San Cristóbal, Oct. 1 to Dec. 3, 1817.

82   *Gaceta de México*, no. 1340, Nov. 5, 1818.

83   PCRun, Apr. 25, 1820.

Chapter 7. As the World Turned

1   Stites, *Four Horsemen*.

2   On the politics of Iguala, see Arenal Fenocchio, *Un modo de ser libres*.

3   See Plan de Iguala, February 24, 1821, accessed digitally on the website of the Library of Congress, Washington, DC, https://loc.gov/rr/Hispanic

/Mexico/iguala. The original is in the Library of Congress, Law Library, KGF 7505.3 1821.

4   On the pivotal events of 1808, see Tutino, *Mexico City, 1808*, especially chaps. 9–10.

5   The essential analysis of the role of the military in Iguala is Moreno Gutiérrez, *La trigarancia*.

6   See Tutino, *Mexico City, 1808*, pt. 1, "City of Silver."

7   Ocampo, *Las ideas de un día*.

8   The key study is Ávila, *Para la libertad*.

9   Serrano Ortega, *Jerarquía territorial*.

10 See Van Young's brilliant and detailed political biography, *A Life Together*.

11 Poinsett, *Notes on Mexico*.

12 Ward, *Mexico in 1827*, 2 vols.

13 Poinsett, *Notes on Mexico*, 16–23, quote on 19.

14 Poinsett, *Notes on Mexico*, 52–56, quote on 55.

15 Poinsett, *Notes on Mexico*, 76–77.

16 Poinsett, *Notes on Mexico*, 79–86.

17 Poinsett, *Notes on Mexico*, 91–93.

18 Poinsett, *Notes on Mexico*, 140–41.

19 Poinsett, *Notes on Mexico*, 142.

20 Poinsett, *Notes on Mexico*, 151–53.

21 Poinsett, *Notes on Mexico*, 142–43.

22 Ward, *Mexico in 1827*, 2 vols.

23 Ward, *Mexico in 1827*, 2:172–80, quote on 180.

24 Ward, *Mexico in 1827*, 2:206–18.

25 Ward, *Mexico in 1827*, 2:220–23.

26 Ward, *Mexico in 1827*, 2:223–26.

27 Ward, *Mexico in 1827*, 2:238–39.

28 Ward, *Mexico in 1827*, 2:239–40.

29 Ward, *Mexico in 1827*, 2:241–42.

30 Ward, *Mexico in 1827*, 2:244–54.

31 Ward, *Mexico in 1827*, 2:261–63.

32 Ward, *Mexico in 1827*, 2:266–69.

33 Ward, *Mexico in 1827*, 2:273.

34 Ward, *Mexico in 1827*, 2:275.

35   Ward, *Mexico in 1827*, 2:279.

36   Ward, *Mexico in 1827*, 2:280.

37   Ward, *Mexico in 1827*, vol. 2, Book V, "Personal Narrative," 171–280.

38   Ward, *Mexico in 1827*, 1:vi.

39   Ward, *Mexico in 1827*, 1:x.

40   Ward, *Mexico in 1827*, 1:x.

41   Ward, *Mexico in 1827*, 1:23.

42   Ward, *Mexico in 1827*, 1:23–26.

43   Ward, *Mexico in 1827*, 1:xv.

44   Ward, *Mexico in 1827*, 1:124–49.

45   Ward, *Mexico in 1827*, 1:150.

46   Ward, *Mexico in 1827*, 1:150–259.

47   Detailed in Salvucci, *Politics, Markets*.

48   Salvucci, *Politics, Markets*, 28–99.

49   Ward, *Mexico in 1827*, 1:360–64, quote on 364.

50   Ward, *Mexico in 1827*, 1:364–65.

51   Ward, *Mexico in 1827*, 1:365–69.

52   Ward, *Mexico in 1827*, 1:370–92.

53   Ward, *Mexico in 1827*, 1:292–94, quote on 293.

54   Ward, *Mexico in 1827*, 1:394.

55   Ward, *Mexico in 1827*, 1:395–96.

56   Ward, *Mexico in 1827*, 1:428–38.

57   Ward, *Mexico in 1827*, 1:439.

58   Ward, *Mexico in 1827*, 1:447.

59   Ward, *Mexico in 1827*, 1:456.

60   Ward, *Mexico in 1827*, 1:468–75.

61   Ward, *Mexico in 1827*, 1:475.

62   Ward, *Mexico in 1827*, 2:12–38, quotes on 16, 23, 37.

63   Ward, *Mexico in 1827*, 2:38.

64   Ward, *Mexico in 1827*, 2:55–56.

65   Ward, *Mexico in 1827*, 2:56–57.

66   Ward, *Mexico in 1827*, 2:57.

67   Ward, *Mexico in 1827*, 2:64–68; Randall, *Real del Monte*, offers a close analysis of a key venture.

68   On Zacatecas, the essential study is H. Cross, "Mining Economy of Zacatecas."

69   See Brading's classic *Miners and Merchants*; Tutino, *Making a New World*; Tutino, *Mexico City, 1808*: Valle Pavón, *Finanzas piadosas*; and Valle Pavón, *Donativos, préstamos*.

70   See Tutino, *Mexican Heartland*, chaps. 6 and 7.

71   Best detailed and analyzed in Ávila, *Para la libertad*.

72   The great exception is the classic work of Benson, *Provincial Deputation in Mexico*.

73   "Constitución Federal de los Estados Unidos Mexicanos," Oct. 4, 1824, in Suárez Muñoz and Jiménez Gómez, *La ideología republicana en Querétaro*, full text, 51–94, quotes on 55–56.

74   H. Cross, "Mining Economy of Zacatecas."

75   Brading, *Miners and Merchants*; Tutino, *Mexico City, 1808*.

76   The details, without my emphasis on deflection, are in Sims, *La expulsión*; and Sims, *The Expulsion of Mexico's Spaniards*.

77   On the Parián riots, see Arrom, "Popular Politics in Mexico City." On politics, see Costeloe, *La primera república*; and Anna, *Forging Mexico*. On regime finance, see Hernández Jaimes, *La formación de la hacienda pública*.

78   On Bustamante and Alamán in the 1930s, see Andrews, *Entre la espada y la constitución*.

79   David Weber's classic studies, *The Spanish Frontier* and *Bárbaros*, are essential. On California, see Hackel, *Children of Coyote*. On ties to New Spain's silver capitalism, see Tutino, *Making a New World*.

80   Velasco Ávila, *La frontera étnica*, chap. 3.

81   The text of the treaty is reproduced in Velasco Ávila, *La fróntera étnica*, 373–76.

82   This synthesizes Velasco Ávila, *La frontera étnica*, chaps. 4–6; on secession and slavery, see Lack, *Texas Revolutionary Experience*.

Chapter 8. Independent Guanajuato

1   On the politics of independent Guanajuato, the essential study is Serrano Ortega, *Jerarquí territorial*.

2   On silver to 1810, see Tutino, *Making a New World*, table D.1. On flows after 1810, see appendix B, table B.1, B.2.

3   Poinsett, *Notes on Mexico*, 186–88.

4   Poinsett, *Notes on Mexico*, 188–89.

5   Poinsett, *Notes on Mexico*, 192.

6   Poinsett, *Notes on Mexico*, 199–200.

7   Poinsett, *Notes on Mexico*, 200–201.

8   Poinsett, *Notes on Mexico*, 201–2.

9   Poinsett, *Notes on Mexico*, 202.

10   Poinsett, *Notes on Mexico*, 207, 210.

11   Poinsett, *Notes on Mexico*, 212.

12   Poinsett, *Notes on Mexico*, 216, 218.

13   Poinsett, *Notes on Mexico*, 214.

14   Poinsett, *Notes on Mexico*, 222.

15   Poinsett, *Notes on Mexico*, 233.

16   Poinsett, *Notes on Mexico*, 236.

17   Poinsett, *Notes on Mexico*, 236–46.

18   Poinsett, *Notes on Mexico*, 247, 250–51.

19   Poinsett, *Notes on Mexico*, 259–60.

20   As soon would happen across Mexico. See Tutino, *Mexican Heartland*, chap. 6.

21   This analysis is based on AGN-BN, vol. 554, Puerto de Nieto accounts, 1820–21 to 1825–26.

22   JSE, Mar. 18, 1822; JSE, Sep. 23, 1823; JSE, Dec. 10, 1824.

23   JSE, June 23, 1825; JSE, Oct. 4, 1825.

24   CM-DJC, caja 651, legajo 12, July 20, 1817.

25   CM-DJC, c. 651, l. 14, Dec. 28, 1818.

26   CM-DJC, c. 651, l. 4, May 1, 1823.

27   CM-DJC, c. 651, l. 41, June 4, 1823.

28   CM-DJC, c. 651, l. 12, May 15, 1823.

29   CM-JCP, c. 653, l. 61, June 15, 1825.

30   CM-JCP, c. 652, l. 54, Nov. 4, 1824.

31   CM-JCP, c. 653, l. 63, Dec. 23, 1825.

32   CM-JCP, c. 652, l. 52, May 1, 1824.

33   CM-JCP, c. 652, l. 56, May 7, 1824.

34   CM-JPC, c. 652, l. 61, July 31, 1824.

35   CM-JPC, c. 653, l. 58, Mar. 8, 1824.

36   This limited participation is detailed in Serrano Ortega, *Jerarquía territorial*.

37   Montes de Oca, *Memoria, 1825*, 21.

38   Montes de Oca, *Memoria, 1825*, 22.

39 Montes de Oca, *Memoria, 1826* 2.

40 Montes de Oca, *Memoria, 1826,* 21–22.

41 Montes de Oca, *Memoria, 1825,* 13–14.

42 Montes de Oca, *Memoria, 1825,* plan 1.

43 Montes de Oca, *Memoria, 1826,* no. 2.

44 Montes de Oca, *Memoria, 1825,* 11–12.

45 Montes de Oca, *Memoria, 1825,* 8.

46 Montes de Oca, *Memoria, 1826,* 17.

47 Montes de Oca, *Memoria, 1826,* 17–18.

48 On the Sierra, see Tutino, *From Insurrection to Revolution,* chap. 7; on discourses of barbarism, see Tutino, *Mexican Heartland,* chaps. 6 and 8.

49 Montes de Oca, *Memoria, 1827,* 18.

50 Ward, *Mexico in 1827,* 2:420–22.

51 Ward, *Mexico in 1827,* 2:424, 429, 434.

52 Ward, *Mexico in 1827,* 2:432–33.

53 Ward, *Mexico in 1827,* 2:441–42.

54 Ward, *Mexico in 1827,* 2:459–61.

55 Berlandier and Chovel, *Diario de viaje,* 21–22.

56 Berlandier and Chovel, *Diario de viaje,* 26–28.

Chapter 9. Querétaro After Insurgency

1 Telmo Primo, *Querétaro en 1822.*

2 Telmo Primo, *Querétaro en 1822,* 34.

3 Telmo Primo, *Querétaro en 1822,* 32, 36–37.

4 Telmo Primo, *Querétaro en 1822,* 34–36.

5 Telmo Primo, *Querétaro en 1822,* 29.

6 Poinsett, *Notes on Mexico,* 176–79.

7 Poinsett, *Notes on Mexico,* 181.

8 Poinsett, *Notes on Mexico,* 181.

9 See Tutino, *Making a New World,* chaps. 2, 4, 6, 8.

10 Poinsett, *Notes on Mexico,* 182.

11 Poinsett, *Notes on Mexico,* 183.

12 Poinsett, *Notes on Mexico,* 184.

13 Poinsett, *Notes on Mexico,* 185.

14 Poinsett, *Notes on Mexico,* 186.

15   CPP, Nov. 22, 1820; JSE, Feb. 3, 1821.

16   Recorded in AGN-BN, vol. 554, La Griega accounts, 1820–1821.

17   JSE, Mar. 1, 1820; CPP, Nov. 22, 1820.

18   All this and what follows comes from analysis of AGN-BN, vol. 554, La Griega accounts, 1820–1826.

19   AHQ-NV, vol. 21, Jan. 24, 1823.

20   AHQ-NV, vol. 23, Jan. 24, 1825.

21   AHQ-NV, vol. 19, Jan. 27, 1821.

22   AHQ-NV, vol. 19, Feb. 23, 1821.

23   AHQ-NV, vol. 20, Nov. 27, 1822.

24   AHQ-NV, vol. 21, Dec. 13, 1823.

25   AHQ-NV, vol. 22, Feb. 14, 1824.

26   AHQ-NV, vol. 19, Mar. 30, 1821; AHQ-NV, vol. 20, Jan. 8, 1822; AHQ-NV, vol. 21, Apr. 15, 1823.

27   AHQ-NV, vol. 22, June 19, 1824.

28   AHQ-NV, vol. 22, Nov. 4, 1824.

29   AHQ-NV, vol. 20, Nov. 27, 1822; AHQ-NV, vol. 21, Nov. 5, 1823; AHQ-NV, vol. 22, Nov. 14, 1824; AHQ-NV, vol. 22, Nov. 4, 1824.

30   AHQ-NV, vol. 21, Aug. 23, 1823.

31   AHQ-NV, vol. 22, Feb. 14, 1824.

32   AHQ-NV, vol. 22, Feb. 14, 1824.

33   AHQ-NV, vol. 23, Jan. 24, 1825.

34   AHQ-NV, vol. 23, Feb. 25, 1825; AHQ-NV, vol. 23, Apr. 16, 1825.

35   AHQ-NV, vol. 24, Feb. 14, 1826.

36   AHQ-NV, vol. 24, Mar. 4, 1826.

37   AHQ-NV, vol. 24, Jan. 13, 1826.

38   AHQ-NV, vol. 24, Apr. 7, 1826.

39   AHQ-NV, vol. 24, Jul. 11, 1826; AHQ-NV, vol. 24, Nov. 14, 1826.

40   AHQ-NV, vol. 24, Feb. 10, 1826.

41   AHQ-BD, 1822–1826.

42   AHQ-P, 1826, San Pedro de la Cañada.

43   AHQ-P, 1826, Santa Rosa.

44   AHQ-P, 1826, Juriquilla, San Miguelito, La Solana, Santa Catarina, Monte Negro, Buenavista, Jofre.

45   See Tutino, *Mexican Heartland*, chap. 2.

46   Appendix C, table C.1. Except for a few cases, clearly noted as linked to other cited texts, all appendix references link to this volume.

47   Appendix C, table C.2.

48   Appendix C, table C.3.

49   Appendix C, table C.4.

50   Appendix C, table C.5.

51   Appendix C, table C.6.

52   Appendix C, table C.7.

53   Ward, *Mexico in 1827*, 2:415–16.

54   Ward, *Mexico in 1827*, 2:416–18; on Querétaro's rise to eminence, see Tutino, *Making a New World*, chaps. 1, 3, 6, 8.

55   Ward, *Mexico in 1827*, 2:418.

56   Ward, *Mexico in 1827*, 2:420.

57   AHQ-NV, vol. 25, Mar. 13, 1827.

58   AHQ-NV, vol. 25, Aug. 25, 1827.

59   AHQ-NV, vol. 25, Aug. 1, 1827; AHQ-NV, vol. 26, Feb. 13, 1828; AHQ-NV, vol. 27, June 3, 1829.

60   AHQ-NV, vol. 27, June 3, 1829.

61   AHQ-NV, vol. 26, Feb. 13, 1828; AHQ-NV, vol. 27, June 3, 1829; AHQ-NV, vol. 28, Oct. 18, 1830.

62   AHQ-NV, vol. 28, Sep. 22, 1830.

63   AHQ-NV, vol. 25, Jan. 30, 1827; AHQ-NV, vol. 26, June 12, 1828.

64   AHQ-NV, vol. 27, Mar. 14, 1829.

65   AHQ-NV, vol. 27, Mar. 18, 1829.

66   AHQ-NV, vol. 22, Mar. 26, 1824.

67   AHQ-NV, vol. 22, Mar. 24, 1824.

68   Tutino, *Making a New World*, 338, 377.

69   AHQ-NV, vol. 27, Apr. 1, 1829.

Chapter 10. Mexico in the Wake of Revolution

1   Fernández de Recas, *Mayorazgos*, 404–5; *Gazeta de México*, Aug. 26, 1815; *Gazeta de México*, Oct. 31, 1820.

2   Tutino, *Mexico City, 1808*, 155; *Diario de México*, Feb. 11, 1816; *Gazeta de México*, June 20, 1820.

3   Tutino, *Mexico City, 1808*, 207; *Gazeta de México*, Apr. 26, 1820.

4   Ladd, *Mexican Nobility*, 189; Tutino, *Mexico City, 1808*, 51, 160, 194; *Diario de México*, Dec. 28, 1813; Museo Nacional de Antropología, Mexico City, microfilm, San Luis Potosí, roll 32; *Gazeta de México*, Jan. 13, 1820; *Gazeta de México*, Oct. 4, 1821.

5   Ladd, *Mexican Nobility*, 153–60.

6   Harris, *Mexican Family Empire*.

7   On the Santiagos, see Tutino, *Mexican Heartland*, chaps. 2–4; Tutino, *Mexico City, 1808*, chaps. 2–3; and Tutino, "Power, Class, and Family."

8   On the junta, see *Gazeta de México*, Oct. 4, 2021; on Santiago family economic challenges, see PCR, vol. 173, June 27, 1818; PCR, vol. 185, Mar. 18, 1818; PCRun, 1820.

9   On the Atengo estates, see Tutino, *Mexican Heartland*, chaps. 2, 3, and 7; on the 1820s, see Kanter, *Hijos del Pueblo*, chap. 7.

10 Tutino, *Mexican Heartland*, chap. 4.

11 PCRun, f.d. 1825: Mar. 24, 1825; Apr. 1825; May 2, 1825; PCR, vol. 185, Apr. 19, 1826; PCR, Nov. 15, 1826.

12 PCRun, f.d. 1811, documents and letters; PCRun, f.d. 1833: Feb. 25, 1833; Nov. 26, 1834, to May 17, 1835; PCRun, f.d. 1835: Feb. Mar. 7, 1835.

13 See the letters in Romero de Terreros, "La condesa escribe."

14 *Gazeta de México*, Nov. 2, 1819.

15 PCRun, Apr. 25, 1820.

16 *Gazeta de México*, Oct. 4, 1821.

17 *Gazeta de México*, Mar. 2, 1822; *Gazeta de México*, Sep. 14, 1822.

18 PCRun, Jala docs., 1836, 118–19.

19 Randall, *Real del Monte*, 73, 212.

20 PCR, vol. 172, 1819; PCRun, Jala docs., 1836, 155.

21 PCRun, Jala docs., 1836, 145–51.

22 PCR, vol. 203, Oct. 26, 1827.

23 PCRun, Jala docs., 1836, 137–43.

24 PCR, vol. 201, Mar. 21, 1834; PCRun, Aug. 4, 1836.

25 PCRun, Jala docs., 1836, 156–58.

26 PCR, vol. 201, Mar. 2, 1838.

27 PCRun, f.d. 1811, 1839.

28 Romero de Terreros, *Antiguas haciendas*, 201.

29 CPP, Apr. 8, 1821.

30 CPP, Nov. 15, 1821; CPP, Dec. 19, 1821.

31   CPP, Jan. 23, 1822.

32   CPP, May 20, 1822; CPP, Aug. 26, 1822; Ladd, *Mexican Nobility*, 130–31.

33   CPP, Oct. 18, 1823.

34   CPP, Oct. 13, 1824; Oct. 20, 1824; CPP, Nov. 15, 1824.

35   JSE, Dec. 1, 1824.

36   JSE, Dec. 13, 1825; JSE, Sep. 2, 1826.

37   AGN-BN, vol. 554, Obra Pía accounts, 1820–21 to 1825–26.

38   JSE, 215–57, Feb. 27, 1828; CPP, Nov. 12, 1828.

39   JSE, Nov. 26, 1828.

40   JSE, May 29, 1830; CPP, July 14, 1832; CPP, Dec. 2, 1840.

41   AHQ-NV, Sep. 22, 1830.

42   AHQ-NV, Apr. 8, 1839.

43   JSE, Sep. 20, 1830; JSE, Jan. 3, 1831; JSE, 248, Apr. 4, 1832; CPP, Mar. 11, 1834;
        CPP, Sep. 30, 1835.

44   CPP, Nov. 20, 1833; CPP, Nov. 26, 1833.

45   CPP, Nov. 26, 1833; CPP, Dec. 11, 1833.

46   CPP, Jan. 15, 1834; CPP, Jan. 28, 1834.

47   CPP, vol. Mar. 11, 1834.

48   CPP, Mar. 18, 1834.

49   CPP, May 30, 1837.

50   CPP, July 7, 1837.

51   CPP, Aug. 13, 1837.

52   CPP, May 22, 1838.

53   CPP, May 20, 1838.

54   CPP, June 4, 1839.

55   CPP, Mar. 3, 1840.

56   CPP, June 23, 1840.

57   CPP, 1841–1844.

58   CPP, Jan. 9, 1841.

59   CPP, May 1, 1841; CPP, May 5, 1841.

60   CPP, July 22, 1841; CPP, Oct. 20, 1841; CPP, Oct. 25, 1841.

61   CPP, Jan. 28, 1843; CPP, Feb. 18, 1843.

62   CPP, Apr. 8, 1843.

63   CPP, Apr. 10, 1843; CPP, May 4, 1843; CPP, May 28, 1843; CPP, June 28, 1843;
        CPP, July 11, 1843; CPP, July 12, 1843; CPP, July 19, 1843; CPP, Aug. 2, 1843.

64   CPP, Aug. 2, 1843; CPP, Aug. 9, 1843; CPP, Aug. 19, 1843; CPP, Aug. 23, 1843; CPP, Aug. 26, 1843; CPP, Sep. 30, 1843.

65   CPP, Oct. 13, 1843; CPP, Oct. 15, 1843.

66   CPP, Oct. 10, 1843; CPP, Jan. 17, 1844; CPP, Apr. 4, 1844; CPP, Apr. 20, 1844.

67   CPP, Sep. 11, 1844.

68   CPP, 1844–1845; Bazant, *Cinco haciendas mexicanas.*

69   I rely on Calderón de la Barca, *Life in Mexico*, integrating published text and private letters.

70   Calderón de la Barca, *Life in Mexico*, 92, 420.

71   Calderón de la Barca, *Life in Mexico*, 93, 108–9.

72   Tutino, *Mexican Heartland*, chap. 2; Tutino, *Mexico City, 1808*, chap. 2.

73   Calderón de la Barca, *Life in Mexico*, 112, 113–14, 117, 120, 125–26.

74   Calderón de la Barca, *Life in Mexico*, 195–96.

75   Calderón de la Barca, *Life in Mexico*, 197.

76   Calderón de la Barca, *Life in Mexico*, 199–202.

77   Calderón de la Barca, *Life in Mexico*, 202–3.

78   Calderón de la Barca, *Life in Mexico*, 150.

79   Calderón de la Barca, *Life in Mexico*, 219–20.

80   Calderón de la Barca, *Life in Mexico*, 290–91.

81   Calderón de la Barca, *Life in Mexico*, 506.

82   Calderón de la Barca, *Life in Mexico*, 505, 507.

83   Calderón de la Barca, *Life in Mexico*, 522.

84   On estates and communities at Chalco, see Tutino, *Mexican Heartland*, chaps. 7 and 8.

85   Calderón de la Barca, *Life in Mexico,* 422–23. On the Fagoagas, see Pérez Morales, *Familia, poder, riqueza.*

86   Calderón de la Barca, *Life in Mexico*, letters, Oct. 23, 1841.

87   On Chalco and the wider heartland, see Tutino, *Mexican Heartland*, chap. 7.

Chapter 11. A New Bajío, 1830–1845

1   See figures in Tutino, *Making a New World*, appendix D, table D.1; and Tutino, *Mexican Heartland*, table A.8.

2   Appendix B, tables B.1 and B.3.

3   On British capital and local mine operators at Guanajuato, see Velasco Ávila et al., *Estado y minería*, 98–153, 223–33.

4   Appendix B, table B.4.

5   Appendix B, tables B.1 and B.5.

6   Monroy, "Las minas de Guanajuato," 395.

7   Appendix B, table B.6.

8   See the import figures in Herrera Canales, *El comercio exterior*, cuadro 11, p. 34.

9   The sequence is detailed in Potash, *Mexican Government*, 12–38, the classic study of Mexico's early industrialization.

10 See Potash, *Mexican Government*, 38–51, on the founding of the bank.

11 *Registro Oficial*, Año 2, Tomo IV, no. 55, Feb. 24, 1831, Acámbaro report, Jan. 5, 1831.

12 *Registro Oficial*, Año 2, Tomo IV, no. 3, Feb. 11, 1831, Salvatierra report, Jan. 3, 1831.

13 *Registro Oficial*, Año 2, Tomo V, no. 2, May 2, 1831, Yuriria report, Jan. 17, 1831.

14 *Registro Oficial*, Año 2, Tomo IV, no. 40, Feb. 9, 1831, Valle de Santiago report, n.d.

15 *Registro Oficial*, Año 2, Tomo IV, no. 39, March 8, 1831, Silao report, Dec. 31, 1830.

16 *Registro Oficial*, Año 2, Tomo V, no. 8, May 8, 1831, Penjámo report, Feb. 20, 1831.

17 *Registro Oficial*, Año 2, Tomo V, no. 21, May 31, 1831, Querétaro report, May 11, 1831.

18 AHQ-NV, vol. 30, Feb. 14, 1832.

19 Potash, *Mexican Government*, 67–71.

20 Biographical details come from Ratz, *Tras las huellas de un desconocido*, 101–9; on Rubio in San Luis Potosí, see Sims, *Expulsion of Mexico's Spaniards*, 145.

21 On regional minting, see Lerdo de Tejada, *El comercio exterior*, cuadro no. 35, note 20; on Tampico exports, see Prieto, *Indicaciones*, Resumen General, 1827, 1828, following p. 308.

22 On trade at San Luis Potosí and Rubio's role, see Cañedo Gamboa, "Merchants and Family Business."

23 Appendix B, table B.1.

24 Ratz, *Tras las huellas*, 101–9.

25 Loyola Vera, *Sistemas hidraúlicas*, 165.

26 Loyola Vera, *Sistemas hidraúlicas*, 169–70.

27 Loyola Vera, *Sistemas hidraúlicas*, 166–68.

28 Appendix D, tables D.1 and D.4.

29 Raso, *Notas, 1845*, 63.

30 Chávez Orozco and Florescano, *Agricultura e industria textil*, documents, 192–251.

31 Appendix D, table D.1.

32 Raso, *Notas, 1845*, 69–70.

33 Appendix D, table D.3.

34 Tutino, *Making a New World*, 341.

35 The 1840s import figures are in Lerdo de Tejada, *El comercio exterior*, cuadro 45. On Alamán's efforts, see Tutino, *Mexican Heartland*, chap. 6; and Van Young, *Life Together*.

36 Lerdo de Tejada, *El comercio exterior*, cuadro 47.

37 Lerdo de Tejada, *El comercio exterior*, cuadro 48.

38 AHQ-NV, vol. 22, Nov. 4, 1824.

39 AHQ-NV, vol. 29, May 28, 1831.

40 AHQ-NV, vol. 33, Sep. 30, 1835.

41 AHQ-NV, vol. 42, May 7, 1845.

42 AHQ-NV, vol. 29, Mar. 26, 1831.

43 AHQ-NV, vol. 29, Aug. 29, 1831.

44 AHQ-NV, vol. 31, Dec. 6, 1833.

45 AHQ-NV, vol. 38, Dec. 30, 1842.

46 AHQ-NV, vol. 39, Apr. 29, 1842.

47 AHQ-NV, vol. 42, Sep. 20, 1843.

48 See AHQ-NV, vol. 29, June 10, 1831; AHQ-NV, vol. 30, Dec. 30, 1833; AHQ-NV, vol. 31, Jan. 5, 1833; AHQ-NV, vol. 32, May 5, 1834; AHQ-NV, vol. 33, May 13, 1835.

49 AHQ-NV, 31, vol. Oct. 26, 1833.

50 AHQ-NV, vol. 20, Jan. 8, 1822.

51 AHQ-NV, vol. 24, Feb. 14, 1826.

52 AHQ-NV, vol. 31, Jan. 3, 1833.

53 AHQ-NV, vol. 40, Oct. 23, 1843.

54 AHQ-NV, vol. 29, Mar. 20, 1831; AHQ-NV, vol. 33, Jan. 2, 1835; AHQ-NV, vol. 32, Mar. 24, 1834; May 6, 1835; AHQ-NV, vol. 34, Mar. 11, 1836.

55 AHQ-NV, vol. 31, Nov. 5, 1833.

56 AHQ-NV, vol. 33, Oct. 1835.

57 AHQ-NV, vol. 36, May 8, 1839.

58 AHQ-NV, vol. 34, Apr. 17, 1836.

59 AHQ-NV, vol. 35, Dec. 29, 1837.

60   AHQ-NV, vol. 39, April 1, 1842.

61   AHQ-NV, vol. 31, Sep. 18, 1833.

62   AHQ-NV, vol. 34, Dec. 24, 1836.

63   AHQ-NV, vol. 38, Jan. 22, 1841.

64   AHQ-NV, vol. 40, Feb. 18, 1843; AHQ-NV, vol. 40, Feb. 22, 1843.

65   AHQ-NV, vol. 40, Feb. 3, 1843; AHQ-NV, vol. 40, Feb. 27, 1843.

66   AHQ-NM, vol. 2, Mar. 23–28, 1843.

67   AHQ-NV, vol. 41, Aug. 7, 1844.

68   AHQ-NV, vol. 36, Jan. 28, 1839.

69   AHQ-NV, vol. 36, Jan. 30, 1839.

70   AHQ-NV, vol. 36, Feb. 18, 1839.

71   AHQ-NV, vol. 36, Apr. 18, 1839.

72   AHQ-NV, vol. 36, Oct. 22, 1839.

73   AHQ-NV, vol. 36, Dec. 23, 1839.

74   AHQ-NV, vol. 37, Feb. 29, 1840.

75   AHQ-NV, vol. 37, Mar. 6, 1840.

76   AHQ-NV, vol. 38, Apr. 6, 1841.

77   AHQ-NV, vol. 37, Dec. 29, 1840.

78   AHQ-NV, vol. 39, Feb. 21, 1842.

79   AHQ-NV, vol. 40, Nov. 13, 1843.

80   AHQ-NV, vol. 40, Dec. 21, 1843.

81   AHQ-NV, vol. 40, Jan. 14, 1843.

82   AHQ-NV, vol. 40, Sep. 13, 1843.

83   AHQ-NV, vol. 40, Jan. 14, 1843; AHQ-NM, vol. 4, Sep. 12, 1845.

84   AHQ-NV, vol. 1, Jan. 8–10, 1842; AHQ-NM, vol. 3, Jan. 19, 1844.

85   AHQ-NV, vol. 41, Jan. 26, 1844; AHQ-NV, vol. 41, Aug. 22, 1844.

86   AHQ-NM, vol. 4, Mar. 1–3, 1845.

87   See Tutino, *Mexico City, 1808*; and Tutino, *Mexican Heartland*, chaps. 5–7.

88   AHQ-NV, vol. 42, April 23, 1845, fol. 75–80v.

89   AHQ-NV, vol. 38, Oct. 5, 1841; AHQ-NV, vol. 39, Sep. 16, 1842.

90   AHQ-NM, vol. 1, Jan. 10, 1842.

91   AHQ-NM, vol. 1, July 12, 1842.

92   AHQ-NM, vol. 2, Jan. 17, 1843.

93   AHQ-NM, vol. 2, Dec. 19, 1843.

94   AHQ-NM, vol. 4, Apr. 17, 1845.

95   AHQ-NM, vol. 3, Feb. 7, 1844.

96   Raso, *Notas, 1845,* 4.

97   Raso, *Notas, 1845,* 39.

98   Raso, *Notas, 1845,* 28.

99   Raso, *Notas, 1845,* 34.

100   Appendix A, tables A.2 and A.3.

101   Raso, *Notas, 1845,* 100.

102   Appendix A, table A.4; appendix D, table D.2.

Chapter 12. A New Capitalism, 1845–1860

1   See Torget, *Seeds of Empire,* a work strong on Texas, limited on Mexico.

2   There are endless studies of the war. The best is Guardino, *Dead March.*

3   See Hämäläinen, *The Comanche Empire*; and Delay, *War of a Thousand Deserts.*

4   Granados, *Sueñan las piedras.*

5   A case I made in *Mexican Heartland,* chap. 6.

6   The best detail is in Cypher, "Reconstituting Community."

7   See Fowler, *Santa Anna of Mexico*; and Van Young, *Life Together.*

8   On the Ayutla insurgency, the key study is Guardino, *Peasants, Politics.* On politics, see Sinkin, *Mexican Reform.*

9   Appendix B, table B.2.

10   Monroy, "Las minas de Guanajuato," quote on 104.

11   Appendix B, tables B.6 and B.7.

12   Monroy, "Las minas de Guanajuato," 397.

13   Velasco Ávila et al., *Estado y minería,* 141–47.

14   Monroy, "Las minas de Guanajuato," 397–98; Macías, "El retorno a Valenciana," 646.

15   Monroy, "Las minas de Guanajuato," 398.

16   Appendix B, tables B.2 and B.6.

17   Montes de Oca, *Elogio funeral.*

18   Montes de Oca, *Elogio funeral,* 12–13, 16.

19   Macías, "Retorno a Valenciana," 647–53.

20   Tutino, *Making a New World,* appendix C, table C.26; appendix D, table D.1.

21   Appendix A, table A.6; appendix B, table B.2.

22   Muñoz Ledo, *Exposición,* 11–12.

23   Muñoz Ledo, *Exposición*, 15–18.

24   Muñoz Ledo, *Exposición*, 20.

25   Muñoz Ledo, *Exposisión*, 23.

26   Muñoz Ledo, *Exposición*, 41, 44.

27   Muñoz Ledo, *Exposición*, 53–59.

28   Muñoz Ledo, *Exposición*, 66.

29   Muñoz Ledo, *Exposición*, 75.

30   Muñoz Ledo, *Exposición*, 79.

31   Romero, *Noticias*.

32   Romero, *Noticias*, 165–66.

33   Romero, *Noticias*, 166.

34   Romero, *Noticias*, 167.

35   Romero, *Noticias*, 168.

36   Romero, *Noticias*, 169.

37   Romero, *Noticias*, 171–72.

38   See Chowning, "Catholic Church and the Ladies."

39   Romero, *Noticias*, 172–73.

40   Romero, *Noticias*, 173.

41   Appendix D, table D.4.

42   AHQ-NM, vol. 7, June 1848.

43   Loyola Vera, *Sistemas hidraúlicas*, 172–92.

44   Appendix D, table D.5.

45   Appendix D, table D.6.

46   AHQ-NV, vol. 43, July 31, 1846; AHQ-NM, vol. 7, April 15, 1848; AHQ-NM, vol. 10, June 10, 1849.

47   Appendix D, tables D.7 and D.8.

48   Appendix D, tables D.5 and D.8.

49   Prieto, *Viajes*.

50   Prieto, *Viajes*, 91–92.

51   Prieto, *Viajes*, 93–95.

52   Prieto, *Viajes*, 96.

53   Prieto, *Viajes*, 98–99.

54   Prieto, *Viajes*, 105.

55   Prieto, *Viajes*, 111.

56   Prieto, *Viajes*, 99.

57   Prieto, *Viajes*, 109.

58   Prieto, *Viajes*, 113.

59   Prieto, *Viajes*, 142.

60   Prieto, *Viajes*, 146.

61   Prieto, *Viejas*, 146–49.

62   Prieto, *Viajes*, 115–16.

63   Prieto, *Viajes*, 133.

64   Prieto, *Viajes*, 163–64.

65   Prieto, *Viajes*, 165.

66   Prieto, *Viajes*, 191–92.

67   Prieto, *Viajes*, 113–15.

68   Prieto, *Viajes*, 112–13.

69   Reina, "Las leyes de reforma de 1856"; the Querétaro law is noted on p. 316.

70   AHQ-NM, vol. 5, Oct. 10, 1846; AHQ-NM, vol. 6, July 9, 1847; AHQ-NM, vol. 6, Nov. 15, 1847; AHQ-NM, vol. 6, Nov. 23, 1847.

71   AHQ-NV, vol. 43, Dec. 21, 1846.

72   AHQ-NV, vol. 43, July 9, 1846; AHQ-NV, vol. 44, Sep. 13, 1847; AHQ-NM, vol. 6, Jan. 14, 1847; AHQ-NM, vol. 6, Apr. 16, 1847; AHQ-NM, vol. 6, Apr. 21, 1847; AHQ-NM, vol. 8, Aug. 2, 1848; AHQ-NM, vol. 11, Apr. 9, 1850; AHQ-NM, vol. 11, Apr. 11, 1850; AHQ-NM, vol. 14, Oct. 27, 1851; AHQ-NM, vol. 15, Jan. 22, 1852.

73   AHQ-NM, vol. 7, Mar. 2, 1848; for a similar lease of a valuable *huerta*, see AHQ-NM, vol. 11, Aug. 22, 1850.

74   The sales are in AHQ-NM, vols. 5–14, 1846–1851.

75   AHQ-NM, vol. 6, Apr. 27, 1847.

76   AHQ-NM, vol. 6, Oct. 1, 1847.

77   AHQ-NM, vol. 10, May 19, 1849.

78   AHQ-NM, vol. 10, Dec. 6, 1849; AHQ-NM, vol. 10, Dec. 7, 1849.

79   AHQ-NM, vol. 12, Sep. 3, 1850.

80   AHQ-NM, vol. 12, Oct. 9, 1850.

81   AHQ-NM, vol. 13, Mar. 21, 1851.

82   AHQ-NM, vol. 14, July 23, 1851.

83   AHQ-NM, vol. 14, Aug. 19, 1851.

84   AHQ-NM, vol. 5, May 19, 1846; AHQ-NM, vol. 6, May 1847; AHQ-NM, vol. 6, Oct. 1847; AHQ-NV, vol. 44, Oct. 1, 1847.

85   AHQ-NV, vol. 44, Nov. 15, 1847.

86   AHQ-NM, vol. 12, Jan. 5, 1850.

87   AHQ-NM, vol. 15, Feb. 16, 1852.

88   AHQ-NM, vol. 14, Dec. 3, 1851.

89   AHQ-NM, vol. 14, Dec. 3, 1851.

90   AHQ-NV, vol. 43, Oct. 7, 1846; AHQ-NV, vol. 43, Oct. 15, 1846.

91   AHQ-NM, vol. 7, Apr. 27, 1848.

92   ANQ-NM, vol. 10, July 3–10, 1849; AHQ-NM, vol. 11, Feb. 17, 1850.

93   AHQ-NM, vol. 17, Mar. 29, 1854.

94   AHQ-NM, vol. 5, Dec. 11, 1846; AHQ-NM, vol. 8, Dec. 1, 1848.

95   AHQ-NM, vol. 9, Mar. 1, 1849; AHQ-NM, vol. 14, Aug. 25, 1850; AHQ-NM, vol. 21, March 13, 1855.

96   AHQ-NM, vol. 21, Apr. 25, 1855.

97   AHQ-NV, vol. 44, Apr. 7, 1847.

98   AHQ-NM, vol. 7, June 14, 1848; AHQ-NM, vol. 16, Aug. 2, 1852; AHQ-NM, vol. 16, Aug. 10, 1852.

99   Prieto, *Viajes*, 90.

100   Balbontín, *Estadística*, 8–9.

101   Prieto, *Viajes*, 209–11.

102   Prieto, *Viajes*, 214–17.

103   Prieto, *Viajes*, 233–34.

104   Prieto, *Viajes*, 240.

105   Prieto, *Viajes*, 241–77.

106   Prieto, *Viajes*, 286–87.

107   Prieto, *Viajes*, 289–90.

108   Prieto, *Viajes*, 292.

109   Prieto, *Viajes*, 293–353.

110   Appendix D, table D.9.

111   AHQ-NM, vol. 11, May 27, 1850; AHQ-NM, vol. 11, June 27, 1850; AHQ-NM, vol. 14, Nov. 8, 1851; AHQ-NM, vol. 18, Sep. 21, 1853; AHQ-NM, vol. 22, July 31, 1854.

112   Balbontín, *Estadística*, 3–4.

113   AHQ-NV, vol. 43, Jan. 23, 1846.

114   AHQ-NM, vol. 11, Apr. 22, 1850; AHQ-NM, vol. 12, Sep. 17, 1850.

115   AHQ-NV, vol. 44, Jan. 16, 1847.

116   AHQ-NM, vol. 8, Aug. 25, 1848.

117   AHQ-NM, vol. 13, Feb. 10, 1851.

118   AHQ-NM, vol. 16, Oct. 18, 1852.

119   AHQ-NM, vol. 18, July 18, 1853.

120   AHQ-NM, vol. 20, Dec. 13, 1854.

121   AHQ-NV, vol. 43, July 18, 1846.

122   AHQ-NM, vol. 9, Apr. 27, 1849.

123   AHQ-NM, vol. 17, Jan. 27, 1853.

124   AHQ-NM, vol. 20, Sep. 4, 1854.

125   AHQ-NM, vol. 20, Sep. 21, 1854; AHQ-NM, vol. 20, Oct. 20, 1854.

126   AHQ-NM, vol. 20, Dec. 11, 1854.

127   "Romero y López," *Enciclopedia histórica*.

128   Romero, *Noticias*, 175–79.

129   Romero, *Noticias*, 180–81.

130   Romero, *Noticias*, 182–86.

131   Romero, *Noticias*, 184–86.

132   Romero, *Noticias*, 187–92.

133   Romero, *Noticias*, 196–97.

134   Romero, *Noticias*, 197–99.

135   Romero, *Noticias*, 199–200.

136   Romero, *Noticias*, 201–4.

137   Romero, *Noticias*, 205–7.

138   Romero, *Noticias*, 208–10.

139   Romero, *Noticias*, 211.

140   Romero, *Noticias*, 211–12.

141   Romero, *Noticias*, 211–18.

142   Romero, *Noticias*, 219–20.

143   Romero, *Noticias*, 222–23.

144   Romero, *Noticias*, 232–34.

145   Romero, *Noticias*, 224–27.

146   Romero, *Noticias*, 226–30.

147   Romero, *Noticias*, 234–37.

148   Romero, *Noticias*, 237.

149   Romero, *Noticias*, 238.

150   Romero, *Noticias*, 239–40.

151   Appendix D, tables D.9 and D.10.

152   This is the focus of Tutino, *Mexico City, 1808*.

153   See Chowning, *Catholic Women*, chaps. 2–4.

154   See Weber, *Economy and Society*.

Conclusion

1   On the US empire turning to claim Texas, see Rothman, "Union, Capitalism, and Slavery."

2   Ngai, *Chinese Question*, offers a powerful new social history of gold and the California discoveries, tracing how the collapse of China's economy after the end of silver flows led to a worldwide diaspora of Chinese peoples.

3   See Lin, *China Upside Down*; Allen, *British Industrial Revolution*; Parthasarathi, *Why Europe Grew Rich*; Beckert, *Empire of Cotton*; and Baptist, *Half Has Never Been Told*.

4   New Spain's northward thrust is detailed throughout Tutino, *Making a New World*. On new openings, for Texas, see Velasco Ávila, *La frontera étnica*; and Torget, *Seeds of Empire*; on New Mexico, the classic study is Weber, *Mexican Frontier*; on California, see Hackel, *Children of Coyote*; on the greater west, Hyde, *Empires, Nations, and Families*, offers a sweeping vision, hardened a bit in Johnson, *Broken Heart of America*.

5   This understanding is reflected in Guardino, *Dead March*.

6   Tutino, *Mexican Heartland*, 190–96, grounded in Wyllie, *Mexico: A Report on Its Finances*, 381–83 (first published in London in 1844)—plenty of time for US emissaries to know before 1846.

7   Guardino, *Dead March*, 311–12, written before Tutino, *Mexican Heartland*, noted Wyllie's work.

8   Guardino, *Dead March*.

9   I make the argument in greater detail in Tutino, *Mexican Heartland*, chap. 6.

10   Tutino, *Mexico City, 1808*, based on Valle Pavón, *Donativos, préstamos y privilegios*.

11   Countryman, *American Revolution*, offers a concise synthesis; A. Taylor, *Internal Enemy*, links the wars for independence and 1812 to the social transformations emphasized here.

12   See Archer, *Army in Bourbon Mexico*; and Castro Gutiérrez, *Nueva ley y nuevo rey*.

13   This is the focus of Tutino, *Mexico City, 1808*.

14   This is emphasized throughout Guardino, *Dead March*.

15   This becomes one more confirmation, with a twist, of Findlay and O'Rourke's emphasis in *Power and Plenty* that military power has long been and remains key to global capitalisms.

16 On the larger war, see Guardino, *Dead March*. On popular resistance in Mexico City, see Granados, *Sueñan las piedras*.

17 Tutino, *Mexican Heartland*, tables A.13 and A.14.

18 Ashworth, *Republic in Crisis*.

19 For the biggest picture, see Hahn, *Nation Without Borders*; for a close gendered vision, see Manning, *Troubled Refuge*.

20 González Navarro, *Anatomía del poder en México*.

21 Breña, *Primer liberalismo español*.

22 See Hale, *Mexican Liberalism*.

23 Guardino, *Peasants, Politics*.

24 See Sinkin, *Mexican Reform*; Bazant, *Alienation of Church Wealth*; and Tutino, *Mexican Heartland*, chaps. 6 and 8.

25 The key and classic study is Bazant, *Alienation of Church Wealth*.

26 Dabbs, *French Army in Mexico*; Pani, *Para mexicanizar el segundo imperio*; Pani, *Una serie de admirables acontecimientos*.

27 See Foner, *Reconstruction*; White, *Railroaded*; and Hahn, *Nation Without Borders*.

28 Appendix B, table B.2.

29 See the debates between Lucas Alamán and Tadeo Ortiz de Ayala in Tutino, *Mexican Heartland*, chap. 6.

30 Import figures are in Herrera Canales, *El comercio exterior*.

31 On labor around Mexico City, see Illades, *Hacia la república del trabajo*; and Trujillo Bolio, *Operarios fabriles*.

32 On Chalco, see Tutino, *Mexican Heartland*, chap. 8.

33 The essential overview of this time of conflict is Falcón, *Las naciones de una república*; on privatizations and conflicts near the capital, see Tutino, *Mexican Heartland*, chaps. 6, 8, and 9; on adaptations at Papantla, see Kourí, *Pueblo Divided*; Pérez Montesinos, *Landscaping Indigenous Michoacán*, offers a new vision of contested developments just south of the Bajío.

34 Tutino, *Mexican Heartland*, chap. 9.

35 Stauffer, *Victory on Earth or in Heaven*.

36 This is detailed in chapters 6 and 10. The larger emphasis comes from Barrington Moore's classic *Social Origins of Dictatorship and Democracy*.

37 Chowning, *Catholic Women*.

38 See appendix B, table B.2, and appendix E, tables E.7 and E.8.

39 Appendix B, table B.2.

40 Preciado de Alba, *Guanajuato*, 27–28; my analysis builds on Preciado de Alba's essential work.

41   Landa Fonseca, *Querétaro*, 71–76.

42   Preciado de Alba, *Guanajuato*, 30–34.

43   Appendix B, table B.2; appendix F, tables F.4 and F.6. For Romero, see chap. 12.

44   Appendix F, table F.1.

45   *Seminario Oficial del Gobierno de Guanajuato*, Jan. 6, 1861, p. 4, in Preciado de Alba, *Guanajuato*, 35.

46   Appendix E, table E.10.

47   Preciado de Alba, *Guanajuato*, 36–43.

48   Preciado de Alba, *Guanajuato*, 59–59; on silver minted in 1863, see cuadro 4, p. 103.

49   Preciado de Alba, *Guanajuato*, 84, 135, 149.

50   Preciado de Alba, *Guanajuato*, 97.

51   *El último mohicano* 1, no. 2 (January 1, 1865): 4, quoted in Preciado de Alba, *Guanajuato*, 98.

52   *El Monarquista* 1, no. 6 (February 19, 1965): 4, quoted in Preciado de Alba, *Guanajuato*, 96.

53   Appendix B, table B.2.

54   Diez de Sollano, *Nociones sobre la disciplina eclesiástica*.

55   Diez de Sollano, *Primera carta pastoral*.

56   Diez de Sollano, *Tercera carta pastoral*.

57   Preciado de Alba, *Guanajuato*, 77–81.

58   Sánchez Rangel, *La empresa*, 23–24.

59   Sánchez Rangel, *La empresa*, 6–34.

60   Preciado de Alba, *Guanajuato*, 98.

61   Preciado de Alba, *Guanajuato*, 97, 127, 133, 157, 178,

62   Diez de Sollano, *Sexta carta pastoral*.

63   Diez de Sollano, *Séptima carta pastoral*, quotes on 9.

64   Preciado de Alba, *Guanajuato*, 140, 161–63.

65   Preciado de Alba, *Guanajuato*, 165–66.

66   Landa, *Querétaro*, 90–93, quote on 92.

67   Antillón, *Memoria leída*, 1867.

68   Diez de Sollano, *Décima carta pastoral*; Diez de Sollano, *Duodécima carta pastoral*; Diez de Sollano, *Décimatercera carta pastoral*.

69   See Stauffer, *Victory on Earth or in Heaven*.

70   Diez de Sollano, *Décimo cuatro carta pastoral*.

71   Sánchez Rangel, *La empresa*, 34–70.

72   Antillón, *Memoria leída, 1873*; mining production in cuadro 18; tax revenues in cuadro 30.

73   See Appendix E, table E.4; Appendix D, table D.10.

74   Sánchez Rangel, *La empresa*, 38–41.

75   Landa Fonseca, *Querétaro*, 95–100.

76   Soto González, *Hércules*.

77   Domínguez, *Catecismo elemental*.

78   Appendix F, table F.1.

79   Appendix F, tables F.1 and F.11.

80   On silver, see appendix B; on national industry, see Tutino, *Mexican Heartland*, tables A.14 and A.15.

81   On the turn to gold, see Velasco Ávila et al., *Estado y minería*, 287–312.

82   See the figures in Tutino, *Mexican Heartland*, tables A.12–15.

83   The classic study is Pletcher, *Rails, Mines, and Progress*, complemented by Coatsworth, *Growth Against Development*.

Epilogue

1   I engaged these changes from the perspective of Mexico City and its nearby communities in *The Mexican Heartland*; here I rethink them in the context of the Bajío revolution and the transformations it spawned.

2   Sinkin, *Mexican Reform*; Perry, *Juárez and Díaz*; Coatsworth, *Growth Against Development*.

3   On Díaz' regime, see Guerra, *Mexico*; on regional social control, see Reina, *Rebeliones campesinas*; on local policing, see Tutino, "Entre la rebelión y la revolución."

4   Sánchez Rangel, *La empresa*.

5   For a powerful photographic record of life and labor at La Luz mines facing productive decline after 1900, see Pardo Hernández and Sánchez Rangel, *Mineral de la Luz*.

6   Soto González, *Hércules*.

7   See Miller, *Landlords and Haciendas*.

8   See Chassen López, *From Liberal to Revolutionary*; Fowler-Salamini, *Working Women*; and Lurtz, *From the Grounds Up*.

9   Kourí, *Pueblo Divided*; Kates, "Persistence of Maya Autonomy."

10   Wells, *Yucatán's Gilded Age*; Wells and Joseph, *Summer of Discontent*.

11   Velasco Ávila et al., *Estado y minería*.

12   Gómez Serrano, *Aguascalientes.*

13   The classic study is Bernstein, *Mexican Mining Industry.*

14   On oil, see Brown, *Oil and Revolution*; Santiago, *Ecology of Oil*; and Garner, *British Lions.*

15   See Montejano, "Mexican Merchants."

16   Vergara, *Fueling Mexico*, details how the dearth of coal limited Mexican industry before the coming of oil. On how access to coal fueled Monterrey's industrial rise, the key study is Fernández, "Revolution in the Industrial City."

17   This understanding of Monterrey relies on Fernández, "Revolution in the Industrial City."

18   Gómez-Galvariatto, *Industry and Revolution*, is a key study.

19   On population, see appendix F, table F.11; on rural transformations, see Tutino, *Mexican Heartland*, chaps. 6 and 9; on nutrition, the essential study is López Alonso, *Measuring Up.*

20   All detailed in Tutino, *Mexican Heartland*, chaps. 6–8.

21   See Tutino, *Mexican Heartland*, chap. 9, building on Womack, *Zapata*; and Ávila Espinosa, *Los orígenes del zapatismo.*

22   This is synthesized in Tutino, *Mexican Heartland*, chap. 10.

23   On women sustaining insurgency and facing violence in the heartland, see Tutino, *Mexican Heartland*, chap. 9; on women among Villistas, see Reed, *Insurgent Mexico.*

24   See Tutino, *Mexican Heartland*, chap. 10, building on Fernández, "Revolution in the Industrial City." On international context, the classic is Katz, *Secret War*; on Villa, Katz, *Life and Times*, is essential.

25   On promise and deflection, see Katz, *Secret War*, and Knight, *Mexican Revolution.*

26   Markiewicz, *Mexican Revolution.*

27   Brown, "Why Foreign Oil Companies Shifted."

28   Córdoba, *La ideología.*

29   See López Alonso, *Measuring Up.*

30   This synthesizes Tutino, *Mexican Heartland*, chaps. 11–12; the key to Cárdenas is Gilly, *El cardenismo.*

31   See Vaughan, *Cultural Politics in Revolution*; and Fallaw, *Religion and State Formation.*

32   The turn is outlined in Tutino, *Mexican Heartland*, chap. 11.

33   Gereffi, *Pharmaceutical Industry.*

34   Hewitt de Alcántara, *Modernizing Mexican Agriculture.*

35 Gómez-Galvariatto, *El pan nuestro.*

36 See Tutino, "Americas in the Twentieth-Century World"; and Tutino, "Power, Marginality, and Participation."

37 On struggles leading to 1968, see Coral, "Mexico City Middle Class"; and Zolov, *Last Good Neighbor.* On political responses and social challenges, see Walker, *Waking from the Dream.*

38 Szekely, *La economía política del petroleo.*

39 On the turn to globalization and its early impacts, see Haber et al., *Mexico Since 1980.*

40 LaBotz, *Mask of Democracy.*

41 De Janvry, Gordillo, and Sadaulet, *Mexico's Second Agrarian Reform.*

42 On the second Zapatista rising, see Womack, *Rebelion in Chiapas*; and Stephen, *Zapata Lives.*

43 See Tutino, "Revolutionary Capacity of Rural Communities."

44 See Wright, *Death of Ramón González*; Veloz, *Even the Women Are Leaving*; and Minian, *Undocumented Lives.*

45 On the long rise and recent dominance of the drug economy, see Smith, *Dope.*

46 On US promoters, purveyors, and communities in drug capitalism, the most human revelations come in the works of Sam Quiñones: *Dreamland* and *The Least of Us.*

47 Tutino, *Mexican Heartland*, chap. 9, details men's turn to violence, first upon each other, then striking women and children as patriarchal production dissolved from the 1890s, all before men turned to revolution after 1910; part III explores the larger collapse of patriarchy after 1970 and the endless violence on women as no equitable resolution has come. For details, see Gutmann, *Meanings of Macho.*

48 Fitting, *Struggle for Maize*, offers a revealing analysis of families facing challenge and change.

49 Warman, *Corn and Capitalism.*

BIBLIOGRAPHY

Archives

AGI: Archivo General de Indias, Seville, Spain
AGN: Archivo General de la Nación, Mexico City, Mexico
    AGN-BN: Bienes Nacionales
    AGN-OG: Operaciones de Guerra
AHN: Archivo Histórico Nacional, Madrid, Spain
AHQ: Archivo Histórico de Querétaro, Querétaro, Mexico
    AHQ-BD: Bautismos, Difunciones
    AHQ-NM: Notarías Maldonado
    AHQ-NV: Notarías Vallejo
    AHQ-P: Padrones
CM: Casa Morelos (Archive of the Archbishopric of Michoacán), Morelia, Michoacán
    CM-DJC: Diocesana, Justicia, Correspondencia
    CM-JCP: Justicia, Correspondencia, Parroquial
PCR: Papers of the Condes de Regla, Washington State University Library, Pullman, Washington
    PCRun: Uncataloged files (when consulted in 1973)
UTB: Benson Latin American Library, University of Texas, Austin, Texas
    UTB-G: García Collection
    CPP: Conde de Peñasco Papers
    JSE: José Sánchez Espinosa Papers
    (CPP and JSE were recataloged and refiled several times as I consulted them from the 1970s into the 2000s; I cite by date written—the one enduring identification)

Books and Periodicals

Agraz García de Alba, Gabriel. *Epigmenio González Flores: Patriota y mártir insurgente.* Gobierno de Jalisco, 2007.
Ajofrín, Francisco de. *Diario de viaje que por orden de la sagrada Congregación de Propaganda Fide hizo a la América septentrional en el siglo XVIII.* Real Academia de la Historia, 1958.

Alamán, Lucas. *Historia de Méjico*. 5 vols. Editorial Jus, 1968–69.

Alcaide Aguilar, José Fernando. *La hacienda de "Cienega de Mata" de los Rincón Gallardo*. Universidad de Guadalajara, 2004.

Allen, Robert. *The British Industrial Revolution in Global Perspective*. Cambridge University Press, 2009.

Anderson, Fred. *Crucible of War: The Seven Years War and the Fate of Empire in North America, 1756–1766*. Knopf, 2000.

Andrews, Catherine. *Entre la espada y la constitución: El General Anastasio Bustamante, 1780–1853*. Universidad Autónoma de Tamaulipas, 2008.

Anna, Timothy. *Forging Mexico, 1821–1833*. University of Nebraska Press, 1998.

Antillón, Florencio. *Memoria leída por el C. gobernador del estado libre y soberano de Guanajuato, general Florencio Antillón, en la solemne instalacion del quinto Congreso constitucional, verificada el 15 septiembre e 1873*. Ignacio Escalante, 1875.

Antillón, Florencio. *Memoria leída por el ciudadano general Florencio Antillón, gobernador interino del estado de Guanajuato*. Albino Chagoyan, 1867.

Archer, Christon. *The Army in Bourbon Mexico, 1760–1810*. University of New Mexico Press, 1977.

Arenal Fenocchio, Jaime del. *Un modo de ser libres: Independencia y constitución en México, 1816–1821*. Colegio de Michoacán, 2002.

Arrom, Sylvia. "Popular Politics in Mexico City: The Parian Riots, 1828." *Hispanic American Historical Review* 68, no. 2 (1988): 245–68.

Ashworth, John. *The Republic in Crisis, 1848–1861*. Cambridge University Press, 2012.

Ávila, Alfredo. *En nombre de la nación: La formación del gobierno representativo en México*. Taurus, 2002.

Ávila, Alfredo. *Para la libertad: Los republicanos en tiempos del imperio, 1821–1823*. Universidad Nacional Autónoma de México, 2004.

Ávila Espinosa, Felipe. *Los orígenes del zapatismo*. Colegio de México, 2001.

Balbontín, Juan María. *Estadística del Estado de Querétaro en los años de 1854 y 1855*. Vicente Torres, 1876.

Baptist, Edward. *The Half Has Never Been Told: Slavery and the Making of American Capitalism*. Basic Books, 2014.

Baroni Boissanos, Ariana. *La formación de la estructura agraria en el Bajío colonial, siglos XVI y XVII*. La Casa Chata, 1990.

Barr, Juliana. *Peace Came in the Form of a Woman: Indians and Spaniards in the Texas Borderlands*. University of North Carolina Press, 2007.

Bazant, Jan. *The Alienation of Church Wealth in Mexico*. Cambridge University Press, 1971.

Bazant, Jan. *Cinco haciendas mexicanas: Tres siglos de vida rural en San Luis Potosí, 1600–1900*. Colegio de México, 1975.

Beckert, Sven. *Empire of Cotton*. Knopf, 2014.

Benavides Martínez, Juan José. *De milicianos a soldados del rey: Milicianos y sociedad en San Luis Potosí, 1767–1824*. Universidad de Sevilla, 2014.

Benson, Nettie Lee. *The Provincial Deputation in Mexico: Harbinger of Provincial Autonomy, Independence, and Federalism.* Rev. ed. University of Texas Press, 1992.

Berlandier, Jean Louis, and Rafael Chovel. *Diario de viaje de la Comisión de Límites.* Juan Navarro, 1850.

Bernstein, Marvin. *The Mexican Mining Industry: A Study of the Interaction of Politics, Economics, and Technology, 1890–1950.* SUNY Press, 1964.

Berthe, Jean Pierre, ed. *Las nuevas memorias del Capitán Jean de Monsegur.* Universidad Nacional Autónoma de México, 1994.

Boxer, C. R. *The Golden Age of Brazil, 1695–1750: Growing Pains of a Colonial Society.* University of California Press, 1966.

Brading, D. A. "La estructura de la producción agrícola en el Bajío de 1750 a 1850." *Historia mexicana* 22, no. 7 (1973): 197–237.

Brading, D. A. *Haciendas and Ranchos in the Mexican Bajío, 1680–1860.* Cambridge University Press, 1978.

Brading, D. A. *Miners and Merchants in Bourbon Mexico, 1763–1810.* Cambridge University Press, 1971.

Brading, D. A. *El ocaso del virreinato: Testimonios documentales.* Universidad Nacional Autónoma de México, 1996.

Braudel, Fernand. *Civilization and Capitalism, 15th–18th Centuries.* 3 vols. Translated by Sian Reynolds. Harper and Row, 1982–1984.

Braudel, Fernand. *Out of Italy: Two Centuries of World Domination and Demise.* Europa Editions, 2019.

Breña, Roberto. *El primer liberalismo español y los procesos de emancipación de América, 1808–1824.* Colegio de México, 2004.

Brooks, James. *Captives and Cousins: Slavery, Kinship, and Community in the Southwest Borderlands.* University of North Carolina Press, 2002.

Brown, Jonathan. *Oil and Revolution in Mexico.* University of California Press, 1993.

Brown, Jonathan. "Why Foreign Oil Companies Left Mexico for Venezuela in the 1920s." *American Historical Review* 90, no. 2 (1985): 362–85.

Burnard, Trevor, and John Garrigus. *The Plantation Machine: Atlantic Capitalism in French Saint Domingue and British Jamaica.* University of Pennsylvania Press, 2016.

Calderón de la Barca, Fanny. *Life in Mexico.* Edited and annotated by Howard and Marion Hall Fisher. Doubleday, 1964.

Cañedo Gamboa, Sergio Alejandro. "Merchants and Family Business in San Luis Potosí, Mexico: The Signs of an Economic Upsurge, 1820–1846." PhD diss., University of California, San Diego, 2011.

Carrillo Cázares, Alberto. *Partidos y padrones del obispado de Michoacán, 1680–1685.* Colegio de Michoacán, 1996.

Castro Gutiérrez, Felipe. *Nueva ley y nuevo rey: Reformas borbónicas y rebeliones populares en Nueva España.* Colegio de Michoacán, 1996.

Castro Rivas, Jorge, and Mathilde Rangel López. *Relación histórica de la Intendencia de Guanajuato, 1787–1809.* Universidad de Guanajuato, 1998.

Castro Rivas, Jorge, Mathilde Rangel López, and Rafael Tovar Rangel. *Desarrollo socio demógrafico de la ciudad de Guanajuato durante el siglo XVII*. Universidad de Guanajuato, 1999.

Cayuela Fernández, José Antonio, and José Ángel Gallego Palomares. *La Guerra de Independencia: Historia bélica, pueblo y nación en España, 1808–1814*. Universidad de Salamanca, 2008.

Chassen López, Francie. *From Liberal to Revolutionary Oaxaca: The View From the South, Oaxaca, 1867–1911*. Pennsylvania State Press, 2004.

Chávez Orozco, Luis, and Enrique Florescano. *Agricultura y industria textíl en Veracruz, siglo XIX*. Universidad Veracruzana, 1965.

Chowning, Margaret. "The Catholic Church and the Ladies on the Vela Perpetua: Gender and Devotional Change in Nineteenth-Century Mexico." *Past and Present* 221, no. 1 (2013): 197–237.

Chowning, Margaret. *Catholic Women and Mexican Politics, 1750–1950*. Princeton University Press, 2023.

Clark, Christopher. *Revolutionary Spring: Europe Aflame and the Fight for a New World, 1848–1849*. Crown, 2023.

Coatsworth, John. *Growth Against Development: The Economic Impact of the Railroads in Porfirian Mexico*. Northern Illinois University Press, 1981.

Colombini y Camayori, Francisco María de. *Querétaro triunfante en los caminos del Pueblito: Poema histórica-sagrada en cuatro cantos de; a sagrada imagen de Nuestra Señora de Pueblito*. Zuñiga y Ontiveros, 1801.

Cook, Sherburne, and Woodrow Borah. *Essays in Population History, 3 vols*. University of California Press, 1971–1979.

Coral, Emilio. "The Mexico City Middle Class, 1940–1970: Between Tradition, the State, and the United States." PhD diss., Georgetown University, 2011.

Córdoba, Arnaldo. *La ideología de la revolución Mexicana: La formación del nuevo estado*. Ediciones Era, 1972.

Cortés, Hernán. *Relación de 1520*. Edited by Luis Fernando Granados. Grano de Sal, 1922.

Costeloe, Michael. *La primera república federal de México, 1824–1835*. Fondo de Cultura Económica, 1975.

Countryman, Edward. *The American Revolution*. Rev. ed. Hill and Wang, 2003.

Crosby, Alfred. *The Colombian Exchange: Biological and Cultural Consequences of 1492*. Greenwood Press, 1972.

Cross, Elizabeth. *Company Politics: Commerce, Scandal, and French Visions of Indian Empire in the Revolutionary Era*. Oxford University Press, 2023.

Cross, Harry. "The Mining Economy of Zacatecas, Mexico, in the Nineteenth Century." PhD diss., University California, Berkeley, 1976.

Cypher, James. "Reconstituting Community: Local Religion, Political Culture, and Rebellion in Mexico's Sierra Gorda, 1846–1880." PhD diss., Indiana University, 2007.

Dabbs, Jack Autry. *The French Army in Mexico, 1861–1871*. Mouton, 1963.

de Janvry, Alain, Gustavo Gordillo, and Elizabeth Sadaulet. *Mexico's Second Agrarian Reform: Household and Community Responses*. Center for U.S.-Mexican Studies, UCSD, 1997.

de la Teja, Jesús Frank. *San Antonio de Béjar: A Community on New Spain's Northern Frontier*. University of New Mexico Press, 1995.

de la Torre Villar, Ernesto. *La Constitución de Apatzingán y los creadores de la nación mexicana*. Universidad Nacional Autónoma de México, 2010.

Deans-Smith, Susan. *Bureaucrats, Planters, and Workers: The Making of the Tobacco Monopoly in Bourbon Mexico*. University of Texas Press, 1992.

Delay, Brian. *War of a Thousand Deserts: Indian Raids and the U.S.-Mexican War*. Yale University Press, 2008.

Diario de México. Mexico City, 1808–1817.

Diez de Sollano, José María. *Nociones sobre la disciplina eclesiástica*. Andrade y Escalante, 1857.

Diez de Sollano, José María. *Primera carta pastoral del Obispado de León*. Mariano Rodríguez Velazquez, 1864.

Diez de Sollano, José María. *Tercera carta pastoral que el illmo. señor obispo de Leon dirige a su venerable clero y fieles discesanos*. Felipe María Conejo, 1864.

Diez de Sollano, José María. *Sexta carta pastoral . . . 1866*. Pablo Gómez, 1866.

Diez de Sollano, José María. *Séptima carta pastoral . . . contra protestantismo*. Pablo Gómez, 1866.

Diez de Sollano, José María. *Décima carta pastoral . . . Monzón*, 1870.

Diez de Sollano, José María. *Duodécima carta pasoral . . . Monzón*, 1872.

Diez de Sollano, José María. *Décimotercera carta pastoral . . . Monzón*, 1873.

Diez de Sollano, José María, *Décimocuatro carta pastoral . . . Monzón*, 1874.

Domínguez, Juan de Dios. *Catecismo elemental de geografía y estadística del Estado de Querétaro*. Escalante, 1873.

Dubois, Laurent. *Avengers of the New World: The Story of the Haitian Revolution*. Harvard University Press, 2004.

Dunn, Richard. *The Rise of the Planter Class in the English West Indies*. University of North Carolina Press, 1972.

Falcón, Romana. *Las naciones de una república: La cuestión indígena y el congreso mexicano*. Congreso de la Unión, 1999.

Fallaw, Ben. *Religion and State Formation in Post-Revolutionary Mexico*. Duke University Press, 2013.

Fernández, Rodolfo. "Revolution in the Industrial City: Monterrey, Mexico, 1890–1920." PhD diss., Georgetown University, 2014.

Fernández de Recas, Guillermo. *Mayorazgos de la Nueva España*. Porrúa, 1965.

Ferrusca Beltráa, Rita. *Querétaro: De pueblo a ciudad, 1665–1733*. Archivo Histórico de Querétaro, 2004.

Fick, Carolyn. "From Slave Colony to Black Nation: Haiti's Revolutionary Inversion." In Tutino, *New Countries*.

Fick, Carolyn. *The Making of Haiti: The Saint Domingue Revolution from Below.* University of Tennessee Press, 1990.

Findlay, Ronald, and Kevin O'Rourke. *Power and Plenty: Trade, War, and the World Economy in the Second Millennium.* Princeton University Press, 2007.

Fitting, Elizabeth. *The Struggle for Maize: Campesinos, Workers, and Transgenic Corn in the Mexican Countryside.* Duke University Press, 2017.

Florescano, Enrique. *Precios del maíz y crisis agrícolas en México, 1708–1810.* Colegio de México, 1969.

Flynn, Dennis, and Arturo Giraldez. "Born with a Silver Spoon: The Origins of World Trade in 1571." *Journal of World History* 6, no. 2 (1995): 201–21.

Folsom, Rafael. *The Yaquis and the Empire: Spanish Imperial Power and Native Resilience in Colonial Mexico.* Yale University Press, 2014.

Foner, Eric. *Reconstruction: America's Unfinished Revolution, 1865–1877.* Rev. ed. Harper, 2014.

Fowler, Will. *Santa Anna of Mexico.* University of Nebraska Press, 2007.

Fowler-Salamini, Heather. *Working Women, Entrepreneurs, and Mexican Revolution: The Coffee Culture of Córdoba, Veracruz.* University of Nebraska Press, 2013.

Gaceta de México/Gaceta del Gobierno de México. Mexico City, 1784–1835.

García, Pedro. *Con el cura Hidalgo en la Guerra de Independencia.* Fondo de Cultura Económica, 1982.

Garner, Paul. *British Lions and Mexican Eagles: Business, Politics, and Empire in the Career of Weetman Pearson in Mexico.* Stanford University Press, 2019.

Gereffi, Gary. *The Pharmaceutical Industry and Dependency in the Third World.* Princeton University Press, 1976.

Gilly, Adolfo. *El cardenismo: Una utopía mexicana.* Cal y Arena, 1994.

Giraldez, Arturo. *The Age of Trade: The Manila Galleons and the Dawn of the Global Economy.* Rowman and Littlefield, 2015.

Gómez-Galvariatto, Aurora. *Industry and Revolution: Social and Economic Change in the Orizaba Valley, Mexico.* Harvard University Press, 2013.

Gómez-Galvariatto, Aurora. *El pan nuestro: Una historia de la tortilla de Maíz.* Colegio de México, 2024.

Gómez Serrano, Jesús. *Aguascalientes: Imperio de los Guggenheim.* Fondo de Cultura Económica, 1982.

González Gómez, Imelda. *El tobacco virreinal: Monopolio de una costumbre.* Universidad Autónoma de Querétaro, 2002.

González Navarro, Moisés. *Anatomía del poder en México, 1848–1853.* Colegio de México, 1977.

Graham, Jonathan. "Environmental, Social, and Political Change in the Otomí Heartland: A Hydraulic History of the Ixmiquilpan Valley." PhD diss., Yale University, 2018.

Granados, Luis Fernando. *En el espejo haitiano: Los indios del Bajío y el colapso del orden colonial en América Latina.* Ediciones Era, 2016.

Granados, Luis Fernando. *Sueñan las piedras: Alzamiento occurido en la ciudad de México, 14, 15, 16 de Septiembre 1847.* Ediciones Era, 2003.

Guardino, Peter. *The Dead March: A History of the Mexican American War*. Harvard University Press, 2017.

Guardino, Peter. *Peasants, Politics, and the Formation of Mexico's National State, 1800–1857*. Stanford University Press, 1997.

Guarisco, Claudia. *Los indios del valle de México y la construcción de una nueva sociabilidad política, 1770–1833*. Colegio Mexiquense, 2003.

Guerra, François-Xavier. *Mexico: Del antiguo regimen a la revolución*. Fondo de Cultura Económica, 1988.

Guerra, François-Xavier. *Modernidades e independencies: Ensayos sobre las revoluciones hispánicas*. Fondo de Cultura Económica, 1997.

Guevara Sanginés, María, *Guanajuato diverso: Sabores y sinsabores de su ser mestizo*. Ediciones La Rana, 2001.

Gutiérrez, Ramón. *When Jesus Came the Corn Mothers Went Away: Marriage, Sexuality, and Power in New Mexico, 1500–1845*. Stanford University Press, 1991.

Gutmann, Matthew. *The Meanings of Macho: Being a Man in Mexico City*. University of California Press, 1996.

Haber, Steven, et al. *Mexico since 1980*. Cambridge University Press, 2008.

Hackel, Stephen. *Children of Coyote, Missionaries of San Francisco: Indian-Spanish Relations in Colonial California*. University of North Carolina Press, 2005.

Hadley, Philip. *Minería y sociedad en el centro minero de Santa Eulalía, Chihuahua, 1709–1750*. Fondo de Cultura Económica, 1979.

Hahn, Stephen. *A Nation Without Borders: The United States and Its World in an Age of Civil Wars, 1820–1910*. Viking, 2016.

Hale, Charles. *Mexican Liberalism in the Age of Mora, 1821–1853*. Yale University Press, 1968.

Hale, Charles. *The Transformation of Liberalism in Late Nineteenth-Century Mexico*. Princeton University Press, 1988.

Hämäläinen, Pekka. *The Comanche Empire*. Yale University Press, 2008.

Hamill, Hugh. *The Hidalgo Revolt: Prelude to Mexican Independence*. University of Florida Press, 1968.

Hamnett, Brian. "Anastasio Bustamante y la guerra de independencia, 1810–1821." *Historia mexicana* 28, no. 1 (1979): 515–46.

Hamnett, Brian. *Roots of Insurgency: Mexican Regions, 1750–1824*. Cambridge University Press, 1986.

Hamnett, Brian. "Royalist Counterinsurgency and the Continuity of Rebellion: Guanajuato and Michoacán, 1813–1820." *Hispanic American Historical Review* 62, no. 1 (1982): 19–48.

Harris, Charles. *A Mexican Family Empire: The Latifundio of the Sánchez Navarro Family, 1765–1867*. University of Texas Press, 1975.

Hernández, Jorge. *La soledad del silencio: Microhistoria del santuario de Atotonilco*. Fondo de Cultura Económica, 1991.

Hernández Jaimes, Jesús. *La formación de la hacienda pública mexicana y las tensiones centro-periférico*. Colegio de México, 2013.

Herr, Richard. *Rural Change and Royal Finances in Spain at the End of the Old Regime*. University of California Press, 1989.

Herrejón Peredo, Carlos. *Del sermón al discurso cívico*. Colegio de Michoacán, 2003.

Herrejón Peredo, Carlos. *Hidalgo: Maestro, párroco, insurgente*. Fomento Cultural Banamex, 2011.

Herrejón Peredo, Carlos. *Hidalgo: Razones de la insurgencia y biografía documental*. Secretaría de Educación Pública, 1987.

Herrejón Peredo, Carlos. *Morelos: Revelaciones y enigmas*. Colegio de Michoacán, 2017.

Herrera Canales, Ines. *El comercio exterior de México, 1821–1845*. Colegio de México, 1977.

Hewitt de Alcántara, Cynthia. *Modernizing Mexican Agriculture: Socioeconomic Implications of Technical Change*. UN Research Institute for Social Development, 1976.

Higgins, Kathleen. *"Licentious Liberty" in a Brazilian Gold Mining Region: Slavery, Gender, and Social Control in Eighteenth-Century Sabará*. Pennsylvania State Press, 1999.

Hyde, Anne. *Empires, Nations, and Families: A New History of the North American West, 1800–1860*. HarperCollins, 2012.

Ibarra, Antonio. *Mercado e institución: Redes de negocios y crisis colonial; Gujadalajara en el siglo XVIII*. Universidad Nacional Autónoma de México, 2017.

Illades, Carlos. *Hacía la república del trabajo: La organización artisanal en la Ciudad de México, 1856–1876*. Colegio de México, 1996.

Inikori, Joseph. "The Volume of the British Slave Trade, 1655–1807." *Cahiers d'Etudes Africains* 128 (1992): 643–88.

James, C. L. R. *Black Jacobins: Toussaint L'Ouverture and the Saint Domingue Revolution*. Rev. ed. Random House, 1963.

Johnson, Walter. *The Broken Heart of America: St. Louis and the Violent History of the United States*. Basic Books, 2020.

Jonas, Raymond. *Hapsburgs on the Río Grande: The Rise and Fall of the Second Mexican Empire*. Harvard University Press, 2024.

Kamen, Henry. *The War of Succession in Spain, 1700–1715*. Indiana University Press, 1969.

Kanter, Deborah. *Hijos del Pueblo: Gender, Family, and Community in Rural Mexico, 1730–1830*. University of Texas Press, 2010.

Kates, Adrienne. "The Persistence of Maya Autonomy: Global Capitalism, Tropical Environment, and the Mexican State, 1880–1950." PhD diss., Georgetown University.

Katz, Friedrich. *The Life and Times of Pancho Villa*. Stanford University Press, 1998.

Katz, Friedrich. *The Secret War in Mexico*. University of Chicago Press, 1981.

Kourí, Emilio. *A Pueblo Divided: Business, Property, and Community in Papantla, Mexico*. Stanford University Press, 2004.

Knight, Alan. *The Mexican Revolution*. 2 vols. Cambridge University Press, 1986.

LaBotz, Dan. *Mask of Democracy: Labor Suppression in Mexico Today*. South End Press, 1999.

Lack, Randolph. *The Texas Revolutionary Experience: A Political and Social History, 1835–1836*. Texas A&M University Press, 1992.

Ladd, Doris. *The Mexican Nobility at Independence, 1780–1826*. University of Texas Press, 1975.

Landa Fonseca, Cecilia. *Querétaro: Una historia compartida*. Gobierno del Estado, 1992.

Lane, Kris. *Potosí: The Silver City That Changed the World*. University of California Press, 2019.

Lerdo de Tejada, Miguel. *El comercio exterior de México desde la conquista hasta hoy*. Rafael Rafael, 1853.

Lin, Man-Huang. *China Upside Down: Currency, Ideology, and Society, 1808–1850*. Harvard University Press, 2006.

López-Alonso, Moramay. *Measuring Up: A History of Living Standards in Mexico, 1850–1950*. Stanford University Press, 2012.

López Austin, Alfredo, and Leopoldo López Luján. *Mexico's Indigenous Past*. Translated by Bernardo Ortíz de Montellano. Oklahoma University Press, 2001.

López Lara, Ramón. *El obispado de Michoacán en el siglo XVII*. Fimax, 1973.

Lovejoy, Paul. *Transformations in Slavery: A History of Slavery in Africa*. 3rd. ed. Cambridge University Press, 2012.

Loyola Vera, Antonio. *Sistemas hidraúlicas en Santiago de Querétaro, siglos XVI–XX*. Gobierno del Estado, 1999.

Lurtz, Casey. *From the Grounds Up: Building an Export Economy in Southern Mexico*. Stanford University Press, 2019.

Lynch, John. *Spain under the Hapsburgs*, vol. 2, *Spain and the Americas, 1598–1800*. Blackwell, 1969.

Macías, Carlos. "El retorno a Valenciana: Las familias Pérez Gálvez y Rul." *Historia Mexicana* 36, no. 4 (1987): 643–59.

Mangan, Jane. *Trading Roles: Gender, Ethnicity, and the Urban Economy in Colonial Potosí*. Duke University Press, 2005.

Manning, Chandra. *Troubled Refuge: Struggling for Freedom in the Civil War*. Knopf, 2016.

Marichal, Carlos. *La bancarrota del virreinato: Nueva España y las finanzas del imperio español, 1780–1810*. Fondo de Cultura Económica, 1999.

Markiewicz, Dana. *The Mexican Revolution and the Limits of Agrarian Reform, 1915–1940*. Lynn Rienner, 1983.

Melville, Eleanor. *A Plague of Sheep: Environmental Consequences of the Conquest of Mexico*. Cambridge University Press, 1994.

Miller, Simon. *Landlords and Haciendas in Modernizing Mexico: Essays in Radical Reappraisal*. CEDLA University of Amsterdam, 1995.

Minian, Ana Raquel. *Undocumented Lives: The Untold Story of Mexican Migration*. Harvard University Press, 2018.

Molina del Villar, América. *La Nueva España y el matlazahuatl*. Colegio de Michoacán, 2001.

Monroy, Pedro. "Las minas de Guanajuato: Memoria histórica descriptiva de este distrito minero." *Anales del Ministro de Fomento de la República Mexicana* 10 (1888): 69–748.

Montejano, David. "Mexican Merchants and Teamsters on the Texas Cotton Road, 1862–1865." In Tutino, *Mexico and Mexicans*.

Montes de Oca, Carlos. *Memoria que el gobernador del estado de Guanajuato formó . . . respective al año de 1825*. Imprenta del Supremo Gobierno, 1826.

Montes de Oca, Carlos. *Memoria que el gobernador del estado de Guanajuato formó . . . respective al año de 1826*. Martin Rivera, 1828.

Montes de Oca, Ignacio. *Elogio funeral de la Señora doña Francisca de Paula Pérez Gálvez*. Cornejo, 1868.

Moore, Barrington. *Social Origins of Dictatorship and Democracy: Lord and Peasant in the Making of the Modern World*. Beacon Press, 1966.

Moreno Gutiérrez, Rodrigo. *La trigarancia: Fuerzas armadas en la consumación de la independencia: Nueva España, 1820–1821*. Universidad Nacional Autónoma de México, 2016.

Morin, Claude. *Michoacán en la Nueva España del siglo XVIII: Crecimiento y desigualdad en una sociedad colonial*. Fondo de Cultura Económica, 1979.

Muñoz Ledo, Octaviano. *Exposición . . . sobre la conducta política que observe en el gobierno del estado durante la última revolución*. Fernández de Lara, 1853.

Murphy, Michael. *Irrigation in the Bajío Region of Colonial Mexico*. Westview Press, 1986.

Ngai, Mai. *The Chinese Question: The Gold Rushes in Global Politics*. Norton, 2021.

Ocampo, Javier. *Las ideas de un día: El pueblo mexicano ante la consumación de la independencia*. Colegio de México, 1969.

Olveda, Jaime. *De la insurrección a la independencia: La guerra en la region de Guadalajara*. Colegio de Jalisco, 2011.

Ortiz Escamilla, Juan. *Calleja: Guerra, botín y fortuna*. Universidad Veracruzana, 2017.

Ortiz Escamilla, Juan. *Guerra y gobierno: Los pueblos y la independencia de México*. Universidad de Sevilla, 1997.

Osante, Patricia. *Orígenes del Nuevo Santander*. Universidad Nacional Autónoma de México, 1997.

Osorno, Fernando. *El insurgente Albino García*. Fondo de Cultura Económica, 1982.

Pani, Erika. *Para mexicanizar el segundo imperio*. Colegio de Mexico, 2001.

Pani, Erika. *Una serie de admirables acontecimientos: México y el mundo en la época de la Reforma, 1848–1867*. Educación y Cultura, 2013.

Pardo Hernández, Berenice, and Miguel Sánchez Rangel. *Mineral de la Luz: La obra fotográfica de John Horgan Jr. en México*. La Rana, 2010.

Parthasarathi, Prasannan. *Why Europe Grew Rich and Asia Did Not: Global Economic Divergence, 1600–1850*. Cambridge University Press, 2011.

Pérez Montesinos, Fernando. *Landscaping Indigenous Mexico: The Liberal State and Capitalism in the Purépecha Highlands*. University of Texas Press, 2025.

Pérez Morales, Laura. *Familia, poder, riqueza y subversion: La familia Fagoaga novohispana, 1730–1830.* Universidad Iberoamericana, 2003.

Pérez Rodríguez, Gustavo. *Xavier Mina, el insurgente español: Guerrillero por la libertad de España y México.* Universidad Nacional Autónoma de México, 2018.

Perry, Laurens Ballard. *Juárez and Díaz: Machine Politics in Mexico.* Northern Illinois University Press, 1979.

Platt, Stephen. *Imperial Twilight: The Opium War and the End of China's Last Golden Age.* Knopf, 2018.

Pletcher, David. *Rails, Mines, and Progress: Seven American Promoters in Mexico, 1867–1911.* Cornell University Press, 1958.

Poinsett, Joel Robert. *Notes on Mexico Made in the Autumn of 1822.* John Miller, 1825.

Pomeranz, Kenneth. *The Great Divergence: China, Europe, and the Making of the Modern World Economy.* Princeton University Press, 2000.

Potash, Robert. *Mexican Government and Industrial Development: The Banco de Avío.* Rev. ed. University of Massachusetts Press, 1983.

Powell, Philip Wayne. *Mexico's Miguel Caldera: The Taming of America's First Frontier, 1548–1597.* University of California Press, 1977.

Powell, Philip Wayne. *Soldiers, Indians, and Silver: The Northward Advance of New Spain, 1550–1600.* University of California Press, 1952.

Preciado de Alba, Carlos Armando. *Guanajuato en tiempo de la intervención francesa y el Segundo Imperio.* Universidad de Guanajuato, 2007.

Prieto, Guillermo. *Indicaciones sobre el origen, vicisitudes y estado que guardan actualmente las rentas generales de la federación Mexicana.* Ignacio Cumplido, 1850.

Prieto, Guillermo "Fidel." *Viajes de orden suprema.* Gobierno del Estado de Querétaro, 1986.

Quiñones, Sam. *Dreamland: The True Tale of America's Opiate Epidemic.* Bloomsbury, 2015.

Quiñones, Sam. *The Least of Us: True Tales of America in the Time of Fentanyl and Meth.* Bloomsbury, 2021.

Radding, Cynthia. *Wandering Peoples: Colonialism, Ethnic Spaces, and Ecological Frontiers in Northwestern Mexico.* Duke University Press, 1997.

Randall, Robert. *Real del Monte: A British Silver Mining Venture in Mexico.* University of Texas Press, 1972.

Raso, José Antonio del. *Notas estadísticas del Departamento de Querétaro . . . año de 1845.* Imprenta de Lara, 1848.

Ratz, Konrad. *Tras las huellas de un desconocido: Nuevos datos y aspectos de Maximiliano de Hapsburgo.* Siglo XXI, 2008.

Reed, John. *Insurgent Mexico.* International Publishers, 1969.

Registro Oficial del los Estados Unidos Mexicanos. Año II (1831).

Reina, Leticia. "Las leyes de reforma: Inicio o culminación de un proceso?" In *Juárez: Historia y mito,* edited by Josefina Vázquez. Colegio de México, 2010.

Reina, Leticia. *Rebeliones campesinas en México, 1819–1906.* Siglo XIX, 1980.

Rincón Frías, Gabriel. "Testamento de don Juan Caballero y Ocío." *Investigacion* 5, no. 1 (1985).

Rionda Arreguín, Isauro. *La Compañía de Jesús en la provincia guanajuatense, 1590–1767.* Universidad de Guanajuato, 1996.

Rodríguez Frausto, Jesús. "La Universidad de Guanajuato en su origen." In *Guanajuato: La cultura y el tiempo*, edited by Mariano González Leal. Colegio del Bajío, 1980.

Romero, José Guadalupe. *Noticias para formar la historia y estadística del obispado de Michoacán . . . 1860.* Vicente García Torres, 1862.

Romero de Terreros, Manuel. *Antiguas haciendas de México.* Porrúa, 1956.

Romero de Terreros, Manuel. "La condesa escribe." *Historia mexicana* 1, no. 3 (1952): 456–67.

"Romero y López, José Guadalupe." In *Enciclopedia histórica y biográfica de la Universidad de Guadalajara*, vol. 2, *1821–1861*.

Rothman, Adam. "Union, Capitalism, and Slavery in the 'Rising Empire' of the United States." In Tutino, *New Countries*.

Salvucci, Richard. *Politics, Markets, and Mexico's "London Debt," 1823–1887.* Cambridge University Press, 2009.

Sánchez Rangel, Oscar. *La empresa de minas de Miguel Rul, 1865–1897.* La Rana, 2005.

Santiago, Myrna. *The Ecology of Oil: Environment, Labor, and the Mexican Revolution, 1900–1938.* Cambridge University Press, 2006.

Schwartz, Stuart. "Indian Labor and New World Plantations: European Demand and Indian Response in Northeastern Brazil." *American Historical Review* 83, no. 1 (1978): 43–79.

Schwartz, Stuart. *Sugar Plantations and the Formation of Brazilian Society: Bahia, 1550–1835.* Cambridge University Press, 1986.

Schwartz, Stuart, ed. *Tropical Babylons: Sugar and the Making of the Atlantic World.* University of North Carolina Press, 2004.

Serrano Contreras, Ramón María. "La ciudad de Santiago de Querétaro a fines del siglo XVIII." *Anuario de estudios americanos* 30 (1973): 489–555.

Serrano Ortega, José Antonio. *Jerarquía territorial y transición política: Guanajuato, 1790–1826.* Colegio de Michoacán, 2001.

Sims, Harold. *La expulsión de los españoles de México.* Fondo de Cultura Económica, 1974.

Sims, Harold. *The Expulsion of Mexico's Spaniards, 1821–1830.* University of Pittsburgh Press, 1991.

Sinkin, Richard. *The Mexican Reform, 1855–1876: A Study in Liberal Nation Building.* University of Texas Press, 1979.

Smith, Benjamin. *The Dope: The Real History of the Mexican Drug Trade.* Norton, 2021.

Somohano Martínez, Lourdes. *La versión histórica de la Conquista y la organización política del pueblo de Querétaro.* Instituto Technológico de Estudios Superiores de Monterrey, 2003.

Soto González, Fidel. *Hércules: Industrialización y clase obrera en Querétaro, 1838–1877*. Centro Estatal para la Cultura y las Artes, 2004.

Stauffer, Brian. *Victory on Earth or in Heaven: Mexico's Religionero Rebellion*. University of New Mexico Press, 2021.

Stein, Barbara, and Stanley Stein. *Edge of Crisis: War and Trade in the Spanish Atlantic, 1789–1808*. Johns Hopkins University Press, 2009.

Stein, Barbara, and Stanley Stein. *Crisis in an Atlantic Empire: Spain and New Spain, 1808–1810*. Johns Hopkins University Press, 2014.

Stein, Stanley, and Barbara Stein. *Apogee of Empire: Spain and New Spain in the Age of Charles III*. Johns Hopkins University Press, 2003.

Stephen, Lynn. *Zapata Lives: Histories and Cultural Politics in Southern Mexico*. University of California Press, 2002.

Stern, Steve. *The Secret History of Gender: Women, Men, and Power in Late Colonial Mexico*. University of North Carolina Press, 1995.

Stites, Richard. *The Four Horsemen: Riding to Liberty in Post-Napoleonic Europe*. Oxford University press, 2014.

Streeby, Shelley. *American Sensations: Class, Empire, and the Production of Popular Culture*. University of California Press, 2002.

Suárez Muñoz, Manuel, and Juan Ricardo Jiménez Gómez, eds. *La ideología republicana en Querétaro, 1823–1835*. Instituto de Estudios Constitucionales, 2009.

Szekely, Gabriel. *La economía política del petroleo en México, 1976–1982*. Colegio de México, 1983.

Taylor, Alan. *The Internal Enemy: Slavery and War in Virginia, 1772–1832*. Norton, 2013.

Taylor, William. *Drinking, Homicide, and Rebellion in Colonial Mexican Villages*. Stanford University Press, 1979.

Telmo Primo, Pedro. *Querétaro en 1822*. Edited by Pedro Flores. Vargas Rea, 1944.

Terán, Martha. "1809: Las relaciones entre los indios y los criollos de la ciudad de Valladolid de Michoacán, en el intento de formar una junta soberana de la provincia." *Historias* 68 (2007): 33–51.

Terán, Marta. "La Virgen de Guadalupe contra Napoleón Bonaparte: La defensa de la religion en el obispado de Michoacán entre 1793 y 1814." *Estudios de historia novohispana* 24 (1999): 91–133.

Tone, John. *The Fatal Knot: Guerrilla Resistance in Navarre and the Defeat of Napoleon in Spain*. University of North Carolina Press, 1995.

Torget, Andrew. *Seeds of Empire: Cotton, Slavery, and the Transformation of the Texas Borderlands, 1800–1850*. University of North Carolina Press, 2015.

Torres, Eugenio Martín. *El beneficio de la plata en Guanajuato, 1686–1740*. Presidencia Municipal, 2002.

Trouillot, Michel-Rolph. *Silencing the Past: Power and the Production of History*. Rev. ed. Beacon Press, 2015.

Trujillo Bolio, Mario. *Operarios fabriles en la Ciudad de México, 1864–1884*. Colegio de México, 1997.

Tutino, John. "The Americas in the Twentieth-Century World." In Tutino and Melosi, *New World Cities*.

Tutino, John, "De Hidalgo a Apatzingán: Insurgencia popular y proyectos políticos en Nueva España, 1811–1814." In *La insurgencia mexicana y la Constitución de Apatzingán*, edited by Ana Carolina Ibarra et al. Universidad Nacional Autónoma de México, 2014.

Tutino, John. "Entre la rebellion y la revolución: Compresión agrarian en Chalco, 1870–1900. In *Entre lagos y volcanes: Chalco-Amecameca, passado y presente*, edited by Alejandro Tortolero. Colegio Mexiquense, 1993.

Tutino, John. *From Insurrection to Revolution in Mexico: Social Bases of Agrarian Violence, 1750–1940*. Princeton University Press, 1986.

Tutino, John. *Making a New World: Founding Capitalism in the Bajío and Spanish North America*. Duke University Press, 2011.

Tutino, John. *The Mexican Heartland: How Communities Shaped Capitalism, a Nation, and World History, 1500–2000*. Princeton University Press, 2018.

Tutino, John. *Mexico City, 1808: Power, Sovereignty, and Silver in an Age of War and Revolution*. University of New Mexico Press, 2018.

Tutino, John, ed. *New Countries: Capitalism, Revolutions, and Nations in the Americas*. Duke University Press, 2016.

Tutino, John. "Power, Class, and Family: Men, Women, and Power in the Mexico City Elite, 1750–1810." *The Americas* 39, no. 3 (1983): 359–81.

Tutino, John. "Power, Marginality, and Participation in Mexico City, 1870–2000." In Tutino and Melosi, *New World Cities*.

Tutino, John. "Querétaro y los origenes da la nación mexicana: Las políticas étnicas de soberanía, contrainsurgencia e independencia." In *Mexico a la luz de sus revoluciones*, edited by Laura Rojas and Susan Deeds. Colegio de Mexico, 2014.

Tutino, John. "The Revolutionary Capacity of Rural Communities: Ecological Autonomy and Its Demise." In *Cycles of Conflict, Centuries of Change: Crisis, Reform, and Revolution in Mexico*, edited by Elisa Servín, Leticia Reina, and John Tutino. Duke University Press, 2007.

Tutino, John. "The Revolution in Mexican Independence: Insurgency and the Renegotiation of Property, Production, and Patriarchy, 1810–1855." *Hispanic American Historical Review* 78, no. 3 (1998): 467–517.

Tutino, John, and Martin Melosi, eds. *New World Cities: Challenges of Urbanization and Globalization in the Americas*. University of North Carolina Press, 2019.

Urquiola Permisan, José Ignacio. *Trabajadores de campo y ciudad: Las cartas de servicio como forma de contratación en Querétaro, 1588–1609*. Gobierno del Estado, 2001.

Valle Pavón, Guillermina del. *Donativos, préstamos y privilegios: Los mercaderes y mineros de La ciudad de México durante la guerra anglo-española, 1779–1783*. Instituto Mora, 2016.

Valle Pavón, Guillermina del. *Finanzas piadosas y redes de negociación: Los mercaderes de la Ciudad de México ante la crisis de Nueva España, 1804–1808*. Instituto Mora, 2012.

Van Young, Eric. *Hacienda and Market in Eighteenth-Century Mexico: The Rural Economy of the Guadalajara Region, 1680–1820*. Stanford University Press, 1981.

Van Young, Eric. *A Life Together: Lucas Alamán and Mexico, 1792–1853*. Yale University Press, 2021.

Van Young, Eric. *The Other Rebellion: Popular Violence, Ideology, and the Struggle for Mexican Independence*. Stanford University Press, 2001.

Vaughan, Mary Kay. *Cultural Politics in Revolution: Teachers, Peasants, and Schools in Mexico, 1930–1940*. University of Arizona Press, 1997.

Velasco Ávila, Cuautehmoc, et al. *Estado y minería en México, 1767–1910*. Fondo de Cultura Económica, 1988.

Velasco Ávila, Cuauhtemoc. *La frontera étnica en el noreste mexicano: Los comanches entre 1800 y 1841*. CIESAS, 2012.

Veloz, Larisa. *Even the Women Are Leaving: Migrants Making Mexican America*. University of California Press, 2023.

Vergara, Germán. *Fueling Mexico: Energy and Environment, 1850–1950*. Cambridge University Press, 2021.

Vergara Hernández, María Josefa. *Testimonio*. Gobierno del Estado de Querétaro, 1987.

Verlinden, Charles. *The Beginnings of Modern Colonization*. Translated by Yvonne Freccero. Cornell University Press, 1970.

Vilaplana, Hermenegildo de. *Histórico y sagrada novenario de la milagrosa imagen de Nuestra Señora del Pueblito*. 1765. Reprint, Abendaño y Valdes, 1840.

Walker, Louise. *Waking from the Dream: Mexico's Middle Classes after 1968*. Stanford University Press, 2013.

Ward, H. G. *Mexico in 1827*. 2 vols. Henry Colburn, 1828.

Warman, Arturo. *Corn and Capitalism: How a Botanical Bastard Grew to Global Dominance*. Translated by Nancy Westrake. University of North Carolina Press, 2003.

Weber, David. *Bárbaros: Spaniards and Their Savages in the Age of Enlightenment*. Yale University Press, 2005.

Weber, David. *The Mexican Frontier, 1821–1846: The American Southwest Under Mexico*. University of New Mexico Press, 1982.

Weber, David. *The Spanish Frontier in North America*. Yale University Press, 1992.

Weber, Max. *Economy and Society: A New Translation*. Translated by Keith Tribe. Harvard University Press, 2019.

Wells, Allen. *Yucatán's Gilded Age: Haciendas, Henequen, and International Harvester, 1860–1915*. University of New Mexico Press, 1985.

Wells, Allen, and Gilbert Joseph. *Summer of Discontent, Seasons of Upheaval: Elite Politics and Rural Insurgency in Yucatán, 1876–1915*. Stanford University Press, 1996.

White, Richard. *Railroaded: The Transcontinentals and the Making of America*. Norton, 2011.

Wobeser, Gisela von. *Dominación colonial: La consolidación de Vales Reales, 1804–1810*. Universidad Nacional Autónoma de México, 2003.

Womack, John. *Rebellion in Chiapas: An Historical Reader*. New Press, 1999.

Womack, John. *Zapata and the Mexican Revolution*. Knopf, 1968.

Wright, Angus. *The Death of Ramón González: The Modern Agricultural Dilemma*. Rev. ed. University of Texas Press, 2005.

Wyllie, Robert Crichton. *Mexico: A Report on Its Finances*. A. H. Bailey, 1844.

Wyllie, Robert Crichton. *México: Noticias sobre su hacienda pública bajo el gobierno español y después de la independencia*. Ignacio Cumplido, 1845.

Zeláa é Hidalgo, José María. *Glorias de Querétaro*. Zuniga y Ontiveros, 1803.

Zolov, Eric. *The Last Good Neighbor: Mexico in the Global Sixties*. Duke University Press, 2020.

Note: page numbers followed by *f* refer to figures.

Manila, xix, 26, 47, 79, 135, 367

manufacturing, 34, 44, 156, 189, 193, 237, 335; in Querétaro, 31, 267, 306, 360–61; textile, 34, 187, 300; tobacco, 54, 76

Marfil, 213, 235, 330; militia, 109

Marqués de San Miguel de Aguayo, 273–74

Masons, 205, 225

Maximilian of Hapsburg, 18, 364, 370, 372, 376–79, 381

medical capitalism, xxi, 398

Mejía, Tomás, 349, 373–75, 379

Mellado: chapel, 39f; mines, 108, 200, 213, 377

Meneses, José, 277–78

merchants, 48, 50–51, 53, 81, 199, 208, 257–58, 268, 322, 333, 336, 344, 359; African, xix, 6, 34; British, xx, 9, 47, 50–51, 194, 197; Chinese, xix, 26; European, 12, 27; Indian, 6; Italian, 26; Mexico City, 33, 49, 70; Querétaro, 29; Spanish, 71, 197; US, 51, 194, 197

mercury, xvii, 29, 38, 49, 70, 103, 108, 112–13, 201, 213–14; poisoning, 39; price of, 116, 380

Mesa de los Caballos, 119–21

Mesoamerica, xvi–xviii, 12, 23–26, 95, 397–98, 467n2, 467n6; frontier with North America, 368

mestizos, 128, 133, 137, 217, 240, 260–62; death rates of, 55

Mexica (Aztecs), xvi, 24–27, 30, 136

Mexican capitalism, 4, 19, 209, 363

Mexican independence, xx, 2–4, 98–100, 149, 181–85, 191, 243, 365–66, 477; army and, 197; Comanches and, 208; Hidalgo and, 85, 87, 89, 93, 102; Mina and, 122; Montes de Oca and, 227; Morelos and, 115; Telmo and, 237; war for, 200, 290, 326, 366, 503n11

Mexico City, xiii, xv–xvii, 26, 58, 61, 68, 70–71, 77, 79–80, 90, 95, 105, 154, 156, 169, 269, 281–82, 286, 309, 311, 388, 340, 393, 397, 506n1; Azcárate and, 207; bullion and, 108, 117, 372; Calderón de la Barca and, 290; Council, 176, 273, 276; Encarnación Convent, 52; Espinosa y Navarijo and, 57; Fagoaga sisters and, 327; financiers, 27, 33, 38, 51, 122, 199, 202; French troops and, 375; Hidalgo and, 76, 87, 89; High Court in, 63, 82, 178; industry

and, 382; Inquisition, 82, 85; maize and, xix, 276; merchants, 29, 35, 37, 49, 51, 70, 122, 199, 202; Mezquital and, 157, 170; mint, 38, 115, 187–88; Napoleon's invasion of Spain and, 65–66, 85; National Palace, 188f, 190, 205; oligarchs in, 10, 14, 46, 49, 51, 183–85, 272–73, 289, 306, 317; Our Lady of Guadalupe and, 28, 35, 325; Parián, 164, 190, 205, 287, 487n77; Peñascos and, 160–62, 164; Poinsett and, 187, 211; political debates in, 7, 13, 136; Prieto and, 332–33, 336, 344; pulque and, 171–73, 175, 273, 276; Querétaro and, 24–25; silver and, 34, 108, 114, 118, 202, 367; taverns, 171–73, 175; tobacco factory, 53–54; US invasion and, 325, 368–69; Ward and, 190–91, 199

mezcal, 165, 167, 169, 354

Mezquital, 96, 116, 157–58, 170–73, 176–78, 371, 482n1; independence in, 182; insurgencies, 104, 158, 171, 173, 176; pulque estates in, 286; rape in, 480n94

Michoacán, 66, 71, 83, 99, 131, 305, 328, 357, 368, 378, 391; diocese, 85, 93; Purépecha, 371; rancheros in, 382; religious wars, 308

migrants, 19, 30, 32, 185; Mesoamerican, xviii, 27–29, 397; Spanish, 36, 71, 205

militias, 48, 65–66, 71, 75, 88, 93–94, 109, 140, 144, 160, 162, 188, 237, 243, 246, 257, 279, 353, 366; Calleja's, 96, 158; censuses of, 59, 137, 259–60, 262; estate, 147, 247, 253; loyal, 89, 106–7; patriotic, 104

Mina, Francisco Javier, 13, 104, 121–26, 152, 168, 169, 479n88; manifesto of, 480n91

mine operators, 29, 33, 40, 46, 49, 52, 91, 108, 115, 200–203, 377; bankrupt, 182; financiers and, 38, 44, 201; Mexico City mint and, 115–16

Mining Tribunal, 70, 76, 130, 373

Miramón, Miguel, 350, 374, 379

missions, 32, 45, 206; Jesuit, 5, 45

Molino Colorado estate, 301–2

Molino de Flores estate, 275–76

monarchy: French, 6, 50; Iturbide's, 211, 214; Hapsburg, 370, 379; Spanish, 51, 65, 67, 70, 178, 181, 184

wool/woolens, 25, 27, 53, 156–57, 165–67, 173, 208, 214, 234, 239, 267, 271, 299–300, 306, 335, 355; *obrajes* and, 36, 53, 42–43, 165, 322, 332; Querétaro, 304–5, Puebla and, 191, 193

workers, 5, 7, 29, 31, 34, 44, 54, 59, 115 123, 140, 151, 159, 167, 169, 208, 249, 261–62, 393, 395; British, 194; cloth making and, 27, 53, 300–302, 304–5, 360, 371, 331–32, 381; day, 145, 150, 243, 248; estate, 215, 238, 263–64, 275, 283–85, 341, 387; at La Griega, 240–41, 243–44, 246; Hércules's, 323, 379; Hispanic, 222, 244; indigenous, 259; labor rights and, 390, 392; mine, 38, 40–41, 46, 48–49, 52, 91, 93, 103, 108–9, 115–16, 171, 198, 201–2, 213, 232, 234–35, 296–98, 327, 330–31, 364, 377, 380; NAFTA and, 396; Otomí, 64, 138, 244, 246; at Puerto de Nieto, xiii, 221. *See also* alquilados; *buscones*; mine workers

workshops, xviii, 27, 53, 84, 126, 236–37, 299–301, 305, 335, 357; textile, xiii, 23, 31, 38, 81, 138, 156, 300–301, 304, 351 (*see also obrajes*)

Xalpa, 106, 121, 125–27, 177, 258, 346, 353
Xichú, 118, 140, 252, 342, 349, 351, 358
Xochimilco, 187, 190–91

Yaqui, 45, 387, 469n41
yellow fever, 186, 191, 367
Yermo, Gabriel de, 65, 161
Yuriria, 252, 300, 351, 357

Zacatecas, xv, 24, 43, 90, 119, 166, 301, 352, 368, 386, 487n68; mining silver at, xvi–xviii, 25–26, 31–32, 36, 44, 49, 107, 156, 196, 200–201, 204, 296, 302, 355; minting and, 372, 375
Zapata, Emiliano, xxi, 389–91, 395, 398
Zavala, Lorenzo de, 203–4, 276
Zitácuaro, 93, 104, 106–7, 109–12

www.ingramcontent.com/pod-product-compliance
Lightning Source LLC
Chambersburg PA
CBHW020446270326
41926CB00008B/507